Comparative Law

This book presents a fresh contextualised and cosmopolitan perspective on comparative law for both students and scholars. It critically discusses established approaches to comparative law, but also presents more modern ones, such as socio-legal and numerical comparative law. Its contextualised approach draws on examples from politics, economics and development studies to provide an original contribution to topics of comparative law.

Mathias Siems is Professor of Commercial Law at Durham University.

The Law in Context Series

Editors: William Twining *(University College London),*
Christopher McCrudden *(Queen's University Belfast) and*
Bronwen Morgan *(University of Bristol)*

Since 1970 the Law in Context series has been at the forefront of the movement to broaden the study of law. It has been a vehicle for the publication of innovative scholarly books that treat law and legal phenomena critically in their social, political and economic contexts from a variety of perspectives. The series particularly aims to publish scholarly legal writing that brings fresh perspectives to bear on new and existing areas of law taught in universities. A contextual approach involves treating legal subjects broadly, using materials from other social sciences, and from any other discipline that helps to explain the operation in practice of the subject under discussion. It is hoped that this orientation is at once more stimulating and more realistic than the bare exposition of legal rules. The series includes original books that have a different emphasis from traditional legal textbooks, while maintaining the same high standards of scholarship. They are written primarily for undergraduate and graduate students of law and of other disciplines, but will also appeal to a wider readership. In the past, most books in the series have focused on English law, but recent publications include books on European law, globalisation, transnational legal processes, and comparative law.

Books in the Series
Anderson, Schum & Twining: *Analysis of Evidence*
Ashworth: *Sentencing and Criminal Justice*
Barton & Douglas: *Law and Parenthood*
Beecher-Monas: *Evaluating Scientific Evidence: An Interdisciplinary Framework for Intellectual Due Process*
Bell: *French Legal Cultures*
Bercusson: *European Labour Law*
Birkinshaw: *European Public Law*
Birkinshaw: *Freedom of Information: The Law, the Practice and the Ideal*
Brownsword & Goodwin: *Law and the Technologies of the Twenty-First Century*
Cane: *Atiyah's Accidents, Compensation and the Law*
Clarke & Kohler: *Property Law: Commentary and Materials*
Collins: *The Law of Contract*
Collins, Ewing & McColgan: *Labour Law*
Cowan: *Housing Law and Policy*
Cranston: *Legal Foundations of the Welfare State*
Darian-Smith: *Laws and Societies in Global Contexts: Contemporary Approaches*
Dauvergne: *Making People Illegal: What Globalisation Means for Immigration and Law*
Davies: *Perspectives on Labour Law*
Dembour: *Who Believes in Human Rights?: The European Convention in Question*
de Sousa Santos: *Toward a New Legal Common Sense*

Diduck: *Law's Families*

Fortin: *Children's Rights and the Developing Law*

Ghai & Woodham: *Practising Self-Government: A Comparative Study of Autonomous Regions*

Glover-Thomas: *Reconstructing Mental Health Law and Policy*

Gobert & Punch: *Rethinking Corporate Crime*

Goldman: *Globalisation and the Western Legal Tradition: Recurring Patterns of Law and Authority*

Harlow & Rawlings: *Law and Administration*

Harris: *An Introduction to Law*

Harris, Campbell & Halson: *Remedies in Contract and Tort*

Harvey: *Seeking Asylum in the UK: Problems and Prospects*

Hervey & McHale: *Health Law and the European Union*

Holder & Lee: *Environmental Protection, Law and Policy*

Jackson and Summers: *The Internationalisation of Criminal Evidence*

Kostakopoulou: *The Future Governance of Citizenship*

Lewis: *Choice and the Legal Order: Rising above Politics*

Likosky: *Transnational Legal Processes*

Likosky: *Law, Infrastructure and Human Rights*

Maughan & Webb: *Lawyering Skills and the Legal Process*

McGlynn: *Families and the European Union: Law, Politics and Pluralism*

Moffat: *Trusts Law: Text and Materials*

Monti: *EC Competition Law*

Morgan: *Contract Law Minimalism*

Morgan & Yeung: *An Introduction to Law and Regulation: Text and Materials*

Norrie: *Crime, Reason and History*

O'Dair: *Legal Ethics*

Oliver: *Common Values and the Public–Private Divide*

Oliver & Drewry: *The Law and Parliament*

Picciotto: *International Business Taxation*

Probert: *The Changing Legal Regulation of Cohabitation, 1600–2010*

Reed: *Internet Law: Text and Materials*

Richardson: *Law, Process and Custody*

Roberts & Palmer: *Dispute Processes: ADR and the Primary Forms of Decision-Making*

Rowbottom: *Democracy Distorted: Wealth, Influence and Democratic Politics*

Scott & Black: *Cranston's Consumers and the Law*

Seneviratne: *Ombudsmen: Public Services and Administrative Justice*

Siems: *Comparative Law*

Stapleton: *Product Liability*

Stewart: *Gender, Law and Justice in a Global Market*

Tamanaha: *Law as a Means to an End: Threat to the Rule of Law*

Turpin and Tomkins: *British Government and the Constitution: Text and Materials*

Twining: *Globalisation and Legal Theory*

Twining: *Rethinking Evidence*

Twining: *General Jurisprudence: Understanding Law from a Global Perspective*

Twining: *Human Rights, Southern Voices: Francis Deng, Abdullahi An-Na'im, Yash Ghai and Upendra Baxi*

Twining & Miers: *How to Do Things with Rules*
Ward: *A Critical Introduction to European Law*
Ward: *Law, Text, Terror*
Ward: *Shakespeare and Legal Imagination*
Wells and Quick: *Lacey, Wells and Quick: Reconstructing Criminal Law*
Zander: *Cases and Materials on the English Legal System*
Zander: *The Law-Making Process*

International Journal of Law in Context: A Global Forum for Interdisciplinary Legal Studies

The *International Journal of Law in Context* is the companion journal to the Law in Context book series and provides a forum for interdisciplinary legal studies and offers intellectual space for ground-breaking critical research. It publishes contextual work about law and its relationship with other disciplines including but not limited to science, literature, humanities, philosophy, sociology, psychology, ethics, history and geography. More information about the journal and how to submit an article can be found at http://journals.cambridge.org/ijc.

Comparative Law

MATHIAS SIEMS

CAMBRIDGE
UNIVERSITY PRESS

CAMBRIDGE
UNIVERSITY PRESS

University Printing House, Cambridge CB2 8BS, United Kingdom

Cambridge University Press is part of the University of Cambridge.

It furthers the University's mission by disseminating knowledge in the pursuit of education, learning and research at the highest international levels of excellence.

www.cambridge.org
Information on this title: www.cambridge.org/9780521177177

© Mathias Siems 2014

First published 2014

Printed in the United Kingdom by CPI Group Ltd, Croydon CR0 4YY

A catalogue record for this publication is available from the British Library

ISBN 978-1-107-00375-0 Hardback
ISBN 978-0-521-17717-7 Paperback

Contents

List of tables   *page* xiv
List of figures   xv
Preface   xvii
List of abbreviations   xix

1 Introduction   1
    A. Why compare laws?   1
      1. How to slide into comparative-law thinking   1
      2. The purposes of comparative law   2
    B. What belongs to comparative law?   5
      1. Status quo: no fixed canon   5
      2. The 'law' discussed in this book   6
      3. The three dimensions of 'comparative law in context'   7
      4. Conclusion: the structure of this book   9

Part I Traditional Comparative Law   11

2 The comparative legal method   13
    A. The typical structure of a comparative paper   13
      1. Preliminary considerations   13
      2. The description of laws   16
      3. The comparative analysis   20
      4. Critical policy evaluation   22
      5. An example from comparative tort law   24
    B. Functionalism and universalism in particular   25
      1. Functionalism: origins, use and consequences   25
      2. Comparative law's interest in finding commonalities   28
      3. The example of the Common Core project   31
    C. Critical analysis   33
      1. The simplistic approach   33

2. The focus on Western countries 35
3. The critics of functionalism 37
4. The policy evaluation 39
D. Conclusion 40

3   Common law and civil law 41
A. Terminology and origins 41
B. Juxtaposing civil and common law 43
1. Legal methods and sources of law 44
2. Courts and civil procedure 48
3. Comparative contract law 58
C. Critical analysis 64
1. Diversity in continental Europe 64
2. Differences between England and the US 65
3. Western law instead of civil v. common law? 68
D. Conclusion 70

4   Mapping the world's legal systems 72
A. Background and purpose 72
B. Classifying countries 74
1. Bases for classification 74
2. Review of main classifications 75
3. Main commonalities 79
C. Critical analysis 80
1. Overemphasis of differences 80
2. Overemphasis of similarities 82
3. Disregard of hybrids 85
D. Conclusion 93

Part II   Extending the Methods of Comparative Law 95

5   Postmodern comparative law 97
A. From George W. Bush to postmodernism 97
B. Deep-level comparative law 98
1. Law as reflecting jurisprudential concepts 98
2. Law as embedded in culture 101
3. Law as requiring immersion 105
4. Law as legal pluralism 107
C. Critical comparative law 108

1. Law as discourse		109
2. Law as politics		114
D. Conclusion		116

6 Socio-legal comparative law — 119

A. Setting the scene	119
1. Legal culture and comparative law	119
2. The causality problem in socio-legal research	121
B. Civil litigation, courts and lawyers	127
1. Civil litigation and other forms of dispute resolution	127
2. Litigation rates in the US, England, Germany, the Netherlands and Japan	128
3. Further research on judges, lawyers and the public	132
C. Substantive law 'in action' and society	136
1. Comparative commercial law	136
2. Comparative criminal law	140
D. Conclusion	144

7 Numerical comparative law — 146

A. Measuring the impact of foreign legal ideas	147
1. Cross-citations between courts	147
2. Measuring foreign influence related to academic research	154
3. Measuring the influence on foreign statute law	156
B. Measuring similarities and differences	159
1. Formal features of the legal system	160
2. Substance of legal rules	164
C. Measuring the quality of legal rules and institutions	167
1. Measuring legal rules	168
2. Measuring courts and other legal and political institutions	172
3. Surveying perceptions about law and its enforcement	176
4. Combined approaches	179
D. Conclusion	186

Part III Global Comparative Law — 189

8 Legal transplants — 191

A. Conceptual research on legal transplants	191
1. The rationales for legal transplants	191
2. The way legal transplants 'work'	195
3. Further variants of legal transplants	200

    B. Legal transplants throughout history   201

        1. Legal transplants in continental Europe   202
        2. Colonialism and post-colonialism   205
        3. Transplants in non-colonial countries: all that different?   211
        4. The globalisation of human rights law   214

    C. Conclusion   220

9   Fading state borders   222

    A. Setting the scene   222

        1. The 'end of history' and the 'end of state'?   222
        2. The role of public and private international law   224
        3. Forces for convergence, regionalisation and transnationalisation   230

    B. Convergence of laws   233

        1. Terminology and typology   233
        2. The examples of constitutional and company law   234
        3. Discussion: normative and positive   238

    C. Regionalisation   242

        1. Terminology and typology   242
        2. The European Union as an example of regional integration   244
        3. Discussion: towards multi-level governance   247

    D. Transnationalisation   249

        1. Terminology and typology   249
        2. Examples from transnational commercial law   251
        3. Discussion: is private law-making legitimate?   255

    E. Conclusion   258

10   Comparative law and development   260

    A. The evolving ideas of 'law and development'   260

    B. Development and the rule of law   265

        1. Terminology, typology and purpose   265
        2. The rule of law in China, Russia and Afghanistan   269

    C. The critics of 'law and development'   275

        1. Law does not 'work'   276
        2. Against 'top-down' approaches   277
        3. Western law out-of-context   279
        4. The 'wrong' legal rules and institutions   281

    D. Conclusion   282

Part IV   Comparative Law as an Open Subject   285

11   Implicit comparative law   287

A. Introduction to comparative research in social sciences   287

   1. Main rationales for a comparative approach   287
   2. Main types of comparative research   288
   3. Methods, continued: history, logic and concepts   289
   4. Choice of units of comparison   291

B. Comparative studies of states and their components   292

   1. Determining 'the best' form of government   293
   2. Comparing 'the state in action'   295
   3. Classifying and evaluating policy choices   297

C. Comparative studies of societies and cultures   301

   1. Understanding differences and similarities between legal systems   302
   2. Showing legal universalities and singularities   305
   3. Measuring legal mentalities and their relevance   309

D. Conclusion   312

12   Outlook   313

A. Further directions of 'implicit comparative law'   313

B. Revisiting 'explicit' research in comparative law   314

C. Conclusion   316

References   318
Index   401

Tables

1.1	The purposes of comparative law in this book	*page* 3
1.2	Focus of general comparative law books	6
1.3	Overview of main areas of law and legal systems covered in this book	7
2.1	Similarities and differences	38
4.1	Overview of legal family classifications across time	76
6.1	Criteria which can foster legal adaptability	123
6.2	The relationship between law and religion	125
6.3	Potential relationships between political economy and imprisonment	144
7.1	Overview of topics and methods of numerical comparative law	147
7.2	Number of cross-citations in civil and criminal law (all cited)	151
7.3	Negative binomial regression with dependent variable number of cross-citations in matters of civil and criminal law	153
7.4	The top ten words of the Draft Common Frame of Reference (DCFR), compared with four domestic codes	157
7.5	Matrix on differences in shareholder protection 2005 (max 10, min 0)	165
7.6	Shareholder rights around the world (extract)	169
7.7	Duration of court proceedings to evict tenant (to collect cheque) (extract)	175
7.8	Measuring access to justice in a refugee camp in Nepal	178
7.9	WJP Rule of Law Index, selected countries (min 0, max 1)	182
7.10	Legal systems ranked in terms of ease of doing business (extract)	183
8.1	Standard case and variants	201
9.1	Convergence forces	231
9.2	Convergence and divergence in shareholder protection (1970–2005)	236
10.1	Possible functions of the rule of law and examples	269

Figures

1.1 The three dimensions: areas of law, legal regimes and methods   *page* 8
4.1 Possible classification of BRIC countries   88
7.1 Bar chart on cross-citations between supreme courts   152
7.2 'Foreign Laws' in *Harvard Law Review*   155
7.3 'Westernisation' of shareholder protection in Central and Eastern
Europe (Czech Republic, Latvia, Slovenia) (10 variables)   159
7.4 How often has the BGH cited its own decisions?   162
7.5 How often has the CA cited its own decisions?   163
7.6 Shareholder protection network of strongest 15 per cent ties   166
9.1 International law as the 'law of globalisation'   226
12.1 Relationship between 'comparative law', 'law' and 'other
comparative disciplines'   316

Preface

In a well-known Irish joke a foreigner asks a local how to get to a particular place, but only receives the advice that 'if I were you, I wouldn't start from here'. Of course, in reality (and without teleportation) one has to start from the place where one is at present. Applying this trite insight, 'traditional comparative law' is still a suitable starting point for a general book on comparative law. However, this book also aims to lead the reader somewhere else, namely to a deeper and more interdisciplinary perspective. This is not to claim that traditional approaches have become obsolete, but, just as one cannot ignore past achievements, neither can one disregard new approaches and topics of comparative law.

It is hoped that this strategy has led to a book that fills a notable gap in the literature. This is not to deny that significant comparative legal research has been produced in recent years, though the focus and format of the present book is different from previous ones as (i) it deals with general questions of comparative legal method, in contrast to detailed micro-comparisons of particular rules and countries, (ii) it provides a comprehensive treatment of the state of art of comparative law, in contrast to monographs that discuss particular aspects or methods of comparative law, and (iii) it is a single-authored coherent text, in contrast to books that comprise collections of articles on topics of comparative law.

As a consequence, this book is targeted at a wide audience. In the first instance, it may be appreciated by readers who are specifically interested in comparative law, be they students, academics or others. Secondly, however, comparative law is too important to be left to comparative lawyers! In today's world, even lawyers whose main interest lies in particular domestic legal systems frequently come across foreign sources of law, making familiarity with core topics of comparative law indispensible. Moreover, this book aims to show that comparative law is often closely related to other comparative fields, such as comparative politics, sociology, economics and development; thus, comparative scholars in these fields may also benefit from this book.

Research for this book started in autumn 2009. I want to thank the universities where I have held permanent and visiting positions in recent years. These were, on the one hand, the University of East Anglia and Durham University in the

UK, and, on the other hand, the Riga Graduate School of Law in Latvia, the Central European University in Hungary, the Interdisciplinary Center in Israel, Waseda University in Japan, Shanghai Jiao Tong University and the China University of Political Science and Law in China, the Center for the Study of Law and Society at UC Berkeley and Fordham Law School in the US, and the British Institute of International and Comparative Law and the Institute of Advanced Legal Studies in the UK.

I also want to thank many friends and colleagues who have provided me with extremely helpful feedback on parts of this book: in alphabetical order, Uchenna Anyamele, John Bell, Jacco Bomhoff, Nick Foster, Martin Gelter, Carsten Gerner-Beuerle, Nicholas Hoggard, Jaakko Husa, Hatice Kubra Kandemir, Dionysia Katelouzou, Mariana Pargendler, Daniel Peat, Robert Schütze, Melih Sonmez, and Po Jen Yap. I also thank the editors of the Law in Context series, in particular William Twining, as well as Cambridge University Press, in particular Sinead Moloney, for their patience, encouragement and support. My particular thanks go to the Leverhulme Trust as it awarded me the Philip Leverhulme Prize 2010 in order to undertake research for this book.

Of course, all remaining mistakes are my own. I would be grateful for any feedback, whether of a supportive, neutral or critical nature. This book is accompanied by a website (www.comparinglaws.blogspot.com), which provides additional information on the topics of this book.

Mathias Siems
Durham

Abbreviations

AFTA	ASEAN Free Trade Area
AU	African Union
BCBS	Basel Committee on Banking Supervision
BEEPS	Business Environment and Enterprise Performance Survey
BGB	German Civil Code
BGH	German Federal Supreme Court
CA	Court of Appeal of England and Wales
CARICOM	Caribbean Community
CBR	Centre for Business Research (University of Cambridge)
CDF	Comprehensive Development Framework
CEDAW	Convention on the Elimination of Discrimination against Women
Cemac	Monetary and Economic Community of Central Africa
CEPEJ	European Commission for the Efficiency of Justice
CISG	Convention on Contracts for the International Sale of Goods
CJEU	Court of Justice of the EU
CoE	Council of Europe
DCFR	Draft Common Frame of Reference (EU)
EBRD	European Bank for Reconstruction and Development
ECCAS	Economic Community of Central African States
ECCU	Eastern Caribbean Currency Union
ECHR	European Convention on Human Rights
ECtHR	European Court of Human Rights
ECJ	European Court of Justice
ECOWAS	Economic Community of West African States
EFTA	European Free Trade Association
EU	European Union
FATF	Financial Action Task Force
GCC	Gulf Cooperation Council
HDI	Human Development Indicators
ICC	International Chamber of Commerce
ICCt	International Criminal Court

ICJ	International Court of Justice
IFRS	International Financial Reporting Standards
ILO	International Labour Organization
IMF	International Monetary Fund
IOSCO	International Organization of Securities Commissions
IPCC	Intergovernmental Panel on Climate Change
ISDA	International Swap and Derivatives Association
ISO	International Organization for Standardization
LL M	Master of Laws
MERCOSUR	Mercado Común del Sur
NAFTA	North American Free Trade Association
NGO	Non-governmental organisation
OAS	Organization of American States
OECD	Organisation for Economic Development
ODIHR	Office for Democratic Institutions and Human Rights
OHADA	Organisation pour l'Harmonisation en Afrique du Droit des Affaires
OSCE	Organization for Security and Co-operation in Europe
PECL	Principles of European Contract Law
QCA	Qualitative Comparative Analysis
ROSCs	Reports on the Observance of Standards and Codes
SII	Structural Impediment Initiative
SE	Societas Europaea (European Company)
UCC	Uniform Commercial Code
UDHR	Universal Declaration of Human Rights
UN	United Nations
UNASUR	Union of South American Nations
UNCITRAL	UN Commission on International Trade Law
UNCTAD	UN Conference on Trade and Development
UNDEF	United Nations Democracy Fund
UNDP	UN Development Programme
Uemoa	West African Economic and Monetary Union
UNIDROIT	International Institute for the Unification of Private Law
USAID	United States Agency for International Development
WBES	World Business Environment Survey (World Bank)
WBGI	World Bank Governance Indicators
WEF	World Economic Forum
WHO	World Health Organization
WJP	World Justice Project
WTO	World Trade Organization
ZERP	Zentrum für Europäische Rechtspolitik (University of Bremen)

1

Introduction

'Lawyers are professionally parochial. Comparative law is our effort to be cosmopolitan'.[1] This statement may seem exaggerated, but there is also a good deal of truth in it. Most lawyers are almost entirely trained and specialised in the law of their domestic jurisdiction. Thus, as soon as lawyers leave the borders of their own country, they may feel as if they are stranded on a foreign planet. Learning about comparative law aims to address this problem. But where do you start? Which method do you apply? And is it really feasible to learn about all laws of the world?

It is the aim of this introductory chapter to set the scene for thinking and learning about comparative law. It deals with the questions 'why compare laws?' in Section A and 'what belongs to comparative law?' in Section B. The chapter also explains the focus of the present book – as well as its apparent limitations.

A. Why compare laws?

1. How to slide into comparative-law thinking

Becoming interested in comparative law often happens quite naturally. Let us assume that a lawyer from country A has to deal with a tricky legal problem and a particular set of domestic legal rules applicable to this problem. Someone suggests that it may be helpful to consider the experience of the neighbouring country B. After some research, our lawyer finds a similar, but not identical, rule in B's law and starts wondering why there is this slight but distinct difference.

Thus, she feels that she has to examine the background of the domestic and foreign legal rules in more detail. For instance, she may find out that the two countries share a common legal history but that, at some stage, country B had modified its law based on the model of another legal system, country C. She may also have doubts about the relevance of the difference between countries A and B. Yes, the text of the law reads differently, but perhaps courts apply it in a similar way, or there may be extra-legal factors that lead to a similar result. Or,

[1] Merryman 1999: 10. Similar, Lawson 1977: 73 (value of comparative law like 'escaping from prison into the open air'); Hantrais 2009: 9 (for comparative research more generally). For cosmopolitanism and law see also Glenn 2013; Glenn 2009.

perhaps, she may have to go further and examine other parts of B's legal and socio-economic system in order to understand why B's legal rules differ from her own ones.

Comparing both provisions, our lawyer from country A also wonders whether country B's law may not be preferable. But then she hesitates. Is it really possible to say that one country has better legal rules than another one, or could it not be the case that the legal differences just reflect differences between these two societies? And if we really think that country A should follow country B's path, how should this be done? Perhaps it may be feasible if A's courts applied its law in such a way as to make it similar to B's. Or would it be better if A's legislature changed its law accordingly? Or, if we are really confident that B's law is preferable, why not suggest international harmonisation of the law according to B's model?

All these questions immerse our lawyer deep within many topics of comparative law. It can also be seen that a comparative project may start with a hunch and curiosity, but quickly moves into interdisciplinary and policy issues. Moreover, it shows the need to examine more systematically what benefits research in comparative law can have.

2. The purposes of comparative law

Comparative lawyers frequently discuss the objectives of comparative law. Though they often use somehow different classifications,[2] it is most appropriate to distinguish between three main categories: knowledge and understanding, use of comparative law at the domestic level, and use at the international level.

Table 1.1, below, presents these three categories together with further sub-categories, as they will be explained in the following. Moreover, it indicates that all of these categories will re-emerge at different points in the subsequent chapters of this book.

(a) Knowledge and understanding

The view that comparative law has an intrinsic purpose emphasises its role in legal research and education. Knowledge of foreign laws is valuable where these laws are relevant for the domestic legal system – for example, where the domestic law is of a plural legal nature.[3] In other cases, knowledge of foreign laws can make lawyers or law students reflect on their own laws. It may often be something of a shock to learn that features of the law, previously taken for granted, do not exist in other parts of the world. For instance, a continental European lawyer may be astonished to learn that in England they do not have

---

[2] See, e.g., Mousourakis 2006: 7–15; Dannemann 2006: 401–6; Glenn in EE 2012: 65–74; Bogdan 1994: 27–39; Head 2011: 22–5; Örücü 2007: 53–6; Kamba 1974: 490–505; Constantinesco 1972: 331–431. Similar to the three categories here: Lundmark 2012: 12–4; Chodosh 1999: 1067. Most other scholars also highlight a plurality of purposes, but see also ch. 5 at C 1, below.

[3] See ch. 5 at B 4, below.

Table 1.1 The purposes of comparative law in this book

Main category	Sub-categories	Related to themes addressed in chapters of this book			
(a) Knowledge and understanding	Knowing foreign laws	2 A	3	7 C	8 B
	Understanding context	6	11		
	Global concepts of law	2 B	4	10	
(b) Practical use at national level	Legislative comparative law	8	9 B	11 B	
	Judicial comparative law	7 A			
	Advising on foreign law	9 D	10 B		
(c) Practical use at international level	Unification of law	9 A	9 C		
	Other convergence	7 B	9 B	9 D	
	Idealist comparative law	5	10 C		

Codes, whereas an English lawyer may be deeply puzzled by the one-sentence style of French court judgments.[4] So, the lawyer exposed to foreign experiences may develop a deeper, and potentially more critical, perspective of her own law and the choices its legislators and courts have made.

Going beyond mere knowledge of foreign legal rules, comparative law broadens the understanding of how legal rules work in context. This also often happens quite naturally. If a comparative researcher identifies unexpected similarities, she may want to find out whether there are any common historical roots or recent globalising trends of which she had been unaware. And, if there are unexpected differences, she may want to explore the political, cultural and socio-economic reasons that may explain them. It may also be the case that such understanding of the embeddedness of legal rules fosters tolerance towards other societies and legal traditions.

The aspiring comparatist may progress to develop a more general intrinsic interest in the legal systems of the world. This may afford the insight that the Western (or Eastern etc.) idea of law is not universal, as well as affording a more general appreciation of the diversity of legal rules across the world. A comparatist may also develop an understanding of law as a general phenomenon, with individual legal systems existing as mere variations on the same theme. For instance, she may try to identify a common core of legal rules, or may try to develop general concepts of jurisprudence that incorporate ideas from different parts of the world.[5]

(b) Practical use at domestic level

Comparative law can also be a means to diverse ends at the domestic level. A frequent suggestion is that comparative law can be an important aid to

---

[4] For these examples see also ch. 3 at B, below.
[5] For all these points see also ch. 2 at B 2 and ch. 5 at B 1, below.

the legislator. Foreign laws can provide models of how well different sets of legal rules work in addressing a particular problem or in pursuing a particular policy. This suggestion may be driven by the idea of regulatory competition, since law-makers may be keen on attracting firms and investors. But any reform project needs also to consider the limitations of transplanting foreign models, as frequently discussed in the legal and social policy literature.[6]

It is also possible for judges to make use of foreign law. In some instances, conflict of law rules may require them to do so, but in other cases, too, judges may wish to take foreign ideas into account. Such judicial comparative law can aim modestly to inspire judges with alternative ways of approaching a particular problem, but it can also go further, especially if they openly follow a particular foreign model (though a potential problem of such receptiveness may be that the context of the foreign law may be different, and there may also be concerns of national sovereignty).[7]

Furthermore, other practising lawyers (solicitors, barristers, attorneys, advocates etc.) may make use of comparative law. Apart from situations where foreign law is applicable, many international business transactions require a skilful choice between different laws, or how they may be combined. Knowledge and understanding of different approaches to law can therefore be crucial in order to provide appropriate legal advice.

(c) Practical use at international level

At the international or supranational level, legislators may use comparative law when they deal with questions of whether and how unification of the law can be achieved. If the decision is taken to unify a particular field of law, the negotiating states may want to compare existing domestic laws in order to decide whether to choose the lowest common denominator, the most common approach, a compromise solution with a combination of legal rules, the 'best solution' – however this may be defined – or a general solution that comprises the existing models.[8] This solution can then be the basis for an international treaty, a supranational act (such as an EU Directive) or a form of 'soft law'. Alternatively, a comparative analysis may lead to the recommendation not to unify the law, for instance, because different legal cultures are irreconcilable, or because the costs of unification outweigh its benefits.

Other actors may also foster common rules, making use of comparative law. Judges who apply international or supranational law often need to consider the diverse domestic origins of these rules. It is also possible that some judges wish to develop common solutions, even without such international rules. Furthermore, the international business and legal community may develop

---

[6] For law see ch. 8, below. For social policy see Hantrais 2009: 120.

[7] For further details see ch. 7 at A 1, below.

[8] Cf. Pistor 2002: 108 (national model, lowest common demonitor, or synthetic concept); Dannemann 2012: 109–113 (middle ground, going up one level, going down one level, or stepping outside).

similar responses to legal problems, even where the domestic laws stay diverse. Thus, the frequent use of terms and concepts such as 'transnational governance' and 'convergence of legal systems' emphasises that there is more than formal unification to be considered at the international level.[9]

Comparative law is also not only of practical interest for lawyers. As the world is becoming more and more interconnected, the translation of laws, judgments and legal scholarship is of crucial importance. This is a challenging task since legal terminologies are closely related to the underlying legal systems. Thus, legal translation requires not only excellent skill in the languages in question, but also knowledge of comparative law.[10]

Finally, one can have an idealist understanding of the international use of comparative law. The knowledge of foreign law and its underlying cultures and societies can improve international understanding, and, as a result, possibly help to create a peaceful and just world.[11]

B. What belongs to comparative law?

1. Status quo: no fixed canon

According to Harold Gutteridge, a literal interpretation of the term 'comparative law' is impossible since is does not have its own subject-matter, such as contract or family law.[12] This problem is also reflected in the status quo of comparative law. While general books on subjects such as contract or family law are bound to deal with more or less the same topics, the situation in comparative law is potentially confusing. Table 1.2 presents the main topics of seven general comparative law books,[13] published in English.[14] The words 'high', 'medium' and 'low' indicate to what extent these books deal with methodological questions, legal families (such as civil and common law) and specific areas of law.

It can be seen that the focus of these books differs considerably. On the one hand, there are the books by Gutteridge, Örücü and Nelken, and Bogdan that have a strong focus on method (column 1). So, according to these authors,

---

[9] For details see ch. 9, below.

[10] See, e.g., Goddard 2009; Mattila 2006: 16–7. For the role of languages in comparative law see also ch. 2 at A 2 (b), below.

[11] Khan and Kumar 1971: 16–21. Most emphatically Wigmore 1928: viii ('May this volume contribute to a better understanding of other peoples, and thus help toward greater intelligence and mutual toleration in world-affairs!').

[12] Gutteridge 1946: ix.

[13] Not included are books on comparative legal cultures or traditions (e.g. Ehrmann 1976; Glenn 2010a), books on cases and materials (e.g. Mattei et al. 2009; Riesenfeld and Pakter 2001), as well as encyclopaedias and collections of articles.

[14] For general comparative law books published in French see, e.g., Cuniberti 2011; Legrand 2011; Legeais 2008; Fromont 2005; Jauffret-Spinosi and David 2002; Vanderlinden 1995; in German: e.g. Zweigert and Kötz 1996; Constantinesco 1971–1983 (also published in French); in Italian: Varano and Barsotti 2010; Ajani 2006; Gambaro and Sacco 2002 (also published in French); Losano 2000; Mattei and Monateri 1997; Sacco 1990.

Table 1.2 Focus of general comparative law books

	1. Method of comparative law	2. Legal families and traditions	3. Comparing specific areas of law
Gutteridge 1949	medium	medium-low	low
David 1985	low	high	low
Zweigert and Kötz 1998	medium-low	medium	high-medium
de Cruz 2007	medium-low	medium-low	high
Örücü and Nelken 2007	high	low	medium
Bussani and Mattei 2012	medium	medium	medium
Bogdan 2013	medium	medium	low

comparative law is a label for applying a comparative method to legal research, which may also be called 'comparative study of law' or 'comparative legal studies'.[15] On the other hand, David, Zweigert and Kötz, and de Cruz have a more substantive focus (columns 2 and 3). Thus, here, comparative law is regarded as a body of knowledge.[16]

Which approach is preferable? Given the diversity of economic research, it is often said that economics can only be defined as being 'what economists do'.[17] Similarly, comparative law is what comparative lawyers do.[18] Therefore, it is not suggested that one of the options illustrated in Table 1.2 is 'the correct' one. Still, since it is clear that 'nobody can compare everything in the world of laws',[19] a selection had to be made.

2. The 'law' discussed in this book

The main focus of the present book will be on the method of comparative law, not specific legal families or areas of law. That said, these latter topics will not be ignored.

The concept of legal families stems from the view that we can group the legal systems of the world into separate traditions, each with its distinct common features. Such an approach is relevant for comparative law since, if successful, it can elucidate differences and similarities between legal systems. However, the role of legal families has diminished in recent years. Thus, in the present book,

---

[15] Gordley and von Mehren 2006: xvii. See also Hall 1963: 7; Varga 2007: 101 (contrasting the English term with the French term 'droit comparé', meaning 'law that is compared').

[16] For the discussion see de Cruz 2007: 231–2; Nelken 2007a: 12; Constantinesco 1971: 217 ('rechtsvergleichende Methode' oder 'vergleichende Rechtswissenschaft?').

[17] Backhouse et al. 1997.

[18] See also Adams and Bomhoff 2012: 4 ('comparative law as disciplined practice'); Glanert 2012: 69 (on subjective nature of methods, referring to Heidegger).

[19] Frankenberg 1985: 430. Similar Khan and Kumar 1971: 36 ('the total area of what can be described as comparative law is boundless, and everyone planning a course of such description is faced with a threshold problem of selection').

Table 1.3 Overview of main areas of law and legal systems covered in this book

Areas of law	Chapter	Legal systems
Civil procedure,	3 B 2	England, France, Germany, US
litigation and courts	6 B	England, Germany, Japan, Netherlands, US
	7 A 1	England, Germany and others
Contract law	3 B 3	England, France, Germany
	9 C 2, 3	EU harmonisation
Tort law	2 A 5	England, France, Germany, New Zealand, US
Family law	6 A 2 (b)	Christian and Islamic legal traditions
Commercial law	6 C 1	France, Germany, Italy, UK, US, Muslim countries
	9 D 2	International and transnational laws
Company law	7 B 2, C 1	Eastern European legal systems, US and others
	9 B 2	Various (and conceptual)
Criminal law	5 B 2	European countries, US, Muslim countries
	6 C 2	European countries, US and others
Constitutional law	8 B 4	Various, including international human rights
	9 B 2	Various (and conceptual)
	11 B	France, US and others
Customary law, rule of	4 C	China, Latin American and African countries
law and legal culture	5 B 1	England, France
	10 B, C	China, Russia, Afghanistan and others
	11 C	Africa, East Asia and the West

two chapters deal with legal families in detail,[20] but they are not seen as the general 'macro-structure' for the entirety of comparative law.

Comparisons of specific areas of law can be useful and interesting. Yet, a general book on comparative law cannot provide such a comprehensive comparative treatment of all areas of law, and thus it is preferable to leave such detailed studies to specialised monographs, articles and encyclopaedia. It is, however, useful to provide examples to illustrate the use of comparative law in different fields. As Table 1.3 shows, there has also been an attempt to include a good mixture of examples from different parts of the world.

Methodological questions feature prominently in this book. Since comparative law can serve a variety of purposes, it is suggested that a plurality of methods can be used in a fruitful way. However, special emphasis is given to the interdisciplinary dimension of comparative research, as the following explains.

3. The three dimensions of 'comparative law in context'

In the recent literature there are frequent statements urging comparative lawyers to become more interdisciplinary. For instance, according to Mary Ann

---

[20] See ch. 3 and ch. 4, below.

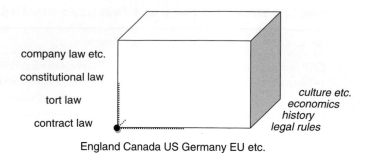

company law etc.

constitutional law

tort law

contract law

culture etc.
economics
history
legal rules

England Canada US Germany EU etc.

Figure 1.1 The three dimensions: areas of law, legal regimes and methods

Glendon and colleagues, 'comparative law is by its very nature an interdisciplinary field'; according to Ugo Mattei, 'sophisticated comparative scholarship can be produced only by interdisciplinary efforts'; and, according to John Reitz, 'since law is but a part of the seamless whole of human culture, there is in principle scarcely any field of study that might not shed some light on the reasons for or significance of similarities and differences among legal systems'.[21]

The relationship between comparative law and interdisciplinary approaches can also be presented in a visual way. Figure 1.1, above, suggests that knowledge about law can be thought of as a three-dimensional space. The *height* refers to areas of law, such as constitutional, company, tort or contract law. The *width* refers to differences between legal regimes. These may be countries, but also supranational regimes such as the EU or rules of transnational law.[22] The *depth* addresses different approaches to legal knowledge. For instance, a lawyer may not only be familiar with the legal rules in her field of expertise, but may also know something about the underlying history, economics and culture of the law.

Many lawyers, both in practice and academia, are primarily interested in one 'dot'. For instance, in Figure 1.1 the 'main dot' and the dotted lines represent an English contract lawyer with a secondary interest in tort and company law, some expertise in Canadian and US contract law, and some knowledge of the history of contract law. This lawyer may then regard everything else as 'too foreign', be it because it refers to a different area of law, a foreign country or an unfamiliar method.

However, it is crucial for a comparatist to appreciate all three dimensions and how they relate to each other. For instance, a cautious researcher may start

---

[21] Glendon et al. 2008: 11; Mattei 1998: 717; Reitz 1998: 627. See also Samuel 2012: 190 (comparatist has 'by definition to be interdisciplinary'); Mousourakis 2006: 39 (interdisciplinary and comprehensive approach); Peters and Schwenke 2000: 832 (full understanding requires a comprehensive and interdisciplinary approach); Twining 2000b: 45 (idea of autonomous disciplines is philosophically dubious); Hall 1963 (on comparative law and social theory).

[22] For the latter see ch. 9 at C and D, below.

with a limited project comparing a specific question of English and Canadian contract law. Yet, in the course of her research she may have no choice but to broaden her investigation: for instance, it may be the case that the topic which is part of contract law in England is dealt with by tort law in Canada. Or, perhaps, the English law on this issue has been influenced by EU law drawing on continental European models and therefore she realises that she needs to study these jurisdictions. And, then, our comparatist may want to explain the differences between the jurisdictions in question which typically requires the consideration of the countries' history, economy, culture etc.

It is not suggested that every other discipline is always relevant. Sometimes it is said that comparative lawyers should regard themselves as social scientists. According to Geoffrey Samuel, it is crucial that comparative lawyers 'work within a spirit of enquiry rather than authority', meaning that they should be social scientists not 'theologians'.[23] Others, such as Pierre Legrand and David Nelken, refer to fields of humanities, such as philosophy, history and literary theory.[24] But how precisely other disciplines are able to contribute to comparative legal research also depends on the actual research question; to quote David Nelken, '(i)t may seem obvious that economics has an affinity with private law, and that political science will be most relevant to the sphere of administrative and constitutional law, whilst psychology has more to offer for family law'.[25]

4. Conclusion: the structure of this book

Comparative law is a 'strange animal'. Thus, it was necessary to explain the aim and scope of the present book in some detail. Based on these considerations, the structure of this book is as follows: Part I deals with 'traditional comparative law'. It critically discusses the main approach of twentieth-century comparative law, in particular universalism and functionalism, and the distinction between legal families. Part II is called 'extending the methods of comparative law'. This part addresses new approaches challenging traditional comparative law, such as critical, socio-legal and numerical comparative law. Part III is on 'global comparative law'. It deals with topics such as legal transplants, convergence of legal systems and the relationship between comparative law and development. Part IV goes further in presenting 'implicit comparative law'. This refers to comparative research in other fields, such as, politics, economics and anthropology that, implicitly, also addresses similarities and differences between legal systems.

As a result, the contextual nature of the book appears in the following form: Part I looks at *past* approaches to comparative law and how these approaches

---

[23] Samuel 2008: 314; 2007: 235.
[24] Legrand 2006b: 371; Nelken 2007a: 16. See also ch. 5, below.   [25] Nelken 2007a: 17.

have been challenged by contextual research. Parts II and III explain how at *present* other disciplines make comparative law richer by using new methods and extending it to new questions. In Part IV it is proposed that *future* comparative law can even go further by integrating the research of other disciplines, even if this is not yet classified as comparative law.

Part I
Traditional Comparative Law

Comparative law has a long history. Sometimes it is said to be as old as law itself,[1] but, in looking for a precise origin, views range, for instance, from Aristotle's comparison of constitutions in the third century BC, to comparisons between Roman, canonical and customary sources in the sixteenth century, to Montesquieu's comparison of political systems in the eighteenth century.[2] More narrowly, the development of comparative law as an academic discipline is somehow clearer, with 1861, 1869 and 1900 offered as possible dates of birth.[3] The background of this development was that the emergence of nation states and the enactment of codes in nineteenth-century Europe led to the initial need for legislative comparative law and, subsequently, to the opportunity of comparisons between these new national laws.[4]

Thus, what is often called 'traditional comparative law' started at the beginning of the twentieth century and has continued to be influential until now, as distinguished from postmodern and critical approaches.[5] Using such a category does not mean that there are no differences within the group of traditional comparative lawyers. Every comparative lawyer is shaped by her background: by, for example, the legal systems she is trained in, or the domestic law of her main field of expertise. Still, there are a number of core themes that are typically seen as belonging to the main substance of traditional comparative law. For example, William Twining speaks about the country, and the Western tradition of micro-comparison; Reza Banakar sees as its central ideas the concept of legal families, harmonisation of laws, and the relationship between law and the state; and Pierre Legrand identifies its 'doxa' with the functional approach by Zweigert and Kötz.[6]

---

[1] Eörsi 1979: 17.   [2] Glenn in EE 2012: 65–6. See also Donahue 2006: 3.

[3] See Gutteridge 1949: 16–7 (publication of Maine's Ancient Law in 1861); Twining 2000b: 36 (foundation of French Society of Comparative Legislation and Maine's appointment to the Oxford Chair of Historical and Comparative Jurisprudence in 1869); Sacco 2000 (first International Congress of Comparative Law held in Paris in 1900).

[4] David 1985: 3; Glenn in EE 2012: 65–6.

[5] See Schieck 2010; Riles 1999: 231; also Kiikeri 2001: 42–4 (traditional, value-based and instrumental comparative reasoning). See also Part II, pr., below.

[6] Twining 2000a: 184; Banakar 2009: 73; Legrand 2005: 632.

This Part critically discusses the main elements of traditional comparative law. It starts with Chapter 2 on the established method of comparative law. Chapter 3 deals with the distinction between civil and common law countries and Chapter 4 turns to the division of the world into legal families more generally. Overall, the aim is to assess the benefits and pitfalls of the traditional approach. It is not the purpose to dismiss it as such but, rather, to show how this approach has evolved and for which functions it remains useful, while also illustrating its limits and how recent scholarship has challenged some of its core assumptions.

2

The comparative legal method

It is one of the aims of this book to challenge traditional comparative law and promote alternative approaches. Yet, to start with, it is useful to discuss the 'comparative legal method' of traditional comparative law in some detail. For this purpose, Section A outlines how, according to traditional comparatists, a comparative legal analysis should be conducted. Section B focuses on two of the most important concepts on which this method is based: functionalism and universalism. A critical analysis follows in Section C, and Section D concludes.

A. The typical structure of a comparative paper

Traditional books and articles on comparative law often provide guidance, or even a blueprint, on how a comparative analysis should be conducted.[1] Most of these guidances are fairly similar, though the precise number of suggested steps depends on how some of those are grouped together. The following distinguishes between four steps. First, a comparative analysis starts with preliminary considerations, deciding on the research question and the choice of legal systems. Second, the comparatist has to describe the laws of these countries. Third, she has to compare them, in particular exploring the reasons for unexpected similarities and differences. Fourth, she should critically evaluate her findings, possibly also making policy recommendations.

1. Preliminary considerations

(a) Possible research questions

Not all comparisons that involve legal questions are part of comparative law. For example, it is not about comparing past laws with current laws or about comparing how different areas of law deal with a particular issue within the

---

[1] E.g. Zweigert and Kötz 1998: 1–47; de Cruz 2007: 242–5; Reitz 1998; Husa 2007; Kamba 1974: 511–2; Örücü 2006a: 37–40; Örücü 2007: 447–9; Constantinesco 1972: 137–8; Dannemann 2006: 406–19.

same country, nor about comparing law with other academic disciplines.[2] Still, this leaves open many possibilities. Thus, one may adopt a wide view and allow anything that could also be a topic for a micro-legal analysis of domestic law.[3] Such an approach is followed by some comparatists who, for instance, suggest that one can start with a question about the structure of the legal system (e.g. prevalence of case law or statutory law), law's institutions and actors (courts, solicitors etc.), different forms of legal reasoning, particular legal rules or concepts, or the court decisions of two or more countries.[4]

A well-known example examining courts is John Dawson's book on *The Oracles of the Law*. It compares, amongst others, the role of the judiciary in England and France. Based on a historical analysis, Dawson finds that in the decentralised court system of England a small group of judges has gradually become the dominant influence for the development of the law. Conversely, in France, a more centralised court structure led to excessive judicial interference and subsequently, as a reaction by the legislature, to its restriction by way of codification.[5]

A problem with such an approach arises if a particular legal system does not possess the institution or rule the comparatist plans to analyse. For example, what shall a researcher do if she wants to compare the commercial courts of two countries but finds out that, in one of them, commercial disputes are predominantly dealt with by non-legal forms of dispute resolutions? Or, what shall she do if she is interested in formal requirements for contracts, but in one legal system there are none?

The answer many comparative lawyers give is that a comparative analysis should not start with a particular legal topic, but with a functional question. For example, in the situations mentioned in the previous paragraph, the comparatist should have asked how commercial disputes are solved, or how the law protects the parties of a contract from unexpected consequences,[6] avoiding any legal terms in the description of this problem. The recommendation is therefore that a real life, socio-economic problem should be the starting point. In the words of Ernst Rabel, 'we compare the solutions produced by one state for a specific factual situation, and then we ask why they were produced and what success they had'.[7] Since such legal functionalism is seen as one of the most

---

[2] See McEvoy 2012: 145–9 (calling these diachronic, internal and hereogeneous comparisons); Zweigert and Kötz 1998: 8. But see also Bogdan 1994: 38 (comparison between French law in the fifteenth century and today may be part of comparative law).

[3] For the distinction between micro-legal and macro-legal analysis, not specifically related to comparative law, see Siems 2008b.

[4] Lundmark 2012: 19–24; Örücü 2007: 447; Graziadei 2003: 100; Merryman 1999: 484; Kamba 1974: 509; Markesinis 2003: 44 (on comparing cases); Bomhoff 2012 (on comparing legal reasoning).

[5] Dawson 1968. For these topics see also ch. 3 at B, below.

[6] Example from Zweigert and Kötz 1998: 34.

[7] As translated in Gerber 2001: 199. See also Markesinis 2003: 35–45 and Markesinis and Fedtke 2009: 37–42 (defending Rabel's Method).

important features of traditional comparative law, it will be discussed in more detail below.[8]

(b) Countries to be examined

The core interest of traditional comparative law is in the laws of countries. Thus, this typically excludes inter- and supranational laws on the one hand, and regional and municipal laws on the other. A number of considerations determine the legal systems a comparatist plans to examine. A fairly obvious point is the availability of primary and secondary resources on these legal systems. Usually, it is good advice to start with primary resources, i.e. legislation and court decisions, published in the original language. This means that preference should be given to countries whose language the comparatist is able to read. Secondary resources, such as academic books and articles, should also be consulted, in particular in legal systems where institutional writers or doctrinal scholarship play an important role.

Another inevitable question is how many legal systems should be included. At least for the purposes of a single paper, traditional comparative lawyers tend to favour a limited number in order to focus on the actual comparison (explained below), since choosing a large number of countries may just lead to parallel country studies.[9] A frequent suggestion is that three may be a good number. Just choosing two countries may overemphasise the contrast between these legal systems, whereas with three the comparatist may be nicely able to show what determines both similarities and differences. For instance, a comparison between English, German and Indian law may be fruitful in showing in which respects the common legal heritage of England and India may be more or less relevant than the shared European features of English and German law. Just choosing two countries can also lead to false results. For example, a US lawyer who compares US and Japanese law may characterise certain differences from his own law as 'typically Japanese'. But, then, many parts of the codified Japanese law are based on German law: thus, adding Germany to the analysis can provide a more accurate assessment.[10]

A difficult question is to assess in advance how the choice of legal systems may influence the results in which the comparatist is interested. Andrew Huxley uses the example that 'while a comparison of chalk with cheese must necessarily highlight the question of edibility, a comparison of chalk with marker pens will focus on legibility'.[11] Thus, at the stage of choosing the legal systems, the comparatist already needs to anticipate what type of differences and similarities she may be able to identify.

---

[8] See B 1, below.

[9] Gutteridge 1949: 74; Hall 1963: 33; Hantrais 2009: 145, 155 (for comparative studies in general).

[10] For these examples see Dannemann 2006: 411 and Nelken 2010: 30. Similarly, for comparative studies in general see Macfarlane 2004: 105.

[11] Huxley 1997: 1924–5.

A related consideration is as to the types of legal systems that should be included in the comparison. Traditional comparative lawyers favour legal systems which are neither too similar nor too different. Often this leads to a comparison between Western common and civil law countries.[12] Conversely, a comparison of two common law countries, say England and Ireland, may be uninteresting since in many respects these legal systems still share the 'common law as a whole'.[13] Traditional comparative lawyers are also hesitant to compare legal systems which are too different since this would lead to comparisons between 'apples and oranges'.[14] Thus, traditionalists typically do not consider non-state law or 'radically different legal systems' from Africa or other parts of the developing world.[15]

Sir Basil Markesinis and Jörg Fedtke make the further suggestion to focus on the major legal systems of the world since 'legal systems enjoy differing degrees of sophistication and richness of material'.[16] This seems to be in line with the mainstream general comparative law books,[17] which, for example, often have large sections on German and French law, but only short ones on smaller jurisdictions such as Luxembourg or Switzerland. Yet, for comparative research on specific topics, such a restriction cannot be regarded as the mainstream view; for instance, in an article on a topic of comparative banking law, Swiss and Luxembourg law may be well be very interesting to compare.

2. The description of laws

(a) Finding the right perspective

Different perspectives may be adopted for describing a foreign legal system. First, the comparatist may analyse it from her own perspective, i.e. from that of her own legal system; second, she could aim to adopt the viewpoint of the other legal system; or, third, she could try to take a neutral stance. Traditional comparatists agree that the first approach is not the right one as we should not impose our own preconceptions on other legal systems.[18] Peter de Cruz illustrates this point as follows:

> Europeans and Americans must be constantly aware, when studying non-Western legal systems and cultures, that they must not approach or appraise these systems from their Western viewpoints or judge them by European or American standards. For example some Western lawyers concluded in the 1970s that China has no legal system because she has no attorneys in the American or European sense, no independent judiciary, no Codes, and, since the Cultural Revolution, no system of legal education. Yet, this is surely to judge a non-Western system by Western

---

[12] For details on common law/civil law see ch. 3, below.   [13] See de Cruz 2007: 232–3.
[14] See also Valcke 2004: 720 (comparison of 'apples and airplanes', though technically possible, entirely fruitless).
[15] See also B 1 (c), below.   [16] Markesinis and Fedtke 2009: 50. See also Markesinis 2003: 50.
[17] See ch. 1 at B 1, above.   [18] Zweigert and Kötz 1998: 35; Bogdan 1994: 41.

standards, rather like the Western visitor who assumed that there was no 'proper' music played in China because he did not see any Western instruments in the Chinese concert hall he visited.[19]

With respect to the other two options, opinion is divided. Sometimes it is said that one should adopt an interior point of view, with the consequence that the comparatist should try to present the legal materials in the same manner as a lawyer of the foreign legal system in question.[20] Others take the view that the functional method provides comparatists with a neutral way of analysing how legal systems address certain socio-economic problems.[21] We will return to this debate at later stages of this book.[22]

(b) To translate or not to translate?

There is a related disagreement on the question of whether or not to translate foreign legal terms. The affirmative view presents this question as a pragmatic one. As it cannot be assumed that everyone reads all of the languages of countries covered in a comparative study, the translation of terms may simply be a necessity in order to make foreign legal concepts and ideas accessible.[23] If it is not straightforward to translate, the comparatist may also create neologism or develop 'a socio-legal Esperanto which abstracts from the language used by members of different cultures'.[24] Further help may be provided from translation studies,[25] multilingual legal systems,[26] and websites such as the EU inter-institutional terminology database.[27]

The counter-view is keen on not misrepresenting foreign law, suggesting to keep the original foreign legal terms.[28] For example, if, in a paper published in English, terms such as 'equity' or 'trust' are used for related concepts in French or German law, this may mislead someone who is not familiar with the conceptual differences between common and civil law countries.[29] An article on appeal proceedings takes a similar position, with the title suggesting that the terms 'cassation', 'revision' and 'appeal' 'should not be translated'.[30] Moreover, as far

---

[19] De Cruz 2007: 223. For law in China see also Ruskola 2003; Peerenboom 2003: 61–3.

[20] Bogdan 1994: 45, 47; Bell 1995: 20 (allow phenonomena to speak for themselves).

[21] Zweigert and Kötz 1998: 10. For further details see B 1 below.

[22] See, e.g., C, below and ch. 5, below.

[23] Örücü 2007: 426; Markesinis and Fedtke 2009: 44 ('Some colleagues . . . cringe at these efforts to anglicise sensibly foreign law. Our own view has always been that if we do not attempt them, we shall never benefit from foreign law nor will foreign lawyers ever see their legal ideas spread further than their national boundaries.').

[24] Nelken 2007a: 124.

[25] See de Groot in EE 2012: 541–2; Husa 2011a: 23; Pozzo 2012: 102–3.

[26] See, e.g., Lemmens 2012: 316; Gambaro 2007; Cao 2007.

[27] Available at http://iate.europa.eu/.   [28] De Cruz 2007: 220; Sacco 1991: 19.

[29] See ch. 3, below. For the distinction between concept and term see Mattila 2006: 108–9; cf. also Pozzo 2012: 94–5.

[30] Geeroms 2002.

as Western scholars deal with non-Western legal systems, using Western-derived legal terms and concepts is even seen as a 'fundamental mistake'.[31]

But it is also possible to try to reconcile these apparently conflicting views. On the one hand, it is clear that questions of translation are related to further differences between the corresponding countries. Thus, in order to understand properly a particular foreign legal term, the comparatist may find it useful to engage with differences between languages by, for example, drawing on research on comparative legal linguistics.[32]

On the other hand, there is the question of how to deal with foreign terms in practice. In a comparative paper, the use of foreign terms may often be a matter of presentation: for instance, the comparatist may simply clarify her translation by way of putting the original term in brackets when it is used for the first time. Teaching comparative law, it can also be useful to mention the original terms before translating them, thus also teaching students a few words of the foreign language in question.[33]

It is also suggested that the reader ought not to be underestimated. For instance, if the French term 'juge' is translated into English as 'judge', no one would assume that this means that the legal position of a French judge is exactly identical to an English one. In this respect the situation is also not different from a comparison between two countries that have the same language: say, a paper on English and US law would use the term 'judge' for both legal systems without meaning to imply that there are no differences between them.

(c) The positive law and beyond

In substance, it seems to be clear that the comparatist has to consider all law relevant for her research question. Of course, legal theorists and philosophers disagree on the precise meaning of the term 'law'. But, then, legal traditions too differ as to what precisely law is. Thus, traditionally, it is recommended that the comparatist not get stuck in philosophical or terminological debates, but be pragmatic, and treat as law that which the people of the legal system in question view as law.[34] This includes statute law, case law and customary law. It is also said that legal systems must be studied in their entirety because, across countries, problems may be addressed by different areas of law. To provide an example, the right of the surviving spouse to share in the division of property may be found in property law, family law or the law of succession.[35]

Getting the positive law of a foreign legal system right can be challenging: to quote Ernst Rabel, 'in their explorations on foreign territory comparatists may come upon natives lying in wait with spears'.[36] In particular, this is the case if

---

[31] Ainsworth 1996: 20 (for Chinese law). See also Ali 2011: 228 (for corresponding views about Islamic law).

[32] Mattila 2006; Galdia 2009. See also Pozzo 2012.

[33] Ali 2011: 221 (for teaching Islamic law to Western students).

[34] Cf. Tamanaha 2000: 313.   [35] Bogdan 1994: 49.

[36] As translated in Zweigert and Kötz 1998: 36.

the study concerns diverse legal systems, because, quoting Stathis Banakas, the comparatist 'studying different laws outside the context of their own culture is like a colour-blind painter: what he paints is foggy shapes and lines only'.[37]

Moreover, even traditional comparatists suggest that, in addition to the positive law, a number of further aspects need to be considered. First, a comparative study should not only describe legal rules but also explain their underlying theories and conceptions as well as scholarly writings.[38] Second, the comparatist has to illuminate the historical, cultural, social and economic context of the law in order to show why particular legal rules exist in a particular place.[39] Third, she has to consider the law in action since, following the functional perspective, it matters whether law is really able to address a particular socio-economic problem. Fourth, in addition, functionalism requires consideration of the fact that societies are juridified to a different extent. Thus, a comparative study also has to consider non-legal forms of social control and dispute resolution.[40]

It seems to be the case that the latter three aspects may get a comparatist deep into interdisciplinary and empirical research. Yet, it is doubtful how far traditional comparative law has moved in this direction. In the first half of the twentieth century, books by John Henry Wigmore[41] included photographs and images, stories of everyday life, biographies and other forms of illustrative presentations in order to visualise and experience legal reality, but mainstream comparative law has not treated his work as serious scholarship.[42] Today, traditional comparatists also express the view that fully engaging in interdisciplinary analysis may just not be attainable as lawyers lack the appropriate training in these disciplines.[43]

A final point a comparatist has to consider is whether she wants to address these three additional aspects in the descriptive section of her comparative paper. On the one hand, this can make sense because the positive law is closely related to its underlying theories, history and context. On the other hand, it is not uncommon to present a comparative analysis as refuting certain myths. In an article by Mark Ramseyer it is even said that:

> comparative law is . . . a bit like a good Hitchcock: Things are rarely what they are perceived to be. The task of comparative law is not merely to describe these widely held perceptions, but to look behind them.[44]

---

[37] Banakas 1993–94: 153.   [38] Husa 2006: 1115.

[39] Bogdan 1994: 43; Zweigert and Kötz 1998: 36; Mousourakis 2006: 49–53.

[40] Zweigert and Kötz 1998: 38; Vogenauer 2006: 872; Bogdan 1994: 54.

[41] Wigmore 1928 (on world's legal systems); Wigmore 1941 (accounts of trial scenes, though without visualisations).

[42] Cf. Riles 2001; Riles 1999; Twining 2000a: 143. See also Wigmore 1941: v ('Reader! this work is not offered to you as a piece of scientific research, but mainly as a book of informational entertainment.').

[43] Lemmens 2012: 311, 323. But see also the research discussed in Part II, below.

[44] Ramseyer 1984–85: 645.

Thus, it can be a useful way of presentation to keep the descriptive part focused on the black letter law, and use everything else for the subsequent comparative analysis, possibly challenging the relevance of the positive law.

3. The comparative analysis

(a) Identifying variation

It is often complained that work called 'comparative law' lacks a proper comparison. According to Linda Hantrais, such work is often 'confined to the presentation of meticulously detailed parallel descriptions of national legal codes and systems'; Pierre Legrand contends that comparatists often 'do not compare; they assemble'; and William Ewald writes that comparative law seems to be 'animated by the Muse Trivia – the same Goddess who inspires stamp collectors, accountants, and the hoarders of baseball statistics'.[45]

Indeed, to do comparative law, and not just 'foreign law', the description of laws has to be followed by the identification of similarities and differences.[46] This should, however, not be done in a pedantic fashion, providing a catalogue of all variations. A frequent approach is to distinguish between formal and functional aspects. The formal dimension addresses the content of legal rules. In addition, it can be interesting to consider further aspects, such as on which sources of law these rules are based, differences in legal style and legal concepts. The functional dimension of the traditional approach asks how the law actually works, in particular whether the legal rules are able to address the socio-legal problem which was the starting point of the comparative study.

Based on this distinction, traditional comparatists often claim that – at least in private law – there may only be formal differences, but that, functionally, legal systems are fairly similar.[47] Thus, traditional comparative law has the tendency to identify that, at a practical level, law is relatively universal. This is, however, very contentious, as discussed later in this chapter.[48]

(b) Explaining variation

The second step of the comparative analysis is to explain the differences and similarities between the legal systems in question.[49] Particular consideration should be given to unexpected results, namely, when relatively similar countries have relatively different laws, and vice versa. In both instances, a wide range of explanatory factors may need to be considered.

---

[45] Hantrais 2009: 35; Legrand 1999: 3; Ewald 1995a: 1961 (and ibid. 1983: 'telephone-book approach'); also Legrand 2005: 707 and Riles 1999: 281 (pure data collection can be left to domestic lawyers).

[46] Kamba 1974: 511–2; Örücü 2007: 447–9; Markesinis and Fedtke 2009: 352.

[47] Zweigert and Kötz 1998: 40.   [48] See B 2 and C, below.

[49] Kamba 1974: 511–2; Örücü 2007: 447–9; Bogdan 1994: 68–77; Khan and Kumar 1971: 2 (the guiding principle for comparative law 'should not be a "what" but a "why"').

To explain differences, a useful approach is to take into account all three major fields of scholarship, i.e. humanities, social and natural sciences. To start with humanities, historical factors may explain the different paths legal systems have taken and how those are reflected in the precise language of the law. The comparatist may also examine the relationship between different legal rules and philosophical, cultural, ethical and religious factors. With respect to social sciences, the comparatist may find that different legal rules reflect different socio-economic factors, for example, the dominant sector of the economy (agriculture, manufacturing, services), the employment rate and the openness towards trade and investment.[50] Politics is also likely to matter because legal rules may be related to differences in law-making procedures and political economy. Regarding natural sciences, some legal rules may be influenced by the geography and the climate of the countries in question, whereas ethnic differences may only play a role in rare cases.[51]

Two further explanations are sometimes suggested but it is preferable to avoid them. First, in the nineteenth century, Sir Henry Maine and other comparatists took the view that legal systems went through a natural process of legal evolution: in primitive societies it was based on ad hoc decisions of the sovereign, which was followed by the evolution of customary law, and finally progressive societies developed advanced and rational forms of law.[52] Yet, today, such 'comparative historical reconstruction'[53] is not regarded as acceptable as it marginalises traditional legal systems, and has an implicit ethnocentric and (neo-)colonial bias.[54] Second, the concept of legal families is still popular today, and attempts are made to use it to explain legal differences. For instance, it has been said that '(l)egal reasoning in the UK differs fundamentally, at least in theory, from legal reasoning in France or Germany, because the UK (with, to a certain extent, an exception for Scotland) belongs to the common law family'.[55] Such a statement is, however, tautological, because whether a country belongs to a particular legal family is determined by its way of legal thinking;[56] thus, it cannot be at the same time a factor explaining such differences.

With respect to legal similarities, many of the same factors play a role. For instance, parallels in history, culture, society, politics and geography may all show why two countries have similar legal rules. An interesting point of discussion is whether legal similarity is contingent on a 'genealogical' (or filial) relationship between legal systems.[57] For instance, a frequent topic of

---

[50] But note that it is often difficult to show a causal relationship; see ch. 6 at C and ch. 11 at B 3, below.

[51] A possible example may be a comparative study into the law relating to a certain disease whose prevalence differs between ethnic groups (e.g. skin cancer). But see also ch. 4 at B 2 (for past justifications of legal families).

[52] Maine 1861. See also ch. 10 at A, below.   [53] Frankenberg 1985: 427.

[54] Riles 1999: 228; Menski 2006: 88; Bennett 2006: 652.   [55] Hage in EE 2012: 533.

[56] See ch. 3 at B, ch. 4 at B, below.   [57] Cf. Samuel 2009: 41.

comparative law is the idea of 'legal transplants', which have spread from some jurisdictions to the rest of the world.[58] But such historical links may well have weakened. By contrast, in today's world it is often a matter of institutional design that determines whether countries have similar rules: for example, the fact that they belong to the same regional organisation, such as the EU.[59] Moreover, a functional view assumes that the actual result of legal rules is often similar across countries, even where there is no apparent relationship between them. Thus, in this view, a comparative analysis may uncover this 'natural' universalism of the law.[60]

4. Critical policy evaluation

(a) Should this be part of comparative analysis?

The first chapter of this book explained that there can be various reasons to do comparative law.[61] As one of them is to get a better understanding of the legal world, comparative lawyers with a core interest in this reason may not be too keen on engaging in policy evaluations. But, as explained, help for national and international law-makers is frequently also seen as one of the purposes of comparative law. So, in principle, some policy evaluation may be provided: but how far should the comparatist go?

Peter de Cruz expresses some doubts, as 'the comparatist is not seeking to be judgmental about legal systems in the sense of whether he believes them to be "better" or "worse" than any other given system'. But, then, de Cruz also adds that it is acceptable to evaluate 'the efficacy of a given solution or approach to a legal problem in terms of that particular jurisdiction's cultural, economic, political and legal background'.[62] Thus, overall, his answer is a cautious and limited 'yes', similar to other comparative lawyers.[63]

Other comparatists are even more willing to engage in applied comparative law.[64] For example, Konrad Zweigert and Hein Kötz hold 'that the comparatist is in the best position to follow his comparative researches with a critical evaluation', and add that '[i]f he does not, no one else will do it'.[65] It is not a coincidence that such a positive view is taken by proponents of a functional perspective of comparative law, since this approach tends to emphasise the

---

[58] See ch. 8, below.
[59] Lalenis et al. 2002: 49 (common institutional design vs. common descent).
[60] See B, below.   [61] See ch. 1 at A 2, above.   [62] De Cruz 2007: 224.
[63] Bogdan 1994: 78–9; Örücü 2007: 450; Constantinesco 1972: 323–5.
[64] Already Wigmore 1928: 1120 ('comparative nomothetics'); Gutteridge 1949: 9. See also Finnegan 2006: 102–3 (for law and development); Pardolesi and Granieri 2012 (aim of comparative law to devise norms); Bellantuono 2012 (proposing a 'comparative legal diagnostics'); Nelken 2010: 5, 11–18 (for work on comparative criminal justice that has a 'normative agenda').
[65] Zweigert and Kötz 1998: 47. Similar Grossfeld 1990: 4 ('making a pile of bricks and then leaving them unused', citing Julius Binder).

technical and rational nature of the law in order to fulfil certain socio-economic purposes.

(b) Possible recommendations

If we accept that policy evaluations are possible, the first and most cautious step is to use the comparative analysis for a critical evaluation of one's own law. A good example is a book by Sir Basil Markesinis and colleagues on the tortious liability of statutory bodies: taking five English cases on this topic, the authors discuss how the cases would be solved under French and German law, which is then followed by a critique of the English approach.[66]

More generally, a comparative analysis can be used to treat the law of a foreign country as a test case of what may happen if the domestic law were changed accordingly.[67] Thus, in principle, it is possible that the comparatist may be able to suggest law reform in order to improve the fairness or efficiency of the law. However, foreign models will not always be suitable, because they may only work in the socio-economic context of the other legal system. To illustrate this point, Michael Bogdan uses the example of a law-maker who is keen on slowing down population growth. Policy options may be to introduce unrestricted abortion, to withdraw subsidies to families with more than two children, or to raise the minimum age of marriage. But, then, not all of these legal tools may be effective: for instance, raising the minimum age does not work if premarital relationships are common and accepted.[68] Moreover, even if a particular tool is indeed the most effective one in achieving a particular result, the foreign model may be rejected since the means of achieving this result may be seen as unacceptable.[69]

In principle, the same approach could be applied in order to offer advice on possible reform of the foreign legal system. Models from other countries may be used, taking into account differences in context. The comparative lawyer is, however, well advised to think twice before suggesting that a foreign country should follow the comparatist's own law. It is not unlikely that she will be accused of applying her own values in considering what is best for others,[70] an accusation often made in the context of lawyers (and economists) urging legal improvements in developing countries.[71]

A further type of recommendation would be to unify the law. This raises a number of questions, such as, do the benefits of unification outweigh its costs, which model should be chosen, and how should the unification be implemented (by formal harmonisation or soft law)? These questions will be addressed later in this book.[72]

---

[66] Markesinis et al. 1999.   [67] Zweigert and Kötz 1998: 15.   [68] Bogdan 1994: 80–1.
[69] See Nelken 2010: 22 (in the context of comparative criminal justice). See also the discussion about legal transplants in ch. 8, below.
[70] Bogdan 1994: 79.   [71] For details see ch. 10, below   [72] See ch. 9 and ch. 11, below.

5. An example from comparative tort law

This section illustrates the traditional comparative method by way of an example, based on Zweigert and Kötz' chapter on strict liability.[73] Zweigert and Kötz' approach is similar to the one outlined in this part, though they do not slavishly follow the four-step procedure. The starting point is the social problem that a victim has suffered damages, but that it is impossible to show that this has been the result of someone else's fault. The main examples are traffic or industrial accidents. Over the last two centuries, this problem has become more severe since technological progress had the side effect of increasing the risks of such damages. As all of these incidents can occur across countries, such a functional starting point is seen as rewarding in comparative tort law.[74]

The descriptive sections of Zweigert and Kötz deal with German, French, English and US law in detail, with shorter sections on Austria, Switzerland and Italy. Manufacturer liability is addressed in a separate part, starting with US law and then dealing with the way it influenced the EU Directive on this topic. The style of this descriptive phase is that of a diligent mainstream comparative analysis: the text examines the statutory and case law, and it refers to secondary documents published in the native languages of all of the four main jurisdictions. Foreign terms are usually translated, but occasionally the original terms are added in brackets.

In substance, the main findings are as follows: over time, in Germany, a number of special statutes on strict liability have been enacted for certain types of accidents, though these statutes often provide for a *force majeure* exception and limit the amount of damages payable. German courts have shown reluctance to go beyond these pieces of legislation. The French development was distinctly different: in 1930, the Cour de Cassation decided, in the case of *Jand'heur*,[75] that a vague general provision of the French Civil Code (art. 1384) can be interpreted as providing for strict liability. Thus, there has been less need for special statutes.[76] In England and the United States, case law has also played an important role. In 1868 the House of Lords held in *Rylands* v. *Fletcher* that someone was strictly liable for damage caused by the escape of a thing from his or her land.[77] There have been some extensions of this principle, though English courts have been more reluctant to generalise *Fletcher* than US courts,[78] and legislation has been enacted for some cases, such as traffic accidents.

Zweigert and Kötz provide a few, but not many, comments explaining the differences between the legal systems. For instance, they note that the relative importance of strict liability in the US may be related to procedural reasons

---

[73] Zweigert and Kötz 1998: 646–84. See also Faure in EE 2012: 1–20; Reimann 2003 (on liability for defective products).

[74] See generally van Boom 2012: 18.

[75] Chambres Réunies of the Cour de Cassation, 13 February 1930, S 1930, I 121.

[76] But see also Faure in EE 2012: 9 (for the no-fault accident compensation system in France).

[77] *Rylands* v. *Fletcher* [1868] UKHL 1, (1868) LR 3 HL 330.   [78] See also Wagner 2006: 1032.

fostering liability claims (jury trial, class actions, lawyers' fees).[79] Furthermore, as is not untypical for traditional comparative law, Zweigert and Kötz find that all of the legal systems have seen a similar development of introducing and extending strict liability. Thus, we have an example of functional equivalence, of legal systems using different tools to achieve a similar result.

The final section of Zweigert and Kötz' chapter critically evaluates the legal systems. Surprisingly, the innovative law of New Zealand, which had not been discussed earlier, is introduced here. This illustrates the problem with a focus on major jurisdictions.[80] New Zealand's law on accidents is interesting because, in 1974, it decided to shift from tort law to public compensation: almost all personal injury claims are now compensated by a social security scheme with private actions being barred from courts.[81] Zweigert and Kötz are sceptical about such an approach, since tort law also has to fulfil an important deterrence function. This point could have invited a comparative treatment of deterrence by way of administrative or criminal sanctions,[82] yet Zweigert and Kötz are mainly interested in the social problem of compensating the victim. There are also no references to interdisciplinary or empirical research, such as the economics of tort law.[83] Since Zweigert and Kötz' book was written two decades ago, no discussion was provided regarding whether and how European harmonisation of tort law could proceed.[84]

B. Functionalism and universalism in particular

Functionalism and universalism are two of the core elements of traditional comparative law.[85] For this reason, the following deals with these concepts in more detail, in particular their origins and operation. A discussion of the 'Common Core project' will provide a practical illustration.

1. Functionalism: origins, use and consequences

(a) The attractiveness of functionalism elsewhere

In sociology and anthropology, the main discussion about functionalism took place in the 1940s to 1960s. For instance, Talcott Parsons suggested that the balance of social systems depended on the way they satisfied certain needs.[86] Walter Goldschmidt's comparative functionalism took a similar starting point – the social needs of societies – but in addition he also claimed that the institutions addressing these needs were fairly similar across societies.[87] Functionalism has

---

[79] On these points see also ch. 3 B 2, C 2, below. Faure in EE 2012: 7 also suggests that this could compensate for less developed provision of social security in the US.

[80] See 1 (b), above.   [81] For a recent overview see Struck 2008.   [82] See, e.g., Whittaker 2005.

[83] For empirical data see, e.g., Faure in EE 2012: 13–4; Reimann 2003: 803–6. For a law and economics perspective see, e.g., Shavell 1987.

[84] For this point see, e.g., van Dam 2013: 126–64.

[85] As already indicated at A 1 (a) and 3, above.

[86] Parsons 1951. See also Husa 2003: 431; Husa 2013: 7–8 .   [87] Goldschmidt 1966.

not been without its critics and it has gradually made way for cultural and hermeneutic approaches.[88] Yet, even today some books and articles on comparative methods appreciate the potential benefits of functionalist approaches. For instance, the main attractiveness of the concept of functional equivalence is said to lie in the fact that dissimilar units of analysis can be grouped into meaningful categories.[89] More specifically, functionalism may be of help for the analysis of non-Western societies, since it may be shown that informal structures within these societies fulfil functions equivalent to the state in the Western world.[90]

In legal research, functionalist approaches have also frequently been suggested. Legal historians who study ancient legal doctrines and institutions, seemingly obscure today, may want to examine the function that these doctrines or institutions used to fulfil.[91] Private international law often requires the characterisation of a foreign legal doctrine, which may make it necessary to identify a functional equivalent in domestic law.[92] Legal sociologists are said to be interested in the way legal rules 'function' in the real world.[93] And legal translators may try to identify which legal institution of the target language has the same function as the origin one.[94]

(b) The popularity of functionalism in comparative law

While some comparative lawyers have identified various kinds of functionalism,[95] others regard it more pragmatically as a 'rule-of-thumb'.[96] In the following, not all nuances of the discussion can be explored. There is also wide agreement as to the core element of functional comparative law: namely, that a socio-economic problem should be the starting point of a comparative analysis.[97] The main advantage of such an approach is that it provides the necessary link between the different rules that legal systems tend to employ. Thus, the shared purpose of these rules is the common denominator ('tertium comparationis') which allows comparability of these legal systems.[98] Moreover, this functional method is regarded as preferable to a strong positivist approach, which would simply juxtapose different legal rules and come to the conclusion that 'these legal systems differ because they were enacted by different States'.[99] In addition, functionalism is said to counter the tendency to assume that foreign legal systems must have the same type of rules as one's own country.[100]

In the last two decades the functional method has also received support from law and economics scholars. Here, one can start with the way different legal systems deal with a particular problem and then compare these approaches in terms of economic efficiency. For example, consider the differing approaches

---

[88] See Michaels 2006: 354.   [89] Hantrais 2009: 77.   [90] See Macfarlane 2004: 98.
[91] Gerber 2001: 192.   [92] Muir Watt in EE 2012: 703–4.
[93] Zweigert and Kötz 1998: 45. For socio-legal comparative law see ch. 6, below.
[94] Husa 2011a: 223–4; Mattila 2006: 265–7.   [95] Michaels 2006; Örücü 2004a.
[96] Husa 2013: 17. See also Husa 2011c (functionalism as facilitating analogies).
[97] See already A 1 (a), above.   [98] Bogdan 1994: 58–9; Brandt 2007: 409.
[99] Valcke 2004: 730–1.   [100] Örücü in EE 2012: 560.

of English and French law to the purchase of a stolen good by a bona fide purchaser.[101] English law protects the original owner of the stolen good and French law the bona fide purchaser. In order to determine the economic effect of the different laws, one has to compare the costs generated by taking care of the good, which matters for French law, with the costs for investigations of the ownership of the title, which matters for English law. Since, typically, it is more expensive to investigate a foreign title than to take care of one's own property, it may be concluded that the French solution is more efficient than the English one.

(c) Limitations set by functionalism

Functionalism, as understood by most comparative lawyers, requires comparability. So, in general terms, the first limitation is that 'incomparables cannot be usefully compared and in law the only things which are comparable are those which fulfil the same function'.[102] Thus, functionalism can even exclude a comparison of fairly similar rules, namely if in the countries in question they fulfil different functions.

Second, certain legal systems may need to be excluded from a comparative analysis. It is frequently said that comparisons must be between alikes, i.e. legal systems must be in the same stage of legal, political and economic development.[103] Thus, traditional comparative lawyers often only compare the laws of Western countries. This is seen as having the advantage of controlling for the stage of development since it makes it easier to explore the remaining differences amongst a baseline of similarity in terms of the countries' history, society, economy and ideology.[104]

Accordingly, political differences may make some comparisons fruitless. For instance, it may not be possible to come up with a functional research question that would compare the antitrust law of market economies with something similar in the few remaining socialist legal systems.[105] It is also frequently said that it may usually not be fruitful to compare Western legal systems with 'radically different legal cultures', in particular from the developing world, perhaps with the exception of some technical legal rules, such as the law related to traffic accidents.[106] For instance, an English comparatist interested in building societies would not want to look at the Afghan law on this matter since, presumably, 'Afghanistan does not practice anything like the English mode of buying houses

---

[101] For this example see Ogus 2006: 45–7. But note that in some cases the bona fide purchaser may be protected under English law, see Smith 2013: 415. For further examples see Adams 1995 (on cost allocation and role of judges); Mattei 1997a: 138 (on how legal systems deal with problem of building on someone else's land).

[102] Zweigert and Kötz 1998: 34.   [103] De Cruz 2007: 226–7; Sacco 1991: 6; Gutteridge 1949: 73.

[104] Cf. Smelser 1976: 66 (on Durkheim and Mill's method of difference); Dannemann 2006: 411; Van Hoecke and Warrington 1998: 533 (specifically for a comparison of European countries).

[105] Sacco 1991: 6; Bogdan 1994: 62–4 (differentiating between political goal and function).

[106] Cf. Hall 1963: 102–3; Riles 1999: 244; Smelser 1976: 66 (citing Durkheim: 'if one includes all sorts of societies and civilisations one ends up with tumultuous and summary comparisons').

by instalments'.[107] And Sir Basil Markesinis and Jörg Fedtke even go as far as saying that the laws of less developed systems are 'more appropriately left to anthropologists and sociologists rather than to lawyers proper'.[108]

Third, certain areas of law are seen as less suitable for a comparative analysis than others because they are heavily influenced by distinct cultural values and socio-political peculiarities.[109] On the one hand, contract and tort law are regarded as good areas for comparative research since the real-world problems are fairly similar across countries. On the other hand, the traditional majority view has its doubts about comparative family and constitutional law. Family law is seen as closely related to 'sentiments and traditions', 'power structures', 'psychological influences' and 'moral considerations' which are often specific to particular nations.[110] Thus, the cultural bases of family law may be too diverse to engage in an actual comparison, going beyond juxtaposition of similarities and differences.[111] In the mid-twentieth century, it was considered that constitutional law suffered from a similar problem since political structures and values were just too different, thus limiting the usefulness of a functional approach.[112] And, even for today's Western democratic societies, it is said that a comparative constitutional analysis assumes a shared understanding of political, social and economic functions of the state that cannot be taken for granted.[113]

However, some comparatists do provide functional examples from these areas of law. For instance, in family law a functional question would be how to help an impoverished spouse after the termination of marriage: alimony, family support or state security?[114] And in constitutional law the question about the way human rights are protected can be seen as a functional one.[115] But the same author of this example also indicates that the 'mixture of institutions and principles' by which the separation of powers, the rule of law, and democracy are pursued illustrates the limits of a functional comparison on those questions.[116]

2. Comparative law's interest in finding commonalities

(a) Parallels in philosophy and other fields

The idea that certain laws and legal concepts are common to all human beings has been a frequent topic of philosophy and jurisprudence.[117] The Aristotelian

---

[107] Lawson 1977: 65.   [108] Markesinis and Fedtke 2009: 46.

[109] Gutteridge 1949: 32, 73 and the following footnotes.

[110] Citations in Bradley in EE 2006: 263. See also Bradley in EE 2012: 315–7.

[111] See Bradley in EE 2006: 259; Krause 2006: 1101, 1110.   [112] Gutteridge 1949: 29.

[113] Teitel 2004: 2576, 2581. See also Tushnet 2006a: 1230; Schweber in Kritzer 2002: 353–6.

[114] Örücü 2006a: 33. See also the critical discussion of diverse methods in comparative family law in Nicola 2010.

[115] Saunders 2009: 13 (with possible answers: written constitutional law, incorporation of international human rights norms or unwritten rules). For functionalism in constitutional law see also Jackson 2012: 62–6.

[116] Saunders 2006: 123.

[117] For the following see, e.g., Gordley 2003; Menski 2006: 132–47; Goldman 2008: 12; Schrage and Heutger in EE 2012: 509; Peters and Schwenke 2000: 803; Gutteridge 1949: 2; David 1985: 2. See also ch. 5 at B 1, below.

tradition of general jurisprudence aims to identify universal principles of natural law, and Christians developed the idea of a universal divine law. Since the enlightenment, such an endeavour has also been driven by a humanist desire to identify eternal principles of justice. More recently, other perspectives have been put forward to support the idea of universal principles of law. For instance, these principles can be identified by way of rational reasoning or by way of showing a universal organic evolution of the law.

The question about a universal law is an obvious point of interest for comparative lawyers. In addition, comparatists have taken notice of claims about the universality of other phenomena. For example, Yoshiyuki Noda considered Carl Jung's concept of psychological archetypes. According to Jung, all human beings are shaped by these archetypes. Noda advances the idea that there may be something similar in law: an unconscious shared legal mentality, which he calls 'protodroit'.[118] Similarly, Vivian Grosswald Curran highlights the impact of Johann Wolfgang von Goethe's vision of a single humanity of European thought, in particular the search for universal, unifying principles, which Goethe called 'Urphänomene'.[119] In the context of legal translation, Curran also refers to Noam Chomsky's controversial idea of a universal grammar. Chomsky challenges the conventional view that all languages are unique; rather he takes it that all languages share deep structures, making it possible to identify universal rules of human grammar.[120]

(b) Universalism and comparative law

Legal universalism may be regarded as a problem for comparative law since complete uniformity would make comparisons obsolete. Yet, in reality, if one goes beyond an extreme naturalist conception of the law,[121] it is clear that legal rules are not completely uniform across the world. Thus, comparative lawyers have sought to establish how universalist ideas and comparative law can be linked.

An initial suggestion may be to identify how far commonalities of legal rules confirm or rebut universalism.[122] The likely result of such an approach would be a rebuttal of universal legal rules since even the laws of fairly similar countries often differ in at least some details. The response of comparative lawyers has been that functional uniformity may be more important than the precise formal rules. Thus, functionalism and universalism are seen as complementing each other.[123] Often traditional comparative law also has the explicit aim of identifying functionally equivalent legal rules, i.e. that 'we must

---

[118] Noda 1975. See also Bogdan 1994: 97.

[119] Curran 1998a: 72. See also Markesinis 2009 (for Goethe's aspiration to create a 'world literature').

[120] Curran 2006: 679–80, 685. More generally on universality in language and grammar see Berry et al. 2011: 195–9.

[121] Term by Valcke 2004: 721.

[122] See Clark 2012: 12; Esquirol 2001: 219; Peters and Schwenke 2000: 803; Banakas 1993–94: 116.

[123] See Michaels 2006: 345; Graziadei 2003: 109.

try to overcome obstacles of terminology and classification in order to show that foreign law is not very different from ours but only appears to be so'.[124]

Going even further, some comparatists suggest that, empirically, similar practical problems lead to similar results across the world. The most well-known formulation of this idea is by Zweigert and Kötz:

> if we leave aside the topics which are heavily impressed by moral views or values, mainly to be found in family law and in the law of succession, and concentrate on those parts of private law which are relatively 'unpolitical' we find that as a general rule developed nations answer the needs of legal business in the same or in a very similar way. Indeed it almost amounts to a '*praesumptio similitudinis*', a presumption that the practical results are similar.[125]

It should be noted this statement is only made for developed countries. In particular, traditional comparative law is often only interested in a comparison between developed common and civil law countries. Here, differences between common and civil law are said 'to be found rather in form than in substance'.[126] Thus, as the *praesumptio similitudinis* indicates, the results are often equivalent.

The question remains why this presumption is valid. Possibly, it matters that all law-makers have a similar aim, namely, to increase the wealth of their countries.[127] Furthermore, the tendency of traditional comparative law towards uniformity has been the subject of a more psychological interpretation. After the Second World War, comparative law was dominated by continental Europeans and Jewish emigrants to the US, and it is said that both of these groups may have had the understandable tendency to emphasise the commonalities of people from different countries, races and religions.[128]

However, it can also be noted that the search for commonalities was already a topic of earlier comparatists. John Henry Wigmore's comparative research of the first part of the twentieth century has been called a 'discovery of endless examples of universal legal ideas'.[129] The tendency towards uniformity was also apparent at the first International Congress of Comparative Law in 1900. Statements by Raymond Saleilles and Édouard Lambert, the two leading French comparatists of that time, illustrate this point. Saleilles called on comparative law to 'ascertain the principles which are common to all civilised systems of law'.[130] Lambert took a similar, though geographically more narrow, view in suggesting that the laws

---

[124] Markesinis 1993: 443. Similarly Ehrmann 1976: 11.

[125] Zweigert and Kötz 1998: 40. Similarly Merryman 1999: 9 (on civil and common law: 'as a rule one can expect the two groups of legal systems to produce similar results in like cases'); Nottage 2010 (two paths leading to the same goal).

[126] Goff 1997: 746. For details of the common/civil law divide see ch. 3, below.

[127] Faust 2006: 846.

[128] Curran 1998a: 68; Curran 1998b: 666. But see also Markesinis 2000: 45 (for the émigrés to England: 'temptation to present themselves as being more English than the English').

[129] Riles 2001: 108, 126. On Wigmore see also A 2 (c), above.

[130] Saleilles 1900: 397 ('droit commun de l'humanité civilisée') as translated in Gutteridge 1949: 5. See also Jamin 2002; Zweigert and Kötz 1998: 3; Hall 1963: 17, 44.

of continental European countries should converge, since differences were not attributable to the political, moral or social qualities of the different countries, but merely to historical coincidences or to temporary circumstances.[131] Thus, both of these pleas anticipate the approach of twentieth-century mainstream comparative law: a focus on Western countries, a functional perspective, and a call for unification of the law. It is also interesting to see that Saleilles directed his statement more to academics, whereas Lambert referred to the need for legislative convergence, reflecting the frequent view that comparative law should not shy away from making policy recommendations.[132]

3. The example of the Common Core project

According to David Gerber '[t]he value and importance of the Common Core project may well place it among the defining achievements in the history of comparative law'.[133] In the context of this book, this project is also a good example of functionalism, universalism and mainstream comparative law.

The term 'common core' originates from a project organised by Rudolf Schlesinger at Cornell University, dealing with the formation of contract from a comparative perspective.[134] The main approach was as follows. A working paper asked country experts how their legal systems would solve a list of factual problems. These answers were used to produce a general report showing emerging themes of agreement (the 'common core'), and the subsequent parts of the two-volume book reported details of the legal systems, while not producing the initial working paper.

In the mid-1990s this approach was picked up by European academics interested in comparative contract, tort and property law. Due to the location of the annual meetings this endeavour was initially called Trento project, then Turin project and today it is usually referred to as the Common Core project. A number of comparative books deriving from this project have been published.[135] In addition, the Common Core website and further books provide explanations and reflections on the method used.[136]

The structure of the Common Core books is similar to the traditional approach to comparative law. As to the preliminary points, the Common Core follows the recommendation to start with a social problem by way of using hypothetical cases. It mainly covers European legal systems. Only in the introductory and concluding chapters do some of the books include information on

---

[131] Lambert 1905 (his contribution to the congress of 1900). See also Lambert 1903.
[132] See A 3, above.   [133] Gerber 2004: 1001.
[134] Schlesinger 1968. See also Mattei et al. 2009: 98–100; Örücü 2007: 435–6.
[135] List at www.cambridge.org/aus/series/sSeries.asp?code=CCEP. See also Siems and Cabrelli 2013 (applying a similar method to comparative company law).
[136] See www.common-core.org/ at the main heading 'The Project' (sub-headings 'The Initial Project', 'Approach', 'Answering Questionnaires'). See also Bussani and Mattei 2007; Bussani and Mattei 2002; Bussani and Mattei 2000.

the laws of other countries, most often the United States.[137] The restriction to Western, in particular to European, countries is seen as having the benefit of assuming a common conception of law, society, politics and religion.[138] This mirrors the limitations set by functionalism in terms of legal systems and areas of law.

The main parts of the books present the solutions to the hypothetical cases, the country experts having been asked to describe how the cases would be solved in their legal system. In addition, the organisers of the Common Core project explain that they are not only interested in the actual results, but also (i) how, in a particular legal system, different elements of statutory law, case law, and scholarly writings interact with and potentially contradict each other, and (ii) how policy considerations, values, economic and social factors, and the structure of the legal process may affect the solution to the case.[139] In some books of the Common Core project, these two elements appear under separate headings within the country solutions.[140] Yet, most studies are not fundamentally different from the paradigms of the traditional comparative method.[141] According to the traditional method, comparatists should also analyse different sources of law.[142] Most case solutions of the Common Core project also focus on the positive law without references to non-legal factors or empirical research on how problems are actually solved. Thus, the overall approach of the Common Core is fairly 'legal' and 'practical', evident also in the publisher's advertisement that it is a series 'to assist lawyers in the journey beyond their own locality'.[143]

Short chapter conclusions and separate chapters in the final parts of the books compare the countries' solutions. This is done in the spirit of functionalism and universalism. The title 'Common Core' already refers to this aim. Moreover, the project website indicates that the project seeks to unearth that which is already common in the EU Member States, and that 'common core research is a very promising hunt for analogies hidden by formal differences'.[144]

A cautious approach is followed with respect to policy recommendations. In contrast to other projects, no attempt is made to offer suggestions for a future European Civil Code.[145] Yet, it is again useful to consult the project website, which states that 'this kind of research should be very useful for and deserve more attention from official institutions that are encharged to draft European legislation' and that their 'task is part of building a common European legal

---

[137] E.g. Möllers and Heinemann 2008: 67–88; Brüggemeier et al. 2010: 38–72.

[138] Website, above note 136 (sub-heading 'The Initial Project').

[139] Website, above note 136 (sub-headings 'Approach' and 'Answering Questionnaires'). These are called descriptive and metalegal formants. On legal formants see also C 1, below.

[140] E.g. Brüggemeier et al. 2010.

[141] For a similar assessment see Frankenberg 2006a. See also Ewald 1995a: 1981 (on the Cornell project).

[142] See A 2 (c), above.   [143] See www.cambridge.org/aus/series/sSeries.asp?code=CCEP.

[144] Website, above note 136 (sub-headings 'The Initial Project' and 'Approach'). See also Mattei 1997a: 144; Mattei et al. 2009: 98–100.

[145] See ch. 9 at C 2, below.

culture'.[146] So, a not-so-hidden agenda is clearly part of the Common Core project.

C. Critical analysis

Not long ago it was said that the literature contained few serious discussions about the methodology of comparative law.[147] Yet, this has changed. The traditional method of comparative law has frequently been challenged and alternative approaches have been suggested. The remainder of this chapter addresses this criticism; the alternatives follow in Part II of this book.[148]

1. The simplistic approach

A first general point of criticism challenges the very idea of a blueprint.[149] Since comparative law serves various purposes, a plurality of methods may be used in a fruitful way.[150] It has also been said that the best approach may depend on, amongst others, the legal systems in question, the subjective abilities of the researcher and the affordability of the costs.[151]

A riposte may be that the restrictions set by the traditional method mean that, under these restrictions (e.g. start with a functional question, focus on Western legal systems), the blueprint does usually work. But, then, another line of criticism can be raised, namely, that the traditionalists miss interesting topics. For example, if we accept functionalism, is it not unsatisfactory that we cannot compare certain countries and areas of law? And is it really the ideal starting point only to allow functional questions, and not, for instance, a comparison of legal institutions, values, categories, concepts, ways of reasoning or languages?[152] In particular, it may be suggested that these latter factors can be the 'tertium comparationis' that links diverse legal systems.

It can also be useful to have a theoretical chapter preceding the actual comparative analysis. For example, an economic-oriented comparative lawyer may first develop an efficient model, and then compare how and why actual legal systems differ from it.[153] Such an approach is also suggested in other comparative studies: for example, in comparative politics it is said that concepts should precede and guide the collection of the necessary materials.[154]

---

[146] Website, above note 136 (sub-headings 'The Initial Project' and 'Approach').

[147] Merryman 1999: 3.

[148] This includes 'critical comparative law' which goes beyond merely being critical about the traditional comparative method (discussed here).

[149] See A pr., above.

[150] Siems 2005: 537; Husa 2011b: 127; Husa 2007; Husa 2003: 425. For the purposes of comparative law see ch. 1 at A 2, above.

[151] Gutteridge 1949: 72; Palmer 2004.

[152] Samuel 2008: 319; Sacco 1991: 16 (comparing the language of the civil codes of the former Western and Eastern Germany).

[153] Mattei 1997a: 182. See also Kovac 2011 (on comparative contract law and economics).

[154] Rose 1991: 447–8; Hantrais 2009: 72, 76.

Moreover, is an explicit comparison really necessary for comparative law? In comparative studies more generally, it is said that descriptive words such as 'democratic' or 'densely populated' are implicit comparisons.[155] Similarly, studies of foreign law can be an implicit comparison because the comparatist is bound to use terms and concepts of her own legal system as points of reference.[156]

The traditional comparative method is also criticised for being too narrowly focused on the positive law.[157] Law needs institutions that enforce it. Enforcement is a well-known problem where, due to high levels of corruption, state law is 'thin'.[158] But, according to John Bell, comparatists should also consider the role of institutions more generally:

> In short, that means that we cannot be content to present rules without some reference to the organisational setting, the procedural context and the conceptual structure within which legal problems emerge and the rules are operated. This is not necessarily a call for socio-legal or even 'law-in-context' work, but it does require thought at least about the legal embeddedness of the legal problems as they present themselves in the different countries studied.[159]

Rodolfo Sacco offers another perspective on the limitations of a purely positivist analysis.[160] His main idea is that law is an aggregate of various 'legal formants'. Comparative law should consider not only legislation but also court decisions and legal scholarship, regardless of whether a particular legal system regards the latter as sources of law. Comparatists should also illuminate how these legal formants interact and compete with each other, thus resisting the usual temptation of domestic lawyers to establish the correct solution to a particular problem.[161]

Sacco, in addition, introduces the term 'cryptotype' to comparative law. This refers to the unformulated elements of legal formants: for instance, the mentality, ideology or other shared premises of law-makers, judges or legal scholars.[162] Similarly, Ugo Mattei and colleagues illustrate this idea as follows:

> At home, every experienced lawyer is a 'practicing anthropologist', to use an expression coined by the late Jerome Frank. By living and practicing in one's own community, a person becomes intuitively aware of the way in which legal institutions actually work; but when one tries to penetrate into a foreign system,

---

[155] Smelser 1976: 3. See also ch. 11 at A 2, below.

[156] Ruskola 2002: 192; Twining 2000a: 187–8. See also Twining 2000b: 57 ('comparative study is more like a way of life than a method').

[157] Grossfeld 2003: 180; Örücü 2007: 61.   [158] Glenn 2003: 96.

[159] Bell 2011: 170. See also Bell 2006a; Somma 2006: 37 (relating analysis of institutions to political problems).

[160] Sacco 1991; Sacco 1990: 47–74. See also Graziadei 2003: 116; Mattei 2001: 251; Mattei et al. 2009: 219–223; Monateri 1998: 841.

[161] Similarly Hyland 2009: 106 ('comparative law considers the law . . . as a collective fabric of justification').

[162] Sacco 1991: 384–7; Sacco 1990: 155–9.

no such intuition or experience is available to serve as a guide. The comparative law student who recognizes this handicap is well on the way to overcoming it.[163]

Beyond this specific point, a more general response to the traditionalists is that they are negligent with respect to the cultural and socio-economic context of the law. This is said to be particularly relevant for comparisons of very different legal systems,[164] though it is also a frequent general assertion of the recent comparative law literature.[165]

What follows from this line of criticism? It raises important points but not all of them are entirely fair. Whilst it is true that traditional comparative law often tends to be fairly positivist, this is not a necessary consequence of the main traditional method of functionalism. Rather, a comparative analysis that starts with a functional question would have to address not only the law, but also the way it is enforced and how it is related to non-legal solutions.[166] It is also clear that traditional comparative research does not support a shallow description of statutory law, but asks comparatists to examine carefully the complexity of legal rules in terms of court decisions and scholarship. Yet, it remains a valid point of criticism that the limitations of the traditional method potentially exclude a great deal of interesting research. This will also become apparent in the following more specific objections.

2. The focus on Western countries

The country-level analysis of traditional comparative law is based on the premise that legal systems are distinguished by nation states. This 'Westphalian' conception of law, stemming from the Peace of Westphalia of 1648, is, however, frequently regarded as outdated.[167] Since international, transnational or regional legal orders play a crucial role today, there is no reason why one should not also compare, for instance, differences between international regimes or between regional and federal unions.[168] Furthermore, the focus on states disregards the role of non-state law. In non-Western countries, legal systems are often said to be pluralist, where state law is only one of many legal orders, while in the West, too, there is increased interest in private forms of regulation.[169] All of this poses challenges that comparative law should take into account. Yet, at the same time, one should not go as far as saying that countries do not matter anymore. Their precise role also depends on the area of law: in some fields of commercial law

---

[163] Mattei et al. 2009: 175.   [164] Van Hoecke and Warrington 1998: 510.

[165] See ch. 1 at B 3, above.   [166] De Coninck 2010: 336. See also A 2 (c) and 3 (b), above.

[167] See Nelken 2001: 32; Glenn 2003: 91, 93. See also Part III, below.

[168] E.g. Guzman 2008: 119–81 (e.g. comparing form, substance and scope of international regimes); Mamlyuk and Mattei 2011 ('comparative international law' as dealing with the relationship of various international instruments); Goldstein 2001 (comparing the EU with the US, the seventeenth-century Dutch Republic and Switzerland). See also ch. 9 at C, below (on regionalism).

[169] For further details see ch. 4 at C 3, ch. 5 at B 4, ch. 9 at D, below.

it is hardly feasible to ignore the international dimension, whereas, for other areas of law, it may still be justifiable to focus on the country-level.

The disregard of non-Western countries by traditional comparative law is more difficult to excuse. With respect to the assertion that these countries are too different to be comparable, it can be objected that, in today's globalising world, non-Western societies often use terms and concepts not fundamentally dissimilar to those from the Western world.[170]

But even assuming that countries from the South and East are still very different from the West, the functional method can offer a feasible tool of comparison. For instance, consider a course on 'Law in Radically Different Countries' that was taught at Stanford University in the 1980s.[171] This course dealt with the legal systems of the US, China, Egypt and Botswana, and, despite the 'radical differences', it did use common problems such 'how does society deal with a promise made, relied on but not kept?' or 'what happens when someone with property, who holds office and has social status dies: who gets all of these things?'. Of course, the way radically different legal systems deal with these legal questions will be very diverse. But that is not a problem as such: it can be interesting to explain this diversity, and it can also be revealing to find and explore similarities in legal systems which in other respects are very different.[172]

In terms of method, a comparison of very different countries often makes interdisciplinary research necessary. Whereas comparison between Western legal systems can take certain cultural similarities as given, a comparison of inheritance law across Western, Eastern and Southern legal systems (as in the Stanford course) has to consider more closely the extent to which these legal rules are shaped by different value systems, family traditions, religious beliefs etc. Applying the traditional framework, it is possible for the researcher to address these points in the comparative stage of her research, i.e. after having described and juxtaposed the legal systems in question. However, such a structural separation of law and context may not always be advisable:

> [T]here is no one method of comparative law but a large variety of methods to compare laws, fitting the different objects of a given comparative project. For example, if we wish to compare the land law of Mali with the land law of Afghanistan, two legal cultures in which a thick component of the legal system is neither written nor dominated by a formalized legal profession as in Germany or the US, we might find useful or even unavoidable to an ethnographic or an anthropological method in the study of comparative law . . .[173]

This more anthropological perspective also means that the comparatist has to be aware of her own preconceptions, avoiding an attitude of '[w]e are the Greeks; all others are barbarians'.[174] This is not to say that a comparative analysis

[170] Riles 1999: 251. See also ch. 4 at C 2 (a), below.   [171] Gibbs 1981. See also Barton et al. 1983.
[172] See also Nelken 2007a: 26; Örücü 1999: 25; Bogdan 1994: 18; Graziadei 2003: 120.
[173] Mattei et al. 2009: 48–9.   [174] Demleitner 1998: 653 (citing Karl Llewellyn).

of radically different legal systems can be entirely neutral, as some traditional comparative lawyers may require.[175] Rather, the comparatist should be aware of what the 'unstated norm' of her analysis is: for instance, whether research on US and Indian family law approaches the specifics of Indian family law from a US perspective, or vice versa.[176]

To conclude, non-Western legal systems can be part of a comparative analysis, and they should not be marginalised into area studies.[177] Of course, the precise choice of countries depends on the topic of the analysis. For instance, if someone is interested in a specific technical detail of capital markets law, it can make sense to focus on Western countries, whereas a more general analysis of how businesses are financed may well analyse legal systems from different parts of the world.

3. The critics of functionalism

A first line of attack criticises the functionalist's focus on similarities. On the one hand, this criticism concerns the endeavour to identify functional equivalents. Here the objection is that it may be equally rewarding to look for functional dissimilarities (or 'disequivalence'), despite formal differences. For example, in divorce law, many legal systems understand the concept of 'irretrievable breakdown of marriage', but the precise application ranges from fault-based systems to divorce by consent.[178] Or, in administrative law, many countries limit the freedom of the state based on the 'principle of proportionality', but differ in the precise extent to which judges can interfere.[179] In particular, such examples of formally similar but functionally different rules are likely to occur when legal rules have been transplanted from abroad (say, within a particular legal family), but do not match perfectly with the conditions of the domestic society.[180] Table 2.1, below, tries to illustrate this point.

On the other hand, frequent criticism has been raised against the presumption of functional equivalents. Such a presumption is rejected by comparatists who aim to be 'objective and neutral as between similarity and difference'.[181] A further criticism is that the underlying concept of universalism is itself culturally conditioned, having emerged and been developed at particular points in time in European legal history.[182] Finally, and more generally, the 'difference theory' rejects the search for shallow similarities. This is embedded in a critical postmodern conception of comparative law, as discussed in detail later on in this book.[183]

---

[175] See A 2 (a), above.   [176] Cossmann 1997: 536. See also ch. 5, below.

[177] For the latter point Mattei 1997b: 8. See also Menski 2006: 264 (research on Indian constitution should be joined work with Indologists).

[178] Antokolskaia 2007: 251.   [179] See, e.g., Barak 2012; Sandulli 1998.

[180] For legal transplants see ch. 8, below. For legal families see ch. 3 and ch. 4, below.

[181] Michaels 2006: 369. See also ch. 5 at C 1, below.

[182] Menski 2006: 132. Generally see also B 2 (a), above.   [183] See ch. 5 at C, below.

Table 2.1 Similarities and differences

| | | Formal | |
		Similarity	Difference
Functional	Similarity	Socio-economic similar countries of same legal family	Socio-economic similar countries of different legal families ('functional equivalents')
	Difference	Socio-economic different countries of same legal family ('functional dissimilarities')	Socio-economic different countries of different legal families

A second key criticism – and a criticism closer to the core of comparative functionalism – is that it is regarded as unacceptable to assume that all societies face the same social problem.[184] Human needs are not universal, but are conditioned by their environments. This is obvious if one thinks about different natural environments, but it also applies more broadly. The factual situation may be identical in two countries, but this does not necessarily imply that both societies (and law-makers) feel the need to provide legal rules on this issue. For instance, whether adultery is regarded as a 'problem' the legal system should address depends on moral, cultural and religious values, which differ across the world. Thus, it is said that societies have distinct priorities, and that it is unacceptable to impose an external measure on them, such as expecting them to deal with a particular issue.[185]

Third, the very idea that law serves particular functions has been challenged. A strict version of functionalism has to assume that there is a clear sequential order: a social problem arises, courts or legislators respond to it, which in turn has the effect of solving the problem. Yet, such a view fails to consider that legal rules often arise in a complex process of historical path-dependencies, cultural preconditions and legal transplants, and that legal rules also shape the problems of society.[186] Moreover, law does not necessarily serve an explicit function. Law-makers may have responded to conflicting aims or they may just offer a certain legal framework, being indifferent to how it is used. There can also be dysfunctional laws, symbolic laws, or laws that may not have a particular function though being perfectly explainable by a county's culture.[187]

---

[184] Örücü 2007: 51–2; Nelken 2007a: 22–3; Adams and Griffiths 2012: 284; Brandt 2007: 419; de Coninck 2010: 327: Husa 2003: 438; Hyland 2009: 69–73; Constantinesco 1983: 54–8.

[185] Nelken 2003b: 814; Glenn 2007: 95; Ruskola 2002: 190; Husa 2003: 438.

[186] For this relationship see also ch. 6 at A, below.

[187] For all of these points, see, e.g., Cioffi 2009: 1525; Husa 2011a: 220; Graziadei 2003: 100, 118; Michaels 2006: 354; Brandt 2007: 415.

In this respect, functionalism also runs the risk of misunderstanding non-Western legal systems, since the top-down approach, whereby state law achieves particular social ends, is very much a Western creation.[188]

Where do these lines of attacks leave functionalism? Some of them raise important objections, but it is submitted that they do not discredit functionalism as a whole. It is true that functionalism tends to focus on, or even assume, similarities over differences. Yet, comparatists have long distinguished between integrative and contrastive comparisons,[189] and it is not a priori better or worse to prefer one over the other. Critics show, however, that functionalism may not work very well in some areas of law, or with respect to legal systems, where we cannot say that law really has a well-defined purpose. We may, therefore, be left to using a functional starting point for comparisons mainly between Western countries in areas such as contract and tort law, a limitation also acknowledged by the traditionalists.

4. The policy evaluation

Attempts at policy evaluation in traditional comparative law are fiercely attacked by some postmodern approaches, which emphasise profound differences between legal cultures: '[t]here cannot be a "better" law. The very notion is fallacious. Who could finally and definitively say what it is?'[190] It is interesting to see that similar counter-arguments have also been raised more generally. In the mid-1980s, some US academics expressed support of the German model of civil procedure, given the more active role of the judge in the German civil trial than in the US one; yet, the majority of US lawyers responded that the institutional arrangements of civil procedure were so deeply embedded in US society and culture that it would not be appropriate to change them.[191]

More pragmatically, the question is how exactly comparative law can help us to find a 'better' solution. For example, a problem faced by the Common Core research is that, whilst it may identify a majority solution, the mere fact of a majority solution does not explain why it should be regarded as the best one.[192] Favouring one solution over another one also raises the objection that this is just too subjective.[193] However, this should not be the final word. Following the quantitative turn in other social sciences, empirical tools have emerged in order to test which types of rules are best able to achieve particular goals. This is an important innovation, though such an approach is not without problems, as later chapters will explain.[194]

---

[188] Twining 2007: 75–6. See also ch. 10 at C 2, below.
[189] Schlesinger 1995: 481; Mattei et al. 2009: 69.
[190] Legrand 2006b: 448. For postmodernism see ch. 5, below.
[191] For the debate see, e.g., Maxeiner et al. 2010: 17; Maxeiner et al. 2011; Stiefel and Maxeiner 1994; Chase 2002; Bryan 2004. For civil procedure see also ch. 3 at B 2, below.
[192] Smits 2010b: 36.   [193] Hill 1989: 105.   [194] For details see ch. 7 and ch. 11, below.

D. Conclusion

The traditional comparative legal method has the benefit that it provides some guidance to the way a comparative analysis should be conducted. However, this chapter has also shown that critics raise a number of valid objections. To some extent, these points of criticism 'merely' highlight the limitations of the traditional method, in particular that it is not perfectly suitable for all areas of law and all countries of the world. In addition, the critics deserve credit for exploring various aspects of the comparative methodology. Thus, it is suggested that a researcher that applies the traditional method needs to justify why this approach is seen as the most suitable for her topic. Most importantly, many points of criticism highlight the relevance of context and interdisciplinarity for comparative legal research, which will be explained further in Parts II and IV of this book.

Most of the examples of present chapter concerned comparisons between two or more countries on specific legal topics (e.g. strict liability in tort law[195]). These 'micro-comparisons' can be distinguished from 'macro-comparisons' which deal with legal systems as a whole.[196] Of course, both types overlap since macro-comparisons typically include analyses of specific topics. But, in addition, the 'macro-comparatist' may aim to provide a more general assessment about the similarities and differences between the legal systems of her study. This often makes use of legal families: for example, when comparing English, French and German law, it may be the case that we observe that the latter two countries are particularly close since both of them are civil law countries (as opposed to England, being a common law country). This will be the topic of the next two chapters.

---

[195] See A 5, above.

[196] Zweigert and Kötz 1998: 4–5. In addition, one can talk about 'meso-comparisons' when a comparison concerns a particular area of law, Constantinesco 1983: 81.

3

Common law and civil law

Most of the general books on comparative law have detailed chapters on 'legal families', some of them using terms such as 'legal traditions' or 'legal cultures'.[1] The core idea of legal families is that the diversity of the world's legal systems is not random, but that groups of countries share common features in terms of legal history, legal thinking and positive rules. Recently, this idea of legal families has also become popular among economists and political scientists, often calling them 'legal origins'.[2]

Chapter 4 of this book discusses attempts to classify all legal systems of the world. Before doing so, Chapter 3 starts with a critical analysis of the distinction between common and civil law countries. The reason for this is that, according to traditional comparative law, this distinction is the 'most fundamental and most discussed issue in comparative law',[3] as common and civil law are said to 'constitute the basic building blocks of the legal order' and to be 'the dominant legal systems of the world'.[4]

Before going into details, Section A clarifies the terminology and origins of the common/civil law divide. Section B explains the core substantive differences. Particular emphasis is given to questions of sources of law, legal methods and court proceedings; a smaller section deals with comparative contract law. Section C provides a critical analysis. Section D concludes.

A. Terminology and origins

The words 'common law' and 'civil law' have multiple meanings. In the current context, they are meant to refer to 'labels' given to groups of legal systems in terms of similarities and differences. Broadly speaking (details below) common law countries are legal systems whose law is based on English law, whereas civil law countries are those influenced by continental European traditions.

---

[1] See ch. 1 at B 1, above. Some also use the term 'legal systems' though this is misleading since it can also refer to the law of a single country. See Constantinesco 1983: 76–7.
[2] See ch. 11 at B 3, below.   [3] Mattei 1997a: 70.
[4] Palmer in EE 2012: 591 and Barnes 2005: 680.

Some of the other meanings are related to this distinction. Within a common law country, we can distinguish between 'common law' and 'equity', the latter being those types of claims that had not been part of the original forms of action (more below). The term 'common law' can also refer to the case law of a common law country, as distinguished from statute law that tends to be of more modern origins.[5] Moreover, the term 'common law' can simply refer to the law that a wider range of people have in common, as distinguished from local laws.[6] Finally, within a particular legal system, 'civil law' can refer to fields such as contract and tort law, distinguishing it from criminal and public law.[7]

In order to understand the civil/common law divide, it useful to outline the origins of both legal families.[8] This is not entirely straightforward. The civil law tradition is based on Roman law which, in its ancient form, used to follow a casuistic style, something today more associated with the common law. In the early sixth century AD the Eastern Roman Emperor Justinian commissioned a synthesis of the Roman law. This Corpus Juris Civilis from 533 AD became influential again in the eleventh century with the revival of Roman law in continental Europe (also called: 'reception'). Three distinct features are worth highlighting. First, universities supported the reception of Roman law, thus explaining the frequent description of the civil law as 'learned law'. Second, the received Roman law was a common law ('ius commune') that transcended national borders, replacing or at least supplementing local customary laws. Third, judicial enforcement of the law was kept under the strict control of the state in order to prevent corruption and guarantee uniform application of the law.

This version of the civil law changed with the emergence of the nation states in the eighteenth and nineteenth centuries. States began to codify the Roman law, often mixed with local laws, in order to create a unified national law. The most important of these new codes was the French Code Civil of 1804, often seen as a symbol of the modern civil law tradition. The Civil Code is drafted in an abstract fashion while also aiming to be understandable for the common public ('as simple as the Bible').[9] This contrasts with the German Civil Code of 1900, whose style is more conceptual and professorial. Thus, the codification movement led to the divergence of laws in continental Europe. However, it also facilitated the spread of the civil law across the world. In parts, this happened through the colonial empires of the European countries. Moreover, some countries, such as Japan and Turkey, voluntarily transplanted major codes of the civil law countries.[10]

---

[5] Zweigert and Kötz 1998: 188.   [6] See Glenn 2005 and C 1, below.

[7] See van Rhee and Verkerk in EE 2012: 140; Mattila 2006: 110, 221–2. But note that in common law countries administrative sanctions may also be called 'civil sanctions', as distinguished from criminal ones.

[8] For the following see, e.g., Glenn 2010a: 126–55, 225–48; Gordley and von Mehren 2006: 3–63; Dam 2006; Head 2011; Djankov et al. 2003b: 605–6.

[9] Ehrmann 1976: 26.   [10] For details see ch. 8 at B, below.

The origins of the common law appear to be clearer. In 1066, following the Norman conquest of England, William the Conqueror was crowned King of England. William and his successors used a feudal system of land ownership and a new court system to control the country and to unify the law. The legal system was based on standardised forms of action ('writs'), which became the basis of the common law. Courts were centred in London, but travelling judges also operated in other parts of the country. In court proceedings, the fact finding was left to juries in order to facilitate acceptance of the royal justice in the local population.

Initially, the royal influence on the legal system was strong. However, when, in the seventeenth century, King James I attempted to make use of his feudal powers in claiming ownership of the entire land, Parliament intervened, and a stronger protection of property rights and a more independent judiciary emerged.[11] Gradually, judges also delivered more elaborate judgments, thus transforming the procedural origins of the 'writs' into more substantive rules; as a result, it has famously been said that '[t]he forms of action we have buried, but they still rule us from their graves'.[12] As with the civil law, colonisation meant that this approach to law spread to other parts of the world, such as the United States, Australia and India.

B. Juxtaposing civil and common law

It would not be feasible in one chapter to provide a summary of all the possible differences and similarities between all possible civil and common law countries. Yet, it is also submitted that this is not necessary, according to the traditional mainstream of comparative law. First, most legal scholars agree that certain subjects are at the core of the common law/civil law divide, namely, sources of law and legal method, legal styles and techniques, and institutions and procedure.[13] This is the focus of the following section, which also outlines how these differences are reflected in one more specific area of substantive law (contract law). Second, while civil and common law countries may be found in all parts of the world, their typical features are mainly seen as a result of a few countries' influence. With respect to the civil law, French and German law are said to have influenced all countries regarded as civil law countries today, and, with respect to the common law, English law and more recently US law have

---

[11] Klerman and Mahoney 2007; Beck and Levine 2005: 254–8. Similarly Shapiro 1981: 104; Glenn 2010a: 256–8.

[12] Maitland 1936: 2.

[13] Vogenauer 2006: 873; Dannemann 2006: 393; Glenn 2010b: 610. Details, e.g., in Lundmark 2012; Barner 2005: 686–731; Smits 2002a: 73–94; van Caenegem 2002: 38–53; Pejovic 2001; Tetley 2000: 701–7. Specifically on comparative civil procedure Maxeiner et al. 2010; Maxeiner et al. 2011; Chase and Hershkoff 2007; Chase and Varano 2012; Koch 2003; Garapon and Papadopoulos 2003; Hadfield 2008: 50–8.

done the same.[14] It is therefore possible to focus on these four legal systems. The aim here is to present a fair description of the mainstream view – with a critical analysis provided in the subsequent section.

1. Legal methods and sources of law

(a) The role of statute law and its interpretation

In the civil law world, the main codes for civil law, commercial law, criminal law, civil procedure and criminal procedure emerged in the nineteenth century. Codification efforts are not unknown to common law countries. In the mid-nineteenth century the American lawyer David Dudley Field drafted a Code of Civil Procedure which was initially adopted by the state of New York, and which has influenced today's Federal Rules of Civil Procedure and the corresponding state laws.[15] With respect to substantive law, some US states have a Civil Code (e.g. California, Montana), and the model law of the Uniform Commercial Code (UCC) has been adopted by all US states with only slight modifications.[16] In pre-independence India, codification concerned procedural rules as well as substantive law.[17] These laws have also impacted on the laws of other British colonies (e.g. in Africa).[18]

Yet, there is a significant difference between these common law codifications and the ones in civil law countries. The main codes of civil law countries follow the idea of the Enlightenment to provide a clear, coherent, systematic, self-contained and complete treatment of particular branches of law.[19] Though modern pieces of legislation may also deal with particular issues in a more ad hoc fashion, law-makers can still be seen today as keen to keep the idea of codes alive. For instance, France set up a Commission Supérieure de Codification in 1989, which has led to the introduction of new codes and the redesign of old ones.[20] In the common law world, the UCC has been influenced by a civil law style of drafting legislation.[21] However, this is the exception, since codifications in common law countries are mostly consolidations of previous case law with only some attempt to systematise the topics.[22]

With respect to the substance of modern legislation, it has been said that continental European law-makers tend to focus on public-interest regulation, whereas in the common law the focus is on market-failure regulation.[23] There may also be a link between this difference and the more pronounced role of

---

[14] See also ch. 8 at B, below on legal transplants.

[15] Weiss 2000: 505–6; Zweigert and Kötz 1998: 242–3; von Mehren 2010: 10.

[16] See www.law.cornell.edu/uniform/ucc.html.

[17] E.g. Criminal Procedure Code 1861; Civil Procedure Code 1908; Penal Code 1860; Contract Act 1872.

[18] See Menski 2006: 462 and ch. 8 at B 2 (a), below.

[19] Weiss 2000: 456–66; Curran 2006: 683; Legrand 1995: 15–6, 27.

[20] See Steiner 2010: 38.   [21] Steiner 2010: 42. See also Whitman 1987.

[22] See Menski 2006: 242 (for the Indian codes).   [23] Ogus 2004: 149.

litigation in common law countries, since litigation favours the use of property rights in order to deal with externalities, whereas civil law countries may prefer strict rules.[24] Similarly, it can be suggested that civil law countries tend to be 'policy-implementing' and not merely 'conflict-solving', and therefore more activist social welfare providers.[25]

The interpretation of the civil law codes has experienced a significant shift in the last two centuries. The French Civil Code of 1804 stated (and still states) that 'judges are forbidden to decide cases submitted to them by way of general and regulatory provisions'.[26] The background of this provision was that previous French courts (the 'Parlements') tended to obstruct reform by announcing general rules binding on all courts. Thus, the Civil Code had the aim of enforcing a strict separation of power, and to disallow judicial law-making: the law should be applied exactly the way it is written in the Code.[27] However, throughout the nineteenth and twentieth century it became clear that such a narrow and literal interpretation was not feasible.[28] Today, a common tool of civil law interpretation is to consider the historical background of the law in order to give full effect to the intention of the law-maker ('exegetical method'). If a provision is ambiguous and the will of the law-maker is not clear, the interpretation may also be based on the objective purpose of the law ('teleological method'). The purpose of the law is particularly relevant for provisions drafted in general terms. Exceptionally, it may also be justifiable to interpret provisions extensively or even to apply them by way of analogy, if this is necessary to give full effect of the law.[29] This is explicitly authorised in some modern codes, such as the Swiss Civil Code, which states that if the Code 'does not furnish an applicable provision, the judge shall decide in accordance with customary law, and failing that, according to the rule which he would establish as a legislator'.[30]

In the common law, traditionally, statutory interpretation focuses on the text ('literal rule'), unless this would lead to an absurd result ('golden rule') or would not sufficiently address the defect the law had sought to remedy ('mischief rule'). But, similar to the civil law, interpretation has gradually shifted from wording to legislative history and purpose.[31] Still, it matters that, traditionally, the main source of the common law is case law. Thus, as statute law is regarded as the exception, statutory interpretation tends to be narrower in common than in

---

[24] Mattei 1997a: 64.

[25] Distinction based on Damaška 1986: 71–96, 147–80. For research on different types of welfare states see ch. 11 at B 3, below.

[26] Code Civil, art. 5 (as translated at www.legifrance.gouv.fr/).

[27] See Legrand 1995: 11–2; Vogenauer in EE 2012: 830–1 (also on the alleged statement by Napoleon when the first commentary on the Code was published: 'Mon Code est perdu!').

[28] For the following see Steiner 2010: 69, 73; Hage in EE 2012: 530–1; Van Hoecke and Warrington 1998: 501–2; Vogenauer 2006: 884; Zimmermann 2001: 176.

[29] See Mattei et al. 2009: 579; Gutteridge 1949: 94.

[30] Civil Code (Zivilgesetzbuch), art. 1(2) (as translated in Ehrmann 1976: 111).

[31] Samuel in EE 2012: 178–9; Bell 2006a: 334–6; Hermida 2004: 343. See also MacCormick and Summers 1991.

civil law countries. This is also reflected in the way many statutes are drafted, since interpretation sections and detailed provisions aim for laws that indicate precisely how they should be applied. Moreover, while in civil law countries judges are keen to anchor their reasoning on the codified law, common law judges are said to refer to statutory law in a more ad hoc fashion, even where a particular topic is heavily codified.[32]

(b) The role of courts

Judicial law-making presents the reverse picture. In the common law, trials not only have the function of solving an individual conflict, but court decisions are a means to develop the law 'from below'. This has had a distinctive influence on the law. The common law is reactive since 'it awaits the interpretive occasion'.[33] The reliance on cases also means that the specific facts of each case are carefully considered. In the words of Lord Macmillan, it follows that '[a]rguments based on legal consistency are apt to mislead, for the common law is a practical code adapted to deal with the manifold diversities of human life'.[34] Given the lack of comprehensive codifications, knowledge of history is also said to be more important than in civil law countries.[35]

Moreover, since previous cases are regarded as binding precedents, judges apply law made by themselves.[36] Thus, the law tends to evolve gradually, as can be seen in traditional fields of common law such as equity and torts. Common law judges are also willing to show judicial creativity in establishing policies for matters of social controversy, and they are said to be relatively open to arguments from economics and other social sciences.[37] In addition, judges of common law countries are praised for being 'market-wise' – for instance, in guaranteeing the freedom of contract.[38] It has also been said that the protection of individual rights and freedoms by these fiercely independent legal professionals has precluded violent intrusions of political power.[39]

Judges in civil law countries reason very differently. As the previous section explained, they have more discretion in interpreting statutory law. But once this is completed, they are said just to be law-appliers. In 1921 Roscoe Pound put it as follows:

> [T]he theory of the codes in Continental Europe of the last century made of the court a sort of judicial slot machine. The necessary machinery had been provided in advance by legislation or by received legal principles and one had but to put in the facts above and take out the decision below. True, the critic says, the facts do not always fit the machinery, and hence we may have to thump and joggle the machinery a bit in order to get anything out. But even in extreme cases of this

---

[32] See Lundmark 2012: 80 (contrasting the situation in Germany and California).
[33] Legrand 1999: 69.
[34] *Read* v. *J. Lyons and Co.* [1946] 2 All E R 471 at 478 (HL).   [35] Mattei et al. 2009: 404.
[36] Shapiro 1981: 69. For precedents in common and civil law countries see 2 (f), below.
[37] See Bell 2006a: 334–6; Faust 2006: 857; Nelken 2003b: 827.
[38] Arruñada and Andonova 2008.   [39] Mattei and Nader 2008: 181.

departure from the purely automatic, the decision is attributed, not at all to the thumping and joggling process, but solely to the machine.[40]

This mirrors statements made today. The civil law judge is seen as keen to follow legal reasoning based on syllogism: first, identifying the legal rule and how it should be interpreted; second, subsuming the facts within these legal rules; and, third, applying the consequence of the legal rule.[41] Thus, in contrast to the common law, the facts of the case are only relevant as far as they relate to the legal rule in question. Similarly, as far as precedents are used, the focus is on the principles of law, not the factual details of the previous cases.

Overall, the method of civil law judges may therefore be criticised as positivist, mechanical and uncreative.[42] More sympathetically, it may be described as seeking to respect the decisions of the legislator, and applying the law in a rational and predictable matter.[43] The institutional structure of courts reinforces this approach: judges are civil servants on a judicial career path and within an institutional hierarchy.[44] They also have to deal with a high workload of cases, thus making unavoidable the normal focus on implementing, not developing, the law.[45]

(c) The role of legal scholarship

A discussion of legal scholarship points towards another reason why the civil and common law traditionally differ. Historically, the civil law tradition is associated with the concept of 'learned law'.[46] In particular, German law professors are said to have had a strong influence on the character of German law, contrasting it with judges in England and the legislator in France.[47]

On the one hand, this concerns the influence of scholarship on legislation and the way it should be interpreted. It has been said that the Pandectists, i.e. the Roman lawyers of nineteenth-century Germany, essentially wrote the Civil Code of 1900.[48] Similarly, the reform of the German Civil Code from 2002 was based on reports produced by law professors.[49] With respect to statutory interpretation, legal scholars usually take the lead. In Germany and in other civil law countries professors write multi-volume detailed annotated guides on the main codes. Monographs, textbooks and journals also deal extensively with the interpretation of statutory law. Often, then, what emerges is a predominant view ('herrschende Lehre' in Germany, 'la doctrine' in France) that is almost as important as the positive law.[50]

---

[40] Pound 1921: 170–1.
[41] Maxeiner et al. 2010: 33, 241; Smits 2002a: 82; Legrand 1999: 76; Lundmark 2012: 284.
[42] Merryman and Pérez-Perdomo 2007: 38; Curran 2001b: 74–5; Andenas and Fairgrieve 2006: 22.
[43] Bell 2006a: 144, 170 (for Germany).   [44] See 2 (c), below.
[45] Bell 2006a: 103 (for France).   [46] See A, above.
[47] See van Caenegem 1987; also van Caenegem 2002: 44–5; Shapiro 1981: 147.
[48] Shapiro 1981: 147.   [49] See Bundesminister der Justiz 1992.
[50] See Mattei et al. 2009: 442; Hermida 2004: 342.

On the other hand, civil law scholarship impacts on courts. Prior to the codification of German law, judges asked law professors to advise on the law.[51] Today, the courts of civil law countries closely consider academic writings, even if this is not regarded as a source of law, and judges are not always allowed to cite them.[52] In return, law journals usually provide substantive sections on case reports. Since French judgments are written in a very condensed style, it is also essential that legal academics explain in short commentaries how these judgments relate to previous cases and scholarship.[53]

In the common law world, scholarship and practice are less intertwined than in civil law countries. Historically, it may matter that the forms of action of the common law have invited reasoning by analogy but not, as in the civil law, the desire to construct law as an abstract legal science.[54] Moreover, Geoffrey Samuel observes that, more recently,

> the narrow perspective of the legal profession and the judiciary in the common law world has stimulated a certain section of the academic community to turn away from the study of positive law. Such academics have, instead, seen themselves more as social scientists or philosophers taking as their object of study 'law'.[55]

Yet there is also some interaction between legal scholars and law-makers. In England, the Law Commission, which prepares legislation, usually has some law professors as its commissioners.[56] Doctrinal legal research also takes great interest in case law and it has even been said that the quality of the common law depends on a strong relationship between legal scholars and judges.[57]

2. Courts and civil procedure

(a) Which types of courts exist?

Civil law countries tend to have different courts for different areas of law. This dates back to Roman law which strictly distinguished between the matters of the state and those of the individuals.[58] Initially, courts were mainly concerned with matters of the individuals, i.e. private law, as well as with criminal law. Thus, in civil law countries, on the one hand, there are regular (or ordinary) courts on private and criminal law. On the other hand, there is often a variety of specialised courts. For instance, Germany has specialised courts for administrative law, labour law, social security law, tax law, plus a federal constitutional court. In France the Conseil d'Etat is the highest court in public law, though with a more restricted constitutional function than its German counterpart.[59] Since French ordinary courts cannot decide on matters concerning the state, lower-instance

---

[51] See Vogenauer 2005.   [52] See Sacco 1991: 346 and 2 (e), below.
[53] See Steiner 2010: 191; Bell 2006a: 83. See also 2 (e), below.   [54] Samuel in EE 2012: 187.
[55] Samuel in EE 2012: 187. See also Siems and MacSithigh 2012.
[56] See www.justice.gov.uk/lawcommission/about/who-we-are.htm.
[57] Braun 2006: 666–70.   [58] D.1.1.1.2 (Ulpian 1 institutionum).
[59] For constitutional courts and judicial review see also ch. 8 at B 4 (a), below.

administrative courts were established in 1987.[60] In addition, there are other specialised courts – for instance, for commercial and labour matters.

Traditionally, common law countries distinguished between courts for 'common law' (in a narrow sense) and 'equity', depending on the forms of action used.[61] Today, this distinction is largely obsolete since a competent court would not dismiss a claim on this basis. In the US and some other common law countries, the two types of courts have also been merged.[62] In England and Wales, however, the High Court has different divisions, and the jurisdiction of the Queen's Bench (or King's Bench) and the Chancery Court can still be related to the actions of common law on the one hand and equity on the other.

Common law countries did not use to distinguish between courts for private and public law. For instance, in matters of civil liability, the state was, and often still is, just a normal party in courts of general jurisdiction. Yet, in the twentieth century, public and administrative law emerged as distinct fields of academic research.[63] In the UK there are now also specialised tribunals for administrative law, as well for other matters (e.g. employment disputes).[64] However, this has not led to a separate line of courts as in Germany and France, since tribunal decisions can be appealed to the courts of general jurisdiction. It has also been suggested that, in any case, legal counsel (solicitors, barristers etc.) specialise in particular fields, thus providing a substitute for the more specialised courts of civil law countries.[65]

With respect to appeal courts, there is traditionally also said to be a civil/common law divide. In civil law countries, the possibility of appeal tends to be more extensive: the first level of appeal courts may not only re-examine the law but also the facts. Then, a second appeal to a higher court may be possible, whereby German law follows a 'revision model' and French law a 'cassation model'. The French model only allows the higher court to quash the decision of the lower court and refer it to a new assessment, whereas in the German model it is possible for the higher court to replace the lower court's decision.[66] In today's common law countries, there are also often multiple levels of courts. For example, in 1875 the Court of Appeal of England and Wales was created, allowing a further appeal to the Supreme Court of the UK (formerly, the Judicial Committee of the House of Lords). Yet, in the common law tradition, appeals cannot be used to re-examine the facts, and it is often at the discretion of the courts whether to grant permission of appeal.[67]

The difference in the propensity to allow appeals is closely linked to other characteristics of civil and common law. Civil law countries tend to have

[60] Mattei et al. 2009: 534–5.
[61] Van Rhee and Verkerk in EE 2012: 143. See also A, above (on common law and equity).
[62] Van Rhee and Verkerk in EE 2012: 143, 151.
[63] See Allison 1996: 1, 19–23, 81–2 (stimulated by continental European contacts).
[64] See www.justice.gov.uk/about/hmcts/tribunals/.   [65] Lundmark 2012: 212.
[66] Bobek 2009: 36; Unidroit 2003: 4–5.   [67] Bobek 2009: 36, 42; Chase and Varano 2012: 235.

career judges who work within a hierarchy (see (b), below), thus emphasising accountability and making it plausible for senior judges to re-examine the work of junior ones. In the common law, typical traditional features include the use of juries and the requirement of oral proceedings (see (b) and (c), below), making it difficult for appeal courts to re-establish the facts.[68] Another typical feature of the common law is the binding effect of precedents (see (f), below), which fosters uniformity of law without the need to allow appeals in all but exceptional cases.[69]

(b) Who exactly is 'the court'?

Here, a first distinction can be made according to the number of judges on a particular court. Traditionally, civil law courts tend to decide by way of panels of judges, whereas individual judges are more prevalent in common law courts.[70] Yet, the precise structure of the court also depends on the type of the case. For instance, it is likely that in both legal families important appeal cases will be decided by a panel of judges, and routine cases at the courts of first instance by a single judge.

Second, the education and careers of judges are said to be fundamentally different in civil and common law countries. Mirjan Damaška also relates this to the way state authority is administered: in the civil law, the organisation of authority follows a hierarchical (vertical) ideal, with professional judges and a 'legalist' application of the law (see also (e), below). The common law, by contrast, follows a coordinate (horizontal) ideal, with judges and juries as the protagonists of such a decentralised system.[71]

To elaborate, in the civil law family, the concept of 'learned law' means that university education is essential in order to transmit 'the science of law'.[72] Of course, not everyone who studied law can become a judge. In France, prospective judges have to pass special exams and attend training at one of the judicial colleges. The German model is somehow different since both university and practical legal education are uniform for all prospective lawyers, but only the best graduates have the option to become judges. It is a commonality of civil law countries that judges are appointed at a young age, leading to a lifetime civil-service career as judges.[73]

Traditionally, in the common law model, there has been no special training; rather, in the English tradition, experienced barristers are appointed as judges. Thus, it is said that such an appointment is seen as a 'badge of quality', producing persons who 'have strong personal independence' and 'the capacity to think and

---

[68] See Zekoll 2006: 1332; Samuel in EE 2012: 173.
[69] See Bobek 2009: 42.   [70] Bell 2006a: 30.
[71] Damaška 1986. Similar Milhaupt and Pistor 2008: 183 (matrix according to centralised/decentralised and coordinative/protective legal systems).
[72] See Lawson 1977: 98. See also A, above.
[73] Dodson and Klebba 2011: 9; Guarnieri and Pederzoli 2001: 14.

act as good lawyers'.[74] English and US judges are also frequently involved in non-judicial tasks – for instance, as wise men in expert commissions.[75] But there may also be further complications: notably in the US, there is a great variety of forms of appointments, including the use of elections.[76]

In addition to professional judges, juries or lay judges play a role in both civil and common law countries, but it is usually said that they are more prevalent in the latter ones. In the common law tradition, juries used to be responsible for fact finding in both civil and criminal cases. Today, civil law juries have disappeared in most common law countries, with the notable exception of the US where the jury is seen as a key element of American culture and democracy.[77] Still, the prior prevalence of the jury is regarded as important in all common law countries, because imagining a 'phantom jury' can aid understanding of the core features of the common law trial, such as the principle of orality and the trial as a single event (see (c), below).[78] In England and Wales, lay judges also play an important role in lower courts in matters of criminal and family law.[79]

In civil law countries the use of juries has varied, while being confined to criminal trials. Germany abolished the jury for criminal trials in 1924 and replaced it with a system of community judges ('Schöffen'), whereas other civil law countries recently introduced juries for some criminal trials.[80] France still uses jurors for severe criminal offences at the Assize Court ('cour d'assises'). In civil law cases, both Germany and France have lay judges in specialised courts (e.g. labour and commercial courts). These are usually expert or representative judges – for instance, in labour courts, they are representatives of the social partners.[81] A difference from juries is that professional and lay judges are part of a mixed panel. This means that lay judges not only decide on matters of facts, but also on matters of law, while also not being insulated from judicial influence.[82]

(c) What is the main form of civil proceedings?

A common law trial is traditionally a single oral event at which all evidence is received. These concepts of concentration and orality are a consequence of the more frequent use of juries in common law countries (see (b), above). In civil

---

[74] Lawson 1977: 98 (first quote); Bell 2006a: 374 (second one), 35 (third one). See also Garoupa and Ginsburg 2011 (suggesting hybrid between career and recognition judiciaries as most efficient model).

[75] Lee 2011: 540; Bell 2006a: 357; Holland in Kritzer 2002: 788–90.

[76] Dodson and Klebba 2011: 9; Garoupa and Ginsburg 2011: 414 (overview of diverse mechanisms of appointment to US state supreme courts).

[77] See C 3, below.   [78] Samuel in EE 2012: 173 ('jury fantome').

[79] Blank et al. 2004: 24; Glendon et al. 2008: 193–7. See also Nolan 2009: 47 (in US low-level crimes dealt with by single-judge courts); Ehrmann 1976: 103 (France abolished Justices of Peace in Fifth Republic).

[80] Reamey 2010: 709–10 (in particular in Eastern Europe).

[81] Bell 2006a: 89, 151, 351–2.   [82] Reitz 2009: 858.

law countries, by contrast, written proceedings tend to be more prevalent, written documents preferred to oral testimony, and the trial divided into multiple procedural steps.[83] This piecemeal method of trying cases still exists today; yet, there have also been some changes.

The nineteenth and twentieth centuries saw a tendency towards oral proceedings in civil law countries.[84] For example, contemporary German law encourages courts to have a single hearing.[85] But there is also a general global trend to speed-up trials, and law-makers may even be urged to do so, since the right to a fair trial implies no undue delay in court proceedings.[86] Thus, in both civil and common law countries, out-of-court settlement and alternative forms of dispute resolution have been fostered, and fast track proceedings for simple cases have been introduced.[87]

Still, the difference remains that, under the common law concept of the trial as a single event, there has to be more extensive pre-trial preparation than in continuous proceedings. Today, the clearest example are the pre-trial discovery rules of US law, where parties are under extensive obligations to disclose possible evidence to the other side. Yet, these rules were only introduced in 1938, and, in the English version of the common law, pre-trial discovery is less important.[88] In civil law countries, there are more limited forms of discovery – not necessarily restricted to the pre-trial stage – but there are also other mechanisms, such as shifts in the burden of proof or rules of substantive law (e.g. strict liability), to address imbalances of information.[89]

(d) What are the roles of judge, parties and lawyers in civil trials?

Starting with the role of the judge, it is traditionally said that the civil law judge is more managerial than the neutral judge of the common law, who is more like 'a neighbour helping the feuding parties in their troubles'.[90] For example, in Germany the judge has a duty to give hints and feedback to the parties.[91] In civil law countries it is also for the judge 'to know the law' ('iura novit curia', 'da mihi factum, dabo tibi ius'), whereas in common law countries the parties need to present the legal arguments in their favour.[92]

---

[83] See generally Unidroit 2003: 4–5; Mattei et al. 2009: 778, 787.

[84] Van Rhee and Verkerk in EE 2012: 151; Cappelletti and Garth 1987: para. 3.

[85] German Code of Civil Procedure (ZPO), s. 272.

[86] E.g. European Convention on Human Rights, art. 6(1); International Covenant on Civil and Political Rights 1966, art. 14(1).

[87] Van Rhee and Verkerk in EE 2012: 148, 151–1; Chase and Varano 2012: 223.

[88] See Maxeiner et al. 2010: 147; Zekoll 2006: 1330.

[89] Mattei et al. 2009: 763; Maxeiner et al. 2010: 177–8. See also Chase and Varano 2012: 224–5 (on recent extensions of procedural duties of disclosure in France and Germany).

[90] Adams 1995; Van Rhee and Verkerk in EE 2012: 143 (also noting that under the Romano-canonical procedure judges were more passive); Ehrmann 1976: 91 (for the quote).

[91] Mattei et al. 2009: 749, 752 (in France possible but not required).

[92] See Mattei et al. 2009: 747.

A possible explanation for this difference is that civil and common law procedures focus on different categories of cases: the civil law, but not the common law, is mainly aimed at cases that involve small amounts of money, where parties need more guidance from the judge.[93] Alternatively, it can be suggested that the difference relates to different conceptions of government. In the civil law, the law-maker desires that judges implement its policies; thus, court proceedings should not be left only to the parties. Conversely, the common law has the character of a more reactive system, since the trial has the main aim of providing justice in the individual case (see also (e), below).[94]

In England, the 1999 Rules of Civil Procedure have given judges more powers in order to speed-up trials. Thus, its position is said to have shifted from that of a 'neutral umpire' to that of a 'focussed interrogator'.[95] But there are still differences between common and civil law judges. With respect to the US, it has been said that both the system of elected judges, and the high number of cases, mean that judges would have neither the skills nor the time to engage in active case management.[96] There is also some resistance to any move away from the model of the relatively passive judge, since this is seen as most consistent with a high level of judicial independence (see (b), above).

Turning to role of the parties, the common law trial follows an adversarial system in which parties (and their lawyers) are actively involved, performing some tasks which, in the civil law model, are performed by the court.[97] With respect to the civil law countries, it is today accepted that it would not be appropriate to downplay the role of the parties and call civil trials 'inquisitorial'. Parties play an important role: they initiate the trial and determine its subject-matter, they present evidence and they have the rights crucial for a fair trial.[98] Sometimes, trials are also very adversarial in practice. However, in comparison, it is believed that civil law trials are less confrontational and more likely to promote compromise than common law ones.[99] James Maxeiner and colleagues illustrate the mutual competitive nature and the remaining differences with the analogy that US civil proceedings 'are likened to football matches and American judges to passive football referees' and German ones 'to athletics contests, such as high jump, where referees direct contestants in their competition'.[100]

More specific differences between the roles of judge and parties can be seen in the law of evidence. In the common law model, parties are said to be in charge of the interrogation of witnesses, the designation of expert witnesses,

---

[93] Kötz 2003: 76–7; also Kötz 2010: 1252 (for contract law).   [94] Zekoll 2006: 1332–3.

[95] Bell 2006a: 307. For similar trends in other common law countries see Chase and Varano 2012: 222.

[96] See Kravets 2010. See also note 76, above.   [97] Van Rhee and Verkerk in EE 2012: 141.

[98] Van Rhee and Verkerk in EE 2012: 146, 151; Zekoll 2006: 1330; Cappelletti and Garth 1987: paras. 28, 43; Maxeiner et al. 2010: 143.

[99] Bell 2006a: 134.   [100] Maxeiner et al. 2010: 190.

the presentation of documents etc.[101] Yet, due to the (previous) prevalence of juries (see (c), above), there are also a number of restrictions, such as bans on hearsay evidence and suggestive questions, in particular in the US and to a lesser extent in England.[102] In civil law countries, the parties can submit evidence, but it is mainly the judge who is responsible for fact-finding and establishing the truth.[103] Thus, the judge takes a greater role than in common law countries: for instance, it is for the judge to interrogate witnesses and to designate expert witnesses, with party involvement differing between countries.[104] Due to the absence of juries in civil trials, most types of evidence are permissible, and it is at the court's discretion to evaluate its credibility.[105]

Finally, there are differences in the role lawyers play in relation to their clients, the court and the state. A preliminary consideration is whether countries have a unitary or a divided profession. The latter is today often associated with England: here, only barristers can represent clients in higher courts, whereas solicitors deal with all other matters. Yet, this division is not specific to the common law, because its origins can be traced to the advocates and procurators in Roman law.[106] Most of today's civil law countries have, however, merged the two professions,[107] and the same has happened in some common law countries, such as the US.

A broad civil/common law divide can be found in terms of the 'gatekeepers' of the legal profession.[108] In civil law countries the state tends to play a larger role: it may use a system of state exams (as in Germany and Japan), and/or it may require a degree from a – typically state-funded – university in order to become a lawyer. In the common law tradition it may not be technically necessary to have a law degree, though today that would be usually the case. The actual qualification as a lawyer is usually in the hands of the legal profession itself, with only some state oversight.

These differences are reflected in the relationship between lawyer and client. In common law countries, it is usually accepted that the lawyer's clear focus is on the client's interest. A good example are the rules on costs and fees in the US: each party pays its own costs (called 'American rule'), but client and lawyer can agree that the latter is only entitled to remuneration if he or she wins the case ('no-win no-fee' or contingency fee arrangement). Yet, this cost and fee structure is not a general feature of all common law countries: in England, the losing party has to pay the costs of the trial (called 'English rule'), and the

---

[101] See Dodson and Klebba 2011: 10; Mattei et al. 2009: 798. But see Andrews 2010: 105 (since 1998 single joint expert or court-appointed expert possible under English law).
[102] Mattei et al. 2009: 758; Zweigert and Kötz 1998: 274–5; Glendon et al. 2008: 250.
[103] Damaška 2010: 17.
[104] Unidroit 2003: 4–5; Dodson and Klebba 2011: 10; Mattei et al. 2009: 781, 798; Kern 2007: 28 (for cross-examination in Germany and France).
[105] Mattei et al. 2009: 758; Zweigert and Kötz 1998: 274–5.
[106] Clark 2012: 370–4; Clark 2002: para. 27.
[107] Clark 2002: paras. 30–31; Chase and Varano 2012: 218.
[108] Based on Anderson and Ryan 2010.

permissibility of contingency fees is fairly diverse across the world.[109] As far as there is a split of the legal profession, barristers have a stronger duty to the judicial system than solicitors.[110]

Lawyers in civil law countries are also required to act in the best interest of their clients, but, being a 'free profession', in addition there is a strong emphasis on public responsibility.[111] In German law, it is explicitly said that lawyers are 'independent agents of the administration of justice'.[112] There are also frequent restrictions in codes of conduct enacted by the legal professions. For instance, continental European lawyers may face stricter standards for personal advertising and publicity than common law lawyers.[113]

(e) How are judgments written?

Where judges decide in panels (see (a), above), the question arises as to whether the court speaks with one voice, or whether there can be individual concurring or dissenting opinions. In general, civil law courts use the first option, occasionally making an exception for constitutional courts, whereas common law courts use the second.[114] This is in line with institutional and methodological differences, since the common law judge tends to have a more independent individual position within the court organisation, and the civil law judge tends to aim for an objective and impersonal finding of the law (see (b), above).

Differences in the style of judgments can also be related to the differences in legal reasoning. Common law judgments give a detailed account of the facts, and the reasoning is inductive, discursive and pragmatic.[115] Thus, its attractiveness may be that the judgment can inform us 'what is really going through a judge's mind when he [or she] is trying a case'.[116] Because of the role of precedents (see (f), below), common law judgments may also provide a detailed treatment of previous cases. Traditionally, no references are made to academic writings, but this is slowly changing in English courts.[117] With respect to the United States, the decisions of the Supreme Court can be seen as a special case, since its clerks often provide judges with detailed references not only to previous cases, but also to the academic literature.[118]

The style of judgments in civil law countries reflects their more deductive mode of reasoning, as well as the prevalence of a specialised career judiciary. It has been described as more formalistic, austere and abstract than in common law countries.[119] Policy arguments may be concealed through such reasoning.[120]

---

[109] See Hodges et al. 2010: 132–3 and C 2, below.
[110] Compare, e.g., Code of Conduct of the Bar of England & Wales 2004, ss. 302, 303 with the Solicitors Regulation Authority Code of Conduct 2011.
[111] See Shapiro 1990: 697.   [112] Federal Lawyer's Act (BRAO), s. 1.
[113] See Garoupa 2004 (contrasting Europe and the US).
[114] See Zekoll 2006: 1332; Mattei et al. 2009: 556–60.
[115] See Vogenauer 2006: 894; Mattila 2006: 85.   [116] Markesinis 1994: 610.
[117] See Markesinis 1994: 621–2.   [118] See Peppers 2006; Petherbridge and Schwartz 2012.
[119] Hermida 2004: 342; Vogenauer 2006: 894; Komarek 2011: 26.
[120] Markesinis 1994: 613. See also 1 (b), above.

There is also less emphasis given to facts, indicating a concept of justice which is more concerned with general principles than with the specifics of each individual case.[121] With respect to further details, a distinction needs to be made between German and French judgments, with some other civil law countries using a mixture between these models.[122]

The most distinctive feature of German judgments is their academic style.[123] The reasoning of simple cases in lower courts is somehow akin to common law judgments, though the summary of the facts tends to be more condensed. This is different in legally more complicated cases. German courts often use a strictly logical approach, employing various levels of analysis with many headings and sub-headings (I, II, III, 1, 2, 3, a, b, c, aa, bb, cc etc.). The language is fairly technical, making frequent references to the positive law, often by way of chains of articles or sections ('Paragraphenkette').[124] Moreover, there are frequent citations of previous decisions, though often without a detailed discussion of the precise facts and findings of those precedents, a practice even described as an 'uncritical use of headnotes'.[125] Academic writings are also frequently referred to. The latter may surprise lawyers from other legal traditions, but, when asked about it, German judges even respond that they 'genuinely consult these writings' and pay attention to the views of academics.[126]

French judgments, by contrast, contain no references to the academic literature. Traditionally, there have also been no references to previous cases. And, in total, the judgment may just be a few lines, hardly ever more than one page. The justification for such an approach is that the shortness of a judgment provides clarity,[127] similar to the French codes which are also deliberately drafted in a short but clear style. Others have called this way of writing judgments 'cryptic' and, since the late 1970s, the Paris Court of Appeals has provided more extensive explanations.[128] Still, the style of the Cour de Cassation, the highest court in matters of civil and criminal law, has remained unchanged.

This French style has puzzled US comparative lawyers. Michael Wells took the starting point that US lawyers expect 'reason and candor' in judicial decisions in order to guarantee fairness and legitimacy. Yet, French opinions written in 'an uninformative syllogism of a few hundred words' show that this correlation may not be as important as Americans think.[129] Mitchell Lasser's analysis was interested in the discourse not reported in the formalistic French judgments. He observed that policy-oriented discourse takes place in France as well, but that it

---

[121] Komarek 2011: 26; Curran 2001a: 87.

[122] See Forster 1995: 153–7 (for a general comparative overview); Monateri 2003 (for Italy).

[123] See also Mattila 2006: 85; Monateri 2003: 584 ('theoretical activism').

[124] Also noted by Markesinis 1994: 620.

[125] Zweigert and Kötz 1998: 264. See also Lundmark 2012: 363 (on empirical study of the frequency of citations in 1980s).

[126] Markesinis 1994: 609.   [127] See Monateri 2003: 584.

[128] See Steiner 2010: 171, 182; Lasser 2009a: 4; Mattila 2006: 85; Glendon et al. 2008: 145–6.

[129] Wells 1994.

is separated from the judgments ('bifurcation'). Evidence of this discourse can be found in the reports of the reporting judge and the opinions of the advocate-general, published in some cases. Thus, in Lasser's view, the differences between the US and France are about judicial mentalities, not the existence of substantive deliberation.[130]

(f) What effects do judgments have?

In both civil and common law countries, judgments are binding between the parties of the trial ('res judicata'). Thus, subject to appeals, there shall be no second trial on the same issue between the same parties ('inter partes'). Details differ between countries,[131] but the more interesting distinction is that some legal systems allow 'class actions', which have effect for everyone within the class who does not opt-out. A predecessor of class actions, 'group litigations', had existed in medieval England but they were gradually abolished throughout the nineteenth century.[132] In the US, however, the idea survived and it regained importance in modern times, since, today, single incidents can often harm many people (e.g. industrial accidents, investment frauds).[133] In civil law countries, other means, such as the involvement of public authorities or consumer organisations, have typically been used to tackle such problems.[134] Recently, in some civil law countries, limited forms of class actions have been introduced; yet, it is not clear to what extent they can really work in countries without US style law firms and contingency fees.[135]

With respect to the more general effect of judgments, it is a typical feature of common law countries that judgments not only decide individual cases but are precedents for future ones ('stare decisis').[136] This has the benefit of ensuring consistency and predictability, in the absence of comprehensive codifications. At the same time, the reasoning from case to case can ensure that the law is adaptable to changing circumstances.[137] The way this process works is that judges have to distinguish between factual differences, while also distinguishing between the ruling of a case (the 'ratio decidendi') and further elaborations (the 'obiter dicta') of judgments.[138] Thus, despite binding precedents, it may be argued that this process of reasoning gives judges considerable freedom, and in the US in particular it is frequently said that the importance of stare decisis should not be overemphasised.[139]

In civil law countries the traditional starting point is that previous court decisions are not binding and that case law is not a source of law.[140] In the French

---

[130] Lasser 2009a. See also Lasser 1998.   [131] See, e.g., Chase and Varano 2012: 227–9.
[132] For details see Yeazell 1987.   [133] See generally Zekoll 2006: 1358.
[134] See Hodges 2010; Chase and Varano 2012: 230–1.
[135] Milhaupt 2009: 843 (for South Korea); Mullenix 2010: 59 (mere formal convergence).
[136] Samuel in EE 2012: 175; Dodson and Klebba 2011: 13. But for its history see Hondius 2007.
[137] For this dual purpose see Fernandez and Ponzetto 2012.
[138] See Samuel in EE 2012: 175–6.   [139] See, e.g., Hondius 2007.
[140] For the debate in France see Steiner 2010: 85–6; Dawson 1968: 422. For changes in the importance of precedence in civil law countries see Marchenko 2011: 292–3.

tradition, the main reason for this is that the Napoleonic Codes had precisely the aim of preventing judges from making law.[141] In Germany, the strong tradition of legal scholarship may also play a role in promoting national uniformity, without binding precedents.[142] Yet, this is not the full picture. In some civil law countries, there are special laws that make decisions of supreme courts binding.[143] Moreover, it is argued that the persuasive authority that decisions of higher courts have in practice can be regarded as akin to precedents.[144]

This is not to say that the effect of precedents is identical in civil and common law countries. A study on precedents, coordinated by Neil Mac-Cormick and Robert Summers, illustrates this point. This research was based on country reports, drafted according to precise guidelines in order to facilitate comparisons.[145] Though overall the study finds some convergence, MacCormick and Summers conclude that common and civil law countries still tend to differ. Common law courts discuss precedents in detail in order to identify the 'ratio decidendi', and to give careful consideration of the facts. Conversely, it is common in civil law countries for the ruling of court to be reduced to the principles of law, with the facts of this decision having no further role to play in future cases.[146] Another important difference is that civil law courts often look for a series or group of decisions before they conclude that this line of reasoning should be followed.[147]

(g) Conclusion

The civil and common law divide is not always clear-cut. Yet, overall, this section has shown that courts operate differently in civil and common law countries. Moreover, the individual points of variation are not somehow arbitrary, but they often complement each other. As the frequent references between the different sub-sections have illustrated, topics such as the structure of courts, the prevalence of career judges, the use of juries, the form of civil proceedings, the role of judges in trials, the methods that judges use, and the style and the effect of their judgments are all closely interrelated. Thus, it may be said that, here at least, civil law on the one hand and common law on the other seem to be relatively coherent 'bundles' that cannot be mixed.

3. Comparative contract law

(a) Introduction

Contract law is regarded as a popular topic for comparative lawyers, since legal systems tend to share the initial division of this area of law into questions such as

---

[141] See 1 (a), above, and Hondius 2007: 16.   [142] See Mattei 1997a: 24.

[143] For Germany see Federal Constitutional Court Act (BVerfGG), s. 31(1).

[144] Maxeiner et al. 2010: 38; Bell 2006a: 69; Komarek 2011.

[145] See MacCormick and Summers 1997: 13–4.

[146] MacCormick and Summers 1997: 536–8. See also Curran 2006: 702; Curran 2001b: 74–5; Legrand 2003: 289–90 (against case-book approach to German law since it denies the experience of the Germanness in German law).

[147] MacCormick and Summers 1997: 538. See also Mattei et al. 2009: 619; Steiner 2010: 98.

contract formation, non-performance, and remedies, while also being different enough to make a comparison interesting.[148] A prominent feature of the books on comparative contract law is the division between common and civil law countries, with the main focus on English, French and German law.[149]

In part, this distinction is a reflection of different sources of law.[150] In common law countries, the starting point of contract law is typically case law, with statute law playing an increasingly important, though conceptually secondary role. An analysis of contract law in civil law countries typically starts with the civil codes, while not denying the role of case law and special statutes (e.g. on matters of consumer protection). In addition, the role of scholarship is seen as playing an important role in civil law countries: for instance, it has been said that scholars are to French contract law what judges are to the English one.[151] But there are also said to be differences in the substance of legal rules and concepts. The following illustrates those differences by way of three main topics of contract law.

(b) Contract formation

Most contracts are concluded by way of offer and acceptance, and this is indeed a starting point in both civil and common law countries. Yet, at a conceptual level, in common law countries contracts are defined in an objective way, since they require an exchange of promises, whereas in civil law countries more emphasis is put on the subjective element of a meeting of minds.[152] A similar divide exists in the interpretation of contracts: in the interest of legal certainty, common law countries use an objective starting point, whereas in civil law countries preference is given to the intention of the parties.[153] Of course, neither of these approaches is pure, so it may well be argued that the eventual results are often similar.[154]

A further prominent difference is the doctrine of consideration, which has developed in common but not civil law countries. This means that a valid contract requires that the parties agree to exchange something of value.[155] It is not necessary that the consideration is fair or adequate, but, if there is no consideration, in particular in the case of gifts, there can be no contract. Gifts are, of course, recognised in common law countries, but to make a binding promise

---

[148] Farnsworth 2006: 901.

[149] See, e.g., Kadner Grazio 2009 (focus on England, US, France, Germany, Italy, Switzerland); Levasseur 2008 (focus on England, US, France, Germany, Louisiana, Québec); Klimas 2006 (focus on England, US, France, Germany, Lithuania, Louisiana, Québec); Marsh 1994 (focus on England, France, Germany). See also Gordley and von Mehren 2006: 413–551 and Zweigert and Kötz 1998: 323–536 (both focus on England, US, France, Germany).

[150] See, e.g., Beale 2013: 323–5.   [151] Valcke 2009b: 81.

[152] Beale 2013: 320; Hermida 2004: 350–1; Legrand 1999: 3–4; Gordley and von Mehren 2006: 63 (for the background of the 'will theory').

[153] See, e.g., Herbots in EE 2012: 425–31.

[154] Barnes 2008; Van Hoecke 2004: 181, 189; Siems 2004a.

[155] See Gordley in EE 2012: 216–22; Gordley and von Mehren 2006: 421 (for the controversial historical background).

it has to be put in a deed. By contrast, civil law countries have no problem treating gifts as contracts but, then, the civil codes often impose formalities, such as a notarial deed, to make such a contract binding. Thus, we can say that the results are functionally similar. In a possible discussion between an English and a French lawyer about gifts, Rodolfo Sacco illustrates this as follows:

> [T]he two lawyers will claim that the difference between the two systems lies in the following: that the formal gift is valid in England because it is not a contract and therefore does not come under the law of consideration, while the formal gift is valid in France because it is a contract and therefore must be binding; that furthermore informal donation is not valid in either country and that delivery of a movable operates the transfer of ownership with the purpose of making a gift . . . [Thus] they will claim that the operating rules are analogous in the countries just quoted; and that however the phenomena are explained by techniques, concepts, dogmatic apparatus completely opposite in the various countries.[156]

(c) Good faith and pre-contractual duties

Another dividing factor is that in civil but not in common law countries, there is said to be a general principle of good faith in contract law. This principle has various dimensions. In terms of concluded contracts, good faith may be used to ensure fairness, though civil law countries also recognise the principle of good morals to strike down unfair contractual provisions. Moreover, even before a contract is concluded, parties have to act in a way that takes the interests of the other side into account. In German law, there is an explicit provision in the Civil Code stating that a pre-contractual relationship is a legal relationship under the law of obligations, with the result that the principle of good faith is applicable.[157] Pre-contractual liability is also possible in other civil law countries, where it may also be based on a general principle of fairness (as in the Netherlands) or tort law (as in France).[158]

In common law countries, good faith in contract law is a controversial topic. Although in 1766 Lord Mansfield referred to good faith as the governing principle applicable to all contracts and dealings,[159] and although the term good faith is sometimes used in specific cases,[160] traditionally, English law has not endorsed it as a general principle.[161] It has been said to be too uncertain, or even unworkable in practice, and inconsistent with values of a market economy since it gives undefined and unfettered discretion to judges to decide cases with subjective notions of morality and fairness. Good faith in pre-contractual

---

[156] Sacco 2001: 186–7. See also Sacco 1991: 350–8.
[157] German Civil Code (BGB), s. 311(2). See also Siems 2002.
[158] For more details see Cartwright and Hesselink 2009.
[159] *Carter* v. *Boehm* (1766) 3 Burr 1905 at 1909 (97 ER 1162 at 1164).
[160] Details in Piers 2011.
[161] For the following: *Walford* v. *Miles* [1992] 2 AC 128 at 138 per Lord Ackner; Thomson 1999; Goode 1998: 19–20.

negotiation is also regarded as being irreconcilable with the freedom of contract, and the adversarial position of the parties to negotiate the most favourable bargain and to look after their own interests, without need to act in an altruistic manner.

Yet, some legal tools of common law countries are similar to good faith.[162] A traditional technique is to use the concept of 'implied terms' to reach a result that is fair and just. More recently, some common law courts, though not the English ones, take it that there can be an equitable relief against procedural or substantive unconscionable bargains.[163] Legislation has also provided special rules on consumer protection, and some modern laws of common law countries actually do use the term 'good faith' in contract law.[164] How far this concept has properly 'arrived' in the common law is, however, a matter of debate. Gunther Teubner called its transplantation to the common law a 'legal irritant', since such an abstract and open-ended principle is seen as 'a unique expression of continental legal culture'.[165] This is confirmed by research showing that, in the judicial practice of English and US courts, good faith is only 'a weak interpretative tool'.[166] Specifically, there is no inclination to use good faith in order to establish duties in pre-contractual negotiations.[167]

Returning to the situation in civil law countries, it would, however, also be misleading to overemphasise the role of good faith. In Germany, for instance, the freedom of contract, the adversarial position of the parties and market economy are the main principles of contract law, and only under exceptional circumstances does the principle of good faith require that other policy reasons prevail. Good faith is also not about morality, nor does it give unfettered discretion to judges. German courts do not use good faith to allow the legal consequences of contract or statute in a single case to be superseded by a supposedly more equitable solution; rather, they employ it to develop categories and rules which can then be applied in a reliable way to individual cases.[168]

Thus, the extent to which there are differences in the results between legal systems depends on the specific circumstances. One of studies of the Common Core project investigated how European legal systems solved thirty cases dealing with good faith. It was found that eleven cases led to the same result, in nine there was general but imperfect harmony, and, in ten, significant disharmony of results, with English law often, but not always, pursuing a path separate from the legal systems of the continent.[169]

---

[162] See Piers 2011: 152–62; Valcke 2009b: 77.

[163] For Australia, New Zealand, Canada and the US see, e.g., Chen-Wishart 1989; Kiefel 2000: 693–5.

[164] See Mason 2000. For the US see also Uniform Commercial Code (UCC), s. 1–201.

[165] Teubner 1998: 19. For legal transplants as 'irritants' see also ch. 8 at A 2 (c), below.

[166] Pistor 2005: 259–61.   [167] See McKendrick 1999.

[168] Similar Kötz 2010: 1245 ('number of distinct rules').

[169] Zimmermann and Whittaker 2000. For the Common Core see also ch. 2 at B 3, above.

(d) Contractual remedies

In the field of contractual remedies one also finds frequent references to differences between civil and common law countries. The following provides three examples.[170]

First, a fundamental question is whether the main remedy is specific performance or damages. In civil law countries, the starting point is that each party can force the other to perform the contractual obligation; thus, 'one does not buy a right to damages, one buys a horse'.[171] In particular, this is the case when performance can be ensured by the handing over of an existing good, whereas rules of civil procedure may exclude enforcement to perform in nature in other cases, such as individual services.[172] The line of reasoning in common law countries is precisely the opposite. According to Oliver Wendell Holmes, 'the duty to keep a contract at common law means a prediction that you must pay damages if you do not keep it – and nothing else'.[173] Thus, one is generally free to refuse performance, provided that one then becomes liable to compensate the other party. This is supported by economic arguments since it allows an 'efficient breach of contract'.[174] But there are also exceptions to this rule: for instance, in US law, 'specific performance may be decreed where the goods are unique or in other proper circumstances'.[175] Thus, it is possible, but not necessary, that, in practice, civil and common law countries reach the same result.

Second, and similarly, there is a different starting point for the question of whether a claim for damages requires any fault on the part of the other side. Fault is typically required in civil law countries, in particular in Germany, though there is often a shift of the burden of proof.[176] Other civil law countries, in particular France, more frequently distinguish between different types of contract, and exclude damages only in the case of *force majeure*.[177] In the common law, the starting point is strict liability. For example, in an English case involving the liability of a laundry, it was stated:

> The laundry company undertakes, not to exercise due care in laundering the customer's goods, but to launder them, and if it fails to launder them it is no use saying 'I did my best. I exercised due care and took reasonable precautions, and I am very sorry if as a result the linen is not properly laundered.'[178]

However, this is not the entire picture because there are many cases where the principle of strict liability does not apply.[179] It has therefore been said that, in both civil and common law countries, often intermediate solutions prevail, such

---

[170] For further topics see, e.g., Torsello in EE 2012: 754–76; Treitel 1988.
[171] Jones 1983: 452.   [172] See Lando and Rose 2003.
[173] Holmes 1897: 462.   [174] See, e.g., Shavell 2006; Siems 2003: 51–3.
[175] Uniform Commercial Code, s. 2–716. Similarly, the case law in England: *Co-operative Insurance Society Ltd* v. *Argyll Stores (Holdings) Ltd* [1998] AC 1.
[176] German Civil Code (BGB), s. 280(1).   [177] See Zweigert and Kötz 1998: 499–502.
[178] *Alderslade* v. *Hendon Laundry* [1945] 1 All E R 244 at 246 (CA) per Lord Greene, MR.
[179] See Zweigert and Kötz 1998: 503–5.

as adjusting the burden of proof, requiring fault but on the basis of an objective standard of care, or distinguishing between different types of contracts.[180]

Third, civil and common law countries tend to differ in their treatment of penalty clauses. In principle, civil law countries allow penalty clauses. Courts have, however, some means of control. For instance, in German law a penalty that is 'disproportionately high' may be reduced to a reasonable amount, and in French law the penalty can be reduced or increased if it is 'manifestly excessive or derisory'.[181] Common law countries distinguish between penalty and agreed damages clauses because agreeing on a penalty would be against the doctrine of consideration. A clause which requires a party that has broken the contract to pay a sum which is extravagant in relation to the likely loss is invalid as a penalty; but a clause which represents a genuine pre-estimate of the likely loss is a valid liquidated damages clause.[182] Although this prohibition of penalties has become less restrictive,[183] insertion of a penalty clause into a contract is still a risky enterprise.

(e) Conclusion

The differences outlined in this section can be seen as interconnected. The main feature of the contract law of common law countries is that it places strong emphasis on the predictability of the results of a case – for instance, in favouring an objective approach to contract interpretation while rejecting the principle of good faith and reducing the scope of specific performance. By contrast, the contract law of civil law countries, for instance, its subjective interpretation and the principle of good faith, has been related to Kantian principles of personal freedom of will and personal responsibility, as well as ideas of natural law.[184]

These differences between common and civil law may be regarded as remarkable since Western societies are fairly similar.[185] But it is also possible to relate those legal differences to socio-economic ones. For instance, it has been said that 'the English law of contract was designed for a nation of shopkeepers', while 'the French system was made for a race of peasants'.[186] Or to put it in a more elaborate way:

> [D]ifferences may be explained by the fact that English courts hear more cases involving shipping, international trade and financial services than courts on the continent. The atmosphere is naturally more bracing, so that if a choice has to be

---

[180] Grundmann 2009.   [181] German Civil Code (BGB), s. 343(1); French Code Civil, art. 1152.

[182] *Dunlop Pneumatic Tyre Co. Ltd* v. *New Garage & Motor Co. Ltd* [1915] AC 79.

[183] *Philips Hong Kong* v. *Attorney-General of Hong Kong* (1993) 61 Build LR 41 (Privy Council).

[184] Banakas 2008: 546. See also Moss 2007: 1 (in contract law emphasis on certainty in common law countries and on justice in the specific case in civil law ones).

[185] Bell 1995: 23.

[186] Kahn-Freund et al. 1979: 318. See also Kötz 2010: 1251 ('Of course, "shopkeepers" might have to be replaced these days by "hard-nosed business executives" and "peasants" by "consumers"').

made between the justice in the individual case and the security of the transaction, the latter is the favoured option.[187]

A contentious aspect of this statement is that law is seen as simply following social and economic circumstances. This has been a frequent topic of socio-legal approaches to comparative law, to be discussed later in this book.[188]

C. Critical analysis

The previous section has aimed to provide a fair picture of the common/civil law divide, neither overemphasising the differences between these two legal families, nor downplaying the variety within them. At the same time, these caveats have already indicated that calling a country 'civil law' or 'common law' may only have a limited explanatory value. The following provides further reasons to be sceptical.

1. Diversity in continental Europe

The legal systems of continental Europe cannot be regarded as uniform modern versions of Roman law. Modern civil law countries may have rules which are precisely the opposite of Roman law – for instance, in allowing specific performance.[189] Moreover, there is considerable diversity between civil law countries. One can start with saying that there were different 'common laws' in Europe (*droit commun* in France, *gemeine Recht* in Germany, *derecho commún* in Spain etc.), which did not disappear with the reception of Roman law.[190] In addition, the received commonalities became weaker with the emergence of nation states, since national codifications gradually modified the Justinian version of Roman law.[191]

Thus, for instance, it has been said that, in the substantive law, '[t]he differences between French and German law may be as great, or even greater, than those between French and English, or German and English law'.[192] As to the operation of courts, it has also been found that there is 'no single pattern', due to the way the diverse structures of the judiciary, the government, the legal community and wider society are interrelated.[193] Accordingly, there are also differences in judicial style, where one may identify not a clear divide, but a spectrum of open to closed legal reasoning, starting with England, then Germany, then the Netherlands, and finally France.[194]

Consequently, most classifications distinguish at least between a Romanist and a Germanic model of continental civil law.[195] A common way of differentiation is whether the main codes of a country are akin to the French or the German

---

[187] Zweigert and Kötz 1998: 510.   [188] See ch. 6, below.
[189] See Mattei et al. 2009: 880; Zimmermann 1996: 591.   [190] Glenn 2005; Glenn 2013: 112–25.
[191] See A above and ch. 8 at B 1, below.   [192] Zimmermann 2001: 113.
[193] Bell 2006a: 2.   [194] Jagtenberg and de Roo 2009: 304–5.   [195] See ch. 4 at B, below.

models. Moreover, some taxonomies have a separate category for the Nordic countries, since they differ from other continental legal systems in not having adopted comprehensive codes. Naturally, things become even more complex when one considers non-European countries, as Chapter 4 will explain.

2. Differences between England and the US

Just as England and the United States may be 'two nations separated by a common language',[196] their two legal systems are also said to be 'separated by a common law'.[197] Two versions of this divergence are suggested. On the one hand, some point towards the mixed nature of US law because it has rejected many common law principles and has adopting those from the civil law.[198] On the other hand, there is the position of American exceptionalism. Most prominent is Robert Kagan's view that the 'American way of law' follows a strict version of 'adversarial legalism', which is different from all other legal systems: not only those of civil law countries, but also England.[199] A similar result may follow from the fact that, due to EU law, 'English law is gradually becoming less English',[200] whereas the US has retained many elements of the original English common law.

In detail, it is possible to identify a number of significant differences between the substantive law of England and the US. The constitutional structure of both countries is very different: the US has a written constitution and is a federal country. US law has also put a stronger emphasis on human rights as a result of the struggle for independence and the influence of the French Revolution.[201] This may also explain why US tort law is more protective, for instance, in cases of violations of privacy.[202] In addition, Kagan mentions further differences: in the US, criminal sanctions are more severe, social insurance is less important, while the tax rate is lower than in other developed countries.[203]

There are also differences in terms of courts, civil procedure and legal thought. In some of these areas, the US can be regarded as more 'civilian' than England. The Code of Civil Procedure, drafted by David Dudley Field, and the Uniform Commercial Code, a result of work by Karl Llewellyn, are said to have been partially influenced by the civil law.[204] In terms of sources of law, extensive legislation – possibly similar to civil law countries – is today regarded as a typical feature of US law.[205] And, with respect to the doctrine of precedent,

---

[196] Referring to the Oscar Wilde quote, 'We have really everything in common with America nowadays except, of course, language' (*The Canterville Ghost*, 1887).

[197] Curran 1998a: 55.   [198] Glenn 2010a: 263.   [199] Kagan 2001; Kagan 2007.

[200] Cooke 2004: 273.   [201] See von Mehren 2010: 6; Mattei et al. 2009: 67.

[202] Garoupa and Gómez Ligüerre 2011: 329–32. See also Reimann 2003: 837–8 (for product liability).

[203] Kagan 2001; Kagan 2007. For the harshness of US criminal law see also ch. 5 at B 2 (a) and ch. 6 at C 2 below.

[204] Van Rhee and Verkerk in EE 2012: 142; Whitman 1987.

[205] Glenn 2010a: 263. Though civil law legislation may be more principled, see B 1 (a), above.

it is said that US judges usually have more flexibility than their English counterparts.[206]

Yet, more often the emphasis is on US exceptionalism – or, if put from a European perspective, on the idea that 'the English judiciary appears to be more like the Continental system(s) than it is like the American'.[207] Most of these differences are related to the fact that, in US civil procedure, the jury still plays an important role, in contrast to England and other legal systems. It follows that US law uses more extensive pre-trial discovery, since a jury trial needs to be a single event. The trial itself follows a strong adversarial tradition controlled by the parties and their lawyers (e.g. when it comes to questioning witnesses). Today, this is not only different from continental European courts, but also English ones, where judges can manage cases more actively than in the past.[208]

In the US judicial process, it is crucial for parties to be able to afford the best lawyers since, in contrast to other countries, legal aid for civil cases is usually not available.[209] Such a 'privatised model' is also apparent from the way fees and costs are allocated.[210] Since in the US even the winning party has to pay its own costs, the involvement in trials can be very expensive. The possibility of contingency fees can reduce this risk; such arrangements, however, also confirm the strongly competitive nature of the US judicial process. In addition, the possibility of class actions has the effect that winning a case may not only be about getting justice, but also about making a profit. What emerges, therefore, is that the US approach encourages 'litigant activism', whereas the loser-pays rule and the lack of contingent fees and class actions in England reduce the incentive to file 'novel suits'.[211]

Turning to judges, it is also possible to present a strong contrast between the US and England (as well as other European countries). In the US, it is regarded as essential that the selection of judges is democratically legitimised, say, by way of election or political appointment. Thus, political, social and moral values often play a crucial role. In England, by contrast, the focus is on professional qualifications. It has also been argued that the English system has moved to a model of a career judiciary: one starts as a barrister, then becomes a 'recorder', and eventually a judge.[212] All of this also has the consequence that the English judiciary is more homogenous and less political than its US counterpart.

---

[206] Atiyah and Summers 1991: 113–34; Posner 1996: 90. See also B 2 (f), above.

[207] Posner 1996: 36. Similarly Kern 2007: 90; Andrews 2010: 98. For the following see Parker 2009; Garoupa and Gómez Ligüerre 2012: 335–40; Vorrasi 2004; Unidroit 2003: 5.

[208] See B 2 (d), above.

[209] See Maxeiner et al. 2010: 48 and Cappelletti and Garth 1987: para. 63 (on the access to justice movement and the welfare model of civil procedure).

[210] Mattei and Nader 2008: 146. See also B 2 (d), above.

[211] These terms are from Kagan 2001: 9 and Posner 1996: 34, 90.

[212] Posner 1996: 30 (classifiying barristers as akin to junior judges); Bell 2006a: 298.

Furthermore, the political function of US judges can be seen in their role 'as guardians of the constitution'.[213] Most importantly, they can review legislation. Thus, judges are central players in a politically fragmented system, despite controversy over the limits to judicial activism. In the English tradition, judicial review of legislation is not possible, since judges should respect the primacy of parliament.[214] The more cautious approach of English judges can also be observed more generally. English judges tend to reason formally by, for instance, relying on previous case law and interpreting statutory law in a narrow fashion. By contrast, American judges are said to be less reluctant to engage openly with policy arguments and to decide on ethically, politically or scientifically sensitive topics.[215]

A similar division can be seen in legal thought more generally. It has been noted that, in the nineteenth century, German ideas about teaching law at universities were influential in the US.[216] Yet, the twentieth century has seen significant changes in US legal thinking, with the main trends and schools being legal realism, law and society, law and economics, and empirical legal studies. Thus, Susan Bartie contends that, today,

> the main point of distinction is that in America there is a growing band of scholars who proclaim that the discipline can abandon its link with the profession and should boldly shape its interdisciplinary studies to meet broader conceptions of the law.[217]

Here, too, the US is therefore the exception because legal thinking in England as well as in continental Europe tends to be more focused on black letter law.[218] This is not to deny that there have also been some developments in Europe. It has, for instance, been said of the UK that today's legal scholarship is more varied and lively than fifty years ago.[219] Still, comparing three of the major law journals of England, Germany and the US, Reinhard Zimmermann rightly observes that

> the briefest comparative glance at the Law Quarterly Review reveals that in approach, outlook and focus it is much closer to the Juristenzeitung than to the Harvard Law Review.[220]

Overall, the theme that emerges is that there are significant differences between the legal systems of the US on the one hand, and those of England and other European countries on the other. According to Kagan, these legal differences are so deeply entrenched in political structures and legal cultures that no changes

---

[213] von Mehren 2010: 6.
[214] For further discussion on judicial review see ch. 8 at B 4 (a), below.
[215] Atiyah and Summers 1991; MacCormick and Summers 1991.
[216] Mattei et al. 2009: 67.   [217] Bartie 2010: 367. See also Edwards 1992.
[218] See Grechenig and Gelter 2008; Posner 1996: 21.
[219] Twining 1997: 338–9. See also Siems and MacSithigh 2012: 670–1.
[220] Zimmermann 1996: 584.

can be expected.[221] Even if this goes too far, it can be seen that the features distinguishing US from English law are closely connected. Thus, we are not talking about some minor variation, which can be found between all members of the same legal family; rather, it can be misleading even to start with the assumption that English and US law are fundamentally similar.

3. Western law instead of civil v. common law?

The emphasis on the common/civil law divide can disguise the commonalities shared by Western legal systems. Relevant general factors[222] include concepts and ideas such as nation states, capitalism, liberal values, individualism, and a joined intellectual, cultural and scientific heritage from Greek and Roman philosophy, Christianity and the Enlightenment. Factors more specific to law include individual human rights, the rule of law, a positive and rational law, a specialised legal profession with judges and lawyers, and the separation between law and religion. It may therefore be justified to speak of a comprehensive Western legal tradition, being different from the laws of religious and tribal communities and dysfunctional states.

More specifically, it is too simplistic to say that the civil law, but not the common law, is based on Roman law. On the one hand, no contemporary legal system is entirely based on Roman law. According to Reinhard Zimmermann, 'it is not easy to think of a legal rule derived, directly or indirectly from Roman law and expressed exactly the same way in all European codes'.[223] Even core civil law countries such as France and Germany are not only a product of Roman law but also of their own local traditions.[224] On the other hand, considerable evidence of Roman law can be found in common law countries. For instance, in Patrick Glenn's description of English law, there are repeated references to Roman law such as the relevance of canon law, the Roman origins of trust law, and the influence of Pothier and the French codes in England.[225] Another point to mention is the use of legal Latin and legal French in England.[226]

There has also been extensive research on the convergence between civil and common law countries.[227] This discussion about convergence goes beyond legal families, by, for instance, showing how international, transnational and regional laws, as well as other influencing factors, have changed domestic legal systems.[228] But, more specifically, convergence has been identified in the areas

---

[221] Kagan 2007. But for convergence see ch. 9 at A 3 and B, below.

[222] For the following see, e.g., Glenn 2010b; Mousourakis 2006: 66–7; Zimmermann 2001: 111; Husa 2004: 26–7; Goldman 2008: 16; Van Hoecke and Warrington 1998: 502–3; Ziegert 2004: 149; Kinoshita 2001: 32; Gambaro and Sacco 2002: 51 ('occidental law'). See also Wieacker 1990 (for a common European legal culture).

[223] Zimmermann 2001: 114.   [224] See 1 above and ch. 4 at C 3 (a), below.

[225] Glenn 2010a: 239, 269–70, 272. See also Markesinis 2000: 38–42.   [226] Mattila 2006: 228.

[227] See, e.g., Van Hoecke and Warrington 1998: 499–501; Worthington 2011: 349; Markesinis 2000 and the following notes.

[228] See ch. 9, below.

that are seen as determinant for the civil/common law divide: civil procedure, legal methods and sources of law.[229] Thus, it is worth revisiting some of those topics as they relate to the roles of legislation, courts, and legal academics, in both legal families.

With respect to legislation, the distinction of countries with or without codes has lost its relevance. In civil law countries, the main codes are no longer seen to be the most significant sources of law, and common law countries are said to have reached the 'age of statutes'.[230] The legislative style in civil and common law is also more mixed than it is traditionally assumed. In some areas of law, such as tax law or land law, precise and detailed rules are used in both legal families. Other pieces of legislation are drafted in a more principled fashion, not only in the civil law, but also the common law, as frequent words such as 'reasonableness', 'equitable', and 'unfair' show.[231] In terms of statutory interpretation, the proposition that there is a clear civil/common law divide has also been challenged. In the last few decades, English courts have moved away from a narrow interpretation, for instance, in allowing analogies of statutory provisions.[232] In a comprehensive study on statutory interpretation in France, Germany and England, Stefan Vogenauer has also shown that, despite different starting points, all three legal systems use a similar mix of formal and value-oriented arguments.[233]

Turning to courts, the main criticism is that the common/civil law divide mischaracterises the way the judiciary works in today's civil law countries. According to Martin Shapiro, it is 'fundamentally incorrect' to assume that the civil-law judge simply applies a set of complete and self-explanatory rules in a mechanical way.[234] Similarly, according to Sir Basil Markesinis and Jörg Fedtke, it is not accurate to describe the judicial function of civil-law judges as 'narrow, mechanical, and uncreative';[235] rather, here too they are the 'oracles of law'.[236] Particular reference can be made to the importance of general clauses in civil law countries, such as the principle of good faith: here, akin to common-law case law, courts develop the law incrementally.[237] This point can also be reversed; referring to the common law, Hein Kötz asks:

> Would the balance of power between Parliament and the judges be altered if the German rule were introduced in England by way of statute? I do not believe so. In both countries judges operate under fairly broad principles, and in both countries the practitioner must eventually look at the precedents in order to find out what a court is likely to say in a difficult case.[238]

---

[229] See B 1 above. For convergence in civil procedure see Chase and Walker 2010; Dodson and Klebba 2011. For sources of law see Zweigert and Kötz 1998: 201; Zimmermann 2001: 177–85; also Reimann 2002: 677.

[230] Worthington 2011: 359. For a critical view of the 'age of statutes' see Calabresi 1985.

[231] For further examples see Kötz 1987: 4–5.   [232] Kötz 1987: 10–1. See also Voermans 2011.

[233] Vogenauer 2001.   [234] Shapiro 1981: 126–56.

[235] Merryman and Pérez-Perdomo 2007: 38.

[236] Markesinis and Fedtke 2009: 182–3. This refers to Dawson 1968.

[237] See Zimmermann 2001: 176.   [238] Kötz 1987: 6–7.

As to the role of legal scholars, a strict common/civil law divide fails to consider that legal thought has long extended across the borders. Duncan Kennedy identifies three globalisations of legal thought: classical legal thought (1850–1914), based on the German concept of 'legal science'; the social (1900–68), mainly driven by French scholarship on the limits of positivism; and policy analysis, neo-formalism and adjudication from US legal scholarship (since 1945).[239] Of course, this does not deny differences. Yet, overall, it is plausible to conclude that, today, legislators, courts, and scholars play a joined role in both civil and common law countries, not least because all three groups depend on each other.[240]

Finally, the distinction between civil and common law can mislead in pointing towards presumed differences in substantive law. For instance, it has been said that both legal families 'divide private law into large legal fields, such as property, tort, and contracts, among others, and analyse these fields in a similar way', and that 'there is probably as much diversity among the responses of civil law systems to various legal issues as there is between civil law and common law countries'.[241] These are fairly general statements, but many more specific examples can also be provided – for example, that 'civil and common law do not differ fundamentally in the types of trust-like arrangements that they permit',[242] that in commercial contract law they can even 'be considered as one legal tradition',[243] and that the common/civil law divide does not play a role for new legal topics, such as internet law.[244]

D. Conclusion

The concluding sections on civil procedure and contract law in civil and common law identified some interconnected similarities between the rules of countries of the same legal family.[245] Yet, the more general conclusion has to be a more sceptical one. It has been said that 'comparison all too often proceeds through misleading or exaggerated dichotomies and binaries'.[246] The foregoing discussion has shown that this is also a recurrent problem for the distinction between civil and common law countries. This is not to deny that legal systems differ in various ways. Thus, criticising the civil/common law divide is not meant to imply that there are no differences, but, rather, that it can be misleading to regard this divide as the main tool to understand them: for example, it would

---

[239] Kennedy 2003a. See also ch. 8 at B 1 (b), below.

[240] For the interdependency see Shapiro and Stone Sweet 2002: 174–5.

[241] Hermida 2004: 343; Glendon et al. 2008: 50.

[242] Mattei 1997a: 175. See also Zimmermann 2001: 167 ('it can hardly be maintained that a wall of incomprehension separated English trust from the law of the Continent. Rather the trust appears to be the specifically English variation of a common European theme.').

[243] Hermida 2004. For further examples see Constantinesco 1983: 131–2.

[244] Marchenko 2011: 298.

[245] See B 2 (g) and 3 (e), above. Cf. also Bell 1995: 28 (on the coherency of legal traditions).

[246] Freeden and Vincent 2013: 10.

be too risky to start with the presumption that, say, just because a particular legal rule of contract law says something for France that is probably also how it is for Germany.

The present chapter focused on Western countries, in particular France and Germany as civil law countries, and England and the US as common law ones. If one considers other parts of the world, the limitations of the civil and common law families are likely to become even more striking. To be sure, here, other categories also play a role. Accordingly, the next chapter provides a more general discussion about the benefits, limitations and pitfalls of classifying the world into distinct legal families.

4

Mapping the world's legal systems

The division between civil and common law countries discussed in Chapter 3 is a major building block for mapping the world's legal systems. In addition, a number of further categories have been suggested. Section A discusses why scholars attempt to classify the world's legal system at all. Section B provides examples of how precisely this has been done in the twentieth and early twenty-first centuries. The critical analysis of Section C challenges the usefulness of these classifications for comparative law, and Section D concludes.

A. Background and purpose

Classifications are common in many academic disciplines. In the natural sciences, the most prominent example is the Linnaean taxonomy of animals, plants, and minerals, originally developed in 1735 by Carl Linnaeus. This taxonomy is also said to have inspired 'the comparative lawyer as a zoologist' to classify legal systems.[1] Yet, in substance, the various taxonomies of the social sciences are closer to comparative law, since some of those categories mirror the legal families explained in the next section.

For example, in linguistics, one can distinguish between language families, such as Indo-European, Afro-Asiatic, and Sino-Tibetan, each having various offspring.[2] Classifications of religions may start with the main categories of Abrahamic, Indian and East Asian religions, or list them by the number of adherents to, say, Christianity, Islam, Hinduism etc.[3] With respect to cultures, various classifications are possible. A prominent example is by Samuel Huntington, who identified eight civilisations: Western, Confucian, Japanese, Islamic, Hindu, Slavic-Orthodox, Latin American and African.[4]

There are also frequent classifications of political and economic systems. With respect to politics, an initial distinction can be drawn between presidential and parliamentary republics, and constitutional and absolute monarchies, and there

---

[1] Mattei et al. 2009: 258; also Glenn 2006: 423; Constantinesco 1971: 257; Varga 2007: 97.
[2] See www.ethnologue.com/browse/families. See also http://wals.info/languoid; Constantinesco 1983: 435–41.
[3] See www.adherents.com/Religions_By_Adherents.html.
[4] Huntington 1993; Huntington 1996. See also ch. 11 at C 1, below.

are also more sophisticated classifications of the electoral systems of the world.[5] Until the end of the Cold War, it was also common to distinguish between 'three worlds' of capitalist, communist and non-aligned countries;[6] today, one suggestion is that countries can be classified into eight worlds, considering economic policies as well as wealth.[7] An alternative distinction is based on political power: here Immanuel Wallerstein's historical research is influential, suggesting that the 'world system' is composed of countries of the core, the semi-periphery and the periphery.[8] This produces a result which is akin to the frequent distinction of the development literature between developed countries, transition economies (emerging economies, newly industrialised countries) and developing countries (less developed countries).[9]

Since taxonomies seem to be feasible in these fields, it may simply be the case that 'so too the comparatist can classify laws by reducing them to a limited number of families'.[10] Such a 'just do it' approach may also draw a parallel to more pedestrian activities: in the words of Jacques Vanderlinden, 'classifying legal systems is similar to reorganising the books in our library, or the knives in our kitchen'.[11]

In addition, more substantive reasons can be suggested as to why comparative lawyers attempt to map the legal systems of the world. First, the main rationale mentioned in the literature is that classifications facilitate the description and understanding of foreign laws. A researcher who analyses legal systems that are known to share common features can focus on the remaining differences.[12] Similarly, there is a benefit when learning about foreign laws:

> If one has for instance become acquainted with English law, the need arises for knowledge of legal rules in New Zealand, one can avoid having to study New Zealand law from the beginning; since the New Zealand legal system is based upon English law, it is sufficient to concentrate on the relatively few significant differences between the two legal systems.[13]

A necessary caveat is that classifications only provide an initial picture, often used for pedagogical and didactic purposes.[14] Legal families are bound to be 'a loose conglomeration of data', 'a rough and ready device' or a 'first roughly

---

[5] IDEA 2008. See also ch. 11 at B, below.

[6] A study that related these categories to other differences was Sawyer 1967–68.

[7] Economides and Wilson 2001: 115 (US/EU/Japan, other OECD countries, newly industrialised economies, semi-industrialised countries, newer newly industrialised economies, former Soviet Union countries, remaining communist countries, sub-Saharan Africa).

[8] E.g. Wallerstein 1979. See also Economides and Wilson 2001: 56–7.

[9] For a good overview see Nielsen 2011.

[10] David 1985: 18. See also Husa 2011b: 112 ('paralleling the comparative study of law with scientific disciplines').

[11] Vanderlinden 2002: 162.

[12] Hertel 2009: 128. Similarly Twining 2000a: 152, 178.   [13] Bogdan 1994: 38.

[14] Husa 2004: 19; Bogdan 1994: 85; David 1985: 21; Mousourakis 2006: 59.

sketched map'.[15] Thus, as one goes deeper into a comparative analysis, complications and qualifications of the national legal systems mean that one has to go beyond the initial taxonomy.[16]

Methodologically, this is not at all unusual. For example, such an approach can be related to Karl Popper's view that scientific knowledge grows by way of 'conjectures and refutations'.[17] Since legal family classifications can never be a perfect fit to the real world, they can be seen as, more or less refined, conjectures. But, it is then also the task of the comparative researcher to critically scrutinise these conjectures in order to gain a fuller picture of the legal world.

The second reason for mapping legal systems is that being part of the same legal family does not 'just' mean that legal systems have a set of legal rules in common: it can also be a 'matter of self-identity', or even an attempt at 'insulation' from foreign influence.[18] For example, for lawyers from Hong Kong, being part of the common law may help them to maintain a difference from mainland China, as English lawyers may like to use the common law to show that they are different from continental European countries. A similar relationship may also be observed in the civil (or mixed) character of the laws of Quebec and Scotland within Canada and the United Kingdom.[19]

Third, legal families can help predict the success of legal transplants. If two legal systems are based on similar conceptual understandings of the law, the transfer of a rule or institution between these countries is more likely to be successful than across legal families.[20]

Fourth, classifications may be used to show how legal similarities and differences are related to non-legal ones. For example, in economic geography, a distinction is made between spatial, institutional, cultural, organisational and relational proximity.[21] Geographers are primarily interested in the spatial aspect, and lawyers in the institutional one. But if one combines those taxonomies, it may be possible to say whether legal traditions are conditioned by spatial or other non-legal circumstances.

B. Classifying countries

1. Bases for classification

Jaakko Husa explains that the various taxonomies of legal families are based on:

---

[15] Glenn 2010a: 15–6; Zweigert and Kötz 1998: 72; Husa 2011b: 116.

[16] Mattei et al. 2009: 260; Zweigert and Kötz 1998: 72.

[17] Popper 1963. See also Glenn 2010a: 1–3 (referring to Popper's 'rational theory of tradition').

[18] Mattei et al. 2009: 263; Monateri 2012: 9.

[19] For England see Monateri 2012: 9. For mixed legal systems see C 3 (a), below.

[20] Mattei 1997b: 5; Esquirol 2001: 223; Berkowitz et al. 2003a: 167; Berkowitz et al. 2003b: 163; also Lalenis et al. 2002 (for policy transfers). See also ch. 8 at A 2 (d), below.

[21] Coe et al. 2010: 147–8.

history, ideology, legal style, legal argumentation and thinking, codification level of law, judicial reasoning, structural system of law, structure of court system, spirit and mentality of legal actors, training of lawyers, law's relation to religion and to politics, the economical basis of law, the background philosophy of legal thinking, the doctrine of sources of law, the empirical effectiveness of formal legal rules, the role of tradition in law, paradigmatic societal beliefs about law, etc.[22]

These criteria do not always lead to a clear-cut division of legal systems. Thus, to classify countries means making a decision about some common aspects that matter, while disregarding others.[23] Methodologically, two approaches may be distinguished. On the one hand, it can be said that, historically, legal systems have evolved into distinct 'real types' of legal families; notably, this is the case for the way the division of common and civil law countries is usually presented.[24] On the other hand, some comparative lawyers have developed 'ideal types' of legal families – for instance, referring to possible sources of law, which are then applied in order to classify countries.[25]

However, these starting points are less different than they appear. The historical reasoning does not mean that legal classifications are permanent. It is clear that 'legal systems never are, they always become'.[26] Thus, classifications are bound to be subject to change, not dissimilar to classifications of economic or political systems.[27] With respect to the ideal types, it is evident that their criteria are chosen in a way as to reflect differences between the actual legal systems of the world. Moreover, as the proponents of this view use criteria that are 'permanent' or 'determinant', not merely 'incidental or fungible',[28] here, too, historical contingencies play an important role. The following classifications will also show that most classifications have led to relatively similar results.

2. Review of main classifications

Table 4.1 displays how academics have tried to map the legal families of the world.[29] The first two examples, both from the first decades of the twentieth century, employed classifiers that would not be approved by today's comparatists, while the actual categories are not entirely different from modern

---

[22] Husa in EE 2012: 492–3. See also Vanderlinden 1995: 328 (identifying 14 criteria used in literature).

[23] Peters and Schwenke 2000: 826.   [24] See ch. 3 at A, above.

[25] Vanderlinden 1995: 338–355 (customary, doctrinal, jurisprudential, legislative and religious legal systems); similar Vanderlinden 2002: 169, 178; also Constantinesco 1971: 266–7 and 1983: 270–431 (determinant elements of legal systems); also referring to 'ideal types' are Bavinck and Woodman 2009: 208; Luts 2011: 49.

[26] Mattei 1997b: 14; Mattei and di Robilant 2001: 1075.

[27] See A above. See also Constantinesco 1983: 477, 521; Husa 2004: 31 (distinguishing legal families as 'strengthening/established' and 'weakening/unestablished').

[28] Luts 2011: 41; Constantinesco 1983: 241. See also Mattei 1997b: 15.

[29] For good overviews see also Pargendler 2012b; Varga 2010; Husa in EE 2012: 493–8; Constantinesco 1983: 88–157.

Table 4.1 Overview of legal family classifications across time

	France, Italy, Spain, Belgium; Latin America	Germany, Austria, Switzerland, Greece	Nordic countries, or mixed legal systems (RSA etc.)	England, Ireland, US, Canada, Australia, Singapore, Hong Kong	Russia; Eastern European & Central Asian countries, Cuba	North Africa, Middle East, Pakistan, Malaysia, Indonesia	Israel	India	Japan, China, Mongolia, (South) Korea, Thailand, Vietnam	Sub-Saharan Africa
Sauser-Hall 1913	Law of the Arian (Indo-European) people	Law of the Arian (Indo-European) people	Law of the Arian (Indo-European) people	Law of the Arian (Indo-European) people	Law of the Arian (Indo-European) people	Semitic	Semitic	Indo-European	Mongelic	Barbarous people
Wigmore 1928	Romanesque	Germanic		Anglican	Slavic	Islam	Hebrew	Hindu	Japanese / Chinese	(Seven historical legal systems)
Arminjon et al. 1951	French	German	Scandinavian	English	Russian	Islamic		Hindu		
Schnitzer 1961	Roman	German		Anglo-American	Slavic	Religious laws (Islamic, Jewish, Christian)	Religious laws (Islamic, Jewish, Christian)	Afro-Asiatic laws	Afro-Asiatic laws	
Derrett 1968	Roman			English		Islamic	Jewish	Hindu	Chinese	African
David 1950	Western				Soviet	Muslim		Hindu	Chinese	
David 1982/85	Romano-Germanic	Romano-Germanic	Romano-Germanic	Common law	Socialist	Other forms of social order (Muslim, Indian, Far East, Africa)	Other forms of social order (Muslim, Indian, Far East, Africa)	Other forms of social order (Muslim, Indian, Far East, Africa)	Other forms of social order (Muslim, Indian, Far East, Africa)	Other forms of social order (Muslim, Indian, Far East, Africa)
Zweigert and Kötz 1996/98	Romanistic	Germanic	Nordic	Common law		Islamic		Hindu	Japanese / Chinese	
Mattei 1997b	Professional law / Civil law	Professional law / Civil law	Professional law / Mixed systems	Professional law / Common law	Political law / Law of transition	Traditional law / Islamic	Traditional law	Traditional law / Hindu	Traditional law / Far Eastern	Political law / Law of development
La Porta et al. 1998	French legal origin	German legal origin	Nordic legal origin	English legal origin	Socialist legal origin	French legal origin	English legal origin	English legal origin	German legal origin	English or French legal origin
Saidov 2003	Romano-Germanic	Romano-Germanic	Mixed systems	Common law	Socialist	Religious and traditional laws	Religious and traditional laws	Religious and traditional laws	Roman Germanic	Religious and traditional laws
De Cruz 2007	Civil law	Civil law	Hybrid legal systems	Common law	Socialist system	Other types of law	Other types of law	Common law	Eastern Legal Conceptions	
Gaenn 2010a	Civil law	Civil law		Common law	Civil law	Islamic	Talmudic	Hindu	Confucian	Chthonic

ones. Georges Sauser-Hall based his taxonomy on racial characteristics. He distinguished between the law of the Aryan or Indo-European people (for European countries, India and America), the law of the Semitic people (for the Middle East), the law of the Mongolic people (including China and Japan), and the law of barbarous people (mainly Africa).[30] John Henry Wigmore, by contrast, tried to illustrate different legal traditions by way of an impressionistic and pictorial method to comparative law.[31] The legal families are more specific than Sauser-Hall's ones, while they also point to broader categories: Romanesque and Germanic (as civil law), Anglican (as common law), Islam, Hebrew and Hindu (as religious legal systems), plus the specific cases of Slavic, Japanese and Chinese law.[32] In addition, Wigmore included historical legal systems, such as Egyptian, Mesopotamian and Celtic law.

After the Second World War, the interest in comparative law increased, and most general books were structured according to legal families. Pierre Arminjon, Boris Nolde and Martin Wolff based their taxonomy on a combination of legal history, sources of law, technique, terms, concepts, and culture, focusing on topics of private law.[33] This led to groups of French, German, Scandinavian, English, Russian, Islamic and Hindu legal families. Adolf Schnitzer followed an even stronger historical approach.[34] Thus, his treatment starts with the 'law of the primitive people' and the 'law of ancient culture', but then also turns to the familiar groups of Roman, German, Slavic and Anglo-American law. The subsequent category on religious law deals with Jewish, Christian and Islamic law. In addition, there is a broad category of Afro-Asian law with short sections on various legal systems. The book edited by Duncan Derrett also follows a historical perspective with chapters on Roman, Jewish, Islamic, Hindu, Chinese, African and English legal systems. The choice of these legal systems is justified by saying that these are ones which have a long history but which, in a modified version, still exist today.[35]

The main comparative law books of the second part of the twentieth century were the ones by René David, and Konrad Zweigert and Hein Kötz. The treatment of legal families in David's books has changed throughout the various editions. Initially, economic, political, philosophical and religious similarities were seen as the main criteria. This led to a major distinction between Western and Soviet law,[36] supplemented by chapters on Islamic, Hindu and Chinese legal systems. The more recent editions provide more emphasis on legal technique. This is not meant to refer to particular legal rules, but to the 'constant and more

---

[30] Sauser-Hall 1913.
[31] Wigmore 1928. See also ch. 2 at A 2 (c) and B 2 (b), above.
[32] Similar was already Esmein 1905 (Roman, Germanic, Anglo-Saxon, Slavic and Islamic law; based on history, geography, religion and race).
[33] Arminjon et al. 1951.   [34] Schnitzer 1961.   [35] Derrett 1968: xiii–xiv.
[36] The same distinction was made by comparative lawyers of the socialist countries: e.g. Eörsi 1979: 45 (distinction between legal families based on socio-economic system as a whole); Oksamytnyi 2011: 61 (distinction between socialist and bourgeois legal systems).

fundamental elements' that may determine whether 'someone educated in the study and practice of one law will then be capable, without much difficulty, of handling another'.[37] As a result, the distinction between Romano-Germanic civil law and English common law became more prominent, with further chapters on socialist law and other legal systems.[38] After the fall of communism, a new edition replaced socialist with Russian law.[39]

From the outset, the book by Zweigert and then Zweigert and Kötz focused on the divide between common law and (Romanist, Germanic and Nordic) civil law.[40] Smaller sections have dealt with Chinese, Japanese, Islamic and Hindu law and, before the fall of communism, with the socialist legal family. These legal families are mainly based on different legal styles in private law, and, specifically, on the legal systems' history, their characteristic modes of thought, distinctive institutions, variations between sources of law, and the ideologies of the law.[41]

With the books by David, and Zweigert and Kötz, a consensus seemed to emerge. Yet, since the mid-1990s, two new classifications have been suggested. The one by Ugo Mattei offers a distinctly different starting point, his main categories being 'rule of professional law', 'rule of political law' and 'rule of traditional law'.[42] In Europe and North America, for example, the legal arena is distinct from the political and religious one; these countries belong to the rule of professional law, with the sub-categories civil law, common law and mixed legal systems. The rule of political law refers to countries where the legal system is weak due to the power of the ruling elite. Mattei includes in this group the transition economies and developing countries of Eastern Europe, central Asia, Latin America and Africa – while also noting elements of professional and traditional law. Finally, the rule of traditional law includes the Islamic legal systems as well as India and China – while acknowledging elements of professional and political law in the latter two countries.

The opposite approach to Mattei's is the classification adopted by Rafael La Porta and colleagues. The latter are financial economists who use the categories of 'legal origins' as variables in quantitative studies.[43] They take the view that all legal systems of the world can be captured by common law (English legal origin), civil law (German, French and Nordic legal origin) and socialist law.[44] To classify countries, the main consideration is whether, according to a book on foreign law,[45] the main codes of these legal systems are based on a particular

---

[37] David 1985: 20–1.

[38] Similar Ehrmann 1976: 13–9 (families of Romano-Germanic, common law, socialist, non-Western laws).

[39] Jauffret-Spinosi and David 2002.

[40] The first edition was Zweigert 1969.   [41] Zweigert and Kötz 1998: 67–8.

[42] Mattei 1997b. Similar Oksamytnyi 2011: 66–75 (Western, Eastern and ideological legal systems).

[43] Summarised in La Porta et al. 2008. See also ch. 7 at C 1 and ch. 11 at B 3, below

[44] Note that La Porta et al. 1998 only examined forty-nine Western countries. The category of 'socialist law' was used in later studies, e.g. Djankov et al. 2003a.

[45] Reynolds and Flores 1989. See also www.foreignlawguide.com/.

model. This may sound very crude but it can be related to the fact that the imposition of codes is a proxy for colonial or quasi-colonial influence. In this respect, it has also been said that:

> [i]f you want to understand why a country has a particular legal system, look at the nationality of the last soldier who departed its shores.[46]

Retaining the category of socialist law for Russia and her neighbouring countries is also less unusual than it may appear. In the comparative literature it is said that patterns of socialist legal thought remain strong in Russia,[47] and that there may well be a 'socialist legal tradition without socialism'.[48] Akmal Saidov and Peter de Cruz have also kept the category of socialist law.[49] Furthermore, these books classify some non-Western countries as being part of common or civil law: Saidov allocates Japan to the Romano-Germanic legal family, and de Cruz India to the common law. As a basis for distinguishing legal families, both Saidov and de Cruz follow a similar mix of history, sources of law, and legal style as Zweigert and Kötz.

The final book to mention is by Patrick Glenn, now in its fourth edition.[50] With the exception of one modification (replacing the Asian with the Confucian legal tradition), the categories have remained unchanged. Most of them are similar to the ones of the previous literature, in particular Derrett's book. Glenn and Derrett also share a historical perspective keen on providing a balanced treatment of all legal traditions, whereas, in most of the other books cited here, civil and common law are dominant.

3. Main commonalities

There are a number of constant features in the legal family classifications of the last one hundred years. Most prominent is the divide between civil and common law, usually based on an analysis of legal styles, sources of law and institutional features.[51] Often, within the civil law, a distinction is made between the French-Roman and the Germanic sub-families. As far as a category of mixed legal systems is included, this is usually limited to a small number of countries such as Scotland and South Africa that have been influenced by both civil and common law traditions.[52] The Scandinavian countries are most often classified as Germanic civil law; yet, it has also been argued that their model of the welfare state and the close interaction between their law-makers justify a separate and relatively uniform Nordic legal family.[53]

The precise borders between civil and common law and the rest of the legal world are not entirely clear. Extreme views would be that either civil and

---

[46] Yoram Shachar, as cited in Feeley 1997: 94.   [47] Butler in EE 2012: 783.
[48] Uzelac 2010: 377.   [49] Saidov 2003; de Cruz 2007.   [50] Glenn 2010a.
[51] See also ch. 3 at B, above.   [52] For further details see C 3 (a), below.
[53] See, e.g., Husa et al. 2008; Bernitz 2007; Zweigert and Kötz 1998: 276–85.

common law are together part of a Western legal family distinct from all other legal cultures, or that all legal systems of the world have followed the models of civil or common law countries. The predominant view takes an intermediate position: civil and common law are most prominent in the West, but have also gained some influence in other parts of the world.

Furthermore, many of the taxonomies have a category with Russia and some of its neighbouring countries. In the times of the Soviet Union, this could be justified by the impact of the political system on the law. Today, it is not always clear whether the basis is the communist legacy, the autocratic political system of some of these countries, or specifics of a Slavic legal culture.[54] Frequently, there are also categories based on Islamic and Hindu law, closely linked to the corresponding religious traditions. With respect to the rest of the world, many taxonomies use geographic classifiers, such as East Asian and African law, based on the assumption that there is something specific about these cultures that is also reflected in their laws.

C. Critical analysis

It has been said that 'great divides are tempting organizing techniques'.[55] At the same time, classifications are bound to simplify. Thus, these simplifications may be criticised for overemphasising the differences between categories, underemphasising the differences within these categories, and ignoring hybrids. All these points have been directed against legal families.

1. Overemphasis of differences

There is no denying that there are differences between legal systems. The notion of legal families may therefore have the benefit of making aspiring comparatists aware of such differences. However, there is also the risk of a mistaken black-and-white thinking. We have already seen that Western civil and common law have more in common than divides them.[56] It is also possible to highlight similarities between the legal systems of the West and of other parts of the world. For instance, it is possible to draw parallels between the common law and Islamic law, since both legal traditions are based on a decentralised system of institutions.[57] There is also an extensive debate about the relationship between Western and East Asian legal systems, as discussed in the following.

Most taxonomies have a category of East Asian law (or Far Eastern or Confucian law). This legal family is said to be markedly different from Western

---

[54] See, e.g., Fekete 2011: 48 (referring to a deep institutional scepticism but also high expectations in terms of social justice); Butler 2011 (possible 'renaissance of Slavonic law' due to continuing influence of customs).

[55] Marcus 2010: 521.   [56] See ch. 3 at C 3, above.

[57] Makdisi 1999: 1696–717; Rosen 2000: 38–68; Rosen 2006: 40–1 (contrasting it to the civil law, being centrally controlled, and traditional legal systems). Similar Ziegert 2004: 149.

conceptions of law. Law is seen as less important, as society is primarily based on personal relations and networks. In the Confucian terminology, this also means that consensus, harmony and goodness ('li') are preferred to formal standards and regulations ('fa').[58] If disputes arise, the main aim is to ensure that no one loses his or her face.[59] Thus, extra-judicial means are preferred to a 'struggle for law' with winners and losers.[60] Overall, such collectivism means that concepts such as individual rights, the rule of law and formal legal reasoning are regarded as alien.[61] As far as there is law, the focus is on criminal law, which is obeyed as a mere external force, 'like children who fear parental punishment'.[62] Conversely, contract law is seen as unimportant, since signing a contract does not imply a formal obligation but merely the continuation of negotiations.[63]

Such a picture may be helpful for an aspiring comparatist who had assumed that all countries of the world have a similar understanding of the law. Yet, the apparent danger is that it would also mislead her. Once she visits a country such as China or Japan, she would be surprised to find out that these legal systems have codes and statutes akin to Western countries,[64] and that at universities law is taught in a positivist fashion akin to continental European universities.[65] Moreover, when she visits a law firm or a court, a lawyer or judge may start a technical discussion about details of the positive law (such as the concept of piercing the corporate veil in company law),[66] which may make her wonder whether Western and Eastern legal cultures are really as irreconcilable as they had appeared to her.

More specifically, Chinese legal culture has changed considerably in recent decades. In the increasingly differentiated Chinese society, morals and custom can no longer meet the interest in a stable order; the need for legal rules is therefore increasing, and there is a growing emphasis on law in the population.[67] For instance, firms want to use well-drafted contracts, and judicial enforcement of contractual rights has become more common.[68] There have also been a number of institutional changes. In the last two decades, the number of lawyers has been exploding.[69] According to the ideas of the Chinese leadership,

---

[58] Zweigert and Kötz 1998: 282–3.

[59] See Pattison and Herron 2003: 482, 490. For the corresponding view in cultural studies and cross-cultural psychology see ch. 11 at C 1, below.

[60] Ehrmann 1976: 45.

[61] Van Hoecke and Warrington 1998: 506. For Japanan see Maslen 1998.

[62] Cf. Ruskola 2002: 189.

[63] Pattison and Herron 2003: 460, 491, 508; Zweigert and Kötz 1998: 284. See also Menski 2006: 520 (traditional Chinese private law only based on customs).

[64] See also ch. 8 at B 3 below (on legal transplants in China and Japan).

[65] See Menski 2006: 56–7, also 470 (for Africa), criticising the 'positivist ideology'.

[66] Based on my experience visiting the Shanghai Supreme Court in January 2011.

[67] Dam 2006: 12–3; also Peerenboom 2003: 50–5 (criticising Mattei's classification of China as a 'traditional legal system').

[68] See the empirical study by Clarke et al. 2008.   [69] Data in Clarke et al. 2008.

market economy and the rule of law are also compatible not only with capitalism and democracy, but also with socialism of the Chinese type.[70] Because of this, and because of changes following the accession to the World Trade Organization (WTO) in 2001, there has been a professionalisation of the judicial system.[71]

All of this shows that the view that there is 'law in the West' but 'culture in the East' can be highly misleading. For example, it is clear that in Western legal systems contractual conflicts are often solved without the involvement of lawyers or courts.[72] With respect to East Asia, the idea of a distinctly different legal family can lead to a stereotyped view of these legal systems. Teemu Ruskola has discussed this problem under the heading of 'legal orientalism': what Western lawyers write about China tells us more about their own legal ideology than about Chinese law.[73] This does not mean that the picture presented of law in China is necessarily a negative one: there can also be a 'fervid idealisation', or even a hallucination, of a society that does not need law.[74] More often, however, it is said that the concept of legal families is used so as to favour one's own conception of law. It can lead to an 'exoticization of legal cultures', where the West is seen as the centre and the developing world as the periphery.[75] This may have the deeper purpose of legitimising the Western supremacy of law, by way of constructing the identities of 'us' and 'them'.[76] And if these groups of legal systems are seen as incompatible, such an approach may even contribute 'to conflictual and antagonistic relations between peoples and laws'.[77]

Overall, the orientalism debate illustrates the problem of thinking that others are essentially different from us. Of course, one should also not do the reverse in presuming that 'they are just like us'.[78] Hence, we turn to the problem that legal family classifications also overemphasise similarities.

2. Overemphasis of similarities

Chapter 3 already provided two examples of overemphasising similarities: the civil law family of continental European countries is fairly diverse (as is also apparent in distinctions between a Romanist and a Germanic model), and England and the United States follow fundamentally different paths in many legal questions.[79] The following deals with the legal systems of Africa, Asia and Latin America, and how their suggested classifications can mislead us.

---

[70] See Chen 1999: 136.
[71] For further discussion about the rule of law in China see ch. 10 at B 2, below.
[72] Macaulay 1963. See also Charny 1990; Deakin and Michie 1997.
[73] Ruskola 2002: 189. See also Ruskola 2013. The term 'orientalism' derives from Said 1979. For legal orientalism see also Darian-Smith 2013: 48–51.
[74] Ruskola 2002: 217 (but see also 299). Some use the term 'reverse orientalism' for such an idealisation, see Gaudreault-DesBiens 2010: 176.
[75] Muir Watt 2006: 595.   [76] Monateri 1998: 832. See also Monateri 2012.
[77] Glenn 2006: 431.   [78] Cf. Nelken 2006: 949.   [79] See ch. 3 at C 1 and 2, above.

(a) African and Asian legal systems

Some of the classifications, such as La Porta et al.'s, allocate the legal systems of all African and Asian countries to either the civil or the common law. This leads to surprising results; for example, in the La Porta studies, Iran, Saudi Arabia and Yemen are seen as common law countries. Other researchers are more cautious, but here too it is frequently suggested that, for instance, India is regarded as common law and Japan as German civil law. These classifications are usually based on the colonial influence of European countries, and, in some cases, such as Japan, voluntary copying of some of the major codes.[80]

Legal scholars specialised in these countries tend to regard such classifications as unacceptable. Paradigmatic is Werner Menski's book on the legal systems of Asia and Africa. Having explained the religious dimensions of the Indian legal system, Menski rejects its classification as a common law country.[81] Similarly, with respect to Africa, he writes that African traditions have not been super-seded by modern laws, that African laws are not mere copies of Western ones, and that 'one must ask how much effect less than a century of colonial domination could have had on many peoples of Africa'.[82] Furthermore, socio-legal and critical comparative lawyers bring forward that classifying non-Western countries as either civil or common law is too positivistic and Eurocentric since it disregards the law as experienced beyond the courtroom as well as the deeper structures of those non-Western legal cultures.[83] Finally, even two more traditional comparatists say about the spread of the common law:

> [T]his might lead one to the conclusion that in the areas of Africa which were previously under British rule most legal relations today are governed by the rules of English Common Law. This conclusion would be wholly erroneous. The fact is that to much the largest part of the African population the Common Law is almost of no practical significance; the legal relations of Africans, in contract and land matters as well as family and succession matters, are principally governed by the rules of customary African law, and in many regions also by the rules of Islamic law.[84]

It follows that such classifications are not helpful because they would indicate a similarity between legal systems that have very little in common. The alternative is therefore to seek categories that would better capture the specifics of these legal systems. Here, the countries of Asia and Africa are frequently classified as African law, (East) Asian law, or even Afro-Asian law.[85] Yet, such geographic categories are usually not more than a definition of an area study. In the books cited in the previous section, these terms are often just headings which are immediately followed by a discussion of individual legal systems, raising doubts about the value of these categories.

---

[80] See B, above, and ch. 8 at B, below.   [81] Menski 2006: 203.
[82] Menski 2006: 464. See also ch. 8 at B 2, below.
[83] Friedman 1997: 36; Baxi 2003: 49; Frankenberg 1985: 442.
[84] Zweigert and Kötz 1998: 230.   [85] See B 2, above.

Some attempts have, however, been made to relate these geographic categories with more substantive classifications. For example, it may be a characteristic feature of African legal systems that lawyers and law-makers are less influential, since customary law (or folk law) still plays an important role.[86] With respect to Asia, some scholars have also developed substantive classifications, such as that of a Confucian legal family.[87] Yet, it is not clear how meaningful these categories are. The differences between, say, all African countries are so profound that any description of these legal systems as a single group is bound to overemphasise similarity.[88] Moreover, the reference to a common culture may play a role in some instances, but it is not necessarily the case that cultural proximity also translates into a legal one.[89] For instance, China, North Korea, and South Korea are all countries influenced by Confucian thinking, but their legal systems are very different. In addition, it can be objected that classifications referring to cultural or religious characteristics are unsatisfactory in re-stating the categories of other disciplines,[90] whereas the legal-family categories have precisely the aim of identifying distinct approaches to law.

(b) Latin America

In the late nineteenth and early twentieth centuries, Latin American comparatists often classified their legal systems as 'sui generis'.[91] Today, however, Latin American countries are usually seen as being part of the French version of the civil law, since they were influenced by the French codes in private, criminal and procedural law, with additional but more limited influence from German, Portuguese and Spanish law.[92]

Yet, recent research has shown that just calling the legal systems of Latin America 'French civil law' does not do them justice. An article by John Henry Merryman on 'the French deviation' addressed how French judges had soon disregarded the strictness of the civil code, creating judge-made law (even though it was not officially called that way). In contrast to this, the courts of the former colonies did not regard it as acceptable to deviate from the strong separation of powers between legislators and judges.[93] A similar point is made by Patrick Glenn (not limited to these countries):

[I]n creating large states, large corporate structures, large labour organizations, large legal professions – in short, large institutionalized elites in all directions, western law provides all the disadvantages of a large, wooden house in a warm, humid climate. It may be beautiful, and well-designed, but be subject to many

---

[86] See Sacco 1995: 456; Twining et al. 2006: 128; Glenn 2010a: 63 (but also 83–4: no pure chthonic traditions in the world today).
[87] See 1, above.   [88] Menski 2006: 383; Bogdan 1994: 88.
[89] Similarly Mattei et al. 2009: 270; Chase and Walker 2010: lxi (distinction between modern and non-modern legal systems).
[90] See A, above.   [91] See Pargendler 2012b: 1046, 1049.
[92] See Zweigert and Kötz 1998: 115.   [93] Merryman 1996. See also ch. 3 at B 2, above.

forms of internal rot. To survive, it requires protection beyond the structure itself and if this is neglected, or impossible, the structure will not last.[94]

The question remains why Latin American legal systems have stuck to a formal version of the French codes. Here, Jorge Esquirol's research is helpful, and can be summarised briefly as 'Latin American societies are not European, only their jurists pretend to be'.[95] Esquirol contends that Latin American lawyers are deliberately 'legalist' in insulating law from an illiberal society. Thus, facing the tension between the European ideal of law and the Latin American social, political, cultural and economic particularities, it is not seen as necessary to change the former 'fiction of Europeanness' but, rather, it is hoped that society will eventually catch up.

But research has also explored how Latin American law is not limited to the European codes any more. Matthew Mirow's article on the 'the Code Napoleon buried but ruling in Latin America' illustrates this tension. On the one hand, the French Code has lost in importance in the twentieth century due to external and internal changes. The former denotes the influence of US positive law, legal culture and politics; the latter refers to specialised subject-matter legislation, changes to the codes, and the growth of case law. On the other hand, the Code still rules since it 'continues to serve a taxonomic function as the intellectual superstructure upon which all legal thought is built'.[96]

Overall, this short discussion shows that just calling Latin American countries 'French civil law' is not helpful.[97] Rather, to get a proper understanding of law in Latin America, various topics need to be addressed, such as, how complete was the influence of the French positive law in different areas of law, how has the law been applied and how has it been insulated from society, and how have legal rules been changed in the last two centuries? We will revisit these topics in the chapter on 'legal transplants'.[98]

3. Disregard of hybrids

(a) Mixed legal systems

Hybrids are often equated with mixed legal systems, but the latter is only one of its sub-categories. In contrast to other forms of hybridity (see the following sections), here it is the entire legal system that deserves to be called mixed. In principle, any type of mixture may be conceivable. However, following the focus of traditional comparative law on common and civil law, the term mixed legal systems is often limited to legal systems which have been strongly

---

[94] Glenn 2010a: 281.

[95] Esquirol 1997: 470. See also Esquirol 2003 and Esquirol 2008 (challenging common misconceptions about law in Latin America).

[96] Mirow 2005: 191. See also Mirow 2004.

[97] For a similar conclusion see López-Medina 2012: 360.

[98] See ch. 8 at B 2, below. See also ch. 6, below (on the relationship between law and society).

influenced by both of these legal families.[99] Typically, this is the result of historical developments: say, a country was initially part of the common law but was then occupied or influenced by a civil law country (or vice versa).

As far as the comparative literature deals with these mixed legal systems,[100] the main examples are Israel, Louisiana, Quebec, Puerto Rico, Scotland, South Africa and Sri Lanka.[101] However, it may be suggested that this list should be significantly longer since, after the Second World War, many civil law countries have been influenced by US law. Reference was already made to Latin America. Another example is Japan: between 1890 and 1900, Japan copied large parts of the five major German codes, but these legal transplants have not fully persisted. For example, the Japanese corporate law has been substantially changed since the Second World War, in particular due to American influence. The same is true for other areas of trade and business law.[102]

Legal scholars have also tried to identify mixed legal systems that go beyond the mixture of civil and common law. A comprehensive example of this are the maps found on the website Juriglobe of the University of Ottawa.[103] It uses the categories civil law, common law, Muslim law and customary law, and allows mixtures between them. Most African and Asian countries are regarded as being mixed between common or civil law and Muslim or customary law. In the case of mixtures, the website also indicates the dominant category. For instance, Iran is regarded as Muslim law with elements of civil law, whereas Iraq is seen as civil law with elements of Muslim law. Overall, this taxonomy confirms the importance of the civil/common law categories, since more than 55 per cent of the world's population live in a country where the civil law is dominant, and 15 per cent in a country where the common law is dominant.[104] It can also be seen that, according to these categories, more than half of the legal systems of the world are regarded as mixed.[105]

The mixture of Western legal traditions and customary law, say in Africa, has also been a general topic of comparative and anthropological legal research. It is helpful to distinguish four types of customary law.[106] 'Living customary law' is the original unwritten version of customary law. Colonial powers often dismissed it as not 'proper law', and after independence many of the new leaders saw it as an obstacle to consolidate their power over the entire country. Still, living customary law may have survived at the local level – for instance, as

---

[99] Palmer 2008 (as 'the traditional view'). See also Palmer 2012.   [100] See B 2, above.

[101] See the World Society of Mixed Jurisdiction Jurists, at www.mixedjurisdiction.org/. In addition, Kim 2010: 705 refers to Botswana, Cameroon, Cyprus, Guyana, Jordan, Lesotho, Malta, Mauritius, Namibia, the Philippines, Saint Lucia, Somalia, Seychelles, Thailand, Vanuatu, and Zimbabwe.

[102] See ch. 8 at B 3, below. See also Matsuo 2004: 50 (Japan as a mixed legal system). For the position of Japan see also Oda 2009: 3–4.

[103] See www.juriglobe.ca/eng/ and Fathally and Mariani 2008. For a general discussion about 'maps of law' see Bavinck and Woodman 2009. For 'mapping law' see Twining 1999.

[104] Koch 2003: 2.   [105] See du Plessis 2006: 482.

[106] Following Ubink and van Rooij 2011. Similar Menski 2006: 473–81.

regards family relationships.[107] In addition, more generalised written versions of customary practices have emerged. This can be 'textbook customary law', where academics or state officials have tried to consolidate the customary practices of a particular people.[108] It can also be 'codified customary law', where the state has incorporated customary practices into legislation. Yet, there have also been doubts about the authenticity of such customary law, since national law-makers may lack knowledge of local customary practices – or they may even transform them as to serve international business interests.[109] Finally, 'judicial customary law' is about the way judges make use of living, textbook and codified customary law. Details depend on many further questions, such as the relationship between tribal and state courts, the basis on which judges decide cases, and their actual willingness to consider traditional values.[110] But overall, it can be seen that mixtures of Western and customary law can appear in a variety of forms, which would necessitate many further sub-categories of mixed legal systems.

Furthermore, the Ottawa map does not consider that most legal family taxonomies distinguish between French, German and Nordic civil law countries. Thus, many legal systems in Central and Eastern Europe can be regarded as mixed civil law countries. For example, traditionally, Lithuanian law tended to be influenced by French law, and Latvian law by German law. Yet, after regaining independence in 1990, both legal systems have re-drafted their laws in a comparative fashion, being influenced by both German and French legal traditions, by Nordic law, and partly also by advisers from the US.[111] In addition, here, as elsewhere in Central and Eastern Europe, it may still be possible to identify some aspects of a socialist legal culture as far as judges and law professors have retained their posts and parts of their ideology.

Mixtures are even more complex in parts of the world where there have been various sources of influence. For instance, it has been said of Thailand that:

> it has had in its modern texture a real mixture of sources such as English Law, German Law, French law, Swiss Law, Japanese Law and American Law . . . alongside historic sources in existence since 1283, such as rules from indigenous culture and tradition, customary laws and Hindu jurisprudence, still to be found in some modern enactments.[112]

More generally, it has been suggested that, in South-East Asia, Islamic, Chinese, Hindu, indigenous customary and European legal norms all play a role, and

---

[107] See, e.g., Read 2000: 190–3; Bennett 2006: 664–5, 662, 666; Odinkalu 2006: 154; Moore 1986b: 35.

[108] Cf. Donovan 2008: 79–87 (as 'applied anthropology'); Bennett 2006: 646.

[109] See Riles 2006: 788 ('invented tradition'); Snyder 1981 (on Senegal: transformation to serve interests of world capitalism).

[110] See, e.g., Faundez 2011: 28–30 (on Bolivian constitution of 2009 recognising indigenous courts); Keep and Midgley 2007: 29 (on 'ubuntu-botho' in South African case law).

[111] See Siems 2007a: 65.

[112] Örücü 2004b: 364; also Örücü 2008: 39. One could also add Buddhist law: see Sucharitkul 1998.

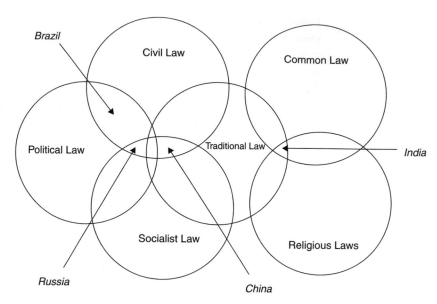

Figure 4.1 Possible classification of BRIC countries

that therefore the idea of legal families 'makes no sense whatsoever'.[113] At the very least, such complex mixtures show that one has to abandon the idea that there has to be 'one correct' taxonomy of legal families. By way of example, Figure 4.1, above, illustrates the position of the BRIC countries (Brazil, Russia, India and China), using all of the main taxonomies of Table 4.1. It can be seen that these four legal systems belong to two or three legal families. Such a mixed classification can be useful for the purpose of comparison. For instance, comparing Brazil and China, there is similarity due to the joined civil law affiliation, while the other categories are different (socialist and traditional for China, and political for Brazil). This does not imply that a comparatist has to endorse all these classifications, though at least they offer a useful conceptual framework to discuss why, say, for Brazil the political element may not be the decisive one.[114]

Finally, even England, France and Germany may be regarded as mixed.[115] It was already mentioned that English law has been influenced by Roman law.[116] France and Germany can also be called mixed legal systems because, apart from Roman law, both the 'droit coutumier' of tribes from Northern France and Germanic sources of law influenced their laws.[117] Moreover, there has always

---

[113] Harding 2001: 200; Harding 2002: 49. See also Mattei et al. 2009: 255–7 (traditional, religious, colonial, post-independence law and perhaps socialist or Americanised law in Africa).

[114] As also contemplated by Mattei 1997b: 33.

[115] Zimmermann 2001: 158; Örücü 2004b: 363; Donlan 2011 (project on 'remembering legal hybridity').

[116] See ch. 3 at C 3, above.

[117] See, e.g., Zweigert and Kötz 1998: 75, 139; Zimmermann 2001: 159; Glenn 2007 and Glenn 2010a: 87–9 (on interaction between Western and chthonic law).

been some exchange of legal ideas and concepts on commercial topics.[118] Thus, the notion of mixed legal systems can indeed have a destructive force in showing that there are no pure legal families.

(b) Horizontally divided legal systems

Another form of hybridity is that the mixture concerns differences between regions of a particular legal system. Then, it is also said that legal systems are 'horizontally divided' or 'bijural'. Again, we can start with the legal families of common and civil law. Cameroon has, through colonisation, been influenced by both English and French law. Yet, in contrast to mixed legal systems, the division is spatial, with English common law having been influential in the North and South West, and French civil law in the other parts of the country.[119] Other possible examples are the UK, the US and Canada, with mixed legal systems in Scotland, Louisiana and Quebec and common law in the other parts. It can also be suggested that the EU is bijural, since it has members from both common and civil law jurisdictions.[120]

Horizontal divisions can also relate to religious, customary and political laws. For example, in Nigeria, some Islamic law is applied in the predominantly Muslim northern states but not in the predominantly Christian southern ones.[121] The relationship between Western and customary law in Africa (see the previous section) can also appear as a horizontal division because the former may be influential in the big cities, whereas customary law may be dominant in rural areas.[122] Similarly, in countries of transition, it may be the case that Western laws have become influential in some of the metropolitan regions but not elsewhere. China is a possible example.[123] Thus, overall, the phenomenon of horizontally divided legal systems may be more frequent than it is usually assumed.

(c) Vertically divided legal systems

Fairly common is a vertical division between areas of law, which may also be called 'legal polytheism'.[124] In order to distinguish between such a division and mixed legal systems, Esin Örücü's 'salad bowl analogy' is a helpful device. Örücü distinguishes between bowls where the ingredients are a purée (also called 'covert mixtures'), where they are clearly visible ('Italian salad bowls'), and where they are clearly separate ('English salad plate').[125] Mixed legal

---

[118] Vagts 2000: 598–9. See also Mattei et al. 2009: 434 (since Roman law, as civil law, was unsuitable for business transactions).

[119] See Cameroon Legal Systems, at www.hg.org/article.asp?id=7155.

[120] See generally Breton and Trebilcock 2006, while Breton et al. 2009 refer to them as 'multijural' (defined as 'coexistence of two or more legal systems or sub-systems with a broader normative legal order to which they adhere').

[121] See Ostien and Dekker 2010.

[122] See International Council of Human Rights 2009: 10; Mamdani 1996: 11–2 (using the term 'bifurcated state').

[123] See also ch. 10 at B 2, below.   [124] Ehrmann 1976: 30 (for common law and equity).

[125] Örücü 2007: 180; Örücü 2008: 47, 52.

systems – as discussed in the first sub-section – are the first two types of 'bowls' since the entire system is in-between legal traditions. In the present section we are interested in the 'English salad plate' option, where one or more areas of law follow their own logic.

Most taxonomies focus on topics of civil procedure, in particular as regards the distinction between civil and common law countries.[126] With respect to criminal procedure, it has sometimes been said that here the common/civil divide is even sharper,[127] but most scholars express the view that generalisations are problematic, since we observe convergence between the adversarial model – traditionally associated with common law countries – and the inquisitorial model – traditionally associated with civil law ones.[128] As such a trend can also be found in civil procedure,[129] the legal family affiliation may be fairly similar in both areas of law. Yet, this is different if we go beyond Western legal systems. In some Muslim countries, private adjudication is dealt with by courts similar to the Western world, but criminal procedure, as well as criminal law, are distinct, being based on Islamic law. Thus, for these countries, we can talk about vertically divided legal systems.

A division also exists between public and private law. In constitutional law, the basic political structures – such as democratic or autocratic, or federal or unitary – play a key role and may justify distinct classifications. In addition, factors such as whether there is a written constitution, a separate constitutional court, or a case-based approach to human rights, lead to categories different from the common/civil law divide.[130] In administrative law, a division may be made between the US and Germany on the one hand, and England and France on the other, since the former two countries have general laws on administrative procedure, whereas in the latter two it is mainly judge-made law.[131] It can also be interesting to turn to substantive features of public law. Here, it may matter that private law often used to extend across borders (e.g. the received Roman law), whereas the development of public law has been more dependent on national borders. Thus, it has been suggested that classifying legal systems in public law may be less meaningful than in private law.[132]

In private and commercial law, too, complications need to be considered, though often the distinction between mixed and vertically divided legal systems is not entirely clear. For instance, South Africa and Sri Lanka are usually called mixed legal systems, but one could also regard them as vertically divided because

---

[126] See ch. 3 at B 2, above.   [127] Chase and Walker 2010: lix.

[128] See Reamey 2010; Roberts 2007: 353; van der Walt 2006: 52–3; Weigand in EE 2012: 271–3; Mattei et al. 2009: 852.

[129] See ch. 3 at C 3, above.

[130] Summary of discussion in Jackson 2012: 55–8. See also Shapiro and Stone Sweet 2002: 168 (constitutional law almost invariably becomes case law); Komarek 2011: 8 (in US fundamental difference between common law and constitutional adjudication).

[131] Ziller in EE 2012: 746–7; Dam 2006: 122.

[132] Bell 2006c: 1266. See also Ackerman 2010 (contrast between common and civil law 'is a non-starter').

some areas of law, such as property law, are based on civil law rules, whereas commercial law is predominantly based on common law ones.[133] As far as Muslim countries are concerned, contract law is often a blend of different variants of Western law and Islamic law; in company law, there may be both Western forms of companies and Islamic partnerships available; and family law may be predominantly based on Islamic law.[134] Most of Chinese private and commercial law is a mix as well, but there are differences in detail: contract law is a mix of the former Socialist law, German law and the international sales law (CISG), company law is primarily based on a German model but with some US influence, and securities regulation is predominantly influenced by the US.[135] In India, a codified version of the common law is the basis for contract and tort law, but in family law things get complicated (even disregarding the Islamic law applicable to the Indian Muslims): though its origins lie in classical Hindu law, it gradually changed due to its consolidation by British lawyers under colonialism, its codification after independence and the case law by modern Indian courts.[136]

In commercial law more generally, a formal distinction can be made between countries that do and do not have a commercial code: most civil law countries (e.g. Germany and France) would belong to the former category, but there are also civil law countries that have incorporated commercial law topics into their civil codes (e.g. Italy and Switzerland).[137] It may also be possible to classify according to the international commercial laws that countries follow:

> Take the law of international sales. Is it really the Germans with their Bürgerliches Gesetzbuch versus the Americans with their Uniform Commercial Code? Or is it rather the Germans and the Americans as members of the United Nations Convention on Contracts for the International Sale of Goods (CISG) versus the English who have not ratified it? Or is it perhaps the Germans and the English as EU members (and thus signatories to the Rome Convention) versus the Americans? Or is it perhaps all these countries as members of the WTO (and thus beneficiaries of its free trade regime) versus those nations who are not?[138]

The picture that may therefore emerge is that it is fairly common for legal systems to have divided identities. Yet, any specific area of law is also embedded in the entire legal system.[139] Thus, just because a country adopts a set of rules for a particular topic, does not mean that it would be justified to talk about a vertically divided legal system, in particular since the main bases for

---

[133] See Kim 2010: 711; also Zimmermann and Visser 1996.

[134] See ch. 8 at B 2 (b), below; cf. also Mattei 1997b: 16 ('The same system may belong to the rule of traditional law if we consider family law, while belonging to the rule of professional law as far as commercial law is concerned').

[135] See Siems 2007a: 66.

[136] See, e.g. Menski 2006: 246–54; Glenn 2010a: 297 ('much of the great corpus of hindu law is now said to be obsolete').

[137] See, e.g., Mattei et al. 2009: 421–2, 438–9; Siems 2004c.   [138] Reimann 2001: 1114.

[139] This point is emphasised by Whitman 2005b: 394 (e.g. on similarities between criminal law, privacy, hate speech and workplace harassment law).

classifications are the general features of legal systems and not specific legal rules.[140] Still, the differentiations between areas of law show that legal systems tend to have various shades, disregarded by the broad categories of legal families.

(d) Parallel legal systems

The previous sections already dealt with some aspects of the relationship between Western laws and customary/religious laws. It was said that there may be genuine mixtures of these two forms of law, or that legal systems may be horizontally or vertically divided. A further possibility is that of parallel legal systems.[141] Such parallelism arises when a legal system applies the rules of different legal traditions to different persons. A good example is the family law of countries such as India, where different legal regimes are applicable to Hindus, Muslims and Christians.[142]

Another case of parallelism arises where – on a purely domestic level[143] – citizens can choose between different legal regimes. This may be explicitly provided for: for instance, Western and customary/religious courts have co-existed in some countries of Africa and the Middle East, though the recent trend is to merge these two court systems.[144] But even if that is not the case, there may be de facto choice between the official and an informal legal order. The latter orders can be found across the world and are often independent of national borders. Frequently discussed examples are the law of the Romani people ('Gypsy law'), the law of the Quaker community, the law of squatter settlers in Brazil, and the norms of religious communities.[145]

Transnationality is also a common feature of business and commercial law. It is possible that such laws have become part of the positive law (e.g. the CISG, as explained in the previous section). But there is also the view that, for some rules of transnational governance, national borders have become irrelevant. A good example of this are the Incoterms, clauses drafted by the International Chamber of Commerce (ICC), which are applied in many international business contracts. This point will be addressed in detail later on, in the context of globalisation and comparative law.[146]

Overall, the prevalence of these parallel legal systems shows that many laws are not based on geographical borders. Thus, this variant of hybridity challenges

---

[140] See B 1, above.

[141] Oksamytnyi 2011: 62; also Moore 2005: 49 (dualistic legal systems).

[142] See Menski 2007: 195–6; Fyzee and Mahmood 2008: 1 (noting that due to the personal scope the term should be 'Muhammadan law' not 'Islamic law'). But see also Ali 2011: 211–2 (Shari'a law, Muslim law, Islamic law, or Muhammadan law?).

[143] As distinguished from questions of conflict-of-laws. See ch. 9 at A 2 (b), below.

[144] See Menski 2006: 477 (on Africa); Masud in Kritzer 2002: 1347–9 (on various Muslim countries). See also Faundez 2011: 34 (for Mozambique).

[145] For the first three examples see Weyrauch 2001; Bradney and Cownie 2000; Santos 2004: 99–162. See also ch. 5 at B 4, below (on legal pluralism).

[146] See ch. 9 at A 1 and D, below.

the core belief that one can develop taxonomies of legal families comprising particular countries.[147]

D. Conclusion

The present and the previous chapter have shown that classifications into legal families often do not provide an accurate picture. This does not come as a surprise given the nature of such taxonomies. To quote Patrick Glenn, it is clear that:

> ... the separation we seek to bring about, for purposes of clarity and recognition, is immediately challenged by information which is inconsistent with the separation we have chosen.[148]

The question remains, however, whether thinking about legal families does not cause more harm than good. Legal families have the didactic aim of facilitating the understanding of the world's legal systems.[149] Yet, in many instances, a comparatist can be misled by such categories because she may assume stark differences (or similarities), whereas in reality there are similarities (or differences), or a mixed picture.

It is also perfectly possible to conduct comparative legal research without using the notion of legal families. To illustrate, Chapter 3 started with a comparison of civil procedure and sources of law in common and civil law countries. Yet, as it is the established practice of traditional comparative law, this comparison focused on just a small number of countries (France, Germany, England and the US), since it is believed that the laws of these countries have influenced neighbouring countries, former colonies and other legal systems.

Thus, a preferable alternative is to examine differences in civil procedure and sources of law as follows: the starting point is a comparison between France, Germany, England and the US (not using the concepts of common and civil law). Subsequently, one can discuss how the laws of these legal systems have influenced other parts of the world. This influence can be direct (say, French law to Spain), or indirect (say, French law to Latin America via Spanish law), and it may also be said that some legal systems have been influenced by multiple foreign legal systems (say, Latin American legal systems by French and US law). Thus, the result is something akin to a tree-like model, which shows how some legal systems have influenced others.[150]

In addition, it has to be considered that legal systems are not just influenced by legal transplants, because the claim of mere copying would disregard the ongoing influence of their pre-transplant law and the post-transplant period, in which the transplanted law may be altered or applied differently from the

---

[147] For a similar point see Twining 2000a: 150, 181; Twining 2007: 73.   [148] Glenn 2010a: 362.
[149] See A, above.   [150] For this idea see also Örücü 2004b; Örücü 2007: 175–6.

origin country.[151] Thus, to get to a proper understanding of the legal world, the comparatist has to be prepared to find the unexpected, i.e. unexpected differences between similar countries and unexpected similarities between different ones.[152] It is suggested that legal families do not help in developing such curiosity.

[151] For 'legal transplants' see ch. 8, below.
[152] For the law and society relationship see also ch. 6, below.

Part II
Extending the Methods of Comparative Law

It is common to distinguish traditional from 'other forms of comparative law'.[1] The latter approaches are not a single school,[2] but have in common the disapproval of the legalism and doctrinalism associated with the traditionalists. To illustrate, consider the following apparently harmless statement:

> As Japan belongs to the German legal family, both German and Japanese commercial law provide that in case of a sale between traders, the buyer shall, upon taking delivery of the subject matter, examine it without delay (German Commercial Code, s. 377; Japanese Commercial Code, s. 536).[3]

The previous part already dealt with the reference to legal families,[4] but non-traditionalists may also raise a number of further and more general objections against this statement. They recommend that comparative lawyers should 'prolong [their] puzzlement' and should 'not jump to easy conclusion'.[5] Thus, first, the mere comparison of legal rules is regarded as insufficient. At the very least, comparative law needs to be based on an understanding of the theories and values underlying legal orders. So, in the example, the similarity between the German and Japanese law may only be superficial, whereas deep-level comparative law could highlight profound differences. Second, a rule-based comparison gives no consideration of the real-world sense in which these rules operate in both countries. Thus, socio-legal research would need to be conducted. Third, comparative law, as well as legal research in general, traditionally did not embrace the use of quantitative tools prevalent in other scientific disciplines. But there is no reason why this should not be done. Thus, for instance, referring to these latter two objections, comparatists may want to compare how often courts in Japan and Germany have actually applied the provision in question.

---

[1] Husa 2003: 445.

[2] But see Markesinis and Fedtke 2009: 359 (wondering 'which academic school was gaining the upper hand: Hein Kötz, Ulrich Magnus, Walter van Gerven or Reinhard Zimmermann, one might argue, versus Duncan Kennedy, Ugo Mattei, Pierre Legrand or Annelise Riles? That is four on either side, so is it a draw?').

[3] Modified example from Siems 2007b: 140–1.

[4] See ch. 3 and ch. 4, above.   [5] Cotterrell 2006: 723.

These three 'extensions' to the method of comparative law are addressed in the following chapters on postmodern, socio-legal and numerical comparative law. The view taken in this book is that these relatively new approaches to comparative law are valuable, but that not everything traditional should be abandoned, nor is everything new necessarily a way forward.[6] In addition, the subsequent Parts III and IV show that changes to comparative law are not only trigged by these new ideas, but also by the 'globalisation' of the law and the growing interest in comparative legal topics by non-legal researchers.

[6] Similarly Peters and Schwenke 2000: 803, 829; Husa 2003: 445.

5

Postmodern comparative law

Some traditional comparative lawyers denounce postmodern comparative law as 'incomprehensible'.[1] Indeed, it is often fairly complex. Yet, this chapter aims to show that it is possible to make it comprehensible. Section A introduces the term 'postmodernism' while being aware of its ambiguities. Sections B and C, on deep-level and critical comparative law, discuss six variants of postmodern comparative law in detail. Section D continues the analysis of these approaches, while also relating them to other chapters of this book.

A. From George W. Bush to postmodernism

The former US president George W. Bush (junior) observed that '[n]ot everybody thinks the exact same way we think. Different words mean different things to different people.'[2] Of course, Bush meant to say that even the same words (not different ones) can mean different things to different people. This can be contrasted with the naive attitude that the same words always mean the same thing to different people, or a more optimistic one that different words can mean the same thing to different people. Further permutations of this sentence would keep the final part constant at 'the same', leading to the statements that the same (or different) words can mean the same (or different) things for the same people.

Postmodern comparative lawyers have a general interest in the way words and concepts are understood at home and abroad, and, thus, potentially all of these eight permutations. More specifically, however, following postmodernists in other fields, they focus on differences[3] – namely, that apparently similar words and concepts often have different meanings in different legal systems. Thus, the main purpose of comparative law is not to find common denominators between legal systems but to appreciate their complexity. This is in line with the view that 'one cannot understand a place without seeing how it varies from others',[4] but postmodern comparative law often goes further. It emphasises that the identity

---

[1] See below at note 121.   [2] Cited in Roberts 2007: 360.
[3] Antokolskaia 2006: 31 (with references to Derrida and Foucault).
[4] Lawson 1977: 73 (not a postmodernist).

and self-knowledge of the researcher crucially determines the understanding of the foreign law and, thus, also the judgement of similarity or difference.[5] In particular, the neutrality assumption of traditional comparative law is rejected: as there is no 'view from nowhere',[6] the postmodernist is said to start 'from the premise that reasoning, language and judgement are determined by inescapable and incommensurable epistemic, linguistic, cultural and moral frameworks'.[7]

Yet, this should not be seen as a closed definition, as the term 'postmodernism' is notoriously ambiguous. For instance, it is also associated with cultural studies, a rejection of functionalism, a prevalence for local narratives,[8] and an emphasis on 'plurality, intersubjectivity, experience, situated knowledge, hermeneutics, [and] hybridity',[9] all referring to trends that started in the mid to late twentieth century.

The topics discussed in this chapter can be related to these trends – for instance, they emerged in a similar period, they reject the functionalism of comparative law, they often favour local specificity to generalisations, and they emphasise the role of culture, plurality and subjectivity in law. But, this chapter also understands 'postmodern comparative law' in a pragmatic way, namely as an umbrella term for six more specific approaches, grouped under the main headings of 'deep-level' and 'critical' comparative law.

B. Deep-level comparative law

The term 'deep-level comparative law'[10] refers to the criticism that the traditional method of comparative law only achieves a relatively shallow understanding of differences and similarities. This can be distinguished from the more openly 'critical' approaches, which take the position that the traditional method leads to flawed results. But what exactly does 'deep-level' refer to? The following section distinguishes between four approaches, though there are some overlaps between them, and thus the attribution of particular scholars to any one of these categories is not entirely straightforward.

1. Law as reflecting jurisprudential concepts

Linking legal philosophy and comparative law is not a new endeavour. For example, in 1951, Roscoe Pound wrote a short article suggesting a philosophical method to comparative law.[11] In the mid-1970s, Wolfgang Fikentscher produced a five-volume work on comparative methods of law. It dealt with four legal families – ancient and religious, Romanic, Anglo-American and central European – and analysed their methods of law based on jurisprudential and

---

[5] See van Erp 1999; Cotterrell 2012: 39.   [6] Nelken 2010: 10.
[7] Peters and Schwenke 2000: 802. See also Mattei and di Robilant 2001.
[8] Calhoun et al. 2002: 351, 413–4.   [9] Eberhard 2009: 68.
[10] Borrowed from Van Hoecke 2004. See also Watt 2012 ('comparison as deep appreciation').
[11] Pound 1951: 2.

philosophical streams of thought. For example, the section on central Europe includes detailed discussions of Kant, von Savigny, Puchta, von Jhering, Hegel, Marx and others.[12] In a more recent monograph, Fikentscher examines 'modes of thought' more generally, distinguishing between pre-axial age, East and South Asian, Western, Muslim, Marxist and National Socialist modes of thought. This book goes beyond a jurisprudential approach, in particular drawing on anthropological research.[13] Yet, a review by a well-known anthropologist strongly criticises the idea that the global variety of modes of thought can be condensed into five types.[14]

Returning to the title of this section, William Ewald advocates that comparative law needs to become less technical and more jurisprudential. He suggests a transformation of comparative law into 'comparative jurisprudence' with a core interest in the 'principles, concepts, beliefs, and reasoning that underlie the foreign legal rules and institutions'.[15] Thus, the main focus is neither on black letter doctrines nor on external socio-legal aspects of how law works, but it is to understand the 'cognitive structure' of the legal system from the inside.[16] For instance, a comparatist interested in the German law of obligations may start with its Roman origins, but then it is also important to understand the specific German and European intellectual context; thus, Ewald asks the comparatist to study the ideas of legal thinkers such as von Savigny, Puchta, Windscheid and Gierke, but also Kant and Herder, since the former cannot be understood without having a grasp of the ideas of the latter.[17]

A frequent example is to relate differences between common and civil law to jurisprudential and philosophical ideas. For this purpose, Hugh Collins notes that the civil law tradition reflects Cartesian logic – considering the style of the French Civil Code in particular, as well as idealist philosophical traditions and the Enlightenment – whereas the common law has been influenced by utilitarianism and 'intellectual traditions that emphasise empiricist philosophies which stress the importance of observation, particular facts and even common sense'.[18]

Catherine Valcke follows Ewald's terminology of 'comparative law as jurisprudence', referring to the ideas underlying the positive law.[19] She illustrates this approach by studying the differences between the French and English law of contract formation. French law aims to establish the actual subjective intention of the parties, whereas English law uses an objective concept, incorporating that which the parties reasonably have (and can be taken to have) intended. Valcke relates this aspect of the law to different philosophical and political conceptions about the relationship between the individual and the state:

---

[12] Fikentscher 1975–77.   [13] Fikentscher 2004. See also Fikentscher 2009.
[14] Moore 1996. See also ch. 11 at C 1, below.   [15] Ewald 1998: 705.
[16] Ewald 1995a: 1930, 1947–8.   [17] Ewald 1995a: 1996, 2101, 2107.
[18] Collins 2008: 156, 178. See also ch. 3 at B 1, above.
[19] Valcke 2004: 731; also Valcke 2012 ('getting inside contract law'). See also Husa 2009.

The individual in Rousseau's state of nature is, somewhat like contractual intention at French law, exclusively empirical, whereas the individual in Hobbes's and Locke's states of nature, somewhat like contractual intention at English law, combines an empirical and a normative dimension.[20]

Akin to this is Geoffrey Samuel's approach to comparative law, which asks us to identify the 'internal structures of legal knowledge'.[21] For instance, he considers the difference between English and French government liability law. In England the claimant has to prove fault, but not in France. This is said to be related to different concepts about the relationship between the individual and the community:

> In France the emphasis is on the community as a *persona* with its own *intérêt général;* each time an individual citizen is damaged as a result of some activity in the public interest it is unjust, given the constitutional principle of equality, that it should be the individual who bears the cost of the activity. In England, in contrast, a government body is seen simply as an ordinary *persona* with its own individual interest to protect.[22]

These authors have in common their use of a conceptual approach in order to explain differences between legal systems. Yet, it is also possible to 'go deeper' in order to find common structures. This has often been a topic of 'general jurisprudence', notably John Austin's concern for an 'exposition of principles, notions and distinctions common to all systems of law'.[23] Similarly, Jerome Hall suggests that one of the aims of comparative law is to identify concepts that legal systems have in common despite differences in specific rules, the ultimate aim being a 'transnational theory of what is common in all legal systems'.[24]

To provide two more specific examples, Martin Shapiro's study on courts had the explicit aim of moving beyond descriptions towards 'a more general theory of the nature of judicial institutions'. He found that, across countries, courts do not only solve conflicts, but they also have many political functions, such as setting social policies or providing legitimacy to government and politicians.[25] In a number of books, George Fletcher has aimed to develop universal concepts of criminal law. Though the surface structure of the law is admitted to be diverse across countries, Fletcher finds a 'universal grammar', since criminal law everywhere is shaped by the same conflicts and controversies.[26]

---

[20] Valcke 2009a: 86.

[21] Samuel 1998: 827. In his writings Samuel also frequently refers to Berthelot's 'schemes of intelligibility', e.g. Samuel 2004: 73; Samuel 2007: 106.

[22] Samuel 1998: 824 (footnotes omitted). For this topic see also Fairgrieve 2003.

[23] Austin 1885: 1073. A different use of this term is advocated by those who do not subscribe to such universalism: e.g. Tamanaha 2011c; Tamanaha 2001; Twining 2009a: xiv.

[24] Hall 1963: 59, 62. Similarly Klami 1981: 21 (comparative law as empirical test of legal theory).

[25] Shapiro 1981: vi, viii, 17–36.

[26] Fletcher 2007 with references to his earlier works. See also Mikhail 2009 (on the worldwide prohibition of homicide as example of a 'moral universal').

The question that remains is how much these conceptual approaches differ from traditional comparative law. Traditionalists suggest that a comparative analysis should start with a description of the laws, which is then followed by an explanation of similarities and differences.[27] It is clear that, in this latter phase, concepts and theories play an important role. Thus, it seems to be that the difference is mainly a formal one: either start with a black-letter analysis of the law followed by more jurisprudential concepts, or adopt a jurisprudential approach from the very beginning.

However, it can also be suggested that this difference may well matter. It may be reasonable to start with theories and concepts, since these tend to be older than the concrete legal norms.[28] Moreover, in many papers of traditional comparative law, it seems that the comparatist puts all her efforts into a detailed description of the legal rules, with the explanatory part becoming a mere supplement: thus, there may be some need to follow an approach that puts less emphasis on a mere description of legal rules. Further details, of course, depend on the precise topic that a comparatist aims to analyse: while for many topics it is helpful to consider the general values of a legal order, this link may be weaker for more modern and technical fields of law (e.g. environmental standards or tax rates).

2. Law as embedded in culture

(a) Positive approaches

Since the 1950s, the humanities and social sciences are said to have experienced a shift from materialism, universalism and ideology to culture-bound approaches ('cultural turn').[29] This also had an impact on legal scholarship. Postmodern legal scholars take the view that law should not mainly be seen as a technical tool to fulfil certain functions. Rather, we are told, that 'to consider law, one cannot fail to see it as part of culture', or that law is 'first and foremost, a cultural phenomenon, not unlike singing or weaving'.[30]

The view of law-as-culture has become a prominent feature in the comparative law literature. In a number of articles, Bernhard Grossfeld and collaborators examined how the mutual influence of law and culture shapes differences between legal systems.[31] Culture is understood broadly: to start with, it is about the written text and language. For example, a comparison between Chinese law and that of a Western legal system needs to consider that the Chinese language uses more concrete words than Western languages.[32] It also requires an immersion into the 'milieu and social setting' that affect the convictions of the

---

[27] See ch. 2 at A, above.   [28] Klami 1981: 26.
[29] Sarat and Simon 2003: 1–2; Hantrais 2009: xi, 73; Nelken 2012: 313.
[30] Rosen 2006: 5; Legrand 1999: 5.
[31] Grossfeld and Eberle 2003: 295. See also the following notes and Grossfeld 1990.
[32] Grossfeld 2005: 173. See also Hiller and Grossfeld 2002 (on comparative legal semiotics); Gaakeer 2012: 259–60 (different language versions as different modes of thought).

law-maker and its interpreters.[33] In addition, Grossfeld and colleagues mention other 'invisible powers' that comparative lawyers should consider. 'Invisible' does not mean that these powers cannot be identified, but that they are usually taken for granted: for example, whether and how law forms and reflects history, geography, philosophy and ideology.[34]

As literature and film studies are part of culture studies, it has also been suggested that comparative literature and film studies can be revealing for comparative lawyers.[35] To be sure, a novel or a film with a law-related plot is unlikely to present an accurate description of this legal system, yet it can offer important insights, since it may illustrate and reflect the legal attitudes and aspirations prevalent in a particular country. It has also been suggested that these insights may help to identify 'virtual' transplants – for example, when individuals of foreign countries believe that trial proceedings in their own country are akin to those watched in Hollywood movies.[36]

Other scholars have referred to connections between law and religious studies and traditions. At a general level, there are said to be strong methodological and epistemological similarities between law and theology since both create their 'own abstract constructions' which do not necessarily depend on external realities.[37] A more specific example is provided by Gary Watt. He speculates about a parallelism between the English trust, on the one hand, and the dualism of the Church of Rome and the Church of England in sixteenth-century England on the other: namely, that the possibility of splitting the asset into a legal and an equitable title, and this religious dualism, are both seen as 'a creative expression of a culture of divided unity'.[38]

In some legal systems, and for some areas of law, a cultural view may be particularly relevant. For example, Menachem Mautner starts his book on the 'law and the culture of Israel' with the observation that Israeli law reflects 'the struggle over the shaping of the Jewish culture and identity'.[39] Writing about Russia, Uriel Procaccia takes the position that the widespread antipathy towards contracts is related to the fact that elements of Western European culture – such as individualism, materialism, rationalism and humanism – have not been well received in Russia.[40] It is also evident that an understanding of the rules of traditional societies requires a cultural and anthropological perspective.[41]

Criminal law and criminal procedure in particular have both been subjects of the cultural approach to comparative law. For example, in order to understand

---

[33] Eberle 2009: 458; Grossfeld and Eberle 2003: 293, 306, 309.

[34] Grossfeld and Eberle 2003: 292; Eberle 2009: 452–3; Eberle 2007: 97.

[35] Olson 2010; Dellapenna 2008; Samuel 2012: 189–90. See also Watt 2012: 84 ('aspect of law that is art'); Legrand 2006b: 368 (even fantasies sustained by a culture are a valuable clue for comparatist); Procaccia 2007 (using pictures and other illustrations, somehow akin to Wigmore, see ch. 2 at A 2 (c) and B 2 (b), above).

[36] Nelken 2006: 940; Mattei and Nader 2008: 208.   [37] Samuel 2012: 174, 188–90.

[38] Watt 2012: 101–2.   [39] Mautner 2011: 1.

[40] Procaccia 2007. For similar views about Japan and China see ch. 4 at C 2 (a), above.

[41] See, e.g., Moore 2005: 86, 100; Geertz 1983 and ch. 11 at C, below.

why in the US someone can be jailed for minor crimes that in Europe would only result in a fine, one may consider that the US policy reflects 'strong Christian values based on Old Testament retribution'.[42] There may also be 'two different visions of human moral nature', since the concept of human evil may be immanent in US criminal law, but not in its German counterpart.[43] Specifically with respect to capital punishment, it has been argued that understanding it purely as a means of crime control misses the point: the death penalty is deeply embedded in the cultural life of the US, whereas the abolishment of the death penalty has become part of the European identity.[44]

It has also been suggested that criminal trials should equally not be seen in purely functional terms. David Garland speaks about 'a rhetoric of symbols, figures, and images by means of which the penal process is represented to its various audiences'.[45] As regards differences between jurisdictions, Lawrence Rosen contrasts Western and Islamic criminal trials. In the West, the trial is restricted to the facts that are relevant for the law in question. In the Islamic trial, by contrast, the character, background and social relationships of the accused are treated as at least as important. It is therefore crucial to understand that cultures may have different preferences as regards the information seen as relevant for the application of the law.[46]

All of this sounds very plausible. Yet, there are also a number of potential problems. At a practical level, it may be difficult for a comparatist to be fully familiar with the entire culture of each of a country's legal systems that she aims to examine. Thus, there is the risk of imposing unrealistic standards, a problem that can also arise for other variants of postmodern comparative legal research.[47]

More fundamentally, there is the risk of treating a country's culture and law as 'coherent woven wholes', or even 'hermetic, closed, immutable entities'.[48] Consequently, if asked why a particular country has a particular law, one could simply provide the meaningless 'explanation' that this is just the way this country's culture deals with a particular situation. Such reasoning would also be circular: 'culture is as much a consequence as a cause of behavior: if anything, it is not culture that explains behavior, but rather behavior that defines culture'.[49] This does not deny the role of culture. But it is also possible that different cultures can have similar laws, and similar cultures different ones. Thus, the comparatist should be open as to the precise role that cultural factors can play in a particular legal question.

---

[42] Eberle 2009: 484.   [43] Kleinfeld 2011.

[44] Boulanger and Sarat 2005; Girling 2005. For socio-legal approaches see ch. 6 at C 2, below.

[45] Garland 1990: 17. See also Garland 2001 (for crime control more generally); Marrani 2010 (comparing the symbolic position of the judge in England and France).

[46] Rosen 2006: 99–100, 109–10; also, ibid., 26 (in the West judges should not bring their own moral values into their decisions). On Islamic justice and culture more generally see Rosen 2000 and Rosen 1989 (fieldwork research of qadi courts in Morocco).

[47] See further C 2, below.   [48] Riles 1999: 241; Peters and Schwenke 2000: 814.

[49] Law 2011a: 1432. See also Nelken 2007a: 123; Nelken 2010: 50–1.

(b) Normative approaches

Beyond the aim of explaining other legal systems, cultural aspects are sometimes used in a normative manner. One variant is the 'cultural constraints argument', which argues that differences between legal systems are 'unbridgeable', since laws are embedded in 'unique national cultures'.[50] Legal diversity is then presented in a positive way. Understanding that law is culture-specific should lead to respect, tolerance and appreciation of difference.[51] Roger Cotterrell also relates this to multicultural societies: in both cases, communication becomes richer 'with perceptions of difference being part of the richness'.[52]

However, there is the apparent risk of cultural relativism. If we always had to appreciate foreign laws as being part of another country's culture, this would also embrace cruel and dictatorial laws which do not deserve to be appreciated.[53] But the question, then, is whether a view of law-as-culture may be used for the opposite purpose, namely to challenge a particular legal model. Horatia Muir Watt seems to make this suggestion, that law is a 'contextualised cultural phenomenon' and that comparative law is a way of questioning legal norms.[54]

More controversially, this normative point has been made by Mary Ann Glendon, writing, amongst others, about the abortion laws of the United States and Western Europe (as they were in the late 1980s[55]). Referring to Plato, Glendon takes the position that law is not only about legal rules, but that it 'tells stories' about attitudes and behaviours. It follows that comparative law has a 'pedagogical claim' when the experience of other countries shows deficiencies of our attitudes and behaviours.[56] Glendon contends that this is precisely what can be said about the 'excessively liberal' US abortion law:

> A Martian trying to infer our culture's attitude toward children from our abortion and social welfare laws might think we had deliberately decided to solve the problem of children in poverty by choosing to abort them rather than to support them with tax dollars.[57]

Reviewers of Glendon's book have noted that it is somehow ironic that she uses the concept of 'law as storytelling', developed by the political left and

---

[50] Antokolskaia 2007: 256 (for family law). See also Grossfeld 1990: 41 (uniqueness of legal systems).

[51] Menski 2006: 11, 26; Menski 2007: 189 (aim to 'construct plurality-conscious models of handling legal diversity'); Darian-Smith 2013: 108–9 (epistemological diversity needed); Cotterrell 2006: 712.

[52] Cotterrell 2007: 136.   [53] Peters and Schwenke 2000: 819.

[54] Muir Watt 2000; also Muir Watt 2012 (specifically dealing with the field of global governance). Similarly Samuel 2008; Fletcher 1998.

[55] For data on the development of the abortion laws of 186 countries between 1960 and 2009 see Finlay et al. 2012 (overall finding liberalisation).

[56] Glendon 1987. See also Glendon et al. 2008: 8 ('power and duty to make a critical evaluation what he or she discovers through comparison'); Glendon 2007 (re-stating the reference to Plato).

[57] Glendon 1987: 55.

radical feminism, to suggest a shift to a more conservative abortion law.[58] The more substantive point of criticism is that Glendon makes a policy suggestion on a controversial issue, but avoids openly discussing politics and the non-philosophical context of the law.[59] These points are useful to note, since both will re-appear in the subsequent sections on critical and socio-legal comparative law.

3. Law as requiring immersion

Both the cultural view and the one discussed in this section have in common the view that law is not seen as something that can plainly be understood as fulfilling certain functions. However, recommending 'immersion' into a foreign legal system may have the advantage that it does not start with a pre-defined concept of culture.

An example of such an approach is Richard Hyland's work, which calls it 'the interpretive method'.[60] To illustrate it, Hyland draws a parallel between comparative law and comparative literature: for instance, a researcher of novels from different countries that all relate to the Second World War would not start with a functional question, but would analyse the novels as they are.[61] In his comparative study of the law of gifts, Hyland accordingly recommends that:

> we think of gift law in the context of the world that jurists imagine for its operation, the purposes gift norms are designed to achieve, and the effects these norms are imagined to have. There is no need to consider beforehand the extent to which that world is real or whether the norms have any particular effect or function.[62]

John Bell's approach is similar, using the term 'immersion' explicitly. He too suggests that we should understand legal systems on their own terms.[63] This means, taking the 'insider's view on legal systems', i.e. becoming the 'voice of that system, albeit with a non-native accent'.[64] It should be added, however, that Bell also suggests that the description of foreign laws can be accommodated to make them understandable to the local audience.[65] This is not an uncommon recommendation: for instance, in a comparative law book written explicitly for the Indian market, one might expect the Indian point of view to influence the presentation of the subject.[66]

---

[58] Bartlett 1987. Glendon's 'pro-life' position also became more prominent later on, notably when she was US ambassador to the Vatican in 2008–9.

[59] Cohen 1989: 1270; Fineman 1988: 1443.   [60] Hyland 2009: 106. See also Hyland 1996.

[61] Hyland 2009: 116.   [62] Hyland 2009: 106.

[63] Bell 2006a: 41. See also Bell 2001: 17; Valcke 2012: 25.

[64] Bell 2011: 168. Similarly Hall 1963: 33, 67 (comparative law as 'humanistic legal sociology', understanding law from an internal perspective).

[65] Bell 2011: 171.

[66] Khan and Kumar 1971: 46. Similar Lemmens 2012: 317, 321 (bridge between foreign law and domestic audience).

Vivian Grosswald Curran discusses the concept of immersion in detail. She acknowledges that 'total immersion' is impossible, since one's own legal culture will inevitably influence one's interpretation of foreign law.[67] Still, the comparatist as an 'outsider' should have precisely the aim of understanding the insider's view, and this:

> necessitates acts of imagination, for the leap into a foreign mentality necessarily involves a leap of imagination, no matter how steeped the comparatist may be in the target country's legal culture. An act of imagination must occur in the penetration by the legal comparatist of foreign legal cultures, as the comparatist begins to understand new categories, new patterns of interpretation.[68]

It is interesting to note that Curran uses the term 'legal culture' in the present context of law as requiring immersion. This is akin to the use of 'legal culture' by others – for example, Csaba Varga's reference to legal culture as the ideas, value preferences and moral foundations of the law.[69] Yet, legal culture is also employed in the context of socio-legal comparative law, namely as far as it relates to the way law is applied in practice. Of course, both meanings overlap, since the application of the law depends on the deeper meaning legal rules have in a particular society. Pragmatically, it has also been suggested to include both elements within the meaning of legal culture.[70]

The final example is Igor Stramignoni, who suggests applying Heidegger's concept of 'poetry' to comparative law. Poetry, as understood by Heidegger, refers to 'what really lets us dwell', and with this the 'comparatist-poet' will be equipped to tell 'what difference the law makes' and develop a 'poetic awareness of difference' between legal systems.[71] This encouragement to reflect on differences is also found in Curran's research. Following Isaiah Berlin, she stresses that humans define their identities by way of being different from others. Thus, a comparative approach is essential to make legal reasoning intelligible to members of one's own legal system, as well as others.[72]

The writings by these authors are important in stressing the limits of functionalism. However, it is difficult to see the need for immersion as a specific tool for comparative legal research. Even when a researcher only deals with one country, it is necessary not to remain at the surface level of the positive law but to become immersed into that legal system. Thus, while the view of law as requiring immersion is useful as general guidance for all legal research, it does not provide a specific comparative tool. This conclusion does not necessarily

---

[67] Curran 1998a: 90.

[68] Curran 1998a: 64. See also Dannemann 2006: 392 and Cotterrell 2003: 151 (parallel to 'thick description' in anthropology).

[69] Varga 2007 (with references to his earlier work).

[70] Sunde 2010: 26 (institutional and the intellectual structure of legal culture); Bell 2001: 2–5 (ideological and practical aspects of culture); also Merry 2010: 48–52 (practices of legal institutions, public attitudes and beliefs about the law, legal mobilisation, legal consciousness). See also ch. 6 at A 1 (a), below.

[71] Stramignoni 2002: 760, 763.   [72] Curran 1998b: 667; Curran 1998a: 46–8.

mean that there is something wrong with this approach: indeed, a number of comparatists have expressed the view that we should think about comparative law as a variant of legal research more generally, not a unique and distinct method.[73]

4. Law as legal pluralism

The views discussed up to now aim to develop an understanding of statute or judge-made law which is more meaningful than that of traditional comparatists. However, it is also an important feature of deep-level and postmodern comparative law that it argues that law has to be understood in a wide sense: namely, as legal pluralism. Such a view also reflects research in other academic fields dealing with topics such as cultural, social, structural, political and socio-economic pluralism.[74]

Legal pluralism is difficult to define precisely, but the following statement by Franz von Benda-Beckmann and colleagues may be a representative summary:

> Legal orders or single rules may be rooted in different sources of legitimacy, such as age-old tradition, religion, the will of the people, or agreements between states. The coexistence of such legal forms in the same social field (however defined) is generally called 'legal pluralism'.[75]

Thus, legal pluralists reject the view that only the state can make law, or even regard this as a 'myth'.[76] Legal pluralism is seen as the rule since the social order is typically based on a variety of sources of normativity.[77] These sources can exist at the level of nation states, but this is not necessarily the case. Indeed, it may be argued that modern societies 'no longer aspire to one set of apparently solid moral and cultural values';[78] thus, these multiple formal and informal sources may be as prevalent at the sub-national and supranational level.[79]

Clear examples of legal pluralism are found where customary law plays an important role, in particular in tribal communities of developing countries, but also in the laws of groups and communities such as the Quakers, Romani, Native Americans and religious organisations.[80] Thus, in the first instance, the pluralism is one between state and non-state legal orders. Second, a plural

---

[73] E.g. Adams and Griffiths 2012; Lemmens 2012: 304–5, 313; Bell 2011. But see also ch. 12 at C, below.

[74] Moore 1986b: 20–2.

[75] Von Benda-Beckmann et al. 2009a: 2; also Griffiths 1986 (as strong form of legal pluralism). A good source of information is the website of the Commission on folk law and legal pluralism at www.commission-on-legal-pluralism.com/.

[76] Menski 2006: 115, 183.

[77] Moore 2005: 1; Mattei 1997a: 105, 107, 119.   [78] Banakar 2011: 24.

[79] See, e.g., Moore 2005: 307; Twining 2007: 85; Griffiths 2009a: 166. See also ch. 9 at C and D, below.

[80] For these examples see, e.g., Weyrauch 2001; Bradney and Cownie 2000; Cooter and Fikentscher 1998; ch. 9 at D 1, below.

situation occurs since these local and personal non-state laws are not pure any more, but interrelated with the other legal domains, including the ones of state law.[81]

In addition, legal pluralists are keen on emphasising that, even in mainstream Western legal systems, pluralism is ubiquitous. This should not be seen as a surprise since, in medieval Europe, canon, Roman, feudal, royal and urban laws, as well as laws based on religious, ethnic and commercial affiliation, all co-existed in the same territory.[82] Today, too, Western law is seen as a combination of human design and human experience, since law obtains its legitimacy 'from within the cultural, private societies of peoples and not just the public, external, political constitution of the state'.[83] To provide two more concrete examples: first, it is said that, in Europe, legal pluralism has re-emerged due to the overlapping normative orders of the national legal systems, the European Union and the European Convention on Human Rights.[84] A quite different second example is the law on assisted suicide: here, apart from the positive criminal and medical law, a pluralist understanding of the law also includes the guidelines of medical associations and public prosecutors, and how these are translated into social practice.[85]

An apparent problem is how far it is feasible for a comparative researcher to consider everything that can contribute to social order – for instance, whether also to include means such as 'language, customs, moral norms, and etiquette'.[86] Yet, this is not a problem that is specific to legal pluralism, since even traditional comparative law would not be blind to these factors as far as they can be regarded as functional equivalents.[87] Thus, as far as relevant and possible, pluralist notions of law should be included in comparative legal research.

C. Critical comparative law

The term 'critical comparative law' is occasionally used in the literature, but often without a precise definition.[88] This is not implausible, since the corresponding 'critical legal studies' of US scholarship is seen as a movement, not a

---

[81] Griffiths 2009b: 503.
[82] Goldman 2008: 38; Berman 2009: 227. See also Glenn 2013: 17–34; Tamanaha 2008: 377–81.
[83] Goldman 2008: 51. See also Easterly 1977: 209.
[84] Husa 2012 (who also calls this 'polynomia'). See also Smits 2013 (for private law).
[85] See Adams and Griffiths 2012. The underlying book is Griffiths et al. 2008.
[86] Tamanaha 2001: 180; also Tamanaha 2008: 390–1 (criticising legal pluralism as a 'troubled concept'); Tamanaha 1993b (even calling it a 'folly').
[87] See ch. 2 at A 2 (c), above.
[88] See, e.g., Frankenberg 1985: 434 (for hidden political agenda of Western-centric approach of comparative law); Twining et al. 2006: 2 (reference to the 1997 Symposium on New Approaches to Comparative Law, published in the *Utah Law Review*); Somma 2006 and Somma 2007 (mainly as 'fight' against positivism); Merino Acuña 2012 (referring to the 'Frankfurt school'). But also Örücü 1999: 131–2 ('transfrontier mobility of law and reciprocal influence between systems'), though this may also be seen as part of mainstream comparative law.

fixed canon. Much the same can be said about other critical theories, such as literary theory. Thus, it seems most appropriate to use the term critical comparative law in a pragmatic way: namely, as all comparative legal research related to such critical approaches.

1. Law as discourse

The notion of law as discourse followed the rise of literary theory and related postmodern scholarship in the second part of the twentieth century. A core element of these approaches is the belief that a particular subject is shaped by our own preconceptions and the language we use to describe it.[89] Thus, understanding human communication is seen as crucial while recognising that objective and universal knowledge is impossible. With respect to the method of comparative law, it follows that:

> there is no getting outside the dominant discourse of law, and thus no foreign worlds for the comparativist to discover. All that can be done, then, is to deconstruct the ambiguities and indeterminacies within the dominant discourse, including the internal contradictions in its assumptions about the character of foreign law.[90]

The view of law as discourse is therefore relativist in seeking to 'celebrate plurality', and in exposing differences between 'us' and 'them', while rejecting the view of law as an instrument of solving problems or of finding commonalities between legal systems.[91]

Main proponents of this approach to comparative law are Mitchel Lasser, Günter Frankenberg, Nora Demleitner and Pierre Legrand.[92] In one of Lasser's methodological papers, he asks comparatists to 'understand discursive and conceptual patterns' in order to gain access to the 'ideolects of foreign legal actors'.[93] Naturally, this is not an easy task, but Lasser does not want to overemphasise the cognitive problems of understanding foreign law: in principle, these problems also apply to domestic legal systems, and the growing transnationalisation of legal science may weaken the 'inside/outside' distinction.[94] More specifically, Lasser examined how literary theory can help us in our understanding of French and US court judgments.[95] For example, referring to concepts developed by Roman Jakobson, Lasser explains that French judgments can be read as suffering from a 'contiguity disorder' because they are unable to combine considerations (here: law and policy), whereas US judgments suffer from a

---

[89] See, e.g., Coe et al. 2010: 48–50; Schneider 1995: 627.   [90] Riles 1999: 246.

[91] See McCrudden 2007: 373–4; Menski 2006: 11; Riles 2006: 807.

[92] Further examples may be Schneider 1995 (deconstructionist approach); Teitel 2004: 2584 (dialogical method); Somma 2007 (applying a hermeneutical approach).

[93] Lasser 2003: 203, 222.   [94] Lasser 2003: 215, 218, 222.

[95] For the following Lasser 1998, in particular 748–50.

'similarity disorder' since they are unable to say anything without knowing the context.[96]

Frankenberg is sceptical as to whether we can 'go native' and understand foreign legal cultures. He advocates a critical approach to comparative studies that is sensitive 'to the relationship between the self and the other'.[97] Thus, it is important to recognise the subjectivity of knowledge, in particular to be aware of one's own cultural ties and biases. With this, Frankenberg admits, that the critique may well turn into a tragedy:

> [T]he tragic comparatist seems to be well aware of the limits and defects of her home law and her intellectual situation. Confined to the borders of a national legal regime and the parochial nature of the corresponding legal education, the tragic self dresses casually and bemoans a state of 'consecrated ignorance' of foreign laws and of her own alienation.[98]

More optimistically, Demleitner sees that the aim of comparative law is to 'help us understand how another person conceives of the world'. Without such understanding, comparative law will merely confirm stereotypes about legal systems and cultures.[99] Conversely, the correct approach will not only identify but respect foreign legal cultures since 'difference often drives creativity'.[100]

Last but not least, Pierre Legrand's research deserves special attention. Legrand is one of the most prolific – but also one of the most controversial – contemporary comparatists. A significant proportion of his research is openly confrontational, characterising the traditional comparative literature as positivistic, superficial, and as providing a mere illusion of understanding of other legal systems.[101] Some of these critiques are the topics of subsequent parts of this book, such as the rejection of legal transplants, harmonisation and convergence.[102] With respect to the traditional method of comparative law, the functionalist search for similarities is called an 'instrumental dissolution of specific cultural forms into generic strategic effects, an enterprise of totalization, and a "theological" project'.[103] Legrand also criticises the positivist comparatists for feeling equipped to make normative assessments about the superiority of particular legal rules.[104] As regards recent projects, the Common Core publications are described as 'snippety compilations' that accumulate 'selected titbits extracted largely from legislative texts and appellate judicial decisions'.[105] And reviewing the *Oxford Handbook of Comparative Law*, Legrand writes:

---

[96] But this is not seen as the complete picture since judicial discourse also takes place in the unofficial sphere not expressly mentioned in judgments. See ch. 3 at B 2 (e), above.

[97] Frankenberg 1985: 441. See also Frankenberg 2012b: 177–8.

[98] Frankenberg 1997: 266 (footnotes omitted).   [99] Demleitner 1999: 741.

[100] Demleitner 1999: 746. See also Demleitner 1998: 652.   [101] E.g. Legrand 2011; Legrand 2005.

[102] See ch. 8 at A 2 (b) and ch. 9 at B 3 and C 3, below, in particular on Legrand 1996 and Legrand 1997b.

[103] Legrand 2005: 705.   [104] Legrand 2006b: 394. See also ch. 2 at C 4, above.

[105] Legrand 2005: fn 159. For the Common Core see ch. 2 at B 3, above.

This book evidences pathologies not unfamiliar to the field of comparative legal studies: a compulsion for lists and an obsession with size . . . Salient contributions were thus entrusted to friends and to friends of friends . . . Variations on the theme of discipleship include a defence of functionalism, or of comparative studies at the level of the lowest common denominator, and a 37-page chapter on comparisons as studies in similarities or differences which, astonishingly, excludes meaningful treatment of philosophical, anthropological, sociological and linguistic texts.[106]

With respect to the final point, Legrand is particularly interested in the writings of Heidegger, Gadamer and Derrida.[107] According to these, the interpretation of text is a complex undertaking that requires an understanding of the relationship between 'the self' and 'the other'. This leads to a focus on textual analysis for criticism and deconstruction, since a non-textual starting point cannot be assumed. In addition, Legrand seems to be influenced by culturalist ideas that societies are as unique as individuals.[108] For comparative law it follows that we should understand 'law in its fullest sense',[109] meaning:

how foreign legal communities think about the law, why they think about the law as they do, why they would find it difficult to think about the law in any other way, and how their thought differs from ours.[110]

For these features, Legrand often uses terms such as the 'cognitive structure of the law', the 'collective mental programme' of legal cultures, and, most frequently, 'legal mentalities'.[111] According to Legrand the result of such considerations is that there are deep differences between countries: every legal system is singular[112] and comparing them is like comparing different 'world versions'.[113] Yet, this is not to mean that these national legal mentalities are holistic: whereas for some questions it may be worth looking at the French legal community as a whole, for others, one may just examine the attitudes of local lawyers. Moreover, it is clear that, even at the individual level, identities are often complex:

Any individual partakes in a seemingly infinite array of ascertainable cultural formations. One can be a labour lawyer in Poitiers while being a woman, a Belgian expatriate, a European, a militant of Amnesty International, a breeder of Siamese cats regularly entering international competitions, and a long-standing member of the *Parti socialiste*.[114]

Overall, however, Legrand's writings focus on how countries and legal families differ. Here, he takes the position that civil and common law are based on irreducibly different ways of understanding: it is not possible for a civil-law

---

[106] Legrand 2007b. See also Legrand 2011: 19 (criticising the 'encyclopedism' of comparative law).
[107] References in Legrand 2011; Legrand 2006c: 523. See also Glanert 2012.
[108] See Brandt 2007: 430.   [109] Legrand 2007a: 222.   [110] Legrand 2005: 707.
[111] Legrand 1996: 60. See also Samuel 2008: 292.   [112] Legrand 2006c.
[113] Cf. Caterina 2004 (who argues against this position).
[114] Legrand 2006b: 376 note 43. See also Legrand 1996: 63.

lawyer to think like a common-law lawyer, or vice versa.[115] This does not mean that the former cannot understand the latter. However, this is merely an imagination in the former's own terms,[116] while, for instance, a civil-law lawyer 'can never understand the English legal experience like an English lawyer'.[117] Finally, similar to Demleitner, Legrand takes the view that a comparatist must be someone who values and, even cherishes, diversity.[118] Differences are seen as a matter of 'national and cultural identity' and as 'the expression of the human capacity for choice and self-creation'.[119] Thus, it cannot be said that the law of a particular country is superior, since we may 'simply have two narrative construals of reality that are both intrinsically valid'.[120]

In the assessment of Legrand and the other law-as-discourse comparatists, three types of criticism can be distinguished. First, some have disapproved of their writings on the basis that they cannot be put to practical use. For instance, Sir Basil Markesinis and Jörg Fedtke express the view that the need for applied legal research will not allow 'comparative law falling into the hands of philosophers, anthropologists, and incomprehensible "post-modernists"'.[121] Unsurprisingly, Legrand takes the opposite position:

> The vocation of comparative work about law is intrinsically scholastic and its agenda is, therefore, incongruent with that of practitioners or lawmakers seeking to elicit epigrammic answers from foreign laws.[122]

However, both positions are too extreme. As we have seen earlier, comparative law can validly fulfil a number of purposes, some more academic and some more practical.[123] Thus, in the current context, it would not be appropriate to reject something merely because it leans towards the academic side of comparative law.

Second, the strong emphasis on the limits of understanding foreign law is open to criticism. There is no denying that preconceptions influence our understanding, but this does not mean that it is impossible to learn new things. Thus, legal systems should not be seen as 'closed frameworks' that foreigners can never enter.[124] A possible reply may be that we can only acquire a partial knowledge about a foreign legal system. But, then, domestic lawyers face the same problem. Every lawyer, be it a practitioner or an academic, only has

---

[115] Legrand 1999: 11, 64.

[116] See Legrand 2009: 221 (other law 'can only ever be intelligible to me on my terms'); Legrand 2003: 244 (describing himself as 'someone who is free to imagine oneself as either a common-law or a civil-law lawyer').

[117] Legrand 1996: 78.   [118] Legrand 1999: 11; Legrand 2002: 62; Legrand 2003: 287.

[119] Legrand 1998b: 225, 229; Legrand 2001b: 1050.

[120] Legrand 1999: 78. See also Legrand 2009: 220.

[121] Markesinis and Fedtke 2009: 69; also ibid., 54; Markesinis 2003: 51–4. Specifically, they refer to Mattei and di Robilant 2001.

[122] Legrand 2007a: 222. Similarly Sacco 1991: 2 ('the effort to justify comparative law by its practical uses sometimes verges on the ridiculous').

[123] See ch. 1 at A 2, above. On legal research more generally see Siems and MacSithigh 2012.

[124] Similarly Peters and Schwenke 2000: 816.

incomplete knowledge of the legal rules and the way these are applied in his or her own legal system.[125] Thus, since complete understanding is an illusion,[126] knowing something about domestic law and about foreign law merely differs in degree not in kind.

Moreover, one can make the case that, in some instances, being a foreigner may even be helpful. It was already mentioned that a comparatist may be the best person to communicate a foreign legal order to the local audience of her own country.[127] But the comparatist's advantage can also be a more general one. The foreign lawyer's outsider perspective can illuminate features of the law that internal observers would not realise: for example, showing the 'constructed nature' of the way domestic lawyers portray their legal system.[128] Similarly, according to George Fletcher, anthropological research may be praised for writing about foreign law in a way that 'no native would write about it'.[129] Stephen Smith starts by saying that authors such as Ibsen, Shaw and Joyce were better understood abroad than at home. With respect to law, Smith suggests that:

> the significance of a certain law or legal doctrine is often best understood precisely by taking them out of its local context. In the same way that locals often fail to appreciate what they have in their own backyard until tourists arrive, domestic lawyers, fully immersed in the local legal culture, are not always best positioned to appreciate what is significant about their law.[130]

Third, the emphasis on differences can be seen as problematic. Since the discourse-oriented comparative lawyers are influenced by literature and cultural studies, it is interesting to note that here too it is often regarded as possible to identify unexpected similarities. For instance, in comparative literature it is not uncommon to search for universal archetypes that transcend time and place.[131] Furthermore, the deconstructive method in particular may precisely aim to challenge binary oppositions of both traditional and structuralist Western thinking.[132]

For comparative law, the view that the differences of any two legal systems are irreconcilable would have the consequence that such an analysis would just have two chapters, one written by someone trained in the legal tradition of the first country, the other written by someone trained in the legal tradition of the second one. Thus, we would lack the ability to make generalisations, which is a precondition for comparative law.[133] Furthermore, from a methodological

---

[125] Edge 2000: 11.   [126] Van Hoecke 2004: 173; Antokolskaia 2006: 35.

[127] See B 3, above.   [128] Kessler 2011: 132; also Laithier 2009: 15.

[129] Fletcher 1998: 691.   [130] Smith 2010: 348.

[131] See contributions in Saussy 2006. For the counter-view see Apter 2013. See also Samuel 2012: 178 (references to research for universal themes in comparative mythology).

[132] Schneider 1995: 629, 634–5 (with references to Claude Lévi-Strauss' structuralism and Jonathan Culler's deconstruction).

[133] Merryman 1999: 491; Siems 2007b: 140.

point of view, it is difficult to argue why one should start with a presumption of difference. Rather, a preferable position is to be open to both similarity and difference (a point which, of course, can also be raised against the presumption of similarity in traditional comparative law).[134]

More specifically, it is often an exaggeration to claim that there are fundamental differences between countries or legal families. Legrand's views on this matter have been related to the historical school of thought of von Savigny who believed that a country's law is the manifestation of a common consciousness formed over centuries: thus, every people have a unique law.[135] Yet in today's world, legal rules and cultures are often subject to change due to circumstances that are not specific to a particular country or region.[136] There is also the problem that putting too much weight on the characteristics of, say, English v. French law (or common v. civil law) risks viewing legal systems (or families) as all-embracing solid units. This can lead to a disregard of many other factors that determine similarities and differences (e.g., different dynamics in specific areas of law; the role of the EU).[137] Thus, the main problem of the law-as-discourse comparative law is that it challenges the superficiality of the positivist tradition while making broad generalisations about differences between legal traditions, which can do more harm than good.[138]

2. Law as politics

The US critical legal studies movement of the 1970s contested the established division between law and politics. When traditional lawyers pretended that law can be applied in a logical and neutral way, this was seen as pure rhetoric in order to disguise hidden agendas, and that in fact law always has a political and ideological dimension.[139]

Turning to comparative law, political or ideological factors can, on the one hand, be used to explain similarities and differences. Such a political dimension is obvious when one compares the constitutional law of countries with different political systems, and ideology is likely to be a decisive factor for areas such as immigration and labour law.[140] But these factors can also be relevant elsewhere. For instance, whether a legal system provides for pre-contractual liability may depend on whether a communitarian social ideology is prevalent in the country in question.[141] It has also been suggested that modern family laws are less a

---

[134] See Lemmens 2012: 322; Cotterrell 2012: 39; Bell 2011: 174; Nelken 2010: 32 and ch. 2 at B 2 (b), above.

[135] Palmer 2004: 10; Mautner 2011: 33. See also ch. 6 at A 2 (a), below.

[136] See also Part III, below.

[137] Cotterrell 2007: 139–140; Cotterrell 2003: 150; Karhu 2004: 84; Riles 2006: 798.

[138] See also the critique of legal families in ch. 3 at C and ch. 4 at C, above.

[139] See, e.g., Hutchinson and Monahan 1984; Tushnet 1991.

[140] See, e.g., Kennedy 2012: 39, 42.

[141] Fletcher 1998: 694. For pre-contractual liability see also ch. 3 at B 3 (c), above.

reflection of culture but of political determinants, such as a particular ideological position.[142]

On the other hand, politics can be used in a more normative way. Brenda Cossmann is open about:

> putting the question of political agendas onto the agenda of comparative law... We are attempting to contribute to the debate about how law can be used, if at all, in women's struggle for social change – to debates about how law can be used to begin to destabilize hierarchical gender identities in India. We make no claims to neutrality in our work, but rather begin from an explicitly and unapologetically political location.[143]

Political views are also frequent in the discussion about postmodernism, hegemony and comparative law. Critical studies see it as a main feature of the postmodern world that today's capitalism works to the sole benefit of multinational corporations and their supporting elites.[144] Here, 'law' also plays a role. For instance, Western legal influence and the use of comparative law are said to have a hidden political agenda to the detriment of the poor and oppressed in developing countries.[145] In this literature, it is therefore suggested that law should not be seen as depoliticised and neutral; rather, it is necessary to reconnect law with politics in order to make use of its 'emancipatory' and 'counter-hegemonic' potential.[146] Later chapters of this book will return to these topics, for instance, in the context of legal transplants, and comparative law and development.[147]

David Kennedy's article on 'New Approaches to Comparative Law: Comparativism and International Governance' deserves special attention. Amongst others, Kennedy shows how political attitudes determine the views of comparative lawyers.[148] This can be seen in both the cultural and the technocratic forms of comparative law. According to Kennedy, the cultural variant is interested in private law, legal cultures and area studies. Here, a left-wing comparatist is said to hold the view that national differences in legal culture and legal rules, in particular in the field of private law, should be left intact, and that local cultures should inform the universal one, whereas a right-wing comparatist supports the standardisation and codification of private law, as well as the use of legal transplants in order to reduce the transaction costs set by local cultures. The technocratic variant is directly concerned with topics of international economic law, harmonisation and development. Here, Kennedy identifies a left-wing view with an approach that is, on the one hand, supportive of international law but, on the other hand, regards the WTO as a system that suppresses differences

---

[142] Bradley in EE 2012: 314–31.   [143] Cossmann 1997: 542.
[144] E.g. Harvey 1989a; Jameson 1991.
[145] Frankenberg 1985: 434; Peters and Schwenke 2000: 822; Santos 2004: 192–3.
[146] Santos and Rodriguez-Garavito 2005: 15, 17; Santos 2004: 351.
[147] See ch. 8 at A 2 (c) and ch. 10 at C, below.
[148] For the following see Kennedy 1997: 594, 606–12.

and cultural specificity. A right-wing view, then, favours internationalisation as a bargain process between countries, while supporting a system of regulatory competition in which universal rules of the neoliberal variant emerge.

Kennedy also discusses how comparative law can benefit from a closer alignment with international law. Comparative lawyers tend to attribute legal rules to historical commonalities and legal borrowings, whereas international lawyers are interested in international governance, that is, to build the 'normative or institutional conditions for international public order'.[149] But that should change:

> [I]f we are to rejuvenate comparative law, criticize or claim the discipline, we should do so not simply by interrogating the methods and limits of its own project, but should also see comparative law in relation to the broader problems of governance in which it plays, often unwittingly to be sure, a number of important roles. And we should see comparativists as people with projects – political, professional, and personal projects of cosmopolitan governance.[150]

Finally, Kennedy indicates the contribution comparative lawyers can make to the governance debate. In line with other postmodern comparatists, their task is mainly seen as highlighting differences: for example, comparative law may show how international governance can accommodate cultural differences, or where unification of the law is not appropriate.[151]

Assessing the law-as-politics approach, it may be argued that some of its elements are not unfamiliar to traditional comparative law. Traditionalists may consider political factors at the stage of a comparative analysis that seeks to explain the variation of legal rules.[152] Most traditional comparative lawyers also take it that policy recommendations can be part of a comparative analysis.[153] Yet, these recommendations tend to be about technical details of the law, not fundamental political questions. Thus, law-as-politics offers the lesson that comparatists should not shy away from these big questions.

It is also valid to reflect on the politics of comparative legal research itself. It is revealing how Kennedy shows that the choices comparatists make are not the ones of entirely neutral academics, but are shaped by their political views. It is also plausible to suggest that a more openly political comparative law could make comparative law more relevant in the context of global governance.

D. Conclusion

The postmodern approaches to comparative law illustrate that there is considerable diversity in the way comparative law can be approached. They also

---

[149] Kennedy 1997: 549 and 583, 601–5.   [150] Kennedy 1997: 551.
[151] For details Kennedy 1997: 614–33.   [152] See ch. 2 at A 3 (b), above.
[153] See ch. 2 at A 4 (a), above.

stimulate methodological awareness, in particular as they highlight the limitations of traditional comparative law. This is not to say that traditional methods have become obsolete; yet, there are, at least, five possible shortcomings that postmodernists have identified.

First, traditional comparatists have a tendency to regard similarities between legal systems as more plausible and interesting than differences. Yet, there is no reason why, a priori, this should be the case. Second, traditionally, comparative law tends to focus on black letter rules, whereas postmodernists highlight that, amongst others, history, culture and politics are often of crucial importance. They also use the concept of legal pluralism to show that even Western legal orders do not only consist of black letter law. Third, postmodern approaches teach us that functionalism is often problematic since law may, to put it as a modest criticism, not always be geared towards certain functions. Fourth, these points can also impact on the way a comparative paper is structured. For instance, if a pure description of the positive law is highly misleading, a comparatist may not want to defer the deeper analysis to the explanatory phase,[154] but use 'immersion' as a primary tool of analysis. Fifth, traditional comparative law is sensitive to problems of 'getting the foreign law right';[155] yet, the postmodern approach shows that it is also necessary to go further and consider how biases and preconceptions influence our understanding of foreign legal systems.

Thus, postmodern approaches to comparative law are valuable. But they should not be the final word on the methods of comparative law, because they too leave a number of shortcomings that lead directly to the subsequent topics of this book. For example, some postmodernists claim that legal systems and cultures are fundamentally different. But, then, in order to make such statements, would it not be necessary to present data that show, or do not show, that there are indeed such differences (see Chapter 6 and Chapter 7, below)? Moreover, is it not worth examining whether globalising trends have changed these established divisions (see Part III, below)? In particular, is it not equally interesting to explore curious similarities – for instance, by way of analysing the prevalence and functioning of legal transplants (see Chapter 8, below)?

In addition, postmodern comparative law tends to regard differences between legal systems as worth preserving. But, then, why is this the case? Could it not be that cultures and societies have already converged to a significant degree, and that the law just needs to catch up (see Chapter 9, below)? Specifically, there is the need to examine the role of law in development: so, is it the case that foreign legal influence disrupts local legal cultures, or could this not be precisely what some countries need in order to develop a legal system 'fit' for the modern world (see Chapter 10, below)?

These questions also show that further tools are needed to assess the operation of comparative law in context. Help may come from other disciplines. For

---

[154] See ch. 2 at A 3 (b), above.   [155] See ch. 2 at A 2, above.

example, politics and economics are interested in law as well – yet, in contrast to traditional legal research, not in a pure description of legal rules, but often in a normative analysis. And other disciplines such as psychology and anthropology can help us in evaluating more precisely how far different mentalities hinder cross-border understanding (see Chapter 11, below).

6

Socio-legal comparative law

A great variety of studies use socio-legal approaches to comparative law. Some of them are based on quantitative data, some on qualitative data, and some use mixtures of both.[1] Moreover, an understanding of socio-legal comparative law faces a number of conceptual challenges, in particular, the complex relationship between law and society. Thus, at the outset, Section A sets the scene and explains the scope and aims of socio-legal comparative law. The subsequent Sections B and C discuss socio-legal research on civil procedure, commercial and criminal law, referring to examples from various countries and regions. Section D concludes.

A. Setting the scene

Two elements characterise socio-legal comparative law. First, it replaces the formal understanding of 'law', attributed to traditional comparative law, with a socio-legal one – often using the term 'legal culture'. Second, it reflects on whether and how law and society are related in a causal way. Both will be discussed in this section.

1. Legal culture and comparative law

(a) The meanings of legal culture

The term (legal) culture is criticised for its vagueness.[2] Yet, alternatives, such as (legal) mentalities, formants, traditions, ideologies or styles,[3] are hardly more precise. It is also possible to identify a number of specific building blocks of legal culture. To start with, the term legal culture goes beyond the 'law in books' in considering the 'law in action'.[4] David Nelken illustrates this as follows:

---

[1] The examples of B and C 1, below, are mainly quantitative; the ones of C 2 mainly qualitative. More generally see D and ch. 11 at A 2, below.

[2] Cotterrell 1997; Glenn 2004: 20. See also Piché 2009: 105 (on different definitions); Nelken 2004b: 118–9 (use of indicators or interpretation of cultural meaning); Sunde 2010 (see ch. 5 at B 3, above).

[3] See Nelken 2007a: 115.   [4] See Ehrmann 1976: 4; Blankenburg and Verwoerd 1988: 9.

Knowing more about differences in legal culture can actually save your life! One well-travelled colleague who teaches legal theory likes to tells a story of the way crossing the road when abroad requires good knowledge of the local customs. In England, he claims, you are relatively safe on pedestrian crossings, but rather less secure if you try to cross elsewhere. In Italy, he argues, you need to show about the same caution in both places; but at least motorists will do their best to avoid actually hitting you. In Germany, on the other hand, or so he alleges, you are totally safe on the zebra crossing. You don't even need to look out for traffic. But, if you dare to cross elsewhere, you risk simply not being 'seen'.[5]

It has also been attempted to establish the importance of law in society by way of collecting and comparing data on litigation rates.[6] In addition, legal culture is not only about concrete actions, but also about the attitudes of the public towards the law. Thus, it is potentially fruitful to use cross-country surveys in order to compare legal cultures.[7]

Lawrence Friedman calls these aspects relating to the behaviours and views of the general public 'external legal culture'. By contrast, 'internal legal culture' refers to the persons who make the law, in particular the attitudes of legislators, judges and practising lawyers.[8] With respect to the latter group, it is also important to consider the institutional setting of the legal system. For instance, this may refer to the number of lawyers in a particular country, the structure of courts, the appointment of judges and the way legal education and training are organised.[9]

Finally, legal culture is not only about formal institutions of law-making and law enforcement. Often, other ways of achieving social order may be as important as, or more important than, formal law.[10] Thus, one also needs to consider informal types of social control and dispute resolution, and, again, the structure of these institutions and the habits and attitudes underpinning them.

(b) The spatial levels of legal cultures

Following both traditionalists and postmodernists,[11] a tempting starting point is to say that legal cultures differ at the levels of legal families and countries. With respect to legal families, such reasoning reflects that most classifications incorporate elements of legal culture, such as legal style and the operation of courts.[12] It is also not implausible to assume that the common political framework of the nation state will shape a country's legal culture.[13]

---

[5] Nelken 2004a: 3. See also Nelken 2012: 311–3.

[6] See B 1, below.　　[7] See also ch. 7 at C 3 and ch. 11 at C 3, below.

[8] Friedman 1975. See also Nelken 2007a: 112; Nelken 2004a: 4; Cotterrell 2006: 719; Cotterrell 2001: 74 (internal-external distinction sociologically doubtful since law part of society); Bell 2001: 12–3 (preferring distinction between institutional and non-institutional actors).

[9] See Ehrmann 1976: 9; Nelken 2007b: 11.　　[10] See, e.g. Nelken 2007b: 11; Nelken 1995: 438.

[11] See Part I and ch. 5 at B and C, above.　　[12] See ch. 4 at B 1, above.

[13] See Nelken 2012: 315–7; Nelken 2007b: 12; Nelken 2004b: 120–1 (also referring to other units of legal culture).

But neither connection is a necessary one. On the one hand, it can be said that legal culture goes beyond theses scales. For instance, Lawrence Friedman suggests that today we may have a 'legal culture of modernity' or even 'world legal culture', transgressing the borders of countries and legal families.[14] Jan Smits also takes the view that it is possible to overcome national legal cultures: identifying legal culture as 'mental software', it becomes clear that legal culture is not acquired automatically by way of birth or nationality, and it is feasible that 'mental programming' can accommodate different cultural perceptions.[15]

On the other hand, focusing on legal families and countries may be inaccurate in assuming that the legal culture of a particular legal family or country is uniform.[16] With respect to legal families, the previous part of this book discussed the apparent risk of overemphasising similarities.[17] With respect to the country level, it may, for instance, be shown that legal cultures differ according to areas of law: for example, there may be distinct career paths for civil, criminal and administrative judges. It can also be said that legal pluralism is widespread in all legal systems.[18] At a more general level, the problem may be described as one of 'invented cultures'. In anthropology and cultural studies, it is observed that the coherence and uniformity of cultures is often less real than it is a result of ideology, rhetoric and imagination – and it is not unlikely that this may also be the case for legal cultures.[19]

This discussion about similarities and differences is similar to the one in traditional and postmodern comparative law. Yet, socio-legal comparative law has the advantage of being able to provide empirical data to support or refute similarities between, say, countries of the same legal family. In addition, socio-legal comparatists are not only interested in descriptive questions, but also in causalities, as explained in the next section.

2. The causality problem in socio-legal research

(a) The mirror view and its critics

The mirror view of law and society assumes that law reflects the society in question. One variant of this view suggests that law is a product of a society's history. The well-known positions of Montesquieu and von Savigny relate this mirror to countries; they argue that there is an organic connection between a particular people – its beliefs, culture, morals, as well as its social, political and economic forces – and its legal system.[20] But it is also possible to use

---

[14] Friedman 1994, but also Friedman 2001: 354 (most lawyers 'firmly rooted in their own legal habits and traditions'). See also Part III, below (on global comparative law).

[15] Smits 2007b.   [16] Nelken 2007a: 117; Nelken in EE 2012: 487.

[17] See ch. 3 at C 1 and 2 and ch. 4 at C 2, above.   [18] See ch. 5 at B 4, above.

[19] Nelken 2007a: 114; Nelken 2007b: 15 referring to Kuper 1999; Hobsbawm and Ranger 1983; Anderson 1983.

[20] See Antokolskaia 2006: 37–9; Ewald 1995b; Nelken 2003a: 448. For Montesquieu see also ch. 11 at B 1, below.

other scales: for instance, it may be shown that the practice of a particular local court reflects the specifics of this place; or it may be the case that all European legal systems are seen as a mirror of the interwoven histories of European countries.

Another version is that law mainly reflects society as it is today. This can be based on a Marxist understanding, which holds that, in capitalist societies, economic forces are paramount, shaping the legal rules to accommodate the interests of the capitalist class.[21] Today, this version of the mirror view is more often phrased in a more general way: namely that law reflects the needs of current society,[22] that law changes over time in response to social developments,[23] and that law is the result of felt social needs.[24] Thus, the main point is that the law-as-mirror-of-history view risks seeing law as a 'frozen phenomenon', which it is evidently not.[25]

The question is, however, what determines how quickly law is able to respond to new or changing circumstances. Identifying these determinants of 'legal adaptability' is not always straightforward. For example, consider the preference towards professional or lay judges. On the one hand, professional judges may be more knowledgeable and notice that certain legal concepts are outdated. On the other hand, it is also possible that lay judges foster adaptability because they may not bother with formal legal arguments in the first place.

There is also the problem which types of criteria need to be considered. A paper by Thorsten Beck and colleagues uses variables on the strictness of judicial legal justification as proxies for legal adaptability.[26] Based on data from eighty countries, this leads to the result that the law is more adaptable in common law than in civil law countries. Such a view is shared by other scholars, indicating that the civil law countries' greater reliance on formal legal rules, and the more bureaucratic nature of the judiciary, lead to greater autonomy of the law than in common law countries.[27]

But it is too narrow only to focus on the role of courts. A more meaningful catalogue needs to take into account the legislature, legal practice, academics and the general public of a particular place. This is illustrated in the non-exhaustive list of criteria in Table 6.1 on whether and how law mirrors aspects

---

[21] Cf. Bogdan 1994: 69–70.

[22] See Graziadei 2003: 100, 118; von Wangenheim 2011: 741 (referring to neo-institutional research on property rights).

[23] Nelken 2002; Ehrmann 1976: 38.   [24] Friedmann 1959: 3–23.

[25] See Kurkchiyan 2009: 360; also Banakas 1993–94: 125 (a particular legal culture 'may be swept aside by the winds of political and economic change'); Sunde 2010: 24 ('legal culture is in constant flux').

[26] Beck et al. 2003: 664 with data from Djankov et al. 2003a: 465 (variables on complaint must be legally justified; judgment must be legally justified; judgment must be on law not on equity).

[27] Lundmark 2012: 40, 101–7; Garcia-Villegas 2006: 346 (both comparing civil law countries with the US); cautiously also Hadfield 2008 (distinguishing between open and closed judicial regimes). Generally on the civil/common law divide see ch. 3, above.

Table 6.1 Criteria which can foster legal adaptability[1]

1. Legislature and administration	– Balanced federal structure – Swift law-making (including delegated legislation) – Research by natural and social sciences taken into account – Foreign ideas taken into account – Evaluation of existing laws – Feedback by interested parties possible – Democratic structures – Competent, heterogeneous, responsive, open-minded and honest politicians and civil servants – Freedom of contract, choice of laws, arbitration, and self-regulation possible – Principled legislation – Adaptability-friendly regulation of courts, advocates, legal academia, and general public (see 2.–5., below)
2. Courts	– Legal actions simple, cheap, and quick – Flexible interpretation, analogies, customary and case law possible – Parties or experts can actively take part in proceedings – Precedents not binding – Judgments published – Appointment of judges who can foster innovation – Promotion does not reward legal conservatism – Independent judges
3. Advocates	– Sufficient number of lawyers (no 'closed shop') – Contingency fees possible – Liability towards clients possible – Creative contract drafting
4. Legal academics	– Innovative forms of interpretation favoured – Factual impact of law taken into account – Foreign law taken into account – Innovative legal thinking supported (e.g. by appropriate grading systems, appointments, promotions) – Successful exchange with general public and law-makers (legislature, judges, advocates)
5. General public	– Freedom of speech – Culture of discussion – Pluralist society – Knowledge of foreign languages and cultures – Interest in political questions – Culture of learning and thinking – Scientific research respected

[1] Based on Siems 2006: 397 (with further explanations).

of current societies. It is then also clear that it is too simplistic just to speculate about differences between civil and common law countries.

Yet, there is also the view that law is largely autonomous of past and present social structures. The main line of reasoning is that it is not society as a whole but mainly the internal discussion between judges, law professors and other legal experts which determines the substance of legal rules.[28] It has also been suggested that legal discourses have their own dynamics and legal systems, as sub-systems of modern society, and their own forms of self-reproduction.[29]

Such autonomy of law is said to be supported by specific examples. Some of those concern the longevity of legal rules. For instance, the mirror thesis would seem to be refuted by the fact that Germany and France use their century-old civil codes, and England case law which is even older, whereas everything else has changed in the last centuries (political systems, industrialisation, technology, internationalisation etc.).[30] Moreover, comparative law is said to teach us that very different societies may have fairly similar law, whereas similar societies may have very different ones. For example, due to legal transplants, the civil codes of France and Germany have spread to other regions of the world, often with only small modifications,[31] while in Europe, countries such as England, Scotland and the Netherlands may be regarded as similar in sociological terms, albeit that their laws are very different.[32]

An initial problem with this line of reasoning is that it is based on a very narrow and positivist conception of law: perhaps the wording of particular sections of the French Civil Code has been unchanged for two hundred years, and perhaps these sections are indeed identical to, say, the Civil Code of Mali, but this does not mean that the way the law actually operates is identical.

A more fundamental objection is that the critics of the mirror view tend to focus on fairly technical areas of law, such as general contract law, which may indeed be relatively time-independent and easy to transplant. Other types of law are clearly not independent of society. For instance, the law on industrial accidents depends on the industrialisation of the country in question. Family law may be another example because legal changes have often followed cultural ones, for instance, with respect to cohabitation and homosexuality. Of course, it is also possible that the causal relationship is reversed and that law is used as a tool of engineering.[33] For instance, the law-maker may favour a particular industry or may want to provide a more liberal family law because it aims to initiate changes to the economic and cultural structure of the society in question. Thus, it is worth examining these potential causalities in more detail.

---

[28] See generally Antokolskaia 2006: 38; Graziadei 2003: 124; Menski 2006: 110; Tamanaha 2001: 74 and the following references.

[29] Teubner 1998: 22; Deakin and Carvalho 2011; King 1997: 125 (all with references to Niklas Luhmann).

[30] This example is from Siems 2006: 405. More generally see Watson 2007.

[31] See Graziadei 2003: 120; Tamanaha 2001: 107 and ch. 8, below (on legal transplants).

[32] Sacco 2001: 182.   [33] Dalhuisen 2004: 113; Nelken 2003a: 451.

Table 6.2 The relationship between law and religion

Categories	Tentative examples
1. religion → law	– family law of Christian countries – restrictions on consumer credit in legal systems influenced by Christian rejection of usury
2. religion → no law	– no law on financial derivatives in some Muslim countries – no law on opening hours of shops in some orthodox Jewish communities
3. law = religion	– family law in some Muslim countries – prohibition of interest for credit in some Muslim countries
4. law → effect on religion	– law of non-profit organisations – tax law (e.g. church tax)
5. law → religion influences the effect of the law	– effect of absence of common family name influenced by Christian values – effect of favourable business law influenced by Protestant work ethic
6. law ←→ religion	– laws against religious symbols (niqab etc.) – liberal abortion laws and evangelical Christians

(b) Illustrating possible causalities

Law and society may interact in various ways. The following uses law and religion in order to illustrate some of these possible causal relationships.[34] Equivalent examples could be provided for other relationships, such as law and culture, law and economics, etc.

The first category is the one that puts the 'law in context' in trying to identify the factors that make the law.[35] As far as a causal relationship can be established, this would also confirm the view that, at least in some aspects, law is a mirror of society. Harold Berman has examined the specific case of law and religion in detail, tracing the influence of Gregorian church-state reforms and of the Protestant reformation on secular law.[36] Table 6.2, above, provides two specific examples, family law and consumer credit, where Christian values may still play a role in many legal systems. This is not meant to imply that these legal rules only reflect Christian values, indeed it has also been suggested that usury prohibitions were (or still are) typical for many small-scale societies with their need for reciprocity.[37]

---

[34] Another question is whether it is possible to proof such a causal link. See D and ch. 11 at B 3, below.

[35] Nelken 2007a: 21.

[36] Berman 1983; Berman 2006. See also Berman 1974. For further references on the role of religion for Western law see Darian-Smith 2013: 324.

[37] Moore 1986b: 26. See also Rubin 2010 (comparing the evolution of interest bans in Christianity and Islam).

Second, it is also possible that religion has the opposite effect, namely that there is no law on a particular topic. The examples of Table 6.2 show that this can be the result of two very different reasons. In the first example there is no law on financial derivatives because Islam is said to ban gambling: so, here the religious rule and the lack of law complement each other. The second example is meant to refer to a situation where strong religious beliefs already have the effect that shops stay closed on religious holidays.[38] Thus, here, law and religion are supplements: since religious conventions effectively influence behaviour in a particular way, legal rules are not seen as necessary. To be sure, it is not always clear that, without religion, a corresponding law would have been enacted. For example, adultery is seen as a taboo in many religions: thus, on the one hand, it may be thought that, given this religious sanction, law is not necessary.[39] On the other hand, in Western European societies, this religious taboo has largely disappeared, without leading to the desire to introduce laws against adultery.

The third category refers to a situation where religion is part of the law (or law part of religion[40]). The examples – family law and credit in some Muslim countries – are similar to the ones of the first category, but there is the crucial difference that in the third category there is no strict separation of law from religion, as is in today's Western legal culture.[41] To be sure, this division between religion as an element of the law and as an influencing factor of the law is not always clear-cut. For example, the secularisation of the law of marriage in the Christian world has been a gradual process, still ongoing in some countries.[42] And, with respect to Islamic law, it would be misleading to regard it simply as 'God's law', since it also contains many 'man-made elements'.[43]

The next two categories both turn to the 'context in law', showing how law can have an impact on the outside world.[44] In the fourth category, the question is how the law impacts on religion, with two examples on the way religious organisations may be structured and financed. The causal relationship is more complex in the fifth category. The first example is about the question of whether the strength of family ties is weakened if married couples keep their own names. This fear was expressed in Germany when it abandoned the prerequisite of a common family name. Yet, the case of Latin American countries may indicate that, possibly due to strong Christian values, family ties can remain

---

[38] See also Mautner 2011: 121–5 (for the relationship between ultra-Orthodox Jews and the Israeli state); Glenn 2010a: 109, 119–20 (for the extensive scope of the orthodox variant of the Talmudic tradition).

[39] See H. Aoki 2001: 139 (on research by Nobushige Hozumi).

[40] See the category in Berman 1974 (law as a dimension of religion); also Hirschl 2011 (with eight models of state and religion relations).

[41] See Banakar 2011: 18; Head 2011: 237. See also Glenn 2007: 186 (Islamic law as 'composite science of law and morality').

[42] See Antokolskaia 2007: 244–5.

[43] Menski 2006: 279–83. Moreover, Muslim countries often do distinguish between state law and religious norms: see An-Na'im 2008.

[44] Nelken 2007a: 21.

strong without a common family name.[45] The second example refers to Max Weber's controversial view that legal rules and a favourable work ethic, which is attributed to Protestantism, can foster economic development.[46]

Sixth, there are cases where there is conflict between law and religion, leading to the question of how religious believers try to reconcile these duties.[47] Table 6.2 provides two topical examples with liberal laws on the one hand (allowing abortion and banning full-face coverage) and conservative religious beliefs on the other.

Many of these causal relationships between law and society, here illustrated by the example of law and religion, are topics of socio-legal comparative law. In addition, some of these themes will re-appear in other chapters of this book. For example, the question about the effect of the law is of natural interest to comparative law and development, and it has also been explored in empirical studies by financial economists.[48]

B. Civil litigation, courts and lawyers

As socio-legal research is interested in 'law in action', one of the key topics of its comparative counterpart has been the examination of similarities and differences in civil litigation, in particular litigation rates, the number of lawyers and judges, and the ease of litigation. This is addressed in this section; questions of substantive law follow in the subsequent one.

1. Civil litigation and other forms of dispute resolution

Comparative research on the use of civil litigation is a frequent topic of socio-legal research. In the 1970s, John Henry Merryman and colleagues collected time-series data on litigation rates and types of claims in a number of European and Latin American jurisdictions.[49] Yet there was only limited analysis of these data. To be fair, it is not easy to say with certainty why there is more litigation in some jurisdictions than in others. Presumably, differing attitudes towards litigation play a role. For example, a well-known book by Laurent Cohen-Tanugi argues that, in the US, litigation is seen as more positive – since it is more democratic – than in France and other European countries.[50] Research for the 2006 Congress of the International Academy of Comparative Law has, amongst others, tried to explore whether it is perceived as a stigma to be sued in civil litigation. Such a stigma was found to be prevalent in China, Japan, Chile and Sweden, but not in the US or most European countries.[51]

---

[45] See Dannemann 2006: 398.   [46] See ch. 11 at C 1, below.
[47] Weber 2008 (original from 1905). For Weber see also ch. 11 at C 1 (b), below.
[48] See ch. 10 and ch. 11 at B 3, below.
[49] Merryman et al. 1979. See also Merryman 1999: 503; Twining 2005: 230.
[50] Cohen-Tanugi 1985. See also Cohen-Tanugi 1996.   [51] See Mattei 2007: 8.

Another line of research is to compare data on cases filed, resolved and pending per judge, on the time to resolve a case, and on clearance and congestion rates. Maria Dakolias examined these issues for a number of Latin American and selected other jurisdictions. For example, it was found that in Chile the average of cases per year is 5,000, whereas in the US it is 1,300, in France 277 and in Germany 176.[52] These are striking differences in workload that may invite deeper analysis of potential determinants, for instance, the availability of expedited proceedings, exemptions to provide reasoned opinions, assistance by administrative staff or paralegals, organisational inefficiencies etc.

Comparative data on civil litigation in the developing countries of Africa and Asia are less frequently discussed. Following statements of traditional comparatists, this may have something to do with the fact that its population largely lives under an indigenous legal tradition that would not be called 'law' in the Western world.[53] This sounds like an 'orientialist' stereotype,[54] but, considering socio-legal research, there is evidentially some truth to it. According to studies on different African countries, between 75 and 90 per cent of all disputes are settled by customary forms of justice.[55] And, if countries leave citizens the choice between civil and religious courts, data from Indonesia show frequent preference for the latter ones.[56] There has also been fieldwork research in Niger showing that judicial enforcement is of secondary importance, since law is seen as 'a process for establishing a *modus vivendi* for a community and is inextricably interwoven with family relations, community relations, history, and spiritual beliefs'.[57]

One may question whether these customary traditions of dispute resolution can survive in an increasingly globalised world.[58] Yet, at the same time, there is a trend away from litigation towards 'privatisation of adjudication' in the developed world.[59] In Europe, law-makers have fostered the use of mediation and arbitration,[60] and the globalisation of business relationships has promoted alternative dispute resolution in international commerce, to be discussed later in this book.[61] The importance of alternative forms of dispute resolution is also relevant to the following section, examining litigation rates in selected developed countries in more detail.

2. Litigation rates in the US, England, Germany, the Netherlands and Japan

Do litigation rates differ between the US and England, Germany and the Netherlands, and Japan and Western countries? Research on these country relationships

---

[52] Dakolias 1999. See also Buscaglia and Ratliff 2000: 61 (on the joint empirical work by Dakolias and Buscaglia).

[53] David 1985: 31; Zweigert and Kötz 1998: 66.

[54] For legal orientalism see ch. 4 at C 1, above.   [55] Studies cited in Ubink and van Rooij 2011.

[56] See K. von Benda-Beckmann 2009 (also comparison between different regions).

[57] Kelley 2007: 17.   [58] Pimentel 2011. See also ch. 10 at B (on rule of law reforms).

[59] Resnik 2010. See also van Aeken 2012.

[60] See Jagtenberg and de Roo 2009: 313–4.   [61] See ch. 9 at D 2, below.

is interesting since it may confirm or refute the relevance of legal families.[62] Such research has also attempted to understand the determinants for differences in litigation rates.

Litigation rates are considerably higher in the United States than in England. A core study on this topic was by Patrick Atiyah, who found that in 1983/84 there were twenty times as many suits for medical malpractice and even 350 times as many product liability suits in the US as in England.[63] A possible explanation may be differences in national character, Americans being more aggressive, the English being more restrained and fatalistic.[64] Yet, in both jurisdictions, many routine disputes are handled without the involvement of courts. Thus, it may be more significant that in particular areas of law, such as the ones of Atiyah's study, class actions and punitive damages are more readily available in the US than the UK.[65]

It is also helpful to consider the availability of alternative institutions. Rebecca Sandefur's analysis of remedies for civil justice distinguishes between formal institutions (courts, administrative agencies and ombudsman services) and 'auxiliaries'. With respect to the latter institutions, she explains that the monopoly on legal advice is stronger in the US than in the UK. Furthermore, there are more national advice providers in the UK, in particular the Citizens' Advice Bureaux with more than 3,000 locations. Other national and local auxiliaries are also available in both countries, though they are only competent for some types of disputes.[66] The data of Sandefur's research confirm that in the UK it is more common to use auxiliaries, whereas in the US it is more common to go to courts or to 'do nothing'.[67]

Research on litigation rates in Germany and the Netherlands (as well as other civil law countries) has also tried to explain differences in apparently similar legal systems. The main studies were conducted by Erhard Blankenburg and colleagues in the 1980s and early 1990s. For example, Blankenburg reports the number of adversarial procedures of civil courts of first instance: Austria, Belgium and West Germany are seen as litigation prone, with 5,020, 4,800 and 3,561 procedures per 100,000 inhabitants, whereas in France, Italy and the Netherlands, litigation is more often avoided, with 1,950, 1,640 and 1,430 such procedures.[68] Other studies compared the German state of North Rhine Westphalia with the Netherlands. Since both are similar in terms of size, population, industrial structures, Blankenburg assumed that the conflict potential should be similar in both regions, yet, again, there was more

---

[62] See ch. 3 and ch. 4, above. Specifically for the US and England see ch. 3 at C 2, above. For East Asia see ch. 4 at C 2 (a), above.

[63] Atiyah 1987.

[64] Posner 1996: 108–9. More sceptical as regards such differences Markesinis 1990b.

[65] Ramseyer and Rasmusen 2010. Also differentiating between types of claims Kritzer 2008.

[66] Sandefur 2009: 965.   [67] Sandefur 2009: 969.

[68] See Blankenburg 1997: 46; Blankenburg 1992: 103 (also with data that include summary debt enforcement, which produces a similar division).

litigation (as well as more judges and lawyers) in the German state than in the Netherlands.[69]

A number of explanatory factors were contemplated but eventually dismissed. First, Blankenburg regards the substantive law of both countries as fairly similar.[70] Thus, here, one does not encounter the problem of, say, comparing countries with extensive and little employment protection.[71] Second, Dutch courts are not seen as fundamentally different from German ones, since they are based on a composite of the French and the German traditions.[72] Third, Blankenburg refers to a study on attitudes towards legality, which found that the Dutch and Germans have fairly similar views about obeying the law.[73] Fourth, legal aid is not seen as a contributing factor, since it only accounts for a small proportion of cases in both countries.[74]

Thus, what does explain the difference between the Netherlands and Germany? Blankenburg argues that the lower number of lawyers in the Netherlands is a result of the more pronounced infrastructure of the alternatives to courts. For example, some conflicts, such as road accident claims, are handled by public agencies, while in Germany they lead more often to civil litigation.[75] Similarly, in the Netherlands, but not in Germany, divorce proceedings can be handled without court involvement.[76] There are also a number of quasi-judicial bodies which function as a filter to litigation in the Netherlands: conciliation commissions take care of many conflicts between landlords and tenants, and employment disputes may require permission from the local labour bureau in order to proceed.[77] Finally, according to Blankenburg, it is significant that the monopoly to give legal advice is more liberal in the Netherlands than in Germany, thus explaining the greater role of organisations such as consumer associations and trade unions in taking care of disputes in an informal way.[78]

David Nelken challenges this emphasis on alternatives to civil litigation.[79] Blankenburg seems to concur with the functional starting point of traditional comparative law, namely that there are certain social problems which need to be addressed by everyone. But this is not self-evident, since what is regarded as a 'problem' may well differ across countries.[80] Thus, the focus on structural alternatives to litigation at the 'supply side' may miss the role of cultural factors at the 'demand side'. This debate about the relationship between structural and

---

[69] Blankenburg and Verwoerd 1988.   [70] Blankenburg 1997: 64; Blankenburg 1994: 791.
[71] See Blankenburg 1992: 105 (for the US and Europe); Blankenburg and Rogowski 1986 (for Germany and the UK).
[72] Blankenburg 1994: 790.
[73] Blankenburg 1998: 19. The study is Gibson and Caldeira 1996, further discussed in ch. 11 at C 3, below. See also Hertogh 2010: 164 (challenging Blankenburg's assessment).
[74] Blankenburg 1997: 61; Blankenburg 1998.
[75] Blankenburg 1997: 45; Blankenburg and Verwoerd 1988.   [76] Blankenburg 1997: 45.
[77] Blankenburg 1997: 57–8. See also Blankenburg 1994: 797; Jettinghoff 2001: 110–1.
[78] See Blankenburg 1997: 54, 56 (also on differences in lawyer fees).
[79] For the following see Nelken 1997. Similar Hertogh 2010: 165.
[80] See ch. 2 at C 3, above.

cultural arguments also re-appears in the socio-legal research about litigation rates in Japan.

Accordingly, the final example concerns the question of whether there is anything special about Japan. The usual starting point is that its rate of litigation is considerably lower than in that of other developed countries. This was already found in one of the aforementioned articles by Blankenburg, according to which the other developed countries had between 1,400 and 5,100 adversarial civil cases per 100,000 inhabitants per year, whereas in Japan this number was only 500.[81] This initial difference has also been confirmed by other researchers.[82]

For a long time, the most frequent explanation was that the low Japanese litigation rate is due to their ideal of a 'harmony culture', an ideal that prefers conciliation and other informal means of settling a controversy, rather than open conflicts.[83] Thus, suing or being sued may be socially discouraged or even stigmatised.[84] This may also be a general feature of the East Asian legal culture, since in China, too, formal litigation is often said to be avoided for cultural reasons.[85] It may also confirm the category of an East Asian (or Confucian) legal family that rejects the Western 'struggle for law' with winners and losers.[86]

However, this line of reasoning has been challenged on a number of grounds. To start with, it is likely that it is not simply culture, but also the institutional availability of alternatives, that matters. For example, in Japan, a divorce does not necessarily require court involvement, but can be realised by an entry on the family registry in the competent administrative office.[87] There is also a special law on civil conciliation that incorporates an arbitral procedure into civil litigation: when one of the parties requests it, the court sets up an arbitral committee with one judge and two commissioners. This is a popular way of solving disputes.[88]

Moreover, institutional characteristics of the courts and the legal profession may explain the low rate of litigation. This point has most prominently been made by John Haley.[89] According to his research, there is no social or cultural hostility towards law in Japan; rather, litigation is very costly and time-consuming, and it may even be difficult to find a lawyer, since the number of lawyers is kept low by way of a strict judicial exam system. This leads to the question of why the Japanese law-maker installed such measures. Frank Upham argues that the Japanese power elite were not keen on citizens asserting their rights, thus creating the 'invented tradition' of weak legal

[81] Blankenburg, above note 68.

[82] See, e.g. Wollschläger 1997; Wollschläger 1998, but see also the following notes.

[83] See, e.g. Mayeda 2006: 572; Nelken 2007a: 113; Law 2011a: 1430; Abe and Nottage in EE 2012: 462.

[84] See also text to note 51, above.

[85] Menski 2006: 548.   [86] See ch. 4 at C 1 and 2 (a), above.

[87] See Ramseyer and Rasmusen 2010: 11 (contrasting it with US law).

[88] See Oda 2009: 67; Clark 2002: para. 278; Zweigert and Kötz 1998: 301.

[89] E.g. Haley 1978; Haley 1998; Haley 2002; also Oda 2009: 5 (reporting recent survey that 80% of respondents refer to time and costs for hesitance to engage in litigation).

consciousness.[90] Mark Ramseyer points towards the close control and supervision of the judiciary by the dominant political party (the LDP). A side-effect of this influence was that the outcome of civil litigation could be predicted relatively easily; parties could therefore rationally negotiate on this basis without the need for judicial involvement.[91] Haley reaches the same conclusion regarding the high degree of predictability of litigated outcomes, though he notes that, although judges are not regarded as 'political lackeys', it matters that they are a group of fairly homogenous 'faithful public servants'.[92]

Another objection to the 'harmony culture' reasoning is that, recently, litigation has played a more pronounced role in Japan. This can be seen in specific areas of law. Eric Feldman, for instance, provides examples from health policy. When, in the 1980s, legal conflicts arose over HIV contaminated blood, individual claims and an innovative judiciary played a crucial role, akin to similar events in the US and in France.[93] Feldman also shows that medical malpractice litigation has risen from fewer than 100 new claims per year in the 1970s to more than 1,000 in the year 2005.[94] Another example is company law: since the 1990s, the number of derivative actions has risen sharply. The most likely explanations for this development are changes to the law, such as a reduction of court fees in 1993, but possibly also the globalisation of companies and investments.[95] Finally, a study by Tom Ginsburg and Glenn Hoetker provides more general evidence of 'Japan's turn to litigation'. They find that, since the 1990s, litigation has increased by approximately 40 per cent, attributing it to the growing number of lawyers, the reform of civil procedure in 1996, as well as economic circumstances.[96]

Overall, the three examples (UK/US, Germany/Netherlands, Japan/West) teach us that one has to be careful about making too confident assumptions about the relationship between litigation rates and legal cultures. It is also important to note that cultural and structural determinants for litigation are mutually interdependent: on the one hand, structures may be a reflection of cultural values, but, on the other hand, cultures can also change, which may, in part, be determined by structural decisions.[97] If both factors change, as has happened in Japan, it is therefore difficult to assess what exactly accounts for the variation in litigation rates.

3. Further research on judges, lawyers and the public

Apart from the litigation rates, the personnel of the civil process have been a frequent topic of comparative socio-legal research.[98] A good starting point

---

[90] Upham 1998. See also Upham 1987.   [91] Ramseyer 1988; Ramseyer and Rasmusen 2003.
[92] Upham 2005, in particular at 273 (comparing those views).
[93] Feldman 2000a; see also Feldman 2000b.
[94] Feldman 2009.   [95] See Siems 2008a: 216–7.
[96] Ginsburg and Hoetker 2006; also Oda 2009: 79 (data on increase of lawyers).
[97] See Nelken 1997: 87.
[98] For an extensive treatment see Abel and Lewis 1988. See also Shapiro 1990.

seems to be to compare the number of judges and other practising lawyers across jurisdictions. Yet, this is not a straightforward task. For example, with respect to 'judges', one may want to focus on professional judges, since only they may have the proper legal qualifications to be a judge. But, then, such data may be misleading since, in some countries, judicial functions are performed by lay judges (or magistrates, justices of peace etc.). However, including lay judges may lead to the objection that they are akin to jurors. But then, including jurors may overstate the numbers for countries with jury systems. In addition, the division between judges and other lawyers may not be straightforward. For example, in a comparison between England and the US, Richard Posner assumes that English barristers are not like US attorneys-at-law, but more like junior judges in the US system, since the 'English bar is almost an apprenticeship for becoming a judge'.[99]

With respect to the term 'lawyer', the main problem is whether to include everyone who studied law or only persons who are qualified to represent clients. Choosing the first approach would appear to inflate the numbers in countries, such as France, where it is common to study law without having the intention of a legal career in a narrow sense.[100] But only including qualified lawyers may raise the objection that the standards for passing this hurdle are very diverse across countries. For instance, in most countries, it requires a number of years of practical training, but not in the US; and, in most countries, the majority of candidates have a fair chance of passing the bar exam, but this was – and, to some extent, still is – different in Japan.[101] Things get even more complicated if one considers religious or customary legal systems: for example, some Muslim countries may have 'Western' lawyers, but also a parallel profession that practises before Sharia courts.[102]

None of these points speak against comparative socio-legal research on the number of judges and lawyers, though it has to be made very clear what the numbers really show.[103] Moreover, presenting such data may aim precisely to identify substitutes and complements between legal professions in different countries: for example, a low number of judges and lawyers may invite further research in the relevance of informal methods of dispute resolution.

Turning to actual data,[104] a comparison between European and North American countries is often said to lead to the result that there are more judges per capita in continental Europe than in the US, the UK and Canada, and that there are more practising lawyers in the latter countries; consequently, there is a higher ratio of judges to other practising lawyers in continental

---

[99] Posner 1996: 22.   [100] See Steiner 2010: 202.

[101] Abe and Nottage in EE 2012: 472–4; Aronson 2012.   [102] See Clark 2002: para. 35.

[103] See Galanter 1993: 77–9 (on dubious claims that the US is home to 70 per cent of the world's lawyers); also Twining 2009a: 247 and Ehrmann 1976: 56 (on problems of defining the term 'lawyer').

[104] Apart from the following footnotes see CEPEJ 2012: 146–54, 309 (professional and non-professional judges and lawyers in Europe); Pérez-Perdomo and Friedman 2003 (data on Latin American countries); Galanter 1993: 104–7 (various countries).

Europe.[105] These differences are usually attributed to the more active role that judges tend to play in civil law countries, since, in the common law, many of these tasks are said to be performed by the lawyers representing their clients.[106] However, as a general trend, it can also be observed that, throughout the twentieth century, the number of lawyers (as well as law students) has risen in both civil and common law countries, which may be attributed to the rise of capitalism and the modern state.[107]

It is also worth revisiting the countries discussed in the previous section. With respect to England and the US, Richard Posner reports that, when considering judges in a mere literal sense, the ratio of lawyers to judges is similar. But if one treats English barristers as akin to junior judges (as indicated above), the English rate drops to the rate of France and Germany.[108] This seems to be in line with the lower rate of litigation in England. Posner also suggests that England can manage a smaller legal system, since English law is clearer than US law, and because it has fewer judicially enforceable rights.[109] However, adding Germany and the Netherlands to this picture does not confirm the positive correlation between a higher ratio of lawyers to judges and more litigation, since this ratio is higher in the Netherlands than in Germany.[110] Considering the absolute numbers, however, we find that Germany has more judges and lawyers per capita than the Netherlands, thus being in line with the higher rate of litigation.[111] Finally, with respect to Japan, the main problem is the aforementioned definition of lawyers: if one only includes qualified lawyers, the per capita number of lawyers is considerably lower than in Western countries (and thus in line with the hypothesis, Japan having a low rate of litigation), but this changes if one includes everyone 'who performs lawyerly functions'.[112]

A wealth of further comparative data, whether quantifiable or not, can be collected on judges and lawyers. For example, it is interesting to compare the salaries of judges, which shows, for example, that they tend to be higher in England than in continental Europe.[113] The selection and recruitment of judges also tends to be diverse: this can invite an analysis of the applicable legal rules, but it may also invite a more empirical examination of the influence of politics

---

[105] Clark 2002: paras. 73, 137; Clark 2012: 383; Van Rhee and Verkerk in EE 2012: 141; Blankenburg and Verwoerd 1988: 14; Posner 1996: 28; Maxeiner et al. 2010: 79–80.

[106] Van Rhee and Verkerk in EE 2012: 141–2; Posner 1996: 29; Blankenburg and Verwoerd 1988: 14. See also ch. 3 at B 2 (d), above.

[107] Clark 2012: 337, 340, 380–1 (on Europe, US, Japan and Latin America); Pérez-Perdomo and Friedman 2003: 8, 10 (on Latin America); Shapiro 1990: 684, 709. See also Clark 2002: para. 98; Clark 2012: 394–6 (declining resistance against huge law firms in civil law countries).

[108] Posner 1996: 28.   [109] Posner 1996: 83.

[110] Blankenburg and Verwoerd 1988: 14 (comparing the Netherlands with the German state of North Rhine Westphalia).

[111] Blankenburg 1997.

[112] Childress 2007. See also Maxeiner et al. 2010: 79–80 (on South Korea showing a lower per capita number of lawyers, judges and lawyers per judges than in the US and Germany).

[113] Bell 2006a: 39; CEPEJ 2012: 262–72.

in the appointment process.[114] A related question is whether personal ideologies affect the decisions of judges. For this purpose, a comparative analysis of court decisions is fruitful, as far as judges deliver individual opinions.[115] If this is not the case, one may conduct interviews in order to find out how judges think about the relationship between law and politics.[116] Turning to lawyers, questionnaires have been used to explore the views of the legal profession on EU law.[117] Another study has empirically examined contracts on attorney fees in the US, showing that parties often tend to adopt the loser-pays fee structure dominant in other parts of the world.[118] There is also interesting comparative research on the sociology of legal professions, including, for instance, the influence of transnational lawyers, to be discussed later in this book.[119]

A final point possible to consider is the 'user side' of the judicial process, in particular the debate about 'access to justice' and 'ease of litigation'. Researchers have examined a variety of reasons as determining access to justice.[120] Some of these concern details of the positive law, for instance, the provision of legal aid, the availability of small claim procedures and class actions, the rules on costs and fees, and the right to free legal representation. It is also possible to approach this debate from a socio-legal perspective: for instance, one can collect comparative data on legal aid and costs of litigation.[121] Chris Hodges and colleagues have used a functional approach in order to compare the precise costs that would arise in a number of hypothetical cases. Their results seem to confirm some of the differences in litigation rates, discussed in the previous section,[122] while noting that there may also be non-financial impediments, such as a lack of awareness of legal remedies. Another problem related to access is that of legal delay.[123] Here, a case-based study funded by the World Bank has examined the duration of trials and enforcement in 109 countries. It also identified how many procedural steps were necessary in each of these countries, with the plausible result that the number of steps is positively correlated with the duration of judicial proceedings.[124]

Is it possible to say which country has more accessible courts? A non-empirical book on the judiciary of five countries contends that the US and Germany are

---

[114] See CEPEJ 2012: 248–50; Jacob et al. 1996: 390, 395.

[115] See Weinshall-Margel 2011 (comparing the supreme courts of Israel, Canada and the US).

[116] See Sturgess and Chupp 1988: 255–537.

[117] Örücü 2007: 442–8.   [118] Eisenberg and Miller 2013.

[119] See ch. 9 at D 2 (final section), below.

[120] The first major study was Cappelletti et al. 1978/79. For a recent overview of different strategies see Barendrecht 2011. For a comparative book see Wrbka et al. 2012.

[121] See, e.g., CEPEJ 2012: 63–77 (data on budget for legal aid, legal aid per inhabitants and per GDP, number of legal aid cases, annual amount of court fees etc.); Posner 1996: 76–9 (data on cost of litigation).

[122] Hodges et al. 2010 (e.g. typically lower costs of litigation in Germany than in England and in the Netherlands).

[123] See, e.g., Krishnan and Kumar 2011 (for comparison between Indian states); Buscaglia and Ratliff 2000: 57 (selected data for developing countries).

[124] Djankov et al. 2003a. For the more contentious claims of these studies see ch. 7 at C 2, below.

at the high-end of accessibility, Japan at the low end, and France and England in the middle.[125] A socio-legal and more general project of Dutch academics has constructed an index in order to measure access to justice.[126] This project seeks to capture the costs of justice, the quality of the procedure and the quality of the outcome by way of surveys. A number of these questions are fairly general: for instance, 'was the procedure fair?' or 'did the outcome solve your problem?'. Thus, this study is closely related to more general measurements of legal rules and institutions, to be discussed in the subsequent chapter on 'numerical comparative law'.[127]

C. Substantive law 'in action' and society

Any area of substantive law is open to socio-legal comparative research. The following provides examples from commercial and criminal law. Both subsections start with the question of how the positive law is applied in practice. Subsequently, following the discussion on potential causal relationships,[128] it is shown how societal factors may shape the law, and how, in turn, law may shape society.

1. Comparative commercial law

(a) How the law is applied

Many areas of private and commercial law invite analysis of how the positive law is applied in practice. This is particularly interesting where choices are left to private parties, for instance, where the law only provides default rules. In a comparative context, one can then examine how differences and similarities in the positive law are related to the way it operates in practice across countries.

The first example is from comparative contract law. It is often thought that contracts tend to be wordier in common law than in civil law countries.[129] Comparative socio-legal research is relatively rare, but an empirical study by Alessandro Arrighetti and colleagues has examined contractual drafting in Germany, Italy and the United Kingdom in some detail.[130] They conducted sixty interviews on 'contracts between original equipment manufacturers and suppliers of component parts', and evaluated these findings both quantitatively and qualitatively.

The questions of this study included topics related to the form, duration and substance of contracts. For instance, Arrighetti and colleagues report that

---

[125] Jacob et al. 1996: 397–9.

[126] Tilburg Institute for Interdisciplinary Studies of Civil Law and Conflict Resolution Systems 2009. See also www.measuringaccesstojustice.com.

[127] See ch. 7 at C, below.   [128] See A 2, above.

[129] See, e.g., Mattila 2006: 236–8 (main reason: English courts interpret terms more literally); Kötz 2010: 1247 (due to default rules in civil law); Lundmark 2001; Lundmark 2012: 67–74; Hill and King 2004. See also Kitagawa 2006: 240, 251–2 (contracts in Japan shorter and simpler than in the US).

[130] Arrighetti et al. 1997. See also Deakin and Michie 1997.

91 per cent and 84 per cent of the German and British interviewees indicated that they 'always' (as opposed to 'sometimes' or 'never') used legally binding contracts, whereas in Italy these were only 58 per cent. A similar picture emerges when one considers specific clauses of contracts: for example, the majority of German and British contracts had clauses on retention of title, protection of intellectual property rights and limitation of liability but only a minority of the Italian ones. All of this was attributed to the real, or perceived, weakness of the Italian court system.

The study also reported on the role of trade associations in contractual drafting and its relationship to law and law enforcement. In Germany, there were 'general conditions of business' that applied to entire industries, but they also followed the guidance of the codified law to perform in good faith. In Italy the role of trade associations is important in practice, though their influence was more informal, given the deficiencies in the court system. For the United Kingdom we have to distinguish between previously nationalised sectors and other private firms: firms that belonged to previously nationalised sectors tended to draft detailed contracts, reflecting the desire of the former state corporations for uniform rules, whereas other firms made their own agreements often including informal understandings. Overall, it can therefore be seen that differences in contractual practices are closely related to the legal system, but also reflect the influence of trade associations and other socio-economic factors.

Second, comparative company law is often approached from a socio-legal perspective. A relatively straightforward line of research is to consider certain countable events related to company law. For instance, company law typically provides different types of companies, it allows mergers and takeovers, and it enables shareholder suits. Accordingly, it can be interesting to find out how often certain types of companies are incorporated, merged or sued in different jurisdictions.[131]

A more challenging question concerns the relationship between corporate governance at a country-level and at a firm-level. The country-level can refer to certain socio-cultural characteristics that are specific to the way companies are run in a particular country. Moreover, legal systems use different tools of corporate governance. For instance, some of them require a division between supervisory and management board (e.g. Germany), whereas in others companies have just a single board of directors (e.g. in the US). But many further questions about the running of companies are left to the individual firm. The empirical examination of these features is a major topic in academic and non-academic research on corporate governance. A number of professional advisers use documents, such as the articles of association or annual reports of companies, in order to rate factors such as investor protection across firms.[132] In academic research, most prominent is the study by Paul Gompers and colleagues, which uses twenty-four rules to construct a governance index for the

---

[131] See, e.g., Wymmersch 2009; Armour et al. 2009c.
[132] E.g. www.standardandpoors.com/about-sp/gamma/en/eu; www.gmiratings.com.

level of shareholder rights in US firms, and there has also been research on firm-level corporate governance in other countries.[133]

A common view is that the country and firm level of corporate governance are substitutes. For instance, if a particular legal system is weak in terms of investor protection, companies themselves may be keen on providing adequate mechanisms in order to attract international investment. There is some empirical evidence supporting this view, based on data from emerging markets where law and law enforcement may often be inadequate. The counter-view doubts the capacity of firm-level corporate governance to substitute for a weak institutional framework. Thus, the relationship between firm- and country-level governance may be complementary, and there is also some empirical support for this view, based on data from East Asian companies.[134]

(b) How the law shapes society – and vice versa

Even more challenging is the question of whether company and commercial law shape society – or whether there is the reverse causal relationship. Comparative company law offers a detailed discussion of this problem. To start with, mainstream research tends to use categories similar to the general division into legal families.[135] On one side, there is the Anglo-Saxon common law model. This is seen as pursuing a market-based approach, where the shareholders' individual interests are to the fore. Moreover, in these countries, capital markets are seen as more developed, so that interest in shares is broader and shareholder ownership is often dispersed. In civil law countries, by contrast, it is claimed that concentrated ownership structures mostly prevail in joint-stock companies. Since management cooperates with the dominant shareholders, relations within the company count more than control through the markets. This 'insider model' is to be explained by the fact that banks and employees hold a strong position. The firm is accordingly run not primarily in the interests of shareholders, but of all stakeholders in the undertaking.

So, assuming this close link between company law and financial markets is accurate,[136] how can it be explained? One view – popular in business and finance studies[137] – stresses that law 'matters' for financial development. For instance, common law countries are seen as having 'good law' in protecting investors, which motivates people to invest in shares. This explains the importance of their financial markets, a proxy for which is the higher degree of dispersed shareholder ownership. In civil law countries, by contrast, investor protection is seen as inferior, and therefore financial markets are less developed.

Michael Bogdan suggests that, '[f]rom a lawyer's viewpoint, it is extremely satisfying that the importance of law as a pre-condition of desirable economic

---

[133] Gompers et al. 2003; MacNeil and Xiao 2006 (for the UK); von Werder et al. 2005 (for Germany).

[134] For references to these studies see van Essen et al. 2013.

[135] This paragraph draws on Siems 2008a: 29.

[136] For this claim see ch. 7 at C 1 and ch. 11 at B 3, below.   [137] See ch. 11 at B 3, below.

and social development is now generally recognized'.[138] But many legal scholars tend to be more sceptical about this alleged causal relationship between law (cause) and finance (effect). A linear, causal relationship may overlook the legal systems' own internal dynamics of self-reproduction.[139] Furthermore, if there is causality, it can also go the other way. For instance, there are examples which show that only after the number of investors and the importance of the capital market increased was shareholder protection strengthened.[140]

There are also other considerations that are frequently adduced in order to explain variation in company and commercial laws. Nick Foster emphasises the fact that legal differences are not mere technicalities, but historically and culturally conditioned. For example, comparing France and England, he explains that the more restrictive French laws on security interest, and the higher minimum capital requirements, reflect different attitudes to commerce.[141] Others point towards the way legal systems are influenced by political structures and events. For example, Mark Roe takes the view that, in the second part of the twentieth century, a strong emphasis on shareholder protection and capital markets – dominant in the US and the UK – was seen as incompatible with social-democratic ideas in continental Europe.[142] Similarly, Katharina Pistor relates differences in company and financial law to the literature on comparative capitalism, namely the distinction between liberal and coordinated market economics.[143] In a book on *Law and Capitalism*, Katharina Pistor and Curtis Milhaupt also refer to differences in the degree of centralisation of law-making and enforcement, expecting more centralisation in civil than in common law countries. However, using case studies of individual countries, they also show that regulatory responses to financial crises may depart from these different starting points.[144]

Differences in political economies are also frequently mentioned in order to contextualise the common/civil law divide in other fields of private and commercial law. For example, according to James Whitman, civil law countries tend to favour the interests of consumers, and common law countries the interests of producers, which is seen as reflecting differences in politics and values.[145] John Reitz, too, refers to common and civil law, while also indicating that the UK is sometimes closer to the European continent than the US.[146] In one of his papers, Reitz discusses the relevance of political economy in understanding differences in contract law, showing that common law countries tend to be more market-centred and civil law countries more state-centred. This includes regulatory aspects of contract law such as employment at will, price

---

[138] Bogdan 2009: 33. 　[139] See A 2 (a), above.

[140] Coffee 2002; Cheffins 2008. 　[141] Foster 2007. 　[142] E.g. Roe 1993; Roe 2000.

[143] Pistor 2005. See also Pistor 2009 and ch. 11 at B 3, below.

[144] Milhaupt and Pistor 2008.

[145] Whitman 2007. See also Cotterrell 2007: 149–51; Whitman 2003b: 329–34.

[146] Reitz 2009: 857. See also Reitz 2002 (on role of the political economy in limiting convergence).

controls, and consumers' cancellation rights, but also includes the doctrine of consideration and the default remedy for breach of contract.[147]

Adding the commercial law of Muslim countries to the picture confirms the mutual interdependence between law and society. Timur Kuran's book *The Long Divergence: How Islamic Law Held Back the Middle East* initially seems to argue that the deficiencies of Islamic law, such as the absence of corporations and credit, explain the lack of economic growth in many countries of the Middle East.[148] Yet, one can also start with the reverse causal relationship. Islamic law emerged in a pre-industrial, local economic environment where laws allowing for small-scale businesses and transactional arrangements were entirely sufficient.[149] Thus, a preferable line of reasoning is that it is not the inherent nature of Islamic law as such that is the problem, but the fact that it has not evolved so as to accommodate the need for large-scale production, capital accumulation and business entities found in the Western world.

A tempting explanation for this lack of legal evolution may be the static nature of a law based on religion. However, Islamic law, too, has evolved: for instance, countries of the Middle East have transplanted significant parts of Western business laws, and one may also refer to the recent design of Sharia-compliant forms in banking and finance.[150] Thus, according to Kuran, incomplete reforms, low trust, and high levels of corruption explain why Muslim countries do not have an up-to-date legal system that stimulates development.[151] Of course, one may further respond that there are considerable differences between Middle Eastern countries in terms of legal and economic development, inviting more detailed comparative socio-legal research on the countries of this region.

2. Comparative criminal law

(a) How the law is applied

According to James Whitman, comparative research on criminal punishment shall not focus too much on the text of the laws, but needs to determine 'whether behaviors that are nominally forbidden are in fact prosecuted'.[152] In addition, it matters whether prosecutions result in actual convictions, what precise sentences are imposed, and how these are executed.[153] All of these aspects of how the law is applied in practice can lead to interesting socio-legal comparisons. For example, imprisonment is a possible sanction around the world, yet comparative incarceration data show remarkable differences.[154] Similarly, with respect to the Islamic law of countries such as Saudi Arabia,

---

[147] Reitz 2007; Reitz 2012. For the latter points see also ch. 3 at B 3, above.
[148] Kuran 2010a. See also Kuran 2005.   [149] N. Foster 2010: 30.   [150] See ch. 8 at B 2, below.
[151] Kuran 2010a: 194. Similarly Ayres and Macey 2005.   [152] Whitman 2005a: 31.
[153] For comparative statistics see Pakes 2012: 68–71 (but criticising simple 'bean counting').
[154] See, e.g., the documents of the International Centre for Prison Studies, available at www. prisonstudies.org/ (World Prison Briefs and Publications). See also Nelken 2010: 56–70 (for a general discussion); Hamilton and Sanders 1992 (comparing the US and Japan).

Western observers are often upset by sanctions such as stoning and the cutting off of a hand, but it has to be asked how far these sanctions are actually applied in practice.[155]

The present section focuses on capital punishment as a paradigmatic case of comparative criminal law. Since the 1970s, more and more countries have formally abolished the death penalty. In addition, organisations such as Amnesty International use the category of being 'abolitionist in practice' for countries where there have not been any executions for more than ten years. According to data from 2012, in total 140 countries have abolished the death penalty in law or in practice, while 58 countries remain 'retentionist'.[156] Two well-known countries with capital punishment are the US (though not all states) and China. But here, too, the number of executions has declined in the last fifteen years.[157]

There has also been significant interest in the process between the prosecution of a crime punishable by death and the execution of the sentence. Naturally, the fairness of the trial is essential due to the irreversible nature of this sanction, as is the fairness of the death row experience and the process of execution.[158] For instance, the reports by Amnesty International include case studies on all of these problems, supplemented by comparative observations.[159]

(b) How the law shapes society – and vice versa

Can harsh criminal punishment reduce the crime rate? Such a view may be based on a simple belief of criminal law as deterrent. But even if it is regarded as unlikely that individuals can accurately predict possible sanctions, criminal law may still be able to influence behaviour by way of 'habit formation'.[160]

The value of comparative research is that it can provide information on the possible effects of relatively harsh or lenient criminal laws. However, to be robust, such research has to include control variables on other factors that may influence differences in crime rate. This can be challenging, even if one only considers relatively similar jurisdictions. For example, research on the death penalty has often made use of variations between the US states. Yet, the results do not tend to be reliable. In criticising a 2007 newspaper article, which claimed that 'each execution saves more than 70 lives', Gebhard Kirchgässner showed how easy it is to choose econometric techniques either supporting or rejecting the deterrence hypothesis.[161] It is also revealing to compare the homicide rate

---

[155] See generally Bassiouni 1997.
[156] Amnesty International 2013. See also Hood and Hoyle 2008: 40–65 and Zimring 2003: 16–41 (on the abolitionist movement and its progress).
[157] For the US see Berry 2011: 1019; Sarat and Martschukat 2011: 1–6 (also decline in public support). For China see Johnson 2010.
[158] Hood and Hoyle 2008: 215–77 and 155–86.
[159] E.g. Amnesty International 2013. See also www.handsoffcain.info.
[160] Hood and Hoyle 2008: 321.
[161] Kirchgässner 2011. See also Hood and Hoyle 2008: 329–33.

between the US and Canada, since both rates have tended to move in the same direction while laws on the death penalty differed sharply.[162]

These types of questions also relate to research in criminology and moral philosophy. Explaining crime is one of the interests of criminologists, and law is part of this picture (though not necessarily at the centre). In addition, comparative criminology can reveal how levels of crime are related to topics such as crime prevention, the process of the criminal justice system, and the internationalisation of crime.[163] Moral philosophy would take another angle on law's influence on the crime rate. For example, even if it were found that capital punishment reduced the crime rate, one may take the moral point of view that it is not 'right' for the state to kill the perpetrator. Or, alternatively, if it were shown that capital punishment did not reduce the crime rate, one may take the moral point of view that retribution demands the death penalty.[164]

This leads to a more general question of why countries differ in the harshness of punishment. A good starting point is the debate about differences in criminal punishment between the US and Europe, in particular as regards the availability of the death penalty.

One set of reasons follows the view that legal systems mirror their histories.[165] For example, David Garland links the racially motivated lynchings in the nineteenth-century southern states of the US with their relatively frequent use of the death penalty today.[166] Referring to a similar period, according to James Whitman, the US situation can be explained by the fact that forms of punishment such as hanging, which had been reserved for persons of the lowest social status, were gradually generalised to the upper classes. In continental Europe, by contrast, equal treatment meant that the more lenient treatment of the aristocracy, based on the wish to respect the perpetrator's honour, became the general approach.[167] It is also possible to focus on events that happened in the twentieth century. Here, Europe may be regarded as a special case, the argument being that the abolition of the death penalty was a reaction to the atrocities of the two World Wars. A more contentious reasoning is that modernity has marched further along either in Europe or in the United States, with scholars disagreeing on whether a harsh criminal law is or is not typical for 'late modern societies'.[168]

Alternatively, there are a variety of reasons why current factors may be decisive. It has already been mentioned that postmodernists tend to explain differences in capital punishment, as well as the harshness of punishment in

---

[162] Donohue and Wolfers 2006: 799.   [163] See, e.g., Nelken 2000; Nelken 2010; Nelken 2011.

[164] Cf. Hood and Hoyle 2008: 350–82 (death penalty as a question of opinion or principle).

[165] See generally A 2 (a), above.

[166] Garland 2007. See also Zimring 2003: 89–118 (referring to the legacy of lynch mobs); Garland 2001 (for crime control in the US and the UK more generally).

[167] Whitman 2003a (referring to both law and application of punishment in general).

[168] References in Kleinfeld 2011: 5. See also ch. 11 at C 1 below.

general, with the more pronounced role of Christian values in today's US than in Europe.[169] There is also some quantitative empirical work that has confirmed the relevance of religion.[170] But the more general question of whether differences in criminal sanctions reflect differences in opinions and values does not provide a clear answer. While, in general, public attitudes seem to be correlated with the harshness of punishment, the abolition of the death penalty in Europe often occurred despite public opinion supporting it.[171]

Thus, tangible features of current societies may be more important. A tempting explanation could be that the higher crime rate in the US is accountable for its harsher punishment,[172] but, then, punishment should also have some effect on the crime rate, so the causal relationship may not be clear. There is some empirical support for the relevance of inequality and ethnic diversity.[173] Sociologists have also suggested that criminal punishment is related to more complex social practices, such as workplace and household discipline, the organisation of labour markets, and the welfare state.[174]

Another potentially important cause are political structures. Andrew Hammel takes the view that the existence of a cohesive group of elites and a centralised political system account for the fact that the abolition of the death penalty happened in Europe but not in the US. Since, across countries, the general public often supports the death penalty, the role of European elites is seen as crucial for its abolition. Conversely, in the US, the federal system and the democratically elected judges lead to greater receptiveness to more diverse social groups.[175] This view is shared by other researchers, who also suggest a link between the greater democratic responsiveness of officials and harsher punishment, comparing the US with Europe.[176]

Adding Asian countries to the discussion presents some variations to these possible explanatory factors.[177] Many Asian legal systems still allow the death penalty, yet it can be shown that economic development and democratisation have led to its abolition in some countries, and to a decline in executions in others (e.g. in India, Taiwan, South Korea, and Japan). The highest number of executions can mostly be found in communist or authoritarian political regimes (e.g. in China, North Korea, Vietnam, and Myanmar). Conversely, cultural factors seem to be less important. Moreover, as far as capital punishment has, de iure or de facto, been abolished, this was often on the initiative of political elites, with public opinion still in favour of it (e.g. in Hong Kong and South Korea).

Beyond the debate about the death penalty, work by Michael Cavadino and James Dignan analyses the relationship between political economies and

---

[169] See ch. 5 at B 2, above.   [170] Greenberg and West 2008.
[171] See Nelken 2010: 67–8; Kleinfeld 2011: 6.   [172] See Boulanger and Sarat 2005: 4–6.
[173] Jacobs and Carmichael 2002 (based on comparison between US states).
[174] See Whitman 2005a: 20.   [175] Hammel 2010. See also Berry 2011.
[176] See Whitman 2005a: 28; Whitman 2003a: 14–5; Berry 2011: 1023.
[177] For the following see Johnson and Zimring 2009.

Table 6.3 Potential relationships between political economy and imprisonment

1. political economy → crime rate →	punishment
2. political economy ←→ general culture → public opinion →	punishment
3. political economy → media culture → political and public opinion →	punishment
4. political economy → political culture → political opinion →	punishment
5. political economy ←→ political institutions →	punishment

the harshness of punishment more generally. It explains the high incarceration rates in the US with neoliberal politics, whereas, in continental Europe the more inclusive economic and social policies point towards the aim of resocialisation.[178] To be sure, this is unlikely to be the only reason that explains differences in incarceration rates. For example, crime levels may differ due to cultural and religious reasons, and the effectiveness of criminal procedure may also play a role.[179]

Cavadino and Dignan have also developed models of how the political economies of 'neoliberal', 'conservative corporatist' and 'social democratic' countries may be reflected in different rates of imprisonment.[180] Table 6.3 illustrates the potential causalities. Cavadino and Dignan regard a combination of the models 2 and 5 as most plausible. Contrasting the five models, it also seems likely that there are diverse ways causalities operate across the world. This is a challenge for comparative socio-legal research, while it also offers the opportunity to illuminate such potential differences. It also shows that the initial illustration of possible causalities[181] can be further differentiated in terms of the precise interaction between the various non-legal elements (society, culture, politics etc.) that influence the law.

D. Conclusion

By definition, socio-legal comparative law not only considers the positive law but also other data related to society. These other data may be qualitative or quantitative. Choosing one or the other type of data can have an impact on the results of the comparative analysis.[182] Qualitative comparative socio-legal research tends to focus on the details of particular legal systems and therefore differences between legal systems, akin to postmodern comparative research. By contrast, quantitative comparative socio-legal research may be better able to show similarities between apparently very different legal systems, in this respect akin to its traditional counterpart.

---

[178] Cavadino and Dignan 2006. See also Lacey 2011 (convergence unlikely to happen); Wacquant 2009 (US-style neoliberalism as main cause for harsh punishment).

[179] Nelken 2009: 297–301 (in particular on Italy). See also ch. 5 at B 2, above.

[180] For the following see Cavadino and Dignan 2011.

[181] See A 2 (b), above.   [182] Cotterrell 2012: 48. See also Nelken 2010: 42.

In addition, quantitative research often has the ambition of showing causal relations. This is of particular interest for the debate on whether comparative law confirms or refutes the theory that law mirrors society.[183] However, the research discussed in this section has illustrated that causalities are often too complex to prove clear causal links. In particular, it seems to be a general feature of the law that it tends to be in a mutually interdependent relationship with society. It has also been said that 'the more deeply legal rules are embedded in their context, the more difficult it becomes to suggest, let alone prove, causal links'.[184] Thus, socio-legal comparative lawyers tend to be careful in making claims about distinct causal relationships. Other researchers, in particular economists, are often less hesitant, as will be explained in more detail in later chapters.[185]

Overall, it is clear that applying socio-legal methods to comparative research has many benefits. For example, it can help in showing whether alleged differences between legal families are just technicalities, or whether they are correlated to real-life data such as the frequency of litigation, the strength of financial markets, and crime rates. It can also improve our understanding of the relationship between law and society – for instance, whether societal factors may substitute for deficient laws.[186] Socio-legal comparative studies will also re-appear in the discussion about globalisation and comparative law in Part III of this book, as it requires an understanding of the socio-economic dimension of globalisation.[187] There is also a clear link to 'implicit comparative law', addressed in Part IV, since studies of socio-legal comparative law that emphasise the socio-legal aspect may not be fundamentally different from comparative research in sociology, politics or economics dealing with legal issues.

---

[183] See ch. 6 at A 2, above.   [184] Dannemann 2006: 399.
[185] See ch. 7 at C 1 and ch. 11 at B 3, below.   [186] See, e.g., C 1 (a), above.
[187] See also the recent book by Darian-Smith 2013 developing a 'global socio-legal perspective'.

7

Numerical comparative law

According to Lord Kelvin (1883) '[w]hen you can measure what you are speaking about and express it in numbers, you know something about it; but when you cannot measure it, when you cannot express it in numbers, your knowledge is of the meagre and unsatisfactory kind'.[1] Lord Kelvin was a natural scientist but today many social scientists would agree that quantitative approaches are central to scientific progress. Legal researchers have joined in relatively late, but there is now also a growing field of 'empirical legal studies', applying statistical methods to legal questions.[2]

Numerical comparative law in a wide sense may refer to any quantitative research related to comparative law. Yet, in the following, two topics are excluded since they are addressed in other chapters. Quantitative comparative research about socio-legal data, such as litigation and crime rates, was already dealt with in the previous chapter. Moreover, economic research that uses law as an explanatory variable is only considered here as far is it concerns the coding of the law; the question of a possible causal relationship follows in the chapter on implicit comparative law.[3]

So, what is covered in the present chapter? Section A shows how numbers can be used to measure the impact of foreign and comparative legal ideas; in particular, it presents research on how often and for which reasons court decisions cite foreign courts. Section B discusses how to measure similarities and differences between legal systems, thus supplementing the traditional and postmodern research on this issue. Section C turns to attempts to measure the quality of legal rules and institutions. Section D concludes.

As a result, the three main sections of this chapter are structured according to core topics of comparative law. An alternative structure could be based on the main methods used in studies of numerical comparative law: conducting surveys, counting empirical facts, and coding legal rules. As the overview in Table 7.1 shows, and as the following will explain, these three methods can be used for any of the three topics.

---

[1] See Merton et al. 1984.   [2] See, e.g., Lawless et al. 2009.
[3] See ch. 11 at B 3, below. Other examples in ch. 10 at A, below.

Table 7.1 Overview of topics and methods of numerical comparative law

	Conducting surveys	Counting empirical facts	Coding legal rules
Measuring the impact of foreign legal ideas (A)	A 1, 3	A 1, 2	A 3
Measuring similarities and differences (B)	B 2	B 1	B 2
Measuring the quality of legal rules and institutions (C)	C 3	C 2	C 1

A. Measuring the impact of foreign legal ideas

One of the aims of comparative law is to get lawyers interested in rules and concepts from other legal systems.[4] The success of this endeavour may be measured by way of counting how often courts cite the courts from other jurisdictions. Moreover, one can count references to words and persons indicating the influence of foreign ideas, or try to develop measures of legal transplants.

1. Cross-citations between courts

(a) The non-quantitative discussion about judicial comparativism

There has been a good deal of non-quantitative research on whether courts should and do consider the case law from other jurisdictions. Thus, the following starts with the normative and positive non-quantitative debate before turning to quantitative research on cross-citations.

Whether courts should consider foreign case law is particularly controversial in the US.[5] The Supreme Court itself is divided on whether it is legitimate to refer to foreign case law in the interpretation of the US Constitution.[6] The critical view is most prominently expressed by Justice Scalia, namely that 'this Court . . . should not impose foreign moods, fads, or fashions on Americans'.[7] Such a sceptical view may also be shared by some judges in Europe, but explicit criticism of 'judicial comparativism' is more frequent in the literature. Here, the main arguments are that it may circumvent national sovereignty and democratic controls, that it may disregard the context of foreign legal decisions, and that it may invite cherry picking.[8]

The majority of the US Supreme Court takes a more positive view. According to Justice Breyer 'cross-country results resemble each other more and more,

---

[4] See ch. 1 at A 2 (b), above.

[5] See, e.g., Benvenuto 2006; Parrish 2007; Yap 2005 (also on other countries).

[6] The main cases are *Roper* v. *Simmons* 125 SCt 1183 (2005); *Lawrence* v. *Texas* 123 Ct 2472 (2003); *Foster* v. *Florida*, 537 US 990 (2002); *Aktins* v. *Virginia* 536 US 304 (2002).

[7] *Lawrence* v. *Texas* 123 Ct 2472, 2495 (2003) (Scalia J.).

[8] McCrudden 2007: 387–9; Legrand 2006b: 417, 419. For more positive views see, e.g., Hol 2009; Bell 2012.

exhibiting common, if not universal, principles in a variety of legal areas' and reflect 'a near universal desire for judicial institutions that, through guarantees of fair treatment, help to provide the security necessary for investment and, in turn, economic prosperity'.[9]

The literature has also identified a trend towards 'transjudicialism'. For instance, Anne-Marie Slaughter contemplates that the rise in transnational litigation has led to a global community of courts where foreign judges are accepted as fellow professionals.[10] It is also believed that such a process has the effect that comparative legal reasoning can be used to interpret or even to develop transnational rules.[11] Human rights are sometimes discussed as a special case. Here, references to international standards play an important role and we may even observe an emerging 'ius commune of human rights' based on comparative reasoning[12] – and the South African Constitution even provides that courts 'must' consider international and 'may' consider foreign law for the purpose of interpreting human rights.[13]

But does this also mean that courts actually refer to foreign courts more and more frequently? A number of senior judges have participated in the debate on whether and when cross-citations take place. Carl Baudenbacher, a Swiss jurist and President of the Court of Justice of the European Free Trade Association (EFTA), identified examples from Germany, Austria and Switzerland. He related these cross-citations to the common legal tradition of these countries, while also indicating the role of values and social, economic and political realities.[14] Similarly, Guy Canivet, a judge at the French Constitutional Council and the former president of the Cour de Cassation, identified foreign citations in France and, in so doing, he referred to the role of legal families and the level of economic development.[15] Aharon Barak, former president of the Israeli Supreme Court, mainly refers to a common ideology, in particular 'allegiance to basic democratic principles', decisive for the frequent references of the Israeli Supreme Court to the supreme and constitutional courts of the US, Canada, Australia, the UK, Germany and other Western European countries.[16]

With respect to the UK, a book by Lord Bingham, late judge at the House of Lords and one time Lord Chief Justice, explains how they considered decisions from other common law jurisdictions, but occasionally also from further afield. The problem with the latter may be that, as far as the law is codified, the 'judge is unlikely to gain much help from other jurisdictions'.[17] But common

---

[9] Breyer 2003. See also *Printz* v. *United States* 72 521 US 898, 921 (1997) (Breyer J.).

[10] Slaughter 2003: 193.

[11] Jemielniak and Miklaszewicz 2010: 16. For transnational law see also ch. 9 at D, below.

[12] Harding and Leyland 2007: 328. See also Bahdi 2002 (on 'transjudicialism'). See also ch. 8 at B 4, below (on the globalisation of human rights law).

[13] South African Constitution, s. 39(b) and (c). See also J. Foster 2010; Smithey 2001 (with quantitative information on South Africa and Canada).

[14] Baudenbacher 2003: 524.   [15] Canivet 2006.

[16] Barak 2002: 110–4.   [17] Bingham 2010a: 2.

law judges also discuss whether the bond between their jurisdictions may not have weakened. In the well-known British case of *Donoghue* v. *Stevenson*, the House of Lords considered US case law, but even then indicated that 'though the source of the law in the two countries may be the same, its current may well flow in different channels'.[18] More recently, from a US perspective, Justice Scalia referred to such divergence, attributing it to the UK and its 'submission to the jurisprudence of European courts dominated by continental jurists'.[19]

In the academic literature, a number of collaborative projects have discussed the frequency of cross-citations, though typically limited to Western countries. The most ambitious one was a project for the XIVth International Congress of Comparative Law in 1997. The resulting book contains a general report and national reports on Australia, Canada, France, Germany, Greece, Iceland, Israel, Japan, Luxembourg, the Netherlands, the UK, the US, and the EU.[20] Another collaborative book discussed the influence of foreign case law in Austria, France, Germany, the Netherlands and Spain.[21] In a number of books and articles, Sir Basil Markesinis and Jörg Fedtke have discussed judicial recourse to foreign law, with illustrations from Italy, France, Germany, Canada and South Africa.[22] Finally, two groups of researchers have employed a mixture of qualitative, quantitative and conceptual methods for various countries, coordinated by the Hague Institute for the Internationalisation of Law and the International Association of Constitutional Law.[23]

These publications have often also tried to explore when and why foreign courts are cited. For example, the general report to the comparative law congress makes a distinction between citations in terms of necessary comparison, legal rules with an international element, and legal rules of a purely domestic character.[24] Similarly, Markesinis and Fedtke categorise cross-citations according to the judges' presumed motivation, such as the existence of a gap or ambiguity in the local law, the presumed necessity of a harmonised response to a particular legal issue, increased legitimacy either in the face of 'locally expressed fears' or due to evidence that a proposed solution has worked in other systems, or when the interpreted law has an international or foreign source.[25]

---

[18] *Donoghue* v. *Stevenson* [1932] AC 562, 576 (per Lord Buckmaster). More positive Lord Atkin, ibid. at 598 ('It is always a satisfaction to an English lawyer to be able to test his application of fundamental principles of the common law by the development of the same doctrines by the lawyers of the Courts of the United States').

[19] *Roper* v. *Simmons* 125 SCt 1183, 1227 (2005) (Scalia J.).   [20] Drobnig and van Erp 1999.

[21] Canivet et al. 2004. See also Andenas and Fairgrieve 2012.

[22] Markesinis and Fedtke 2005; Markesinis and Fedtke 2006; Markesinis and Fedtke 2009; Markesinis 2006.

[23] For the former see Hol 2012; Gelter and Siems 2012 is also part of this project. For the latter see Groppi and Ponthoreau 2013.

[24] Drobnig 1999. See also Bobek 2013: 21–34 (distinguishing between mandatory, advisable and voluntary use).

[25] Markesinis and Fedtke 2006. See also Andenas and Fairgrieve 2012: 50–8 (developing a typology with seven criteria).

(b) Quantifying cross-citations

Citations of foreign case law are a visible sign of judicial comparativism. There has been a growing effort to evaluate these cross-citations quantitatively. Often, such research has a time dimension. For example, David Zaring examined how often US federal courts referred to foreign case law between 1945 and 2005, finding that the most popular foreign courts are from Canada and Western Europe, but also that the use of foreign decisions is rare and more or less unchanged over time.[26] Esin Örücü searched all decisions of the All England Law Reports published in 1972, 1982, 1992 and 2002. She found between thirty and fifty-seven citations of common law courts, but only three to seven of continental jurisdictions in all four years.[27]

One of my papers examined the decisions of the Court of Appeal of England and Wales (CA) and the German Federal Supreme Court (BGH) for the years 1951 to 2007, aiming to identify whether the citation patterns of the CA and the BGH reflect the conventional comparative perceptions about the English and German legal systems. For instance, the paper addressed how often the CA and the BGH cite the highest national and European courts, and higher foreign courts from different legal families. It was found that, on average, the CA cites other common law jurisdictions in about 16 per cent of its decisions. Citations from the CA to other countries, as well as foreign citations from the BGH, tend to remain under 1 per cent, though in the early twenty-first century there has been a slight increase in German citations to the highest Austrian and Swiss courts.[28]

A joined project with Martin Gelter pursued a more comprehensive analysis of cross-citation in Europe. Using databases from Austria, Belgium, England (and Wales),[29] France, Germany, Ireland, Italy, the Netherlands, Spain, and Switzerland, we hand-collected a dataset of cross-citations between the highest courts in matters of civil and criminal law.[30] We considered 636,172 decisions between 2000 and 2007, and found 1,430 cross-citations. A problem with this number, however, is that some of these highest courts are also competent for matters other than civil and criminal law, for example, administrative or labour law. Thus, we also identified the precise areas of law, and deducted the cases not concerning criminal and civil law. This led to a total of 1,098 cross-citations between these ten courts.

Table 7.2 displays the total number of cross-citations per citing court. In addition, it indicates why the foreign courts have been cited. Interestingly, the

---

[26] Zaring 2006.   [27] Örücü 2007: 417.   [28] Siems 2010a.

[29] In the subsequent text of this chapter the term 'England' is always to be read as referring to 'England and Wales'.

[30] Note that for France, Belgium and the Netherlands we also considered the opinions of the respective Advocates-General, though for France only a sample of them could be incorporated. For the citations of the High Court of Ireland to the Court of Appeal of England and Wales (CA) we had to rely on a random sample of decisions because citations to English courts do not always reveal whether the cited court is really the CA.

Table 7.2 Number of cross-citations in civil and criminal law (all cited)[1]

Citing court is supreme court from...	Reasons to cite foreign court			
	Case history and jurisdiction	International and European	Pure comparative	Total
Austria	13 (14)	53 (57)	423 (431)	489 (502)
Belgium	4 (4)	9 (14)	41 (45)	54 (63)
England	8 (9)	29 (51)	8 (9)	45 (69)
France	11 (11)	2 (2)	5 (5)	18 (18)
Germany	5 (5)	16 (16)	25 (25)	46 (46)
Ireland	1 (1)	24 (84)	209 (382)	234 (467)
Italy	5 (5)	2 (11)	5 (5)	12 (21)
Netherlands	10 (14)	23 (47)	67 (73)	100 (134)
Spain	1 (1)	12 (12)	4 (4)	17 (17)
Switzerland	24 (29)	4 (5)	55 (59)	83 (93)
Total	*82 (93)*	*174 (299)*	*842 (1,038)*	*1,098 (1,430)*

[1] *Source:* Gelter and Siems 2013; Gelter and Siems 2014 (also for the subsequent text).

majority of these citations have been made for purely comparative reasons, i.e. they were not triggered by international or European law or a problem of jurisdiction or conflict of laws. It can also be seen that there are considerable differences in the overall propensity to cite one of the other nine courts: Austria and Ireland do this fairly frequently, but there are less than twenty cross-citations coming from France, Spain and Italy.

It may be suggested that these differences mainly reflect differences in the style in which judgments are drafted.[31] For example, common law judges or the courts in German-speaking countries often write comparatively long opinions with many citations to other cases, whereas in Italy and Spain it is less common to provide detailed references. Thus, in these latter countries, foreign case law may not be disregarded, but 'only' left uncited. To identify such hidden influence, it would therefore be necessary to employ other empirical tools, such as conducting interviews with judges or asking them to participate in a survey.[32] However, in any case, differences in legal style do not explain why there are more cross-citations from Austria and Ireland than from Germany and England. For this, it is necessary to consider the cited courts.

Figure 7.1 shows that the citations from Austria to Germany, and from Ireland to England, dominate the picture: Austria has cited Germany 459 times, and Ireland has cited England 456 times. The other relationships trail behind these two by one order of magnitude: fifty-eight and forty-five citations to Germany

[31] See generally ch. 3 at B 2 (e), above.
[32] For such research see Mak 2011; Flanagan and Ahern 2011.

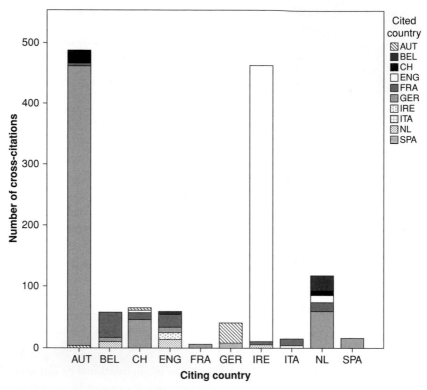

Figure 7.1 Bar chart on cross-citations between supreme courts[1]
[1] *Source:* Gelter and Siems 2012 (also for the subsequent text).

from the Netherlands and Switzerland respectively, forty-one citations from Belgium to France, and thirty-four citations from Germany to Austria. Thus, there is apparently some 'one-way traffic' from smaller to bigger jurisdictions, while one may also contemplate the role of cultural and linguistic proximity. These, and other possible explanatory factors, can also be assessed more formally.

(c) Econometric analysis of cross-citations

Thus, we undertook regression analysis in order to understand the differences between these cross-citations. The 'dependent variable', i.e. the variable that is to be explained, is the number of cross-citations between the ten courts in matters of civil and criminal law. Since this refers to count data (0, 1, 2 etc.), a technique called 'negative binomial regression' was used, with further technical details explained in the paper. A number of reasons, i.e. the 'independent variables', were examined as potentially explaining differences in cross-citations.

Table 7.3 Negative binomial regression with dependent variable number of cross-citations in matters of civil and criminal law[1]

Independent variables		Interpretation of coefficients	
(Constant)	−8.077***	*Change per 1 unit increase*	*Change per standard deviation*
Population of cited country	.0389***	+3.97% per 1 million	+185.11%
Lack of corruption of cited country	.753***	+112.37% per 1 point in index	+130.02%
Same language	1.122*	+207.13% for change to same language	+53.94%
Language skills	2.106***	+721.59% for change from 0% to 100% knowledge of language	+97.01%
Same legal family	.599***	+82.10% for change to same family	+31.41%
Cultural difference	−.956**	−61.57% per 1 point in index	−38.11%
Coordination difference	−1.475*	−77.12% per 1 point in index	−28.91%
Dummies citing court	#***		
Number of observations (N)	90		

[1] Adapted from Gelter and Siems 2013 (also for the subsequent text).

Table 7.3 shows that the independent variables of this model are all statistically significant (indicated by the '*'s).[33] Thus, it can be said that the population of the cited country and a low level of corruption, native languages, language skills, legal families, and cultural and political factors all have a bearing on which courts are likely to be cited. We also tested other variables, such as GDP per capita and geographical distance, which turned out not to be significant. The column 'Change per standard deviation' allows a comparison between the weight of the independent variables: thus, population, corruption and knowledge of the language of the cited court (i.e. native languages and language skills) are more important factors driving cross-citations than legal traditions, culture and politics.

The relevance of the population of the cited country is not really surprising, since even a casual glimpse of our data shows that most citations go from smaller to larger countries. With respect to corruption, it likely matters that the highest courts of the two countries that performed poorly in this index (Italy and Spain) are only rarely cited by the other countries. In substance, the data concerning both the size of population and the absence of corruption may indicate that

[33] Statistical details are beyond the scope of this chapter. The symbols mean: *** significant at the 1% level, ** significant at the 5% level, * significant at the 10% level, # significance denotes highest degree (individual parameter estimates not displayed).

the reputation of a court explains why it is the target of cross-citations. For example, since corruption has an impact on all types of state activities, factors such as the quality of the legislature, courts and law schools may all contribute to the attractiveness of a particular legal system.

Moreover, a particular court may attract citations because its decisions are more easily accessible than others. Language is the main proxy for this – and, as a matter of policy, our results may therefore suggest that courts should strive to make their decisions available in languages that possible foreign readers understand. It is also interesting to see that languages are more important than legal families; thus, for instance, the common language explains more of the cross-citations between Ireland and England than the common law.

2. Measuring foreign influence related to academic research

Adding academic research leads to a number of further questions related to the impact of foreign legal ideas: for example, are foreign academics cited in domestic judgments; are foreign laws or judgments cited in domestic law journals; and have foreign academics had an influence on domestic laws? In particular, it can be interesting to measure the international impact of academic research, since, to quote Jan Smits, the 'most common way in which foreign law permeates national law is through national legal writing'.[34] This may even be the case where the actual law is very different.[35]

Research by Sir Basil Markesinis tried to measure the influence of comparative lawyers on both fellow academics and judges.[36] For example, with respect to Italian comparatists, he observes strong citation networks, in particular due to Sacco and his pupils. Here, as well as in other countries, it also matters in which language a particular piece is published: for instance, British comparatists, as well as Zweigert and Kötz, David, Legrand, and the English articles by Sacco, are occasionally cited in the US literature, but not others. With respect to courts, Markesinis does not find that comparative law is very influential since, even when comparative lawyers are cited, this is often for their non-comparative work. Markesinis believes that this disregard of comparative law is a problem, though he also indicates that being cited should not be seen as a measure of scholarship.

It is also interesting to measure how the impact of comparative law has changed over time. This measure can respond to claims that, on the one hand, comparative law is said to have remained an esoteric subject, which matters

---

[34] Smits 2006b: 517, also 523. See also Faust 2006: 861 (aim of positive economic analysis of comparative law to establish why lawyers in different jurisdictions care, or do not care, about comparative law).

[35] See Kleinheisterkamp 2006: 296 (for the use of foreign legal doctrine in Latin America).

[36] Markesinis 2003: 75–155 and 261–4 (for list of databases and journals searched); updated in Markesinis and Fedtke 2009: 77–120.

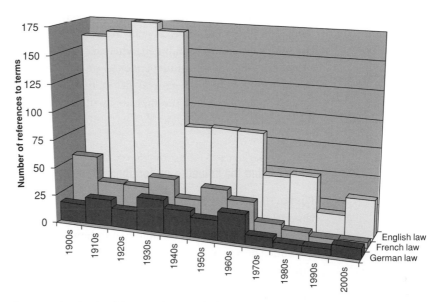

Figure 7.2 'Foreign laws' in *Harvard Law Review*[1]
[1] *Source:* own calculations.

only to a few people with special interests,[37] the likely explanation being that legal education is primarily focused on providing a coherent description of the law as it is applied domestically. On the other hand, there are claims that we can observe a growing interest in comparative law, with the twenty-first century becoming the 'era of comparative law'.[38]

A previous project searched how often foreign words for 'law' (e.g. 'droit', 'Recht') as well as the term 'comparative law' (and the equivalent German term) have been mentioned in two of the main US and German law journals between 1950 and 2006.[39] It was found that in general there has been a decline in the use of all of these words in the US journal. The German data are more ambiguous. In particular, while there is a decline in the French term 'droit', the English term 'law' has been mentioned more frequently, possibly reflecting the shift towards English as the internationally dominant language in legal scholarship.

Figure 7.2 illustrates a related way of collecting and presenting such data. Here, the *Harvard Law Review* is searched for the terms 'English law', 'French law' and 'German law', starting with the year 1900. All three time series show a general downward trend, though in the 2000s there were more references to these terms than in the 1990s. One can also calculate how the relative frequency

---

[37] Reimann 1996: 65; Markesinis 1990a (calling it 'a subject in search of an audience').
[38] Örücü 2004a: 216.
[39] Siems 2007b. The journals were the *Harvard Law Review* and the *Neue Juristische Wochenschrift* (NJW).

of these three terms has changed: at the beginning of the twentieth century there were almost four times as many references to 'English law' than to 'French law' and 'German law' combined, whereas today it is just twice as many. Thus, apparently, the growing independence of US from English law has been a stronger trend than more general factors that some speculate play a role, such as 'parochialism, belief in the superiority of the American Way (ie, arrogance), the lack of language skills, etc'.[40]

3. Measuring the influence on foreign statute law

It is not straightforward to measure the influence on foreign statute law. As far as law-making institutions publish preparatory works, it may be possible to count the number of citations of foreign legal systems. Potential influence may also be quantified by way of opinion polls: for example, a recent US study suggests that Americans 'are surprisingly receptive' to foreign legislative models.[41] Another approach is to measure the actual 'output', i.e. the relevant statute laws. Here, three variants can be distinguished.

First, one may start with a particular law and then try to examine which laws may have influenced it. Table 7.4 illustrates this approach, aiming to calculate the main origin of the DCFR, essentially the draft for a future European Civil Code.[42] The four foreign codes considered are the German Civil Code (BGB), the French Code Civil, the Indian Contract Act and the US Uniform Commercial Code (UCC). It can be seen that six of the top German terms but only four of the top French, Indian, and US terms are in the DCFR's list of most common terms; in particular all top five DCFR terms are part of the German top ten. Thus, it may not be unreasonable to assume that the BGB has been particularly influential.

Examining such similarities in language is in line with non-quantitative research showing how comparing legal languages can illustrate legal transplants.[43] But there are limitations as well. The use of certain words is likely to be influenced by purely linguistic preferences or how the German and French codes have been translated. Since the Indian Contract Act deals with fewer topics than the DCFR and the US UCC with somehow different ones, a more limited overlap is, in any case, to be expected.

Second, it is possible to ask the reverse question, namely, whether particular legal rules have had an impact on other legal systems. For example, international and regional organisations may use numerical benchmarking in order

---

[40] Reimann 1996: 53. See also Garoupa 2011 (on legal parochialism); ch. 3 at C 2, above (for differences between English and US law).

[41] Linos 2013: 36–66. But different for judicial comparative law: Curry and Miller 2008.

[42] Available at http://ec.europa.eu/justice/policies/civil/docs/dcfr_outline_edition_en.pdf. See also ch. 9 at C 2, below.

[43] Pozzo 2012: 90–4.

Table 7.4 The top ten words of the Draft Common Frame of Reference (DCFR), compared with four domestic codes[1]

Rank	Word	Top ten ranks in French, German, Indian and US codes
1	contract	Germany (1), France (9), India (1), US (8)
2	person	Germany (2), France (2), India (3), US (2)
3	party	Germany (6)
4	performance	Germany (9)
5	time	Germany (7), France (8), India (8)
6	obligation	–
7	right	Germany (5)
8	security	US (1)
9	goods	India (2), US (3)
10	debtor	France (3)

[1] *Source:* own calculations. Note: property and family law were excluded; thus, the DCFR was used without books IX, X. The other Codes are: French Code Civil (sections 1101 to 1386–18; and 1582 to 2322), German BGB (books 1 and 2), Indian Contract Act, US Uniform Commercial Code. Common terms such as 'article', 'section' or 'may' have been omitted.

to find out whether they have successfully managed to influence national lawmakers. In the EU, the Commission has a natural interest in monitoring how directives have been implemented and whether recommendations have been taken up by national legislators.[44] A good example from the academic literature is William Carney's article, that analysed the impact of the Model Business Corporation Act on US state law. The general result was that the Model Business Corporation Act led to convergence, because 74.4 per cent of its 142 provisions had been taken over by all US states. Since not all provisions are equally important, Carney also isolated important provisions and found that the Model Business Corporation Act also led to convergence with regard to these provisions.[45]

A more complex reception process was examined by T.T. Arvind and Lindsay Stirton, analysing the reception of the French Civil Code in the German states of the early nineteenth century.[46] Arvind and Stirton coded the way these states had adopted and implemented the French Civil Code, assigning scores of '1', '0.75', '0.5', '0.25' and '0'. Subsequently, they aimed to explain what may account for differences in the degree of implementation of the Code. For this purpose, they used a 'fuzzy-set qualitative comparative analysis' in order to identify necessary and sufficient conditions for the full or partial implementation of

[44] Statistics on the implementation of directives are published in the Internal Market Scoreboard, available at http://ec.europa.eu/internal_market/score/index_en.html and see, e.g., Commission Staff Working Document 2007; Commission Staff Working Document 2008. For quantitative research in the literature see, e.g., Linos 2007.
[45] Carney 1998.   [46] Arvind and Stirton 2010.

the Code.[47] Yet, this was not seen as providing evidence of causation, since questions of causal relationships needed 'the help of the researcher's substantive and theoretical knowledge'. Thus, this approach differs from a fully quantitative method that uses regression analysis to identify robust causal relationships. But regressions can only show statistically significant results when we have a large number of observations and a limited number of explanatory variables. In the situation analysed by Arvind and Stirton, this would not be the case, since they only have fourteen states but eight possible explanatory factors. Thus, their analysis is a good compromise of using some quantitative tools in order to establish possible causal relations, while not claiming that they can provide statistical proof.

Third, a functional approach starts with a question, such as 'what are the possible ways of protecting shareholders?' and then develops an index that translates details of the law into numbers. Subsequently, these numbers can be used to examine similarities and differences between countries (or to evaluate whether particular legal rules are a determinant for economic development).[48] They may also show whether foreign legal systems may have had an impact on the legal rules in question.

Figure 7.3, below, is based on data collected at the Centre for Business Research (CBR) in the University of Cambridge.[49] Inter alia, this project developed a functional ten-variable index on shareholder protection, considering topics such as the independence of board members, the powers of the general meeting, and the prohibition of multiple voting rights. Then, we coded various legal systems according to this index, i.e. assigning values such as '0', '0.5' or '1' depending on the legal rules in question.[50] Subsequently, it is possible to measure how different one country (or a group of countries) is from others: calculating the differences between each variable in the law of a particular legal system, and the same variable in the law of the other countries, and then adding together the absolute values of these differences.

Based on this method, Figure 7.3 indicates the potential influence that Western legal systems had on the law on shareholder protection in three Central and Eastern European countries between 1995 and 2005. It can be seen that, in these ten years, they seem to have adopted provisions from English and French company law, leading to a 10 per cent reduction in the respective difference. German law had already been fairly similar in 1995, and the difference from US law remained relatively unchanged at a high level, thus possibly refuting the

---

[47] The main ones, identified by the paper, are 'territorial diversity, control by Napoleon, central state institutions, a feudal economy and society, liberal (enlightented absolutist) rule, nativism among the governing elites and popular anti-French sentiment'. On the 'fuzzy-set qualitative comparative analysis' see also ch. 11 at A 3, below.

[48] See C 1 and ch. 11 at B 3, below.

[49] See www.cbr.cam.ac.uk/research/programme2/project2-20.htm and B 2 and C 1, below for more details. For the following see Lele and Siems 2007: 37–43; Siems 2008c: 125–35; Siems 2010b; Siems 2010c.

[50] The full text of the index, the dataset and detailed explanations can be found online: see ibid.

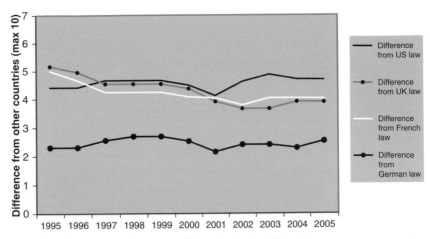

Figure 7.3 'Westernisation' of shareholder protection in Central and Eastern Europe (Czech Republic, Latvia, Slovenia) (10 variables)

argument that there has been an 'Americanisation' of legal systems in recent times.[51] Of course, what precisely triggered these changes cannot be answered with such an approach. Thus, the question of legal transplants in law-making may also invite a qualitative historical analysis, understanding more precisely how foreign political, cultural or economic forces have influenced domestic law-making.[52]

The reverse trend can also be explored, namely, how legal systems that had been fairly similar have gradually diverged. For example, a study by Mark West starts with the observation that in 1950 the US Model Business Corporation Act and the modern Japanese Commercial Code were both based on the Illinois Business Corporation Act of 1933. Using a fifty-year historical database he found that, despite globalisation pressures, these laws had diverged over time, classifying provisions as the same if the functions of the statutes were substantially similar. West also discusses the reasons for the divergence of US and Japanese company laws. His main explanation is that, in the United States, regulatory competition had constantly put pressure on the law-makers to keep their law up-to-date. In Japan, though, usually only exogenous shocks led to statutory change, as there was no pressure from regulatory competition.[53]

B. Measuring similarities and differences

One of the key questions of comparative law is to understand similarities and differences between legal systems – for instance, in terms of whether or not they belong to a particular legal family. This question is related to the topic of the previous section, since foreign influence may lead to an approximation of legal

---

[51] For the latter claim see also ch. 8 at B 1 (b), below.   [52] See ch. 8 at B, below.
[53] West 2001. For regulatory competition see also ch. 9 at A 2 (b), below.

systems. Yet, this is not necessarily the case: for example, it may also be interesting to show legal similarities triggered by similar socio-economic conditions, but without direct interaction. It is also useful to distinguish between possible formal and substantive similarities and differences between legal systems.

1. Formal features of the legal system

An initial question is how much countries rely on formal, as opposed to informal ways, of achieving social order. A possible way to quantify possible differences is the use of cross-country surveys. For example, a book by Thomas Lundmark presents the results of a survey where he questioned lawyers about the completeness, determinability and certainty of their legal systems.[54] Alternatively, one may employ objective measures. For example, Peter Nardulli and colleagues have collected data on the number of legal publications and law schools across countries.[55] As suggested by Donald Black, one may also want to determine a measure for the quantity of law, expected to be inversely related to the extent of informal social order.[56]

Actual attempts to measure the quantity of legal rules have been limited to the codified law. In the 1980s Heinz Schäffer and Attila Racz led a research project on 'Quantitative Analyses of Law – A Comparative Empirical Study: Sources of Law in Eastern and Western Europe'.[57] This project used questionnaires to estimate the total amount of generally binding normative acts, for instance, in terms of pages and the number of single norms. Schäffer and Racz also tried to identify the amount of legal changes within a period of ten years, as socialist governments were expected to be less hesitant in changing existing legal orders.

More recently, Tom Ginsburg and colleagues were interested in whether and how legal systems differ in the 'specificity' of codified law. The first paper called this 'leximetrics', and examined whether in Europe the length of laws implementing EU directives varies systematically across countries.[58] Based on the implementing statutes of directives on product liability, works council, and e-commerce, they constructed a 'statutory specificity index' with the most specific legal system being the UK (i.e. having the longest implementing statutes) and the least specific ones being the Scandinavian countries. Thus, this result may confirm statements by comparative lawyers that, in common law countries, legislation tends to be more detailed in order to make clear that it replaces prior judge-made law.[59]

---

[54] Lundmark 2012: 96–130. Similarly, for judical discretion, Cooter and Ginsburg 1996: 300. On surveys see also C 3, below.

[55] Nardulli et al. 2013. See also www.clinecenter.illinois.edu/research/sid-thematic-legal-infrastructures.html.

[56] Black 1976. But this correlation is disputed: see, e.g., Nelken 2010: 37.

[57] Schäffer and Racz 1990.   [58] Cooter and Ginsburg 2003.

[59] See ch. 3 at B 1 (a), above, and, e.g., Zweigert and Kötz 1998: 268.

Ginsburg and colleagues also examined the specificity of constitutions, using data from most countries of the world.[60] Here, too, civil law countries tend towards shorter texts than common law ones, though, in Latin America, constitutions also tend to be relatively long. As with other statutes, the lengthiness could be the result of a relatively detailed treatment of particular issues, but it is also possible that it is the outcome of a broader scope of topics. Thus, just relying on the length of the text can only provide an initial picture and invites further research on the substance of the constitution.[61] It can also be revealing to explore how the length of constitutions is related to other factors, such as the level of social trust in a particular society.[62]

With respect to similarities and differences between courts, one may simply count and compare the number of court decisions, or say, dissenting judgments across countries,[63] or one may use socio-legal data such as the duration and cost of trials.[64] Another approach is to pursue a content analysis of court decisions. Mark Hall and Ronald Wright provide the following summary of this approach:

> On the surface, content analysis appears simple, even trivial, to some. Using his method, a scholar collects a set of documents, such as judicial opinions on a particular subject, and systematically reads them, recording consistent features of each and drawing inferences about their use and meaning. This method comes naturally to legal scholars because it resembles the classic scholarly exercise of reading a collection of cases, finding common threads that link the opinions, and commenting on their significance. But content analysis is more than a better way to read cases. It brings the rigor of social science to our understanding of case law, creating a distinctively legal form of empiricism.[65]

How exactly may this be done in comparative law? A comparatist may find it interesting to explore whether such an analysis could show differences and similarities in legal methods – for instance, in forms of statutory interpretation. However, linguistic and conceptual differences can make a direct textual comparison across legal cultures difficult. For example, a content analysis of English judgments would search for terms such as 'literal rule', 'golden rule', and 'mischief rule', whereas in Germany the relevant terms would refer to 'Wortlaut' ('wording'), 'Entstehungsgeschichte' ('historical background') and 'Sinn und Zweck' ('purpose').[66]

---

[60] Ginsburg 2010b. See also Elkins et al. 2009; Ginsburg et al. 2012; Melton et al. 2013; and the project website at www.comparativeconstitutionsproject.org.

[61] E.g. Hanretty 2011 (examining how often constitutions explicitly leave matters to ordinary legislation).

[62] Bjørnskov and Voigt 2013. The data are from Voigt 2009a (also finding that common law countries tend to have longer constitutions). See also ch. 11 at C 3, below (for research on relationship between law and trust).

[63] For the first point see A 1 (b), above; for the second one, see, e.g., European Parliament 2012.

[64] See ch. 6 at B 3, above, and see C 2, below.

[65] Hall and Wright 2008: 64. See also Meuwese and Versteeg 2012: 240–4 (on quantitative text analysis and comparative law).

[66] For an attempt to quantify these topics see Siems 2007c.

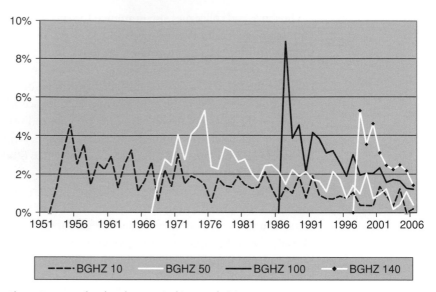

Figure 7.4 How often has the BGH cited its own decisions?

Another interesting question is whether courts differ in the extent to which they make references to the academic literature and other court cases. Usually, it is said that the academic literature is cited more frequently in Germany than in England,[67] whereas it may be assumed that, in a common law country like England, case law is cited more often than in a civil law country like Germany. However, the latter point was not confirmed in a previous paper, already mentioned in the preceding section. Considering the Court of Appeal of England and Wales (CA) and the German Federal Supreme Court (BGH) for the years 1951 to 2007, it counted all court citations for a random sample of fifty-seven decisions per country (one per year). The sample mean of all citations per judgment was 7.26 for the CA and 7.96 for the BGH, and since the standard deviations were relatively high (6.00 and 6.84), one could not reject the hypothesis that the population means were equal.[68]

A related question is whether there are differences in the way courts cite their own decisions. For example, comparing the average age of cited cases in the US and England, Richard Posner observes that the turnover of cases is higher in the US due to the larger pool of recent cases.[69] With respect to the common and civil law divide, it may be suggested that, in the system of case law of the former countries, old decisions are more honoured than in the latter ones. Yet, this is not necessarily the case.

Figures 7.4 and 7.5 show how often and when the German BGH and the English CA cite their own decisions.[70] The general shape of the curves is that

---

[67] See Kötz 1990. See also ch. 3 at B 2 (e), above.   [68] See Siems 2010a: 159.

[69] Posner 1996: 86–7. For more recent research on US courts see Black and Spriggs 2013.

[70] This and the following is from Siems 2010a: 166–8. Four volumes were chosen for each of the courts: with respect to the BGH it was examined how frequently the decisions of the volumes

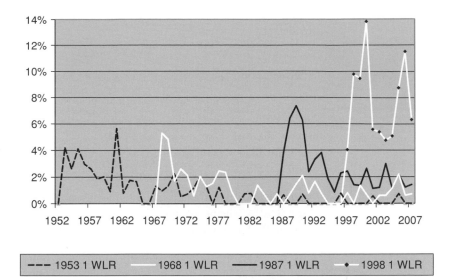

Figure 7.5 How often has the CA cited its own decisions?

there are initially no citations, then a steep rise, and finally a smooth decline. Three reasons can be brought forward in order to explain these developments. First, it is likely that there is an initial 'excitement' about new decisions, but subsequent decisions or law reforms may modify or even reverse their findings. Second, courts may prefer to cite the most recent decision. Thus, in these situations, the original decision is still 'good law', but falls victim to shorthand citation. Third, court decisions reflect the socio-economic problems at that time. As the world constantly changes, it is clear that some of the topics of older decisions become obsolete.

The eight curves of Figures 7.4 and 7.5 do not look entirely identical. Some of the curves reach a considerably higher peak, and some are less skewed than others. In order to identify the reasons for these different shapes, one would have to examine the specific citations of the specific years in a non-quantitative way. Comparing the BGH and CA data, it can, however, be established mathematically that, in both figures, the 'skewness', i.e. the degree of asymmetry of a distribution around its mean, is similar.[71] Thus, in terms of the number of citations of previous case law, it cannot be confirmed that, in England, old decisions are more honoured than in Germany. Yet, this also shows the limitations of such a quantitative approach. A more qualitative assessment may be able to identify a difference, since English courts tend carefully to analyse the facts,

10 (1953), 50 (1968), 100 (1987), and 140 (1998) of the official law reports (BGHZ) have been cited in decisions published in the *Neue Juristische Wochenschrift* (NJW), and with respect to the CA it was traced how often the CA decisions published in volumes (1953) 1, (1968) 1, (1987) 1, (1998) 1 of the *Weekly Law Reports* (WLR) have been cited in other decisions published in the WLR.

[71] For the BGH the numbers are between 0.74 and 2.45 and for the CA between 0.71 and 1.89.

ratio and dictum of previous judgments, whereas German courts often only provide a list of references.[72]

2. Substance of legal rules

Sometimes comparative lawyers seem to get frustrated about the debate of whether there are more differences or similarities between legal systems. For instance, there is said to be a high degree of subjectivity in whether a comparatist is more inclined to perceive differences or similarities.[73] Also, according to Ugo Mattei:

> In the absence of quantitative tools to measure analogies and differences among legal systems, whether common law or civil law are more or less similar depends only on the terms of comparison and on the problems that one is facing.[74]

However, today, quantitative tools are available to make such assessments. A first approach is to use surveys. For example, the Oxford Civil Justice Survey asked 100 participants, predominantly in the legal departments of companies, whether they thought that there was considerable variation in the contract laws and civil justice systems of the EU Member States. With respect to contract laws, 71 per cent answered in the affirmative, and, with respect to civil justice systems, even these were 84 per cent.[75] Of course, this does not prove that there are actually considerable differences. Still, it is interesting to see that such a perception exists, possibly influencing the way businesses operate in other Member States.

Second, one can start with one particular legal system and then examine quantitatively how far it differs from others. For example, William Carney was interested in the differences between EU and US company law.[76] For this purpose, he undertook a taxonomy of the EU company law directives, divided them into 131 provisions, and searched in the laws of the US states for similar provisions. He found that ninety-five provisions were not in effect in any US state, fourteen were in effect in all fifty states, and the remaining twenty-two provisions were adopted by a random number of states. He also observed that the provisions which were in effect in none of the US states mainly consisted of protections for creditors and employees.

Third, if one is interested in the way particular interests are protected, one may also use a functional approach. This has been a popular method in company law. For example, the aforementioned project of the Centre for Business Research at the University of Cambridge has constructed two datasets on shareholder protection.[77] The first dataset was based on a relatively comprehensive index

---

[72] Gelter and Siems 2014. See also ch. 3 at B 2 (e), above.
[73] Antokolskaia 2006: 27.   [74] Mattei 1997b: 41.
[75] See Vogenauer 2008. A related question is whether evidence shows that consumers regard legal diversity as a reason to avoid cross-border contracts: see Low 2012.
[76] Carney 1997.   [77] See already A 3, above, as well as C 1, below.

Table 7.5 Matrix on differences in shareholder protection 2005 (max 10, min 0)

	Germany	France	UK	US	India	Japan	China	
Germany	–	3.0	3.63	4.0	2.88	2.75	0.85	...
France	3.0	–	4.13	3.0	4.13	3.25	3.35	...
UK	3.63	4.13	–	3.63	4.0	4.38	2.78	...
US	4.0	3.0	3.63	–	3.13	2.75	3.65	...
India	2.88	4.13	4.0	3.13	–	2.88	2.03	...
Japan	2.75	3.25	4.38	2.75	2.88	–	2.60	...
China	0.85	3.35	2.78	3.65	2.03	2.60	–	...
....	...	...	...	...	...	...	...	...

of sixty variables for shareholder protection. It was used to code the laws of France, Germany, India, the UK and the US for the period from 1970 to 2005. Then, for instance, one could calculate how the differences between these legal systems have evolved. In one of the papers it was shown that the 1970 data seem to confirm the classification of legal families: French law was relatively similar to German law, but more different from UK, US and Indian law. But this changed in 2005, since, here, the data show that the French law on shareholder protection is now closer to UK law than it is to German law.[78]

The second shareholder protection index has ten variables with twenty-five legal systems coded. This also includes a time-dimension (1995 to 2005),[79] but the following will focus on just the final year and the differences between the twenty-five countries.[80] Thus, the differences between each variable in the law of a particular legal system and the same variable in the law of the other countries have been calculated. Subsequently, the absolute values of these differences were added together. This results in symmetric matrices with 25 columns and rows, indicating the differences between each pair of countries.[81] An extract of these matrices can be found in Table 7.5. For instance, one can observe that the German and Chinese laws on shareholder protection are relatively similar (the difference just being 0.85), whereas the German and US laws are relatively different (the difference being 4.0).

The transformation of these data into matrices opens the possibility of social network analysis. The main interest of social network analysis is to identify, visualise, and compare the relationships between individuals or entities. In the terminology of network analysis, the individuals are called 'nodes', and the relationships are called 'ties' or 'edges'. In the present case, the nodes are the twenty-five countries and the ties are the values on the differences between countries.

[78] Lele and Siems 2007: 38. See also Siems 2010b; Armour et al. 2009a.
[79] See also A 3, above.   [80] This and the following is based on Siems 2010c.
[81] Such an approach of pairs (or dyads) is also used in political science and international relations. See, e.g., Sommerer et al. 2008.

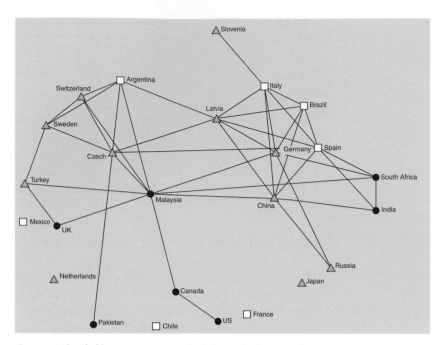

Figure 7.6 Shareholder protection network of strongest 15 per cent ties

For the purposes of deciding when a relationship is close enough to be considered a tie between two countries, a cut-off point has been chosen. Figure 7.6 displays the strongest 15 per cent of the links, i.e. the 45 out of the 300 country-pairs that are most similar to each other. In addition, the network program has shifted the position of nodes according to the strength of their relationships. Thus, countries whose shareholder protection is relatively similar are moved closer together. Different symbols stand for the three legal origins:[82] English legal origin countries have a black spot; French legal origin countries a white box; and German legal origin countries a grey triangle.

Some linkage of countries that share the same legal family can be observed. In the civil law world, there are 'cliques' between Germany, Russia and China; Germany, Latvia, and China; Sweden, Switzerland, and the Czech Republic; and Italy, Brazil, and Spain – meaning that the ties of all countries refer to each other. A chain connects all common countries, with the exception of Pakistan. Pakistan is an outsider since it is the only common law country that does not score well in the shareholder protection index. Likewise, Mexico and Chile have relatively low scores, which explains why they are not connected to other countries. Conversely, France and Japan have higher scores than most other countries, which again makes them different from the rest of the world.[83]

---

[82] Based on the La Porta classifications; see ch. 4 at B 2, above.
[83] For the precise numbers see Siems 2010c: 766.

There are also a number of ties in Figure 7.6 that do not appear to make sense: for instance, the ones between Pakistan and the Czech Republic, Canada and Malaysia, and Spain and India. Most remarkably, the difference between Argentina and the Czech Republic is only 0.25 out of 10 variables. However, such similarities are not implausible. Today, many aspects of shareholder protection are based on an international model of what is regarded as good corporate governance. For instance, the OECD, as well as private initiatives, have drafted standards on how companies should be managed, for instance, on the structure and responsibilities of the board of directors, and on the rights and duties of shareholders.[84] These guidelines were particularly aimed at transition and developing countries. Thus, there is no reason why legal systems as diverse as Argentina and the Czech Republic may not impose similar requirements on, say, disclosure of major shareholder ownership.[85]

Such quantitative research about functional differences is not limited to company law and related fields. For example, a study on civil procedure law claims to have found that common and civil law countries diverged between 1950 and 2000.[86] In a number of papers, Mila Versteeg and colleagues have analysed differences in constitutional laws, using a sixty year dataset covering most countries of the world.[87] They show that, increasingly, a set of provisions appears in nearly all written constitutions. As far as substantive differences are concerned, they construct an ideological ranking of the world's constitutions, showing a clear split between libertarian and statist constitutions. They also examine whether particular models have been influential, with the interesting result that the US Constitution increasingly diverges from the global models. Finally, an econometric paper examines the determinants for constitutional transplants, finding that shared colonial ties, commonalities in religion and legal origin, and competition for foreign aid are statistically significant. The significance of legal origin deserves special attention since, usually, comparative lawyers take the view that the civil/common law divide is less relevant for questions of constitutional law.[88]

C. Measuring the quality of legal rules and institutions

Most challenging is measuring the quality of legal rules and institutions such as courts and administrative agencies. An initial point to consider is who is

---

[84] See, e.g., OECD 2004; Avilov et al. 1999. See also ch. 9 at D 2, below.

[85] In both countries there was a threshold of 5% in 2005. For references see the CBR dataset (see note 49, above).

[86] Balas et al. 2009. This study is related to Djankov et al. 2003a, discussed under C 2, below.

[87] For the following see Law and Versteeg 2011; Law and Versteeg 2012; Goderis and Versteeg 2013; also Law 2011b. See also Meuwese and Versteeg 2012 (discussing the use of quantitative methods in constitutional law more generally). Landman and Carvalho 2010: 78–86 (for quantitative research on 'de jure human rights commitment').

[88] See ch. 4 at C 3 (c), above.

involved in such research. Legal scholars are sometimes sceptical as to whether policy evaluation should be part of comparative law.[89] Economists and political scientists are less hesitant about making such evaluations – as well as quantifying them. In addition, policy actors (governments, international organisations etc.) are interested in assessing how well particular legal rules or institutions 'work'. Of course, policy actors and academics tend to have different incentive structures. Thus, they approach questions of quality from different perspectives, as they belong to different communities with their own interests, approaches and ways of communication.[90]

As regards the data in question, a general distinction is often made between performance and perception data.[91] In addition, one can distinguish whether the aim is to measure the quality of the black letter legal rules, or whether one is interested in institutional structures, such as the operation of courts. A number of studies also combine methods, aiming to achieve 'the best of all worlds'. All of these approaches are discussed in the present section.[92] More briefly, the section addresses how such measurements may be used to show causal relationships. This second step can be relevant in determining the quality of legal rules and institutions, yet it properly belongs to the later chapter on 'implicit comparative law'.[93]

1. Measuring legal rules

The most influential study that tried to measure the quality of legal rules across countries is the article by Rafael La Porta and colleagues on 'Law and Finance'.[94] This study coded the law on shareholder and creditor protection across countries. For instance, with respect to shareholder protection, they used six variables to construct an index for 'anti-director rights'. The variables were defined in a brief and binary way, for instance:

> Proxy by mail allowed: equals one if the company law or commercial code allows shareholders to mail the proxy vote to the firm, and zero otherwise.

Next, La Porta et al. looked at forty-nine countries and each legal measure, and calculated an aggregate score for the strength of 'anti-director rights' for each of the legal systems. Subsequently they grouped the countries into legal origins (i.e. legal families),[95] with the result that common-law countries had the strongest, and French civil-law-countries the weakest legal protection of shareholders (see Table 7.6 below). Finally, they drew on these numbers as independent variables for statistical regressions, finding that good shareholder

---

[89] See ch. 2 at A 4 and C 4, above.
[90] See Hantrais 2009: 122 ('two communities theory').   [91] Kern 2009: 500.
[92] The following is based on Siems 2011.   [93] See ch. 11 at B 3, below.
[94] La Porta et al. 1998.   [95] See ch. 4 at B 2, above.

Table 7.6 Shareholder rights around the world (extract)[1]

Country	Proxy by mail allowed	(Other variables)	Anti-director rights
United Kingdom	1	...	5.0
United States	1	...	5.0
English-origin average	0.39	...	4.0
Belgium	0	...	0.0
France	1	...	3.0
French-origin average	0.05	...	2.33
German-origin average	0.00	...	2.33
Scandinavian-origin average	0.25	...	3.0

[1] La Porta et al. 1998: 1130–1.

protection leads to more dispersed shareholder ownership, which can be seen as an indicator for developed capital markets.

Many subsequent papers by La Porta and other researchers have used a similar method for other areas of law, for instance, in civil procedure, securities regulation, and labour law.[96] This line of research has also become one of the most important trends in contemporary comparative legal and economic scholarship: searches with Google and Westlaw result in many times more hits for 'La Porta et al.' than for 'Zweigert and Kötz',[97] and citation statistics from finance studies provide evidence that they are one of the most influential studies of the last two decades.[98]

These studies have also had an impact beyond academia: for instance, the EU Commission's impact assessment on the Directive on Shareholders' Rights explicitly referred to the 'Law and Finance' article in order to justify their reform proposal.[99] Most importantly, the World Bank has incorporated some of the La Porta et al. studies into its annual Doing Business Reports. It has also extended its scope, supplementing it with some socio-legal data (thus, this Report will be discussed in more detail in the final section, below, on 'combined approaches'). Moreover, such research is not limited to the World Bank. Already in the early 1990s, the OECD developed indicators of employment protection, being regularly updated and having inspired academic research in this field.[100] In addition, the OECD Product Market Indicators deal with regulatory issues

[96] Djankov et al. 2003a; La Porta et al. 2006; Botero et al. 2004. See also the references in Siems 2007a; Siems and Deakin 2010.

[97] See Siems 2007b: 144.   [98] See Durisin and Puzone 2009.

[99] European Commission 2006: 7, 53.

[100] OECD Indicators on Employment Protection, available at www.oecd.org/employment/emp/oecdindicatorsofemploymentprotection.htm. See, e.g., Estevez-Abe et al. 2001 (relevance of firm-specific, industry-specific and general skills depend on employment and unemployment protection).

in the domains of state control, barriers to entrepreneurship, and barriers to trade and investment.[101]

However, the research by La Porta et al., in particular the initial article on 'Law and Finance', has remained very controversial. To start with, this concerns the way they classify all legal systems of the world into distinct Western-based legal origins.[102] There has also been frequent criticism of the coding of legal rules. At a general level, comparative lawyers may object that their approach is by far too simplistic, treating legal systems as mere compilations of information which can be coded and aggregated in a numerical way.[103] More specifically, it has been shown that the legal indices of La Porta et al. do not provide an accurate numerical description of the law of different countries. For instance, numerous coding errors have been identified in La Porta et al.'s coding on shareholder protection.[104] Researchers have also developed methods of not simply aggregating variables of shareholder protection, but of considering how legal rules are related to each other.[105]

Another line of criticism concerns the very limited number of variables; for instance, there are six for 'anti-director rights'. It is doubtful that these are good proxies for the general level of shareholder protection since they do not capture many important aspects of company law.[106] Moreover, the choice of variables suffers from a clear US bias. Thus, the 'Law and Finance' article can be regarded as a form of implicit benchmarking and it may therefore be open to the challenge that it misleads the reader: La Porta et al. claim to measure the quality of legal rules in an objective way, but in reality they only show how much countries deviate from the US model.

A possible rejoinder may be that, despite the US bias, most of La Porta et al. studies have managed to identify a statistically significant effect of law on financial development.[107] Thus, only the interpretation of their results may change: countries do not benefit from any improvements to their legal system, but only from such changes that follow the US model. But, again, this is unsatisfactory. Legal rules operate differently in different institutional environments. The fact that legal transplants from US law may have had a positive effect in some countries leaves open the possibility that they may work in a completely different manner in other parts of the world. It is therefore preferable to acknowledge openly the variety of legal models, and to measure legal rules from a functional perspective.

For instance, following the approach of the Common Core project,[108] a comparative researcher may start with a hypothetical problem in order to examine

---

[101] OECD Indicators on Product Market Regulation, available at www.oecd.org/economy/growth/indicatorsofproductmarketregulationhomepage.htm.

[102] See ch. 4 at C, above.   [103] See Siems 2005.   [104] E.g. Spamann 2010; Cools 2005.

[105] Ferreira et al. 2013 (using a flow-chart in order to code the legal rules that determine whether shareholders can influence the composition of the board of directors).

[106] See Lele and Siems 2007: 19–21.

[107] But see also the discussion in ch. 11 at B 3, below, on the problem of establishing a causal relationship between law and finance.

[108] See ch. 2 at B 3, above.

how this problem would be solved in different legal systems. Alternatively, a comparatist can start with a question such as 'how do legal systems protect shareholders?' and then examine the different tools of different legal systems. Both of these approaches can be used to measure legal rules in a quantitative way. The first one is found in an article by Simeon Djankov, La Porta, and other colleagues on the law and economics of self-dealing.[109] They present a complex hypothetical case of a transaction between two companies to lawyers from seventy-two countries, and ask them to respond to questions such as: which body of the companies has to approve the transaction in question, or how could the transaction's validity be challenged? Then, Djankov et al. code this information using various indices and subindices. Finally, they find that this new dataset predicts stock market development, and generally works better than the initial La Porta et al. index.

The second functional approach has been used in the aforementioned project on Law, Finance and Development at the Centre for Business Research (CBR) in the University of Cambridge.[110] The overall aim of the CBR project was to review the mechanisms by which legal institutions influence financial systems and thereby affect economic development. For this purpose, the CBR researchers constructed time-series indices on shareholder, creditor, and worker protection in twenty-five countries. The selection of the variables considered that the same functional role may be performed in different jurisdictions by rules with different formal classifications. The main aim was, therefore, that the indices should get as close as possible to representing a coherent and meaningful characterisation of the law in any given jurisdiction. Subsequently, the CBR researchers examined the claim that the quality of the law is reflected in a country's financial development, which, however, has only been confirmed in some cases.[111]

Is one of these two techniques preferable? The first approach seems more straightforward, but there are at least two problems. First, evidence on the state of law as seen by practising lawyers is not available on a historical basis. Thus, the case-based approach cannot collect time-series data, making claims about causal relationships between law and finance doubtful. Second, this approach has to assume that the same type of problem exists in all of the legal systems examined. This is far from obvious, since social and economic structures differ widely between countries.[112] Thus, instead of relying on just one case, a comprehensive index is better able to capture how different legal tools may reflect different types of problems.

However, the second approach, too, has its shortcomings: the index construction and the coding of variables may aim to be as objective as possible, but since the legal world is very complex it inevitably involves some subjective

---

[109] Djankov et al. 2008.
[110] See www.cbr.cam.ac.uk/research/programme2/project2-20.htm as well as A 3 and C 2, above.
[111] Summary in Siems and Deakin 2010.
[112] For the critique of functionalism see ch. 2 at C 3, above.

element. Once the data are collected, the most common procedure is to aggregate the numbers of all variables. This, however, raises the question of whether all variables are really equally important. Also, the same variable may play a completely different functional role in different countries, or different variables may play the same role, with their relative importance varying from one context to another.[113] The possible time dimension, though useful, also creates further challenges, since the development of black letter legal rules needs to be supplemented by data that capture changes to the political and social climate.[114]

2. Measuring courts and other legal and political institutions

The measurements by La Porta et al. may also be regarded as unsatisfactory if one takes the view that the most important factor is not the details of the positive legal rules but the quality of political and legal institutions, and, in particular, the strength and quality of law enforcement. This interest in the operation of courts and other institutions partly overlaps with socio-legal comparative law.[115] In the research addressed here, however, the focus is not on interpretation and understanding, but on improving these institutions, and thus developing 'benchmarks' or 'indicators'.[116] Paradigmatic is the following statement from the World Bank's website:

> Measuring the performance of the various elements of the justice sector is crucial for any justice reform. Empirical research and court statistics are key in this context. Benchmarks and comparative data are invaluable tools for justice reform practitioners working on evaluations.[117]

It is difficult to establish what measures are the appropriate ones. At a general level, one can distinguish between input and output measures.[118] For example, input measures may refer to the financial resources provided to a particular enforcement authority, and output measures may aggregate the fines imposed by this authority. Yet it is not clear what comparing input measures tells us about the quality of this enforcement authority, since good financial resources may also just be wasted. But comparing output measures may also be not very meaningful if a particular jurisdiction has more violations of the law simply due to external circumstances.

In detail, the efficiency of courts is a natural point of interest for governments and other policy actors. The Netherlands Council for the Judiciary assigned a study to compare the judicial system of the Netherlands with that in

---

[113] Ahlering and Deakin 2007: 884.

[114] For example, see the time-series on property rights, political liberty and stability by Fedderke et al. 2001; Fedderke and Garlick 2011.

[115] See ch. 6 at B, above.   [116] Davis et al. 2012. See also www.worldbank.org/ljr.

[117] See http://go.worldbank.org/LRFA0Q06E1.

[118] See, e.g., Easterly 2006: 159; Fukuyama 2013: 355–6.

other countries,[119] and the European Commission for the Efficiency of Justice (CEPEJ) undertakes a regular evaluation of the judicial systems of the Council of Europe's Member States.[120] These two studies contain comparative information on the number of lawyers, judges, cases etc., but they also have a clear policy dimension. For instance, the Dutch study includes a performance index calculated by the number of concluded cases per judge and per Euro spent on the judiciary, and the European study reports data such as the public budget allocated to all courts per inhabitant, the level of computerisation of courts, the number of cases violating the right to a speedy trial, and the clearance rate of litigious and non-litigious civil cases.

Two private organisations provide more general quantitative information on political and legal institutions. The Freedom House produces the report on Freedom in the World, which rates from one to seven the political rights and civil liberties of countries.[121] The Political Risk Services has designed a Political Risk Index, including a variable which rates countries from zero to six on law and order.[122] One of the law and order sub-variables examines the independence of the judiciary, based, for instance, on questions such as 'are judges appointed and dismissed in a fair and unbiased manner?' and 'is the judiciary subject to interference from the executive branch of government or from other political, economic, or religious influences?'. In addition, the 'law and order' variable incorporates other data, such as the crime rates of countries.

This combination of legal data with non-legal ones has been criticised.[123] More generally, the critique is similar to that of other indices. On the one hand, this concerns the choice of indicators. Since the variables of the Freedom House and the Political Risk Services use a Western model of law, rights and democracy as a benchmark, they can only tell readers how different other countries are to the West. This is also a topic that will re-emerge in the context of comparative law and development.[124] On the other hand, it is difficult to know whether and how to aggregate data. Here, the criticism is therefore that categories such as 'law and order' and 'rule of law' are 'too broad and fuzzy to contain meaningful information'.[125]

These and other indicators are also discussed in a book chapter on 'the quality of judges' by Sandra Oxner, a retired Canadian judge.[126] Oxner develops her own criteria on issues such as appointment, training, performance, discipline, and dismissal of judges. The Annex of her chapter applies these criteria to

---

[119] Blank et al. 2004: 7.

[120] See www.coe.int/t/dghl/cooperation/cepej/evaluation/. The most recent version is CEPEJ 2012.

[121] See www.freedomhouse.org/report/freedom-world-2013/checklist-questions.

[122] See www.prsgroup.com/ICRG_Methodology.aspx. Other variables, too, include law-related questions: e.g. economists have used the 'expropriation' variable in order to measure the strength of property rights, cf. G. Xu 2011: 343–4.

[123] Davis 2004: 149–50.   [124] See ch. 10 at C 3, below.

[125] Voigt 2009b; also Skaaning 2010.   [126] Oxner 2003.

the judiciary of Canada, Pakistan, the Philippines, South Africa, Trinidad and Tobago, Uganda and the Ukraine. The 'coding' is done with '+' and '−', without aggregating the scores and ranking the countries in question (though it can be seen that Canada performs very well).

There has also been academic research on similar topics in various fields. In political science, scholars are interested in the functioning of institutions of law-making and law enforcement, including courts. For example, with respect to legislators, one can research their 'performance' in terms of number of parliamentary laws passed, and then try to establish whether this is related to similarities in parliamentary models, or more a result of socio-economic developments.[127] And, with respect to bureaucracies, one can develop categories of those factors that account for a professional and effective government.[128]

Research in political science may also involve the use of comparative measurements in order to make policy recommendations. For instance, one of Stefan Voigt's papers is interested in the optimal number of high courts. In terms of expertise, having a number of specialised high courts may be useful, but they may also lead to an incoherent legal system. Using data from 138 countries, Voigt finds that a larger number of high courts never seems to have a positive economic effect, and that, in some instances, the outcome is negative.[129]

In legal research, for example, Howell Jackson and Mark Roe have challenged the view that it is effective private enforcement of investor protection, and not public enforcement, which stimulates financial market development.[130] For this purpose, they used resource-based enforcement data – such as the staffing of securities regulators per population, and their budgets per GDP – as indicators for the strength of public enforcement, finding that it is more important than private liability rules, and about as important as disclosure rules, in explaining financial outcomes.[131]

Two articles by Simeon Djankov and colleagues, all of them economists, deal with the efficiency of courts and the entry procedures of start-up firms across countries.[132] The main focus is on the speed of proceedings. In the article on courts, this relates to the duration of trial and of enforcement in hypothetical cases to evict a tenant for non-payment of rent and to collect a bounced cheque; in the article on regulation of entry, they examine the number of procedures, official time, and official cost that a start-up must bear before it can operate legally. Table 7.7, below, provides an extract from the former article.

In total, the article reports data on 109 countries, but even the data on seven countries can invite a number of observations. The general picture is that the

---

[127] See Pettai and Madise 2007 (data from three Baltic states from 1992 to 2004; finding that the challenges of renewed state-building and EU accession steered them in same direction). See also ch. 11 at B 1, below.

[128] Discussion of possible criteria in Fukuyama 2013.

[129] Voigt 2012. For a more general discussion about specialised courts see Garoupa and Gómez Ligüerre 2011: 321–334.

[130] This relates to La Porta et al. 2006.

[131] Jackson and Roe 2009.   [132] Djankov et al. 2003a; Djankov et al. 2002.

Table 7.7 Duration (days) of court proceedings to evict tenant (to collect cheque) (extract)[1]

	Duration until completion of service of process	Duration of trial	Duration of enforcement	Total duration
China	15 (15)	105 (120)	60 (45)	180 (180)
France	16 (16)	75 (75)	135 (90)	226 (181)
Germany	29 (29)	191 (61)	111 (64)	331 (154)
Poland	90 (90)	720 (730)	270 (180)	1080 (1000)
Uganda	1 (14)	7 (40)	21 (45)	29 (99)
United Kingdom	14 (14)	73 (73)	28 (14)	115 (101)
United States	6 (23)	33 (17)	10 (14)	49 (54)

[1] Djankov et al. 2003a: 494–9.

common law countries (UK, US and Uganda) have quicker proceedings than the civil law ones, which is also the general finding of their study. The normative view that Djankov et al. take is that lengthy proceedings are harmful, since they make the enforceability of contracts more difficult. As they found that the number of procedural steps determines the duration of judicial proceedings, they recommended that countries reduce formalism in civil procedure. This normative dimension of the Djankov study is reinforced by the fact that it found its way into the World Bank's World Development Report 2002,[133] and subsequently also into its Doing Business Reports.[134]

A critical assessment has to address at least three problems. First, Djankov et al. seem to assume that it is good to have cheap courts which decide many cases in a short period of time. But is this really desirable? The apparent danger of this kind of 'justice light' is that the quality of decision suffers. Thus, one could equally make the opposite case, namely, that it is preferable to have a well-funded court system where judges can take their time to decide a few cases as well as possible. Or, considering Table 7.7, if trials take 720 days (Poland), this may be too long, but perhaps seven days (Uganda) may be too hasty.

Second, the aim of the Djankov et al. study is to measure the operation of courts. However, in many countries there are special laws to protect tenants. Thus, merely considering the duration of proceedings does not provide general information on courts, but it may mainly show the strength of tenant protection. In particular, this is apparent for the three continental European countries in Table 7.7, where the duration of proceedings to evict a tenant exceeds the one to collect a cheque.[135] Thus, what would be needed would be a typical case that plays a similar role in such diverse societies as China, France, Uganda, and the US. This leads us back to the problem of functionalism and the limits of using problem cases as a starting point for comparative law.[136]

[133] World Development Report 2002: 117–32.   [134] See 4, below.
[135] For more details see Kern 2007: 12–3.   [136] See ch. 2 at C 3, above.

Third, one may raise doubts about the accuracy of information on the duration of judicial proceedings. Djankov et al. present their results as objective information indicating the number of days proceedings take in various countries. Yet, the data are collected by way of questionnaires sent to lawyers of the Lex Mundi network of law firms.[137] Thus, these statements about the duration of trials indicate the *perceived* duration of trials from the perspective of the lawyers. For example, it could be the case that there are historical contingencies explaining why, in Poland, judges and courts are not popular and therefore, when asked about the duration of trials, lawyers assume that everything takes a long time. Thus, these subjective assessments need to be scrutinised more closely.[138] Of course, using perceptions may also have its advantages, as discussed in the following section.

3. Surveying perceptions about law and its enforcement

Comparative survey methods are frequently used in the social sciences.[139] They are also an important tool for governments and other policy actors. For instance, the EU has an obvious interest in measuring the effectiveness of European integration, and therefore sponsors surveys and other data-collections such as Eurobarometer, Eurostat, the European Social Survey, and the EU Survey of Income and Living Conditions.[140]

Surveys related to questions of comparative law are also not a new phenomenon and often go beyond scholarly work. In 1976, Henry Ehrmann's book on *Comparative Legal Cultures* already reported whether, according to opinion polls, people in England, France, Germany and the US had confidence in their courts.[141] Sandra Oxner explains that, since 1981, the UN has developed comparative standards of judicial independence, sometimes using surveys to measure them.[142] Individual governments are also interested in such data: according to a study by the European Commission for the Efficiency of Justice (CEPEJ), thirty-three out of forty-six Member States of the Council of Europe survey court users or legal professionals in order to assess the functioning of the judicial system.[143] A prominent example of an NGO conducting a comparative survey on a law-related question is Transparency International's Global Corruption Barometer, based on a survey of more than 70,000 households.[144]

Frequently, general surveys also contain questions on legal topics. For example, the World Values Survey, which is based on 256,000 interviews across the

---

[137] See www.lexmundi.com/.

[138] For a similar point see Eisenberg 2009 (criticising the survey of the US State Chamber Institute for Legal Reform on the tort liability systems of US states).

[139] See Hantrais 2009: 26, 49 and ch. 11 at C 3, below.

[140] See Hantrais 2009: 17, 130. There are also corresponding surveys in other regions and at the international level: see, e.g., www.issp.org/ (International Social Survey Programme); www.afrobarometer.org/; www.latinobarometro.org/; www.asianbarometer.org/.

[141] Ehrmann 1976: 51–2.   [142] Oxner 2003: 311, 314.   [143] CEPEJ 2012: 95.

[144] See www.transparency.org/policy_research/surveys_indices/gcb.

world, asks participants to rate from one to four whether they have confidence in their justice system, and whether they think that human rights are respected in their country.[145] Similar, but restricted to European countries, is the European Social Survey. Here, too, there is, inter alia, a question which asks participants to rate on a scale from zero to ten whether they have trust in their legal system:[146] for example, in Germany, Sweden, and the Netherlands the majority of the population considers courts as trustworthy, whereas only a minority does so in France and Belgium, and in Italy, Spain and the United Kingdom there is approximately an equal split.[147]

Academic research, too, has taken an interest in these surveys. Bruno Deffains and Ludivine Roussey have examined what determines the level of trust in judicial institutions, as measured by the World Value Survey. Using data on public resources devoted to the judiciary, they show that investing in such resources pays off.[148] Another project, called Euro-Justis, specifically aims to create indicators that measure confidence in criminal justice.[149] The data collection of these new indicators is conducted as part of the European Social Survey. The overall rationale of this project is that 'the police and criminal courts need public support and institutional legitimacy if they are to operate effectively and fairly',[150] though one could also argue in favour of the reverse causal relationship.

Another academic project with a focus on institutional data is called Measuring Access to Justice.[151] It seeks to capture different elements of justice by way of surveys. For example, the coding of procedural justice is composed of eight questions, such as 'Were you able to express your views and feelings during the process?', 'Was the process objective and unbiased?' and 'Did you find the process fair?'. The aim is to use these indicators for comparative research, focusing on specific circumstances. The example provided on the project website is based on a survey of 300 Bhutanese refugees who experienced crimes in a refugee camp in Nepal. Table 7.8, below, presents the mean results, distinguishing between the quality of the procedure and the outcome, and then various sub-categories of justice.

A further group of surveys is based on the perceptions of firm managers. For instance, the World Bank's World Business Environment Survey (WBES) 2000 surveyed over 10,000 firms in 80 countries. Topics related to law included taxes and regulations, the functioning of judiciary, corruption, collateral

---

[145] See www.wvsevsdb.com/wvs/WVSData.jsp. See also Ivanyna and Shah 2011 (constructing a new governance index based on these data).

[146] See http://ess.nsd.uib.no/.   [147] Loth 2009: 268.

[148] Deffains and Roussey 2012. For a similar result see Green 2011 (expectations-based measures of the World Values Survey tend to have positive effect on wealth).

[149] See www.eurojustis.eu/, in particular the 2011 report available at www.eurojustis.eu/fotoweb/HEUNI_Report_70_revised_09112011.pdf.

[150] Jackson et al. 2011.

[151] Tilburg Institute for Interdisciplinary Studies of Civil Law and Conflict Resolution Systems 2009. See also www.measuringaccesstojustice.com.

Table 7.8 Measuring access to justice in a refugee camp in Nepal[1]

	Dimension	Mean
Quality of the procedure	Procedural justice	3.26
	Interpersonal justice	3.76
	Informational justice	3.49
	Restorative justice	2.75
Quality of the outcome	Retributive justice	2.08
	Restorative justice	2.19
	Utilitarianism	2.27
	Informational justice	2.91

[1] *Source:* www.measuringaccesstojustice.com/index.php/main-parent-page/current-projects/measuring-access-to-justice-in-a-refugee-camp-in-nepal/ (data from November 2010).

requirements, property rights, public services, legal predictability and government intervention.[152] A successor of this survey is administered by the Enterprise Analysis Unit of the World Bank, again covering a broad range of topics, such as corruption, legal infrastructure, and crime. For instance, one of the questions asks participants whether they agree or disagree that the court system of their country is 'fair, impartial and uncorrupted'.[153] The World Economic Forum's (WEF) Global Competitiveness Reports are also based on an executive opinion survey. Participants are asked to rank their legal system from one to seven on questions such as 'is the judiciary independent from political influences of members of government, citizens, or firms?' and 'are property rights clearly defined and well protected by law?'.[154]

A critical analysis of this survey-based research first needs to address who was asked, for it can make a crucial difference to the results: for example, did the survey ask the general public, managers and executives, or a specific group, such as refugees in a camp in Nepal? This also has a normative dimension. For instance, the business surveys may have the bias that the law is only seen as a way of facilitating businesses, potentially disregarding other interests. Second, a similar issue arises for the questions that are included in the survey. For instance, the World Bank studies have been criticised as mainly being interested in the protection of property rights, and not in the equal application of the law.[155] Third, there can be problems with the collection of survey data. Naturally, participants may be reluctant to disclose participation in illegal behaviour,

[152] See http://go.worldbank.org/RV060VBJU0.
[153] See www.enterprisesurveys.org. Another survey, the Business Environment and Enterprise Performance Survey (BEEPS), has been jointly undertaken by the World Bank and the European Bank for Reconstruction and Development (EBRD): see www.ebrd.com/pages/research/economics/data/beeps.shtml.
[154] See www.weforum.org/reports.
[155] Perry-Kessaris 2011. Similarly Krever 2013 (neo-liberal conception of law).

such as corruption.[156] A survey on variables about judicial independence also explains:

> It cannot be completely excluded that some questionnaire respondents pursue their own agenda and have an incentive to make reality fit to it: a loyal citizen could try to make his country look better than it really is, whereas a political activist striving for improvement might try to make his or her country look worse than it really is.[157]

As far as terms such as 'fair' or 'just' are used, there is also the risk that participants understand these terms in a dissimilar way. This is a particular problem for comparative research. Sceptics point out that participants are typically coloured by cultural differences and recent economic performance.[158] Moreover, comparative survey research often has to draft questions in different languages, the problem being that even small lexical and grammatical variations can make a difference.[159]

Fourth, it has been suggested that survey participants often give 'top-of-the-head answers' based on stereotypical views about, say, the government or the judiciary.[160] These answers may therefore be unreliable given the complexity of these institutions – unless one tried to develop more precise indicators that showed how people relate to the justice system.[161] Moreover, examining the impact of legal reforms on perceived corruption,[162] for instance, may not be read as showing that law matters for the level of corruption, since even a 'placebo reform' may have changed the perceptions of the participants. It is therefore difficult to say whether cross-country differences in perceived corruption (or other legal topics) are the result of differences in laws and institutions.

Thus, overall, one has to be sceptical: while surveys can provide interesting information, there are good reasons to be cautious as to whether perceptions can really be used to assess the quality of legal systems across countries.

4. Combined approaches

Scholars and policy actors have combined indicators and approaches in different ways. Some of these combinations are mainly aggregates of data collected by other organisations. For example, in a paper on 'benchmarking competitiveness', Jeffrey Sachs and colleagues constructed indices based on data from the Freedom House, the European Bank of Reconstruction and Development, the Heritage foundation, plus their own survey data.[163] The report on Economic Freedom of the World, published by the Fraser Institute, uses data from the World Economic Forum, the World Bank and the Political

---

[156] Perry-Kessaris 2003: 688.   [157] Feld and Voigt 2003: 505.
[158] Kurtz and Schrank 2007; Hantrais 2009: 82–3.
[159] Hantrais 2009: 78–81. See also ch. 11 at C 3, below.   [160] Toharia 2001: 91, 95.
[161] Hertogh 2010: 153 (as opposed to mere level of trust or confidence).
[162] See the study by Buscaglia 2001.   [163] Sachs et al. 2000.

Risk Services.[164] Well-known is Transparency International's Corruption Perception Index, which draws on seventeen sources, including, again, data from the Freedom House, the Political Risk Services, and the World Economic Forum, inter alia.[165] Most prominent are the World Bank Governance Indicators (WBGI), developed by Daniel Kaufmann and colleagues.[166] The WBGI contain aggregate indicators on voice and accountability, political stability and absence of violence, government effectiveness, regulatory quality, rule of law, and control of corruption, amongst others, and is based on research by the Freedom House, Political Risk Services and Transparency International.

The WBGI play an important role in the promotion of 'rule of law' in developing countries and transition economies.[167] However, it is usually also acknowledged that quantitative data alone are not always sufficient, and that they have to be supplemented by a qualitative impact assessment of the law.[168] This can also be seen in the diagnostic project by the United States Agency for International Development (USAID) on the Commercial Law and Legal Institutions Reform Project in Eastern Europe and Eurasia (C-LIR). The aim of this project was to evaluate the legal reforms after the fall of communism, and the website provides country reports that consist of a score, plus narrative reports on various areas of commercial law.[169]

Studies that combine data collected by various other studies raise the question of which studies to include and how to aggregate the data – the results often being very sensitive to small changes.[170] Moreover, it is preferable to use on primary data. Thus, the following discusses how three projects have combined original data on the coding of legal rules, the measurement of institutional quality, and/or survey data.

A first example is a comparative study by ZERP, an institute at the University of Bremen, Germany, on the conveyancing services market in the EU.[171] The legal rules on selling immovable property are relatively diverse, since, in Southern and Western Europe, notaries play a crucial role ('the Latin notary countries'), whereas in England and Ireland their tasks may be performed by solicitors, with mixed models in the Netherlands and the Nordic countries.[172] In order to analyse the different regulatory systems, the ZERP study constructed indices of legal rules. Using data on the costs of conveyancing services in eighteen countries, it could be shown that countries with a higher degree of regulation also tend to exhibit higher fees. Of course, fees are not the only consideration

---

[164] See www.freetheworld.com/.

[165] For further details see www.transparency.org/research/cpi/overview. In addition, Transparency International produces its own Global Corruption Barometer: see 3, above.

[166] See www.govindicators.org/. For a critical assessment see Thomas 2010.

[167] For comparative law and development see ch. 10, below.

[168] See Taylor 2007: 88.   [169] See http://egateg.usaid.gov/bizclir/.

[170] Hawken and Munck 2011.   [171] ZERP 2007. See also Schmid 2009.

[172] See generally on notaries Clark 2002: para. 42; Mattei et al. 2009: 145, 152; International Union of Notaries, available at www.uinl.org.

that matters for conveyancing services. Thus, the study constructed an 'Overall Service Assessment' variable with sub-variables on choice, quality, certainty and speed. The data for this variable were collected by way of a survey, answered by about 700 persons from twenty-one Member States. But, here again, the result was that a high level of regulation, in particular in the Latin notary countries, leads to low scores in the ranking of those countries.

Unsurprisingly, the Council of Notaries of the European Union was unhappy with these findings. In a press release, it accused the ZERP report of lacking 'the necessary technical accuracy and scientific rigour'.[173] To support this argument, it referred to a study by Peter Murray;[174] however, the latter study was explicitly based on a 'traditional comparative methodology' – thus, it was hardly plausible to attack the more empirical ZERP project for an alleged lack of 'scientific rigour'. In addition, the Council of Notaries was unconvinced by the survey evidence of the ZERP study, since many replies were from persons that were likely to have a conflict of interest, such as real estate agents. A possible response could be that the notaries, too, have a natural conflict of interest. Yet, it also shows more generally that surveys need to consider that different groups may have different preferences, and that it may therefore be crucial for a survey to disclose how the views of these groups differed.

The second example is the Rule of Law Index of the World Justice Project (WJP), a non-profit organisation launched by the American Bar Association. The WJP Rule of Law Index consists of eight factors with forty-eight sub-factors, in total over 400 variables.[175] It is based on a general survey of 1,000 respondents in the three largest cities of each country with data collected from 'qualified respondents', usually lawyers and law professors. Thus, it combines more subjective with more objective data, while not trying to code details of black letter rules. Table 7.9, below, presents an extract of some of the results, highlighting the 'top five' countries for each of the eight factors.

The WJP does not calculate an overall ranking of all countries, but – considering the top five ranks – it can be seen that Denmark, Finland, Norway and Sweden perform best with six top ranks, followed by Australia, the Netherlands, and Singapore with three top ranks, New Zealand with two top ranks, and Austria, Germany, Hong Kong, Japan and the UAE with one top rank. It would also be interesting to see how exactly the general survey data differ from the more objective expert responses – for instance, it is worth considering that, in oppressive political regimes, one may not expect totally honest answers to questions about the quality of political and legal institutions. However, the WJP dataset does not provide further analysis, apart from saying that 'for those questions asked to both groups . . . , the correlation is very high (above 0.8 in most cases)'.[176]

---

[173] See www.cnue-nouvelles.be/en/000/actualites/cp-zerp-29-01-08-en.pdf.
[174] Murray 2007.   [175] See http://worldjusticeproject.org/methodology.
[176] www.worldjusticeproject.org/?q=faq.

Table 7.9 WJP Rule of Law Index, selected countries (min 0, max 1)[1]

	F1	F2	F 3	F 4	F5	F6	F7	F8
Australia	0.88	0.90	0.86	0.84	0.84	0.83	0.72	0.72
Austria	0.82	0.77	0.89	0.82	0.80	0.84	0.74	0.75
Belgium	0.78	0.78	0.84	0.81	0.67	0.70	0.68	0.72
Brazil	0.62	0.52	0.64	0.69	0.54	0.56	0.55	0.49
Canada	0.78	0.81	0.88	0.78	0.84	0.79	0.72	0.75
China	0.36	0.52	0.78	0.35	0.42	0.41	0.43	0.54
Denmark	0.93	0.95	0.91	0.91	0.82	0.85	0.79	0.87
Finland	0.89	0.93	0.92	0.90	0.84	0.82	0.79	0.87
France	0.80	0.80	0.84	0.79	0.75	0.76	0.68	0.69
Georgia	0.48	0.77	0.84	0.61	0.47	0.63	0.61	0.66
Germany	0.82	0.82	0.86	0.80	0.73	0.73	0.80	0.76
Hong Kong	0.73	0.89	0.93	0.71	0.82	0.75	0.71	0.76
India	0.61	0.32	0.39	0.56	0.48	0.41	0.45	0.44
Japan	0.80	0.84	0.89	0.78	0.82	0.87	0.77	0.68
Malaysia	0.57	0.69	0.86	0.50	0.48	0.52	0.57	0.61
Netherlands	0.86	0.93	0.86	0.84	0.90	0.83	0.80	0.80
New Zealand	0.87	0.92	0.87	0.86	0.84	0.82	0.76	0.79
Norway	0.90	0.94	0.87	0.90	0.84	0.83	0.82	0.85
Russia	0.31	0.39	0.49	0.47	0.41	0.45	0.50	0.40
Singapore	0.73	0.91	0.93	0.73	0.67	0.80	0.79	0.87
South Korea	0.66	0.74	0.82	0.76	0.74	0.67	0.72	0.76
Sweden	0.92	0.96	0.89	0.93	0.93	0.89	0.78	0.82
Thailand	0.53	0.41	0.63	0.66	0.50	0.51	0.43	0.59
UAE	0.55	0.74	0.91	0.47	0.44	0.65	0.60	0.75
UK	0.79	0.80	0.84	0.78	0.78	0.79	0.72	0.75
US	0.77	0.78	0.83	0.73	0.77	0.70	0.65	0.65

[1] *Source:* The World Justice Project, Rule of Law Index 2012. The factors are: (1) limited government powers; (2) absence of corruption; (3) order and security; (4) fundamental rights; (5) open government; (6) effective regulatory enforcement; (7) access to civil justice; (8) effective criminal justice. Another factor (informal justice) is not included in the index.

Third, the World Bank's Doing Business Report deserves a more detailed treatment. This report, which is annually updated since 2004, examines eleven areas of law and ranks legal systems accordingly (see Table 7.10).[177] The data are described as 'objective measures of business regulations' – thus differing from the more subjective WJP Rule of Law and related indicators. In detail, most of the sub-categories use codings of legal rules, as developed by La

[177] See www.doingbusiness.org/. The categories are 'starting a business', 'dealing with construction permits', 'getting electricity', 'registering property', 'getting credit', 'protecting investors', 'paying taxes', 'trading across borders', 'enforcing contracts', 'resolving insolvency', and 'employing workers' (the latter not being used for the rankings).

Table 7.10 Legal systems ranked in terms of ease of doing business (extract)[1]

Top 10	Ranks 11–20	Selected countries	Bottom 10
1 Singapore	11 Finland	22 Saudi Arabia	176 Niger
2 Hong Kong	12 Malaysia	24 Japan	177 Côte d'Ivoire
3 New Zealand	12 Sweden	28 Switzerland	178 Guinea
4 United States	14 Iceland	31 Netherlands	179 Guinea-Bissau
5 Denmark	15 Ireland	34 France	180 Venezuela
6 Norway	16 Taiwan	52 Rwanda	181 Congo, Dem. Rep.
7 United Kingdom	17 Canada	91 China	182 Eritrea
8 South Korea	18 Thailand	112 Russia	183 Congo, Republic
9 Georgia	19 Mauritius	130 Brazil	184 Chad
10 Australia	20 Germany	132 India	185 Central African Rep.

[1] Doing Business Report 2013, ranking available at www.doingbusiness.org/rankings (data from June 2012).

Porta and colleagues.[178] Moreover, for some questions, 'time-and-motion indicators' are used: for instance, for questions on the time and duration of incorporating a business, this would include time spent getting licences and enforcing contracts.[179]

These reports have been highly influential. The World Bank uses its numerical benchmarks of legal rules in order to put pressure on developing and transition economies, which often depend on the World Bank's funding. Some countries have also deliberately pursued the strategy of improving their ranks. For instance, the front page of Georgia's main government website advertises Georgia as the 'World's Number One Reformer 2005–2012', Saudi Arabia uses the Doing Business ranking to assert that it has the 'most business-friendly regulatory environment in the Middle East', and Rwanda also promotes its high regional rank and reform efforts.[180]

In the ranking, common law countries perform very well: the top four legal systems all belong to the common law, as do the majority of the top ten countries. For civil law countries, a possible reaction may be to try to 'transplant' the common law. An example of this takes place in Dubai, where the Dubai International Financial Centre (DIFC) was allowed to create its own 'common law courts' for civil and commercial matters, with judges trained in common law jurisdictions.[181]

Alternatively, one can take the view that the ranking shows that the World Bank's method suffers from a common law bias. For example, as Germany,

---

[178] See 1, above.   [179] See 2, above.

[180] See www.georgia.gov.ge/; www.sagia.gov.sa/en/Why-Saudi-Arabia/Key-Benefits--/Easy-Place-To-Do-Business/; www.rdb.rw/media-centre/press-releases/doing-business-2012-report-rwanda-3rd-easiest-place-to-do-business-in-africa-and-2nd-five-year-top-global-reformer.html.

[181] See www.difccourts.ae/. A similar concept is that of 'charter cities': see http://chartercities.org/. See also ch. 8 at B 2 (b), below (for Rwanda's shift from civil to common law).

Japan, and the Netherlands perform very well in the WJP Rule of Law Index (see Table 7.9), the Doing Business rank may seem somehow implausible. Expressive criticism has come from France, challenging the methods and findings of the Doing Business Reports.[182] Apart from details on the choice and coding of legal variables, the criticism concerns the very idea of assessing law with a 'doing business' benchmark:

> French law is humanistic in nature, protecting the rights of the individual. It has played a key role in Europe and throughout the world in the dissemination of fundamental human rights. The Civil Code has inspired the belief that the law is there, first and foremost, to protect social peace and the citizens' freedom and will.[183]

In Germany the associations of lawyers, judges and notaries have set up a website in order to promote German law[184] – apparently in reaction to an initiative by the Law Society of England and Wales promoting England and Wales as 'the jurisdiction of choice'.[185] Moreover, a number of French and German associations, sponsored by their governments, have established a Civil Law Initiative that has produced a report on 'Continental law: global, predictable, flexible, cost-effective'.[186] This report lists a number of reasons why the law and courts of civil law countries may be superior to the common law approach. For instance, one finds the following statements:

> Continental law is characterized by statutes and codification . . . Because of such codification, continental law is accessible . . . In common law countries, the search for the applicable law often requires consulting a long series of court decisions in order to find an appropriate precedent – if one even exists . . . The courts in continental law countries are also required to explain the reasons for their decisions. In contrast, in common law countries, when jury trials are used, juries do not have to give the reasons for their decision. Continental legal systems have adopted a simplified and streamlined law of evidence, which, among other advantages, obviates the slow and costly pre-trial exchanges of evidence conducted under pre-trial discovery.[187]

Thus, inter alia, the civil law is seen as more certain than the common law. For this purpose, the Civil Law Initiative also aims to construct a Legal Certainty Index dealing with the predictability, stability, and security of the law.[188]

---

[182] Report by Association Henri Capitant des Amis de La Culture Juridique Française, available at www.henricapitant.org/node/16; Group on 'attractivité economique du droit', website at www.gip-recherche-justice.fr/aed.htm. See also Michaels 2009a: 773.

[183] Fauvarque-Cosson and Kerhuel 2009: 822.   [184] See www.lawmadeingermany.de.

[185] See www.eversheds.com/documents/LawSocietyEnglandAndWalesJurisdictionOfChoice.pdf.

[186] French/English version available at www.fondation-droitcontinental.org/; German/English version available at www.kontinentalesrecht.de/.

[187] Ibid. at 4, 22.

[188] See www.fondation-droitcontinental.org/jcms/c_12115/index-de-la-securite-juridique and Raynouard and Kerhuel 2011.

Furthermore, even within the World Bank, the Doing Business Report is not beyond criticism. Other departments of the World Bank have been responsible for the World Business Environment Survey (WBES), the Business Environment and Enterprise Performance Survey (BEEPS), and the World Bank Governance Indicators (WBGI) (see above). The Doing Business project has also been the subject of a report by the World Bank's Independent Evaluation Group.[189] This report discussed various shortcomings in the choice of variables and its aggregation. Yet, in the end, it just led to a modest change to the Doing Business Report: since 2010, the 'employing workers' sub-index has been excluded from the ranking; thus, worker protection is no longer seen as negative per se.[190]

Of course, worker protection is not the only topic covered by the Doing Business Report that has advantages and disadvantages. For instance, contrary to the report, entry barriers or other aspects of formality can have a social value,[191] and paying taxes is not only a burden since businesses may benefit from a functioning well-funded government.[192] Another example is secured credit: according to the Doing Business Report secured credit is good since it provides creditors with a quick method of compensation; however, debtors may well be concerned that this sidesteps the need for due process.[193] Of course, such arguments can now also be raised against the Civil Law Initiative: for example, while legal certainty is valuable, it may make the law less adaptable.[194]

Finally, the Doing Business Report is problematic since it does not set the right incentives for countries to enact laws that would substantially improve their legal systems. Three variants of this argument can be distinguished. First, as the examples of Saudi-Arabia, Georgia, and Rwanda show, it is relatively easy to rise in the rankings if a country wants to do so. The reason is that indices of legal rules cannot consider all details of the law but have to rely on proxies.[195] Thus, countries can focus on adopting these specific provisions, while leaving the vast majority of their legal systems underdeveloped.

Second, the World Bank's ranking puts together countries in which the socio-economic, cultural, and natural contexts of the law are completely different. A law-maker may therefore face the dilemma that, whilst it knows that a specific recommendation of the Doing Business Report does not make sense in its country, it may also recognise the importance of the rankings and still adopt this measure – contrary to the public interest.

Third, the Doing Business Report is based on an exaggerated belief in the importance of legal rules. To illustrate, the 2008 report explains that many Italians still live with their parents because the long time it takes to evict tenants leads to an unwillingness to let property. Yet, an Italian observer rightly explains that economic and cultural explanations are, by far, more plausible.[196]

---

[189] World Bank Independent Evaluation Group 2008.
[190] For the discussion see Michaels 2009a: 774–5.
[191] Arruñada 2007: 730. See also 2, above.   [192] Aguilera and Williams 2009: 1427.
[193] Davis 2010.   [194] For the latter see ch. 6 at A 2 (a), above.
[195] See 1, above.   [196] Alpa 2010: 81–82.

Moreover, empirical scholarship has suggested that other aspects, such as politics, culture, and capital account liberalisation, are more important for financial development than legal rules,[197] and there may also be cases where informal dispute resolution is preferred to the formal one[198] – topics to which we return in the context of comparative law and development in the next part of this book.

D. Conclusion

Almost a decade ago, a previous paper, also entitled 'numerical comparative law',[199] found it necessary to discuss the pros and cons of numerical comparative law at a general level, in particular the reductionist dimension of quantitative methods. Today, the focus has moved beyond such general points. As the examples of this chapter have shown, numerical comparative law can contribute to many core topics of comparative law, such as judicial comparative law, legal transplants, legal families, and comparisons as a basis for making policy recommendations.[200]

This does not mean that all of these studies are beyond doubt. In particular, it is not clear whether any one of three methods mentioned in the preface to this chapter (conducting surveys, counting empirical facts, coding legal rules) is the preferable one. Surveys provide interesting insights into perceptions about judicial comparative law, differences between legal systems, and the quality of legal rules. Yet, they have the inherent limitation that the general public, and even lawyers, may have a misleading view about the law and its enforcement. Thus, counting empirical facts may be preferable. For example, this may refer to cross-citations, the quantity of laws, or the number of days it takes to enforce a claim. Yet, here, we have the inherent problem that we cannot be certain what these numbers really tell us; thus, the challenge is the interpretation of possible causes and consequences. Finally, coding legal rules is akin to a black letter approach to law, having the advantage that it may actually tell us what the law is. For instance, this can be used to identify legal transplants, to evaluate the relevance of legal families, or to test whether formal legal rules really matter. Yet, such codings share the same problems as any black letter approach in disregarding the context and operation of the positive law.

Overall, it is therefore suggested that integrated approaches are most likely to provide a meaningful comparative picture. Of course, this does not mean that a comparatist cannot specialise in a particular approach to numerical comparative law. But, in any case, he or she also has to be aware of 'which conclusions can and cannot be drawn from statistics' – as already noted in the concluding paragraph of the 2005 article.[201]

---

[197] See Pagano and Volpin 2001; Stulz and Williamson 2003; Chinn and Ito 2006.
[198] See Buscaglia and Stephan 2005.   [199] Siems 2005.
[200] For non-quantitative research on these themes see A 1 (a), above; ch. 8, below; ch. 3 and ch. 4, above; ch. 2 at A 4, above.
[201] Siems 2005: 540.

Moreover, it is clear that quantitative approaches in law do not work in a vacuum. For example, as the experience of the La Porta et al. studies has shown,[202] misunderstanding the positive law can make corresponding quantitative measurements futile. It can also be useful to combine quantitative and qualitative approaches, thus more fully embracing the methods of other social sciences.[203]

---

[202] See C 1, above.   [203] See further ch. 11, below.

Part III
Global Comparative Law

The term 'globalisation' is not without problems. For example, William Twining warns us that it may foster 'generalisations that are exaggerated, false, meaningless, superficial, or ethnocentric'.[1] There is also the apparent risk of assuming that globalisation is only a recent phenomenon, when in fact one can identify many 'globalisations' throughout human history.[2]

In this book, the term 'global' is used in a pragmatic way to illustrate a number of interlinked topics. Thus, globalisation, as understood here, has various shades. For example, the term covers a variety of scales: some phenomena, such as the internet, may genuinely be global ones, but others may be about trends which are focused on the main economic centres, or on particular regions of the world.[3] There can also be diversity as regards the subject of globalisation. Typically, reference is made to tangible factors, such as the globalisation of trade, finance, production and labour.[4] But it may also be said that globalisation is mainly an intellectual construct, emphasising the impact of the ideas about globalisation.[5] Furthermore, there is variety in the countries and cultures that may be seen as the main drivers of globalisation: frequently, emphasis is put on the Westernisation or even Americanisation of other societies, but there may also be Asian and Islamic forms of globalisation.[6] Finally, things may be even more complex, as a taxonomy by Boaventura de Sousa Santos shows.[7] He distinguishes between hegemonic and counter-hegemonic globalisation, with two sub-categories for both of those. Hegemonic globalisation can be 'globalised localism', where particular local phenomena spread to other parts of the world (e.g. certain features of American culture and lifestyle); alternatively, it can be 'localised globalism', where local patterns change due to the impact of transnational imperatives (e.g. considering the influence of

---

[1] Twining 2009a: xviii.
[2] E.g. Steger 2009 refers to five globalisations (fifth to third millennia BC; fifteenth century AD; 1500–1700; 1700–1970; since 1970s).
[3] See also Hay 2011: 334–5 (globalisation or triadisation; globalisation or regionalisation).
[4] For data see, e.g, McGrew 2011: 297.
[5] See Hay 2011: 341. More generally for the definition of globalisation, see, e.g. Goldman 2008: 26–34.
[6] Glenn 2010a: 52–4.　　　[7] E.g. Santos 2002; Santos 2004.

multinational corporations). The two forms of counter-hegemonic globalisation are cosmopolitanism, and the common heritage of humankind, referring to cross-border solidarity among excluded groups on the one hand,[8] and global concerns such as the protection of the environment on the other.

Globalisation is of natural interest for comparative lawyers.[9] In the following, its various elements will re-appear under three main headings. Chapter 8 deals with 'legal transplants'. This chapter can be seen as an example of the argument that globalising trends are not merely phenomena that came about in the twentieth century, while also showing recent 'Westernisations' and 'Americanisations' of legal systems. Chapter 9 is about 'fading state borders', specifically in relation to the three variants of the convergence, regionalisation and transnationalisation of legal systems. Yet, here, it may also be questioned whether commonalities of legal rules are real global phenomena, and not predominantly an intellectual construct. Chapter 10 on comparative law and development illustrates how we do not only observe 'globalisation of law', but also 'law under globalisation'[10] – for example, how globalisation has an impact on demands for adherence to the rule of law. This chapter also addresses whether a counter-hegemonic form of legal globalisation may be feasible.

Throughout this part, examples are provided from different areas of law, given that the effects and implications of globalisation are likely to vary between them.[11] For example, in a relatively international field such as trade law, it seems reasonable to assume the emergence of transnational legal instruments. In other fields of private law the need for such rules may be less pronounced, but legal transplants may lead to some convergence of legal systems. Public law, too, may not be immune from such developments, but globalising trends may also be challenged as undermining state sovereignty. Similar concerns may arise in other fields of law that have a social dimension: for instance, the globalisation of labour law may lead to fears of a 'race to the bottom'.[12]

---

[8] Thus, this may be seen as 'vernacular', as opposed to 'elitist' cosmopolitanism. For this terminology see Remaud 2013.

[9] Similarly Riles 1999: 275 (task of comparative law to understand concrete artifacts of globalisation); Buxbaum 2009 (comparative law as a bridge between the nation-state and the global economy).

[10] For this distinction see Heydebrand 2001.

[11] See also Mattei et al. 2009: 2 (distinguishing between contract, tort and public law); Twining 2009b (on implications of globalisation for law).

[12] See also ch. 9 at A 2 (b), below.

8

Legal transplants

The literature on legal transplants has achieved a high level of complexity. It is therefore useful to start with an illustrative example. In 2005 the People's Republic of China enacted a new Companies Act that allowed shareholders to file a claim on behalf of the company against its directors ('derivative action'). Since these new rules were, to a large extent, based on the model of US law,[1] one may raise a number of questions, such as: why did China do this? Did the US have any involvement in it? Does this imported legal rule really work in China? Is this typical for the way law reform takes place, and is it advisable to do so?

Some of the literature approaches these topics from a conceptual perspective, whereas others are more interested in the empirical question where and how often legal transplants have occurred. Both perspectives are discussed in Sections A and B of this chapter, with a conclusion following in Section C.

There is also a close relationship between legal transplants and topics of Chapters 9 and 10: convergence of laws and law and development. For instance, in the example above, it seems to be the case that Chinese and US company law converged, and it may also be the case that China enacted this new provision in order to stimulate its economic development. As will be explained in these latter chapters, however, such a relationship between legal transplants, convergence and development may be a typical, but it is not a necessary, one.

A. Conceptual research on legal transplants

The research discussed in this section often distinguishes between different variants of legal transplants: for instance, between the reasons for their adoption and the way they work or do not work. Despite being predominantly conceptual, this research also has a normative dimension in supporting or rejecting at least some types of legal transplants.

1. The rationales for legal transplants

Legal transplants are typically thought of as a smart way of choosing a foreign legal model that has proven to work well. However, this is not the entire picture,

---

[1] See Siems 2008a: 217.

since not only the transplant country ('the importer'), but also the origin country ('the exporter') may have an interest in the transplant. Moreover, it can be the case that some legal transplants are not directly related to the benefits of either of the two countries involved.

(a) Aspired benefits for transplant country

A number of reasons can be advanced for why a country may deliberately adopt a legal rule from another legal system, also known as 'legal borrowing'.[2] The most intuitive category is that the transplant country rationally compares the laws of a number of countries and chooses 'the best one'. This may be a response to changed societal circumstances,[3] or it may have the aim of changing society in a particular way.[4] It may also be the case that the transplant country constantly seeks ways to improve its legal rules and, therefore, is keen on identifying legal rules that have already been successfully 'tested' abroad.[5] In the mid-nineteenth century, the German jurist Rudolph von Jhering put it as follows:

> The reception of foreign legal institutions is not a matter of nationality, but of usefulness and need. No one bothers to fetch a thing from afar when he has one as good or better at home, but only a fool would refuse quinine just because it didn't grow in his back garden.[6]

Today, such 'cost-saving transplants'[7] are often supported by law and economics reasoning. This reasoning is typically based on the construct of a competitive market for legal ideas with a potential drive towards the most efficient legal rules (i.e. a 'race to the top'). However, law and economics also asks us to consider the costs of enacting new laws, or of switching from one set of rules to another one.[8] Thus, similar to a firm's decision on whether to 'make or buy' a certain tool, it can show us when it is more efficient to 'make' one's own law, and when one should 'buy' it from elsewhere (i.e. use a transplant).[9]

A related topic is whether the transplants are or should be directed towards legal rules or policies. For 'applied' or 'legislative' comparative law,[10] the focus is on specific legal rules or their functional equivalents,[11] whereas the political

---

[2] For this terminology see Graziadei 2006: 456–461; Mattei et al. 2009: 241–2.

[3] Eörsi 1979: 564 (calling this 'adaptational reception').

[4] Nelken 2003a: 456 ('geared to fitting an imagined future'). See also Nelken 2001: 20 (relevance for periods of revolutionary and post-revolutionary nation-building).

[5] Michaels 2013a: 34. But see also Grajzl and Dimitrova-Grajzl 2009 (uncertainty may be greater for imported than for home-made law).

[6] As translated in Zweigert and Kötz 1998: 17. Similarly Markesinis 2000: 61 ('I believe there is a tendency, deeply rooted in human nature, to look around and borrow, where possible, good and tested ideas.').

[7] Miller 2003: 845.

[8] See Mattei 1997a: 19, 129–30, 239; Caterina in EE 2012: 191; Ogus 2002.

[9] For this analogy see Michaels 2013a. See also Michaels 2013b (suggesting that in these cases 'one size fits all' may be preferable).

[10] See Örücü 2007: 45–6, 427; de Cruz 2007: 13.

[11] See McBarnet 2002: 100 (distinction between mechanical and functional transplants).

science literature is more interested in international policy transfer and learning. But then these often overlap: for example, political scientists deal with questions such as the transferability of policies between societies, akin to the debate in comparative law on whether and how legal transplants 'work'.[12]

Another type of legal transplant is called the 'legitimacy-generating transplant'.[13] Here, the transplant country may be unable or unwilling to evaluate the potential benefits of all countries of the world. Rather, certain models may be *a priori* more appealing because they are seen as more prestigious, or because they signal a desired turn towards modernity.[14] It is also possible to develop further criteria that play a role. For example, the law-maker of a democratic country may want to consider the perceptions of the general public about rules from particular foreign countries, albeit that these may or may not be justified.[15]

Related to these, but slightly different, are 'entrepreneurial transplants'. This category refers to legal transplants initiated by those groups 'who reap benefits from investing their energy in learning and encouraging local adoption of a foreign legal model'.[16] Thus, it is important to recognise that a transplant may be beneficial to one domestic group, but can have a detrimental effect on another one. This also raises the general question of what is meant by saying that the transplant country chooses 'the best' or 'most efficient' foreign model. Experiences from other countries can be helpful but, given the diversity of possible aims and preferences, they do not provide law-makers with a clear-cut decision on which legal system to choose.

The final category includes those transplants that aspire to benefit both the transplant and the origin country. Such benefits can follow from the aim of reducing the 'transaction costs' that arise from differences between legal systems.[17] Thus, for example, if two countries have different rules on product safety, one of them may decide to transplant the rules of the other country, not because it thinks that these are superior, but to make it easier for firms to accommodate the laws of both countries. It is also possible that the mutual benefits may take the form of an 'imposition by bargaining'[18]. For instance, this is the case when a developed country makes its aid conditional on a developing country adopting certain legal rules, perhaps in order to foster the interests of foreign investors. Thus, here too, both countries aim to benefit economically.

(b) Aspired benefits for origin country

Specifically dealing with the origin country, a general distinction can be made between tangible and intangible benefits. For example, a country may benefit from its laws being transplanted, since a familiar legal system makes it easier

---

[12] See 2, below.   [13] Miller 2003: 854.
[14] See Milhaupt and Pistor 2008: 209; Mattei and Nader 2008: 19–20, 142.
[15] See Linos 2013: 13–35.   [16] Miller 2003: 849–50. See also B 2 (b), below.
[17] Cf. Mattei 1997a: 94, 219; Pistor 2002: 97.
[18] Mattei and Nader 2008: 19–20, 142 (also referring to it as 'subtle extortion').

for its firms to do business with firms from the transplant country. Beyond rules of business law, a country (i.e. its people, politicians etc.) may see it as a tangible benefit if another country follows its values – for instance, by way of transplanting its human rights law. Such a transplant may also be regarded as having intangible benefits, namely that a country is interested in the 'prestige' of having an influential legal system. But, then, having a legal system that is seen as prestigious may, in turn, have tangible benefits: for instance, foreigners may want to buy literature about this legal system, or pay to study at its universities.

Another distinction is between forms of influence. Soft forms of influence may start by simply making the domestic law accessible to foreign readers, by way of, for instance, providing freely available translations of its laws on the web. Going further, a country may start discussions with other countries in order to promote its law – for example, by way of setting up an expert group drafting model laws. A far less 'soft' form of influence – and most contentious – is an 'externally-dictated transplant',[19] sometimes called 'legal imposition' or even 'legal imperialism'.[20] But this type of legal transplant may also have various shades. Upendra Baxi distinguishes between conquest, colonial, cold war, and disciplinary globalisation.[21] Similarly, legal transplants can be the result of different phases of colonial, neo-colonial, or other forms of imposition.[22] It is also possible to take the perspective of the transplant country and order the transplants by the extent to which it still enjoys de facto sovereignty regarding the transplant decision, distinguishing between imposition, transnational commitment, external pressure, prestige generated, and voluntary adoption.[23]

(c) Transplants beyond direct benefits

Legal transplants are not always the consequence of the benefits that they provide for the transplant country, the origin country, or both of them. Often the process that leads to a legal transplant is not a deliberate one; thus, here, it may be better to talk about 'legal circulation', 'cross-fertilisation', 'diffusion' or 'migration'.[24] This terminology also reflects how political scientists think about the transfer of policies – for instance, as they research topics such as the 'diffusion of innovations among the American states' and the 'global diffusion of regulatory capitalism'.[25]

It is difficult to determine when such 'legal diffusion' occurs, since it requires an analysis of the precise historical and cultural circumstances in question. For

---

[19] Miller 2003: 847.   [20] Gardner 1980; Mattei 2003; Mattei et al. 2009: 241–2.

[21] Baxi 2009 (in addition, referring to voluntary and judicial globalisation).

[22] See, e.g. Mattei and Nader 2008: 19–20, 142.

[23] Cohn 2010: 591 (in addition referring to negative fertilisation and novation).

[24] For the different terms used see Perju 2012: 1306–8; Nelken 2002: 30–1. For the term 'legal migration' see also Choudhry 2006.

[25] Walker 1969 (being one of the first studies on policy diffusion); Levi Faur 2005 (also with general references to the diffusion literature). See also Peck 2011 (suggesting a shift to 'policy mobilities'); Campbell 2010: 97–106 (on other models).

instance, it can matter whether countries have a common language, and how easy it is to access the sources and texts of the other legal system.[26] Frequent reference is also made to the role of legal families in stimulating legal diffusion and other types of legal transplants.[27]

2. The way legal transplants 'work'

Scholars disagree on whether and how legal transplants 'work'. This discussion can appear very confrontational, but it is possible to reconcile some of the conflicting views. For example, it seems plausible that the 'working' of legal transplants can differ considerably according to areas of law and countries. Moreover, the term 'work' is not entirely clear: does it mean that the legal transplant operates exactly as in the origin country, or does it refer to good enforcement of the law, or that it fits with the societal needs of the transplant country? The following tries to clarify this debate.

(a) The positive view: they work as in origin country

For the positive view, one has to start with Alan Watson, who is often seen as the founding father of the concept of legal transplants.[28] Watson's view is shaped by being a legal historian and Roman lawyer, in particular his insight that the private law of many countries is significantly based on the reception of Roman law. This is even said to lead to the belief that 'a law student of the time of Justinian, transported to the twentieth century, would find little to wonder at in the civil codes of modern Europe'.[29]

Watson follows that 'borrowing, even mindless, is the name of the legal game'.[30] Such borrowing is not limited to legal rules, since the transplant of Roman law also concerned legal institutions and structures.[31] His main explanation for all of this is that topics of private law are typically not of interest to governments but left to legal experts. Thus, according to Watson, its rules and concepts 'can survive without any close connection to any particular people, any particular period of time or any particular place'.[32]

Such a positive view of legal transplants is shared by comparative lawyers who aim to strengthen the practical value of comparative law: for example, Sir Basil Markesinis encourages us to 'increase intellectual interaction and borrowings'.[33] Beyond comparative law, economists and development organisations often follow an 'instrumentalist' and 'technological' view of the law[34] and therefore support the use of legal transplants in order to solve social or economic

---

[26] MacQueen in EE 2012: 791 (for Scotland). See also Evans-Jones 1998.

[27] See 2 (d), below.

[28] Being the result of Watson 1993 (first edition from 1971), though in 1782 Jeremy Bentham already reflected on 'transplanting laws': see Huxley 2007.

[29] Ewald 1998: 703 (paraphrasing Watson's view).   [30] Watson 2007: 5.

[31] Watson 1994: 2.   [32] Watson 1976: 81. See also ch. 6 at A 2 (a), above.

[33] Markesinis 2000: 49.   [34] Cf. Twining 2002: 42; Twining 2004: 26.

problems, while dismissing opposition as 'parochialism'.[35] This is closely related to Chapter 10 on 'comparative law and development' where these views are discussed in more detail.

(b) The sceptical view: they are largely irrelevant

This positive view is challenged by scholars in the postmodern tradition, notably Pierre Legrand.[36] The basis for Legrand's criticism is that he rejects the view that law is only about the words that can be found in legal texts. Rather, one needs to consider that 'meaning is a function of the application of the rule by its interpreter'.[37] Such interpretation is always subjective and shaped by the larger cognitive framework of a particular country, in particular its culture and mentality.[38]

Following from this, he advocates the 'impossibility of legal transplants'. A legal rule cannot survive the journey from one legal system to another one unchanged: 'as the understanding of a rule changes, the meaning of the rule changes', and 'as the meaning of the rule changes, the rule itself changes';[39] or, to quote Bruno Latour, there cannot be any 'transportation without transformation'.[40] For example, when Watson claims that there are similarities between Roman law and subsequent laws of civil law countries, Legrand regards these similarities as meaningless, superficial, and just rhetorical, since they merely concern words.[41]

But the question remains of whether Watson and Legrand do not merely have a terminological disagreement. Both seem to agree that law-makers do occasionally copy text from other countries, whether you want to call it a 'legal transplant' or not. Going beyond this point, it is not clear whether Legrand rejects the idea that law-makers should consider foreign models. On the one hand, his criticism seems to be focused on the conceptual point that, even when one does consider foreign models, this does not lead to a legal transplant. On the other hand, he also states that legal transplants reflect an attitude that marginalises difference,[42] and such a positive view of legal diversity is indeed typical for postmodern comparative legal scholarship.[43] Yet, there is also the more explicit position that regards legal transplants as harmful.

(c) The negative view: they are often harmful

Foreign cultural influences are sometimes seen as detrimental: take, for example, the criticism of the US influence on eating and drinking habits ('McWorld', 'Coca-Colonization').[44] With respect to legal transplants, two variants of such

---

[35] Buscaglia and Ratliff 2000: 31.
[36] See generally ch. 5 at C 1, above.   [37] Legrand 2001a: 57.
[38] Legrand 2001a: 59 and 68 ('law as a culturally-situated phenomenon').
[39] Legrand 2001a: 61. Similarly Menski 2006: 5 ('law is much more than a body of rules that can simply be imposed on others').
[40] Latour 1996: 118–19.   [41] Legrand 2001a: 63–4.   [42] Legrand 2001a: 65.
[43] See, e.g. ch. 5 at B 2 (b), above.   [44] For these terms Barber 1995; Wagnleitner 1994.

a view can be distinguished. On the one hand, the criticism can refer to the relationship between the transplanted and the previous law. Thus, it may be argued that foreign ideas have 'polluting or disrupting effects' on the domestic legal order,[45] and that legal transplants should really be called 'legal irritants'.[46] On the other hand, the negative effect may refer to the relationship between the transplanted law and the social, economic, cultural and political environment. Taking the view that there are complementarities between the law, society, culture, and political process of a particular country, it follows that one should not simply copy laws from other countries.[47] Thus, according to this view, legal transplants often fail, due, for instance, to lack of enforcement, side-lining, or general unsuitability.[48]

But both of these criticisms go too far. In today's world, there are no 'pure legal systems'; rather, all legal systems have managed to incorporate ideas from various parts of the world.[49] Thus, the general scepticism about foreign influences being irritants is at least an exaggeration. With respect to the lack of 'fit' with current socio-economic and other conditions, one objection to this criticism is that this may sometimes be deliberate, since legal transplants can aim precisely to change the society in question. Yet, it still seems plausible to argue that legal transplants have to consider the different environment of the transplant country. It may therefore be more appropriate to phrase the criticism as one against blind borrowing, but not against reflective learning from abroad.[50]

(d) The differentiated view: they function in a modified way

Thus, most scholars take an intermediate position. A typical statement of this view is that legal transplants are often not a clear success or failure, but rather that the picture is a mixed one.[51] Then, it may also be said that, since neither the success nor failure of a transplant can be assumed, it is most important to choose and design legal transplants as well as possible.[52]

Parallels are often drawn with other phenomena: Marc Galanter points out that laws are like languages, since they can absorb foreign influences while also 'preserving a distinctive structure and flavour'.[53] T.T. Arvind uses the comparison with wine: a type of grape can be transplanted outside its native

---

[45] Gutteridge 1949: 25.   [46] Teubner 1998. See also ch. 3 at B 3 (c), above.

[47] See Ajani 2009: 11 (against instrumental use of law); Ahlering and Deakin 2007 (on institutional complementarities in law). See also ch. 10 at C, below (on law and development).

[48] Cf. Foster 2007: 273–4.

[49] See generally ch. 4 at C, above (on hybrids), as well as B, below.

[50] Similarly Rubin 2000: 108 ('little can be borrowed, but much can be learned, from foreign law'); Peck 2011: 775 ('policy markets: from diffusion to learning').

[51] Nelken 2001: 19; also Nelken 2003a: 442.

[52] See Frankenberg 2012a (suggesting an 'IKEA theory': laws need to be stripped of their social context before they can be recontextualised in the recipient country); Bellantuono 2012 (proposing an explicit 'comparative legal diagnostics'); Xanthaki 2008 (distinguishing between 'transplant concept', 'transplant term' and 'transplant comparative research design'); Örücü 2002 (transposition always in need of refinement).

[53] Galanter 1994: 680.

terrain, but the wine will be a bit different, as is the case for transplanted law.[54] Michele Graziadei cites psychological research, according to which higher mental functions incorporate new into previous material – and legal transplants can be thought of as an example of such a process.[55]

These parallels show that it is crucial to examine how the foreign rules are received in the transplant country. It is even said that the process of legal reform and development is more important than the substance of transplanted rules.[56] For instance, this process may determine how well the old and new elements mix, ranging from complete amalgamation to a situation where domestic and foreign elements remain clearly visible.[57] Specifically, the way a new official law interacts with pre-existing, more informal laws has to be examined: the latter may continue to exist, creating a pluralist legal order;[58] alternatively, the new laws may be used to challenge the previous ones.[59]

Turning to the question of how far the transplant will be identical to the law of the origin country, the best response may be that outcomes differ according to the relevant circumstances. For instance, Margit Cohn has developed such a typology: it starts with the categories where the transplant has been more or less successful: 'full convergence', 'fine-tuning' and 'pro-transplant transposition'. But, it is also possible that the transplant has not been well received, thus, leading to 'counter-transplant cross-fertilisation', 'distortion', 'mutation' or even 'rejection'.[60]

What determines which of those responses occurs? The general line taken is often that the transplant has to 'fit' into previous conditions. Literature in political science has discussed key conditions for the transferability of policies.[61] Countries need to be ideologically and psychologically compatible. Thus, there needs to be agreement on basic policy objectives and values (for example, whether and how social welfare is provided). It also has to be considered that resistance against a foreign policy can arise both at the level of the government and of the general public. Moreover, the implementation of a policy transfer may fail due to politics or socio-economic differences.

The legal literature has identified similar conditions. Katharina Pistor refers to the need to ensure 'complementarities between the new law and pre-existing legal institutions'.[62] She also mentions the relevance of economic differences: for instance, company law rules designed for companies with dispersed shareholder ownership would not work for concentrated ownership structures (and vice versa).[63] Roger Cotterrell distinguishes between two positions: someone who regards 'law as culture' will regard a transplant as successful when the law is

---

[54] Arvind 2010: 66; also Watt 2012: 91–6 ('horticultural metaphor').
[55] Graziadei 2009: 736–7.   [56] Peerenboom 2013.
[57] See also ch. 4 at C 3 (c), above (on Örücü's 'salad bowl analogy').
[58] Mattei et al. 2009: 248, 253.
[59] Tamanaha 2001: 120. See also Menski 2006: 123–4 (on research by Masaji Chiba).
[60] Cohn 2010: 592.   [61] For the following see Hantrais 2009: 133–9; Rose 2005; Rose 1993.
[62] Pistor 2002: 98.   [63] Ibid. 127. See also ch. 6 at C 1 (b), above.

consistent with the environment of the transplant country, and someone who regards 'law as an instrument' will do so when the law has the intended effect.[64] But it may also be said that both types of success are connected, since the effect of a transplant will depend on the way it fits into the society of the transplant country.

Often a distinction is also made between areas of law. Ernst Levy based this view on 'the strength of connection with a people's past', following which he argued that transplants were most difficult in family and succession law, then real property law, and then personal property and contract law.[65] Similarly, according to Otto Kahn-Freund, there is a continuum of legal transplants: some legal rules can be transferred by 'mechanical insertion' while other rules may be rejected, similar to the failed transplant of a kidney.[66] But, according to Kahn-Freund, there is also a time dimension, because trends such as industrialisation, urbanisation, and new technologies have reduced obstacles to legal transplants.[67]

Furthermore, it is necessary to consider the countries involved in the transplantation process. For example, it is said that a developed legal culture may have the capabilities to absorb a legal transplant, and a small jurisdiction may need to rely on transplants in order to develop a new field of law.[68] Frequent reference is made to the role of legal families: if two legal systems are based on similar conceptual understandings of the law, the transfer of a rule or institution between these legal systems is more likely to be successful than across legal families.[69] But, this should not be seen as an absolute barrier. According to T. T. Arvind:

> [N]o legal system is entirely a prisoner of its own past traditions. Informal institutions can be changed, or new ones developed, to conform to those traditions that exist in the country of origin of the transplanted law, or the countries on whose jurisprudence a harmonised law was based.[70]

It seems unlikely that a country is easily able to switch from a civil to a common law tradition, or vice versa.[71] Yet, Arvind's statement rightly shows that copying a particular legal text is often only one of the elements that make a legal transplant 'work'. Though these other elements – such as legal education, methods, and mentalities – cannot be changed overnight, most comparative lawyers agree that here, too, foreign models can be helpful.[72]

---

[64] Cotterrell 2001: 79.   [65] Levy 1950: 244.

[66] Kahn-Freund 1974: 6. But see also C, below.

[67] Kahn-Freund 1974: 9.   [68] Mattei et al. 2009: 227–9.

[69] Mattei 1997b: 5; Esquirol 2001: 223; Berkowitz et al. 2003a: 167; Berkowitz et al. 2003b: 163. See also Örücü 1999: 29 (mismatch may lead to mixed jurisdiction).

[70] Arvind 2010: 81.   [71] For some attempts see B 2 (b), below.

[72] See generally Twining 2002: 20; Sacco 1991: 394. More specifically, e.g. Chiu 2010 (on 'transcultural articulation' of Rawlsian theory of justice in the Han-Chinese cultural context).

An analysis of legal transplants may also challenge the relevance of broad categories, such as legal families. The way countries influence each other's laws is often complex. It has therefore been suggested that tree or wave models can show how legal rules have spread.[73] The apparent parallel approach is that of comparative linguistics, with its interest in how languages interact in more or less complex ways.[74] This parallel can also show unusual developments: for example, that there is not only a 'genetic transmission' of languages, but also that some people have adopted a foreign language, abandoning their mother tongue.[75]

3. Further variants of legal transplants

The foregoing differentiated view on how legal transplants work already indicates that it may be useful to distinguish between types of legal transplants. This differentiation can be further refined, and can include other topics relevant for legal transplants. Margit Cohn has developed a sophisticated typology;[76] another one is by William Twining, as summarised in Table 8.1, below.

Most of Twining's categories can be related to points mentioned in the previous sections. Generally speaking, Twining's 'standard case' is about transplants of positive legal rules that are based on a deliberate choice of the transplant country, and that 'work' as well abroad as at home. But not all of the categories always go hand in hand: for example, Watson's research would usually be associated with the 'standard case', yet, in the category 'agency', he emphasises the role of jurists and other experts, since politicians would not care about details of the law.

Many of these categories also relate to the subsequent chapters. For example, Chapter 9 on 'fading state borders' will deal with the way companies shape the formal and informal law in a globalised economy (see (b), (d), (f) of Table 8.1); and Chapter 10 on 'comparative law and development' will, inter alia, address resistance against legal transplants, contrasting it with the effect that they are supposed to have (see (j) and (l) of Table 8.1).

The remainder of the present chapter examines legal transplants more empirically. The apparent link to the foregoing discussion is that empirical data may confirm or refute some of the conceptual views. For example, Watson's position that transplanted law can have important effects even if it is dysfunctional poses an empirical question, as does the claim that legal transplants show that there is separation between law and society.[77]

---

[73] See Örücü 2007: 173. See also ch. 4 at D, above.
[74] E.g. Labov 2007. See also Sacco 1991: 5; Mattila 2006: 16, 115–17, 259–61 (on interaction between legal languages).
[75] Lundmark 2012: 32 (referring to the USA).
[76] Cohn 2010. See also text accompanying notes 23 and 60, above.
[77] Cotterrell 2001: 75–6; Ewald 1995b: 504.

Table 8.1 Standard case and variants[1]

Topics	Standard case	Variants	In this book
(a) Source-destination	Single exporter to single importer	Single exporter to multiple destinations (or vice versa)	2(d) above B 1(a), 2(a) below
(b) Levels	Municipal to municipal legal system	Other levels (regional, sub-state, transnational etc.)	B 4(a) below ch. 9 below
(c) Pathways	Direct one-way transfer	Complex paths (e.g. reciprocal influence)	2(d) above (and ch. 8 A above) B 2(a), 4(b) below
(d) Formal or informal	Formal enactment or adoption	Informal, semi-formal or mixed	1(a) above ch. 9 below
(e) Objects	Legal rules and concepts; institutions	Any legal phenomena, ideas, methods, practices etc.	1(a), 2(a) above (and ch. 7 above) B 1, 2(b), 3 below
(f) Agency	Government to government	Individuals (e.g. jurists) and groups (e.g. companies, NGOs)	1(a) and (b), 2(a) above B 2, 3(b) below ch. 9 below
(g) Timing	One or more specific reception dates	Continuing process	1(c) above B 2(b), 3 below
(h) Power and prestige	Parent civil or common law to less developed	Reciprocal interaction	1(a), 2(d) above (and ch. 4 above) B 1(b), 2(b) below
(i) Change in object	Unchanged or minor adjustments	Transformation of object	2(a)–(c) above B 2, 3 below
(j) Relation to pre-existing law	Blank slate; gap filling; full replacement	Struggle, resistance; layering; assimilation; surface law	2 (c) and (d) above B 2(b), 3 below ch. 10 below
(k) Diffusion perspective	Technological and instrumental	Ideological, cultural, contextual	2 (a) and (b) above B 1(b), 2(b), 4(c) below
(l) Impact	'It works'	Performance measures; empirical research; monitoring; enforcement	2 above (and ch. 7 above) B 2(b), 3 below ch. 10 below

[1] Based on Twining 2007: 86–7. See also Twining 2004: 17; Twining 2005: 205–7; Twining 2009a: 279.

B. Legal transplants throughout history

Where does your breakfast come from? It may not be untypical, if, to quote the geographer David Harvey,

> [t]he coffee was from Costa Rica, the flour that made up the bread probably from Canada, the oranges in marmalade came from Spain, those in the orange juice came from Morocco and the sugar came from Barbados. Then, I think of all the things that went into making the production of those things possible – the

machinery that came from [West] Germany, the fertilizer from the United States, the oil from Saudi Arabia . . . [78]

Statements by comparative lawyers indicate that a country's law may be similar. Moreover – perhaps in contrast to one's breakfast – this is not only seen as a recent phenomenon. For instance, it has been said that 'every legal system contains imported elements', and that law's evolution 'has always been externally influenced'.[79] But, then, Patrick Glenn also observes that:

> Law drawn from another tradition will originally be identifiable as to its source but the layering of domestic sources over foreign ones will eventually camouflage many distant origins.[80]

Thus, the challenge is to identify precisely what role legal transplants have played throughout history. The first recorded example of a legal transplant is said to go back to the Code of Hammurabi of the seventeenth century BC.[81] It is therefore obvious that a complete historical survey cannot be attempted. Still, the following section discusses some of the main examples, focusing on the rationales for, and the working of, legal transplants. It starts with legal transplants in continental Europe, and then addresses transplants in the colonial and post-colonial world, as well as in countries that have not been part of one of the colonial empires. As an example of constitutional transplants, the final section deals with the diffusion of human rights. It is justifiable to look at human rights diffusion separately, as it concerns the influence of particular ideas, often promoted by international intermediaries, rather than the 'simple' copying of certain legal texts. Moreover, this final section leads us to the topics of the following two chapters (fading state borders; comparative law and development).

1. Legal transplants in continental Europe

(a) Until the mid-twentieth century: not only legislative transplants?

The reception of Roman law is often seen as a prominent early example of legal transplants in Europe.[82] But, focusing on the nineteenth and twentieth centuries, legislative transplants seem to be the predominant paradigm. Some of these transplants have been involuntary – for example, due to the Napoleonic occupations of the early nineteenth century – whereas more recent transplants tend to be voluntary ones.

A popular object of legal transplants has been the French Civil Code. It has been seen as an example of a code that is 'systematic, de-contextualized and a-historical' and therefore relatively easily transplanted.[83] But the impact of the French Civil Code has often been mediated by previous local legal cultures that continued (and continue) to play a role. For instance, in Spain, traditional

---

[78] Harvey 1989b.   [79] Mattei et al. 2009: 240; Cohn 2010: 628.
[80] Glenn 2001: 141.   [81] Watson 1993: 22–4.
[82] See ch. 3 at A and ch. 8 at A 2 (a), above.   [83] Muir Watt 2006: 591.

local laws still have effect in some regions; also, when Spain adopted a civil code in 1889, the local Castilian law was merged with elements of the French model.[84]

Frequently, multiple sources of influence have interacted. Apart from French law, German legislative models also played a role in Italy, Spain, and, in particular, in Portugal.[85] In Germany, a variety of foreign laws were considered for the commercial code of 1861.[86] Greece is also a good example: in the first half of the nineteenth century, its commercial code and code of criminal procedure were influenced by French models, and its criminal code and code of civil procedure by German ones. The civil law remained initially 'Greek' (being based on the Byzantine Hexabiblos), but was replaced by a German-inspired civil code in 1946.[87]

Foreign influence has not been limited to legislative transplants. In the nineteenth century, German lawyers travelled to Greece to give lectures, and Greek lawyers travelled to Germany to study law.[88] German legal doctrine has also been influential in Italian civil law, despite Italy having transplanted the French Civil Code,[89] and it also raised some interest in the common law world.[90] Ugo Mattei explains this influence by arguing that, in the nineteenth century, German law was only partly codified: German conceptual legal thinking, in particular its Roman-inspired civil law, was attractive to other countries since it was not tied to a particular legal text.[91] However, elsewhere, Mattei also explains that the prestige of German law continued in the early twentieth century, thus stimulating some diffusion of its codified law.[92]

The general picture that emerges is that legal transplants between continental European countries have been fairly common. They did not only concern the positive law, but also the deeper structural levels of the 'legal ocean', such as the relevant legal methods and the use of law in society,[93] often mixing various models. It also helped that European countries share a common history and culture. This does not mean that transplants work exactly the same way in the origin and the transplant country (and that is possibly also how it should be),[94] but it usually prevents an outright 'rejection' of the transplant.

(b) The recent period: Americanisation of civil law countries?

Since the Second World War, and in particular since the fall of communism, US law has played a growing role in continental Europe. US transplants concern a

---

[84] See Zweigert and Kötz 1998: 107–8; Guillet 2005 (comparing it with the more limited impact of customary law in Peru).

[85] See Zweigert and Kötz 1998: 104–9.   [86] See Zweigert and Kötz 1998: 51.

[87] See Giaro 2003: 129.   [88] Ibid.

[89] See Mattei 1997a: 110 and more generally Monateri 2003.

[90] See Reimann 1993.   [91] Mattei 1994: 202–3, 215.

[92] See Mattei and Nader 2008: 19–20, 142 (referring to Japan and Turkey).

[93] For the distinction between such structural levels see Sunde 2010: 43.

[94] See Hiller and Grossfeld 2002: 179 (suggesting that judges 'must be creative in applying and interpreting' the transplanted law).

variety of topics. The US law on product liability influenced the EU legislation on this matter.[95] The US concept of a uniform real security right provided a model for European law-makers – which was helped by model laws and guidances of organisations such as the EBRD, UNIDROIT and UNCITRAL.[96] Such indirect influence via the international level can also be seen elsewhere: for example, the US Foreign Corrupt Practices Act 1977 influenced the OECD Anti-Bribery Convention and, by doing so, the legal systems of most European countries.[97] In the field of criminal procedure, the US law on plea bargaining has been partly transplanted to Germany, Italy, France, as well as other countries.[98] This seems remarkable given that plea bargaining is typical for an adversarial system of criminal procedure, as distinguished from the more inquisitorial ones of continental Europe.[99] US models have also triggered institutional changes: for instance, in the use of independent regulatory agencies in the EU and its Member States.[100]

More generally, it has been said that the legal culture in continental Europe has gradually become more American. Indicators are the growing number of US-style casebooks in Europe, European lawyers studying for an LL M at US universities, and large US law firms establishing offices in Europe.[101] As he did previously for the popularity of German law, Ugo Mattei argues that the US legal culture has benefited from the way US scholars try to understand 'law as a phenomenon of social organisation', and are less interested in the local particularities of the formal law.[102] In addition, the wider political and economic context certainly plays a role. As international relations scholars discuss American political hegemony, the legal hegemony of the US may be reflected in changes to legal thinking and consciousness – with or without changes of formal legal rules.[103]

However, claims about Americanisation should not be exaggerated, as previous chapters of this book have shown. In the discussion about legal families, it was said that, in many respects, the US is the exception because legal thinking in Europe tends to be focused on black letter law, which has changed little in recent times.[104] The chapter on socio-legal comparative law discussed the still prevailing use of the death penalty in the US, as opposed to European legal

---

[95] See Mattei 1997a: 86, 132 note 40; Howells in EE 2012: 717; also Reimann 2003 (on convergence of product liability rules around the world). See also ch. 2 at A 5, above.

[96] Uniform Commercial Code, art 9. See van Erp in EE 2012: 652–4.

[97] See Ajani 2009: 5.

[98] Langer 2004 (for Europe and Latin America); Mattei 1997a: 86 (for Italy); Glendon et al. 2008: 264 (for the UK); Grande 2012: 205 (on US as exporter in criminal procedure).

[99] See Feeley 1997: 98–9 and ch. 4 at C 3 (c), above.

[100] See Gilardi 2005: 85. For the EU see http://europa.eu/agencies/index_en.htm.

[101] Mattei 1994: 206; Wiegand 1991; Wiegand 1996.

[102] Mattei 1994: 195–6, 199; also Delmas-Marty 2009: 62 (e.g. referring to role of prestige and adaptable laws).

[103] Mattei and Nader 2008: 81, 83. See also Gilpin 2001: 93 (for international relations).

[104] See ch. 3 at C 2, above.

systems.[105] And the chapter on numerical comparative law presented evidence showing that, between 1995 and 2005, the company laws of Central and Eastern European countries did not become more American.[106]

2. Colonialism and post-colonialism

(a) The colonial world: only common and civil law?

The literature on law and colonisation often identifies different paths of colonisation. A first distinction is between conquered and settled colonies.[107] As far as sparsely inhabited places have been settled, typically, the settlers simply took their laws with them. With respect to legal transplants, the main question is then whether and how the settled communities kept in contact with their countries of origin. Examples may be the relationship between England and Australia, and, to a lesser extent, between England and the United States.[108]

In most of the colonies, however, there was a significant indigenous population. This led to the different colonial strategies, notably the French on the one hand and the English on the other.[109] France is said to have followed the principle of 'direct rule', trying to apply French law universally in its colonies. In contrast, the 'indirect rule' of England (later, the United Kingdom) meant that, in principle, the existing customary law and the role of native chiefs were retained for the local population. The main focus was therefore not on ensuring universal application of English law, but 'merely' on gaining political sovereignty over the occupied territories.

The differences between direct and indirect rule may be related to the distinction between civil and common law.[110] The civil law structure of French law may mean that one can rationally and systematically develop legal rules which can then be applied to people of any culture and religion. The common law, by contrast, is more willing to accept diversity – for example, by making more frequent use of juries.[111] Since law is also seen as something that derives from society, it also seems plausible that the common law would be willing to accept the use of customary law as far as pre-colonial societies remained in place.

However, this binary division is not beyond doubt. The description of French law as universal is about an aspiration, but one can be sceptical whether the entirety of French law could really be effectively transplanted to completely foreign cultures. Though France also tried to pursue a strategy of cultural assimilation – for instance, by way of promoting the French language – it is clear that, in reality, local customs and cultures did not disappear. It was also inevitable that, in practice, the French, too, had to rely on local chiefs and

---

[105] See ch. 6 at C 2, above.   [106] See ch. 7 at B 2, above.   [107] E.g. McPherson 2007: 13.

[108] On the spread of the common law see, e.g. Glenn 2005: 63–84; McPherson 2007. See also ch. 3, above.

[109] See, e.g. Mommsen 1992; Menski 2006: 447–50.

[110] For the relationship between political and legal explanations see Cioffi 2009.

[111] See Easterly 2006: 243.

interpreters:[112] thus, while 'direct rule' may have been the aspiration, the reality was often a different one.

With respect to English law, it is remarkable that some of its typical characteristics of decentralisation and gradual development were not fully transplanted. For example, while juries played a role in some of the settlement colonies to protect Europeans against the native population, there was no desire to transfer such powers to the local population.[113] There was also more reliance on statutory law than in England. Codification was a convenient tool to facilitate the transfer of common law rules: for instance, in India, large parts of the common law were codified and these codes were also transplanted to other British colonies.[114]

Moreover, the line of influence often did not simply go from one colonial power to its colony. In many colonies, more than one Western country left its mark. For example, in South Africa, both English and Dutch influence shaped the law, with the result that some areas of law became more English (e.g. commercial law) and others more Roman-Dutch (e.g. property law).[115] There are also examples where the mixture included an element of choice: for example, when Egypt was under British occupation, the local law-makers decided to look at French law as a source of inspiration and as a deliberate strategy against the British rule.[116]

In addition, there are claims that the Western legal systems are themselves, in part, a product of non-Western ideas. For example, in an article entitled 'Black Gaius', Pier Giuseppe Monateri argues that Roman law is a multicultural product of African, Semitic, and Mediterranean civilisations.[117] Focusing on English law, John Makdisi identified foreign elements in the common law actions and in the trial by jury.[118] Reference can also be made to research by George Makdisi (the late father of John Makdisi), who showed how Islamic educational institutions had an influence on European universities and the English Inns of Court.[119]

Legal rules have also spread within the group of non-Western countries. For example, the comparative legal literature refers to the 'spread of Hindu legal influence in South East Asia', the 'Chinese influence on Korea and Japan' and the 'diffusion of Islamic law'.[120] Many of those sources of influence were related to other forms of proximity, such as associations by way of language, religion, political alliances or patterns of migration.[121] Thus, for many countries, it

---

[112] See Glenn 2010a: 368.   [113] See Roe 2009: 586, 592.

[114] See Menski 2006: 242, 464; Halpérin 2010a and already ch. 3 at B 1 (a), above. See also Mommsen 1992: 10 (on laws specifically designed for colonies).

[115] See ch. 4 at C 3 (c), above.   [116] Shalakany 2001: 168.

[117] Monateri 1999.   [118] Makdisi 1999: 1640, 1676.

[119] Makdisi 1981; Makdisi 1985–86. A related position is Hobson 2004 (considering the origins of Western civilisation more generally).

[120] Harding 2001: 206; Glenn 2010a: 325; Graziadei 2009: 726. On the Chinese influence see also Ruskola 2012: 259, 268–74; Graziadei 2006: 444; Twining et al. 2006: 160 (more sceptical).

[121] Twining 2009a: 16.

is not enough merely to determine how Western legal transplants have been received, but also how the original law has interacted with various forms of foreign influence. The further question is whether independence meant that the former colonies wanted to get rid of the laws imposed by foreign powers – or whether new patterns of legal transplants emerged.

(b) The post-colonial development: everything new?

Most Latin American countries had already gained independence at the beginning of the nineteenth century. At that time, the French Napoleonic Codes were the main source of influence. A previous chapter of this book already discussed the view that Latin American lawyers often stayed overly faithful to the French model of a strict separation of powers between legislators and courts: thus, they applied the codes literally while French judges were (already) more flexible.[122]

But there is more to say about legal transplants in Latin America. Notably it was the case that, after independence, traditions became more mixed. For example, this can clearly be seen in the Brazilian Commercial Code of 1850, which incorporated ideas from both civil and common law countries, often to suit the interests of local elites.[123] Another example is the Chilean Civil Code of 1855, drafted by Andrés Bello: while the main basis for the Chilean Civil Code was the French Civil Code, parts of it were also inspired by traditional Spanish law and elements of German law. Moreover, this Code is an example of a regional legal transplant, since it influenced the civil codes of many other Latin American countries throughout the nineteenth century.[124]

This eclecticism continued with the influence of US law. In the second half of the nineteenth century, Mexico, Brazil and Argentina had already incorporated some concepts of US constitutional law.[125] As in Europe, Americanisation became more pronounced after the Second World War. Examples concern a wide range of legal topics, such as the law of trust, the adversarial model of criminal procedure, pensions, health insurance and other forms of social welfare, as well as legal education and practice.[126] Researchers trying to understand the reason for this shift to the US, have indicated that it has less to do with possible virtues of the common law than with a political decision for free markets and limited state powers,[127] the influence of US advisers and international financial institutions,[128] and the interests of local lawyers trained in the US who returned to their home countries.

---

[122] See ch. 4 at C 2 (b), above.   [123] Pargendler 2012a.

[124] See, e.g. Kleinheisterkamp 2006: 274–6; Mirow 2005: 183–4; also López-Medina 2012: 355 (on the central role of regional dialogue in Latin America).

[125] See Kleinheisterkamp 2006: 268.

[126] Dam 2006: 44 (on the law of trust); Phillips 2007: 915, 926 (on criminal procedure reform in Chile and other countries); Weyland 2004 (on social welfare); Riles 2006: 789–90 (on globalisation of legal profession).

[127] Phillips 2007: 920; López-Medina 2012: 357–8.   [128] See ch. 10, below.

A sociological study by Yves Dezalay and Bryant Garth on Argentina, Brazil, Chile and Mexico examined the latter aspect in more detail, also relating it to the terminology of legal transplants. Here, the importers of US law are said to belong to the cosmopolitan elite of those countries, and directly benefited from them.[129] Thus, the 'logic of those half-failed transplants' is that, on the one hand, they were not generally accepted, but on the other hand, they continued, since they were driven by powerful self-interested parties.[130]

A similar picture – where colonial origins play a continuing role subject to further mixtures – can be identified for the countries that gained independence in the twentieth century. But there have also been a number of variations.

Starting with the constitutional law of African countries, a first point to note is that the very idea of the state is said to be 'an imported device of colonial origins'.[131] The more specific constitutional design was initially based on those of the former colonial powers, yet with the occasional 'rejection' of the initial transplant. For example, though the former English colonies started with a parliamentary model, similar to England, most of them switched to a presidential model, similar to France.[132] Doubts have been expressed as to whether the concept of the separation of power is compatible with the traditional African perception about 'unity of power'.[133] This relates to the wider question about the effectiveness of the state in developing countries – a topic to which we return in Chapter 10 on comparative law and development.

More generally, it is sometimes held that the role of the colonial transplants should not be overstated: indeed, 'one must ask how much effect less than a century of colonial domination could have had on many peoples of Africa'.[134] But there is also the view that emphasises the ongoing influence. For instance, patterns of legal cooperation and law student migration show that lawyers (and aspiring lawyers) of the former colonies continue to associate with the former colonial powers.[135] Here, it also matters that most of the British and many of the French colonies have kept English and French as the official legal language, thus fostering the continuation of the former colonial legal ties.

In Africa, some of the new Acts and codes have also been influenced by Western ideas. In Ethiopia, one of the few African countries that had not been colonised, the Civil Code of 1960 is a clear example of strong influence. It was mainly drafted by the French comparative lawyer René David, who drew on his comparative expertise but mainly followed the French model. His experience also confirms the pragmatic use of legal transplants, outlined earlier in this chapter:

---

[129] Dezalay and Garth 2002. A related study dealt with lawyers in seven Asian countries: Dezalay and Garth 2010. See also ch. 10 at B 1, below.

[130] Dezalay and Garth 2001: 16, 246.   [131] Mattei et al. 2009: 255.

[132] Nijzink et al. 2007: 60–2.   [133] Mancuso 2009: 79 (for Somalia).

[134] Menski 2006: 462. See also ch. 4 at C 2 (a), above.   [135] Spamann 2009: 1845, 1850.

Ethiopia cannot wait 300 or more years to construct in an empirical fashion a system of law which is unique to itself, as was done in two different historical eras by the Romans and the English. The development and modernization of Ethiopia necessitate the adoption of a 'ready made' system . . . [136]

Yet, the Civil Code is said to have had limited effect on the Ethiopian law in practice.[137] This is an experience it shares with transplanted laws in other countries. In some of the former colonies, the Western laws' lack of 'fit' led to new laws legitimising previous customs. For example, in 1997 the Central African Republic recognised polygamous marriage, which had previously been banned by the Western-based Civil Code of 1958.[138] But, then, it may still be said that while details of the law have changed, the Western concept of codified law has not been reversed.[139]

There have also been some examples where countries have deliberately attempted to change their legal family. As a former Belgian colony, Rwanda initially had a French-inspired law; however, in the early twenty-first century, it shifted closer to the common law. This was stimulated by a shift to English as the main official language, and the aim of joining the Anglophone East African Community and the Commonwealth of Nations (which both happened in 2009). Today, Rwanda may be seen as a mixed legal system.[140] Sudan presents a contrasting example. In the 1970s, the government attempted to implement a general shift from common law to French civil law, but this was reversed a few years later. Still, today, there are some civilian elements in Sudanese law, mainly due to Egyptian influence.[141] In addition, Islamic law plays a role, in particular since the *coup d'état* of 1989, and in particular in areas such as criminal and family law.

This leads to the more general question of how far Islamic legal traditions have shaped the law of the Muslim countries of Northern Africa and the Middle East. Ian Ayres and Jonathan Macey take the view that the Muslim world is characterised by an underdeveloped law, since 'legal rules and institutions, once in place, tend to remain static'. They relate this to an apparent lack of legal transplants:

> The unfavorable views of the United States and the West in general among Middle Easterners inevitably contribute to their systematic reluctance to copy what are erroneously viewed as exclusively Western economic philosophies and approaches.[142]

---

[136] David 1963: 188–9.

[137] Menski 2006: 47–8 note 62, and 483–4.   [138] See Mancuso 2009: 80.

[139] Halpérin 2010b (law as union of primary and secondary rules as successful Western transplant). Similarly Humphreys 2010: 119 ('injection of legalism').

[140] See the website of the Faculty of Law of the National University of Rwanda at www.law.nur.ac.rw/.

[141] See Abdelrahman 2004 (on the history of Sudan's contract law).

[142] Ayres and Macey 2005: 426.

Yet, actual developments do not confirm such reluctance, but show a mixture of Western and Islamic traditions. The precise proportion of these elements has often been a matter of debate. In Egypt, the Civil Code of 1949, drafted by Abd al-Razzaq al-Sanhuri, combines elements of French and Islamic law, including the nineteenth-century Mecelle of the Ottoman Empire, which also blended Western and Islamic legal thinking.[143] Some see the French element as dominant and criticise the Code for being unauthentic, alien and ignorant of classic Islamic law.[144] But in Article 1 of the Code there is also a commitment to customs and Islamic law, as far as the Code does not address a particular issue.[145] Thus, it may well be a good compromise.

The Egyptian Civil Code also serves as another example of a regional legal transplant, since both the code and the commentaries on the code have had an impact on other Arab countries.[146] The importance of regional trends is also apparent in the rise of Islamic banking since the 1970s. As Islam does not allow interest payments,[147] distinct forms of contract have been developed that provide alternative means of finance. This has led to some legislative transplants but, predominantly, it concerns contractual practices and religious expert opinions, being in line with Islamic law as a pluralist legal tradition.[148]

Finally, in some of the former non-Muslim Asian colonies, the colonial law has continued to play an important role. For example, while it is possible to identify elements of Hindu law in India, there is no denying that many rules and principles of the received English common law have been retained and are applied in practice. Moreover, Indian law-makers keep considering experiences from England (as well as other common law countries) when they draft new or modify old laws.[149]

In other Asian countries, colonial laws have been largely superseded. Typically, this happened under communist rule. For example, it has been said about Vietnam that 'French colonial legality was . . . easily swept aside by Soviet inspired revolutionary reforms'.[150] Another case is that of multiple colonial powers. For instance, the islands of Micronesia were initially a Spanish colony, and, in the late nineteenth and twentieth centuries, became part of the German and then the Japanese empire. Yet, today's positive law is entirely a product of its more recent history, namely its time as a UN trust territory, administered

---

[143] For the Ottoman model see Foster 2012.

[144] See Shalakany 2001; Mallat 2007: 261–8; Vogel 2006: para. 138.

[145] See also Menski 2006: 350; Vogel 2006: para. 135; Mattei et al. 2009: 380 (laws of Islamic world as post-colonial hybrids).

[146] See Shalakany 2001: 181; Edge 2000: 14; Vogel 2006: para. 136.

[147] To be precise, 'riba', which most scholars equate with interest payments.

[148] See Vogel 2006: para. 140; Mattei et al. 2009: 913–20, also ibid., 378 (problem that codification of Islamic law turns a dynamic and pluralistic tradition into a static and rigid one). In addition, a number of transnational organisations supporting Islamic finance have emerged: see list at www.wdibf.com/organizations.html.

[149] See, e.g., Tamanaha 2001: 110; Glenn 2010a: 312–3.   [150] Gillespie 2006: 15.

by the United States between 1947 and 1986. Thus, the law is a clear US legal transplant – though doubts have been raised about its compatibility with local customs and values.[151]

Overall, the picture that emerges is that legal transplants did not stop with independence. Often (not always) colonial laws were kept and further foreign laws were transplanted, here, too, not always voluntarily. Thus, most of the former colonies today have a mixture of involuntary and voluntary transplants from the West, plus further transplants from neighbouring countries, and indigenous forms of law and order. This should enable transplant countries to choose such legal rules and institutions as really 'fit'. But cherry picking particular legal rules can also be problematic, as can be seen in countries that have never been under colonial occupation.

3. Transplants in non-colonial countries: all that different?

(a) The transplanted formal law

A broad distinction can be made between two phases. In the first phase, comprehensive legal transplants often concerned entire codes. For example, between 1880 and 1922, Japan copied large parts of the French codes – initially – and then the German codes, on criminal law, criminal procedure, civil law, civil procedure, commercial law, and bankruptcy law.[152] While these latter codes were not mere copies of the German ones, they created a legal system that – as regards its formal laws – became part of the German variant of the civil law family.

Turkey is another example. While the Ottoman law of the late nineteenth century included some elements of French civil law,[153] the reforms of the Turkish Republic, established in 1922, led to a more comprehensive Westernisation of the law. The main codes came from Switzerland (civil law, civil procedure, and bankruptcy law) and Germany (commercial law and criminal procedure). This influence also continued, for instance, through translations of Swiss and German legal literature, and through refugees from Nazi Germany who became law professors at Turkish universities in the 1930s and 40s.[154] Some of the refugees also had an impact on the positive law: for example, Ernst E. Hirsch was the main adviser for the Turkish Commercial Code of 1957.

The second phase is characterised by more piecemeal legal transplants, often now from the US. In post-WWII Japan, the US influence was profound and not always voluntary.[155] Initially, the US put pressure on Japan to enact a democratic constitution, though it has also been said that some of those American ideas

---

[151] See Tamanaha 1993a (e.g. referring to the caste system, community sanctions, community ownership rights).
[152] See, e.g., Ramseyer 2009: 1701.
[153] Menski 2006: 355; Mattei 1994: 201; Zweigert and Kötz 1998: 298–91.
[154] Örücü 1999: 81–4; Örücü 2006b: 265.   [155] See, e.g., Kelemen and Sibbitt 2002.

have been misunderstood and mistranslated.[156] Transplants by pressure also occurred later on: for example, in the Structural Impediment Initiative (SII) of the 1990s, the US pressured Japan to make its law more open – for instance, by way of improving investors' rights.[157] Still, it is said that the main structure of Japanese law is closer to the (German) civil law than to the (US) common law.[158]

In other countries, too, we can observe selective but influential US transplants: for instance, in South Korea, the Philippines, Liberia, and Israel.[159] In China, the shift to a market economy has led to an influx of some US law, but also of laws from other Western and Eastern countries, such as Germany, France, Japan, and Taiwan.[160] Recent transplant experience in Turkey is also mixed: as a candidate country it pays special attention to EU law, but there are also some examples of US legal transplants.[161]

(b) The law in practice

Both of these phases are akin to the transplants in continental European and colonial countries: comprehensive transplants in the past, but more selective ones today, often with some transplants from the US. But do these transplants 'fit' better or worse than in other countries? On the one hand, transplants in countries that were not under colonial occupation may work better, since they tend to be voluntary ones. On the other hand, Western legal transplants are more likely to be rejected in non-Western countries, nor have the countries discussed here experienced a diffusion of Western culture through one of the colonial empires.

Starting again with Japan, there is indeed the view that there is only a 'façade of Western law'.[162] Since both the transplanted law, and, indeed, the underlying Western vision of legal rationality, are seen as alien to Japanese culture and society, it is said that Western law has often not been accepted, and that the law in books and in practice diverges widely.[163] Convergence is seen as unlikely, since Japanese legal thinking is held to show a particularly strong path dependency, and even to be unique.[164]

But such scepticism should also not be exaggerated. It was not the case that Japan only copied the legal texts of Western countries. From the very beginning of the process, legal academics and practitioners established close links between Germany and Japan.[165] More recently, legal practice has also moved closer together. The increasing need for international legal advice meant that

---

[156] Inoue 1991. See also Inoue 2002 (for the contentious understanding of the term 'dignity' in the Japanese constitution).

[157] See Siems 2008a: 317.   [158] Mattei et al. 2009: 199. See also ch. 4 at C 3 (a), above.

[159] Mattei et al. 2009: 196; Mattei 1994: 207.   [160] See Siems 2007a: 66.

[161] See, e.g., Kayaalp 2012 (for diffusion of regulatory agencies).   [162] Ehrmann 1976: 47.

[163] See the references in Siems 2008a: 258–9.   [164] See Kitagawa 2006: 249–50.

[165] E.g., through the East-Asian Society (OAG), established in 1873, see www.oag.jp/ueber-die-oag.

since the late 1980s the establishment of foreign lawyers and the setting up of foreign-Japanese partnerships have been eased.[166] Moreover, socio-economic and cultural changes can be seen as forces for legal convergence – where convergence does not only refer to an approximation of the positive law but also to the way it is applied.[167]

The recent reforms in China have triggered similar responses. On the one hand, it has been called a 'myth that Western laws govern the social field to the exclusion of all other law-founding elements'.[168] On the other hand, there is some evidence that hitherto accepted statements about the Chinese understanding of law have to be re-thought. In the Chinese academia, Western conceptions of legal theory and philosophy are debated, and are being adopted to a not inconsiderable extent.[169] There have also been liberalisations for foreign law firms doing business in China,[170] as well as joined academic institutions and programmes.[171] Moreover, a successful reception of foreign law does not exclude variation: for instance, it has been suggested that the principle of good faith, which was transplanted to Chinese contract law, can also incorporate Confucian ideas and values.[172]

In Turkey, the legal transplants of the 1920s were part of a programme to transform society: according to Mahmut Esat Bozkurt, the Minister of Justice of that time, the aim was to free the Turkish nation from 'thirteen centuries of ill beliefs and chaos, close the doors of an old civilisation, and enter the modern civilisation'.[173] However, there have been doubts as to how comprehensive this shift has been. In family law, the Civil Code broke with most (though not all) Islamic traditions, but it is often said that it had limited effect and that customary practices continued.[174] Scholars have also examined how far the transplanted law has taken hold in the rural areas of Turkey. Unsurprisingly, the picture is a mixed one. While informal means of solving disputes continue to play a role, sometimes villagers also make use of the formal legal system, including disputes about family law.[175]

The overall result is that, in non-colonial non-Western countries, the experience of legal transplants shows many similarities to those of colonial and Western countries: laws have been frequently transplanted, affecting the local environment, but not in a naive and mechanical way.

---

[166] See Siems 2008a: 259–60.   [167] See ch. 9 at A 3 and B, below.
[168] Menski 2006: 586. See also ch. 4 at C 2 (a), above.
[169] See Siems 2008a: 261.   [170] See Siems 2008a: 262.
[171] For the China-EU Law School (CELS) see www.cesl.edu.cn/. For a joined programme see, e.g. http://law.sjtu.edu.cn/International/Article120401.aspx. See also ch. 10 at B 2 (on the rule of law in China).
[172] See Wang and Xu 1999: 16.
[173] As translated in Yildirim 2005: 358. See also Özsunay 2011: 5; Örücü 2006b: 265 ('aim was to become European').
[174] See, e.g., Menski 2006: 361–2; Cotterrell 2001: 89; Watson 2007: 9. For the Islamic elements see Yildirim 2005: 359.
[175] Starr 1978. See also Örücü 2006b: 280.

4. The globalisation of human rights law

(a) Human rights and judicial review in Western legal systems

Today, human rights play a role in all parts of the world. Still, it is useful to start with the Western legal systems: France and the United States are often seen as the origin countries of codified human rights.[176] But there are also significant differences between them. Both of their catalogues include civil and political rights. In addition, in France but not in the US, some social and economic rights are provided for, whereas in the US, but not in France, cultural rights of minorities are more readily accepted.

In the nineteenth and twentieth centuries, human rights were incorporated in the constitutions of other continental European countries. Significant US influence can be identified in Germany after the Second World War, and in the Central and Eastern European countries after the fall of communism.[177] But these human rights catalogues are also distinctly 'European'. As in France, they often include social rights, and the German constitution puts much emphasis on dignity as the pre-eminent constitutional value which can be seen as a reaction to the atrocities of the Third Reich.[178] By contrast, the United Kingdom does not have a constitutionally entrenched bill of rights.[179] However, it is subject to the European Convention on Human Rights (ECHR). Thus, today, the situation in the UK has been characterised by a complex evolution that tries to reconcile 'degrees of loyalty to European doctrine and reliance on Commonwealth sources of influence'.[180]

It has also been discussed more generally how the interaction between domestic and European courts has led to the emergence of fundamental rights 'as a lingua franca within and across European jurisdictions'.[181] Here, comparative law has an important role to play: the manner in which human rights laws are formulated gives judges considerable scope of interpretation; more specifically, the European Court of Human Rights (ECtHR) often considers whether a consensus exists in the way human rights are protected at the level of its member states.[182] This may be a challenging task given the differences between civil and common law countries in Europe. Yet, an empirical study has found that legal families are not a significant factor in disagreements between judges.[183] This is an important insight, given the growing internationalisation of human rights. It also confirms the position of this book that the traditional classification of legal families plays only a limited role in many areas of law.[184]

---

[176] For this and the following see Chen 2006: 489–90; Panditaratne 2006: 99; Scoffoni 2006: 76, 90 (also contrasting France with Canada and Spain).

[177] See, e.g., Schneider 2010; Barak-Erez 2009: 480–1.   [178] See, e.g., Whitman 2004.

[179] For comparisons with other common law countries see Goldsworthy 2006; Lee 2011.

[180] Cohn 2010: 583.

[181] Lasser 2009b. See also von Staden 2012 (quantitative analysis of compliance with the judgments of the ECtHR).

[182] See, e.g., Dzehtsiarou 2010; Ambrus 2009 (but lack of consistency and transparency criticised).

[183] Arold 2007a; Arold 2007b.   [184] See ch. 4 at C 3 (c), above.

The question of judicial review of acts of parliament is a potentially controversial one.[185] On the one hand, due to the concept of limited government,
human rights should hold the state accountable, including the law-maker. On
the other hand, it may be argued that, in a democracy, 'activist' and 'political'
judges should not be allowed to challenge the will of the people as expressed by
the primacy of parliament. There may also be other tools to ensure compliance
with human rights: for example, constitutional checks and balances prior to the
moment a law comes into force.

The US Supreme Court allowed judicial review of primary legislation in
a landmark decision of 1803.[186] While in Australia and Israel judicial review
has also been advanced by courts,[187] in most countries it was legislators who
introduced or extended judicial review, often under US influence. Notably
this was the case in Germany, Austria, and Italy after the Second World War,
in Canada in 1982, and in many Central and Eastern European countries
after the fall of communism.[188] Only a few countries have been more hesitant.
Notably this has been the case for the UK, which follows a relatively strict model
of parliamentary sovereignty.[189] Initially, the situation in France was similar,
but in 1958 a limited abstract form of judicial review was introduced, and in
2008 citizens were allowed to file constitutional complaints.[190] In addition, the
ECtHR can review violations of individual rights that occur in its member states.

A distinction remains depending on whether countries have separate courts
for constitutional review.[191] On the one hand, for example, in the US, Sweden
and Switzerland, the same courts deal with questions of constitutional and other
areas of law. On the other hand, there is the model of separate constitutional
courts (or constitutional councils) in, for instance, Austria, Germany, France
and Italy. These are based on Hans Kelsen's position that ordinary courts only
have the task of applying, but not evaluating, parliamentary laws. This has
further consequences, including, for instance, that appointments to a constitutional court require special procedures and that not all constitutional judges
may be qualified lawyers.

Overall, it can be seen that the protection of human rights has become
accepted in the Western world, with legal transplants playing an important
role, though this is not to say that all countries provide the same set of human

---

[185] See, e.g., Kokott and Kaspar 2012: 796–805; Guarnieri and Pederzoli 2001: 13, 150, 186;
Ginsburg 2012: 296–9; Shapiro and Stone Sweet 2002: 138–56.
[186] *Marbury* v. *Madison* 5 US 137 (1803). See also Koopmans 2003: 35, 51–7, 233 (for discussion
about judicial restraint and activism in the US).
[187] See Horwitz 2009: 543, 549.
[188] See Koopmans 2003: 40–4; Mattei et al. 2009: 524; Utter and Lundsgaard 1993; also Ginsburg
2012: 291–5 (distinguishing between three waves).
[189] See Koopmans 2003: 15; Glendon et al. 2008: 66–7; Horwitz 2009: 543 (yet also
'interpretation' of statutes to avoid 'constitutional' problems).
[190] See now art. 61–1 of the Constitution of the Fifth Republic.
[191] For the following see Ferreres Comella 2011; Bell 2006a: 38, 99; Bell 2006b: 258; Tushnet
2006a: 1227, 1242–3; Twining et al. 2006: 135; Kelsen 1942 (comparing Austria and the US).

rights.[192] And despite recent trends to allow judicial review, enforcement mechanisms also differ to a considerable degree. But it may also matter that legislative transplants have been supplemented by judicial ones, as is evident in some of the cross-citations between constitutional and supreme courts in Europe.[193]

(b) Should 'the Western model of human rights' be transplanted?

The concept of human rights is closely linked to the history of Europe and North America.[194] Landmarks for civil and political rights are the English Magna Carta Libertatum of 1215, the Age of Enlightenment (notably the philosophers John Locke, Jean-Jacques Rousseau and Immanuel Kant), the American Declaration of Independence of 1776, and the French Declaration of Human Rights of 1789. The nineteenth and twentieth centuries have also left their marks on human rights: for instance, reactions to the industrial revolution triggered the idea of social and economic rights, and those to Fascism and Nazism the need to protect ethnic and religious minorities.

According to 'cultural relativists', these Western origins mean that human rights are not 'universal' and that they should not be imposed on other cultures.[195] If such imposition occurs, this is sometimes also seen as a 'neo-imperial' endeavour, for example, in promoting property rights that mainly benefit international companies and investors.[196] Indeed, the non-universality of human rights may already be seen in the Western world, given the variation in the availability of economic, social, cultural, and community rights. In other parts of the world, the very idea of individual human rights may be challenged. For example, such formal legal rights may not be appropriate for societies in Africa and the Middle East, which are based on kinship and other group-centred social structures, and where law and religion are not strictly separated.[197] It has also been said that 'Asian values' may be irreconcilable with human rights. For instance, reference is made to the collectivist and communitarian principles in Asian culture, the idea of thinking about what is 'good' (not what is 'right'), as well as 'a deep Asian spiritualism, historical practice of non-violence, and inner respect for the environment'.[198]

---

[192] On the need for 'national margins of appreciation' (initially developed by the ECtHR) see, e.g. Delmas-Marty 2009: 47–51; Glenn 2009: 35; Peerenboom 2006: 39.

[193] See ch. 7 at A 1, above.

[194] For the following see van Genugten 2012: 205–6; Goldman 2008: 227, 233, 301–2; Chen 2006: 506.

[195] See, e.g., Steiner and Alston 2000: 366–402; Kennedy 2002: 114; Menski 2006: 13, 41–2; Fedtke 2008: 50; Cotterrell 2002.

[196] Mattei and Nader 2008: 153; Goldman 2008: 247; Obiora 1998: 673–4; Santos 2002: 44 (as 'globalization from above'). See also ch. 10 at C, below.

[197] Mattei and Nader 2008: 144; Glenn 2010a: 222; Muir Watt 2006: 598.

[198] For these points see Twining 2009a: 199 and Goldman 2008: 232–2; Pangalangan 2006: 347 and Glenn 2010a: 336; Mamlyuk and Mattei 2011: 430. See also Steiner and Alston 2000: 538–53; Bloise 2010: 3.

However, the globalisation of human rights also has its supporters. Human rights may be of Western origin, but this should not lead us to a 'genetic fallacy', as they may well reflect universal human principles.[199] A modified version of this view is that human rights are an expression of modernity and, therefore, in today's world, are transferable to non-Western countries. For example, in many of those countries today, state powers and the forces of free markets make individuals seek the protection provided by human rights. There is also some evidence that, as societies become wealthier, its citizens become more interested in civil and political rights.[200]

A compromise between these two views is that human rights *can* play a role throughout the world, but that they are *not only* of Western origin. According to this view, it is misleading to postulate isolated legal orders and, for instance, a strict dichotomy between European and Asian values.[201] It has also been suggested that the Asian values debate was largely rhetorical, since it was used by autocratic regimes in order to defend their poor human rights record against foreign criticism.[202] More specifically, scholars have shown that human rights are not simply a 'gift of the West to the rest',[203] but that they can also be reconciled with African, Islamic and other traditions.[204] Thus, according to this view, a global ethic and a dialogical human rights discourse are the way forward[205] – not simply one-sided transplants of 'Western' human rights.

(c) The role of human rights in the world

The international regime of human rights, starting with the UN Universal Declaration of Human Rights of 1948 (UDHR), covers civil and political rights, economic, social and cultural rights, as well as some of the 'third generation' rights such as minority rights, women's rights, other group and community rights, as well as a right to development. The UN takes the view that countries have a duty to protect human rights 'regardless of their political, economic and cultural systems',[206] and most of the treaties and protocols have indeed been ratified by the majority of countries in the world.[207]

But some trends show that human rights are not entirely global. For example, comparative studies on the Convention on the Elimination of Discrimination against Women (CEDAW) have explored the difficulties of translating this

---

[199] E.g. Sharma 2006: 244; Headley 2008. See also F. von Benda-Beckmann 2009: 120, 126 (distinction between normative and empirical statements about universality).

[200] Chen 2006: 487, 506; Bloise 2010: 10; Friedman 1996: 85.

[201] Twining 2009a: 42, 414. See generally also ch. 4 at C 2 (a), above.

[202] Twining 2009a: 199.   [203] Baxi 2006b: 33.

[204] Menski 2006: 489 ('clever lies and assertions to the effect that Africa had no indigenous concepts of good governance, and democracy, of human rights, and of justice'); F. von Benda-Beckmann 2009: 118; Twining 2009a: 187, 393, 412.

[205] For these points see, e.g., Goldman 2008: 235–6; Twining 2009a: 430. Similarly Santos 2002 (for a multicultural conception of human rights).

[206] UN General Assembly 1993: para. 5.   [207] Baumgartner 2011: 444.

convention into actual practice at the local level.[208] In addition, many countries of the Middle East have entered reservations to the CEDAW as far as it is seen as incompatible with Islamic principles. Human rights charters have also been developed at a regional level, starting with the ECHR in 1953. Some of those provisions reflect regional traditions: for instance, the African charter includes duties of individuals owed to the family and society.[209]

Quantitative research by David Law and Mila Versteeg has constructed an index of fifty-six provisions on human rights, coding the constitutions of most countries of the world in a sixty-year dataset. They found that, in 1946, the average constitution contained nineteen of these provisions, which rose to thirty-three out of fifty-six in 2006. Moreover, Law and Versteeg report that the availability of judicial review has also increased in this period: from 35 per cent to 87 per cent of all countries.[210] This trend is in line with research by Arne Mavčič who identified precisely which model of judicial review countries pursue.[211] Quantitative research has also tried to identify whether the adoption of new human rights and the availability of judicial review can be attributed to international norm diffusion, or whether these are more a product of domestic developments, with mixed results.[212]

Further, there is some evidence that ratification of human rights treaties leads to lower human rights violations, though this evidence is not very strong, in particular for non-democratic countries.[213] Evidently, the availability of human rights provisions and judicial review does not mean that protection is effective and equivalent throughout the world.[214] At a fundamental level, the problem is that some governments may regard constitutional provisions protecting human rights as merely symbolic and are unwilling to hold themselves accountable. The availability of judicial review may not provide a remedy if access to justice requires the investment of significant financial resources or if judges are not sufficiently independent. Moreover, even when governments and judges are committed to implementing human rights, there is the question of how precisely this is done, since human rights laws often leave considerable scope for interpretation and the balancing of conflicting interests.

Thus, a more valid assessment requires further analysis of how, in particular countries, human rights have been transplanted, and of how well they work.

---

[208] Merry 2006; Ali 2006 (in the context of Islamic forms of adjudication).

[209] See van Genugten 2012: 217–8.

[210] Law and Versteeg 2011: 1195, 1199. See also ch. 7 at B 2, above.

[211] See the data available at www.concourts.net/.

[212] See Elkins et al. 2013 (finding that UDHR and ICCPR triggered some convergence); Ginsburg and Versteeg 2013 (finding that constitutional review is mainly driven by domestic electoral politics). Further references in Landman and Carvalho 2010: 86–8.

[213] Baumgartner 2011; Landman 2008: 246. More positive Simmons 2009.

[214] For the following see Kennedy 2002: 116; Horwitz 2009: 542–5; Klug 2005: 92; Twining 2009a: 297.

For example, the protection of human rights in South Africa and India is said to work reasonably well,[215] but is this a result of legal transplants? With respect to South Africa, one may answer in the affirmative.[216] The bill of rights of the South African Constitution of 1996 has been influenced by its German, US, Canadian, and Indian counterparts. In its application, the South African Constitutional Court has also considered the case law of other countries: for instance, in considering the horizontal effect of human rights, it referred to the German Constitutional Court. By contrast, the strong rights for religious and cultural minorities in the Indian Constitution of 1950 are said to be more closely related to the specific Indian historical context, namely the growing tensions between Hindus and Muslims after gaining independence.[217] But the Indian Constitution can also be seen as following a general trend, since social, economic and cultural rights were also part of the UN Universal Declaration on Human Rights of 1948.

The discussion about the Japanese Constitution of 1947 is similar as regards a provision granting an individual right to receive welfare. On the one hand, it could be something uniquely Japanese that was added to the US model the Japanese law-maker was compelled to follow.[218] On the other hand, this right can be related to the US New Deal legislation of the 1930s, the emerging European welfare states, and the discussions preceding the Universal Declaration on Human Rights in the post-war period.[219] To be sure, none of those provided a constitutionally enshrined right to receive welfare. But then, we must also consider that, in practice, Japanese courts are said to follow a cautious approach in enforcing human rights.[220]

This cautiousness of Japanese courts raises the more general question of whether it shows the uniqueness of 'Asian values', possibly including a general reluctance to resort to litigation.[221] Statements on the lack of effectiveness of human rights protection in Hong Kong and Indonesia[222] may confirm this point. But there are also some counter-examples. The Supreme Court of the Philippines is seen as showing activism, compensating for the deficiencies of politics,[223] and, since the enactment of the South Korean Constitution of 1987, the Korean Constitutional Court is said to exercise 'high equilibrium judicial

---

[215] Singh et al. 2007 (specifically referring to health reforms); Young 2012: 200–7 (Indian Supreme Court as 'engaged court'). But see also Kumar 2011 (on the impact of widespread corruption on human rights in India).

[216] For the following see Fedtke 2008; Moran 2006; Davis 2003.

[217] Baxi 2006a: 385, 394. See also Menski 2006: 268–70.

[218] See Bloise 2010: 21, 24; Shigenori 2006: 146 (comparing it with the US).

[219] See Bloise 2010: 16; Shigenori 2006: 140 (comparing it with Germany); Horwitz 2009: 536.

[220] See Shigenori 2006: 148; Law 2011a: 1440. But also Brown Hamano 1999: 483 (not 'a mere alien transplant that failed').

[221] See (b) and ch. 4 at C 2 (a), above.   [222] See Petersen 2006: 224; Juwana 2006: 365.

[223] See Pangalangan 2006: 360.

review', and is becoming 'a forum for groups seeking to advance social change as well as for individual disputes'.[224]

The overall picture is that, today, human rights do play a role in many parts of the world and that, often, this is due to foreign influence. This finding does not imply that human rights protection is identical throughout the world. Moreover, the case of human rights may be seen as a challenge to the concept of 'legal transplants', because copying the precise text of a particular provision is neither a necessary nor a sufficient condition for the effectiveness of human rights.

C. Conclusion

Legal transplants were crucial for the emergence of legal families in Europe and in the way those models spread to other parts of the world. But legal transplants are also very topical today since, to quote Patrick Glenn, 'nowadays all traditions are in constant contact with one or more of the other legal traditions'.[225] These 'modern' transplants tend to differ from the old ones:

> Transplants are no longer adoptions of entire systems of law in a top-down fashion initiated by colonial forces. Instead, they come in different shapes and sizes, take place serially, and originate in a variety of sources.[226]

This implies, first, that legal transplants are now more often voluntary than in the past. This is not, however, to deny that there can be elements of involuntariness, for instance, if countries feel that they are under international political or economic pressure to implement certain policies. Second, legal families have become less important for contemporary legal transplants. This is not to say that common historical paths may not continue to play a role, but these are now often overlaid by trends of Americanisation, Europeanisation, and internationalisation. Third, there can be different dynamics in different areas of law. While legal transplants can and have played a role in all areas of law,[227] certain foreign models may be more popular in some areas of law than in others, as examples from general private, family, and human rights law have illustrated.

The question remains whether we can say that modern legal transplants typically 'work'. In the past, there have often been cases where legal transplants purely meant copying or translating a particular foreign legal text. Today, however, the main aim tends to be to transfer a particular policy – be it driven by the transplant or the origin country. Thus, the respective country has an interest in the transplanted law working. While this aim could still be unfulfilled, a careful

---

[224] See Ginsburg 2003: 242; Chaihark 2006: 285–6 (on inspiration from German law).
[225] Glenn 2010a: 43.   [226] Cohn 2010: 628. See also A 3, above.
[227] For a similar assessment see Perju 2012: 1311–3; Harding 2002: 45 (for South East Asia). For the counter-view see A 2 (d), above.

comparative analysis – going beyond the text of the positive law – can reduce this risk.

Recent trends related to legal transplants (as well as other concepts) are discussed in the following two chapters. These, too, will show that transplants play an important role, though not in a simple and mechanical way. For example, while typically legal transplants occur at the horizontal level between national legal systems, this chapter also provided some 'verticial' examples, where international hard and soft laws have played a role.[228] Here it can also be suggested that such transfers can create a new normative 'space', distinct from national legal systems.[229] Thus, there is a need to analyse the relationship between the national, international, and possible 'transnational' levels in more detail, as the subsequent chapter will do.

---

[228] See B 1 (b) and 4 C, above and Perju 2012: 1319–20 (distinguishing between horizontal and vertical migration).
[229] Hendry 2013.

9

Fading state borders

The primary interest of traditional comparative law lies in exploring legal differences and similarities between countries.[1] Thus, for this type of comparative legal research the existence of state borders plays an important role. Such borders are also relevant for many postmodern and socio-legal comparatists, as far as it can be said that the people of a particular country tend to share the same culture and values. To be sure, this latter notion of a 'nation state' is of European origins, and it does not work well if, as in many of the former colonies, state borders have been drawn in an arbitrary way.[2]

The more fundamental question, however, is whether we can talk about a decline of the notion of 'state borders' and the implications of such decline for comparative law. The three topics discussed in this chapter share a common ground, in that they challenge the relevance of location and state borders for legal questions. This may be the case because national legal systems have become more similar (convergence, Section B), laws are unified for a group of neighbouring countries (regionalisation, Section C), or the applicable law is not related to a particular country (transnationalisation, Section D). But it can also be suggested that such claims go too far. Thus, this chapter also considers reasons why state borders may still be of central importance today.

It should be noted that the three main topics discussed in this chapter are not independent of each other: regional and transnational laws can be forces for the convergence of legal systems, regional laws are influenced by the rules that the countries of this region have in common, and transnational laws are dependent on the extent to which national legal systems accept and enforce them. Thus, before turning to these three categories, Section A will set the scene and address some of the general issues related to fading state borders.

A. Setting the scene

1. The 'end of history' and the 'end of state'?

The topics discussed in this chapter are closely related to claims of an 'end of history' and an 'end of state'. The 'end of history' refers to the title of publications by Francis Fukuyama who in 1989 took the view that:

[1] See Part I, above. [2] For research on such 'artificial states' see Easterly 2006: 256–7.

What we may be witnessing is not just the end of the Cold War, or the passing of a particular period of post-war history, but the end of history as such: that is, the end point of mankind's ideological evolution and the universalization of Western liberal democracy as the final form of human government.[3]

In a follow-up comment, twenty years later, Fukuyama asserts that there has been a continuing trend towards liberal democracy. Furthermore, he takes the view that cultural values have also been affected: specifically, Fukuyama refers to human rights, accountability of state powers and the rule of law to which non-Western societies have been converging.[4]

With explicit reference to Fukuyama, Henry Hansmann and Reinier Kraakman postulate that the historical differences in company law have faded in favour of approximation to the US model.[5] Similar views have been expressed by others. Jan Dalhuisen calls modern laws 'practical, technical and problem-solving' and notes that they do not differ greatly from country to country.[6] Similarly, Lawrence Friedman takes the position:

> It seems obvious that a French lawyer and an English lawyer would have an easier time comparing notes on, say, urban planning, income tax deductions, or copyright protection for software, than they would discussing legal problems with a lawyer from the days of Henry VIII or Louis XIV, respectively. The legal worlds of those two kings are gone forever.[7]

Others go further: globalisation is not merely seen as a force of approximation but leading to an 'erosion' (or 'retreat', 'decline', 'disaggregation', 'hollowing out') of the state.[8] This claim has a domestic and an international dimension though both also overlap. With respect to the domestic level, the state may be disaggregating since today state functions are often split between various parts, not only between the government, the legislature and the courts but also between regulatory agencies, public-private partnerships, self-regulatory bodies and other non-state entities. This is often called 'governance' (in contrast to 'government'), meaning that instead of mandatory and hierarchical legal norms cooperative and other innovative forms of law-making are used.[9] In addition, the privatisation of law-making challenges the notion that the state has a monopoly of governance power and that there is a strict distinction between the state and society.[10]

---

[3] Fukuyama 1989: 13. See also Fukuyama 1992.

[4] Fukuyama 2010. For human rights see also ch. 8 at B 4, above, and for the rule of law see also ch. 10 at B, below.

[5] Hansmann and Kraakman 2001. See also B 2, below.

[6] Dalhuisen 2004:128.   [7] Friedman 1996: 74.

[8] See, e.g., Santos and Rodriguez-Garavito 2005: 5 ('eroding state power'); Strange 1996 ('retreat of the state'); Mattei 1998: 710 (claims that nation state in serious decline); Berman 2009: 236 (disaggregation of the state); Coe et al. 2010: 216 (hollowing out of the state).

[9] See, e.g., Rhodes 1997; Santos and Rodriguez-Garavito 2005: 5, 272. See also ch. 7 at C 1 and 2, above (on use of indicators).

[10] See Backer 2012: 92–3; Calliess 2012; Tamanaha 2001: 129. For examples in international commercial law see D 2, below.

The disaggregation of the state is also said to continue at the international level. It is seen as the sign of a new 'transgovernmentalism' that not only do governments interact with each other but so do courts, regulatory agencies and other parts of the state.[11] The interdependence of societies also challenges national sovereignty: states have no choice but to collaborate, not only through international treaties, but also through more complex intergovernmental forms of global governance.[12] This includes the use of soft-law which can refer to legal norms that do not have the form of a source of law or to all legal norms which are not enforceable (even if they are in the form of a formal legal source).[13] Due to the lack of a global government, the international sphere may also need to rely on private forms of law and regulation,[14] and given the power of multinational companies, credit agencies, investment funds, audit firms and other private organisations, it is expected that market forces, private regulatory bodies, contracts and arbitration may become the dominant forms of order in a 'borderless world'.[15]

These general claims may sound a bit exaggerated. Thus, the following addresses two more specific themes in order to understand whether and how laws have become more similar, more regional and more transnational. The first one concerns the relevance of private and public transnational law for globalisation and comparative law, and the second one outlines possible forces for convergence, regionalisation and transnationalisation of the law.

2. The role of public and private international law

(a) Public international law

It may be thought that a main reason for a growing similarity of laws is that countries agree on treaties and conventions that envisage the harmonisation of legal rules. Yet, the relationship between public international law and domestic legal systems – and, by implication, comparative law – has become a more complex one.

To start with, domestic laws can be relevant for the understanding of international law. When international laws are drafted based on legal concepts that already exist at the domestic level, the latter can be helpful for the interpretation of the former.[16] Here, it is said that lawyers from common law countries need to consider that the mind-set of international treaties is predominantly 'civilian'

---

[11] See Gordon 2010: 507; Slaughter 1997: 184.

[12] See, e.g., Picciotto 2011; Gilpin 2001: 80, 390, 398; Darian-Smith 2013: 177–8.

[13] Blutman 2010: 606.   [14] Cafaggi 2011: 23. See also D, below.

[15] See Calliess and Hoffmann 2009: 119; Gilpin 2001: 8; Coe et al. 2010: 218; Economides and Wilson 2001: 6. The term 'borderless world' is from Ohmae 1990.

[16] See, e.g., Momirov and Naudé Fourie 2009: 295 (calling this vertical, 'bottom-up' legal comparison). E.g. domestic tort and insurance law have inspired the Vienna Convention on Civil Liability for Nuclear Damage 1997 and the International Convention on Civil Liability for Oil Pollution Damage 1969.

in origin.[17] It is also suggested to consider the role of national courts since those not only enforce international law but may also play a role in creating international rules.[18]

In some cases, international law explicitly requires a comparative approach: for example, the International Court of Justice (ICJ) shall not only apply international conventions and customs but also 'the general principles of law recognized by civilized nations', and the International Criminal Court (ICCt) shall also apply the 'general principles of law derived by the Court from national laws of legal systems of the world'.[19]

These provisions, however, raise a number of problems. First, the terms 'civilised nations' and 'legal systems of the world' are unsatisfactory. Although treating certain countries as more 'civilised' than others was common in the early twentieth century,[20] today it is rightly discredited. It is also hardly feasible to examine the rules in question of all legal systems of the world. Second, therefore, a common approach is to consider representative legal systems, for instance, those seen as the origin countries of the main legal families.[21] Such an approach may also be supported by the criteria of appointment to the ICJ and ICCt, namely that these courts shall represent 'the principal legal systems of the world'.[22] This raises the question, however, whether the focus of traditional comparative law on major legal systems and legal families has not become outdated.[23] Third, it may be doubtful whether principles of national law can really be transferred to the international level. They may work perfectly well in the domestic context but may not be suitable for the international one.[24] Comparative law also teaches us that legal differences are often related to social, economic or cultural ones: thus, given those differences, a principle may just not be transferable.[25] To be sure, it can help that the focus is on 'general principles', not specific rules. This may make it easier to identify common ground, and, then, to adapt the general principles to more specific rules of international law.[26]

The local context is also relevant for the impact that international law has on domestic law. To start with, it can be distinguished whether countries treat international and domestic law as a unity ('monism') or whether they require

[17] Blakesley et al. 2001: 4. But see also Mitchell and Powell 2011: 11 (it depends on who drafted treaty in question); Romano 2003 (suggesting an Americanisation of international litigation); ch. 8 at B 4 (c), above (on 'third generation' human rights, incorporating concepts from non-Western countries).

[18] Roberts 2011 (with examples from Italy and the US).

[19] ICJ Statute, art. 38(1)(c); ICCt Statute, art. 21(1)(c).

[20] See ch. 2 at B 2 (b) and ch. 11 at C 1, above. The formulation goes back to the Statute of the Permanent Court of International Justice (PCIJ) 1920, art. 38(3).

[21] See Ellis 2011: 957; Pellet in Zimmermann et al. 2006: Art. 38, para. 258. See also *Right of Passage over Indian Territory (Portugal* v. *India)* (1957) ICJ Rep 125, 141–42 ('the main systems of law').

[22] ICJ Statute, art. 9; ICCt Statute, art. 36(8)(a).   [23] See ch. 3 at C and ch. 4 at C, above.

[24] Bothe and Ress 1980: 62.   [25] Ellis 2011: 959, 968. See also ch. 6 at A 2 (a), above.

[26] Lauterpacht 1927 (early example for using models derived from domestic private law); Waldock 1962: 56 (for the second statement).

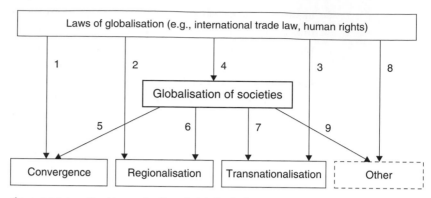

Figure 9.1 International law as the 'law of globalisation'

a transposition of international law into the domestic context ('dualism').[27] Considering the extent of commitment to particular international treaties, it can also be examined whether participation reflects differences between legal families.[28] Moreover, there is the question of how the international law is actually applied. If it is drafted in general terms, such as human rights treaties, a comparative analysis of domestic laws and practices is needed in order to find out how far international law has led to actual uniformity.[29] In this context, it also needs to be considered whether international legal rules are accompanied by an institutional structure, such as an international organisation, possibly also with adjudicative tribunals,[30] and how those may contribute to a global legal culture.

This leads to the more general question about the relationship between globalisation and international law. It has been said that globalisation has impacted on international law since the cooperation of independent sovereign states is now replaced by an interdependence of states.[31] In particular, this is reflected in the fact that complex and dynamic forms of networked and experimental governance have supplemented traditional forms of international law.[32] But international law has also been one of the driving forces for globalisation.

Figure 9.1 illustrates possible causal effects of international law as 'the law of globalisation'[33]. As (1) shows, international laws may directly lead to the convergence of the legal rules of a particular area of law. They may also stimulate regionalisation (2): for example, the World Trade Organization (WTO)

---

[27] See, e.g., Aust 2010: 75–6; Glenn 2013: 240.
[28] Mitchell and Powell 2011 (for commitment to international courts).
[29] See ch. 8 at B 4, above (for human rights) and, e.g., Svensson and Larsson 2009 (study on divergent application of copyright laws).
[30] There is a trend to establish such structures. See, e.g., Koch 2003; Hobe 2002: 384.
[31] Hobe 2002: 386.
[32] See, e.g., de Búrca et al. 2013. For networked governance see also C 3, below.
[33] For this term see Boulle 2009.

allows for regional trade agreements under certain conditions.[34] International law can also be linked to transnational law of a private nature (3): for example, the WTO may endorse private standards, or the World Bank may make funding conditional upon their compliance.[35] In addition, international law can contribute to the globalisation of societies (4): for instance, the WTO framework has the aim to increase cross-border trade and services. These factual developments further contribute to the globalisation of laws, i.e. convergence, regionalisation and transnationalisation (5)–(7).[36] Of course, one should not be naive – or 'hyperglobalist'[37] – in always assuming such causalities. International laws and growing international trade do not automatically lead to uniform rules: for example, it is possible that domestic legal rules remain unchanged ('path-dependence') or that legal changes only benefit the interests of powerful countries ('law under globalisation') (8) and (9).[38] Finally, it is worth noting that Figure 9.1 should not be read as implying that causalities cannot go in the reverse directions: for example, changes at the domestic level fostering the internationalisation of the law.

(b) Private international law

In private international law a broad distinction can be drawn between a 'European' and a (US) 'American model'.[39] The European one aims for policy-neutral rules of private international law agreed on a multilateral basis, which is aimed to determine the applicable law with legal certainty. By contrast, the American approach uses unilateral rules of private international law based on a country's own domestic interests. This is a crude distinction and in reality things are also often mixed, but it offers a useful starting point for examining the relationship between private international law and the topics of this chapter.

As far as private international law has the aim to decide clearly on the applicable law, the problem is how far this can really be achieved. It would not only require internationally uniform rules of private international law but it would also have to be ensured that these are applied in a uniform way. Thus, given this absence of a global private international law, the need for legal certainty can be seen as a driving force for the convergence of substantive laws. Similarly, it has been suggested that private-international-law problems for cross-border businesses are a motivation for transnational law, such as the new *lex mercatoria*.[40]

As far as countries can decide unilaterally which laws they apply, the consequence is often that domestic laws have an effect beyond their borders. Such extraterritoriality can be found in US securities regulation: for example, the US

---

[34] See, e.g., Fazio 2007: 63; Ravenhill 2011: 177, 193–5. Regional arrangements are also acknowledged in Chapter VIII of the UN Charter.

[35] See, e.g., Cafaggi 2011: 42; Ohnesorge 2009.   [36] See also 3, below.

[37] Cf. Hay 2011: 317.   [38] For these two concepts see also B 3, below, and Part III pr., above.

[39] See, e.g., Reimann 2006: 1374–6; Muir Watt 2006: 568.

[40] Juenger 2000. For the *lex mercatoria* see D 2, below.

rules on takeover bids apply if a certain proportion of the target's shareholders lives in the US – regardless of the fact that the companies involved may be foreign and therefore also have to comply with their domestic takeover laws.[41] It can also be the case that it is the jurisdiction of US courts that is extraterritorial. A prominent example is the US Alien Tort Statute. It provides that US courts have jurisdiction 'of any civil action by an alien for a tort . . . committed in violation of the law of nations or a treaty of the United States'.[42] Since the 1980s courts have used this provision on various occasions to decide on compensation for human rights violations that took place in other countries.[43]

The extraterritorial effect of legal rules is not limited to US law. Indeed, it can be seen as a general phenomenon that in an increasingly interconnected world more than one legal system may be applicable.[44] Here, then, one may also identify a trend that European legal standards lead the way for topics such as health, safety and environmental risks.[45] A further twist is that firms may deliberately subject themselves to the rules of more than one legal system: for example, being listed at more than one stock exchange can be aimed at showing that a company not only wants to comply with the lax domestic rules but also the stricter foreign ones (called 'bonding effect'). This may then be described as 'functional convergence' since results become functionally similar between companies from various countries.[46]

Another way to address problems of private international law is to let individuals and companies choose the applicable law, possibly even regardless of spatial circumstances. Such choice of law is usually possible in contract law, though legal systems may require compliance with some mandatory domestic laws, for instance, on consumer protection.[47] In company law the main question is whether firms can freely choose their place of incorporation. Countries that follow the 'incorporation theory' recognise any company that is properly constituted according to the law of another country. By contrast, countries of the 'real-seat theory' seek to prevent the evasion of domestic law by requiring that a company has to be incorporated in the country of its headquarters. Thus, the situation in these countries is similar to those in tax law or labour law, where choice is tied in with being the resident of a country or having your factories or offices there.[48]

The important consequence of such choice is that it can stimulate 'regulatory competition' creating a 'law market', which Erin O'Hara and Larry Ribstein define as:

---

[41] See Siems 2004b. For other questions of securities law see, e.g., Siems 2008a: 274–5.

[42] Alien Tort Statute, 28 USC § 1350.

[43] But see also Kirshner 2012: US courts start backtracking; now also in *Kiobel* v. *Royal Dutch Petroleum Co.*, No. 10–1491 (US April 17, 2013).

[44] See Berman 2009: 235; Grossfeld and Eberle 2003: 296.

[45] Vogel 2012; also Bradford 2012 (as the 'Brussels effect').   [46] See Coffee 1999: 650, 681.

[47] See generally Goode et al. 2007: paras. 2.23–2.36.

[48] For all of this see references in Siems 2008a: 297–303.

... ways that governing laws can be chosen by the mobility of at least some people, firms, and assets and the incentives of at least some states to compete for people, firms and their assets by creating desired laws.[49]

Both the demand and the supply of such a market has been extensively researched for a number of areas of law.[50] On the one hand, the question can be asked which legal systems are most popular and why this is the case. The 'why' question can be a complex one because it cannot simply be assumed that individuals and firms compare the advantages and disadvantages of all legal systems. Rather, it is likely that other factors such as accessibility of information about foreign laws, the reputation of particular legal systems and the quality of its judiciary play a decisive role. On the other hand, it is not clear whether, why and how countries would really compete for the 'best law'. Clear benefits exist in some circumstances, for instance, when countries want to attract tax-paying businesses, but not in others. There is also the possibility that countries may react defensively, for instance, by way of providing rules for 'pseudo-foreign corporations' trying to evade domestic legal rules.[51]

Various connections can be made between regulatory competition and the topics of the present chapter. First, does regulatory competition stimulate legal convergence? Often this is suggested: assuming that a particular legal system is 'better', it seems plausible to say that others may try to imitate it. The direction of this convergence may not be entirely clear, however: for instance, in company law some suggest a 'race to the bottom' since legislators are exposed to pressure from company founders and managements and therefore deregulate the law at the expense of shareholders, creditors or employees. The counter-view stresses that there can be a 'race to the top' because, as with other forms of competition, the market's invisible hand leads to an optimal pattern for corporate governance.[52] But, it may also be suggested that regulatory competition can lead to divergence since competition stimulates innovation and specialisation as well as differentiation of legal systems according to different preferences. So, presumably it depends, as Anthony Ogus explains:

> [C]ompetition should exert pressure for a convergence of legal principles in those areas of law (e.g. contract, property and corporate law) which are predominantly facilitative. That is, because there is largely a homogeneity in the legal product being demanded, actors will search for the legal means of reaching desired outcomes at lowest cost . . . In contrast, it is difficult to predict the impact of competition in relation to interventionist law (for example, tort and regulation). Here the legal product is heterogeneous, because in different jurisdictions it is likely that different preferences will exist as to the levels of protection to be supplied and of the costs which must be incurred.[53]

[49] O'Hara and Ribstein 2009: 65.
[50] See, e.g., Druzin 2009, Vogenauer 2008 and Vogenauer 2013 (for choice of contract law and choice of forum); Schön 2005 (for company and tax law); Siems 2009b (for partnership law).
[51] For the EU and US debate see, e.g., Borg-Barthet 2010: 593–4, 606–9.
[52] See the references in Siems 2008a: 298.   [53] Ogus 1999: 420–1 (footnotes omitted).

Second, regionalisation plays a role as far as the region supports the idea of intra-regional regulatory competition. Notably this is the case in the EU. For example, a series of decisions of the European Court of Justice opened up the possibility of regulatory competition in company law, arguing that corporate mobility is protected by the freedom of establishment of the EU Treaty.[54] Regions may also decide to provide rules that can be chosen alternatively to those of its members: thus, 'horizontal competition' is supplemented by a 'vertical' one.[55] This may also be the case in EU company law since the Societas Europaea (SE) is an additional form of company available to cross-border businesses in the EU. Yet, there is the further twist that the SE is not a uniform type of company but that it differs according to the Member State in which it is incorporated: thus, there are also various types of SEs competing with each other.[56]

Third, in the context of regulatory competition, transnational law can provide additional legal rules to choose. This may be done within the framework of domestic laws: for example, as far as parties enjoy freedom of contract, transnational standard form contracts may become popular. The impact of transnational law may also go further if countries allow the choice of non-state law as a separate legal order.[57] Beyond choice of substantive law, transnational contracts often provide for arbitration – thus, raising questions about the choice between different arbitral tribunals and between those and state courts.[58]

3. Forces for convergence, regionalisation and transnationalisation

A previous book examined the reasons for the convergence in shareholder law in detail. Among the causes for convergence, it drew a distinction between 'convergence through congruence' and 'convergence through pressure'.[59] For Table 9.1, below, these categories have been modified in order to summarise what forces drive convergence of legal systems more generally.[60]

'Convergence through congruence' can arise where the social, political, and economic circumstances become similar internationally. Claims of a 'flat' world may often be exaggerated,[61] but there is also no denying the changes that have occurred. For example, in terms of economic policy, there are more market economies today than before the fall of communism. Economies and societies have also become more integrated, for instance, through modern forms of communication and means of transport.[62] This further contributes to cultural approximations, and it has also been suggested that a transnational modern legal

---

[54] References in Siems 2008a: 300–2.   [55] Fauvarque-Cosson 2007: 3.

[56] See Eidenmüller et al. 2011.   [57] E.g. suggested by Rühl 2013: 295.   [58] See D 2, below.

[59] Siems 2008a: 250–96 (for congruence) and 297–316 (for pressure).

[60] This is not to imply that there is not also a causal relationship that goes in the other direction (i.e. law shaping reality). See already ch. 6 at A 2, above.

[61] Cf. Twining 2009b: 39–40. See also ch. 11 at B 3, below (on varieties of capitalism).

[62] Lee and Olson 2010: 11–35 ('convergenomics').

Table 9.1 Convergence forces

	Specific reasons	How legal systems respond
Convergence through congruence	Convergence of economic policies Internationalisation of the economy and growing interdependencies (e.g. cross-border trade) Internationalisation and growing interdependencies of societies and cultures, e.g. through modern forms of communication and means of transport Internationalisation of private institutions (corporations, investment firms, law firms, NGOs etc.) Convergence and transnationalisation of legal cultures (legal thinking, training, scholarship)	Plausible to assume that the more similar the circumstances, the more similar the corresponding legal rules Communication and cooperation with other countries in law-making increasing International phenomena can indicate need for uniform solutions Path dependencies weakening
Convergence through pressure	Lobbying by companies, in particular multinational corporations (as well as by their shareholders, directors, employees etc.) Lobbying by other interest groups Influence of international organisations Influence of foreign states (including soft power, structural dependence etc.) Regulatory competition and extraterritorial effects of laws become more frequent	International lobbying leads to convergence since desire to reduce transaction costs National lobbying leads to convergence if in same direction Extraterritoriality and regulatory competition can lead to convergence Communication and weakening path dependencies: as for 'convergence through congruence'

culture has emerged with characteristics such as instrumentalism, individualism and legalism.[63]

As far as these circumstances have become similar across countries, it is plausible to assume that the law also becomes more similar, being supported by communication and cooperation between law-makers. For convergence forces that are international phenomena, such as the internet and global commerce, uniform solutions are even more likely. All of this does not deny the relevance of path dependencies accounting for continuing differences between

---

[63] See Friedman 1994; Tamanaha 2001: 127; Cotterrell 2006: 717.

legal systems.[64] Yet, legal systems are not static. Thus, the withering of existing path dependencies can also be a reason for convergence in law.

With respect to 'convergence through pressure' both private entities (companies, law firms, NGOs etc.) and public ones (states, international organisations etc.) play a role. It is also helpful to distinguish between international and national lobbying. As far as influence is targeted at the law-makers of more than one country, convergence is a typical outcome. For example, international organisations will usually advise (or urge) countries to follow the same model of legal rules.[65] A similar outcome is typical for the lobbying of corporations, law firms, business consultants and other private entities: as far as they conduct business in more than one country, uniformity has the benefit of reducing the costs and risks associated with the need to comply with different legal regimes.[66]

The situation is more complicated for domestic lobbying. For instance, if in one country shareholders are the main lobbyists but in another one managers, company laws will stay diverse. Thus, here, convergence depends on the question of whether the power relationship between interest groups becomes more similar across countries.[67] Moreover, under certain conditions, regulatory competition and the extraterritorial effect of laws can lead to convergence, as explained in the previous section.

Despite these forces, full convergence of all legal systems of the world cannot be expected. It is suggested, however, that the convergence forces of Table 9.1 also contribute to the regionalisation and transnationalisation of legal systems. Research on the first topic has identified various reasons why countries of a region collaborate,[68] which can be related to the categories of 'congruence' and 'pressure'. For example, when it is said that interdependence creates demand for regional cooperation and that regions are often formed by countries that have similar political structures,[69] this mirrors the reasons for 'convergence through congruence'. Other theories refer to the internal and external power relationships leading to regional collaboration,[70] akin to the reasons for 'convergence through pressure'. The arguments in favour of transnationalisation are similar: for example, a 'congruence-related' reason is that the growth in cross-border economic activities points towards the use of transnational rules of private law, and a 'pressure-related' one is that these rules may be shaped by the interests of multinational corporations.[71] Of course, all of this only presents a very general picture, thus setting the scene for the following sections.

---

[64] For those see also B 3, below.   [65] See also ch. 10 at A, below.

[66] For the benefits of uniformity see, e.g., Stephan 1999; Zweigert and Kötz 1998: 25; Sacco 2001: 172. But also McBarnet 2002 (practitioners appreciate choice provided by different legal systems).

[67] See B 2, below, for company law.   [68] For details see C 1, below.

[69] See Hurrell 1995: 347, 353.   [70] See Hurrell 1995: 339–44.

[71] For a list of factors see Berger 2000: 98.

B. Convergence of laws

1. Terminology and typology

The term 'convergence of laws' denotes the trend that legal phenomena become more similar. It does not imply that they will become identical. It is also clear that it cannot be assumed that we can predict with absolute certainty that certain legal changes will occur. Still, thinking about convergence is fruitful as it can contribute to a general understanding of the forces which shape legal development.[72]

Convergence of laws is related but not identical to the topics of 'legal transplants' and 'harmonisation'. While legal transplants can contribute to the convergence of legal systems, one can also imagine a situation where a transplant makes the legal systems of the world more dissimilar: say, if initially all countries but one have similar laws on a particular topic, but then half of the countries decide to transplant the law of the outlier, this will lead to the global divergence of legal systems.[73] There can also be convergence without legal transplants, for example, where countries cooperate together to solve a social problem and come up with a solution which is not yet found in any country.[74]

The relationship between harmonisation and convergence is not entirely clear, terminologically. Some regard harmonisation as a deliberate process whereas convergence is considered something that evolves spontaneously.[75] But more frequently convergence is seen as the wider term, thus, it is said that there are different types of convergence, some based on a deliberate programme for legal unification ('harmonisation'), as distinguished from 'natural' or 'evolutionary' convergence.[76] In any case, the non-deliberate forms of unification are usually the more interesting ones to examine since, if confirmed, they may show that formal harmonisation is not always necessary.

The literature has also suggested a number of more specific types of convergence. In political science, Colin Hay distinguishes between various causal chains within the framework of law-making, namely: input, paradigm, policy, legimatory-rhetoric, outcome and process convergence.[77] Similarly, the legal literature, in particular, in company law, has identified various types of convergence: formal, functional, contractual, hybrid, normative and institutional. Ronald Gilson takes it that in company law functional convergence is likelier than formal convergence:[78] while the underlying problems are similar, there are too many obstacles in the way of formal harmonisation, where 'functional' means that a comparable result is produced, with, say, incompetent managers

---

[72] See already Siems 2008a: 229.   [73] For a similar example see Dixon and Posner 2011: 408.
[74] Similar Finkin 2006: 1144 (for international labour law).   [75] Antokolskaia 2006: 21, 23.
[76] Merryman 1999: 26–32; de Cruz 2007: 510. See also Andenas et al. 2011: 576–8 (discussing the terms integration, homogenisation, convergence, unification, and parallelism).
[77] Hay 2004. The following is based on Siems 2008a: 23–4.   [78] See Gilson 2001.

being dismissed, but along different statutory paths. Alternatively, according to Gilson, there may be contractual convergence, where the formal differences may be functionally relevant, but equivalent effects can be reached through contractual arrangements. Paul Rose adds the concept of 'hybrid convergence' where a firm 'escapes' domestic law by shifting its registered seat to another country: here, approximation comes about because firms of various countries are subject to the same rules.[79] Going beyond legal rules, Curtis Milhaupt raises the question of 'normative convergence', referring to extra-legal norms,[80] and David Charny employs the term 'institutional convergence' where de facto the structures in firms become more similar.[81]

All of this makes it clear that the question of whether there is convergence may not lead to a simple yes/no answer. The next section provides two examples where convergence of laws has been suggested, followed by a discussion of possible normative and positive counter-arguments.

2. The examples of constitutional and company law

While constitutional law and company law seem to be very different, convergence in these two areas of law shows a number of parallels. The following section will deal with four core topics: convergence of the main policies, convergence of the actual details of the law, convergence forces and convergence of the law in practice.

First, in both areas of law, it has been found that countries have converged in a number of dominant legal policies. In constitutional law the idea of convergence has been summarised as follows:

> There has been a slow but steady spread of forms of democracy and of at least a minimalist understanding of the rule of law. Increasingly, there is a shared conception of a constitution as an instrument that represents fundamental law, derives its authority from a sovereign people and needs to be taken seriously by the organs of state, at least as far as public and international perception are concerned. In one form or another, the institution of judicial review of the constitutionality of state action, including legislation, is gaining acceptance.[82]

All of this is seen as a result of a process that started in the late eighteenth century, to be precise, due to a growing number of countries with democratic institutions and due to the migration of constitutional ideas based on a democratic model.[83] This does not imply that there are no variations between legal systems. Yet, the clear trend of the last two centuries goes in the direction of democratic political systems, together with the advancement of liberal market economies.

---

[79] Rose 2001: 134–5.   [80] Milhaupt 2001.   [81] Charny 1998: 165.   [82] Saunders 2009: 21.
[83] See Tushnet 2009; Goldsworthy 2006: 116; Ginsburg and Dixon 2011: 2; Gleditsch and Ward 2008 (with data on growing proportion of democracies).

In company law, Henry Hansmann and Reinier Kraakman suggest that the Anglo-American model of corporate governance has won the day.[84] This model is based on the idea of shareholder primacy as the main guiding principle of company law. The opposite models, which leave more flexibility to managers and directors or give more emphasis to the interests of other stakeholders (such as creditors and employees), are seen as incompatible with today's market environment.

But one does not have to agree with Hansmann and Kraakman to show convergence. Previous work explained that the company laws of France, Germany, the UK, the US, China and Japan all reflect a mixture of three types of shareholders.[85] In favour of the model of the 'shareholder as owner', for instance, is the fact that shareholders can in principle freely sell their shares, and are entitled to special rights. In the sense of the 'shareholder as parliamentarian', however, there are also mechanisms intended to enable the company to have an organisation with checks and balances. In view of the company's ability to attract capital, finally, the 'shareholder as investor' enters in, because finance and disclosure related provisions of company law are aimed primarily at them. Though legal systems may lay emphasis on one model type of shareholder, it was found that in all of the six legal systems, the overall legal situation is a hybrid one.

Second, researchers have also shown that the precise texts of written constitutions[86] have converged. It is said to be striking how similar the language of constitutional texts is.[87] Critics of the convergence hypothesis also acknowledge that at least the words of constitutions are often very similar. According to Günter Frankenberg:

> Constitutions across national boundaries, language barriers, epistemic communities, political constellations, and cultural contexts appear to share the same vocabulary, follow similar institutional paths, contain comparable elements, and share a basic design. Read ten constitutions and you know them all, at least you know the most common varieties of constitutional construction.[88]

Legal texts can also be examined in a quantitative way in order to see whether differences have decreased. Studies have accordingly been able to analyse how the constitutions of most of the countries of the world have converged, one series of studies examining the trends starting in 1946, and another one even starting in 1789.[89]

In modern company law, a global model of 'good corporate governance' has emerged that countries are expected to follow. For example, there is evidence

---

[84] Hansmann and Kraakman 2001.   [85] For this and the following see Siems 2008a: 225–6.

[86] Cf. Ginsburg and Dixon 2011: 4–5 (explaining different definitions of 'constitutional').

[87] Goodin 1996: 223.

[88] Frankenberg 2012a: 564. See also Frankenberg 2012b: 185–6; Frankenberg 2006b: 442.

[89] For the former see, e.g., Law and Versteeg 2011: 1164. For the latter see www.comparativeconstitutionsproject.org/. See also ch. 7 at B 2, above.

Table 9.2 Convergence and divergence in shareholder protection (1970–2005)

	France	Germany	India	UK	US
France	–	div.	div.	conv.	conv.
Germany	div.	–	div.	conv.	conv.
India	div.	div.	–	conv.	conv.
UK	conv.	conv.	conv.	–	conv.
US	conv.	conv.	conv.	conv.	–

showing that rules on independent directors, audit committees and derivative actions have been popular legal transplants in recent decades.[90] It is also possible to examine whether there has been convergence in company law in a quantitative way.

Table 9.2 is based on the sixty-variable dataset on shareholder protection collected at the Centre for Business Research at the University of Cambridge.[91] It displays how the relationships between five countries have developed over thirty-five years, in terms of convergence or divergence. It can be seen that in all but three relationships (the ones between France, Germany and India), there has been convergence in shareholder protection. In particular, it is worth noting that the US and the UK laws have converged with the laws of all of the other countries, possibly because topics such as independent directors and audit committees derive from the Anglo-Saxon model of corporate governance.

Third, in both areas of law the convergence can be related to the convergence forces outlined in the previous section. This is self-evident for company law since these forces were identified specifically for the convergence in this area of law. Previous work explained that especially for public companies 'convergence through congruence' acts as a strong convergence force. For example, the increased use of modern forms of communication, approximations in economic policy, company and shareholder structures, increasing cross-border investment and mergers, the liberalisation of capital markets and reforms in pension provisions all account for growing legal similarities. In terms of 'convergence through pressure' it was found that the liberalisation of markets increases the pressure shareholders can exert internationally, whereas 'regulatory competition for company founders' and 'lobbying' play a secondary role.[92]

The convergence of constitutional laws can also be related to reasons of 'congruence'. This link is clear as far as constitutions are seen as 'manifestations of a society's moral commitments'.[93] It can also be said that in many previously poor countries a wealthy middle class, the digital revolution and higher levels of education have contributed to the spread of economic and political rights.[94] But

[90] See Siems 2008a: 134, 195, 222.
[91] See ch. 7 at B 2, above, and specifically Siems 2010b (for the convergence data).
[92] Siems 2008a: 398–9.   [93] Davis and Trebilcock 2008: 905.
[94] See Dixon and Posner 2011: 409–10; Chang and Yeh 2012: 1170–2.

more emphasis is usually put on the impact of 'pressure', widely understood. Private activists and organisations, such as Human Rights Watch, lobby for improved protection of human rights; foreign governments and the international experts of the Venice Commission provide programmes for democracy assistance, in particular in the context of constitutional design for countries in transition; and international and regional organisations exert pressure, for example, the UN (e.g. through its United Nations Democracy Fund, UNDEF), the OSCE (Organization for Security and Co-operation in Europe) (through its Office for Democratic Institutions and Human Rights, ODIHR), the EU (through conditions for trade and aid) and the World Bank and the IMF (through funding conditions).[95] A provision in the Universal Declaration of Human Rights also refers to the protection of rights in a democratic society,[96] and a UN Guidance of the Secretary General from 2010 states that:

> [t]he UN has long advocated a concept of democracy that is holistic: encompassing the procedural and the substantive; formal institutions and informal processes; majorities and minorities; men and women; governments and civil society; the political and the economic; at the national and the local levels. It has been recognized as well that, while these norms and standards are both universal and essential to democracy, there is no one model . . . Indeed, the ideal of democracy is rooted in philosophies and traditions from many parts of the world.[97]

Similar to company law, a further form of pressure is the desire to attract foreign capital, including human capital.[98] In particular, this may induce countries to provide constitutionally enshrined protections of property rights and the rule of law, a topic also to be discussed in the subsequent chapter on 'comparative law and development'.

Fourth, there has also been some convergence beyond the black letter law. A likely objection is that in 'new' democracies constitutional law may often be ineffective due to factors such as a weak civil society, and lack of democratic culture, fully free press and diverse political parties. It can also be the case that courts may not enforce rights and duties as well as in established democracies. However, courts have also played a positive role in the democratisation process in a number of countries: for instance, in South Africa, Ukraine, Pakistan, Taiwan and South Korea.[99] They may also act as substitutes where political institutions are inefficient: for example, in Columbia and India.[100] More generally, with respect to constitutional courts, scholars have observed a rise

---

[95] See, e.g., Cassese 2012: 75–94; Chang and Yeh 2012: 1172–3; Nijzink et al. 2007: 57; Reynolds 2011 (on 'designing democracy'); Keck and Sikkink 1998 (on advocacy networks); www.venice.coe.int/ (for the Venice Commission); http://ec.europa.eu/europeaid/ (for the European Instrument for Democracy and Human Rights, EIDHR, and the Cotonou Agreement); see also ch. 10 at A, below (for IMF and World Bank).

[96] UDHR, Art. 29(2).   [97] UN 2010: 2.   [98] See Law 2008; Tushnet 2009.

[99] See Ginsburg 2010a: 179–88 (distinguishing between upstream triggers of democracy, downstream guarantors, downstream democratic consolidators and judicial irrelevance).

[100] See Landau 2010; Dickson 2008: 12.

in judicial transplants, reflecting the common origins of constitutions and possibly also a universalist understanding of human rights and democracy.[101]

To be sure, not all countries of the world are well-functioning democracies. But developments in the Middle East starting in 2011 ('Arab spring') may indicate pressure to provide meaningful forms of democratic representation. There are also data showing that in Africa support for democracy is growing.[102] Moreover, a controversial 'sequentalist' view holds that even in non-democratic countries 'rule of law' reforms have started a process that will eventually lead to democratic reforms, speculating about future developments in China.[103]

For company law, previous work explained that current and future convergence also involve a 'convergence of law and reality'. When, in the past, provisions of company law were transplanted, the competent courts and authorities, and also the directors and shareholders involved, often lacked the practical experience of how to apply this law. But nowadays 'convergence through congruence' is based on a change in the factual circumstances, so that fewer contradictions between law and facts arise. And in 'convergence through pressure' interest groups lay weight on effective enforcement of the law, so that here too it will not only be formal convergence that will come about.[104]

3. Discussion: normative and positive

In the normative debate about convergence some statements sound fairly extreme. On the one hand, consider Richard Hyland who compared harmonisation to 'the extinction of animal and plant species that results from the destruction of natural habitat', Harold Gutteridge who compared it to a 'demand almost as great a sacrifice as the abandonment of his national speech or religion' and Gary Watt who called global uniformity of laws 'terrifyingly totalitarian'.[105] On the other hand, John Burke asks us:

> Do we really need different rules about M&A between Italy and Kazakhstan? No, we do not. Do we need substantially different prospectus requirements for listing stocks at the LSE and NYSE? Clearly not is the reply. The same may be said of most disciplines of law: contract, tort, property, IP, anti-trust, and company law, including banking law. No legal system should contain a contrarian rule unless otherwise cogently rationalized.[106]

Both positions are, however, too radical, considering the diverse reasons why laws may converge. The critical view fails to consider the benefits of uniform law in terms of reduced transaction costs. It also overlooks the fact that legal

---

[101] See Choudhry 1999: 833–9 and ch. 7 at A 1, above.   [102] See Nijzink et al. 2007: 70–1.

[103] Cf. Carothers 2010: 22 (rejecting this view). See also ch. 11 at B, below.

[104] Siems 2008a: 399–400.

[105] Hyland 1996: 193; Gutteridge 1949: 158; Watt 2012: 99. Similarly Santos 2004: 192; Legrand 2001b: 1037.

[106] Burke 2011.

convergence is something quite natural when extra-legal circumstances converge as well.[107] By contrast, the affirmative view is inappropriate, if cultural, socio-economic or other differences suggest that laws should stay different. It also overlooks the apparent benefit that a multiplicity of legal systems can stimulate legal innovations, at least as far as choice of the applicable law is possible.

More has to be said about the positive question whether it is actually justified to talk about a convergence of legal systems. First, it is possible to point towards reasons why the black letter law of countries do not, and will not, converge. One can start with the suggestion that continuing legal differences reflect that countries will continue to differ in terms of their economies, cultures, societies etc. For example, consider the views that there will be no monistic universal culture but a 'clash' of civilisations, that different forms of market economies do and will persist, and that even multinational companies have deep domestic roots.[108] However, convergence does not imply identity – so it is not inconsistent to suggest convergence and accept that certain differences persist. Thus, the more interesting objection is why the 'convergence forces' may not have an effect on the law. Typically this refers to path-dependencies and uses the following example:[109]

A long time ago, a path was trodden through a wood. Attention was paid to keeping the path far enough away from wolves' dens not to be attacked by wolves. Later, this path was modernised into a road, even though by then no wolves were threatening travellers any longer. This makes various degrees of path dependence clear. First-degree or weak path dependence is present where even today the way through the wood is efficient and contains no needless curves (though it is not the only efficient way through the wood). By contrast, with second- or third-degree path dependencies the route is inefficient from today's point of view. Second-degree or semi-strong path dependence makes it not worthwhile on a cost comparison ripping up the path and building a new road. With third-degree or strong path dependence it is different. Here too, however, the route is not changed, since for instance the road administration has not been convinced of the need to, or resistance from private groups (shopkeepers etc.) stands in the way.

Examples for all three types of path-dependencies can be found in the development of company law. For instance, a weak path dependency exists in so far as the terminology of company laws is different but nonetheless leads to comparable results in terms of shareholder protection, 'harmless mutations' as called by Hansmann and Kraakman.[110] Semi-strong path dependence means that the costs of law reform would exceed their benefits. Here, for instance, one can think of the principle of minimum capital or the separation between

[107] See A 3, above ('convergence through congruence').
[108] Huntington 1993 and Huntington 1996; Hall and Soskice 2001; Doremus et al. 1998.
[109] Based on Roe 1997 as summarised in Siems 2008a: 293–4.
[110] Hansmann and Kraakman 2001: 465–6. See also ch. 2 at B 1 (b), above.

supervisory and management boards, since changing such rules would make it necessary to revise many areas of company law.[111] A strong path-dependence may be assumed for the question whether and how company law should consider the interests of stakeholders, such as employees, since here political considerations may hold legislators back from adopting the most economically efficient solution (whatever this may be).[112]

Path dependencies are also likely to play a role elsewhere. At a general level, it has been suggested that particularities of legal language and concepts can constitute semi-strong path-dependencies and that weak legal adaptability of law-making institutions a strong one.[113] Specifically with respect to constitutional law, lack of convergence may be explained by ideological, cultural and religious differences, possibly also involving resistance against Western values.[114] But this scepticism about rule convergence should also not be exaggerated. For instance, a study on comparative constitutions in Muslim countries found that even countries where Islam is declared to be the state religion tend to have many 'Western' constitutional rights, such as freedom of religion, expression, association and assembly.[115]

Beyond the discussion about path dependencies, scholars have identified more complex forms of legal evolution, for instance, inspired by game theory or a Darwinian theory developed by linguists, with convergence not the necessary outcome.[116] Evolutionary ideas have also been used to show that increased dialogue can stimulate experimentation and more selective transplants.[117] Another logical possibility is that evolution leads to 'polarisation' (or 'dual convergence'), meaning that groups of countries will share very similar laws.[118] But against all of this speaks that, at least in constitutional and company law, the studies cited above have shown that convergence of legal rules does occur. Thus, while not dismissing the possibility of experimentations or polarisations, convergence seems to be a common outcome in some areas of law.

A second question is whether it actually 'matters' that the positive law is converging. Two lines of critique can be distinguished. The first one is closely related to the view that legal transplants are largely irrelevant.[119] As in the transplant discussion, Pierre Legrand is a prominent voice: he takes the view that convergence only exists at a superficial level if one pretends that legal

---

[111] See Siems 2008a: 295.   [112] See Bebchuk and Roe 1999: 150.

[113] See Ogus 2002 (for the former) and Siems 2006 (for the latter).

[114] See, e.g., Schneider 1995 (for impact of politics on German and US constitutions); Figueroa 2011 (for backlash in modern Latin American constitutions); Ginsburg and Dixon 2011: 11–12 (also referring to age of constitutions); Menski 2006: 4, 16, 179, 195 (in particular on religion; not specifically about constitutions).

[115] See Stahnke and Blitt 2005.

[116] Garoupa and Ogus 2006 (for the former); Smits 2011 (for the latter). See also Smits 2002b.

[117] See Saunders 2009: 18, 23; also Muir Watt 2006: 587 (how 'increased awareness of alterity may generate a need for identity and tradition').

[118] See Ginsburg and Dixon 2011: 8; Hay 2011: 320; Hay 2004.

[119] See ch. 8 at A 2 (b), above.

rules are completely unconnected to their cultural environment.[120] This is not to deny that legal change can happen but it materialises in a 'constructive cognitive process' without 'uniformisation' at a deeper level.[121] Such a position is also possible in comparative constitutional law, if one takes the view that a constitution cannot be understood outside its institutional context, or even that it is an expression of 'a particular nation's self-understanding'.[122]

But, again, the counter-argument is that these are certainly valid reasons that there will not be identity of legal cultures, while they may still become more similar. Aspects of legal culture and mentality are not static. This has already been discussed in one of the previous chapters where it was shown that it is misleading to argue that differences between common and civil law are so fundamental that they exclude any exchange of ideas.[123]

The second line of critique argues from a more socio-legal perspective that in practice similar rules often have fundamentally different effects across countries. For example, with respect to constitutional law, it has been said that the role of constitutional and supreme courts is often very different. This can relate to differences in appointment procedures and jurisdiction,[124] but it can also be a result of the courts' adjudication since they may take different views as to the relationship between protecting the constitution and respecting the decisions of law-making institutions (i.e. judicial activism).[125] More fundamentally, the objection is that constitutions pursue very different aims in different parts of the world. Whereas in the West a constitution is predominantly seen as a 'legal' document, in other countries it may be more akin to a manifesto (say, in the remaining socialist countries), an aspirational document (say, in countries in transition), a document to unite the country (say, in countries with ethnic tensions), or to consolidate the powers of the state (say, in countries under external threads), or to please donor countries (say, in the developing world).[126] All of this may suggest that in many countries constitutional protections of human rights and democratic processes are largely irrelevant in practice.[127]

But such a grim picture would be an exaggeration. The convergence forces do not only steer countries towards legal convergence but also towards convergent constitutional practices. There can even be the situation that the formal

---

[120] Legrand 2005: 707–8; Legrand 2001b: 1037; Legrand 1996: 56–8. On Legrand see also ch. 5 at C 1, above.

[121] Legrand 2001b: 1042.   [122] See Tushnet 2006b: 68.

[123] See ch. 5 at C 1, above, and more generally ch. 4 at C, above.

[124] See, e.g., Goldsworthy 2012: 710–4; Dickson 2008: 5; Harding et al. 2008: 12–4.

[125] See, e.g., Goldsworthy 2007; Goldsworthy 2006: 119; Goldsworthy 2012: 709–10; Dickson 2008: 11–3; Harding et al. 2008: 4.

[126] See Frankenberg 2006b: 451–5, 458–9; Frankenberg 2012b: 178–82; Law 2011b: 380; Chao-Chun Lin 2006: 300. See also Rosenfeld 2012 (distinguishing between various models based on 'constitutional identity').

[127] See also Mattei 2002: 276 (in Africa written constitutional document 'entirely irrelevant if the fundamental informal institutional constraints are not created and settled'); Pistor 2002: 113 (on 'creative compliance').

constitutional law is diverse but that common circumstances influence the political reality of countries in a similar way.[128] As was already explained, such 'functional convergence' is also common elsewhere. For example, in company law it may be possible that similar rules are applied differently, but there is also the view that it is more likely that legal rules will remain somehow different but that the practical effects are similar.[129]

There is, however, another major problem concerning both constitutional and company law in practice. The globalisation of economies and societies reduces the power of the state, for example, to influence the way multinational companies operate, with the result that domestic laws on democratic participation, human rights and corporate governance become less relevant.[130] It may therefore be suggested that the real shift is towards regional and transnational law, to which we turn in the next two sections.

C. Regionalisation

1. Terminology and typology

Regionalisation is not a new phenomenon,[131] but regional trade agreements and other forms of regional cooperation only became more widespread after the Second World War, in particular since the 1990s.[132] There exists, however, considerable diversity in this 'new regionalism', as this section will explain.

The terms 'region' and 'regionalisation' require the following clarifications: first, in the present context, we are interested in 'macro-regions', i.e. groups of countries which are in geographic vicinity, as distinguished from 'micro-regions' which are areas within one country.[133] Second, 'regionalisation' is sometimes said to refer to a natural growth of social integration, as distinguished from 'regionalism'.[134] However, it can also refer to the process through which regions emerge,[135] and that is how it will be used in this section. Third, regional agreements may start with the modest aim of 'regional cooperation', but lead to 'regional integration' later on.[136] Yet, for further details, we need to identify more precisely what aims underlie the formation of regions.

---

[128] Pettai and Madise 2007: 50 (on how in the Baltic countries, despite different laws, challenges of state-building and EU accession steered countries in same direction).

[129] See 1, above.

[130] See, e.g., Goodhart 2005: 73–92 (for democracy); Delmas-Marty 2003: 1–27 (for tension between economy and human rights); Siems 2008a: 239–40 (for company law); Fox 2002 (on the limits of national laws in a globalised economy). See also A 1, above.

[131] See Fazio 2007: 41–8 (reference to Lombard league, Hanseatic league, German Zollverein of 1834; Benelux of 1921).

[132] For data see Ravenhill 2011: 187; Duina and Morano-Foadi 2011: 561. See also Duina and Morano-Foadi 2011 (introducing a special issue on regional trade agreements); Mattei et al. 2009: 73–95 (on regional integration). A useful resource for information about regions is the Regional Integration Knowledge System (RIKS), available at www.cris.unu.edu/riks/.

[133] De Lombaerde et al. 2010: 736.   [134] Hurrell 1995.

[135] De Lombaerde et al. 2010: 737, 739.   [136] De Lombaerde et al. 2010: 737 note 24.

Five types of economic regions can be distinguished.[137] First, regional agreements can be limited to one or more specific aims. For example, the aim may be to harmonise legal rules in particular areas of law. This is the case for the Organisation pour l'Harmonisation en Afrique du Droit des Affaires (OHADA), which aims to harmonise business laws for sixteen countries of Central and Western Africa. Second, free-trade areas eliminate tariffs between its members. Examples are the North American Free Trade Association (NAFTA), the Gulf Cooperation Council (GCC) and the ASEAN Free Trade Area (AFTA). Third, customs unions have, in addition, a common external tariff. Examples are the South American unions MERCOSUR and Andean Community. Fourth, a common market is created when further barriers are removed, say, for the free movement of capital and services: for example, the European Union (EU), the Economic Community of West African States (ECOWAS), the Economic Community of Central African States (ECCAS) and the Caribbean Community (CARICOM). Fifth, countries of a monetary union have a single currency, harmonised monetary and possibly also economic policies. These are today often sub-groups of countries belonging to a common market: for the aforementioned examples, these are the Eurozone, the West African Economic and Monetary Union (Uemoa), the Monetary and Economic Community of Central Africa (Cemac) and the Eastern Caribbean Currency Union (ECCU).

Moreover, regional cooperation is not limited to economic cooperation and integration. The EU has achieved some political integration which can be seen as a model for the African Union (AU) and the Union of South American Nations (UNASUR). Further examples of political cooperation are the Council of Europe (CoE), the Organization of American States (OAS) and the Arab League. The CoE, the OAS and the AU have also fostered regional cooperation to protect human rights, namely through the European Convention on Human Rights, the American Convention on Human Rights and the African Charter on Human and Peoples' Rights.

Given the typological variety of regions, it is clear that there are also a variety of reasons accounting for regional cooperation.[138] A first line of reasoning points towards the role of power politics. This may refer to a common threat that countries of a region face (e.g. in the cold war Western Europe facing a threat from the Soviet Union); the belief that in a globalised economy single countries are unable to assure their autonomy towards multinational companies or more powerful countries, possibly leading to protectionist tools (e.g., the South American regions and their relationship to the US); or the ambition of one of the countries of the region to dominate the others (e.g., possibly, Germany in the EU, the US in NAFTA, and Brazil in UNASUR).

---

[137] See, e.g., Economides and Wilson 2001: 164–6; Fazio 2007: 61–3; Ravenhill 2011: 175.
[138] The following structure is based on Hurrell 1995. See also Ravenhill 2011: 179–83, 196–9; Delmas-Marty 2009: 82–5; Duina and Morano-Foadi 2011: 562, 567; Gilpin 2001: 343; Fazio 2007: 53.

More focused on the region itself is the argument that a region provides companies with a larger open market to sell their products and to attract investment (as well as citizens with more choice, more freedom to travel etc.). This is one of the main reasons for the current free trade agreements. A region-focused integration may also be supported by a process that stimulates regional awareness, and such integration may also be triggered by successful models of regional agreements in other parts of the world. In addition, it has been suggested that economic integration may only be an intermediate step if the actual objective is that it will 'spill-over' to other fields and deepen regional political integration. The EU may be seen as the main example of this 'neo-functional' perspective, in particular due to the influence of pro-European institutions such as the European Commission and the Court of Justice.

This 'neo-functional' view has, however, been challenged by the now dominant 'intergovernmental' perspective since even in the EU it is the Member States who are the 'masters of the treaties'. This leads to the final set of explanations that focus on developments at the level of the individual states. Thus, regions are more likely to be expected to arise when the cultural, economic, social and political structures are relatively similar. For instance, this may be seen in the changing membership of the Latin American regions, where Venezuela left the Andean Community in 2006 and joined MERCOSUR in 2012.[139]

2. The European Union as an example of regional integration

The EU is often seen as a model for other regions, and the EU has also supported regionalism in other parts of the world.[140] It is therefore worth outlining the extent to which the case of the EU may be seen as a successful and meaningful form of regional integration.

At a general level, it can be noted that the EU has managed to create a legal order that incorporates elements from various traditions, in particular from both common and civil law countries. For example, this 'hybridisation'[141] can be related to the judgments of the Court of Justice of the EU (CJEU): its concise style of reasoning is akin to French courts, but it also uses a common-law style of relying on precedents and, in substance, has made use of some German concepts, such as the principle of proportionality.[142] More generally, the case law of the CJEU shows how it is possible to use comparative reasoning incorporating ideas from different legal cultures. This is not only done where

---

[139] Namely because Venezuela's president Chavez rejected the 'pro-US position' associated with the Andean community: see http://en.mercopress.com/2011/04/24/venezuela-formally-exits-andean-nations-and-waits-for-mercosur-incorporation.

[140] See, e.g., contributions in De Lombaerde and Schulz 2009.

[141] McEldowney 2010; Husa 2004: 28. Also called 'bijural', Breton and Trebilcock 2006, or 'polynomia', Husa 2012.

[142] See, e.g., Husa 2004: 29; de Cruz 2007: 160–3.

the Treaty obliges the CJEU to consider legal principles common to the Member States,[143] but also in other 'hard cases'.[144]

What explains the EU's success in overcoming the differences between legal traditions? One possible answer is to re-consider the alleged differences between common and civil law: perhaps, even though these legal traditions have distinct features, these are superseded by the more general commonalities in European (legal) culture.[145] Another response refers to distinct features of the EU. If it is taken that judges and other practitioners dominate the common law tradition and scholars and legislators the civil law one, the secret of the EU's success may be that its law is predominantly a 'product of bureaucracy' for which 'economic and social aspects prevail over legal ones' (meaning the differences in style between common and civil law).[146]

This leads to the more specific question of how 'deep' and 'wide' regional integretation has advanced in the EU. Considering the EU as a 'region', its competences are relatively extensive: it has achieved a greater level of economic integration than most other regions and it has also got involved in further areas, such as justice and home affairs, external relations, and environmental and public health matters. But this does not mean that the EU has now as many powers as a federal state. A study comparing the EU with twenty federal states found that the EU provides significantly less legal uniformity than these states.[147] For example, it tends to provide less or no harmonisation for questions of social security, pension, welfare, education, criminal law, private law and the corresponding procedural laws.

Yet, it is also possible to identify parallels between the EU and federal states, in particular the US. For example, the European debate about the relationship between the union and the state level, as well as the relationship between the Member States (i.e. the potential for regulatory competition) often uses the US as a point of comparison.[148] From a US perspective, analogies have also been drawn between the growing role of rights and judicial enforcements and the 'adversarial legalism' of the US: the European courts have played an important role in making EU law justiciable, and the trend towards a rights-based approach is seen as a logical development for a modern and diverse society replacing cooperative and corporatist forms of governance.[149]

But such an assessment may also be somehow misleading because, in addition, the EU has fostered more informal forms of convergence – and these can

---

[143] Treaty on the Functioning of the European Union (TFEU), Art. 340 (for the non-contractual liability of Union organs); Treaty on European Union (TEU), Art. 6(3) (for the protection of fundamental rights).

[144] See, e.g., Kiikeri 2001; Kakouris 1994; Andenas and Fairgrieve 2012: 47–9.

[145] See ch. 3 at C 3, above.

[146] Zenzo-Zencovich and Vardi 2008. For the role of judges etc. see ch. 3 at B 1, above.

[147] Halberstam and Reimann 2012: 23–4 (index from 0 to 10: the EU scores 2.7 whereas the average is 4.4 for the federal states).

[148] E.g. Schütze 2009; Barnard 2000. For regulatory competition see also A 2 (b), above.

[149] Kelemen 2011: 6, 12; also Stone Sweet 2004. See also ch. 3 at C 2, above.

also be related to possible models in the US.[150] Here, the main idea is that 'deep' integration requires not only formal harmonisation of legal rules, but also more informal coordination in fields that have not been harmonised.[151]

A good example for the choices and mixtures between more and less formal forms of harmonisation and convergence is the EU contract law. There has been piecemeal harmonisation of some topics, for instance, through directives on matters of consumer protection. But since complete formal harmonisation would not be feasible, suggestions for a future EU contract law have also emerged as an optional '29th regime' in addition to the contract laws of the twenty-eight Member States. Such rules were initially drafted by a group of academics calling them Principles of European Contract Law (PECL), but the EU Commission has now also suggested a proposal for an optional European sales law.[152] In addition, following up from PECL, groups of academics have added further areas of law, incorporated the existing EU directives and consolidated everything into a Draft Common Frame of Reference (DCFR). The DCFR does look like a draft for a future European Civil Code, though the EU Commission indicates more cautiously that the subsequent Common Frame of Reference (CFR) should be seen as a '"toolbox" or a handbook to be used for the revision of existing and the preparation of new legislation in the area of contract law'.[153] Moreover, there are a number of 'even softer' comparative initiatives to stimulate the Europeanisation of contract law, for example, the Ius Commune Casebooks for the Common Law of Europe and the books of the Common Core project.[154]

All of these latter trends can be seen as part of a more general desire to create a common European legal culture. Though some scholars point towards deep historical similarities between European legal cultures,[155] the dominant view is that efforts have to, and should, be undertaken to make legal education and scholarship more European.[156] There is, however, a 'chicken and egg problem': for instance, law students will want to study the domestic law in their home countries as far as laws still differ between Member States – and these differences will remain as far as distinct national legal cultures impede full legal harmonisation. It is also clear that a European legal culture can hardly emerge without

---

[150] In particular the National Conference of Commissioners on Uniform State Laws (NCCUSL) of the Uniform Law Commission, http://uniformlaws.org/, and the American Law Institute, www.ali.org. See now also the European Law Institute, www.europeanlawinstitute.eu/.

[151] This was initially explained in a White Paper on Governance, suggesting an 'open method of coordination'. See http://ec.europa.eu/governance/governance_eu/nat_policies_en.htm.

[152] Proposal for a Regulation of the European Parliament and of the Council on a Common European Sales Law, COM (2011) 635 final.

[153] See http://ec.europa.eu/justice/contract/cesl/background/index_en.htm. On the DCFR see also ch. 7 at A 3, above.

[154] For the former see www.casebooks.eu/. For the latter see ch. 2 at B 3, above. See also Miller 2011: 3–14 (for different elements of Europeanisation); Hondius 2011 (calling for Europe-wide commentaries); Zimmermann 2006 (for the role of comparative law).

[155] In particular, Wieacker 1990. See also ch. 3 at C 3, above.

[156] Heringa and Akkermans 2011; Fauvarque-Cosson 2007; Smits 2007a. But also Monateri 2012: 18 (calling these 'biased, non neutral political projects').

a more general approximation of cultures in Europe. As Hugh Collins suggests, to succeed, the EU needs to form a denser community of shared interests by way of persuading citizens of the European project.[157]

3. Discussion: towards multi-level governance

European integration has not been without its critics. Some of this criticism is best seen as political, for example, by those who regard the EU as a threat to national sovereignty and democratic representation. Most of the more academic challenges to EU harmonisation are akin to those directed against convergence more generally, for instance, emphasising the value of legal diversity and experimentation.[158] Specifically, however, the harmonisation programme of the EU is seen as a challenge to the common law tradition, in particular as far as it concerns plans for a European Civil Code. Pierre Legrand (again), takes the position that such a code as a 'self-contained and self-referential system' would be an 'act of repression', excluding 'other approaches to legal knowledge' and eliminating 'the common law's world-view'.[159] But, a civil code that would replace existing laws is not on the agenda. It can therefore also be argued that, at present, it is the 'scientific' nature of the civil law that is disrupted by the 'non-systematic interference' of EU laws.[160]

Turning from the normative to the positive, is an analysis of the EU useful towards understanding regionalism more generally? To start with, the possible tensions between civil and common law can also be seen elsewhere. For example, the members of the African regional association OHADA are predominantly French civil law countries. Yet, one of its sixteen members is Cameroon which is geographically split between common and civil law.[161] Since OHADA's uniform laws are written in the style of civil law legislation, this creates a similar tension as one may observe in the EU.[162]

More generally, it can be noted that the EU went through various stages of economic and political integration. The EU may therefore be seen as a model of what other regions may want to do (or may want to avoid): for example, whether or not to go the path of a monetary union. The EU has also developed a sophisticated institutional structure which can be of interest for other regions, as it has been observed that regional trade agreements tend to move from 'less to more institutionalisation'.[163] A particularly interesting point of comparison is the spread of regional courts, where it has been found that there are already eleven 'functioning copies' of the European Court of Justice.[164]

---

[157] Collins 2008: 18.   [158] See, e.g., Deakin 2006; Smits 2010c.

[159] Legrand 1997a: 45, 53, 56; Legrand 1999: 111, 114; Legrand 2006a: 17. See also Legrand 1998a; Legrand 1998b; Legrand 2011: 5; also Teubner 1998 (for good faith as a 'legal irritant' in English law).

[160] Banakas 2008: 545.   [161] See already ch. 4 at C 3 (b), above.

[162] See Mancuso 2008; Moore Dickerson 2010.

[163] Duina and Morano-Foadi 2011: 566.   [164] Alter 2012.

However, here, too, there have been critics: it has been said that the research on comparative regionalism frequently suffers a 'Eurocentric bias' and that it tends to ignore the fact that 'ideas often come from different places', not only the EU.[165] These arguments bear some resemblance to points discussed in the previous chapters, in particular the alleged Eurocentrism of traditional comparative law, the mixture of legal traditions, and the use of legal transplants.[166] As there, the choice of comparators (i.e., here, regions) depends on the precise research question. For example, a comparative analysis of the Andean Tribunal of Justice may want to consider the EU since this court is a close copy of its European counterpart.[167] But an analysis of how the Andean Community deals with specific problems of transition economies in Latin America may want to engage in a comparison with MERCOSUR.

In addition, it needs to be considered that the regional level is embedded in an increasingly 'complex network of national, transnational and international private and public norms', which is said to involve 'a variety of institutions, norms, and dispute resolution processes located, and produced, at different structured sites around the world'.[168] The relationship between the global-international and the regional level can be one where the region simply follows the former standards (e.g. in matters of international human rights). But the question has also been raised whether, in the context of international trade, regionalism is a 'stepping stone' or a 'stumbling block' for more international integration, both economically and politically. The optimists suggest that liberalisation of markets within one region creates a 'domino effect' for global markets. The sceptics, by contrast, see the danger of regions as 'economic fortresses' not being interested in global cooperation and liberalisation any more.[169]

The most significant general trend is, however, the growing privatisation of law. This can be seen at all levels, including the regional one. For instance, it has been said that today regionalism 'involves a rich variety of non-state actors, resulting in multiplicities of formal and informal regional governance and regional networks in most issue areas'.[170] In all instances the relationship between the various state and private levels is crucial. This 'interlegality' is often complex and dynamic, posing challenges to law-makers since they cannot simply rely on setting fixed rules.[171] The understanding of the various levels and their interrelationships is also one of the key challenges for modern comparative and transnational law, as will be further explained in the next section.

---

[165] De Lombaerde et al. 2010: 742; Duina and Morano-Foadi 2011: 565.
[166] See ch. 2 at C 2, ch. 4 at C 3 and ch. 8 at B, above.
[167] See Alter and Helfer 2011; Alter et al. 2012.
[168] Quotes by Ladeur 2004: 95–6 and Snyder 1999: 343 (calling this 'global legal pluralism').
[169] See Ravenhill 2011: 202–6.   [170] De Lombaerde et al. 2010: 732.
[171] See Cottrell and Trubeck 2012; Snyder 1999: 343; Michaels 2009b: 254.

D. Transnationalisation

1. Terminology and typology

In a general sense, 'transnational law' may refer to any law that transcends nation states.[172] It is therefore different from plain domestic laws, but it may include EU law and international law. Yet, more narrowly, the focus is usually not on laws that are only relevant to a particular territory, such as a region. Transnational law also has a different focus than international law since its main concern is not international treaties and conventions that emanate from sovereign states.

Still, transnational law is a broad category that includes various types of legal rules. For example, writing about transnational commercial law, Roy Goode and colleagues define it as rules, from whatever source, which govern international commercial transactions and which are common to at least a significant number of legal systems, including, for instance, unwritten customs, contractually incorporated rules and trade terms promulgated by international organisations, standard term contracts, and restatements of scholars.[173]

More generally, the following variants can be distinguished, based on the private or public level where the transnational element may be found.[174] First, transnational law can emerge at the private level, for example, through contracts between firms which are based in different countries, or through agreements about moral and ethical questions between individuals who belong to the same religious community but live in different countries. Second, non-state organisations may draft rules aimed to be used irrespective of national borders. For instance, these organisations may be industry groups, NGOs, religious organisations, or groups of academics. The audience for their rules can be private parties who adopt them, say, as codifications of trade usages, model contracts or codes of conduct. Such documents can also be model laws with the aim to encourage law-makers to adopt these rules. Third, states and intergovernmental organisations may coordinate laws that have a transnational dimension on an informal basis (possibly also together with private parties). For example, they may agree on recommendations that are aimed at law-makers, courts, individuals or firms. Such agreements can also concern the cooperation of the practical application of the law: for instance, in matters of cross-border law enforcement. Fourth, states and intergovernmental organisations may agree on formally binding laws, such as treaties and conventions, dealing with matters that have a cross-border dimension. This is to be distinguished from other international (or regional) laws that merely aim to harmonise domestic laws.

---

[172] See, e.g., Senn 2011: 197–8; Hantrais 2009: 3; Jessup 1956: 2.

[173] Goode et al. 2007: para. 1.03; also paras. 1.51–1.59. See also Goode 2005: 539; Trakman 2011 (suggesting a plural conception of transnational law).

[174] For similar classifications see Cafaggi 2011: 32–8; Smits 2010a: 2–6; Berman 2009: 230; Friedman 1996: 70.

Transnational law can be found in many areas of law. It has been said that some progress to create a 'world law' has already been made in commercial law,[175] which will be the topic of the following section. Some of the commercial law instruments also relate to other areas of law: for example, property law and secured credit.[176] In other fields of business law (widely understood), transnational trends have been suggested in construction law and sports law.[177] Internet law is also a prominent case since topics such as the decision about top-level domain names, by their very nature, go beyond the borders of one country.[178]

Beyond business law, forms of cooperation in international crime, environmental policy and disaster response law have a transnational nature.[179] Constitutional law is said to operate 'within an increasingly transnational legal environment'.[180] Family law may appear to be more locally embedded but a number of examples can be suggested as well: for instance, relating to problems of conflict of laws aiming to protect the rights of children.[181] A further important example is the law associated with religious communities transgressing national boundaries.[182] Problems can arise between these transnational personal laws and the domestic laws of residence. This issue has become topical for the role of Islam in Europe, for example, in relation to the recent restrictions to wear headscarves or full face veils in some countries.[183]

The relationship between different areas of transnational law can be a complicated one. For instance, it has been suggested that there may be 'asynchrony' due to the different speeds in which these laws develop,[184] as well as the emergence of policy conflicts due to the different rationalities, such as economic and non-economic ones, on which transnational instruments are based.[185] Reconciling such conflicting aims is also an important topic in the context of 'law and development', as discussed in the subsequent chapter.

For comparative law, the emergence of transnational law poses a challenge to the traditional approach of comparing state-based legal orders. It may also be questioned whether established concepts of comparative law are helpful for the understanding of transnational law. This has been doubted for legal transplants,[186] as well as for legal traditions:

---

[175] Gordley and von Mehren 2006: xxi. Similarly Nelken 2007b: 14–5. More sceptical Eiselen 2010: 98 ('no over-arching international trade law or lex mercatoria that will generally apply to international transactions').

[176] See van Erp 2006: 1066–7 (on UNIDROIT Cape Town Convention on International Interests in Mobile Equipement and EBRD Model Law on Secured Transactions).

[177] References in Michaels 2009b: 247.   [178] See, e.g., Botzem and Hofmann 2010.

[179] See, e.g., Roberts 2007: 348 (on international cooperation, coordination and mutual assistance in criminal law); Busch and Tews 2005: 153–64 (on environmental policy); www.ifrc.org/en/what-we-do/idrl/ (disaster law of International Red Cross).

[180] Jackson 2010. See also ch. 8 at B 4 (c), above (on human rights).

[181] References in Reimann 2006: 1377–8.   [182] See, e.g., Twining 2007: 85; Michaels 2009b: 252.

[183] See, e.g., Mattei et al. 2009: 248; Demleitner 1999: 752; also Bowen 2007 (anthropological study of the French position).

[184] Delmas-Marty 2009: 119.   [185] Fischer-Lescano and Teubner 2004: 1004, 1013.

[186] Nelken 2007b: 14.

> [T]he new living law of the world is nourished not from stores of tradition but from the ongoing self-reproduction of highly technical, highly specialized, often formally organized and rather narrowly defined, global networks of an economic, cultural, academic or technological nature.[187]

But it cannot be excluded that legal transplants are relevant: for example, a particular transnational norm may have its origins in one of the domestic legal systems.[188] There is also the possibility that legal traditions are relevant: for example, it may be suggested that common law countries are more receptive to soft forms of transnational law than civil law ones.[189] Thus, this discussion shows that it is useful to turn to one particular area of transnational law in more detail.

2. Examples from transnational commercial law

The idea of a transnational commercial law dates back to the common medieval merchant law ('*lex mercatoria*'). The *lex mercatoria* did not replace local laws but was a separate, though loose, legal order that was created by the merchants themselves, for instance, by way of commercial customs and the creation of financial instruments. In the nineteenth century the codification of commercial laws in Europe made the *lex mercatoria* fade away, despite attempts to keep the international nature of commercial law alive.[190]

After the Second World War, a new (or modern) *lex mercatoria* is said to have emerged – but it is not entirely clear how this term should be understood. A first view, aligned to the informal nature of the old *lex mercatoria*, takes the position that the *lex mercatoria* is about private transnational law-making of commercial actors, in particular standardised contracts and customary private law.[191] However, two types of objections are possible. On the one hand, it may be said that more formal aspects of transnational commercial law are at least as important as these informal ones. For example, this may refer to international conventions and uniform laws and rules, or the role of international commercial arbitration.[192] On the other hand, there is the view that the emphasis on private law-making underplays the continuing role of the state for international commercial law. In particular, it is said that private parties depend on the recognition of private law-making by the state, and need the state when it comes to the enforcement of contractual provisions.[193]

---

[187] Teubner 1997: 7.   [188] For example see ch. 8, B 1 (b) and 4 (c), above.

[189] Fazio 2007: 234. Similarly Gaudreault-DesBiens 2010: 171–2 (for recognition of Sharia-based adjudication in common and civil law).

[190] In particular by Leone Levi, see Gutteridge 1949: 146; de Cruz 2007: 16.

[191] See Zumbansen in EE 2012: 904 ('transnationalists'); Wiener 1999: 161 ('autonomist approach'), also ibid. 20 ('from public to private international governance'); Collins 2011: 3 (associating this with a common law view of the *lex mercatoria*).

[192] See Stone Sweet 2006; Collins 2011: 3 (associating this with the German and French view of the *lex mercatoria*).

[193] See, e.g., Goode 2005: 547 (contracts cannot create law); Stone Sweet 2006: 637 (on enforcement); Zumbansen in EE 2012: 904 ('traditionalists'); Wiener 1999: 161 ('positivist position'). See also 3, below.

Some have attempted to distil and formulate general doctrines of transnational commercial law.[194] Yet, the difficulty is that transnational commercial law derives from various – more or less private and informal – sources. To start with, contractual practice has an increasingly transnational nature. This comprises not just diverse individual contracts. Rather, international corporations and law firms have gradually used more and more similar contracts around the world, often said to be based on an Anglo-Saxon style of drafting.[195] In addition, multinational companies may use the same codes of conduct for dealings with their international business partners. For example, these may specify certain environmental and labour standards in order to respond to concerns from consumers – or because the laws of some of the countries in which they do business require them to comply with those standards anyway.[196]

Codes of conduct may also refer to standards developed by non-state organisations and groups, for example, those of the International Organization for Standardization (ISO) and the various fairtrade associations.[197] Such uniform rules that firms can, but do not have to, use also exist in relation to various other topics of commercial law. Frequent examples are the instruments of the International Chamber of Commerce (ICC): in particular, the Incoterms that clarify certain terms that may be used in international sales contracts as well as the Uniform Customs and Practices for Documentary Credits.[198] More specialised codes or standard contracts are, for example, the Wolfsberg Principles developed by a group of banks to address problems of money laundering, and the master documents by the International Swap and Derivatives Association (ISDA), representing various financial institutions and investment firms.[199]

These instruments already point towards a 'creeping codification' of transnational commercial law.[200] Moreover, this trend can refer to codifications that involve states and intergovernmental organisations. At the most modest level this means involvement in the drafting of a particular instrument but not that this instrument is binding for countries, firms or individuals. An example is the UNIDROIT Principles of International Commercial Contracts. UNIDROIT is an intergovernmental organisation with sixty-three Member States (as of August 2013). The Principles of International Commercial Contracts have, however, not the form of a binding international convention. Rather, they are aimed at the parties of international contracts and arbitral tribunals in order to identify common standards of international business contracts.[201] Other examples are

---

[194] Goode et al. 2007: para. 18.01.
[195] See McBarnet 2002 (on transnational transactions); Moss 2007: 2 (on Anglo-Saxon models); Markesinis and Fedtke 2009: 324 and Goldman 2008: 295 (on importance of in-house lawyers and other practioners).
[196] See Lin 2009 (examples: Gap Code of Vendor Conduct, Wal-Mart Standards for Vendor Partners, HP Supplier Code of Conduct); Eidenmüller 2011: 728.
[197] See www.iso.org/ and www.fairtrade.net/.   [198] See www.iccwbo.org/.
[199] See www.wolfsberg-principles.com/; www.isda.org/.
[200] Berger 2010. See also Michaels 2007 (calling this the 'new new lex mercatoria').
[201] See Goldman 2008: 281, 287.

the UN Global Compact and the OECD Guidelines for Multilateral Enterprises, both being recommendations aimed at multinational corporations.[202]

One step further go international agreements that are implemented into domestic laws but where it is left to firms and individuals whether they want to opt in or opt out of these provisions. The main example is the United Nations Convention on Contracts for the International Sale of Goods of 1980 (CISG), which was prepared by the United Nations Commission on International Trade Law (UNCITRAL). It applies to international sale contracts if the law of one of the contracting parties of the convention (seventy-nine countries in August 2013) would be applicable; yet, parties can exclude or vary the application of the CISG. The CISG is also seen as a successful example of a blend between common and civil law – in terms of its drafting process,[203] its terminology,[204] and its substance, for instance, concerning controversial concepts such as good faith and specific performance.[205] In addition, according to its Article 7, the application of the CISG has to consider its international character and the need to promote its uniform interpretation.

A final category are international agreements which are subsequently implemented into mandatory domestic laws. Such agreements may be international hard law, i.e. conventions and treaties: in the field of international commercial law examples are the various conventions by UNIDROIT and the Hague Conference on Private International Law.[206] However, transnational soft law may also become domestic hard law: for instance, UNCITRAL has drafted a number of model laws on topics such as international credit transfers, electronic signatures and electronic commerce.[207] Furthermore, international soft laws are influential in accounting, banking and securities law, in particular the International Financial Reporting Standards (IFRS), the rules on bank capital adequacy of the Basel Committee on Banking Supervision (BCBS), the recommendation on money laundering of the Financial Action Task Force (FATF), and the principles on securities regulation of the International Organization of Securities Commissions (IOSCO) – noting that some of these have been co-drafted by private groups or sub-state units.[208]

There can also be further hybrids between forms of transnational commercial law. For example, consider the OECD Principles of Corporate Governance.[209]

---

[202] See www.unglobalcompact.org/ and www.oecd.org/corporate/ guidelinesformultinationalenterprises/.

[203] For this see Gerber 2001 (on Rabel's involvement); Herings and Kanning 2008: 260 (on US influence). See also Ogus 2006: 273 (UK opposed CISG since it would result in a diminished role of English law for international transactions).

[204] Eiselen 2010: 104.   [205] See Huber 2006: 940–2; Shapiro and Stone Sweet 2002: 308.

[206] See http://unidroit.org/ and www.hcch.net/.

[207] See www.uncitral.org/uncitral/en/uncitral_texts.html.

[208] See www.ifrs.org/, www.bis.org/bcbs/, www.fatf-gafi.org/, www.iosco.org/. See also Chiapello and Medjad 2009: 460 (on 'co-regulation' in accounting law); Brummer 2010 (on how soft law in international finance is different from hard law of WTO).

[209] See OECD 2004 as discussed in Siems and Alvarez 2014.

The OECD is a group of thirty-four countries (as of August 2013) belonging to the wealthiest of the world but its recommendations are mainly aimed at law-makers in emerging and less developed economies. In addition, they are also intended for private parties as guidance for good practice. Thus, on the one hand, a country may have enacted mandatory rules following the OECD Principles of Corporate Governance. On the other hand, it may have left the implementation of the principles, or parts of them, to the companies themselves – and the companies may then be interested in implementing the principles in order to attract foreign investments.

International commercial arbitration deserves special attention since it may enable parties to 'circumvent' or 'liftoff' from national legal institutions.[210] A variety of transnational instruments can be identified. Most countries of the world have ratified the New York Convention on the Recognition and Enforcement of Foreign Arbitral Awards which ensures that state courts recognise arbitral awards save for a public policy defence.[211] In terms of procedure, the Rules on the Taking of Evidence in International Commercial Arbitration by the International Bar Association apply if parties agree on them.[212] By contrast, the UNCITRAL Model Law on International Commercial Arbitration is addressed at law-makers – and if they follow this model (which many do), it means that parties have considerable freedom to design how disputes are arbitrated.[213]

The use of arbitration further complicates the competition between legal systems. As far as arbitrators compete with state courts, the growing use of arbitration is bound to reduce the number of proceedings at state courts.[214] It has also been shown that revisions of arbitration laws based on the UNCITRAL Model Law have led to more arbitration proceedings in these countries.[215] In addition, one can examine the competition between the major institutional (as opposed to 'ad hoc') arbitration centres, in particular the ICC Court of Arbitration, the International Centre for Dispute Resolution and the London Court of International Arbitration.[216] Turning to the substantive law that arbitrators apply, it has been observed that this is often linked to the domestic law of the place of arbitration.[217] But it also seems likely that disputes that are dealt with

---

[210] Lin 2009: 712; Wai 2002. See also McConnaughay 1999: 453.

[211] See www.uncitral.org/uncitral/en/uncitral_texts/arbitration/NYConvention.html.

[212] See www.ibanet.org/Publications/publications_IBA_guides_and_free_materials.aspx. See also Dodson and Klebba 2011: 18 (on 'mixing' of common and civil law practices in arbitration proceedings).

[213] See www.uncitral.org/uncitral/en/uncitral_texts/arbitration/1985Model_arbitration.html. On its success see Zekoll 2006: 1349; Goode et al. 2007: para. 5.09.

[214] See Hoffmann and Maurer 2010 (data for Germany and the UK). More generally on regulatory competition between litigation and arbitration see Wagner 2013.

[215] Drahozal 2004.

[216] See the International Arbitration Survey 2010, available at www.arbitrationonline.org/research/2010/index.html.

[217] Eidenmüller 2011: 723. Similar for litigation, see Calliess and Hoffmann 2009: 115. On choice of law in arbitration see also Voigt 2008.

by international arbitration make use of substantive principles of transnational commercial law, such as those outlined in the previous paragraphs.[218] Moreover, it has been shown that the close-knit culture of international arbitration influences the reasoning of arbitrators, for example, since they value party autonomy more than state courts would do.[219]

The transnational nature of international commercial arbitration has also been the subject of empirical research by Yves Dezalay and Bryant Garth.[220] Their research draws a broad distinction between two types of arbitrators who compete with each other – but together also foster the use of international arbitration. On the one hand, there are the 'grand old men' of arbitration, often Europeans with an academic background. On the other hand, 'modern technocrats' are more often from the US and keen on pursuing economic interests. In particular, this competition takes place over the use of arbitration in developing and transition economies, where their interests are also supported by local lawyers and arbitrators who have received training in the developed world. These final aspects relate to the more general point that Dezalay and Garth raise in most of their writings, namely the way private actors (arbitrators, lawyers etc.) shape the legal infrastructure across borders.[221]

3. Discussion: is private law-making legitimate?

The main policy question raised by transnational law is whether it gives too much power to private law-making, for instance, in the examples provided in the previous section on transnational commercial law, but also in other areas of law, such as the transnational reach of the norms of religious communities.

The reasons why these private forms of transnational law have emerged relate both to the deficiencies of state laws and to the benefits of private law-making. For instance, on the one hand, it is said that 'national legal systems have failed to keep pace with evolving international practice' and that judges 'simply nationalise disputes'.[222] On the other hand, private law-making is said to 'take into account the needs of international [commercial] relations', it is not 'branded by . . . national origins', and arbitrators and other adjudicators 'stick closer to the parties' agreement'.[223] More general benefits are the liberality and flexibility of private law-making: it more easily allows exceptions in justified cases, enforcement mechanisms can be more varied, and it can be adapted more easily to changing circumstances than state law.[224]

---

[218] See Goode et al. 2007: para. 17.114.

[219] Karton 2013 (based on case analyses and interviews).   [220] Dezalay and Garth 1996.

[221] See, e.g., Dezalay and Garth 2011a (on how international lawyers may be able to bridge economic regulation and human rights); Dezalay and Garth 2011b (on the role they play for the rule of law). See also ch. 8 at B 2 (b), above (for their research on Latin America).

[222] Goode et al. 2007: para. 4.73 and Shapiro and Stone Sweet 2002: 333.

[223] Berger 2000: 91; Chiapello and Medjad 2009: 455; O'Hara and Ribstein 2009: 88.

[224] See, e.g., Berger 2000: 97, 101; Siems 2008a: 388.

But critics, first, point out that there are various practical problems with private law-making in transnational law. Its 'softness' may mean that it is not entirely clear when it is applicable, for example, as far as it includes customary rules. It may also be ineffective given the lack of adequate enforcement.[225] Furthermore, if participants from different countries agree on a common text, this document may only be phrased in very abstract and broad terms with the apparent risk that there are conflicting interpretations around the world.[226] Different languages pose problems if the text is authoritative in more than one language since translations can never match perfectly.[227] And if only one language is used for transnational legal matters (today, typically English), there can be many misunderstandings, for instance, considering how common and civil lawyers may understand a term such as 'equity remedies'.[228] Another problem is that a transnational instrument may not work due to a cultural mismatch. For example, this has been suggested for arbitration: in the developed countries of 'the West' arbitrators may have a common ethic and they may agree with the aim to achieve predictable and clear results, whereas in developing countries of 'the East' there may be insufficient experience in arbitration and the desire for predictable results may be less important than not 'to lose one's face'.[229]

A second line of objections is more directly directed against the legitimacy of private law-making in transnational law. As far as democracies are concerned, the apparent problem is that private law-making undermines the supremacy of parliaments.[230] But the criticism can also be put in a more general way as a problem of accountability: private parties typically act in what is good for themselves without giving consideration to the interests of the common good and outsiders.[231] The risk is therefore that, for example, transnational commercial law is infected with severe power imbalances and inequalities, in particular, since businesses may be better able to exert their influence than consumers, employees and other stakeholders.[232] There may also be problems in other fields. For example, if religious groups decide on matters regardless of state borders, this may risk the fragmentation of modern multicultural societies.[233]

However, these points of criticism need to be qualified, with much depending on how exactly instruments of transnational law are structured and applied. As for its practical aspects, first, there have been various initiatives to foster the communication of court decisions and arbitral awards dealing with instruments

---

[225] See Jordan 2013 (in the context of the global financial crisis of 2008).

[226] See, e.g., Goode et al. 2007: para. 19.04–5 ('creeping re-nationalization of transnational texts'); Legrand 1998c: 250–1.

[227] This is a general problem of multilingual laws: see, e.g., Gambaro 2007; Cao 2007.

[228] Mattila 2006: 250–1; Goddard 2009: 171. See also ch. 2 at A 2 (b), above.

[229] Arvind 2010: 83–4 (for India); McConnaughay 1999: 503–13 (for China and Japan).

[230] See, e.g., Backer 2012: 95–6; Teubner 1997: 3.   [231] Collins 2013: 130–1; Lin 2009: 742–3.

[232] See generally Eidenmüller 2011: 737, 745; Darian-Smith 2013: 53. More specifically Stephan 1999: 780 (on 'pro-bank rules' of the UCP); Siems 2008a: 389 (for corporate governance codes).

[233] Turner 2011: 151, 173.

of transnational law. For example, databases on decisions applying the CISG and the UNCITRAL model laws[234] can reduce divergent applications. A similar effect follows from the transnationalisation of legal scholarship and education, with a number of institutions offering international courses on transnational law.[235] Many of the transnational instruments are also accompanied by institutional structures to support their uniform application. These may provide formal ways of dispute resolution, for example in domain names disputes and in derivative trading,[236] but there are also other structures, such as the CISG-Advisory Council which provides advice on the interpretation of the CISG, and the system of National Contact Points which mediates in disputes about the OECD's Guidelines for Multinational Corporations.[237] Finally, doubts about the effectiveness of transnational soft law need not to be dealt with abstractly. Since its success depends on whether private participants or national legislatures take up such principles, these market forces may bring out whether and to what extent there is a need for this and effective enforcement is guaranteed.[238]

Many of the legitimacy concerns are based on the view that transnational law constitutes an 'autonomous regime' independent of the state.[239] Yet, often the picture is a mixed one. It can be said that the flexibility that private persons and institutions have is only possible if the state has allowed it in advance.[240] Alternatively, the process may be said to be reversed, namely that private self-regulation is subsequently embedded in more formal institutional structures.[241] In any case, on the one hand, domestic legislatures continue to play a crucial role: it is for them to decide whether to recognise private law-making, and how to deal with regulatory conflicts between public and private norms.[242] On the other hand, state courts have to decide on transnational private law-making: for example, whether to use such norms as guidance for the positive law, or whether to oppose them, for instance, on grounds of public policy.[243]

In addition, as far as private law-making does play a role, this should not automatically be seen as illegitimate. There are problems that transcend national borders and therefore call for a transnational (or even global) legal order, but

---

[234] See www.cisg.law.pace.edu/, www.globalsaleslaw.org/index.cfm?pageID=28, www.unilex.info/ and www.uncitral.org/uncitral/en/case_law.html.

[235] For example, see the growing number of universities participating in the Vis Arbitral Moot at www.cisg.law.pace.edu/vis.html.

[236] See www.icann.org/en/help/dndr/udrp/providers and http://dc.isda.org/.

[237] See www.cisg-ac.org/ and www.oecd.org/daf/inv/mne/ncps.htm.

[238] See already Siems 2008a: 389.

[239] See Senn 2011: 199–200; also Moore 1986b: 15 (on anthropologists claiming that international law resembles 'primitive multigroup arenas'), and already A 1 and D 2, above.

[240] Santos 2004: 211; also Wai 2002 (on the role of private international law).

[241] Botzem and Hofmann 2010 (case studies on internet governance and financial reporting).

[242] See, e.g., Wielsch 2012; Bomhoff and Meuwese 2011 (calling the latter the 'meta-regulation of transnational law').

[243] See, e.g., Büthe and Mattli 2011: 205 (on the ISO standards as guidance); Collins 2011 (on the ordre public); Benvenisti and Downs 2012 (on relationship between national courts and transnational private regulatory bodies).

states may be unable to keep pace with these developments.[244] Thus, private transnational law-making can be a necessary 'second-best' solution. The question is then how this can be done in an acceptable way. Here, a first point to consider is that in international commercial law many topics primarily call for special technical expertise: thus, the lack of political legitimacy may not be that significant for the actual result. In other cases, it is important that transnational law does not overlook the interests of important stakeholders. Again, this may lead to a mixture of private and state law-making, for example, requiring that the former fulfils certain requirements of procedural justice and fairness.

These final considerations can also be put in a more general way. The topics discussed in this section are an example of the 'complex network of national, transnational and international private and public norms' mentioned in the previous section.[245] This raises the question of what law-makers should do now: still try to create a uniform law, leave norm conflicts unresolved, allow their agglomeration, or try to integrate them?[246] It is not possible to give a 'one-size-fits-all' answer for all possible circumstances, but recent monographs by Paul Schiff Berman and Mireille Delmas-Marty provide useful guidance. Berman's 'cosmopolitan pluralist approach' suggests procedural mechanism in order to manage multiplicity. This does not aim for uniformity but for a 'productive interaction' among those multiple legal regimes.[247] Delmas-Marty's 'ordered pluralism' also rejects imposed uniformity but accepts the need for a legal order that can tackle the problems of today's world. This should be done in the spirit of pluralism through pragmatic steps, making differences compatible, and with a gradual process towards more and more common rules.[248]

E. Conclusion

In the past, the problem of state borders was mainly described as one of removing legal rules that were 'obstacles to free and cordial intercourse between the nations'.[249] The current trends of convergence, regionalisation and transnationalisation go further – but do they confirm claims about an 'end of state' and an 'end of history'?[250]

---

[244] Friedman 2001: 359 (on the globalisation of risk); Calliess 2007 (on transnational contract law).

[245] See C 3, above.

[246] For these options see Woodman 2008: 37–40 (discussing the relationship between secular and personal religious laws). Even more complex Berman 2012: 152–89 (dialectical legal interactions, margins of appreciation, limited autonomy regimes, subsidiarity schemes, hybrid participation arrangements, mutual recognition regimes, safe harbour agreements, or regime interaction).

[247] Berman 2012. See also Berman 2009.

[248] Delmas-Marty 2009; also Delmas-Marty 2003: 74 ('ordering pluralism'). Similar is the 'convergence through congruence', discussed at A 3, above.

[249] Gutteridge 1949: 156.   [250] See A 1, above.

This chapter has shown that the state is still relevant: naturally, this is the case for convergence since it concerns the way national legal systems react to external changes. It has also been shown that regionalisation and transnationalisation depend on the support of the state. But all three sections also observed a weakening of the state. Thus, traditional approaches to comparative law which mainly focus on comparisons between countries can be misleading because they tend to overemphasise the role of state borders in today's world.

This conclusion also implies that there is some justification in saying that conventional differences between legal systems have become less relevant. But it would also be misleading to talk about an 'end of history'. On the one hand, path-dependencies continue to play a role in accounting for national differences in law and elsewhere. On the other hand, this chapter has shown that the development of law continues to be a dynamic one; even more, it can be said that with the increased 'fragmentation and dispersion' of law it becomes now more likely than ever that 'transformation occurs in both . . . public and private regulatory orders'.[251]

The following chapter addresses 'comparative law and development'. It also offers a further perspective on the topics discussed here. In the present chapter the emergence of 'governance' was seen as a possible reason for a weakening of formal state law.[252] But in the development context there is also the concept of 'good governance', and it is suggested that this 'has given the state a new lease of life even among its strongest adversaries', for example, by way of urging countries to have an effective 'rule of law'[253] – as the following will explain.

---

[251] Senn 2011: 212.   [252] See A 1, above.   [253] Von Benda-Beckmann et al. 2009b: 6.

10

Comparative law and development

There are two ways of understanding the title of this chapter: it could either mean 'comparative law' *and* development, or it could refer to *comparative* 'law and development'. Both variants are addressed in the following. In the sense of 'comparative law' *and* development, the chapter considers how insights drawn from comparative law can assist development policy. This reflects the aim of traditional comparative law to provide policy recommendations, yet it also responds to the criticism that traditionalists tend to shy away from dealing with countries in the developing world.[1]

In the sense of *comparative* 'law and development', it is submitted that there is more than one concept of 'law and development': for instance, one may distinguish between law and economic development and law and human development, or between top-down and bottom-up approaches. The mainstream narrative is that law and development is associated with post-Second World War initiatives led by the US and international organisations such as the World Bank. This chapter will deal with this narrative in some detail, but this is not meant to imply an endorsement of this view.

This chapter is structured as follows: to set the scene, Section A outlines the evolving ideas of law and development. Section B deals specifically with the relationship between the rule of law and development, in particular its 'thin' or 'thick' versions as applied in different countries. Section C turns to the critics of law and development, and Section D concludes.

A. The evolving ideas of 'law and development'

The literature on law and development typically distinguishes between various phases starting in the 1930s or, more frequently, after the Second World War.[2] Yet these ideas can also be characterised in more evolutionary terms, going back further in time.

---

[1] See ch. 2 at A 1 (b), B 1 (c) and C 2, above.

[2] See, e.g., Cooter and Schäfer 2011: 196 (1930–75; 1975–90; 1990–2000; since 2000); Kennedy 2008 (1945–70; 1970–80; 1980–95; 1995–2005); Trubek 2007 (state-led, socialist and neoliberal phases of the last 50 years).

The general notion of 'development' is a prominent feature of the Enlightenment's optimism in shaping the course of history.[3] This can be seen as a predecessor of the view that development often occurs in stages. For example, in the discourse about economic development, the usual process is said to be one where agrarian societies are succeeded by pre-industrial, industrial and finally information societies.[4] In legal research, Sir Henry Maine's *Ancient Law* provided a parallel evolutionary view that related legal development to the level of civilisation: 'primitive societies' were said to have a pre-customary law which then becomes customary law and finally positive law in progressive societies.[5] In particular, Maine famously suggested that societies move from rights and obligations that derive from 'status' to 'contract'.[6] Similarly, but more explicitly, Max Weber related the economic success of the capitalist economies of the West to their formal-rational legal systems supported by professional legal institutions – and distinguished those from forms of order of non-Western countries.[7] In their pure form Maine and Weber's views are today seen as inappropriate and ethnocentric as they assume a superiority of Western laws and institutions.[8] Yet the desire for clear rules, professional institutions and effective enforcement of contracts remains an important element of contemporary approaches to law and development.

In the first three decades after the Second World War external help and an active state were often seen as crucial for economic development. In Western Europe foreign aid from the US, along with the emerging European integration and the positive role of the state in upholding a liberal economic order contributed to the fairly rapid reconstruction.[9] Many Latin American countries pursued a strategy of 'import substitution', meaning the attempt both to foster domestic production and to reduce foreign imports.[10] More specifically related to 'law and development' were US initiatives to promote law reform in Africa and Latin America. Here, the focus was not on the positive rules but on a modernisation of institutions, such as legal education and the legal profession.[11]

This 'first wave' of law and development was, however, not seen as entirely successful, in particular due to the apparent mismatch between the US models

---

[3] See Glenn 2001: 40.   [4] Cf. Gilpin 2001: 176–7; Easterly 2006: 21.

[5] Maine 1861. See also Donovan 2008: 42–4; Zweigert and Kötz 1998: 9; David 1985: 4; Tamanaha 2001: 32; de Cruz 2007: 228.

[6] Maine 1861: 100.

[7] Weber 1978: 641–900 (original from 1922). Weber also refers to the role of religion, e.g., in Weber 2008 (original from 1905). For more details see ch. 11 at C 1, below.

[8] On Maine see, e.g., Menski 2006: 88; Riles 1999: 228; Bennett 2006: 652. On Weber see, e.g., White 2001: 52–3 and ch. 11 at C 1, below.

[9] The role of the state was particularly important in the German 'ordoliberal' model: see Schnyder and Siems 2013.

[10] See, e.g., Prebisch 1959. The view of state-led growth can also be related back to the 1930s: see Cooter and Schäfer 2011: 197.

[11] See, e.g., Kroncke 2012: 492; Paul 2003: vii–xxiii; Trubek and Santos 2006: 5; Dezalay and Garth 2002: 245; Mattei and Nader 2008: 72; Krishnan 2012 (specifically on the reforms sponsored by the Ford Foundation in Africa); also Gardner 1980 (calling this 'legal imperialism').

and the local conditions in Africa and Latin America.[12] It is therefore not clear whether these initiatives really had a positive economic and social effect on the countries in question. In the late 1960s and the 1970s there was also a political backlash against the influence of the United States. This reaction had a strong political dimension: for instance, the 'dependency theory' and the 'world systems theory' argue that the poverty of African and Latin American countries was mainly a result of their exploitation by Western countries.[13] Similar to the dependency theory, though less radical, was the establishment of the UN Conference on Trade and Development (UNCTAD) in 1964 aimed at promoting a 'development-friendly integration of developing countries into the world economy'.[14]

Yet in the late 1970s, with the politics of Reagan in the US and Thatcher in the UK a fairly radical version of economic liberalism became the dominant paradigm. The corresponding economic policy for development has been termed the 'Washington Consensus', referring to the seat of the US Treasury, the World Bank Group and the International Monetary Fund (IMF).[15] Among the typical recommendations of this 'consensus' were the reduction of public spending, the liberalisation of trade and investment, privatisation, deregulation and strong protection of property rights.

The latter two aspects are most directly related to legal rules, but – as a typical feature of recent trends in law and development – they have mainly been shaped by economists (and have often been overlooked by legal scholars).[16] For example, the Peruvian economist Hernando de Soto and his think tank Institute for Liberty and Democracy, on the one hand, emphasise that economic development depends on formal protection of property since informality tends to foster corruption and inefficiencies. On the other hand, they suggest that law should be business-friendly: for example, it should not impose excessive formalities to get a business registered.[17] Similar but more specific suggestions to foster economic development can be found in books by Kenneth Dam and Bob Cooter and Hans-Bernd Schäfer, both referring to the need for secure property rights, rules of investor protection and an effective judicial system.[18] Empirical work by economists claims to have found that those and related reasons are more decisive for economic development than, for example, geographic and cultural differences.[19] Here, the role of law is often phrased in terms of the importance of 'institutions' and 'governance' which includes

---

[12] Trubek and Galanter 1974. See also the literature cited in the previous note.

[13] E.g. Cardoso and Faletto 1979; Wallerstein 1979. See also Merino Acuña 2012.

[14] See http://unctad.org/en/Pages/AboutUs.aspx and UNCTAD 2006.

[15] Williamson 1989. See also Trubek and Santos 2006: 6–7.

[16] Barros 2010: 2 (for de Soto). See also Dezalay and Garth 2002 (on the role of economists in development practice). See also ch. 11 at B 3, below.

[17] See, e.g., de Soto 1989; de Soto 2000; de Soto 2008; and www.ild.org.pe.

[18] Dam 2006; Cooter and Schäfer 2011.

[19] E.g. Acemoglu et al. 2002; Acemoglu et al. 2005; Rodrik et al. 2004. See also Haggard et al. 2008: 208.

political factors such as the accountability of the government and political stability.[20]

International development organisations have played an important part in this phase. When the World Bank and the IMF provide funds to countries, this is often made conditional upon structural improvements of their legal systems.[21] The World Bank and the IMF also produce so-called Reports on the Observance of Standards and Codes (ROSCs) in which they examine whether countries follow international soft laws, such as the OECD Principles of Corporate Governance and the FATF anti-money laundering recommendations.[22] In addition, various parts of the World Bank Group have developed quantitative comparative measures on laws and law enforcement. These were already discussed earlier in this book,[23] notably the Doing Business Report and the World Bank Governance Indicators.

Since the 1990s, however, approaches critical to this consensus started playing a more pronounced role. In 1993 the World Bank established an Inspection Panel which enables private parties to complain about negative effects of projects funded by the World Bank.[24] This is in line with the emergence of compliance committees, inspection panels and dispute settlement bodies in other international groups and organisations.[25] Moreover, in 1998 the World Bank launched a new initiative, called Comprehensive Development Framework (CDF). This CDF emphasises a shift from 'short-term macroeconomic stabilisation and balance-of-payment corrections' to 'longer-term structural and social considerations, such as expanding and improving education and health facilities, maintaining infrastructure, and training a new generation of public officials', all of this being based on a partnership between 'governments, donors, civil society, the private sector and other stakeholders'.[26]

This does not mean that the World Bank has undergone a complete paradigm shift. The articles of agreement of the sub-divisions of the World Bank Group limit their activities: they are not allowed to interfere in the political affairs of the recipient countries, and they shall only ensure that the proceeds are used according to 'considerations of economy and efficiency' but 'without regard to political or other non-economic influences or considerations'.[27] It has also been

---

[20] See also Acemoglu and Robinson 2012 (suggesting that inclusive states produce better laws and institutions); Collier 2007: 135–56 (recommending international legal prototypes to tackle 'bad governance'); Barro 1997 (using political stability as a measure of strong property rights).

[21] See www.worldbank.org/conditionality and www.imf.org/external/np/exr/facts/conditio.htm.

[22] See www.worldbank.org/ifa/rosc.html and www.imf.org/external/NP/rosc/rosc.aspx. For these examples see ch. 9 at D 2, above.

[23] See ch. 7 at C, above.   [24] See www.worldbank.org/inspectionpanel.

[25] See Cassese 2010: 771 and Shapiro and Stone Sweet 2002: 75 (both drawing parallels with previous versions of the French Conseil d'État); de Jong and Stoter: 2009: 312 (on sceptics of the work of the inspection panel).

[26] These quotes are from www.worldbank.org/cdf/. See also Rodrik 2006: 978 (calling this the 'augmented' Washington Consensus).

[27] IBRD Articles of Agreement, arts. 4(10), 3(5)(b). Similar are IDA Articles of Agreement, art. 5(6), 5(1)(g); IFC Articles of Agreement, art. 3(9). See also Danino 2006.

doubted whether the CDF is taken seriously enough since parts of the World Bank Group, in particular, those associated with the Doing Business Report, are said to focus only on economic development and to apply a 'one size fits all' approach.[28] Thus, the current approach of the World Bank is best regarded as a mixed one, as different parts of the group follow different priorities in terms of law and development.[29]

Of course, other countries and organisations also play an important role. The competent government departments, government-sponsored agencies and development banks of developed countries (or some macro-regional organisations such as the EU) not only provide development aid, but also try to influence the laws of recipient countries. This can mean that there is a 'battle of advisors' since every country tends to promote its own legal rules.[30] But there are also similar objectives as far as most Western countries aim to promote human rights and democratic constitutions.[31]

At a global level, the goals of the Millennium Declaration, adopted by the UN General Assembly in 2000, cover a variety of economic and non-economic topics, for example, equality and solidarity, the protection of human rights and the environment ('sustainable development').[32] These aims are also reflected in the UN Development Programme (UNDP), in particular through its Human Development Indicators (HDI).[33] The UN agency for human settlements (UN-Habitat) also urges countries to implement legal reforms that provide 'socially and environmentally sustainable towns and cities', in particular for the world's urban poor.[34]

Wider non-economic interests are also supported by other intergovernmental agencies such as the World Health Organization (WHO), the International Labour Organization (ILO), the Intergovernmental Panel on Climate Change (IPCC), as well as NGOs and other private groups such as Greenpeace, Amnesty International, Oxfam and the World Social Forum.[35] In addition, the balance between economic and non-economic interests is a frequent topic of the World Trade Organization (WTO), albeit, with developed, transitioning and developing countries disagreeing on major policy issues.[36]

---

[28] Faundez 2010; also Rittich 2004: 219; Rodriguez-Garavito 2005: 78 (hard law for business interests but only soft strategies to deal with social concerns).

[29] Sarfaty 2009; Santos 2006: 258–9; Ohnesorge 2009: 1624.

[30] Schimmelfennig 2012 (for rule of law promotion by US, EU, UK, France, Germany). See also ch. 7 at C 4, above.

[31] See also ch. 8 at B 4 and ch. 9 at B 2, above.

[32] See www.un.org/millennium/declaration/ares552e.htm and then the Millenium Development Goals, www.un.org/millenniumgoals/. The concept of sustainable development goes back to World Commission on Environment and Development 1987.

[33] See http://hdr.undp.org/en/statistics/.

[34] See www.unhabitat.org. See also McAuslan 2003: 106–33 (discussing this approach of 'bringing the law back in').

[35] For a good overview see Yeates and Holden 2009.

[36] See, e.g., Lang 2011; Gilpin 2001: 229–32.

The main intellectual basis for this emerging comprehensive view of development comes from Amartya Sen, the winner of the Nobel Memorial Prize in Economic Sciences in 1998.[37] His suggestion is that of 'development as freedom', meaning that the main aim should be to enable everyone 'to be able to do and be'. This requires elementary 'capabilities',[38] not simply income and wealth, but, for example, education, social security, personal liberties, equal opportunities and fairness. A recent report, co-authored by Sen, also refers to subjective well-being ('happiness') as a possible measure of social progress.[39]

Specifically for law and development, Sen's view thus implies that the essence of courts and rights is not primarily to secure existing entitlements but also to provide justice for the poor.[40] As a result, law and justice are not merely seen as a means to another end (say, for economic development); rather, they are an important part of the development process on their own.[41] This final point leads us directly to the relationship between development and the rule of law.

B. Development and the rule of law

1. Terminology, typology and purpose

Recent trends in development policy have often been associated with programmes supporting the rule of law. For example, the rule of law is said to be sponsored by various national, regional, and international organisations and agencies, such as the USAID, the American Bar Association, the European Bank for Reconstruction and Development, the World Bank Group and the UN.[42] Rule of law initiatives are also said to have been well received since they 'enjoy wider acceptance across ideologies, religions and political regimes than democracy and many allegedly universal human rights'.[43] But this is a contentious statement, considering disagreements about the scope of the rule of law.

Most views distinguish between procedural (or formal) aspects on the one hand and substantive ones on the other – though with some doubts on which specific elements should be included.[44] Starting with the procedural aspects, the 'rule of law' can be distinguished from the 'rule by law', the latter meaning that a head of state just uses the law in an opportunistic way in order to implement his or her wishes. By contrast, the rule of law requires that there are

---

[37] Sen 1999. See also Twining 2009a: 219–24; Tamanaha 2011b: 232–3.

[38] For this concept see also Nussbaum 2011 and the website of the Human Development and Capability Association, www.hd-ca.org/.

[39] Stiglitz et al. 2008 (report commissioned by the French government). For legal policy and the growing field of 'happiness studies' see also Huang 2010.

[40] See Armytage 2009: 10.   [41] Sen 2006: 40. See also Sen 2009.

[42] Finnegan 2006: 110; Armytage 2009: 5; Humphreys 2010: 123–38, 155 (in particular on the US and the World Bank).

[43] Peerenboom et al. 2012: 316.

[44] For the following see, e.g., Tamanaha 2004: 91; Trebilcock and Daniels 2008: 29–37; Carothers 2010: 21; Krygier 2012: 235–40; Santos 2006: 258–9; McCorquodale 2010; also Bell 2006c: 1272 (comparing English term with the French 'l'état de droit' and the German 'Rechtsstaat').

clear, transparent, general and prospective laws. In addition, institutions have to apply these laws in a reliable and equal way: for example, the judiciary, the public prosecution, the police and the administrative authorities.[45] These institutions, and their constituents, should not overstep their powers. In particular, this makes it necessary to prevent corruption, usually defined as the abuse of public power for personal gain.[46] The problem of corruption is said to be particularly severe in the developing world since it tends to be reinforced by inequality and poverty.[47]

The rule of law literature often discusses the judiciary in more detail. Frequent topics are the structure of courts, the operation of trials, and the availability of access to justice and effective law enforcement. A typical recommendation is that of judicial independence with various sub-categories suggested, such as internal and external, structural and behavioural, and institutional, personal, functional and financial independence.[48] Less frequently, reference is made to the role of legal education and practising lawyers. But it is clear that without appropriate legal education, however this may be structured, legal institutions cannot function well. Recent research has also elaborated on the role of practising lawyers for the rule of law, not only in terms of representing their clients, but also as brokers between different interests and as local activists representing the interests of the poor.[49]

It is more controversial whether those procedural aspects of the rule of law also include standards about the way laws are enacted. Sometimes it is said that certain principles of 'good governance', such as checks and balances, should be available. Typically this leads to the requirement that law-making should be based on principles of democratic legitimacy.[50] Yet, making democracy a sub-category of the rule of law seems to stretch this term too far. It is also not in line with the approach of international organisations such as the UN and the World Bank which try to promote the rule of law in democratic as well as non-democratic countries.

Beyond formal and procedural aspects, most concepts of the rule of law embrace some topics of substantive law. In one variant this refers to secure property rights,[51] and possibly also some more specific aspects of business law which are seen as pre-conditions for economic development.[52] Such a view may then be associated with the political 'right' and economic liberalism since it mainly benefits business interests and, in an international context, the countries

---

[45] See, e.g., Trebilcock and Daniels 2008.

[46] See, e.g., www.transparency.org/cpi2012/in_detail/.   [47] See Uslander 2008; Kumar 2011.

[48] Peerenboom 2010a: 71; Dam 2006: 106, 111; Andenas and Fairgrieve 2006: 23.

[49] Dezalay and Garth 2011b; Munger 2012 (with references to his previous research). See also Daniels and Trebilcock 2004: 115, 117, 126–7.

[50] E.g. Sarkar 2009: 165 and Humphreys 2010: 204 (both also referring to need to build a civil society).

[51] See Mattei and Nader 2008: 14.

[52] Sarkar 2009: 165 (referring to structural legal reform, e.g., commercial law reform, privatisation, capital market development, and microfinance).

and foreign investors of the developed world.[53] But, today, it is more common to suggest that the rule of law also means something like 'rule of good law'.[54] Typically, this will refer to at least some ideas of 'justice',[55] however this may be defined.

Controversial is the relationship between the rule of law and human rights. The preamble of the Universal Declaration of Human Rights of 1948 states that 'human rights should be protected by the rule of law', from which one may infer that they are not themselves part of the rule of law. But a UN report from 2004 takes the position that the rule of law refers to laws 'which are consistent with international human rights norms and standards'.[56] A book by the late British judge Lord Bingham also includes 'adequate protection of fundamental human rights' as one of the elements of the rule of law.[57] It may also be said that some of the procedural elements of the rule of law, for instance the right to a fair trial, are typically seen as a human right anyway.[58] Naturally, including topics such as freedom of speech and a free press would be more controversial in some parts of the world. But some also extend the rule of law to rights to social welfare, which would then make the rule of law a 'progressive programme'.[59]

These controversies follow from the question about the actual function of the rule of law. Three positions can be distinguished. The first view is a conceptual one, namely that compliance with the rule of law explains why certain countries have been economically successful. This view goes back to Max Weber, who argued that the rationality and predictability of Western legal systems contributed to the rise of capitalism.[60] More recently, the historian Niall Ferguson found the rule of law and representative government to be one of the six 'killer apps' that were key to Western ascendancy, in particular due to private property rights and representation of property-owners in elected legislatures.[61] The same has been shown by quantitative researchers who have examined many of the elements said to belong to the rule of law.[62]

Second, the rule of law may be used as a target that countries are encouraged to achieve. The rationale for this target may be moral or ethical, as far as the rule of law is seen as reflecting universal ideas of justice that have an intrinsic

---

[53] Ohnesorge 2007: 103 ('neoliberal rule of law'); Mattei and Nader 2008 (developed world 'plunders' resources of developing countries); and see C, below.

[54] Shapiro and Stone Sweet 2002: 166.   [55] Tamanaha 2004: 91.

[56] See www.un.org/en/ruleoflaw/index.shtml.

[57] Bingham 2010b. See also McCorquodale 2010: 29.

[58] See, e.g., International Covenant on Civil and Political Rights 1966, Art. 14; European Convention on Human Rights, Art. 6.

[59] Cf. Tamanaha 2011b: 220, 239 (on use of the rule of law by both conservatives and progressives).

[60] See A, above and ch. 11 at C 1, below.

[61] Ferguson 2011. See also Ferguson 2012. The historical variant of the New Institutional Economics also refers to the role of institutions, e.g., North 1990.

[62] References in Haggard et al. 2008: 211; Daniels and Trebilcock 2004: 102; McCorquodale 2010: 38. But note the controversy about the relationship between democracy and development: see ch. 11 at B 1, below.

value,[63] not just 'Western liberal ideas'.[64] But, here too, the main reason may be an economic one. In particular, it has been argued that the World Bank and the US follow a formal definition of the rule of law that values it only for its 'ability to provide a stable investment environment and the predictability necessary for markets to operate'[65] and as a 'necessary precursor for a country's integration into the global economy'.[66]

However, it has also been suggested that the economic aim is like a Trojan horse as these reforms will then 'take on a life of their own'.[67] Organisations have also developed indicators with both ethical and economic elements. Naturally, this is the case for those that try to combine all possible elements of the rule of law, outlined above.[68] The World Justice Project even goes so far in saying that the rule of law can lead to the 'eradication of poverty, violence, corruption, pandemics and other threats to civil society'.[69] But there are also mixed rationalities for the various principles on judicial integrity and independence, drafted by private groups, for instance, groups of judges, but also the UN:[70] here, the aspiration may be that those principles can help economic development,[71] but they are also based on the belief that judicial integrity has an intrinsic value.

Third, criticising such a view, it can be suggested that effectively promoting the rule of law does not mean imposing international 'best practices', but developing rules that are appropriate for the country in question.[72] For example, it has been observed about judicial independence that it is 'an instrumental value, not an end in itself', that 'giving more independence to corrupt judges, makes things worse', and that it is very much a feature of individualist societies with a technocratic model of judicial determination which may not be desired elsewhere.[73] It has also been argued that judicial independence may be weaker (or at least different) in civil than in common law countries since in the former's career judiciaries some monitoring of younger judges is inherently useful.[74] Political differences also play a crucial role: for instance, it has been said that judicial independence is a way to enforce legislative deals in multiparty systems whereas in countries where one party is dominant other forms

---

[63] See Daniels and Trebilcock 2004: 104; Gopal 2009: 54; see also A, above (for Sen).
[64] So Chen 2007: 695 (therefore reluctant to use it for China).
[65] Krever 2011: 288. Similarly Barron 2005: 15 (at the heart formal definition).
[66] Humphreys 2010: 215, also 139–40 (criticising the economic position as being inconsistent with the conceptual origins of the rule of law).
[67] Stephenson 2000: 78.
[68] See in particular the WBGI and the WJP discussed in ch. 7 at C 4, above.
[69] See http://worldjusticeproject.org/sites/default/files/WJP_Index_Report_2012.pdf.
[70] Resources at www.judicialintegritygroup.org/.   [71] E.g. La Porta et al. 2004.
[72] Garapon 2010: 37; Peerenboom 2010a: 72; Hendley 2004: 611 (no 'silver bullet').
[73] For these quotes see Ruskola 2002: 231 note 219 (with reference to Ramseyer 1994); Peerenboom 2010a: 10; Garapon 2010: 44; and Zhu 2010: 57. For the final point see also the empirical work by Licht et al. 2007.
[74] See Guarnieri 2010: 236–7; Shapiro 1981: 151, 156; also Joireman 2004 (presenting quantitative evidence). But there are also differences between common law countries: see Lee 2011.

Table 10.1 Possible functions of the rule of law and examples

Function of rule of law	Example discussed in Section 2	Relevant variant of the rule of law
Explanation for economic development	China, 1980s to 2000s	Mainly formal and thin
International target for countries in transition	Russia, 1990s and 2000s	Mainly substantive and thick
Rules appropriate for country in question	Afghanistan, 2000s	Mainly substantive and thick

of control, such as a career judiciary, are more suitable.[75] And in authoritarian regimes the use of judicial independence may have strategic reasons that are quite different from those in democratic countries.[76]

Thus, instead of international blueprints, the suggestion is that a starting point is asking the question of 'what is wrong?'.[77] Good examples are the initiatives to improve access to justice supported by the United Nations Development Programme on legal empowerment of the poor.[78] Here, what matters is that law reformers identify the relevant problem precisely: for instance, it may then be explored whether weaknesses in access to justice derive from weak procedural protection, poor protective rights, lack of qualified and accessible lawyers, or power imbalances between individuals and multinational corporations.[79]

2. The rule of law in China, Russia and Afghanistan

The following three examples deal with the rule of law developments of China, Russia and Afghanistan in periods of transition, mainly referring to the 1990s and 2000s. These examples serve as convenient test cases for showing the spread of the rule of law idea and whether these reforms can be seen as successful. They are also directly related to the different functions and variants outlined in the previous section, as Table 10.1 illustrates.

The People's Republic of China is most frequently cited as an example for showing that rapid economic development in the last thirty years did *not* require compliance with the rule of law. In particular, it is said to be 'impossible to make the case' that formal legal institutions, such as strong protection of property rights, have contributed to China's economic success.[80] This lack of a rule of

---

[75] Ramseyer and Rasmusen 2003: 125–6.
[76] See further 2, below.   [77] Garapon 2010: 48.
[78] See www.undp.org/legalempowerment/.
[79] See, e.g., Gramatikov and Porter 2011; Dias and Welch 2009; Baxi 2009: 94.
[80] Clarke et al. 2008: 376; also Clarke 2003; Upham 2009; Trebilcock and Veel 2008: 441; Allen et al. 2005; Allen and Qian 2010.

law is distinguished from the use of a 'rule by law', being in line with the pre-Communist preference of Chinese law for coercion and criminal sanctions.[81] Further exploring how Chinese society 'works' and what explains its recent economic progress, frequent reference is made to the role of informal institutions, such as personal connections, business networks, trust and mediation,[82] political decentralisation and the corresponding competition between local governments,[83] the ability and willingness of government officials to solve disputes,[84] as well as the general benefits of stability associated with a strong state committed to economic development.[85]

However, the rule of law has also made some progress in China, at least on a 'thin' version that excludes political rights, Western-style democracy and, for most parts, accountability of the ruling elite.[86] The apparent parallel is to the development of other countries in East and South East Asia. Singapore in particular is often seen as an example of a well-functioning legal system without the need to move further towards a multi-party democracy.[87] A more general study on the role of law in Asian economic development between 1960 and 1995 also found that legal institutions mattered in order to achieve the respective economic policies that these countries were trying to pursue.[88]

For example, modern Chinese business laws have strengthened the protection of shareholders and creditors, and special laws have been enacted to stimulate international investments and joint ventures.[89] A frequent point of discussion is the role of courts and lawyers in modern China. Empirical data show that judicial enforcement has become more important, and that the number of law students and lawyers has increased.[90] Recent research has also rejected 'wholesale denunciations of a lack of judicial independence'.[91] Clearly, one has to distinguish between cases: while in political cases, or in those that involve important socio-economic issues, individual judges may be put under pressure, this is different for the mass of more routine ones.[92] There are also pronounced regional differences, as research has shown that professionalism and independence has grown in Shanghai and other commercial centres.[93] It is also helpful to distinguish between the different elements of judicial independence, for example, trends pointing towards the strengthened role of merit for

---

[81] Cf. Glenn 2010a: 321–3; Mattei and Nader 2008: 72; Ruskola 2002: 189.

[82] See references in previous note.

[83] C. Xu 2011; Daniels and Trebilcock 2004: 108.   [84] Du 2011: 281 (thus, replacing courts).

[85] Du 2011: 267 ('helping-hand regulatory state'); Yulin and Peerenboom 2010: 110, 120. Generally also Gilson and Milhaupt 2011 (on 'economically benevolent dictators').

[86] Peerenboom 2002; Head 2010; more sceptical Lubman 1999.

[87] See, e.g., Silverstein 2008; Harding and Carter 2003.

[88] Pistor and Wellons 1999. But see also C 1, below.   [89] See Yao and Yueh 2009: 754, 756.

[90] Clarke et al. 2008. See also Liebman 2013 (modest growth in caseload).

[91] Peerenboom 2010a: 4.

[92] Yulin and Peerenboom 2010; Guarnieri 2010: 239 (calling this a 'bifurcated structure'). See also Stern 2013 (on environmental litigation, as sitting 'near the boundary of the politically permissible').

[93] Pei et al. 2010; Henderson 2010: 31.

recruitment and promotions but also formal and informal hierarchies that may restrict individual judges.[94]

There is disagreement on why these developments have occurred. First, a cynical response is that non-democratic regimes mainly grant some powers to judges to facilitate the enforcement of controversial policies, to control administrative personnel and to subjugate political opponents.[95] Second, a more positive but equally strategic interpretation is that there is a genuine interest to improve property rights and law enforcement in order to stimulate international trade and investment – and possibly also to respond to the interests of domestic economic elites.[96] Third, it is possible to go further and say that in the increasingly differentiated Chinese society, morals and custom can no longer meet the interest in a stable order, and therefore improvements of the rule of law respond to a more comprehensive emphasis on law in the population.[97]

It seems likely that all three reasons play a role. To be sure, with respect to the second one, it may be objected that the improvements to the rule of law only occurred after or parallel to China's recent economic success. Yet, this does not prove that law plays no role for economic development. Simple causal models overlook the fact that the economy and the law typically co-evolve.[98] It has also been suggested that the sustainability of economic growth in China now depends on improvements to the rule of law: it can reduce its overreliance on export-led growth,[99] and if such improvements were not to happen, entrenched interest groups, such as corrupt officials, may 'block the reform, obstruct development, and even threaten the political stability of the nation'.[100] Thus, the Chinese experience should not be seen as evidence that the rule of law does not matter.

In Russia, by contrast, it may be argued that legal reform based on an international model of the rule of law was supposed to come first. In the early 1990s Russia, as well as the other countries of the former Soviet sphere of influence, faced the challenge of how to move to modern market economies as quickly as possible. The hope was that the rule of law, as apparently successful in Western Europe and North America, could be an important tool. Yet, this has not been a smooth transition.

The fall of communism did not mean that in Eastern Europe and Russia entirely new legal systems had to be created. To some extent, socialist laws and

---

[94] See Peerenboom 2010a: 74–9; Guarnieri 2010: 243.

[95] Ginsburg 2010c: 249–50. For a detailed analysis of courts in authoritarian regimes see Ginsburg and Moustafa 2008; Root and May 2008.

[96] Root and May 2008: 317–8; Arner 2007: 55. See also Harding and Nicholson 2011: 2–4 (on possible reasons for new courts and judicialisation of disputes in Asia).

[97] Dam 2006: 12–3. See also ch. 4 at C 2 (a), above.

[98] For China see Clarke et al. 2008: 378. More generally see Armour et al. 2009b; Siems and Deakin 2010: 135 and ch. 11 at B 3, below.

[99] Kurkchiyan 2010: 1.   [100] C. Xu 2011: 1140; also Dam 2006: 77.

institutions could be modified and, to another extent, countries could return to their pre-communist legal heritage.[101] But it was also inevitable to transplant new laws, in particular on economic matters.[102] Law reform has also addressed institutional aspects, in Russia, for example, leading to new courts, such as the Constitutional Court established in 1991, new administrative bodies such as media complaint councils,[103] as well as an expansion of legal education and training.[104] To be sure, quick institutional reforms are unlikely to work perfectly. Thus, it was also suggested that arbitration could be a temporary substitute,[105] and in company law the Russian legislator explicitly followed the model of a 'self-enforcing law' that aimed to provide shareholder protection with minimal need to resort to courts.[106]

Critics point to various problems of the rule of law in Russia. Some of these are said to be related to the communist or even pre-communist legal heritage of an authoritarian use of law: for instance, that the Tsarist Russia had no tradition of 'law-boundedness' and that the 'rule of law had no place in the Soviet political system'.[107] Blame has also been attributed to the process of transition, such as its disregard of local conditions, its elite-driven, instrumentalist, or even neoliberal nature, and its belief in a 'big bang' in the legal sphere as well as a 'shock therapy' in the economic one, as opposed to the more gradual changes in a country like China.[108]

More specifically, the most frequent points of criticism are: first, some laws are said to be circumvented or disrespected, which may also be seen as a not-so-paradoxical response to a strongly positivist legal tradition that allows limited flexibility in the application of legal rules.[109] Second, corruption is not only said to be widespread in politics and bureaucracy but also in the judiciary.[110] Third, judges are not seen as independent as far as the Kremlin uses criminal trials to persecute political opponents.[111] Fourth, human rights are not sufficiently protected. Despite Russia's ratification of the European Convention on Human Rights, citizens and companies are claimed to be 'subject to arbitrary and capricious interference by the state'.[112]

But some observers also provide a (cautiously) positive assessment. According to Kathryn Hendley, Russia has 'surely moved closer to the ideal of the "rule of law"', given its 'profound institutional reforms' since the fall of communism.[113]

---

[101] See Kühn 2006: 228 (on use of pre-communist legal heritage); Hendley 2004: 607 (legal systems could be 'de-Sovietised'); Bowring 2008: 198–204 (jury system reinstated, returning to previous practice).

[102] Ajani 1995; Waelde and Gunderson 1994.   [103] Kurkchiyan 2009.

[104] Hendley 2009: 251; also van Erp 2007: 400 (for reforms in Eastern Europe).

[105] Rubin 1994.   [106] Based on advice by US academics: see Black and Kraakman 1996.

[107] Kahn 2005: 375, 380; also van Erp 2007: 400; Kurkchiyan 2010: 15.

[108] Glinavos 2010 (for 'neoliberalism'); Peerenboom 2010a: 84; also Peerenboom 2010b (comparing Eastern Europe with China). For the mass privatisations see Boycko et al. 1997. See also Buscaglia and Ratliff 2000: 16–7 (for choice between gradualism and big bang).

[109] Kurkchiyan 2009: 355; Galligan 2003: 1, 7; Kühn 2006: 229.

[110] Kurkchiyan 2007: 75; Hendley 2009: 252.   [111] Edwards 2009; Hendley 2009: 241.

[112] Kahn 2005: 354–5. For more recent assessments see www.hrw.org/europecentral-asia/russia.

[113] Hendley 2006: 347.

Though Hendley does not deny the political influence in high-profile cases, the day-to-day reality of courts and litigants is said to be a different one. Focusing on civil litigation her empirical research found that litigants are most concerned about 'the time, money, and the emotional energy required to see a lawsuit through to its conclusion'.[114] Data also show that the number of civil cases has increased significantly. Thus, the most common problem is the 'avalanche of cases' that courts have to cope with, rather than a general distrust in the Russian legal system.[115]

A more ambiguously positive assessment is the one by Maria Popova. She examined disputes on electoral registration and defamation suits against media companies in Russia and the Ukraine between 1998 and 2004. These were potentially politically contentious cases. Yet, it was found that in Russia courts decided more independently than in the Ukraine. The lack of independence in the Ukraine is explained by the fear of the incumbent government of losing its grip on power. By contrast, the Russian government did not face serious political competition and it could therefore intervene less frequently in the operation of courts.[116]

As a result, a mixed picture emerges, not entirely dissimilar to the Chinese one. The question of whether weaknesses of the rule of law 'mattered' may also invite a similar answer. Clearly, other factors, such as the prevalence of natural resources (oil, gas etc.), have led to economic growth despite these weaknesses, but this does not mean that corruption and other deficiencies of the rule of law do not impede foreign and domestic investment.[117] Finally, the Russian case illustrates a more deliberate attempt than the Chinese one to transplant an international model of the rule of law. Apparently this has not worked perfectly, but it cannot be said for sure whether this is due to the model or factors intrinsic to Russia.[118]

The literature on rule-of-law initiatives in post-2001 Afghanistan also tends to focus on their failures, in particular, the alleged naivety of Western powers and international organisations about transplanting their version of the rule of law to Afghanistan.[119] But, starting with the international agreements and official documents, it can be seen that local conditions were meant to play a prominent role. The Bonn Agreement from December 2001 referred to the aim 'to rebuild the domestic justice system in accordance with Islamic principles, international standards, the rule of law and Afghan legal traditions'.[120] And in the recommendations from the Rome Conference on the Rule of Law in

---

[114] Hendley 2009: 243 (in contrast to fears of political interference, ibid., 249).

[115] Hendley 2013; also Hendley 2009: 243.   [116] Popova 2012.

[117] See Kurkchiyan 2010: 2 (for many entrepreneurs it is still a 'no go zone'). Edwards 2009: 41 (citing a Canadian attorney: 'Until the rule of law is established in Russia, I won't be back').

[118] Cf. Gilpin 2001: 335–6 (on possible reasons on 'what went wrong').

[119] E.g. the contributions in Mason 2011; also Jupp 2013 and Ahmed 2005 (on problems with the new criminal procedure code).

[120] Article 2(2) of the Agreement on Provisional Arrangements in Afghanistan Pending the Re-Establishment of Permanent Government Institutions (Bonn Agreement) of 5 December 2001, available at www.un.org/News/dh/latest/afghan/afghan-agree.htm.

Afghanistan from July 2007 it was stated that rule of law initiatives should be 'consistent with Afghan needs and realities' and that they should 'embrace and engage Afghan legal context, culture, customs and the Islamic foundation of the legal system of Afghanistan'.[121]

More specifically, codified laws were re-introduced, after they had been abolished by the Taliban in 1992. Notably, this led to the constitution of 2004 which emphasises the role of Islam but also observance of the Universal Declaration of Human Rights.[122] In particular, there are provisions on the rights and status of women, not in the least due to influence of foreign officials and other external actors.[123] Other laws were initially drafted with assistance from the Italian government, and those also reflect more general Western influence.[124] Special emphasis has been given to re-establishing a legal infrastructure to apply and enforce state laws. This refers to technical tasks, such as building court houses and prisons, and helping to set up institutions to train judges, prosecutors, lawyers, police and army personnel in the new laws.[125] It also includes field support for the implementation of legal and institutional reforms.[126] Most challenging are changes to legal culture. It is clear that practices and perceptions play a crucial role for establishing the rule of law.[127] A Rule of Law Officer of the US military even phrases this as a 'commitment to indoctrinate both Afghan government officials and the population with the firm belief in the rule of law'.[128] Crucially, this also includes the need to address widespread problems of corruption.[129]

All of this seems to be aimed at a fairly 'thick' version of the rule of law, but subsequent developments suggested a less ambitious approach. The judges of state courts are said to rely 'on nothing more than their own personal intuition', not the newly enacted laws.[130] Moreover, forms of mediation, such as councils of elders, have continued to play an important role in practice. Since these mechanisms are based on traditional cultural standards, they tend to pay no attention to state laws, including the constitution: for instance, the rights of women.[131] The initial expectation may have been that state courts will soon

---

[121] Joint Recommendations available at www.rolafghanistan.esteri.it/NR/rdonlyres/ 49F0C01D-791F-406D-9693-0A782718DF25/0/JOINTRecommendations.pdf.

[122] Namely, Arts. 1 to 3 and Art 7. An English version is available at http://supremecourt.gov.af.

[123] Al-Ali 2011: 80–2. See, e.g., Art. 22 (equal rights) and Art. 44 (foster education for women).

[124] See Hartmann and Klonowiecka-Milart 2011. For the Italian influence see Ahmed 2005; Jupp 2013: 59–61.

[125] See, e.g., United Nations Assistance Mission in Afghanistan (UNAMA), available at http://unama.unmissions.org/; Wyler and Katzman 2010; Jupp 2013: 57–8.

[126] E.g. the NATO Rule of Law Field Support Mission (NROLFSM) and the US Rule of Law Field Force-Afghanistan (US-ROLFF-A), see www.isaf.nato.int/images/media/PDFs/ 110930rolbackground.pdf.

[127] See Krygier 2011. See also C 1, below.

[128] As quoted in Tasikas 2007: 53.   [129] See Islamic Republic of Afghanistan 2008: 146–7.

[130] Jupp 2013: 69 (citing a Prosecutions Caseworker Adviser in 2009).

[131] For this tension see Center for Policy and Human Development 2007: 91–110 and the conference organised by the US Institute of Peace in 2006, materials available at

replace these forms of mediation. Yet, since this did not happen, and since the customary system can help in stabilising the country, traditional forms of mediation are now seen as potentially beneficial as far as some form of collaboration with formal institutions of justice can be achieved.[132]

An even more severe problem is how to deal with provincial, regional and local powers, including the Taliban. Since these powers may have no respect for human rights, democracy, independent courts and other elements of a thick version of the rule of law, any concessions may be seen as a failure.[133] But, realpolitik suggests that they are crucial to social order and state building and that it is equally crucial to address the apparent conflicts between those groups and the government in Kabul. Such an approach may also be confirmed by historical experience showing that throughout its history the central government of Afghanistan had to negotiate and collaborate with such local centres of power.[134] Ideally this would also include a process of transitional justice, but here too there may be a need to be pragmatic since insistence of punishment of all past wrongs may be counter to the need for reconciliation.[135]

It can therefore be concluded that, temporarily, measures to improve human security[136] and to create an effective Afghan state may be more important than having an accountable state with a thick version of the rule of law. Such a development would move Afghanistan closer to the Chinese and Russian models of law and development. As regards the question of whether the rule of law matters for economic development, Afghanistan can be seen as an example for both weak economic development and lack of an effective rule of law, although it does not answer the question on how these factors are connected.

C. The critics of 'law and development'

The first section of this chapter explained that the supporters of law and development are not a uniform group, and the second section outlined different ways of thinking about rule of law reform. Yet, the critics of law and development mainly see the similarities between present and past approaches, in particular referring to the influence of the US, the World Bank, as well as other

---

www.usip.org/rule-law/conference-the-relationship-between-state-and-non-state-justice-systems-in-afghanistan.

[132] See, e.g., Jupp 2013: 77–8 (tribal courts increasingly accepted for minor criminal offences); Martins 2011: 16 (need to strengthen traditional dispute resolution in order to promote security and stability).

[133] Mason 2011. See also Peerenboom et al. 2012: 307 ('downgrading of democracy' in development discourse); Humphreys 2010: 149–62 ('rule of law' becomes mere 'law and order').

[134] See Ahmed 2005: 105–6.

[135] For this tension see, e.g., McAuliffe 2010; Yusuf 2010. Specifically for the situation in Afghanistan see Kfir 2013.

[136] Today, this concept is understood widely, not limited to military actions: see Darian-Smith 2013: 257–63.

Western countries and international organisations.[137] The following discusses their objections and how they relate to more general topics of comparative law.

1. Law does not 'work'

The mainstream view is that law, in particular the protection of property rights, matters for economic development. The basis for this assessment are models as well as qualitative and quantitative empirical evidence.[138] But these findings have been challenged. Proponents of the 'law matters' view are said to ignore the crucial role of culture.[139] For example, the rule of law is said to rely on cultural attitudes, namely a 'prevailing ethic of voluntary compliance with judicial rulings'.[140] More generally, the counter-argument is that social norms, as well as other economic and cultural factors, directly determine behaviour, irrespective of whether they are also channelled through legal rules and institutions.[141] Furthermore, it could be politics that is really decisive since good legal rules may only be a reflection of the 'configuration of interests that drives governmental decision-making'.[142]

The experience of Asian countries is seen as confirming this critique. For example, critics refer to the 'unattractive civil litigation' in South Korea and Taiwan, and Asian-style democracies and autocratic regimes where 'the law exists not to limit the state but to serve its power'.[143] The discussion about the role of the rule of law in China was already mentioned in the previous section but two further statements illustrate this point: in a book from the late 1960s a Chinese lawyer is quoted as saying that 'China has always known that law is not good enough to govern a society. She knew it twenty-five hundred years ago, and she knows it today.'[144] Much the same can be found in the current literature, for instance, when, referring to China, it is suggested that 'in dynamic environments disadvantages of legal mechanisms can outweigh their advantages'.[145]

However, this reasoning does not make law and development obsolete. To start with, these objections are mainly concerned with the question of whether law matters for economic development. Many, however, would say that law also serves the aim of creating a fair and just society.[146] But even focusing on economic development, quantitative research as well as case studies can be used to show either position: that law matters or that it does not.[147] Thus, a

---

[137] E.g. Trubek 2001; Nader 2006.   [138] See A, above and ch. 11 at B 3, below.

[139] See Barros 2010 and the contributions in this book.

[140] Tamanaha 2011b: 223. Similarly Kahn 2003 (rule of law as cultural practice); Carothers 2010: 25 (decisive how citizens relate to state authority and to each other).

[141] Davis and Trebilcock 2008: 897 (summarising this view); also Pistor et al. 2010: 256 (need to consider prevailing social norms).

[142] Goodpaster 2007: 132.

[143] Ohnesorge 2007: 105; Carothers 2006: 5. See also Gilson and Milhaupt 2011; Ginsburg 2000.

[144] Cohen 1968: 4.   [145] Allen and Qian 2010: 141.

[146] See also 4, below.   [147] See also ch. 7 at C 1, above, and ch. 11 at B 3, below.

risk-averse country should be interested in its law since it may at least be possible that sensible law reform stimulates economic development. Another plausible response is that the ambiguity of the evidence only shows that it depends on the precise law, circumstances and desired effect whether or not law matters. Such a position is in line with findings from socio-legal comparative law.[148] It also leads us to the following three counter-arguments dealing with more specific modalities of law and development.

2. Against 'top-down' approaches

Western countries and international organisations are often accused of a 'top-down' approach to law and development, meaning that they try to impose Western or global standards on developing countries. This mirrors the view of critics in development economics who challenge the wisdom of top-down international development, for instance, by way of predominantly relying on foreign aid.[149]

Imposed 'top-down' legal uniformity invites the general criticism that law is not something technical but that a country's legal system reflects its 'common identity' and 'sense of justice'.[150] It can also be seen as undue interference in the national sovereignty and democratic accountability of countries in the developing world. A variant of this criticism by political activists even associates such an approach with post-colonialism and neo-imperialism, referring to top-down law and development as a form of plunder by hegemonic international actors.[151] These hegemonic actors are not only foreign states and international organisations but also multinational corporations. For example, powerful multinationals may be able to impose their interests on the governments of developing countries, or they may even be able to create special legal regimes that operate independently of those of their host countries.[152]

By contrast, these critics point towards the merits of 'bottom-up' approaches which can also include the use of informal forms of laws. The starting point is to understand at the 'micro-level' how law organises everyday life in a given society.[153] For example, writing about judicial reform programmes, these are urged to be 'home-grown and internally driven' with significant participation of the local stakeholders whereas international donors should only play a minor

---

[148] See ch. 6, above.
[149] In particular Easterly 2001; Easterly 2006; Shirley 2008. See also Erbeznik 2011 (for possible negative effects of foreign aid on rule of law reform).
[150] Menski 2007: 210; IUC Global Legal Standards Research Group 2009: 5. See also ch. 5 and ch. 9 at B 3, above.
[151] In particular Mattei and Nader 2008; also Ngugi 2006 (on the World Bank); Brooks 2003 ('new imperialism'); Gardner 1980 ('legal imperialism'); Mattei 2003 ('imperial law'); Riles 2006: 792 (on postcolonialism); Baxi 2003 (on colonialism); Merry 2004: 583 (unequal power similar to colonial laws); López-Medina 2012: 360–5 (examples for political use of rule of law).
[152] See, e.g., Cotula 2011; Ferrando 2013. See also ch. 9 at A 1 and D 2, above.
[153] Banakar 2009: 82.

role.[154] Specifically on informal law, the conceptual position is that of legal pluralism supporting a 'sustainable diversity of laws'.[155] The general advantages of such informality can be summarised as follows:

> In contrast to most state legal institutions in development contexts, these institutions are *of* the community, closer in derivation and proximity, and hence more accessible to members of the community. Its norms and processes, its modes of decision making, are understood by members of the community. The proceedings are less costly, more timely, and often do not require the intermediation of legal professionals. The decision makers are known to or recognized by the community . . . [156]

The literature has also attempted to illustrate more closely how well such informal rules can work, for example, analysing the situation in Southern Sudan and Afghanistan,[157] and with many examples of how specific local groups use informal (as well as formal) law to pursue legitimate interests.[158] In addition, it has been explored how 'bottom-up' approaches can progress to the international level. This has been called 'subaltern cosmopolitanism', for instance, referring to the way NGOs and transnational advocacy networks may stimulate 'emancipation' from 'hegemonic' and 'neoliberal' models of globalisation, law and development.[159]

However, it is suggested that this binary view of bottom-up 'good' and top-down 'bad' is too simplistic. When a problem arises between different local legal orders of the same country, it makes sense to let state law deal with the conflict of those laws.[160] In addition, relying on local customary laws may be impossible for international business transactions since here laws are needed that apply 'over wider spatial, ethnic and class areas'.[161] Traditional customary law can also have substantive drawbacks: it may be 'inherently racial in origin, despotic in operation, and often discriminatory and unfair in outcome', it may be oppressive 'requiring an undesirable degree of conformity', and it may fail to address the 'needs of children, women and the disadvantaged'.[162]

Discrediting everything 'top-down' is also not helpful. As Chapter 8 on legal transplants has shown, the use of foreign models is something quite natural for any legal system of the world. It is also possible that considerations of the local environment support such transplants. For instance, it has been said that the

---

[154] Armytage 2009; also Gopal 2009: 66; Carothers 2006: 4.
[155] Glenn 2011; Glenn 2001: 50; also Menski 2006: 583 (in Asia belief that state is not the only law-making agent). Generally on legal pluralism see ch. 5 at B 4, above.
[156] Tamanaha 2011a: 7; also Gauri 2009 (on benefits of local institutions).
[157] Pimentel 2010; Schmeidl 2011.
[158] Santos and Rodriguez-Garavito 2005 and the contributions in this book.
[159] Santos 2004: 239, 251; Santos and Rodriguez-Garavito 2005; Santos 2005; also Rajagopal 2003.
[160] See also Tamanaha 2011a: 8.
[161] Moore 2005: 49 (referring to Marc Galanter's research on modern India).
[162] Odinkalu 2006: 141; Moore 1986b: 38; Twining 2009a: 358 (quoting Don McKinnon, then Secretary-General of the Commonwealth Secretariat).

citizens of developing countries may appreciate Western laws given that today it is 'impossible for them to live some autochthonous culture in isolation from the rest of the world' – whereas resistance against transplants may mainly come from those who are more interested in their vested interests than the common good.[163] In addition, Western influence may address some of the structural internal problems of developing countries. For example, many African states are said to suffer from clientalism, corruption and state decay;[164] and more generally it has been suggested that the lack of a competitive party system and competitive markets attributes to many problems of the developing world.[165] Thus, change may be welcomed even if it is triggered by foreign influence, including Western-based laws.

To conclude, it is most appropriate to follow the intermediate position that it cannot be generalised whether top-down or bottom-up law reform (or: formal or informal laws) are preferable.[166] Such an approach has also been identified in the recent works of international development agencies, saying to show more interest in legal pluralism, in particular in informal forms of dispute resolution.[167] In addition, since the 2000s, the development discourse has shifted towards 'micro-'approaches, for instance, trying to establish by way of experiments which precise tools are most suitable.[168]

3. Western law out-of-context

As far as law and development is based on models from Western legal systems, another line of criticism is that use of those models may be inappropriate in other parts of the world. On the one hand, this refers to the problem that 'prepacked reforms'[169] pay no attention to the way new and old law, including a country's legal culture and institutions, relate to each other. For example, reforms that strengthen formal property rights are insufficient if institutions (courts, land and commercial registers etc.) do not adequately support and enforce them.[170] If formal property laws are added to informal regimes, this may result in legal confusion, for instance, if it is not clear who the 'real' owner is – or, even worse, if the holder of informal ownership is expropriated without compensation.[171] Furthermore, judicial reforms may not work as expected, for example, due to lack of appropriate training, financial resources and resistance from powerful

---

[163] Michaels 2009a: 790 (for the quote); Nelken 2001: 49 (for the risk to 'romanticise' the idea of resistance).

[164] Van de Walle 2001.   [165] Weingast 2010 referring to North et al. 2009.

[166] Similarly F. von Benda-Beckmann 2006: 63; Kennedy 2003b.

[167] Faundez 2011. See also B 2, above (for Afghanistan).

[168] See, e.g., Banerjee and Duflo 2011 and www.povertyactionlab.org.   [169] Trubek 2007: 238.

[170] Trebilcock and Veel 2008; Prada and Trebilcock 2009. See also G. Xu 2011: 351–5 (on costs and benefits of formal property rights).

[171] G. Xu 2011: 355–8; McAuslan 2003: 64–77; Kelley 2008.

vested interests. This could be seen in the rule of law developments in China, Russia and Afghanistan, but many further examples would also be available.[172]

On the other hand, the imported Western law may 'clash' with the culture of the country in question. In contrast to the position that the law does not have any effect (see 1, above), the view here is that law may have an effect but, from a normative perspective, it is seen as disruptive, dysfunctional and therefore inappropriate. This line of reasoning is based on the thinking that law does not exist in isolation of 'history, culture, human and material resources, religious and ethnic composition, demographics, knowledge, economic conditions, politics [etc.]'.[173] Development agencies and Western countries are therefore accused of overlooking this context-specificity of the law, in particular economists using standardised performance measures of law reform.[174]

But, again, these lines of criticism go too far. Previous chapters have shown that legal transplants and mixtures are common features of most, if not all, legal systems of the world.[175] Thus, the mere fact that a legal idea is 'foreign' does not speak against it. In line with what has been said in previous chapters about changes to legal culture, it is also worth quoting from a policy brief by the World Bank:

> Legal culture is often considered as a given feature of the local environment to which proposed legal reform projects must adapt; many argue that legal and judicial reform programs must be tailored to fit local legal culture or they will fail. Other times, the prevailing legal culture itself may be the object of reform, rather than merely a constraint . . . [176]

The linkage between law and society and how it relates to law and development invites three comments. First, context-specificity may be challenged by those who claim that functional similarities show universalism, and that widespread legal transplants show law's independence from society. Both are frequent claims in comparative law, though they are not the positions of this book.[177] Second, however, it does not seem too far-fetched to identify some global commonalities directly relevant for law and development:

> The battle of the rule of law against arbitrary government takes place in every human society, when those with power seek to expand their discretion (and control), and their subjects resist . . . Struggle for freedom usually begins with the demand for written laws, to constrain the discretion of those in authority, then proceeds to the pursuit of just laws, a much more difficult undertaking.[178]

---

[172] See B 2, above; Chodosh 2005: 68–77 (for India and Indonesia); Lindsey 2007 (various case studies).

[173] Tamanaha 2011b: 219.

[174] Gillespie and Nicholson 2012; Taylor 2007; Mattei and Nader 2008: 47, 89.

[175] See ch. 4 at C 3 and ch. 8, above.

[176] Legal Culture and Judicial Reform, available at http://go.worldbank.org/MESX38R0U0. See also ch. 8 at A 2 (d) and ch. 9 at A 3, above.

[177] See ch. 2 at B and C and ch. 6 at A 2, above.   [178] Sellers 2010: 2.

Even religious laws may be no exception, for example, if it can be shown that there is an Islamic form of the rule of law since Islamic law backs government accountability, access to justice and many fundamental rights.[179] Third, legal reforms using foreign models may be precisely aimed at changing the society in question. To be sure, this is not an easy task since it requires understanding at a 'micro-level' why people behave as they do, and at a 'macro-level' how a country's society may react to possible foreign laws.[180]

4. The 'wrong' legal rules and institutions

The final point of criticism is that the US, the World Bank and others promote legal rules and institutions which are 'not very good'. On a general level, this can be related to its preference for Western laws, in particular in its Anglo-Saxon, i.e. common-law, variant. Such rules may not always be preferable. For example, it has been suggested that the judicial design of civil law countries with more active judges is more suitable for emerging legal systems since the latter countries tend to have an underdeveloped private bar.[181] Beyond common and civil law, strengths and weaknesses can be identified in all legal traditions. For example, according to Patrick Glenn, chthonic law would criticise civil and common law for the way they deal with the environment, Islamic law would criticise them for their treatment of the poor, whereas Western lawyers would criticise Islamic law for their limitations on human expression and speech.[182] Similarly, a policy report by a group of international academic lawyers illustrates the benefits of 'non-mainstream' legal systems as follows:

> Think about the role of workers in the former Yugoslavian corporate governance, or the variety of alternative visions of property in Andean cultures, or the institutional settings that allow the social capital represented by elderly people be put to value in many African societies, or the legal institutions of solidarity and long term commitment in Islamic finance, or the open access to culture and social knowledge in the traditional Asian resistance to intellectual property rights.[183]

Thus, at this general level, it can be said that the diversity of legal systems around the world should provide an incentive to learn from other legal systems. This learning should not be asymmetrical – in particular, it should also include 'reverse learning' from countries who are typically only seen as importers of Western laws.[184]

---

[179] Kuran 2010b; also Ehrmann 1976: 28.

[180] See Seidman and Seidman 2007 and Peerenboom et al. 2012 (without using the terms 'micro' and 'macro').

[181] Koch 2004. See also ch. 2 at C 4, above.   [182] Glenn 2010a: 375.

[183] IUC Global Legal Standards Research Group 2009: 14.

[184] Santos and Rodriguez-Garavito 2005; Nelken 2007a: 35; Hantrais 2009: 15 (for social sciences more generally).

In substance, the main point of criticism is that of one-sided laws promoted by law and development. Frequent themes are the capitalist focus on privatisation, property rights, ease of doing business and the corresponding disregard of resource preservation and social rights.[185] The same is said to happen at the international level where international investors and corporations push for open borders to the detriment of other interests.[186] In all of this, law is seen as a de-political and instrumental tool, not a means of accountability, justice, equity and fairness, or even empowerment of the poor.[187]

These points of criticism raise important concerns, for instance, the usefulness of reverse learning and the need to consider non-economic interests. However, here again, some critics tend to exaggerate. It is misleading to attribute all negative features to Western legal systems and by doing so 're-orientalise' the non-Western legal world. It is also inaccurate to demonise law and development as a whole. As the previous sections of this chapter have shown, there are various nuances: for instance, the work of the UNDP, Sen's 'development as freedom' and thick versions of the rule of law clearly aim for more than 'neoliberal' economic development. This does not deny that there are also examples of one-sided development policy worth criticising.[188] But this should not be seen as a reason to discredit protection of property rights as merely serving business interests since strong property rights can also help citizens against corrupt officials and criminals: here, clearly, 'too little' law is as bad as 'too much'.[189]

D. Conclusion

At times, the law and development discourse tends to be dominated by schematic and absolute claims. For example, consider the views that there are a number of phases of law and development, that there are distinct types of rule of law, that there is evidence that law does or does not work for development, that there is a choice to be made between formal and informal laws, and that law and development does or does not promote 'the right' legal rules.

The position taken in this chapter is that these claims are often misleading. To start with, it has been shown that law and development evolved gradually with various changes in the main actors and in the substance of this process. The discussion about the rule of law identified possible components and motivations, while it was also illustrated, using three examples, that these often overlap with claims about the failures and successes of rule of law reforms difficult to make. The critics of law and development raise a number of valid concerns; yet, they

---

[185] Mattei and Nader 2008: 7, 48; Rose 2010; Santos 2005: 35; Rodriguez-Garavito 2005: 78.
[186] Mattei and Nader 2008: 61, 69; Santos 2005: 34; Muir Watt 2006: 602–3.
[187] Kroncke 2012: 524; Gopal 2009: 56, 60; Legrand 2006c: 528; Gramatikov and Porter 2011 (for the final point).
[188] E.g. the World Bank's Doing Business Report: see ch. 7 at C 4, above.
[189] But see McAuslan 2003: 149.

also tend to exaggerate, thus, their arguments cannot be said as having shown that law is useless or even harmful for development.

A further purpose of this chapter has been to relate the debate about law and development to comparative law. While, in the past, comparatists often excluded developing countries from their analysis, in today's world such an approach is not satisfactory any more. Yet, it is also important to be aware that dealing with countries that face major economic and non-economic challenges requires critical awareness of the core concepts of law and development. The chapter sought to provide such an introduction. At the same time, the more implicit purpose has been to make the case for 'reverse learning' from comparative law. Many topics of comparative law, in particular those discussed in Part III, such as legal transplants, convergence of laws and transnational law, but also other topics, such as the role of legal cultures, legal pluralism and socio-legal comparative law, should be of natural interest for the discussion on law and development.

Part IV
Comparative Law as an Open Subject

Parts II and III of this book discussed new approaches and topics that have entered research on comparative law. These are welcome developments. Yet more can be done, as comparative law is an 'open subject' that can absorb further research not traditionally included. In particular, it is suggested that research in other disciplines that deals with legal topics in a comparative fashion can be regarded as 'implicit comparative law'.

Such a suggestion is in line with some of the general statements found in the literature, arguing that comparative law should become more interdisciplinary.[1] It may also reflect the view that comparative law is not only a legal subject, but that it also belongs to the general comparative sciences.[2] More provocatively, it has been suggested that 'the most interesting . . . comparative legal research has for some time been taking place outside law schools'.[3] But even if one does not agree with this statement, it is at least useful to consider the research of other disciplines on comparative legal topics.

Chapter 11, below, elaborates on the idea of 'implicit comparative law' using examples from comparative politics, economics, sociology, anthropology and psychology. The inevitable limitation is that this cannot be a comprehensive treatment of relevant research from other fields. Thus, Chapter 12 reflects more generally on the direction that comparative law may take in the future.

[1] See ch. 1 at B 3, above.   [2] Cf. Constantinesco 1971: 249.   [3] Muir Watt 2011: 131.

Implicit comparative law

The main theme of this chapter is the research from other disciplines that 'implicitly' deals with topics of comparative law. But to start with, Section A outlines some of the core methodological questions of comparative research in the social sciences, showing both similarities and differences to the methods of comparative law. Subsequently, Section B deals with comparative studies of states and their components, mainly drawing on research from comparative politics and economics. Section C addresses comparative studies of societies and cultures, with examples from comparative sociology, anthropology, and psychology. Section D concludes.

The aim of this chapter is to map how these other comparative fields have produced a remarkable amount of research that should be of interest to comparative lawyers. It should also be noted, however, that the present account of 'implicit comparative law' is highly condensed and selective. Thus, while this chapter can provide a critical introduction into these areas of research, it is clear that it may well be possible to write entire books about the topics in each of its subsections.

A. Introduction to comparative research in social sciences

The comparative method is said to be a tool applicable in all social sciences.[1] Though research traditions are not uniform, there are a number of common themes that most of these comparative studies discuss.

1. Main rationales for a comparative approach

In comparative law, a frequent starting point is to identify the purposes of comparative law.[2] Corresponding discussions can be found in the other comparative social sciences. A broad distinction is made between research that uses comparative information as a tool to understand relations between variables, and comparative research which is interested in particular units for their own sake.[3]

---

[1] Przeworski and Teune 1970: 86. [2] See ch. 1 at A 2, above.
[3] For the following see, e.g., Landman 2002: 891; Azarian 2011: 116–8 with reference to Tilly 1984. Specifically on hypothesis testing Hantrais 2009: 5–6, 49; Smelser 1976: 174.

To start with the latter rationale, a comparatist may engage in a contextual description of a limited number of cases, such as countries, societies or cultures, with an emphasis on the particularities of these units. She may also try to classify countries, to track trends – such as convergences and divergences – or to identify certain phenomena as universal.

By contrast, comparative analysis as a tool is interested in comparative cases in order to test hypotheses. In particular, this may provide evidence for causal relationships, similar to experimental research in the natural sciences. These findings may be valid on a global scale but it may also be found that certain regularities are system-specific. Moreover, such comparisons may be used in order to inform state policy decisions or other choices of any unit of comparison.[4] At a basic level, this may just show the availability of various policy options, but it can also indicate more specifically what consequences certain actions have and what constraints need to be considered.

2. Main types of comparative research

The two rationales outlined in the previous section often correspond to qualitative and quantitative comparative research. Yet, the association is not complete: it can also be suggested that, instead of a binary choice, there is a continuum of methods – from an in-depth analysis to universalist-positivist approaches.[5]

Some take the view that qualitative comparative research can even focus on a single case if this particular case is related to a wider comparative framework – for example, if the aim is to examine whether this case confirms or refutes previous research on other countries or societies.[6] Typically, however, a comparative qualitative study would deal with a limited number of cases in detail, aiming to explain their diversity.[7] Variations in qualitative research, however, complicate the picture. First, it should be noted that comparative qualitative and case-study research are not identical, as, for example, a case study may include quantitative time-series data. Second, qualitative research may also deal with a large number of cases, for instance, where research is aimed at outlining all cultures of the world.[8] Third, while most qualitative researchers are reluctant to draw causal conclusions from case studies,[9] others are specifically interested in possible causal relationships. In particular, this may follow from historical comparative research or a logical analysis of relationships between variables.[10]

Quantitative comparative research, too, can be either descriptive or inferential. Descriptive statistics can provide interesting information on countries and

---

[4] References in Hantrais 2009: ix, 118–20.

[5] Similarly Hantrais 2009: 56–8. See also Goertz and Mahoney 2012 (for the general difference between qualitative and quantitative research in social sciences).

[6] E.g. Landman 2008: 28; Bradshaw and Wallace 1991.

[7] In particular, Lijphart 1971 (distinguishing the comparative from the statistical and the case study method); Sartori 1991: 252 (single case not comparative).

[8] An early example was Spencer 1873-81. For a more recent one see the Human Relations Area Files (HRAF), available at www.yale.edu/hraf/.

[9] See Smelser 1976: 199; Collier and Mahoney 1996.   [10] See 3, below.

other units of comparison. But, usually, inferential statistics that show causal relationships, i.e. regression analysis, are seen as more interesting. Conducting such regression analysis requires a relatively large number of units – say, all countries of the world – in order to identify general patterns. Moreover, in order to be able to establish robust causal relationships, advanced statistical tools may be needed (e.g. panel data analysis).[11]

Which method would a comparatist choose? A first determinant is the type of question she attempts to answer.[12] It is therefore inevitable that research methods differ within the social sciences, since some disciplines are more interested in generalities and others in particularities. Second, the availability of information can exclude certain methods. A frequent discussion in comparative studies is the problem of 'many variables but small N'.[13] For instance, assume that a comparatist has analysed five countries in detail, finding that there are many possible reasons why these countries differ. Here, regression analysis is excluded since it requires the precise opposite, i.e. many observations, or 'large N', but only a limited number of explanatory variables. Third, each method has its advantages and disadvantages. For example, quantitative researchers tend to say that only they can provide hard evidence for certain regularities, whereas qualitative studies are just too subjective. But qualitative researchers may respond that the social world is, in any case, too complex to deduce rules akin to the natural sciences or even mathematics, whereas deep qualitative research may at least help us in the understanding of the world.[14]

As these arguments do not provide an obvious solution, a possible suggestion is to mix methods. Such methodically eclectic 'mixed methods' have recently become more popular, in particular in comparative studies.[15] Applying both quantitative and qualitative methods may enable the researcher to reduce the disadvantages of both methods. What is more, both methods can facilitate each other: for example, qualitative research can generate a hypothesis that can be tested with quantitative data, and any quantitative data also has to be interpreted through use of qualitative information.

3. Methods, continued: history, logic and concepts

According to one school of thought, historical research is fundamentally different from comparative approaches. Exploring a country's history inevitably

---

[11] This refers to a dataset that compares units but also has a time dimension. Statistical details are beyond the scope of this book but see also B 3, below.

[12] Cf. also Dogan 2004: 335 ('For instance, a reply to the question "Is the gap between poor and rich countries increasing?" has to be based on solid statistical data, carefully analysed. On the other hand, when Samuel Huntington asks, "Will more countries become democratic?", the analytical reasoning becomes more important than the statistical evidence').

[13] Smelser 1976: 36; Goldthorpe 1997.

[14] See, e.g., Steinmetz 2004; Hantrais 2009: 97–105 (in particular ibid., 100: 'qualitative researchers know more about less, quantitative researchers know less about more').

[15] See Hantrais 2009: 96; Berry et al. 2011: 279; Widner 1998: 744.

highlights the uniqueness of events; thus, research dealing with more than one country's history may at best be able to juxtapose certain differences.[16]

But, according to others, historical research can at least have an implicit comparative dimension. It can identify historical connections between countries or other units of comparison. For instance, this may be done for reasons of classification.[17] Historical evidence can also help researchers explore how far countries have influenced each other and how far they have remained distinct – for example, in considering the impact of colonialism.[18] Going further, it has been suggested that one can use comparative historical evidence in order to identify causal regularities. Thus, the aim is to develop, and confirm or reject, general theories about events.[19] For example, a researcher may consider a number of historical examples for a particular type of event, and then code the causal factors for each of the examples as 'yes' or 'no', or rank them in terms of importance.[20]

A problem with applying quantitative methods to historical events is that, often, many causal factors play a role, while only a small number of cases are available. The previous section already mentioned this problem of 'many variables but small N' as a general problem in comparative social sciences. For these circumstances Charles Ragin has developed a method called Qualitative Comparative Analysis (QCA) that uses a formalised logical tool, Boolean algebra, in order to identify causal regularities. In a nutshell, QCA means that, with the help of a computer program, it is established which combinations of conditions may be decisive and how these combinations may be simplified. It also involves expert knowledge of the comparative researcher on plausible causal combinations.[21] QCA is therefore a mixture between quantitative and qualitative approaches.

Another response to rich cross-country information is to say that a conceptual approach is needed in order to group diverse phenomena into manageable categories.[22] In particular, a conceptual framework with 'ideal types' may be employed to ascertain which data from different units of comparison can be related.[23] Max Weber's historical and conceptual research, explained later in this chapter, is a good example of such an approach. But concepts are also crucial

---

[16] See Azarian 2011: 116–7; Hantrais 2009: 39; Smelser 1976: 203 ('historians deal with the unique while social scientists look for generalisations').

[17] See Hammel 1980: 150–1; also Hall 1963: 30–1 (historical method used to explain legal families).

[18] See, e.g., Benton 2002 (on colonial cultures and law).

[19] E.g. Kiser and Hechter 1991. See also Mahoney and Rueschemeyer 2003; Skocpol and Somers 1980.

[20] Mahoney 1999. See also van den Baembussche 1989 (reviewing the historical method of the French Annales School).

[21] See, e.g., Ragin 1987; Ragin 1998; also Kogut and Ragin 2006 (applying QCA to reception of legal transplants) and ch. 7 at A 3, above (on research by Arvind and Stirton).

[22] In particular Rose 1991; also Zelditch 1971: 273–88 (on comparability).

[23] See, e.g., Smelser 1976: 54–5.

for quantitative researchers, because theoretical models about the relationship between variables form the basis of understanding what can be tested with comparative quantitative data.

4. Choice of units of comparison

In the social sciences, a great variety of units can and have been compared. A convenient division is one according to scales. For example, these may be political units – starting with villages, towns, cities, to economic zones and other sub-units of countries – to countries and nations, and to macro-regions and other transnational organisations. A more factual approach considers units such as local communities, cultures, societies and organisations, but also broader geographic regions, language groups, networks or even civilisations.[24] These latter groups are likely to be related to the former ones, though it would be contentious to claim that, say, the borders of a particular country tend to correspond to a particular culture or society.[25]

The literature has also identified further complexities. It can be revealing to compare different levels, such as 'mini-states' and 'mega-cities', or macro-regions and 'mega-countries'.[26] Another frequent suggestion is that globalising trends make it necessary to understand the relationship between the levels more closely: for example, whether and how the international level shapes the lower levels, in particular the weakening of the national level.[27] More fundamentally, a 'cosmopolitan view' suggests that it is time to dissolve the 'onion model' of such levels and layers,[28] while others maintain the continuing relevance of more or less autonomous local fields.[29]

Another question concerns which specific units to compare. Following John Stuart Mill, a conventional distinction is between a comparison of very different cases on the one hand, and of very similar ones on the other.[30] According to Mill, the choice depends on the variable of interest, i.e. the variable that the researcher is trying to explain. When units share this variable, it is useful to have very different cases, making it possible to identify the one factor on which all these cases agree as the decisive cause (thus, called 'method of agreement' or 'most different cases'). By contrast, when units do not share this variable,

---

[24] See, e.g., Hantrais 2009: 2, 49, 51, 53, 92; Smelser 1976: 168; Hopkins and Wallerstein 1967. For work on entire civilisations see Toynbee 1934–61 and ch. 4 at A, above.

[25] But see C 2, below.

[26] See Dogan 2002: 85–8 (mini-states and mega-cities); Ebbinghaus 1998 (on EU and vertical analysis with other levels).

[27] See, e.g., Coe et al. 2010: 21; Hantrais 2009: 13, 47; Widner 1998: 741. See also ch. 9 at A 1, above.

[28] Beck and Sznaider 2010: 389. Similarly Glenn 2009; Glenn 2013.

[29] Moore 1986a: 56 (law as 'semi-autonomous social field'). See also ch. 6 at A 2 (a), above.

[30] Mill 2006 (original from 1843). See also Hantrais 2009: 60–61; Hirschl 2006: 48. Mill also suggested two further categories (not discussed here), depending on the degree to which certain phenomena are fulfilled.

choosing similar cases that differ in just one causal condition can explain that this difference is indeed the decisive one (thus, called 'method of difference' or 'most similar cases').

Qualitative research frequently uses the category of 'most similar cases'. In particular, the detailed analysis inherent in qualitative research often means that the researcher only examines a limited number of cases, such as countries that are in the same geographical area or have close historical ties. It is often said that such an approach enables the researcher to engage in a 'controlled comparison', analysing the effect of the remaining differences.[31] But there are also other types of qualitative research. An example of 'most different cases' would be to compare that which unites recent economic success stories from different parts of the world.[32] There are also other suggested criteria: for example, 'prototypical', 'most difficult' or 'outlier' cases.[33]

Today's quantitative comparative research builds on Mill's categories, but rarely makes explicit reference to them. The reason is that, throughout the last century, new tools of statistical control have been developed that can account for both similar and different cases.[34] Thus, the quantitative researcher typically wants to include as many units of comparison as possible. For example, she may wish to engage in a worldwide comparison of all countries, societies or cultures.[35] The advantage of such a comprehensive approach is that it can lead to a truly global finding – whereas comparisons limited to particular regions or cultures may not be generalisable.

To conclude, it can be seen that all topics discussed in this section are closely connected, in particular the aim, the method, and the units of a comparative analysis. Preferences differ across disciplines. Yet, today, most disciplines include, for instance, both quantitative and qualitative forms of comparative research. These topics will be revisited in the following sections, while also the links between areas of comparative law and those of other comparative studies will be shown.

B. Comparative studies of states and their components

Many disciplines compare states and their components, for example, political science, economics, development studies, and sociology. Frequent topics include the search for 'the best' form of government, comparisons of 'the state in action', and assessments of policy choices. These are discussed in the following, preceded by brief explanations of why each of these topics is of interest for comparative law.

---

[31] See, e.g., Hantrais 2009: 88; Guy 1998: 36–41; Hammel 1980: 150.

[32] Landman 2002: 906. See also DeFelice 1986 (against restriction of comparative politics to similar cases).

[33] Hirschl 2006: 53–63.   [34] Bollen et al. 1993: 337.

[35] See, e.g., Dogan 2004: 327 (worldwide analysis); Sartori 1970: 1044 (distinguishing between high, medium and low level categories).

1. Determining 'the best' form of government

Most comparative lawyers take the view that an evaluation about the 'best rules' can, if cautiously made, be part of a comparative analysis.[36] Such evaluations are also frequent in the context of law and development (e.g. in recommendations about rule of law reforms).[37] But, as it is rare that comparative lawyers deal with the seen-as-too-political question about the best form of government, research in comparative politics can be a useful complement. In addition, research on forms of government may aim towards classifications, and is thus related to research into legal families.[38]

In Ancient Greece,[39] Plato, Aristotle, and Polybius classified and compared forms of government. Aristotle's analysis of the constitutions of Greek towns has been particularly influential. He distinguished between the number of rulers on the one hand, and the quality of governments on the other, leading to three 'good' types (monarchy, aristocracy, polity) and three 'corrupt' ones (tyranny, oligarchy, democracy). Yet, Aristotle also indicated that there was not an objectively best form of government, and that differences in government reflected differences in mentality.

In modern times, too, it is not always clear whether the main aim is understanding or evaluation. Montesquieu's book *The Spirit of Laws* is, on the one hand, openly 'relativist', as national legal differences are seen as strongly related to other factors. Notably, Montesquieu suggested that laws do – and should – reflect the climate, geography, culture, and character of a nation.[40] On the other hand, Montesquieu offers some explicit and some implicit critique, in particular where he deals with the distinction between despotic, monarchical and republican governments. He explicitly rejects the despotism that he associates with the Orient, but his book is also interpreted as a 'thinly veiled critique of [the] monarchical absolutism' of eighteenth-century France.[41]

The work by Alexis de Tocqueville provides another example of a positive-normative mix. Writing in the nineteenth century, de Tocqueville's main interest was in the legal and political institutions of the US – for example, its federal structure, its frequent use of juries, and its reliance on case law. While only in some instances did he make explicit comparisons to France and other countries – also relating those differences to cultural ones[42] – de Tocqueville explains in his memoirs that he 'did not write a page without thinking of her' (i.e. France).[43] The preface of de Tocqueville's book *Democracy in America* also indicates the normative dimension of his writings: while France should not 'make a servile

---

[36] See ch. 2 at A 4, above.   [37] See ch. 10 at B, above.   [38] See ch. 3 and ch. 4, above.

[39] See, e.g., Dannemann 2006: 396–7 (on Plato); Sica 2006: xxv (on Polybius); Sica 2006: xxiv; Welzel and Inglehart 2007: 298 (on Aristotle).

[40] Montesquieu 1914 (original from 1748). See also Dannemann 2006: 385; Menski 2006: 86; Moore 2005: 12; Launay 2001: 23; Richter 1969: 133–5.

[41] Launay 2001: 25.

[42] Cf. the discussion in Smelser 1976: 9, 20, 25, 29.   [43] de Tocqueville 1861: 359.

copy' of US institutions, the latter's 'principles of order, of the balance of powers, of true liberty, of deep and sincere respect for right' are explicitly seen as worth borrowing.[44]

More recent research has continued to examine one country from a comparative perspective,[45] while current debates also frequently engage in a more general comparison of various forms of government. Such research tends to be of a quantitative nature. For example, the Polity IV Project provides worldwide data on many political regimes, distinguishing between full democracy, democracy, open anocracy, closed anocracy, and autocracy.[46] These datasets can then be used to show that there is a positive correlation between the level of democracy on the one hand and economic growth, security and safety on the other.[47] To be sure, it is not suggested that there is a perfect correlation. The development of emerging and transition economies provides some counter-examples: for example, China has grown quicker than India, Russia and countries in Latin America.[48] It has also been suggested that weak democracies cause various problems: for example, in comparing such a democracy with a stable 'benevolent autocracy', it may be said that the former is more likely to give into special-interest privileges, and that rulers are more inclined to violate human rights in order to stay in power.[49]

Very controversial is the question of causality. On the one hand, there is the view that economic development often stimulates democracy, i.e. democracy is usually the second step[50] – while it is also clear that other factors, too, play a role in the emergence of democracy.[51] On the other hand, researchers have found that democracy typically leads to long-run prosperity, and that it may also promote peace and reduce conflict.[52]

A potential objection to both of these views is that there are many shades of democracy. Researchers have tried to identify the effects of such differences, possibly enabling some kind of constitutional engineering that predicts the

---

[44] de Tocqueville 1994 (original from 1848): lxv.

[45] E.g. Lipset 1973; Lipset 1996 (on US exceptionalism). See also ch. 3 at C 2, above.

[46] Polity IV Project: Political Regime Characteristics and Transitions, 1800–2010, available at http://systemicpeace.org/polity/polity4.htm. Another example is the project on Varieties of Democracy, https://v-dem.net/. References to further quantitative work in Landman and Carvalho 2010: 66.

[47] See, e.g., Geddes 2007; Przeworski and Limongi 1993.

[48] See, e.g., Gilpin 2001: 329; Linz and Stepan 1996.

[49] Barro 1997: 3; Fein 1987. Similarly Easterly et al. 2006 (for mass killings); ch. 10 at B 2, above (comparing Russia and Ukraine). See also Libman 2012 (for a review of literature on the possible non-linear relationship between democracy and growth); Collier and Levitsky 1997 (for different types of democracies).

[50] Lipset 1959. For more recent debates see, e.g., Landman 2008: 99–129; Zakaria 2003; Rueschemeyer et al. 1992.

[51] See, e.g., Moore 1993 (role of an educated middle class); Beramendi 2007: 759–62 (federal structure); Levitsky and Way 2010 (role of ties to the West); Haber and Menaldo 2011 (discussing research on the role of natural resources).

[52] E.g. Halperin et al. 2010; Feng 2003; Rigobon and Rodrik 2005 (also on the relationship between growth, democracy and the rule of law).

outcomes of certain constitutional structures.[53] Some of those studies examine the effect of specific choices: for example, parliamentarism – as opposed to presidentialism – is seen as fostering political stability as well as economic and human development,[54] and proportional representation – as opposed to majority vote – is seen as leading to larger government spending and more frequent political compromise.[55] Other studies use aggregates: for example, the extent to which a country is a 'consensus democracy' is seen as being associated with less violence and better social welfare,[56] and the extent to which a political structure is 'supermajoritarian' is seen as being positively correlated with policies that are more stable, and yet also with higher levels of income inequality.[57]

A possible problem with these and other categories is that formal constitutional rules and constitutional practice often diverge. Traditionally, lawyers – including comparative lawyers – are mainly interested in the formal rules. But research on how the state 'works' also needs to be considered, as the subsequent section explains.

2. Comparing 'the state in action'

While traditional comparative law tends to be fairly legalistic, it is not uncommon that comparatists also consider the law in practice, be it at a supplementary level or as the core of the analysis.[58] Another reason for examining 'the state in action' is that it can challenge the hypothesis – suggested by some comparative lawyers – that law is independent from politics, making legal transplants straightforward in practice.[59] Moreover, there are specific links between comparative politics and constitutional law. For example, it is suggested that 'comparative constitutional law has to take account of political science to the extent that it explains, at least in part, the context in which the political system operates'.[60] Here, trends in comparative politics also play a role as, since the 1980s, it is said to have become more interested in the way state institutions work. In particular, there has been a shift from emphasising universal relationships to an emphasis on the role of context.[61]

The following addresses three broad topics of 'the state in action'. The first is the way law-making works in different countries. Starting with the role of the parliament, the question of 'legislative power' distinguishes between strong and weak legislators – for example, the US on the one hand and France

---

[53] Sartori 1997: 199. See also Harding and Leyland 2007: 327; Landman 2008: 218–9.
[54] Linz 1990. For the debate see also Fukuyama 2008; Wiarda and Polk 2012: 168–70.
[55] Persson and Tabellini 2003; also Lacey 2008 (relating these to prison sentences).
[56] Lijphart 1999: 244, 258–71, 293–300.
[57] McGann 2007: 193–4. A similar approach is to rank systems in terms of their aggregate number of veto players: see Fukuyama 2007: 29.
[58] See ch. 2 at A 3 (b) and C 3, above.   [59] See ch. 8 at A 2 (a), above.
[60] Harding and Leyland 2007: 322. Similarly Tushnet 2006a: 1229.
[61] See March and Olsen 2006; Mair 1996: 315, 328.

on the other.[62] One may also compare whether parliamentarians are more inclined to public or to private interests,[63] and whether they tend to act in a more partisan or in more a consensus-oriented way.[64] Of course, the law-making process also includes other stakeholders, with the form and intensity of participation differing between countries: for example, it is said that the 'notice-and-comment' rule-making in the US is more open to those interests than the more 'ad hoc' use of civil society committees in Germany and other continental European countries.[65] Furthermore, these input-based topics can be related to the output of the legislative process. Such research may look at the substantive orientation of the law: for example, whether laws favour certain interests, or how government spending compares across countries.[66] Other output measures examine topics such as differences in the style of legislative drafting or in the number of laws enacted.[67]

Second, non-legal comparative research on administrative practices often starts with the problem that rulers may be tempted to appoint friends, family members and political allies to positions of power. The counter-model is that of a professional and politically neutral 'Weberian' civil service,[68] initially associated with Prussia in Germany. The degree of political independence of the bureaucracy is still a frequent topic of comparative public management.[69] But researchers have also developed more elaborative models: for example, by distinguishing those bureaucracies that mainly aim to implement pre-defined programmes from those that aim towards client satisfaction, consumer participation, conflict resolution, and cost-effective results.[70] From a comparative perspective, it can then be observed that some administrative trends have spread across the world, while persisting differences may be related to historical path-dependencies and different conceptions of the state.[71] Trends may also be identified for other administrative questions: for example, research in political science frequently explores the diffusion of independent regulatory agencies from the US to other parts of the world.[72]

Comparative administrative practices are not only a topic of comparative politics and government. Economists (as well as political scientists) have tried to quantify how effectively administrative enforcement operates in different countries, using both input and output measures.[73] Bourdieu and other sociologists have explored the question of who 'really' runs the state, by, for

---

[62] Arter 2007: xvi. See also Fish and Kroenig 2009 (on their Parliamentary Powers Index).

[63] Cf. Siems 2008a: 234–6.   [64] Pedersen 2010: 645.

[65] Streeck 2006 (in particular, on forms of 'corporatism'); Rose-Ackermann 1995.

[66] See, e.g., Pizzorusso 1988: 64–9; World Handbook of Political and Social Indicators, available at www.icpsr.umich.edu/icpsrweb/ICPSR/series/60.

[67] On the former topic see, e.g., Xanthaki 2012; Dale 1988. On the latter see ch. 7 at B 1, above.

[68] For Weber see, e.g., Donovan 2008: 52; Smelser 1976: 117, 120–3 (as distinguished from traditional, or patriachic, and charismatic authority). See also C 1, below.

[69] E.g. Evans and Rauch 1999 (finding a positive effect on growth); Hughes 2003: 17–43.

[70] See Adler and Stendahl 2012: 257.   [71] See, e.g., Hood 2000.

[72] See, e.g., Jordana et al. 2011 and ch. 8 at B 1 (b), above.

[73] See Aubyn 2008. See also ch. 7 at C 2, above.

example, examining the power networks of higher civil service elites in a comparative fashion.[74] Criminologists (as well as other social scientists) have been interested in the way prisons operate, and how the use of prisons relates to social and moral trends.[75] In addition, research on the operation of the police and public prosecution services[76] provides a link to the next category.

Third, it is not only lawyers who are interested in the way courts and judges 'work'. In political science, frequent catch-phrases include that of a 'judicialisation of politics' and a 'politicisation of the judiciary'.[77] For economists, courts are often seen as protectors of property rights, but also as a means to gradually adapt the law to changing circumstances.[78] In detail, such non-legal comparative research may explore the participants of the trial in an empirical way: for example, it may explore how law clerks and 'référendaires' assist the judges of the highest US and EU courts,[79] and whether differences in de iure are reflected in de facto judicial independence.[80] A frequent topic is the judicialisation of constitutional courts: research includes, for example, legal comparisons aggregating information on judicial independence and judicial review,[81] more factual comparisons dealing with judicial activism,[82] and research on what drives – and who benefits from – the rise in judicial power.[83] Comparative criminologists also research a mix of court and adjudication related questions, such as policy transfers in crime control and the spread of 'problem-solving courts', causal factors explaining prison rates, and the relationship between criminal punishment and modern societies.[84]

The judiciary, as well as other lawyers and legal academics, are all said to play an important role in the emergence of 'Western political liberalism', referring to basic legal freedoms, moderate state powers, and a stable civil society.[85] But this possible causal relationship does not necessarily mean that Western political liberalism should be seen as the main aspiration of other parts of the world. Policy choices also include a number of variations within the group of Western countries, as the following explains.

3. Classifying and evaluating policy choices

Classifying countries in terms of policy choices is closely related to the way legal systems are classified into legal families. Neither in comparative law nor in other disciplines are these classifications beyond doubt,[86] but they may have

---

[74] Bourdieu 1996.   [75] Pakes 2012. See also Foucault 1977.

[76] See, e.g., Johnson 2001 (on prosecuting crime in Japan).

[77] Dressel and Mietzner 2012: 396 (on Thailand). See also the subsequent notes.

[78] Djankov et al. 2003a. See also Engert and Smith 2009 and ch. 6 at A 2 (a), above.

[79] Kenney 2000.   [80] Feld and Voigt 2003; also Hayo and Voigt 2007.

[81] Rios-Figueroa and Taylor 2006 (comparing Brazil and Mexico). See also Ferejohn et al. 2007.

[82] Huneeus et al. 2010.   [83] Hirschl 2008; Hirschl 2004; Stone Sweet 2000.

[84] Jones and Newburn 2007 (on policy transfers); Nolan 2009 (on problem-solving courts: e.g. drug courts, domestic violence courts, mental health courts); Nelken 2010: 68–71 (on research on prison rates and related statistics). See also ch. 6 at C 2 (b), above.

[85] Halliday 2010. See also Halliday and Karpik 1998; Halliday et al. 2007.   [86] See ch. 4, above.

the advantage that they correspond to a convenient middle way, that 'rejects the extremes of universalism and particularism'.[87] Moreover, classifications can be seen as test cases to determine which of the respective models is preferable. This relates such research to comparative legal research that aims to evaluate policy decisions, in particular – but not only – in the context of comparative law and development.[88]

In comparative politics, political economy, and social policy, two partly overlapping classifications have been particularly influential. The first one is the distinction between 'three worlds of welfare capitalism' by Gøsta Esping-Andersen.[89] In contrast to previous research on comparative welfare systems, this was not simply based on measures of aggregate spending, but on a variety of substantive policies such as pensions, sickness, and unemployment benefits. The classification by Esping-Andersen distinguishes between the liberal welfare systems of Anglo-Saxon countries, a conservative-corporatist category applicable to most continental European countries, and the social-democratic Scandinavian countries. But, subsequently, it has been argued that Mediterranean countries such as France and Spain deserve a separate category.[90] Also, if one includes countries of the developing world, further categories may be necessary, such as regimes of 'informal security' and 'insecurity'.[91]

These categories should not be thought of as static. Researchers have shown how models of the welfare state have diffused within Europe,[92] and social security is said to have become more than a mere European phenomenon in recent years.[93] Potentially problematic is the impact of economic globalisation on the welfare state. The fear (or aspiration) may be that competitive pressures weaken the provision of welfare in favour of the 'neoliberal' state.[94] But the literature also shows how changes are mediated by cultural traditions and political structures.[95] Whether and how distinctions between welfare states have weakened or strengthened in recent times is therefore, ultimately, an empirical question.[96]

The second main classification is that of 'varieties of capitalism'. According to Peter Hall and David Soskice, the main distinction lies between liberal market economies such as the UK and the US on the one hand, and coordinated (or organised) market economies such as Germany and Japan on the other. A

---

[87] Rose 1991: 447 (for comparative politics).

[88] See ch. 2 at A 4 and ch. 10, above. See also Bellantuono 2012 (calling for a policy-oriented comparative law incorporating research by political scientists and economists).

[89] Esping-Andersen 1990. For other topics see, e.g., Steinmo 1993 (on taxation policy); Holzinger et al. 2008 (on environmental policy). More generally on comparative public policy see, e.g., Clasen 2004; Castles 1993 (using the phrase 'families of nations').

[90] Castles 2004: 26.   [91] Suggested by Wood and Gough 2006.

[92] Manning and Shaw 1999.   [93] Pennings in EE 2012: 805.

[94] Cf. Pedersen 2010 (on research on the institutional competiveness of nations).

[95] E.g. Jreisat 2012; Swank 2002.

[96] See, e.g., Hay 2011: 324–5, 328 (data on state expenditure, workforce employed, and social spending across countries); Hacker 2002 (comparing the US with other countries).

typical feature of the former countries is the use of competitive markets, whereas the latter rely more on collaborative relationships.[97] In addition, the concept of 'institutional complementarities' plays an important role: this implies that the differences between these two groups extend to many institutional features. For example, being a coordinated market economy is seen as related to strong employment protection, support of incremental innovation, sectoral training schemes, coalition governments, and high levels of social welfare.[98] Legal scholars have also suggested that the varieties of capitalism distinction can explain the conceptual differences in many areas of law.[99]

It is sometimes thought that the economic fortunes of the respective countries may show which of the varieties of capitalism wins the day.[100] Others object that it cannot be said that one of the models triumphs. Rather, it is seen as more likely that 'institutional complementarities reinforce differences', that both varieties of capitalism have 'comparative institutional advantages', and that we may rather observe a dual convergence around these two models.[101] It is also worth noting that the division into just two models is not beyond doubt. Hall and Soskice themselves indicate that, within the group of coordinated market economies, we can distinguish between countries with industry-based and group-based coordination.[102] Others suggest further categories: for example, a category of governed market economies, as in today's China,[103] or three categories for the northern, western and southern countries of continental Europe.[104] There are also more radical critics of the varieties of capitalism literature, who refer, for example, to the hybrid nature of many countries (thus, doubting complementarities), the dynamic nature of political economies, and further varieties within the two main models.[105]

Today's comparative economic research on policy choices resembles these two classifications. Considering the history of economic thinking, this is not self-evident: neo-classical economics was (and to a large extent still is) concerned with general theories and models, not variations across countries;[106] Marxist economics, by comparison, regards law as the mere result of economic factors, and so does not take the view that law shapes differences between countries.[107] But the role of legal differences has gradually come to the focus of economists.

---

[97] Hall and Soskice 2001: 6.

[98] Hall and Soskice 2001: 17, 19, 39, 50. See also Hall and Gingerich 2009 (confirming various institutional complementarities with empirical data).

[99] Kennedy 2012: 46–8 (on corporate law, labour law, welfare law, civil procedure); Casper 2001 (on contract law); Tate 2001 (on liability law). See also Pistor 2005 (on link between varieties of capitalism and legal families). See also ch. 5 at C 2, above.

[100] Cf. Gilpin 2001: 175.   [101] Hall and Soskice 2001: 37; Hay 2004. See also ch. 9 at B 2, above.

[102] Hall and Soskice 2001: 34.   [103] See Weiss 2010: 184.

[104] Amable 2003 (Scandinavian welfare state, Rhine capitalism and Mediterranean model, in addition to the market-based Anglo-Saxon model and the meso-corporatist model of Asia).

[105] Campbell 2010: 102–6; Deeg and Jackson 2007; Konzelmann and Fovargue-Davies 2013 (on varieties of liberalism).

[106] See Gilpin 2001: 104.   [107] Cf. Donovan 2008: 47 (law as dependent variable).

For example, theories of endogenous economic growth have considered how institutions can foster innovation and growth.[108] The New Institutional Economics, starting in the 1970s, has addressed, amongst others, how both informal and formal institutions set the rules of the game for the economy, also highlighting the importance of property rights and contract enforcement.[109] In addition, research on developing and transition economies has discussed whether and how such institutions can stimulate economic growth.[110]

Prior to the fall of communism, comparative economics mainly distinguished between capitalist and socialist countries.[111] In the 1990s, a new field of research emerged, often called 'law and finance'.[112] This approach tries to quantify how well the laws of different countries protect certain interests, such as those of shareholders or creditors. The resulting data can then be used to test which legal institutions matter for the growth of financial markets. Such research has also found that the quality of legal institutions varies systematically with the 'origin' of a country's legal system (i.e. whether it falls into the English 'common law', or French, German or Scandinavian 'civil law' systems). It is therefore contended that legal origins determine the financing of corporate growth, and, through that and other channels, the nature of the financial system and ultimately overall economic growth.

This 'law and finance' research has the appeal that it seems to be in line with other findings. The continuing relevance of legal origins, and how those differ, can be explained by the concept of path dependency.[113] This may also explain the better performance of the common law over the civil law world: at a general level, it may matter that case law – being more typical in the former countries – is more efficient than statute law, since it enables a decentralised, bottom-up construction of the legal order.[114] Moreover, it may be of benefit to the common law that it relies more on markets than the state: as the authors of the legal-origin view express it, '[w]hen markets do or can work well, it is better to support than to replace them'.[115] It has also been suggested that economic modelling shows that the adversarial system of common law trials is more efficient than the (alleged) 'inquisitorial' style of civil law countries.[116]

However, this view of the economic superiority of the common law has been successfully challenged. Previous chapters have already explained that the very

---

[108] See Gilpin 2001: 116; Economides and Wilson 2001: 27.

[109] E.g. North 1990: 3; M. Aoki 2001: 5; Williamson 2000: 596. See also Cole 2013 (on various uses of term 'institutions'); G. Xu 2011: 341–2; Milhaupt and Pistor 2008: 18.

[110] See ch. 10 at A, above, and, e.g. Beck and Laeven 2006 (on the experience of transition economies).

[111] Cf. Dallago 2004; Djankov et al. 2003b.

[112] The first paper was La Porta et al. 1998. See also Beck et al. 2003; La Porta et al. 2008; also Siems and Deakin 2010.

[113] See, e.g., Rodrik 2007 and ch. 9 at B 3, above.

[114] See, e.g., Zywicki and Stringham 2011; Mahoney 2001 (with references to Hayek).

[115] La Porta et al. 2008: 327. See also Mahoney 2001: 511.

[116] Massenot 2011. See also ch. 3 at B 2 (d), above.

basis of the law and finance research – the legal origin classifications and the coding and aggregation of legal rules – have crucial flaws.[117] Three more reasons to be sceptical are, first, the 'causality puzzle': does law influence society or vice versa? The plausible response is that there are multiple causal relationships with various feedback mechanisms, making empirical claims, even with the best econometric tools, doubtful.[118] In addition, the dual causality between legal origins and law, on the one hand, and law and financial development on the other, is inconsistent, since the latter but not the former would subscribe to an instrumentalist use of laws.[119] Second, the specific effect of legal origins has been challenged, by showing, for example, that colonial duration, open trade, and political factors such as a competitive party system, political stability, and an effective bureaucracy, are what really drives institutional and economic differences.[120] Third, even assuming such causalities, it can be objected that simple reliance on 'what works' for financial development is insufficient. For example, if one uses measures of low poverty rates and equality as dependent variables, it may well be the case that civil law countries outperform common law ones.[121] And, just asking about 'what works' disregards the fact that legal systems are also about what is 'right'.[122]

As a preliminary conclusion, this also points towards the following lessons about studying other comparative disciplines: on the one hand, the comparative lawyer should be open to other disciplines, which includes an openness towards different methods and a willingness to find unexpected results. On the other hand, as far as other disciplines make claims about genuine issues of comparative law, the comparative lawyer can use her expertise to challenge such views in a constructive way. Ideally, such a dialogue between disciplines would be beneficial to both sides.

C. Comparative studies of societies and cultures

In the previous section, it was not difficult to identify states as the relevant units of comparison, mainly drawing on research in comparative politics and

---

[117] See ch. 3 at C, ch. 4 at C and ch. 7 at C 1, above.

[118] Chong and Calderon 2000. See also M. Aoki 2013: 235–6 ('institutions should be viewed as co-evolving with economic-demographic dynamics rather than determining economic demographic variables in a uni-directional way').

[119] Whytock 2009: 1902. See also Garoupa and Pargendler 2013 (with good summary of critiques of the legal origin theory).

[120] Olsson 2009 (on effect of colonial duration); Klerman et al. 2011 (on identity of colonial power); Rajan and Zingales 2003 (on relevance of free flow of capital and goods); Weingast 2010 and North et al. 2009 (on role of a competitive party system and competitive markets); Roe and Siegel 2011 (on political instability); Charron et al. 2012 (on differences in state infrastructure).

[121] Sachs 2008: 258. See also Kenworthy 2010: 411–15 (on general relationship between institutions and inequality) and ch. 10 at A, above (on Sen).

[122] Cf. Nelken 2010: 26 ('in Anglo-American countries something is right because it works; in other countries a response works because it is right'); Nelken 2007a: 124–5 ('different popular ideas in different countries about the purposes of law and what is to be expected from it').

economics. The present section is mainly based on research in sociology, anthropology and psychology, and here it is more difficult to choose the appropriate point of comparison: the starting point may be the individual human being, but each individual is also part of larger social and cultural structures, raising the questions of how those 'micro' and 'macro' levels are related to each other, and how both relate to state structures.[123] The following presents the diversity of results and methods in three steps: it starts with research on societies and cultures that contributes to an understanding of both differences and similarities between legal systems, followed by research on legal universalities and singularities, and attempts to quantify legal mentalities.

1. Understanding differences and similarities between legal systems

In comparative law, the most frequent position is that there are both similarities and differences between countries. Thus, for example, a comparatist may find that, for a particular legal question, countries A and B are similar, but both are different from country C. This distinguishes such a position from the more radical counter-views that either all legal systems are unique or that all are essentially similar. A corresponding position is taken by many studies that compare societies and cultures.[124] Thus, as far as those studies also deal with legal questions, they are akin to such comparative legal research. In addition, information on cultural or societal factors can be important for the question of whether there are functional similarities despite formal legal differences, also a core topic of comparative law.[125]

The foundational sociological research by Émile Durkheim and Max Weber provides good examples of research that tries to understand differences and similarities between societies, also giving attention to the law. Durkheim famously distinguished between, on the one hand, pre-modern collective societies with mechanical solidarity and a preference for repressive sanctions by way of penal law, and, on the other hand, modern societies with organic solidarity, deriving from an increased division of labour, and a preference for restitutionary sanctions by way of private and commercial law.[126] While recent trends do not confirm that modern (or postmodern) societies use less criminal law,[127] Durkheim's research is still considered ground-breaking in incorporating law as an integrated and conscious part of society, and in fostering an empirical and objective approach to sociology.[128]

---

[123] Cf. Welzel and Inglehart 2007: 303–4 (for the 'ecological' and 'individualistic' fallacies); Berry et al. 2011: 295 (for research finding high correlation between culture at individual and country level); Landman 2008: 19, 41–5 (also for the 'structure-agency problem' in political science).

[124] Cf. Hantrais 2009: 5, 38 ('societal method could be seen as presenting a middle way between the extremes of universalism and culturalism').

[125] See ch. 2 at B 1 (b), above.

[126] Durkheim 1947. See also Donovan 2008: 49–50; Moore 2005: 40–1; Smelser 1976: 78–113.

[127] See ch. 6 at C 2 (b), above.   [128] See Smelser 1976: 46, 74; Tamanaha 2001: 34.

Max Weber's research has equally been both influential and controversial. Weber developed a typology of socio-legal systems, distinguishing between two dimensions: on the one hand, formal and substantive (or informal), and, on the other hand, rational and irrational.[129] It is seen as damaging for a society to be based on irrationality, be it that it is formal – for example, using oracles – or that it is informal – for example, deciding conflicts in an arbitrary way. With respect to rational regimes, Weber prefers the formality of rules to the informality of principles, values and traditions. These 'ideal types' are seen as related to different countries and regions: irrationality is associated with Asian and African cultures, for example, referring to Confucian ethics in China and the 'Khadi justice' of Islamic law. Informal rationality is associated with England, and formal rationality is seen as typical for the modern Roman-based codes of continental Europe. The latter category is then associated with a successful capitalist economy, while Weber also refers to other causal factors related to modern capitalism.[130]

At a general level, Weber has been criticised for the tendency to isolate cultures and to impose Western concepts on the analysis of other parts of the world.[131] More specifically, his disrespect for Chinese and Islamic law has been challenged. Weber's view that only modern Western societies are based on a system of rational law mediated by a professional class of lawyers is seen as inaccurate, since in China too 'technically qualified experts' – here, in Confucian ethics – were essential for creating a stable normative order.[132] The alleged arbitrariness and irrationality of the Khadi justice of Islamic law may be related to the traditional lack of written judgments and appeals, and the particularised way of deciding cases.[133] Yet, it is today widely held that Weber's criticism is inaccurate or even 'orientalist', as Islamic law is also based on doctrines and regularities that consider its historical and socio-cultural context in a non-arbitrary way.[134]

Despite this criticism, Weber's research has remained influential. For example, in today's research, Richard Vogler suggests that different forms of criminal justice can be related to Weberian ideal types, and Roger Cotterrell relates Weberian types of social action to the likelihood of legal transplants in different areas of law.[135] More generally, a Weberian influence can also be

---

[129] For this and the following see Riles 2006: 779–82; Donovan 2008: 52; White 2001: 40–2; Smelser 1976: 116–150. The main work is Weber 1978 (original from 1922).

[130] For example, the 'protestant ethic': see Weber 2008 (original from 1905). Similarly the empirical work by Stulz and Williamson 2003. See also ch. 6 at C 1 (b), above (for research on Islamic law by Kuran).

[131] Gephart 2011: 18. See also White 2001: 52–3.

[132] Qian 2010: 44.   [133] Cf. Shapiro 1981: 194–222; Glenn 2010a: 189.

[134] Nader 2009: 62; Mattei and Nader 2008: 110; Glenn 2010a: 187; Ahmed 2005: 115; Rosen 1989: 18; Shapiro 1981: 194 ('image of a somewhat scruffy Muslim holy man sitting under a tree and deciding cases on a purely ad hoc basis as the morality or equities of the conflict struck him'). For 'legal orientialism' see also ch. 4 at C 1, above.

[135] Vogler 2005 (distinguishing between popular, adversarial and inquisitorial justice); Cotterrell 2001: 82 (traditional, affective, purpose rational and value rational types of action).

identified in the notions of legal families, and how modern laws can stimulate development.[136]

In anthropology, cultural studies and cross-cultural psychology, classifications have also remained relatively popular.[137] Many studies have tried to develop categories of cultures. These may be based on clearly observable characteristics – for example, one may reasonably assume that cultural and linguistic entities are closely related.[138] There is also the prominent view that there are deep cognitive differences between 'Eastern' (i.e. Asian) and 'Western' cultures.[139] More complex substantive typologies distinguish, for instance, between progress-prone and progress-resistant cultures, 'tight' and 'loose' cultures, and 'authority-ranking', 'egalitarian', 'market-pricing' and 'torn' cultures.[140] These studies may also briefly touch on the possible relationship between cultures and institutions (including the law),[141] while the following will elaborate on anthropological classifications that have considered the law in more detail.

Until the 1960s, legal anthropology often distinguished between more and less advanced societies – for example, between 'simple societies with multiplex social relationships and technologically complex societies with single-interest social relationships'.[142] Subsequent anthropologists have suggested more substantive criteria. Some of those relate to cultural and/or geographic categories: for example, Katherine Newman compared the law and economics of pre-industrial societies, distinguishing between food collectors, pastoral societies and cultivators; Clifford Geertz examined how the specifics of Islamic, Indic and Malaysian cultures relate to different legal sensibilities; and Wolfgang Fikentscher suggested the categories of pre-axial, East and South Asian, Western, Muslim, Marxist, and National Socialist modes of thought, including legal thought.[143] Three examples of more law-related categories include Philip Gulliver's distinction between regimes of judicial and political dispute resolution, Paul Bohannan's classification of unicentric, bicentric, and multicentric process models, and Keith Otterbein's distinction between countries that use capital punishments for reasons of 'group survival', 'confrontation' and 'political legitimacy'.[144]

---

[136] See ch. 4 at B 1 and ch. 10 at A, above.   [137] But see also 2, below.

[138] Hantrais 2009: 53. Now discredited are references to race; see Glenn 2010a: 38–9.

[139] Nisbett 2003. Further references in Berry et al. 2011: 17, 122–3, 147–50, 363.

[140] For these examples see Grondona 2000; Triandis 1994: 160; Gannon and Pillai 2010. For further typologies see Chanchani and Theivananthampillai 2004.

[141] See, e.g., Gannon and Pillai 2010: 574 ('Frequently cultural values determine the legal system, the educations system, the political governance system, and the dominant family system, as we would expect. At other times key leaders can change the culture itself to bring it into conformity with the institutions they champion'). See also ch. 6 at A 2, above.

[142] Chodosh 1999: 1097–8 (with reference to Max Gluckman and others).

[143] Newman 1983; Geertz 1983: 169; Fikentscher 2004: 189–466. For Fikentscher see also ch. 5 at B 1, above.

[144] Gulliver 1979; Bohannan 1965; Otterbein 1986 (this was based on the HRAF, see note 8, above).

Comparing religious cultures can also lead to categories with a comparative legal dimension. For example, Jacques Vanderlinden suggests that the Christian, Islamic and Jewish faiths regard revelation as their main source; Buddhist, Confucian and Daoist faiths have legal science; and Hinduism has custom.[145] Other researchers have explained that, in particular, Islamic law and common law share certain similarities: for example, a gradual way of reasoning.[146] Furthermore, developing categories across religions, one may determine, for example, how countries differ in the relationship between state and religion,[147] and whether differences in the extent of religiosity exist and how those are related to the quality of legal institutions.[148]

The more general question remains why, beyond obvious reasons of geography and language, particular cultures and societies are similar. In anthropology, this is often discussed in connection with 'Galton's problem'.[149] It derives from a disagreement between Sir Edward Tylor and Francis Galton at an event in 1889: Tylor presented his anthropological research in order to show deep commonalities between cultures, but Galton objected that these similarities could equally be due to cross-cultural borrowing. In the twentieth century, the concept of cultural diffusion has become a frequent topic of research in social sciences. Sociologists have explored how ideas are communicated and received across societies, identifying, for example, possible channels of communication and stages of adaptation.[150] Economists also use concepts of demand and supply as they relate to ideas,[151] evolutionary psychologists distinguish between genetic and cultural evolution,[152] and critical geographers encourage us to consider the influence of 'discursive paradigms, ideational circuits, institutional frameworks, and power structures'.[153] All of this is of interest for comparative law, as the spread of ideas may lead to socio-cultural changes that, in turn, determine legal changes that, in turn, may explain differences and similarities between legal systems.

2. Showing legal universalities and singularities

In traditional comparative law, there is some support for legal universalities, whereas postmodern comparative law often takes the counter-view of legal singularities.[154] These two views also play a role for a number of further topics of comparative law, such as the transferability of human rights and the

---

[145] Vanderlinden 2002: 181.

[146] Makdisi 1999: 1696–717; Quraishi 2006. See also ch. 8 at B 2 (a), above.

[147] Hirschl 2011: 435–7 (distinguishing between eight models of state and religion relations). See also ch. 9 at D 3 (in particular note 246), above.

[148] Berggren and Bjørnskov 2013 (finding that religiosity is negatively related to institutions).

[149] Naroll 1965. See also Hantrais 2009: 64.

[150] E.g. Rogers 1962; Parsons 1966. See also Twining 2004; Twining 2005. This could also be related to research on migration and law: see, e.g., Coutin 2000.

[151] See Brown 2001.

[152] Boyd and Richerson 1985. See also Du Laing 2011; Berry et al. 2011: 266–7.

[153] Peck 2011: 785.   [154] See ch. 2 at B 2 and ch. 5, above.

globalisation of rules in the context of comparative law and development.[155] It is therefore interesting that some research in anthropology and other social sciences also takes the view that there is some universality in law, whereas others favour singularities. To be sure, as many of those researchers accept that there are both similarities and differences, the contrast between the 'radical' views discussed in this section, and the views discussed in the previous one, should not be overstated.

Anthropology has a natural affiliation with universalities as far as it aims for the 'elucidation of the human condition'.[156] For example, in the late nineteenth century, the comparative legal anthropology of Albert Hermann Post saw, in the legal customs of all cultures, evidence for general forms of human organisation.[157] In the early to mid-twentieth century, Bronislaw Malinowski and Alfred Radcliffe-Brown found that Western and non-Western cultures shared aspirations for order and solidarity, even if some of the latter societies lacked law in a narrow-formal sense.[158] A similar position was taken by Max Gluckman, but, in addition, he also claimed that legal concepts such as ownership, the doctrine of liability, and the logic of judicial reasoning of Western laws could be found in the African societies that he researched.[159]

The problem with such research may be that, traditionally, anthropologists mainly conduct fieldwork in one particular place, being concerned with the in-depth, personal observations of a limited group of persons. Thus, the extent to which such empirical findings can identify what applies to all human beings is doubtful. Some attempts have been made to go further. The long-term project on Human Relations Area Files at Yale University has collected information on a large number of cultures.[160] Specifically related to a legal topic, a project coordinated by Laura Nader and Harry Todd examined dispute resolution in ten societies in different parts of the world. This was based on a standardised data collection method; yet, the resulting book does not contain a conclusion that attempts to identify what features these dispute resolution processes have in common.[161]

Research on human commonalities has, at least, had the impact that, in contemporary anthropology, it is seen as inappropriate to treat certain cultures

---

[155] See ch. 8 at B 4 and ch. 10 at B and C 3, above.

[156] Donovan 2008: xiv.   [157] Post 1884: XI.

[158] Malinowski 1926; Radcliffe-Brown 1951. See also Donovan 2008: 69–78; Caterina 2004: 1529–45 (suggesting an 'innate basis of reciprocity', with references to Malinowski and others); Pospisil 1971: 341 ('there is no basic qualitative difference between tribal (primitive) and civilized law').

[159] Gluckman 1955. See also Donovan 2008: 100–11; Bennett 2006: 650; critical Edge 2000: 9–10 ('over-eager readiness' to interpret customary law of East Africa as akin to English law); Moore 2005: 346 ('customary law was, in fact, so altered a version of indigenous practice that it must be recognised as a composite colonial construction').

[160] See www.yale.edu/hraf/. For a critical summary see Berry et al. 2011: 234–7. A related project, though with a different method and coverage, is the Standard Cross Cultural Sample (SCCS), available at http://eclectic.ss.uci.edu/~drwhite/sccs/.

[161] Nader and Todd 1978. See also Donovan 2008: 135–47, 179–80.

and societies as 'primitive' or 'childlike'.[162] Some contemporary anthropologists, such as Maurice Bloch, also reject the view that 'different cultures or societies have fundamentally different systems of thought'.[163] A further legacy is that cultural differences are not seen as obstacles that can never be overcome. For example, according to Sally Engle Merry, one should not 'misread' culture as hindering the globalisation of human rights.[164] This does not imply that the local context is irrelevant, but that such differences are subject to the 'transnational circulation of people and ideas, . . . transforming the world we live in'.[165]

Some scholars in other disciplines also suggest universalist views with relevance to law. In political philosophy, the idea of a common law of nations is an early example.[166] In comparative criminology, universals may concern cross-cultural approaches to crime prevention.[167] Psychology can also be universal if the 'evidence of shared patterns in the structure of human intelligence or behavior' points towards a 'similarity of social arrangements, including law'.[168] For example, according to Owen Jones and colleagues, it is the 'unique brain signature of the human animal, written by evolutionary processes' that has shaped the architecture of law, as evidenced, for example, in shared institutions of justice and, thus, the shunning of physical aggression, theft, and fraud.[169] In a number of articles, Julie De Coninck also suggests that the findings of behavioural economics can be used to show that physical possession of an object may be a universal factor that is relevant for the structure of property rights.[170]

The particularist counter-view is that it is precisely the aim of comparative research to challenge ethnocentric views that assume that what is familiar is also universal.[171] The emphasis is therefore on how 'spatial specificity' and 'local knowledge' account for legal and other differences.[172] For example, Bruno Latour explicitly rejects the view that social scientists should aim for reduction, and that descriptions can be 'too particular, too idiosyncratic, too localized'.[173] Such a 'relativist' position has also been associated with one of the founding

---

[162] Rosen 2006: 60–1. Similarly Menski 2006: 390 and Grossfeld 2005: 245, for the role of anthropology for comparative law.

[163] Bloch 1977: 279. See also Caterina 2004: 1517–8.

[164] Merry 2003: 68. Similarly Brems 2001.   [165] Merry 2006: 44. See also ch. 8 at B 4 (c), above.

[166] Richter 1969: 142 (discussing Jean Bodin).

[167] See research discussed in Nelken 2010: 19, 28, 40.

[168] Muir Watt 2012: 272. Similarly Berry et al. 2011: 6–8, 11–12, 288–94 (supporting a 'moderate universalism'); Henrich et al. 2010: 62 (rejecting 'radical versions of interpretivism and cultural relativity'). For a more specific example see, e.g., Fiske 1991 (suggesting four elementary mental modes in all cultures). The counter-view is often related to concepts of 'indigenous psychology': see, e.g., Berry et al. 2011:18–20, 286–8, 298; Hantrais 2009: 41.

[169] Jones 2001: 873–4 (for the quote); Robinson et al. 2007 (for the examples). See also Du Laing 2011: 689–92.

[170] De Coninck 2011; De Coninck 2010: 344; De Coninck 2009: 15.

[171] Moore 1986b: 12. Generally see also Rosen 2012: 73; Hantrais 2009: 40; Elder 1976.

[172] Holder and Harrison 2003; Geertz 1983. See also Darian-Smith 2013: 167.

[173] Latour 2005: 137.

fathers of anthropology, Franz Boas, given his scepticism towards universalist ideas.[174] After the Second World War, the American Anthropological Association rejected the concept of universal human rights.[175] Academic writings by Paul Bohannan and E. E. Evans-Pritchard emphasised cultural differences or even uniqueness – for example, Bohannan strongly opposing Gluckman's use of Western legal concepts for non-Western societies.[176] National character studies of specific countries had similar tendencies: for example, Ruth Benedict's book on the nationalism and militarism of Japan in the time of the Second World War.[177]

The politics behind the rejection of universalism is related to the history of anthropological research. In the late nineteenth century, the colonial powers saw anthropology as a useful tool to identify local customs and to use those as a way of administrative control.[178] Thus, it can be suggested that the Western-universalist world vision of anthropology is very much a product of a past age. Since the mid-twentieth century, the problem of a potential Western fieldworker bias has also been extensively discussed. The main distinction is between the perspective of outsiders ('etic') and insiders ('emic'), with the frequent suggestion that the anthropological researcher should try to develop an 'emic' understanding.[179] Yet, becoming a complete 'insider' would be an unrealistic requirement for anthropological researchers of other cultures. Thus, the best possible advice is to be aware of the challenges of cross-cultural research – for example, on how social, linguistic, and ethical differences affect our understanding of different cultures.[180]

In recent years, interpretative and postmodern approaches to anthropology have also been sceptical about 'positivist' claims of universality.[181] This does not deny the role of forces that go beyond particular cultural units: for example, a typical statement may be that 'bounded cultural groups' are also 'embedded in regional and global forces'.[182] In addition, legal anthropology has broadened its field of interest: topics can now concern all types of societies and places, including modern societies and transnational fields; an example of this would include international arbitration and other topics of 'global governance'.[183]

---

[174] Boas 1896 and see Merry 2003: 65; Berry et al. 2011: 230.

[175] American Anthropological Association 1947. Today it follows a more mixed position, see www.aaanet.org/cmtes/cfhr/Committee-for-Human-Rights-Guidelines.cfm.

[176] Evans-Pritchard 1963: 17; Bohannan 1957. For the Gluckman-Bohannan debate see also Donovan 2008: 164–7.

[177] Benedict 1946 (though with brief comparisons with Western countries). For research in psychology see Peabody 1985 (comparing the national characters of six countries).

[178] See Donovan 2008: 59; Mattei and Nader 2008: 102; Tamanaha 2001: 113–5. See also ch. 4 at C 3 (a), above.

[179] See, e.g., Berry et al. 2011: 23–4; Hantrais 2009: 78–9, 100–1; Hyland 2009: 94; Graziadei 2009: 733; Ainsworth 1996: 27, 33.

[180] Books on qualitative cross-cultural research provide such guidance, e.g., Liamputtong 2010.

[181] See Hantrais 2009: 107; Donovan 2008: 20; Darian-Smith 2004: 548.

[182] Darian-Smith 2004: 550.

[183] See generally Moore 2005: 346–67 and for the example see Riles 2008.

It would also no longer be accurate to identify all 'particularists' as having a relativist position, because contemporary anthropologists do not shy away from making policy recommendations. For example, they discuss how to address global and local power structures, and how to improve the situation of the ethnographic informant, but also how to incorporate aspects of culture into the law, and how to use traditions as a defence against injustice.[184] All of this shows that the discussion has moved beyond radical views of universalism and particularism. It may also be said that problems of similarities and differences, as well as universalism and particularism, would properly have to start with empirical information on what individuals think and do across units of comparison – to which we turn next.

3. Measuring legal mentalities and their relevance

The importance of alleged or real differences in legal mentalities is a frequent topic of postmodern comparative law, and it can also be related to many other topics, such as legal families and legal transplants.[185] Trying to measure legal mentalities also overlaps with themes of numerical comparative law.[186] Moreover, the research discussed in the following may not only try to measure how legal mentalities differ, but also to find out how such differences may be related to other socio-economic differences: thus, this also provides a link to socio-legal comparative law.[187]

The general background of many of such measurements is provided by comparative surveys that collect information on a variety of topics such as income, education, work, family relations and crime.[188] Those surveys often include questions with direct relation to law, and the previous chapter on numerical comparative law already discussed some examples, such as the various social and value surveys.[189] Another prominent example is Geert Hofstede's survey-based research on national cultures.[190]

Cross-national surveys face various challenges: the literature discusses, for instance, problems such as the comparability of translations, differences in response styles, and lack of context for broad survey questions.[191] An alternative to surveys is to conduct the same psychological experiments in different societies. Of course, here too, the problem is whether a particular experiment can work across cultures. Still, recent research suggests that there is an urgent need for such studies, as in the past psychologists tended to conduct

---

[184] See, e.g., Moore 2005: 352; Donovan 2008: xi, 2008: 209–30; Mattei and Nader 2008: 202.
[185] See, e.g., ch. 5 at C 1, ch. 4 at B 2, and ch. 8 at A 2 (b) and (d), above.
[186] See ch. 7, above.   [187] See ch. 6, above.
[188] See Hantrais 2009: 26.   [189] See ch. 7 at C 3, above.
[190] See http://geert-hofstede.com/national-culture.html. For other datasets see, e.g., http://usdkexpats.org/theory/schwartzs-culture-model; www-psych.stanford.edu/~tsailab/.
[191] See, e.g., Jowell et al. 2007; Jowell 1998; Hantrais 2009: 78–83; Berry et al. 2011: 106, 114, 293.

experiments mainly with the easiest-to-reach participants, namely Western university students.[192]

It is frequently suggested that research on human behaviour can be helpful for the understanding of legal systems. In the non-quantitative literature, it is, for example, suggested that 'an English judge is not only a judge; she is also English', that the national character of the Germans accounts for their preference for rigid rules, and that different behavioural patterns amongst consumers account for diverse effects of legal rules.[193] Research has also indicated how legal differences may shape behavioural ones: for example, it has been suggested that corrupt legal regimes make people behave in a more friendly way, since they rely on informal networks;[194] and a more general literature also discusses how legal rules become internalised, and how institutions can change identities.[195]

With this background information, the following examples aim to illustrate how researchers have quantified opinions and attitudes relating to legal mentalities. First, it is often discussed that differences in approaches to individualism, as measured by Hofstede, can account for differences in the rule of law and the protection of property rights. For example, James Gibson and Gregory Caldeira's research on European legal cultures found that individualism and support for liberty are positively correlated, and that there are further positive correlations between support for the rule of law and indicators of modernisation.[196] International comparisons usually find that common-law legal systems, in particular the US, are more individualistic and more reliant on the rule of law than other legal families.[197] Research by Amir Licht and colleagues reaches a similar result for differences between corporate governance systems: good shareholder protection correlates with individualism, and both are mainly seen as prevalent in the Anglo-Saxon world.[198]

Second, comparative research on the 'amount of law' can be seen as complementary. Also drawing on the Hofstede data, Amanda Perry-Kessaris observes that countries with a higher score in the category 'uncertainty avoidance' will have more laws than others, but also that laws are potentially underenforced. The UK is seen as a contrasting example as it has a low 'uncertainty avoidance' score, a tendency not to rely on formal statutory law, but an effective rule of law.[199] Research by economists has also considered the role of 'trust', using data from the World Values Surveys, with the finding that distrust leads to more demand for and higher levels of regulation.[200] Psychological studies on different

---

[192] Henrich et al. 2010. See also De Coninck 2011: 725.

[193] Legrand 1999: 73–4; Legrand 1997a: 47; Weatherill in EE 2012: 241.

[194] de Soto 2008: 6.   [195] Schauer 2012: 225; Varshney 2007: 289–90.

[196] Gibson and Caldeira 1996. See also Klasing 2013 (finding that individualism matters for institutional quality).

[197] Licht et al. 2007; Chase 1997: 865; also Ehrmann 1976: 40.

[198] Licht et al. 2005. See also ch. 6 at C 1 (b), above.

[199] Perry-Kessaris 2002: 294–5. See also ch. 7 at B 1, above (for amount of law).

[200] Pinotti 2012; Aghion et al. 2010.

forms of morality also suggest that law and 'non-law' can be substitutes: while secular Western populations have a morality based on justice, personal choice and individual rights, other societies have 'ethics of community' and 'ethics of divinity' with less reliance on law.[201]

Third, one can examine whether forms of government are related to the information collected in value surveys. For example, Eric Posner and Adrian Vermeule were interested in whether populations which have positive views about strong leaders also tend to be non-democratic ones: yet, using the variables of the World Values Survey, such a correlation could not be confirmed.[202] Similarly, another group of researchers did not find that the low trust in legislatures in Latin America, as measured by the Latinbarometer, was related to the type and stability of the political regime.[203] Doh Chull Shin, by contrast, examined attitudes in Asian countries, using the Asian Barometer, and found that the population of autocratic countries, but not democratic ones, supported a 'paternalistic' relationship between the government and the people. This is an important finding, as it can be read as refuting the view that 'Asian values' are bound to lead to particular constitutional rules and structures.[204]

Fourth, there is extensive research on the relationship between crime and criminal punishment and different legal mentalities. Only a few examples can be provided here. Starting with comparative information about crime, an experimental study conducted in five countries found a positive correlation between trust in a society and abstention from theft, while another study did not find that differences between the values of Muslim and non-Muslim countries were strongly related to differences in criminal behaviour.[205] Linking values to actual differences in criminal punishment, another study suggests that the public supports harsher sanctions in countries with relatively soft sanctions, but not in countries with harsher ones.[206] Recent research also conducted an experiment on the frequency of 'antisocial punishment', i.e. a tendency to sanction persons who behave pro-socially, finding that a weak rule of law is one of the significant predictors.[207]

A possible objection to research related to legal mentalities is that, in recent decades, individual identities may have become more loosely connected to the place where people live and work. Yet, in contrast to difference-related statements by comparative lawyers, the research outlined in this section has the advantage that it presents us with scientific tools to test how far global trends have indeed had such an effect. Such research can also improve our understanding on how the 'micro-level' of individual thinking and behaviour is related to the 'macro-levels' of cultures, societies and legal systems.

---

[201] See Henrich et al. 2010: 71–3. See also ch. 6 at A 2, above.
[202] Posner and Vermeule 2012 (on 'tyrannophobia').   [203] Huneeus et al. 2007: 150–1.
[204] Shin 2011. See also ch. 8 at B 4 (c), above (for the Asian values debate in human rights).
[205] Campos-Ortiz et al. 2012; Fish 2011.   [206] Newman 1976/2008.
[207] Herrmann et al. 2008. See also De Coninck 2011: 725–6.

D. Conclusion

This chapter has illustrated that there is a considerable research on comparative law in other disciplines: clearly, comparative law seems to be too important to be left to comparative lawyers! Increasingly, given the availability of electronic publications that may simply be found with search engines on the web, even traditional comparative lawyers have become aware of this fact. But, then, comparative lawyers may be deeply puzzled by the methods and findings of such 'implicit' comparative legal research originating from other disciplines. It was therefore the aim of this chapter to provide a critical introduction to the methods of these comparative disciplines and some of their main research. A number of topics may have been familiar to comparative lawyers: for example, the frequent discussion about universality versus specificity, in particular the different emphasis on either similarities or differences between countries, cultures, societies, or other units of comparison. Other themes may have been less familiar. For example, establishing causal relationships based on comparative legal information is frequent in non-legal research, whereas many comparative lawyers tend to feel more at home in describing and interpreting legal rules from different countries.

But comparative lawyers also have to be aware that other disciplines, even if they use a more scientific method and terminology, hardly provide certainty. There is wide variation in the social sciences, ranging from 'universalist' to 'relativist' views, often (though not always) related to the use of 'robust' quantitative methods on the one hand versus 'deep' qualitative methods on the other. Of course, it is unlikely that one camp gets everything right and the other one everything wrong. Thus, pragmatically, it is suggested that comparative lawyers should adopt a position that tries to incorporate diverse methods and views into their thinking. In so doing, 'implicit' comparative law will become 'explicit'. It can and should also become more 'contextual', as the final chapter of this book will explain in more detail.

12

Outlook

At the beginning of Part IV, it was said that 'comparative law is an "open subject" that can absorb further research not traditionally included'. Moreover, being an open subject means that one has to be sceptical about recommendations to establish a fixed canon of comparative law.[1] Yet, this does not imply a methodological relativism where 'anything goes': treating methods seriously is bound to lead to a reflection about advantages and disadvantages of certain methods. In the present book, the view has been taken that contextual and interdisciplinary approaches to comparative law are a promising way forward. This position is reaffirmed in this final chapter: Section A provides further discussion about 'implicit comparative law', i.e. research in other disciplines that deals with legal topics in a comparative fashion, thus supplementing Chapter 11. Section B revisits the future of 'explicit' comparative legal research (i.e. Chapters 2 to 10 of this book), considering the possible role of other academic disciplines. Section C concludes.

A. Further directions of 'implicit comparative law'

In Chapter 11, it was acknowledged that its account of 'implicit comparative law' was highly selective. In particular, the main examples of this chapter drew on comparative research in the social sciences. The reason for choosing these examples was that, in these fields, there are a number of instances where non-legal researchers have dealt with topics of a genuine comparative legal nature. By contrast, the inspiration that comparative lawyers can get from the humanities and natural sciences is more about non-legal phenomena that can also be of interest to comparative lawyers. For example, in the humanities, there is a large body of literature on textual interpretation[2] that can help comparative lawyers in their understanding of different legal systems. Natural sciences can also be relevant: for instance, it has been suggested that comparative law may consider

---

[1] For such a suggestion see Reimann 2002: 695–7.
[2] For references see Legrand 2011: 17–8 note 2.

work by neurologists in order to understand the 'brain processes of someone engaged in legal reasoning'.[3]

This raises the general question about the relationship between comparative law and other disciplines. This book has mainly considered that other disciplines can be helpful to comparative law, but there should not only be 'one-way traffic'.[4] While in the present non-legal literature there are some references to comparative law, this is often done in a sketchy way. For example, in Linda Hantrais' book on comparative research,[5] some of the main textbooks of comparative law are mentioned, but overall research in comparative politics and sociology is apparently seen as more interesting. More problematically, research by financial economists on the relationship between law and finance uses some concepts of comparative law, such as the divide between civil and common law, but fundamentally misunderstands what these categories mean.[6]

Thus, there is a need to foster cross-disciplinary communication. Of course, this is a general desire, not limited to the relationship between comparative law and other comparative disciplines. The problem is that today's universities are typically compartmentalised into faculties, departments and schools, while researchers are also encouraged to cross the boundaries of academic disciplines.[7] To be sure, there are ways of overcoming this tension: for example, it can be fruitful to establish joined centres, networks and conferences that operate across disciplines. It is suggested that comparative law can be an important element in such initiatives.

The question remains whether the aim should be to develop a generic method of comparative studies. It has been said that, in the past, Auguste Comte, John Stuart Mill, Max Weber, and others tried to engage in 'discipline-free comparative research'.[8] Yet, in Chapter 11, we have also seen that disciplinary preferences for particular types of research often reflect different types of research questions. Thus, it is preferable to say that interdisciplinarity reaffirms methodological pluralism, with possible complementarities between different approaches.

B. Revisiting 'explicit' research in comparative law

Part I on 'traditional comparative law' (Chapters 2 to 4) included some critical remarks on the conventional method of comparative law, notably functionalism. The subsequent discussions in this book have shown that, today, comparative lawyers use a variety of further methods. Additional challenges come from other disciplines, as far as those are typically more empirically oriented. As a result,

---

[3] Hage in EE 2012: 521. See also Pardolesi and Granieri 2012: 16–21 (suggesting similarities between comparative law and natural sciences).

[4] Cf. also Sacco 1990: 161–5 (service of comparative law for social sciences).

[5] Hantrais 2009.   [6] See ch. 4 at B 2, C 2 a, ch. 7 at C 1 and ch. 11 at B 3, above.

[7] See, e.g., Siems and MacSithigh 2012 (specifically on the position of 'law' within the structure of universities).

[8] Hantrais 2009: 24.

while the traditional method still has its scope of application, it is suggested that it is not the 'default option' any more, and that a comparatist needs to justify the method she plans to employ.

The first part also dealt with the notion of distinct legal families, while also challenging its validity. The treatment of 'global' developments has further raised doubts about the view that today's legal world can be securely divided into common law, civil law, and other legal families. Moreover, the debate about differences and similarities, as well as universalism and singularities in other disciplines, points towards the conclusion that one's perception of whether countries belong together in certain groups is often a matter of interpretation. For example, if there are four countries, and they score on a particular measure (min 0, max 1) with (a) 0.35, (b) 0.36, (c) 0.40, (d) 0.50, it could be said that (a) and (b) belong to the same 'family' as the difference is just 0.01, but it is also possible to claim 'universalism' as all countries score between 0.35 and 0.50, or to claim singularities as the four countries do not have identical scores.

Part II on 'extending the methods of comparative law' (Chapters 5 to 7) reflected on the general changes in legal research, which in many countries now also includes postmodern, socio-legal, and numerical methods. It was said that these were welcome developments. Moreover, the subsequent discussion about other disciplines may point towards a further shift. For example, a comparative lawyer may decide not simply to engage in socio-legal comparative law, but to do a sociological study that includes comparative legal information; or she may not simply engage in numerical comparative law, but conduct an econometric analysis that incorporates legal data from various countries.

In appropriate research projects, making this second step can be valuable, but the comparative lawyer does not need to have an inferiority complex. For instance, researchers in economics and other disciplines may tell her that it is essential to prove causal relationships between certain legal differences and social, cultural or economic ones. But the comparative lawyer may then insist that the context and content of the legal rules in question are too complex to claim such a causal relationship. Thus, in this respect, not fully embracing every method from every other discipline is not necessarily a disadvantage. Moreover, understanding the methods from a variety of disciplines can be helpful as it is unlikely that 'positivist' methods, say, always get it right and 'interpretive' ones always wrong (or vice versa).

Part III on 'global comparative law' (Chapters 8 to 10) started with a discussion about legal transplants. While the trend has shifted away from simply copying foreign laws, legal transplants are still a useful conceptual tool. Here, research in other fields can also be helpful, as it can show the availability and advantages of certain policy choices. The subsequent chapters dealing with the fading of state borders and law and development have an even stronger interdisciplinary dimension, as these topics are not rooted in legal questions. There would be various ways in which those topics could be further explored – for example, by linking them to research in geography and international relations.

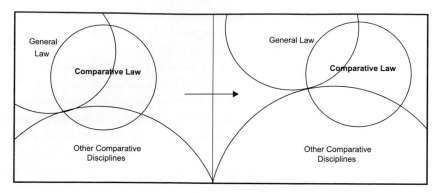

Figure 12.1 Relationship between 'comparative law', 'law', and 'other comparative disciplines'

Contrary to the established approach of comparative law, it can also be rewarding for comparatists to consider differences below the state level more closely, also drawing on research from other disciplines.[9]

Finally, the topics in the third part illustrate the dynamic nature of comparative law. The substance of comparative law is said to be shaped by 'broad intellectual or theoretical trends and movements, by societal developments and the political climate'.[10] In particular, we cannot know for sure how the geopolitical landscape and transnational governance structures will evolve in the future. This reaffirms the need for a comparatist to pay attention to real-world developments, and to how they may impact on the present concepts and tools of comparative law.

C. Conclusion

It was the general aim of this book to steer comparative law into a more contextual direction. In particular, it is suggested that linking comparative law with research in other comparative disciplines is a promising way forward. Figure 12.1, above, illustrates this ambition. It can be seen that shifting comparative law towards other comparative disciplines increases the overlap between those and comparative law. There is also an overlap between comparative law and non-comparative legal research, though it is suggested that this may become a bit smaller. Of course, as the figure illustrates, there also remain questions of comparative law which do not overlap with either of the two other circles.

Typically, comparative lawyers are, in the first instance, trained in law. Thus, the obvious challenge is the lack of familiarity with other comparative disciplines. However, it is not suggested that all comparative legal research has to become fully interdisciplinary. There are different levels of interdisciplinary

---

[9] See, e.g., Mitton 2013 (econometric research on differences between subnations); Greenhouse et al. 1994 (anthropological research on law and community in three US towns).
[10] Peters and Schwenke 2000: 829.

legal research, ranging from basic to advanced types, and which of these types a legal researcher chooses depends on the nature of the problem and her own skills and preferences.[11] It is also suggested that comparative lawyers are specifically equipped for the challenges of learning the unfamiliar. While it is famously said that 'in their explorations on foreign territory comparatists may come upon natives lying in wait with spears',[12] comparative lawyers still try to explore foreign laws. Much the same could be said about the future of comparative law and its relationship to other academic disciplines.

[11] References in Siems 2009a (identifying one basic and three advanced types of interdisciplinary legal research).
[12] Zweigert and Kötz 1998: 36 (quoting Ernst Rabel).

References

Abdelrahman, Omer Ali 2004. *History and Development of the Law of Contract in Sudan (1898–2000)*, PhD thesis, SOAS, University of London.

Abel, Richard L. and Philip S. C. Lewis (eds.) 1988. *Lawyers in Society*, 3 volumes, Berkeley: University of California Press.

Acemoglu, Daron and James A. Robinson 2012. *Why Nations Fail: The Origins of Power, Prosperity, and Poverty*, New York: Random House.

Acemoglu, Daron, Simon Johnson and James A. Robinson 2002. 'Reversal of Fortune: Geography and Institutions in the Making of the Modern World Income Distribution', *Quarterly Journal of Economics*, vol. 117, 1231–94.

Acemoglu, Daron, Simon Johnson and James A. Robinson 2005. 'Institutions as Long Run Causes of Economic Growth', in Philippe Aghion and Steven N. Durlauf (eds.), *Handbook of Economic Growth*, vol. IA, Amsterdam: Elsevier, pp. 385–472.

Ackerman, Bruce 2010. 'Good-bye, Montesquieu', in Susan Rose-Ackerman and Peter L. Lindseth (eds.), *Comparative Administrative Law*, Cheltenham: Edward Elgar, pp. 128–33.

Adams, Maurice and Jacco Bomhoff 2012. 'Comparing Law: Practice and Theory', in Maurice Adams and Jacco Bomhoff (eds.), *Practice and Theory in Comparative Law*, Cambridge: Cambridge University Press, pp. 1–21.

Adams, Maurice and John Griffiths 2012. 'Against Comparative Method', in Maurice Adams and Jacco Bomhoff (eds.), *Practice and Theory in Comparative Law*, Cambridge: Cambridge University Press, pp. 279–301.

Adams, Michael 1995. 'The Conflict of Jurisdictions – An Economic Analysis of Pretrial Discovery, Fact Gathering and Cost Allocation Rules in the United States and Germany', *European Review of Private Law*, vol. 3, 53–94.

Adler, Michael and Sara Stendahl 2012. 'Administrative Law, Agencies and Redress Mechanisms in the United Kingdom and Sweden', in David S. Clark (ed.), *Comparative Law and Society*, Cheltenham: Edward Elgar, pp. 254–89.

Aghion, Philippe, Yann Algan, Pierre Cahuc and Andrei Shleifer 2010. 'Regulation and Distrust', *Quarterly Journal of Economics*, vol. 125, 1015–49.

Aguilera, Ruth V. and Cynthia A. Williams 2009. 'Law and Finance: Inaccurate, Incomplete, and Important', *BYU Law Review*, vol. 9, 1412–34.

Ahlering, Beth and Simon Deakin 2007. 'Labour Regulation, Corporate Governance and Legal Origin: A Case of Institutional Complementarity?', *Law & Society Review*, vol. 41, 865–98.

Ahmed, Faiz 2005. 'Judicial Reform in Afghanistan: A Case Study in the New Criminal Code', *Hastings International and Comparative Law Review*, vol. 29, 93–134.

Ainsworth, Janet E. 1996. 'Categories and Culture: On the "Rectification of Names" in Comparative Law', *Cornell Law Review*, vol. 82, 19–42.

Ajani, Gianmaria 1995. 'By Chance and Prestige: Legal Transplants in Russia and Eastern Europe', *American Journal of Comparative Law*, vol. 43, 93–117.

Ajani, Gianmaria 2006. *Sistemi Giuridici Comparati: Lezioni e Materiali*, 2nd edn, Giappichelli: Turin.

Ajani, Gianmaria 2009. 'Legal Change and Economic Performance: An Assessment', In Antonina Bakardjieva Engelbrekt and Joakim Nergelius (eds.), *New Directions in Comparative Law*, Cheltenham: Edward Elgar, pp. 3–18.

Al-Ali, Zaid 2011. 'Constitutional Drafting and External Influence', in Tom Ginsburg and Rosalind Dixon (eds.), *Research Handbook in Comparative Constitutional Law*, Cheltenham: Edward Elgar, pp. 77–95.

Ali, Shaheen Sardar (ed.) 2006. *Conceptualising Islamic Law, CEDAW and Women's Human Rights in Plural Legal Settings: A Comparative Analysis of Application of CEDAW in Bangladesh, India and Pakistan*, New Delhi: UNIFEM.

Ali, Shaheen Sardar 2011. 'Teaching and Learning Islamic Law in a Globalised World: Some Reflections and Perspectives', *Journal of Legal Education*, vol. 61, 206–30.

Allen, Franklin, Jun Qian and Meijun Qian 2005. 'Law, Finance and Economic Growth in China' *Journal of Financial Economics*, vol. 77, 57–116.

Allen, Franklin and Jun Q. J. Qian 2010. 'Comparing Legal and Alternative Institutions in Finance and Commerce', in James J. Heckman, Robert L. Nelson and Lee Cabatingan (eds.), *Global Perspectives on the Rule of Law*, Abingdon: Routledge, pp. 118–44.

Allison, John W. F. 1996. *A Continental Distinction in the Common Law – A Historical and Comparative Perspective on English Public Law*, Oxford: Clarendon.

Alpa, Guido 2010. *Markets and Comparative Law*, London: BIICL.

Alter, Karen J. 2012. 'The Global Spread of European Style International Courts', *West European Politics*, vol. 35, 135–54.

Alter, Karen J. and Laurence R. Helfer 2011. 'Legal Integration in the Andes: Law-Making by the Andean Tribunal of Justice', *European Law Journal*, vol. 17, 701–15.

Alter, Karen J., Laurence R. Helfer and Osvaldo Saldías 2012. 'Transplanting the European Court of Justice: The Experience of the Andean Tribunal of Justice', *American Journal of Comparative Law*, vol. 60, 629–64.

Amable, Bruno 2003. *The Diversity of Modern Capitalism*, Oxford: Oxford University Press.

Ambrus, Monika 2009. 'Comparative Law Method in the Jurisprudence of the European Court of Human Rights in the Light of the Rule of Law', *Erasmus Law Review*, vol. 2, 353–71.

American Anthropological Association 1947. 'Statement on Human Rights', *American Anthropologist*, vol. 49, 539–43.

Amnesty International 2013. *Death Sentences and Executions 2012*.

An-Na`im, Abdullahi Ahmed 2008. *Islam and the Secular State: Negotiating the Future of Shari`a*, Cambridge, MA: Harvard University Press.

Andenas, Mads and Duncan Fairgrieve 2006. 'Judicial Independence and Accountability: National Traditions and International Standards', in Guy Canivet, Mads Andenas and Duncan Fairgrieve (eds.), *Independence, Accountability and the Judiciary*, London: BIICL, pp. 3–26.

Andenas, Mads and Duncan Fairgrieve 2012. 'Intent on Making Mischief: Seven Ways of Using Comparative Law', in Pier Giuseppe Monateri (ed.), *Methods of Comparative Law*, Cheltenham: Edward Elgar, pp. 25–60.

Andenas, Mads, Camilla Baasch Andersen and Ross Ashcroft 2011. 'Towards a Theory of Harmonisation', in Mads Andenas and Camilla Baasch Andersen (eds.), *Theory and Practice of Harmonisation*, Cheltenham: Edward Elgar, pp. 572–94.

Anderson, Benedict 1983. *Imagined Communities*, London: Verso.

Anderson, Kent and Trevor Ryan 2010. 'Gatekeepers: A Comparative Critique of Admission to the Legal Profession and Japan's New Law Schools', in Stacey Steele and Kathryn Taylor (eds.), *Legal Education in Asia: Globalization, Change and Contexts*, London: Routledge, pp. 45–67.

Andrews, Neil. 2010. 'English Civil Justice in the Age of Convergence', in Janet Walker and Oscar G. Chase (eds.), *Common Law, Civil Law and the Future of Categories*, Markham: LexisNexis Canada, pp. 97–110.

Antokolskaia, Masha 2006. *Harmonisation of Family Law in Europe: A Historical Perspective*, Antwerp: Intersentia.

Antokolskaia, Masha 2007. 'Comparative Family Law: Moving with the Times?', in Esin Örücü and David Nelken (eds.), *Comparative Law: A Handbook*, Oxford: Hart, pp. 241–62.

Aoki, Hitoshi 2001. 'Nobushige Hozumi: A Skillful Transplanter of Western Legal Thought into Japanese Soil', in Annelise Riles (ed.), *Rethinking the Masters of Comparative Law*, Oxford: Hart, pp. 129–50.

Aoki, Masahiko 2001. *Toward a Comparative Institutional Analysis*, Cambridge, MA: MIT Press.

Aoki, Masahiko 2013. 'Historical Sources of Institutional Trajectories in Economic Development: China, Japan and Korea Compared', *Socio-Economic Review*, vol. 11, 233–63.

Apter, Emily 2013. *Against World Literature: On the Politics of Untranslatability*, London: Verso.

Arminjon, Pierre, Boris Nolde and Martin Wolff 1951. *Traité de Droit Comparé*, Paris: Libraire Générale.

Armour, John, Simon Deakin, Priya Lele and Mathias Siems 2009a. 'How Do Legal Rules Evolve? Evidence From a Cross-Country Comparison of Shareholder, Creditor and Worker Protection', *American Journal of Comparative Law*, vol. 57, 579–629.

Armour, John, Simon Deakin, Viviana Mollica and Mathias Siems 2009b, 'Law and Financial Development: What We are Learning from Time-Series Evidence', *BYU Law Review*, 1435–500.

Armour, John, Bernard Black, Brian Cheffins and Richard Nolan 2009c. 'Private Enforcement of Corporate Law: An Empirical Comparison of the United Kingdom and the United States', *Journal of Empirical Legal Studies*, vol. 6, 687–722.

Armytage, Livingston 2009. 'Searching for Success in Judicial Reform: Voices from the Asia Pacific Experience', in Asia Pacific Judicial Forum (ed.), *Searching for Success in Judicial Reform: Voices from the Asia Pacific Experience*, Oxford: Oxford University Press, pp. 3–42.

Arner, Douglas W. 2007. 'Foundations of Financial Development and Economic Growth', in Joseph J. Norton and C. Paul Rogers III (eds.), *Law, Culture and Economic*

Development – A Liber Amicorum for Professor MacLean, London: BIICL, pp. 45–70.

Arrighetti, Alessandro, Reinhard Bachmann and Simon Deakin 1997. 'Contract Law, Social Norms, and Inter-firm Cooperation', *Cambridge Journal of Economics*, vol. 21, 171–95.

Arruñada, Benito 2007. 'Pitfalls to Avoid When Measuring the Institutional Environment: Is Doing Business Damaging Business?', *Journal of Comparative Economics*, vol. 35, 729–47.

Arruñada, Benito and Veneta Andonova 2008. 'Common Law and Civil Law as Pro-Market Adaptations', *Washington University Journal of Law and Policy*, vol. 26, 81–130.

Arold, Nina-Louisa 2007a. *The Legal Culture of The European Court of Human Rights*, Leiden: Nijhoff.

Arold, Nina-Louisa 2007b. 'The European Court of Human Rights as an Example of Convergence', *Nordic Journal of International Law*, vol. 76, 305–22.

Aronson, Bruce 2012. 'The Brave New World of Lawyers in Japan Revisited', *Pacific Rim Law and Policy Journal*, vol. 12, 255–94.

Arter, David 2007, 'Introduction' in David Arter (ed.), *Comparing and Classifying Legislatures*, London: Routledge, pp. xv–xxvii.

Arvind, T. T. 2010. 'The "Transplant Effect" in Harmonization', *International and Comparative Law Quarterly*, vol. 59, 65–88.

Arvind, T. T. and Lindsay Stirton 2010. 'Explaining the Reception of the Code Napoleon in Germany: A fuzzy-set Qualitative Comparative Analysis', *Legal Studies*, vol. 30, 1–29.

Atiyah, Patrick S. 1987. 'Tort Law and the Alternatives: Some Anglo-American Comparisons', *Duke Law Journal*, vol. 36, 1002–44.

Atiyah, Patrick S. and Robert S. Summers 1991. *Form and Substance in Anglo-American Law*, Oxford: Oxford University Press.

Aubyn, Miguel St 2008. 'Law and Order Efficiency Measurement – A Literature Review', Working Paper, available at http://ssrn.com/abstract=1162120.

Aust, Anthony 2010. *Handbook of International Law*, 2nd edn, Cambridge: Cambridge University Press.

Austin, John 1885. *Lectures on Jurisprudence*, 5th edn (edited by Robert Campbell), London: John Murray.

Avilov, Gainan, Bernard Black, Dominique Carreau, Oksana Kozyr, Stilpon Nestor and Sarah Reynolds 1999. 'General Principles of Companies for Transition Economies', *Journal of Corporation Law*, vol. 24, 190–293.

Ayres, Ian and Jonathan R. Macey 2005. 'Institutional and Evolutionary Failure and Economic Development in the Middle East', *Yale Journal of International Law*, vol. 30, 397–428.

Azarian, Reza 2011. 'Potentials and Limitations of Comparative Method in Social Science', *International Journal of Humanities and Social Science*, vol. 1, 113–25.

Backer, Larry Catá 2012, 'Governance Without Government: An Overview', in Günther Handl, Joachim Zekoll and Peer Zumbansen (eds.), *Beyond Territoriality: Transnational Legal Authority in an Age of Globalization*, Leiden: Martinus Nijhoff, pp. 87–123.

Backhouse, Roger, Roger Middleton and Keith Tribe 1997. '"Economics is what economists do", but what do the numbers tell us?', Paper presented at Annual History of Economic Thought Conference.

Bahdi, Reem 2002. 'Globalization of Judgment: Transjudicialism and the Five Faces of International Law in Domestic Courts', *George Washington International Law Review*, vol. 34, 555–603.

Balas, Aron, Rafael La Porta, Florencio Lopez-de-Silanes and Andrei Shleifer 2009. 'The Divergence of Legal Procedures', *American Economic Journal: Economic Policy*, vol. 1, 138–62.

Banakar, Reza 2009. 'Review Essay: Power, Culture and Method in Comparative Law', *International Journal of Law in Context*, vol. 5, 69–85.

Banakar, Reza 2011. 'The Sociology of Law: From Industrialisation to Globalisation', University of Westminster School of Law Research Paper No. 11–03, available at http://ssrn.com/abstract=1761466.

Banakas, Efstathios K. (Stathis) 1993–94. 'The Method of Comparative Law and the Question of Legal Culture Today', *Tilburg Foreign Law Review*, vol. 3, 113–53.

Banakas, Stathis 2008. 'Harmonisation of European Contract Law and General Principles of Contracts: A Common Lawyer's Look into the Future', in Emanuela Navarretta (ed.), *Il Diritto Europeo dei Contratti*, Milano: Giuffrè, pp. 539–59.

Banerjee, Abhijit V. and Esther Duflo 2011. *Poor Economics: A Radical Rethinking of the Way to Fight Global Poverty*, New York: Public Affairs.

Barak, Aharon 2002. 'Foreword: A Judge on Judging: The Role of a Supreme Court in a Democracy', *Harvard Law Review*, vol. 116, 19–162.

Barak, Aharon 2012. *Proportionality: Constitutional Rights and their Limitations*, Cambridge: Cambridge University Press.

Barak-Erez, Daphne 2009. 'The Institutional Aspects of Comparative Law', *Columbia Journal of European Law*, vol. 15, 477–93.

Barber, Benjamin R. 1995. *Jihad vs. McWorld*, New York: Crown, 1995.

Barendrecht, Maurits 2011. 'Legal Aid, Accessible Courts or Legal Information? Three Access to Justice Strategies Compared', *Global Jurist*, vol. 11, issue 1 (Topics), article 6.

Barnard, Catherine 2000. 'Social Dumping and the Race to the Bottom: Some Lessons for the European Union from Delaware?', *European Law Review*, vol. 25, 57–78.

Barnes, Wayne R. 2005. 'Contemplating a Civil Law Paradigm for a Future International Commercial Code', *Louisiana Law Review*, vol. 65, 678–774.

Barnes, Wayne R. 2008. 'The French Subjective Theory of Contract: Separating Rhetoric from Reality', *Tulane Law Review*, vol. 83, 359–93.

Barro, Robert J. 1997. *Getting it Right: Markets and Choices in a Free Society*, Cambridge, MA: MIT Press.

Barron, Gordon 2005. 'The World Bank and Rule of Law Reforms', LSE Working Paper.

Barros, D. Benjamin 2010. 'Introduction', in Benjamin D. Barros (ed.), *Hernando de Soto and Property in a Market Economy*, Farnham: Ashgate, pp. 1–6.

Bartie, Susan 2010. 'The Lingering Core of Legal Scholarship', *Legal Studies*, vol. 30, 345–69.

Bartlett, Katharine T. 1987. 'Storytelling' (book review of *Abortion and Divorce in Western Law* by Mary Ann Glendon), *Duke Law Journal*, vol. 36, 760–8.

Barton, John H., James Lowell Gibbs Jr, Victor H. Li and John Henry Merryman 1983. *Law in Radically Different Cultures*, St Paul: West Publishing.

Bassiouni, M. Cherif 1997. 'Crimes and Criminal Process', *Arab Law Quarterly*, vol. 12, 269–86.

Baudenbacher, Carl 2003. 'Judicial Globalization: New Development or Old Wine in New Bottles?', *Texas International Law Journal*, vol. 38, 505–26.

Baumgartner, Samuel P. 2011. 'Does Access to Justice Improve Countries' Compliance With Human Rights Norms? – An Empirical Study', *Cornell International Law Journal*, vol. 44, 441–91.

Bavinck, Maarten and Gordon R. Woodman 2009. 'Can There be Maps of Law?', in Franz von Benda-Beckmann, Keebet von Benda-Beckmann and Anne Griffiths (eds.), *Spatializing Law: An Anthropological Geography of Law in Society*, Abingdon: Ashgate, pp. 195–218.

Baxi, Upendra 2003. 'The Colonialist Heritage', in Pierre Legrand and Roderick Munday (eds.), *Comparative Legal Studies: Traditions and Transitions*, Cambridge: Cambridge University Press, pp. 46–75.

Baxi, Upendra 2006a. 'Protection of Human Rights and Production of Human Rightlessness in India', in Randall Peerenboom and Albert H. Y. Chen (eds.), *Human Rights in Asia, France, and the US*, London: Routledge, pp. 384–412.

Baxi, Upendra 2006b. *The Future of Human Rights*, 2nd edn, New Delhi: Oxford University Press.

Baxi, Upendra 2009. 'The Renascent Access Nations', in Ayesha Kadwani Dias and Gita Honwana Welch (eds.), *Justice for the Poor: Perspectives on Accelerating Access*, Oxford: Oxford University Press, pp. 77–102.

Beale, Hugh 2013. 'Characteristics of Contract Laws and the European Optional Instrument', in Horst Eidenmüller (ed.), *Regulatory Competition in Contract Law and Dispute Resolution*, Munich: Beck, pp. 313–36.

Bebchuk, Lucian Arye and Mark J. Roe 1999. 'A Theory of Path Dependence in Corporate Ownership and Governance', *Stanford Law Review*, vol. 52, 127–70.

Beck, Thorsten and Ross Levine 2005. 'Legal Institutions and Financial Development', in Claude Menard and Mary M. Shirley (eds.), *Handbook of New Institutional Economics*, Dordrecht: Springer, pp. 251–78.

Beck, Thorsten, Asli Demirguc-Kunt and Ross Levine 2003. 'Law and Finance. Why Does Legal Origin Matter?', *Journal of Comparative Economics*, vol. 31, 653–75.

Beck, Thorsten and Luc Laeven 2006. 'Institution Building and Growth in Transition Economies', *Journal of Economic Growth*, vol. 11, 157–86.

Beck, Ulrich and Natan Sznaider 2010. 'Unpacking Cosmopolitanism for the Social Sciences: A Research Agenda', *The British Journal of Sociology*, 381–403.

Bell, John 1995. 'Comparative Law and Legal Theory', in Werner Krawietz, Neil MacCormick and Georg Henrik von Wright (eds.), *Prescriptive Formality and Normative Rationality in Modern Legal Systems: Festschrift for Robert Summers*, Berlin: Duncker and Humblot, pp. 19–31.

Bell, John 2001. *French Legal Cultures*, London: Butterworths.

Bell, John 2006a. *Judiciaries within Europe: A Comparative Review*, Cambridge: Cambridge University Press.

Bell, John 2006b. 'Reflections on Continental European Supreme Courts', in Guy Canivet, Mads Andenas and Duncan Fairgrieve (eds.), *Independence, Accountability and the Judiciary*, London: BIICL, pp. 253–63.

Bell, John 2006c. 'Comparative Administrative Law', in Mathias Reimann and Reinhard Zimmermann (eds.), *The Oxford Handbook of Comparative Law*, Oxford: Oxford University Press, pp. 1259–86.

Bell, John 2011. 'Legal Research and the Distinctiveness of Comparative Law', in Mark Van Hoecke (ed.), *Methodologies of Legal Research*, Oxford: Hart, pp. 155–76.

Bell, John 2012. 'The Argumentative Status of Foreign Legal Arguments', *Utrecht Law Review*, vol. 8, 8–19.

Bellantuono, Giuseppe 2012. 'Comparative Legal Diagnostics', Working Paper, available at http://ssrn.com/abstract=2000608.

Benedict, Ruth 1946. *The Chrysanthemum and the Sword*, Boston: Houghton Mifflin Co.

Bennett, T. W. 2006. 'Comparative Law and African Customary Law', in Mathias Reimann and Reinhard Zimmermann (eds.), *The Oxford Handbook of Comparative Law*, Oxford: Oxford University Press, pp. 641–73.

Benton, Lauren 2002. *Law and Colonial Cultures: Legal Regimes in World History 1400–1900*, Cambridge: Cambridge University Press.

Benvenisti, Eyal and George W. Downs 2012. 'National Courts Review of Transnational Private Regulation', in Fabrizio Cafaggi (ed.), *Enforcement of Transnational Regulation*, Cheltenham: Edward Elgar, pp. 131–46.

Benvenuto, Osmar J. 2006. 'Reevaluating the Debate Surrounding the Supreme Court's Use of Foreign Precedent', *Fordham Law Review*, vol. 38, 2695–759.

Beramendi, Pablo 2007. 'Federalism', in Carles Boix and Susan C. Stokes (eds.), *The Oxford Handbook of Comparative Politics*, Oxford: Oxford University Press, pp. 752–81.

Berger, Klaus Peter 2000. 'The New Law Merchant and The Global Market: A 21st Century View of Transnational Commercial Law', *International Arbitration Law Review*, vol. 3, 91–102.

Berger, Klaus Peter 2010. *The Creeping Codification of the New Lex Mercatoria*, 2nd edn, The Hague: Kluwer.

Berggren, Niclas and Christian Bjørnskov 2013. 'Does Religiosity Promote Property Rights and the Rule of Law?', *Journal of Institutional Economics*, vol. 9, 161–85.

Berkowitz, Daniel, Katharina Pistor and Jean-François Richard 2003a. 'Economic Development, Legality, and the Transplant Effect', *European Economic Review*, vol. 47, 165–95.

Berkowitz, Daniel, Katharina Pistor and Jean-François Richard 2003b. 'The Transplant Effect', *American Journal of Comparative Law*, vol. 51, 163–204.

Berman, Harold J. 1974. *The Interaction of Law and Religion*, London: SCM Press.

Berman, Harold J. 1983. *Law and Revolution: The Formation of the Western Legal Tradition*, Cambridge, MA: Harvard University Press.

Berman, Harold J. 2006. *Law and Revolution II: The Impact of the Protestant Reformation on the Western Legal Tradition*, Cambridge, MA: Harvard University Press.

Berman, Paul Schiff 2009. 'The New Legal Pluralism', *Annual Review of Law and Social Science*, vol. 5, 225–42.

Berman, Paul Schiff 2012. *Global Legal Pluralism: A Jurisprudence of Law Beyond Borders*, Cambridge: Cambridge University Press.

Bernitz, Ulf 2007. 'What is Scandinavian Law? Concept, Characteristics, Future', *Scandinavian Studies in Law*, vol. 50, 13–29.

Berry, John W., Ype H. Poortinga, Seger M. Breugelmans, Athanasios Chasiotis and David L. Sam 2011. *Cross-Cultural Psychology: Research and Applications*, 3rd edn, Cambridge: Cambridge University Press.

Berry, William W. 2011. 'The European Prescription for Ending the Death Penalty', *Wisconsin Law Review*, 1003–25.

Bingham, Tom 2010a. *Widening Horizons: The Influence of Comparative Law and International Law on Domestic Law*, Cambridge: Cambridge University Press.

Bingham, Tom 2010b. *The Rule of Law*, London: Allen Lane.

Bjørnskov, Christian and Stefan Voigt 2013. 'Constitutional Garrulity and Social Trust', Working Paper, available at http://ssrn.com/abstract=2271580.

Black, Bernard and Reiner Kraakman 1996. 'A Self Enforcing Model of Corporate Law', *Harvard Law Review*, vol. 109, 1911–82.

Black, Donald 1976. *The Behavior of Law*, New York: Academic Press.

Black, Ryan C. and James F. Spriggs II 2013. 'The Citation and Depreciation of U.S. Supreme Court Precedent', *Journal of Empirical Legal Studies*, vol. 10, 325–58.

Blakesley, Christopher L., Edwin B. Firmage, Richard F. Scott and Sharon A. Williams 2001. *The International Legal System*, 5th edn, New York: Foundation Press.

Blank, Jos, Martin van der Ende, Bart van Hulst and Rob Jagtenberg 2004. 'Bench Marking in an International Perspective: An International Comparison of the Mechanisms and Performance of the Judiciary System', available at http://siteresources.worldbank.org/INTLAWJUSTINST/Resources/Benchmarking.pdf.

Blankenburg, Erhard 1992. 'A Flood of Litigation? Legal Cultures and Litigation Flows Before European Courts in Historical and Comparative Perspective', *The Justice System Journal*, vol. 16, 101–10.

Blankenburg, Erhard 1994. 'The Infrastructure for Avoiding Civil Litigation: Comparing Cultures of Legal Behavior in the Netherlands and West Germany', *Law and Society Review*, vol. 28, 789–808.

Blankenburg, Erhard 1997. 'Civil Litigation Rates as Indicators for Legal Culture', in David Nelken (ed.), *Comparing Legal Cultures*, Aldershot: Dartmouth, pp. 41–68.

Blankenburg, Erhard 1998. 'Patterns of Legal Culture: The Netherlands Compared to Neighboring Germany', *American Journal of Comparative Law*, vol. 46, 1–41.

Blankenburg, Erhard and Ralf Rogowski 1986. 'German Labour Courts and the British Industrial Tribunal System. A Socio-Legal Comparison of Degrees of Judicialisation', *Journal of Law and Society*, vol. 13, 67–92.

Blankenburg, Erhard and J. R. A. Verwoerd 1988. 'The Courts as a Final Resort?: Some Comparisons between the Legal Cultures of the Netherlands and the Federal Republic of Germany', *Netherlands International Law Review*, vol. 35, 7–28.

Bloch, Maurice 1977. 'The Past and the Present in the Present', *Man*, vol. 12, 278–92.

Bloise, Joëlle Sambuc 2010. 'International Human Rights Law in Japan: the Cultural Factor Revisited', Working Paper, available at http://ssrn.com/abstract=1715348.

Blutman, Laszlo 2010. 'In the Trap of a Legal Metaphor: International Soft Law', *International and Comparative Law Quarterly*, vol. 59, 605–24.

Boas, Franz 1896. 'The Limitations of the Comparative Method in Anthropology', *Science (new series)*, vol. 4, 901–8.

Bobek, Michal 2009. 'Quantity or Quality? Reassessing the Role of Supreme Jurisdictions in Central Europe', *American Journal of Comparative Law*, vol. 57, 33–65.

Bobek, Michal 2013. *Comparative Reasoning in European Supreme Courts*, Oxford: Oxford University Press.

Bogdan, Michael 1994. *Comparative Law*, Stockholm: Kluwer.

Bogdan, Michael 2009. 'Development Assistance in the Legal Field: Promotion of Market Economy v Human Rights', in Antonina Bakardjieva Engelbrekt and Joakim Nergelius (eds.), *New Directions in Comparative Law*, Cheltenham: Edward Elgar, pp. 33–9.

Bogdan, Michael 2013. *Concise Introduction to Comparative Law*, Groningen: Europa Law Publishing.

Bohannan Paul 1957. *Justice and Judgment Among the Tiv*, Oxford: Oxford University Press.

Bohannan Paul 1965. 'The Differing Realms of the Law', *American Anthropologist*, vol. 67, 33–42.

Bollen, Kenneth A., Barbara Entwisle and Arthur S. Anderson 1993. 'Macrocomparative Research Methods', *Annual Review of Sociology*, vol. 19, 321–51.

Bomhoff, Jacco 2012. 'Comparing Legal Argument', in Maurice Adams and Jacco Bomhoff (eds.), *Practice and Theory in Comparative Law*, Cambridge: Cambridge University Press, pp. 74–95.

Bomhoff, Jacco and Anne Meuwese 2011. 'The Meta-regulation of Transnational Private Regulation', *Journal of Law and Society*, vol. 38, 138–62.

Borg-Barthet, Justin 2010. 'A New Approach to the Governing Law of Companies in the EU: A Legislative Proposal', *Journal of Private International Law*, vol. 6, 589–621.

Botero, Juan, Simeon Djankov, Rafael La Porta, Florencio Lopez-de-Silanes and Andrei Shleifer 2004. 'The Regulation of Labor', *Quarterly Journal of Economics*, vol. 119, 1340–82.

Bothe, Michael and Georg Ress 1980. 'The Comparative Method and Public International Law', in William E. Butler (ed.), *International Law in Comparative Perspective*, Alphen aan den Rijn: Sijthoff & Noordhoff, pp. 49–66.

Botzem, Sebastian and Jeanette Hofmann 2010. 'Transnational Governance Spirals: The Transformation of Rule-making Authority in Internet Regulation and Corporate Financial Reporting', *Critical Policy Studies*, vol. 4, 18–37.

Boulanger, Christian and Austin Sarat 2005. 'Putting Culture into the Picture: Toward a Comparative Analysis of State Killings', in Austin Sarat and Christian Boulanger (eds.), *The Cultural Lives of Capital Punishment*, Stanford, CA: Stanford University Press, pp. 1–45.

Boulle, Laurence 2009. *The Law of Globalization*, Alphen aan den Rijn: Kluwer.

Bourdieu, Pierre 1996. *The State Nobility*, Stanford: Stanford University Press.

Bowen, John R. 2007. *Why the French Don't Like Headscarves: Islam, the State, and Public Space*, Princeton: Princeton University Press.

Bowring, Bill 2008. *The Degradation of the International Legal Order?*, Abingdon: Routledge-Cavendish.

Boycko, Maxim, Andrei Shleifer and Robert Vishny 1997. *Privatizing Russia*, Cambridge, MA: MIT Press.

Boyd, Robert and Peter J. Richerson 1985. *Culture and the Evolutionary Process*, Chicago: University of Chicago Press.

Bradford, Anu 2012. 'The Brussels Effect', *Northwestern University Law Review*, vol. 107, 1–68.

Bradney, Anthony and Fiona Cownie 2000. *Living Without Law: An Ethnography of Quaker Decision-Making, Dispute Avoidance and Dispute Resolution*. Aldershot: Ashgate.

Bradshaw, York and Michael Wallace 1991. 'Informing Generality and Explaining Uniqueness: The Place of Case Studies in Comparative Research', *International Journal of Comparative Sociology*, vol. 32, 154–71.

Brandt, Oliver 2007. 'Conceptual Comparison: Towards a Coherent Methodology of Comparative Legal Studies', *Brooklyn Journal of International Studies*, vol. 32, 405–66.

Braun, Alexandra 2006. 'Professors and Judges in Italy: It Takes Two to Tango', *Oxford Journal of Legal Studies*, vol. 26, 665–81.

Brems, Eva 2001. *Human Rights: Universality and Diversity*, The Hague: Martinus Nijhoff.

Breton, Albert and Michael J. Trebilcock (eds.) 2006. *Bijuralism: An Economic Approach*, Aldershot: Ashgate.

Breton, Albert, Anne Des Ormeaux, Katharina Pistor and Pierre Salmon (eds.) 2009. *Multijuralism: Manifestations, Causes, and Consequences*, Farnham: Ashgate.

Breyer, Stephen 2003. 'Keynote Address', *American Society of International Law Proceedings*, vol. 97, 265–71.

Brooks, Rosa 2003. 'The New Imperialism: Violence, Norms, and the "Rule of Law"', *Michigan Law Review*, vol. 101, 2275–340.

Brown Hamano, Sylvia 1999. 'Incomplete Revolutions and Not So Alien Transplants: The Japanese Constitution and Human Rights', *University of Pennsylvania Journal of Constitutional Law*, vol. 1, 415–91.

Brown, Larry 2001. 'Diffusion: Geographical Aspects', in Neil J. Smelser and Paul B. Baltes (eds.), *International Encyclopedia of Social and Behavioral Sciences*, New York: Elsevier, vol. 6, 3676–81.

Brüggemeier, Gert, Aurelia Colombi Ciacchi and Patrick O'Callaghan (eds.) 2010. *Personality Rights in European Tort Law*, Cambridge: Cambridge University Press.

Brummer, Chris 2010. 'Why Soft Law Dominates International Finance – And Not Trade', *Journal of International Economic Law*, vol. 13, 623–43.

Bryan, Bradley 2004. 'Justice and Advantage in Civil Procedure: Langbein's Conception of Comparative Law and Procedural Justice in Question', *Tulsa Journal of Comparative and International Law*, vol. 11, 521–55.

Bundesminister der Justiz (ed.) 1992. *Abschlußbericht der Kommission zur Überarbeitung des Schuldrechts*, Bonn: Bundesanzeiger-Verlag.

Burke, John 2011, 'One', available at http://eilfe.com/biased-journalism/one/.

Buscaglia, Edgardo 2001. 'An Analysis of Judicial Corruption and its Causes: An Objective Governing-based Approach', *International Review of Law and Economics*, vol. 21, 233–49.

Buscaglia, Edgardo and William Ratliff 2000. *Law and Economics in Developing Countries*, Stanford, CA: Hoover Institution Press.

Buscaglia, Edgardo and Paul B. Stephan 2005. 'An Empirical Assessment of the Impact of Formal Versus Informal Dispute Resolution on Poverty: A Governance-based Approach', *International Review of Law and Economics*, vol. 25, 89–106.

Busch, Per-Olof, Helge Jörgens and Kersin Tews 2005. 'The Global Diffusion of Regulatory Instruments: The Making of a New International Environmental Regime', *The Annals of the American Academy of Political and Social Sciences*, vol. 598, 146–67.

Bussani, Mauro and Ugo Mattei (eds.) 2000. *Making European Law: Essays on the Common Core Project*, Trento: Quaderni del Dipartimento di Scienze Giuridiche.

Bussani, Mauro and Ugo Mattei (eds.) 2002. *The Common Core of European Contract Law: Essays on the Project*, The Hague: Kluwer.

Bussani, Mauro and Ugo Mattei (eds.) 2007. *Opening Up European Law, The Common Core Project*, Bern: Staempfli.

Bussani, Mauro and Ugo Mattei (eds.) 2012. *Cambridge Companion to Comparative Law*, Cambridge: Cambridge University Press.

Büthe, Tim and Walter Mattli 2011. *The New Global Rules: The Privatization of Regulation in the World Economy*, Princeton: Princeton University Press.

Butler, William W. 2011. 'Renaissance of Slavonic Law?', in William E. Butler, Oleksiy V. Kresin and I. S. Shemshuchenko (eds.), *Foundations of Comparative Law: Methods and Typologies*, London: Wildy, Simmonds and Hill Publishing, pp. 331–6 (also in *Journal of Comparative Law*, vol. 5 (2010), 261–4).

Buxbaum, Richard M. 2009. 'Comparative Law as a Bridge Between the Nation-State and the Global Economy: An Essay for Herbert Bernstein', *Duke Law CICLOPs*, vol. 1, 63–78.

Cafaggi, Fabrizio 2011. 'New Foundations of Transnational Private Regulation', *Journal of Law and Society*, vol. 38, 20–49.

Calabresi, Guido 1985. *A Common Law for the Age of Statutes*, Cambridge, MA: Harvard University Press.

Calhoun, Craig, Joseph Gerteis, James Moody, Steven Pfaff and Indermohan Virk 2002. *Contemporary Sociological Theory*, Oxford: Blackwell.

Calliess, Gralf-Peter 2007. 'The Making of Transnational Contract Law', *Indiana Journal of Global Legal Studies*, vol. 14, 469–83.

Calliess, Gralf-Peter 2012. 'Law, Transnational', in Mark Juergensmeyer, Helmut Anheier and Victor Faessel (eds.), *The Encyclopedia of Global Studies*, Thousand Oaks: Sage, pp. 1036–40.

Calliess, Gralf-Peter and Hermann B. Hoffmann 2009. 'Judicial Services for Global Commerce – Made in Germany?', *German Law Journal*, vol. 10, 115–22.

Campbell, John L. 2010. 'Institutional Reproduction and Change', in Glenn Morgan, John L. Campbell, Colin Crouch, Ove Kaj Pedersen and Richard Whitley (eds.), *The Oxford Handbook of Comparative Institutional Analysis*, Oxford: Oxford University Press, pp. 87–115.

Campos-Ortiz, Francisco, Louis Putterman, T. K. Ahn, Loukas Balafoutas, Mongoljin Batsaikhan and Matthias Sutter 2012. 'Security of Property as a Public Good: Institutions, Socio-Political Environment and Experimental Behavior in Five Countries', CESifo Working Paper Series No. 4003, available at http://ssrn.com/abstract=2181356.

Canivet, Guy 2006. 'The Practice of Comparative Law by the Supreme Courts: Brief Reflections on the Dialogue Between the Judges in French and European Experience', *Tulane Law Review*, vol. 80, 1377–400.

Canivet, Guy, Mads Andenas and Duncan Fairgrieve (eds.) 2004. *Comparative Law Before the Courts*, London: BIICL.

Cao, Deborah 2007. 'Inter-lingual Uncertainty in Bilingual and Multilingual Law', *Journal of Pragmatics*, vol. 39, 69–83.

Cappelletti, Mauro et al. 1978/79. *Access to Justice: vol. I, A World Survey* (Mauro Cappelletti and Bryant Garth, eds.), *vol. II, Promising Situations* (Mauro Cappelletti and John Weisner, eds.), *vol. III: Emerging Issues and Perspectives* (Mauro Cappelletti and Bryant Garth, eds.), *vol. IV, The Anthropological Perspective* (Klaus-Friedrich Koch, ed.), Alphen aan den Rijn: Sijthoff and Noordhoff.

Cappelletti, Mauro and Bryant G. Garth 1987. 'Introduction – Policies, Trends and Ideas in Civil Procedure', in *International Encyclopedia of Comparative Law*, Volume XVI Civil Procedure, Tübingen: Mohr Siebeck, ch. 1.

Cardoso, Fernando Henrique and Enzo Faletto 1979. *Dependency and Development in Latin America*, Berkeley: University of California Press.

Carney, William J. 1997. 'The Political Economy of Competition for Corporate Charters', *Journal of Legal Studies*, vol. 36, 303–29.

Carney, William J. 1998, 'The Production of Corporate Law', *Southern California Law Review*, vol. 71, 715–80.

Carothers, Thomas 2006. 'The Rule of Law Revival', in Thomas Carothers (ed.), *Promoting the Rule of Law Abroad: In Search of Knowledge*, Washington: Carnegie, pp. 3–13 (originally published in *Foreign Affairs*, vol. 77, 95–106).

Carothers, Thomas 2010. 'Rule of Law Temptations', in James J. Heckman, Robert L. Nelson and Lee Cabatingan (eds.), *Global Perspectives on the Rule of Law*, Abingdon: Routledge, pp. 17–27.

Cartwright, John and Martijn Hesselink (eds.) 2009. *Precontractual Liability in European Private Law*, Cambridge: Cambridge University Press.

Casper, Steven 2001. 'The Legal Framework for Corporate Governance: The Influence of Contract Law on Company Strategy in Germany and the United States', in Peter A. Hall and David Soskice (eds.), *Varieties of Capitalism: The Institutional Foundations of Comparative Advantage*, Oxford: Oxford University Press, pp. 387–416.

Cassese, Sabino 2010. 'Is there a Global Administrative Law?', in Armin von Bogdandy et al. (eds.), *The Exercise of Public Authority by International Institutions*, Springer: Berlin, pp. 761–76.

Cassese, Sabino 2012. *The Global Policy*, Seville: Editorial Derecho Global.

Castles, Francis G. (ed.) 1993. *Families of Nations: Patterns of Public Policy in Western Democracies*, Dartmouth: Aldershot.

Castles, Francis G. 2004. *The Future of the Welfare State*, Oxford: Oxford University Press.

Caterina, Raffaele 2004. 'Comparative Law and the Cognitive Revolution', *Tulane Law Review*, vol. 78, 1501–47.

Cavadino, Michael and James Dignan 2006. *Penal Systems: A Comparative Approach*, New York: Sage.

Cavadino, Michael and James Dignan 2011. 'Penal Comparisons: Puzzling Relations', in Adam Crawford (ed.), *International and Comparative Criminal Justice and Urban Governance*, Cambridge: Cambridge University Press, pp. 193–213.

Center for Policy and Human Development 2007. *Afghanistan Human Development Report. Bridging Modernity and Tradition: Rule of Law and the Search of Justice*, Islamabad: Army Press, available at http://hdr.undp.org/en/reports/nationalreports/asiathepacific/afghanistan/nhdr2007.pdf.

CEPEJ (European Commission for the Efficiency of Justice) 2012. *European Judicial Systems*, Belgium: Council of Europe, also available at www.coe.int/t/dghl/cooperation/cepej/evaluation/2012/Rapport_en.pdf.

Chaihark, Hahm 2006. 'Human Rights in Korea', in Randall Peerenboom, Carole J. Petersen and Albert H. Y. Chen (eds.), *Human Rights in Asia*, London and New York: Routledge, pp. 265–97.

Chanchani, Shalin and Theivananthampillai, Paul 2004. 'Typologies of Culture', Working Paper, available http://ssrn.com/abstract=1441609.

Chang, Wen-Chen and Jiunn-Rong Yeh 2012. 'Internationalization of Constitutional Law', in Michel Rosenfeld and Andras Sajo (eds.), *The Oxford Handbook of Comparative Constitutional Law*, Oxford: Oxford University Press, pp. 1165–84.

Chao-Chun Lin, Frederick 2006. 'The Implementation of Human Rights Law in Taiwan', in Randall Peerenboom, Carole J. Petersen and Albert H. Y. Chen (eds.), *Human Rights in Asia*, London and New York: Routledge, pp. 298–345.

Charny, David 1990. 'Nonlegal Sanctions in Commercial Relationships', *Harvard Law Review*, vol. 104, 375–467.

Charny, David 1998. 'The German Corporate Governance-System', *Columbia Business Law Review*, 145–66.

Charron, Nicholas, Carl Dahlström and Victor Lapuente 2012. 'No Law without a State', *Journal of Comparative Economics*, vol. 40, 176–93.

Chase, Oscar G. 1997. 'Legal Processes and National Culture', *Cardozo Journal of International and Comparative Law*, vol. 5, 1–24.

Chase, Oscar G. 2002. 'American "Exceptionalism" and Comparative Procedure', *American Journal of Comparative Law*, vol. 50, 277–301.

Chase, Oscar G. and Helen Hershkoff (eds.) 2007. *Civil Litigation in Comparative Context*, St Paul, MN: Thomson and West.

Chase, Oscar G. and Janet Walker 2010. 'Common Law, Civil Law and the Future of Categories: An Introduction', in Janet Walker and Oscar G. Chase (eds.), *Common Law, Civil Law and the Future of Categories*, Markham: LexisNexis Canada, pp. ii–lxviii.

Chase, Oscar G. and Vicenzo Varano 2012. 'Comparative Civil Justice', in Mauro Bussani and Ugo Mattei (eds.), *Cambridge Companion to Comparative Law*, Cambridge: Cambridge University Press, pp. 210–40.

Cheffins, Brian R. 2008. *Corporate Ownership and Control: British Business Transformed*, Oxford: Oxford University Press.

Chen, Albert H. Y. 1999. 'Towards a Legal Enlightenment: Discussions in Contemporary China on the Rule of Law', *UCLA Pacific Basin Law Journal*, vol. 17, 125–65.

Chen, Albert H. Y. 2006. 'Conclusion: Comparative Reflections on Human Rights in Asia', in Randall Peerenboom, Carole J. Petersen and Albert H. Y. Chen (eds.), *Human Rights in Asia*, London and New York: Routledge, pp. 487–516.

Chen, Jianfu 2007. *Chinese Law: Context and Transformation*, Leiden: Martinus Nijhoff.

Chen-Wishard, Mindy 1989. *Unconscionable Bargains*, Wellington: Butterworths.

Chiapello, Eve and Karim Medjad 2009. 'An Unprecedented Privatisation of Mandatory Standard-setting: The Case of European Accounting Policy', *Critical Perspectives on Accounting*, vol. 20, 448–68.

Childress, Steven Alan 2007. 'Lawyers', in David S. Clark (ed.), *Encyclopedia of Law and Society: American and Global Perspectives*, Thousand Oaks: Sage, vol. 2, pp. 930–7.

Chinn, Menzie D. and Hiro Ito 2006. 'What Matters for Financial Development? Capital Controls, Institutions, and Interactions', *Journal of Development Economics*, vol. 81, 163–92.

Chiu, Man-Chung 2010. 'Going Beyond Globalization and Localization: Articulating a Theory of Justice in Han-Chinese Culture', *Law and Critique*, vol. 21, 93–110.

Chodosh, Hiram E. 1999. 'Comparing Comparisons: In Search of Methodology', *Iowa Law Review*, vol. 84, 1025–131.

Chodosh, Hiram E. 2005. *Global Justice Reform: A Comparative Methodology*, New York: NYU Press.

Chong, Alberto and Cesar Calderon 2000. 'Causality and Feedback Between Institutional Measures and Economic Growth', *Economics and Politics*, vol. 12, 69–81.

Choudhry, Sujit 1999. 'Globalization in Search of Justification: Toward a Theory of Comparative Constitutional Interpretation', *Indiana Law Journal*, vol. 74, 819–92.

Choudhry, Sujit 2006. 'Migration as a New Metaphor in Comparative Constitutional Law', in Sujit Choudhry (ed.), *The Migration of Constitutional Ideas*, Cambridge: Cambridge University Press, pp. 1–35.

Cioffi, John W. 2009. 'Legal Regimes and Political Particularism: An Assessment of the "Legal Families" Theory from the Perspectives of Comparative Law and Political Economy', *BYU Law Review*, 1501–52.

Clark, David S. 2002. 'The Organization of Lawyers and Judges', in *International Encyclopedia of Comparative Law*, Volume XVI Civil Procedure, Tübingen: Mohr Siebeck, ch. 3.

Clark, David S. 2012. 'History of Comparative Law and Society', 'Legal Education' and 'Legal Professions and Law Firms', in David S. Clark (ed.), *Comparative Law and Society*, Cheltenham: Edward Elgar, pp. 1–36, 328–61, 362–402.

Clarke, Donald 2003. 'Economic Development and the Rights Hypothesis: The China Problem', *American Journal of Comparative Law*, vol. 51, 89–111.

Clarke, Donald, Peter Murrell and Susan Whiting 2008. 'The Role of Law in China's Economic Development', in Thomas Rawski and Loren Brandt (eds.), *China's Great Economic Transformation*, Cambridge: Cambridge University Press, pp. 375–428.

Clasen, Jochen 2004. 'Defining Comparative Social Policy', in Patricia Kennett (ed.), *A Handbook of Comparative Social Policy*, Cheltenham: Edward Elgar, pp. 91–102.

Coe, Neil M., Philip F. Kelly and Henry W. C. Yeung 2010. *Economic Geography*, Malden, AM: Blackwell.

Coffee, John C. 1999. 'The Future as History: The Prospects for Global Convergence in Corporate Governance and its Implications', *Northwestern University Law Review*, vol. 93, 641–708.

Coffee, John C. 2002. 'Convergence and Its Critics: What are the Preconditions to the Separation of Ownership and Control?', in Joseph A. McCahery et al. (eds.), *Corporate Governance Regimes: Convergence and Diversity*, Oxford: Oxford University Press, pp. 83–112.

Cohen, Jane Maslow 1989. 'Comparison-Shopping in the Marketplace of Rights' (book review of *Abortion and Divorce in Western Law* by Mary Ann Glendon), *Yale Law Journal*, vol. 98, 1235–76.

Cohen, Jerome 1968. *Criminal Process in the People's Republic of China, 1949–63*, Cambridge, MA: Harvard University Press.

Cohen-Tanugi, Laurent 1985. *Le Droit sans l'État*, Paris: PUF.

Cohen-Tanugi, Laurent 1996. 'The Law without the State', in Volkmar Gessner, Armin Hoeland and Casba Varga (eds.), *European Legal Cultures*, Dartmouth: Aldershot, pp. 269–73.

Cohn, Margit 2010. 'Legal Transplant Chronicles: The Evolution of Unreasonableness and Proportionality Review of the Administration in the United Kingdom', *American Journal of Comparative Law*, vol. 58, 583–629.

Cole, Daniel H. 2013. 'The Varieties of Comparative Institutional Analysis', *Wisconsin Law Review*, 383–409.

Collier, David and James Mahoney 1996. 'Insights and Pitfalls: Selection Bias in Qualitative Research', *World Politics*, vol. 49, 56–91.

Collier, David and Steven Levitsky 1997. 'Democracy with Adjective: Conceptual Innovation in Comparative Research', *World Politics*, vol. 49, 430–51.

Collier, Paul 2007. *The Bottom Billion*, Oxford: Oxford University Press.

Collins, Hugh 2008. *The European Civil Code: The Way Forward*, Cambridge: Cambridge University Press.

Collins, Hugh 2011. 'Flipping Wreck: Lex Mercatoria on the Shoals of Ius Cogens', conference paper, available at www.lse.ac.uk/collections/law/projects/tlp/conference.htm (and forthcoming in Stefan Grundmann, Karl Riesenhuber and Florian Möslein (eds.), *Contract Governance*, Oxford: Oxford University Press).

Collins, Hugh, 2013. 'Regulatory Competition in International Trade: Transnational Regulation through Standard Form Contracts', in Horst Eidenmüller (ed.), *Regulatory Competition in Contract Law and Dispute Resolution*, Munich: Beck, pp. 121–41.

Commission Staff Working Document 2007, 'Report on the Implementation of the Directive on Takeover Bids of 21 February 2007', SEC(2007) 268, available at http://ec.europa.eu/internal market/company/docs/takeoverbids/2007–02-report en.pdf.

Commission Staff Working Document 2008, 'Report on the Application by the Member States of the EU of the Commission Recommendation on the Role of Non-executive or Supervisory Directors of Listed Companies and on the Committees of the (Supervisory) Board of 13 July 2008', SEC(2007) 1021, available at http://ec.europa.eu/internal_market/company/docs/independence/sec20071022_en.pdf.

Constantinesco, Leontin-Jean 1971. *Rechtsvergleichung, Band I: Einführung in die Rechtsvergleichung*, Cologne: Carl Heymanns.

Constantinesco, Leontin-Jean 1972. *Rechtsvergleichung, Band II: Die rechtsvergleichende Methode*, Cologne: Carl Heymanns.

Constantinesco, Leontin-Jean 1983. *Rechtsvergleichung, Band III: Die rechtsvergleichende Wissenschaft*, Cologne: Carl Heymanns.

Cooke, Robin 2004. 'The Road Ahead for the Common Law', *International and Comparative Law Quarterly*, vol. 53, 273–86.

Cools, Sofie 2005. 'The Real Difference in Corporate Law between the United States and Continental Europe: Distribution of Powers', *Delaware Journal of Corporate Law*, vol. 36, 697–766.

Cooter, Robert D. and Wolfgang Fikentscher, 1998. 'Indian Common Law: The Role of Custom in American Indian Tribal Courts', *American Journal of Comparative Law*, vol. 46, 287–330 and 509–80.

Cooter, Robert D. and Tom Ginsburg 1996. 'Comparative Judicial Discretion', *International Review of Law and Economics*, vol. 16, 295–313.

Cooter, Robert D. and Tom Ginsburg 2003. 'Leximetrics: Why the Same Laws are Longer in Some Countries than Others', Research Paper, available at http://ssrn.com/abstract=456520.

Cooter, Robert D. and Hans-Bernd Schäfer 2011. *Solomon's Knot: How Law Can End the Poverty of Nations*, Princeton: Princeton University Press.

Cossmann, Brenda 1997. 'Turning the Gaze Back on Itself: Comparative Law, Feminist Legal Studies and the Postcolonial Project', *Utah Law Review*, 525–44.

Cotterrell, Roger 1997. 'The Concept of Legal Culture', in David Nelken (ed.), *Comparing Legal Cultures*, Aldershot: Dartmouth, pp. 13–31.

Cotterrell, Roger 2001. 'Is There a Logic of Legal Transplants?', David Nelken and Johannes Feest (eds.), *Adapting Legal Culture*, Oxford: Hart, pp. 71–92.

Cotterrell, Roger 2002. 'Seeking Similarity, Appreciating Difference: Comparative Law and Communities', in Andrew Harding and Esin Örücü (eds.), *Comparative Law in the 21st Century*, New York: Kluwer, pp. 35–54.

Cotterrell, Roger 2003. 'Comparatists and Sociology', in Pierre Legrand and Roderick Munday (eds.), *Comparative Legal Studies: Traditions and Transitions*, Cambridge: Cambridge University Press, pp. 131–53.

Cotterrell, Roger 2006. 'Comparative Law and Culture', in Mathias Reimann and Reinhard Zimmermann (eds.), *The Oxford Handbook of Comparative Law*, Oxford: Oxford University Press, pp. 709–37.

Cotterrell, Roger 2007. 'Is it so Bad to be Different? Comparative Law and the Appreciation of Diversity', in Esin Örücü and David Nelken (eds.), *Comparative Law: A Handbook*, Oxford: Hart, pp. 133–54.

Cotterrell, Roger 2012. 'Comparative Sociology of Law', in David S. Clark (ed.), *Comparative Law and Society*. Cheltenham: Edward Elgar, pp. 39–60.

Cottrell, Patrick and David M. Trubeck 2012. 'Law as Problem Solving: Standards Networks Experimentation and Deliberation in Global Space', *Transnational Law & Contemporary Problems*, vol. 21, 359–93.

Cotula, Lorenzo 2011. *Law and Negotiating Power in Foreign Investment: Shades of Grey in the Shadow of the Law*, New York: Routledge.

Coutin, Susan 2000. *Legalizing Moves: Salvadoran Immigrants' Struggle for U.S. Residency*, Ann Arbor: University of Michigan Press.

Cuniberti, Gilles (2011), *Grands Systèmes de Droit Contemporains*, 2nd edn, Paris: L.G.D.J.

Curran, Vivian Grosswald 1998a. 'Cultural Immersion, Difference and Categories in U.S. Comparative Law', *American Journal of Comparative Law*, vol. 46, 43–92.

Curran, Vivian Grosswald 1998b. 'Dealing in Difference: Comparative Law's Potential for Broadening Legal Perspectives', *American Journal of Comparative Law*, vol. 46, 657–68.

Curran, Vivian Grosswald 2001a. 'Romantic Common Law, Enlightened Civil Law: Legal Uniformity and Homogenization of the European Union', *Columbia Journal of European Law*, vol. 7, 63–126.

Curran, Vivian Grosswald 2001b. 'Rethinking Hemann Kantorowicz: Free Law, American Legal Realism and the Legacy of Anti-Formalism', in Annelise Riles (ed.), *Rethinking the Masters of Comparative Law*, Oxford: Hart, pp. 66–91.

Curran, Vivan Grosswald 2006. 'Comparative Law and Language', in Mathias Reimann and Reinhard Zimmermann (eds.), *The Oxford Handbook of Comparative Law*, Oxford: Oxford University Press, pp. 675–707.

Curry, Brett and Banks Miller 2008. 'Looking for Law in all the Wrong Places? Foreign Law and Support for the U.S. Supreme Court', *Politics and Policy*, vol. 36, 1094–124.

Dakolias, Maria 1999. 'Court Performance Around the World: A Comparative Perspective', *Yale Human Rights & Development Law Journal*, vol. 2, 87–141.

Dale, Sir William W. (ed.) (1988). *British and French Statutory Drafting*, London: Institute of Advanced Legal Studies.

Dalhuisen, Jan 2004. *Dalhuisen on International Commercial, Financial and Trade Law*, 2nd edn, Oxford: Hart.

Dallago, Bruno 2004. 'Comparative Economic Systems and the New Comparative Economics', *The European Journal of Comparative Economics*, vol. 1, 59–86.

Dam, Kenneth W. 2006. *The Law-Growth Nexus: The Rule of Law and Economic Development*, Washington DC: Brookings Institution Press.

Damaška, Mirjan R. 1986. *The Faces of Justice and State Authority. A Comparative Approach to the Legal Process*, New Haven: Yale University Press.

Damaška, Mirjan R. 2010. 'The Common Law/Civil Law Divide: Residual Truth of a Misleading Distinction', in Janet Walker and Oscar G. Chase (eds.), *Common Law, Civil Law and the Future of Categories*, Markham: LexisNexis Canada, pp. 1–21.

Daniels, Ronald J. and Michael Trebilcock 2004. 'The Political Economy of Rule of Law Reforms in Developing Countries', *Michigan Journal of International Law*, vol. 26, 99–140.

Danino, Roberto 2006. 'The Legal Aspects of the World Bank's Work on Human Rights: Some Preliminary Thoughts', in *World Bank Legal Review: Law and Justice for Development*, Rotterdam-New York: Kluwer Law International, vol. 2, 295–324.

Dannemann, Gerhard 2006. 'Comparative Law before the Code Napoléon', in Mathias Reimann and Reinhard Zimmermann (eds.), *The Oxford Handbook of Comparative Law*, Oxford: Oxford University Press, pp. 383–419.

Dannemann, Gerhard 2012. 'In Search of System Neutrality: Methodological Issues in the Drafting of European Contract Law Rules', in Maurice Adams and Jacco Bomhoff (eds.), *Practice and Theory in Comparative Law*, Cambridge: Cambridge University Press, pp. 96–119.

Darian-Smith, Eve 2004. 'Ethnographies of Law', in Austin Sarat (ed.), *The Blackwell Companion to Law and Society*, Malden MA: Blackwell, pp. 545–68.

Darian-Smith, Eve 2013. *Laws and Societies in Global Contexts: Contemporary Approaches*, Cambridge: Cambridge University Press.

David, René 1963. 'A Civil Code for Ethiopia: Considerations on the Codification of the Civil Law in African Countries', *Tulane Law Review*, vol. 37, 187–204.

David, Réné 1985. *Major Legal Systems in the World Today: An Introduction to the Comparative Study of Law*, 3rd edn (translated by John E. C. Brierley), London: Stevens.

Davis, D. M. 2003. 'Constitutional Borrowing: The Influence of Legal Culture and Local History in the Reconstitution of Comparative Influence: The South African Experience', *International Journal of Constitutional Law*, vol. 1, 181–95.

Davis, Kevin E. 2004. 'What Can the Rule of Law Variable Tell Us About Rule of Law Reforms?', *Michigan Journal of International Law*, vol. 26, 141–61.

Davis, Kevin E. 2010. 'Legal Universalism: Persistent Objections', *University of Toronto Law Journal*, vol. 60, 537–53.

Davis, Kevin E. and Michael J. Trebilcock 2008. 'The Relationship between Law and Development: Optimists versus Skeptics', *American Journal of Comparative Law*, vol. 56, 895–946.

Davis, Kevin E., Benedict Kingsbury and Sally Engle Merry 2012. 'Indicators as a Technology of Global Governance', *Law and Society Review*, vol. 46, 71–104 (partly reprinted in: 'Introduction: Global Governance by Indicators', in Kevin Davis, Angelina Fisher, Benedict Kingsbury and Sally Engle Merry (eds.), *Governance by Indicators: Global Power through Classification and Rankings*, Oxford: Oxford University Press, 2012, pp. 3–28).

Dawson, John P. 1968. *The Oracles of the Law*, Buffalo, NY: William S. Hein.

de Búrca, Gráinne, Robert O. Keohane and Charles F. Sabel 2013. 'New Modes of Pluralist Global Governance', *New York University Journal of International Law and Politics*, vol. 45, forthcoming.

De Coninck, Julie 2009. 'Overcoming the Mere Heuristic Aspirations of (Functional) Comparative Legal Research?, An Exploration into the Possibilities and Limits of Behavioural Economics', *Global Jurist*, vol. 9, issue 4, article 3.

De Coninck, Julie 2010. 'The Functional Method of Comparative Law: Quo Vadis?', *Rabels Zeitschrift für Ausländisches und Internationales Privatrecht*, vol. 74, 318–50.

De Coninck, Julie 2011. 'Reinvigorating Comparative Law through Behavioral Economics? A Cautiously Optimistic View', *Review of Law and Economics*, vol. 7, 711–36.

de Cruz, Peter 2007. *Comparative Law in a Changing World*, 3rd edn, London: Routledge Cavendish.

de Jong, Martin and Suzan Stoter 2009. 'Institutional Transplantation and The Rule of Law: How Interdisciplinary Method Can Enhance the Legitimacy of International Organisations', *Erasmus Law Review*, vol. 2, 311–30.

De Lombaerde, Philippe, Fredrik Söderbaum, Luk Van Langenhove and Francis Baert 2010. 'The Problem of Comparison in Comparative Regionalism', *Review of International Studies*, vol. 36, 731–53.

De Lombaerde, Philippe and Michael Schulz (eds.) 2009. *The EU and World Regionalism: The Makability of Regions in the 21st Century*, Farnham: Ashgate.

de Soto, Hernando 1989. *The Other Path: The Invisible Revolution in the Third World*, New York: Harper and Row.

de Soto, Hernando 2000. *The Mystery of Capital: Why Capitalism Triumphs in the West and Fails Everywhere Else*, New York: Basic Books.

de Soto, Hernando 2008. 'The Rule of Law: An Interview with Gustavo Wensjoe', *Literal*, 5–7.

de Tocqueville, Alexis 1861. *Memoir, Letters, and Remains of Alexis de Tocqueville*, vol. 2, London: Macmillan.

de Tocqueville, Alexis 1994 (1848), *Democracy in America*, New York: Knopf.

Deakin, Simon 2006. 'Legal Diversity and Regulatory Competition: Which Model for Europe?', *European Law Journal*, vol. 12, 440–54.

Deakin, Simon and Fabio Carvalho 2011. 'System and Evolution in Corporate Governance', in Peer Zumbansen and Gralf-Peter Calliess (eds.), *Law, Economics And Evolutionary Theory*, Cheltenham: Edward Elgar, pp. 111–30.

Deakin, Simon and Jonathan Michie (eds.) 1997. *Contracts, Cooperation and Competition*, Oxford: Oxford University Press.

Deeg, Richard and Gregory Jackson 2007. 'Towards a More Dynamic Theory of Capitalist Variety', *Socio-Economic Review*, vol. 5, 149–79.

DeFelice, E. Gene 1986. 'Causal Inference and Comparative Method', *Comparative Political Studies*, vol. 19, 415–37.

Deffains, Bruno and Ludivine Roussey 2012. 'Confidence in Judicial Institutions: An Empirical Approach', *Journal of Institutional Economics*, vol. 8, 351–69.

Dellapenna, Joseph W. 2008. 'Peasants, Tanners, and Psychiatrists: Using Films to Teach Comparative Law', *International Journal of Legal Information*, vol. 36, iss. 1, art. 10.

Delmas-Marty, Mireille 2003. *Global Law: A Triple Challenge*, Ardsley, NY: Transnational Publishers.

Delmas-Marty, Mireille 2009. *Ordering Pluralism: A Conceptual Framework for Understanding the Transnational Legal World*, Oxford: Hart.

Demleitner, Nora V. 1998. 'Challenge, Opportunity and Risk, An Era of Change in Comparative Law', *American Journal of Comparative Law*, vol. 46, 647–55.

Demleitner, Nora V. 1999. 'Combating Legal Ethnocentrism: Comparative Law Sets Boundaries', *Arizona State Law Journal*, vol. 31, 737–67.

Derrett, John Duncan Martin (ed.) 1968. *An Introduction to Legal Systems*, London: Sweet & Maxwell.

Dezalay, Yves and Bryant G. Garth 1996. *Dealing in Virtue: International Commercial Arbitration and the Construction of a Transnational Legal Order*, Chicago, IL: University of Chicago University Press.

Dezalay, Yves and Bryant G. Garth 2001. 'The Import and Export of Law and Legal Institutions: International Strategies in National Palace Wars', in David Nelken and Johannes Feest (eds.), *Adapting Legal Culture*, Oxford: Hart, pp. 241–55.

Dezalay, Yves and Bryant G. Garth 2002. *The Internationalization of Palace Wars: Lawyers, Economists, and the Contest to Transform Latin American States*, Chicago, IL: Chicago University Press.

Dezalay, Yves and Bryant G. Garth 2010. *Asian Legal Revivals: Lawyers in the Shadow of Empire*, Chicago, IL: University of Chicago Press.

Dezalay, Yves and Bryant G. Garth 2011a. 'Introduction: Constructing Transnational Justice' and 'Marketing and Legitimating Two Sides of Transnational Justice', in Yves Dezalay and Bryant G. Garth (eds.), *Lawyers and the Construction of Transnational Justice*, Abingdon: Routledge, pp. 3–12 and 277–95.

Dezalay, Yves and Bryant G. Garth 2011b. 'Introduction: Lawyers, Law and Society' and 'Conclusion: How to Convert Social Capital into Legal Capital and Transfer Legitimacy Across the Major Practice Divide', in Yves Dezalay and Bryant G. Garth (eds.), *Lawyers and the Rule of Law in an Era of Globalisation*, Abingdon: Routledge, pp. 1–16 and 260–6.

Dias, Ayesha Kadwani and Gita Honwana Welch (eds.) 2009. *Justice for the Poor: Perspectives on Accelerating Access*, Oxford: Oxford University Press.

Dickson, Brice 2008. 'Comparing Supreme Courts', in Brice Dickson (ed.), *Judicial Activism in Common Law Supreme Courts*, Oxford: Oxford University Press, pp. 1–18.

Dixon, Rosalind and Eric A. Posner 2011. 'The Limits of Constitutional Convergence', *Chicago Journal of International Law*, vol. 11, 399–423.

Djankov, Simeon, Rafael La Porta, Florencio Lopez-de-Silanes and Andrei Shleifer 2002. 'The Regulation of Entry', *Quarterly Journal of Economics*, vol. 117, 1–37.

Djankov, Simeon, Rafael La Porta, Florencio Lopez-de-Silanes and Andrei Shleifer 2003a. 'Courts', *Quarterly Journal of Economics*, vol. 118, 453–517.

Djankov, Simeon, Edward L. Glaeser, Rafael La Porta, Florencio Lopez-de-Silanes and Andrei Shleifer 2003b. 'The New Comparative Economics', *Journal of Comparative Economics*, vol. 31, 595–619.

Djankov, Simeon, Rafael La Porta, Florencio Lopez-de-Silanes and Andrei Shleifer 2008. 'The Law and Economics of Self-Dealing', *Journal of Financial Economics*, vol. 88, 430–65.

Dodson, Scott and James M. Klebba 2011. 'Global Civil Procedure Trends in the Twenty-First Century', *Boston College International & Comparative Law Review*, vol. 34, 1–26.

Dogan, Mattei 2002. 'Strategies in Comparative Sociology', *Comparative Sociology*, vol. 1, 63–92.

Dogan, Mattei 2004. 'The Quantitative Method in Comparative Research', in Patricia Kennett (ed.), *A Handbook of Comparative Social Policy*, Cheltenham: Edward Elgar, pp. 324–39.

Donahue, Charles 2006. 'Comparative Law before the Code Napoléon', in Mathias Reimann and Reinhard Zimmermann (eds.), *The Oxford Handbook of Comparative Law*, Oxford: Oxford University Press, pp. 3–32.

Donlan, Sean Patrick 2011. 'Remember: Legal Hybridity and Legal History', *Comparative Law Review*, vol. 2, 1–35.

Donohue, John J. and Justin Wolfers 2006. 'Uses and Abuses of Empirical Evidence in the Death Penalty Debate', *Stanford Law Review*, vol. 58, 791–845.

Donovan, James M. 2008. *Legal Anthropology: An Introduction*, Lanham, MD: AltaMira.

Doremus, Paul N., William W. Keller, Louis W. Pauly and Simon Reich 1998. *The Myth of the Global Corporation*, Princeton: Princeton University Press.

Drahozal, Christoper R. 2004. 'Regulatory Competition and the Locations of International Proceedings', *International Review of Law and Economics*, vol. 24, 371–84.

Dressel, Björn and Marcus Mietzner 2012. 'A Tale of Two Courts: The Judicialization of Electoral Politics in Asia', *Governance*, vol. 25, 391–41.

Drobnig, Ulrich 1999. 'The Use of Comparative Law by Courts', in Ulrich Drobnig and Sjef van Erp (eds.), *The Use of Comparative Law by Courts*, London: Kluwer, pp. 3–21.

Drobnig, Ulrich and Sjef van Erp (eds.) 1999, *The Use of Comparative Law by Courts*, London: Kluwer.

Druzin, Bryan 2009. 'Buying Commercial Law: Choice of Law, Choice of Forum, and Network Externalities', *Tulane Journal of International and Comparative Law*, vol. 18, 1–47.

Du, Julan 2011. 'Does China Need Law for Economic Development?', in Michael Faure and Jan Smits (eds.), *Does Law Matter? On Law and Economic Growth*, Cambridge: Intersentia, pp. 265–93.

Du Laing, Bart 2011. 'Bio-Legal History, Dual Inheritance Theory and Naturalistic Comparative Law: On Content and Context Biases in Legal Evolution', *Review of Law and Economics*, vol. 7, 685–709.

du Plessis, Jacques 2006. 'Comparative Law and the Study of Mixed Legal Systems', in Mathias Reimann and Reinhard Zimmermann (eds.), *The Oxford Handbook of Comparative Law*, Oxford: Oxford University Press, pp. 477–512.

Duina, Francesco and Sonia Morano-Foadi 2011. 'Introduction: The Institutionalisation of Regional Trade Agreements Worldwide: New Dynamics and Future Scenarios', *European Law Journal*, vol. 17, 561–7.

Durisin, Boris and Fulvio Puzone 2009. 'Maturation of Corporate Governance Research, 1993–2007: An Assessment', *Corporate Governance: An International Review*, vol. 17, 266–91.

Durkheim, Émile 1947. *The Division of Labor in Society*, New York: The Free Press.

Dzehtsiarou, Kanstantsin 2010. 'Comparative Law in the Reasoning of the European Court of Human Rights', *University College Dublin Law Review*, vol. 10, 109–40.

Easterly, Ernest S. III 1977. 'Global Patterns of Legal Systems: Notes toward a New Geojurisprudence', *Geographical Review*, vol. 67, 209–20.

Easterly, William 2001. *The Elusive Quest for Growth: Economists' Adventures and Misadventures in the Tropics*, Cambridge, MA: MIT Press.

Easterly, William 2006. *The White Man's Burden: Why the West's Efforts to Aid the Rest Have Done So Much Ill and So Little Good*, New York: Penguin Press.

Easterly, William, Roberta Gatti and Sergio Kurlat 2006. 'Development, Democracy, and Mass Killings', *Journal of Economic Growth*, vol. 11, 129–56.

Eberhard, Christoph 2009. 'Law and Anthropology in a "Glocal" World: The Challenge of Dialogue', in Michael Freeman and David Napier (eds.), *Law and Anthropology*, Oxford: Oxford University Press, pp. 67–88.

Eberle, Edward J. 2007. 'Comparative Law', *Annual Survey of International and Comparative Law*, vol. 13, iss. 1, art. 5.

Eberle, Edward J. 2009. 'The Method and Role of Comparative Law', *Washington University Global Studies Law Review*, vol. 8, 451–86.

Ebbinghaus, Bernhard 1998. 'Europe Through the Looking-Glass: Comparative and Multi-Level Perspectives', *Acta Sociologica*, vol. 41, 301–13.

Economides, Spyros and Peter Wilson 2001. *The Economic Factor in International Relations*, London: Tauris.

Edge, Ian 2000. 'Comparative Law in Global Perspective', in Ian Edge (ed.), *Comparative Law in Global Perspective*, New York: Transnational Publishers.

Edwards, Harry 1992. 'The Growing Disjunction between Legal Education and the Legal Profession', *Michigan Law Review*, vol. 91, 34–78.

Edwards, Lynda 2009. 'Russia Claws at the Rule of Law', *ABA Journal*, vol. 59 (July), 38–62.

EE: see Smits, Jan M. (ed.), *Elgar Encyclopedia of Comparative Law*.

Ehrmann, Henry W. 1976. *Comparative Legal Cultures*, Englewood Cliffs, NJ: Prentice Hall.

Eidenmüller, Horst 2011. 'The Transnational Law Market, Regulatory Competition, and Transnational Corporations', *Indiana Journal of Global Legal Studies*, vol. 18, 707–49.

Eidenmüller, Horst, Andreas Engert and Lars Hornuf 2011. 'How Does the Market React to the Societas Europaea?', *European Business Organization Law Review*, vol. 11, 35–50.

Eiselen, Sieg 2010. 'Globalization and Harmonization of International Trade Law', in Michael Faure and André van der Walt (eds.), *Globalization and Private Law: The Way Forward*, Cheltenham: Edward Elgar, pp. 97–136.

Eisenberg, Theodore 2009. 'U.S. Chamber of Commerce Liability Survey: Inaccurate, Unfair, and Bad for Business', *Journal of Empirical Legal Studies*, vol. 6, 969–1002.

Eisenberg, Theodore and Geoffrey P. Miller 2013. 'The English vs. the American Rule on Attorneys Fees: An Empirical Study of Attorney Fee Clauses in Publicly-Held Companies' Contracts', *Cornell Law Review*, vol. 13, 327–81.

Elder, Joseph W. 1976. 'Comparative Cross-National Methodology', *Annual Review of Sociology*, vol. 2, 209–230.

Elkins, Zachary, Tom Ginsburg and James Melton 2009. *The Endurance of National Constitutions*, Cambridge: Cambridge University Press.

Elkins, Zachary, Tom Ginsburg and Beth Simmons 2013. 'Getting to Rights: Treaty Ratification, Constitutional Convergence, and Human Rights Practice', *Harvard International Law Journal*, vol. 54, 61–95.

Ellis, Jaye 2011. 'General Principles and Comparative Law', *European Journal of International Law*, vol. 22, 949–71.

Engert, Andreas and D. Gordon Smith 2009. 'Unpacking Adaptability', *BYU Law Review*, 1553–70.

Eörsi, Gyula, 1979. *Comparative Civil (Private) Law*, Budapest: Akademiai Kiado.

Erbeznik, Katherine 2011. 'Money Can't Buy You Law: The Effects of Foreign Aid on the Rule of Law in Developing Countries', *Indiana Journal of Global Legal Studies*, vol. 18, pp. 873–900.

Esmein, Adhémar 1905. 'Le Droit Comparé et l'Enseignement du Droit', in *Congrès International de Droit Comparé – Actes*, vol. 1, Paris: s.n, 445–51.

Esping-Andersen, Gøsta 1990. *The Three Worlds of Welfare Capitalism*, Princeton, NJ: Princeton University Press.

Esquirol, Jorge L. 1997. 'The Fictions of Latin American Law', *Utah Law Review*, 425–70.

Esquirol, Jorge L. 2001. 'René David: At the Head of the Legal Family', in Annelise Riles (ed.), *Rethinking the Masters of Comparative Law*, Oxford: Hart, pp. 212–35.

Esquirol, Jorge L. 2003. 'Continuing Fictions of Latin American Law', *Florida Law Review*, vol. 55, 31–114.

Esquirol, Jorge L. 2008. 'The Failed Law of Latin America', *American Journal of Comparative Law*, vol. 56, 75–124.

Estevez-Abe, Margarita, Torben Iversen and David Soskice 2001. 'Social Protection and the Formation of Skills: A Reinterpretation of the Welfare State', in Peter A. Hall and David Soskice (eds.), *Varieties of Capitalism: The Institutional Foundations of Comparative Advantage*, Oxford: Oxford University Press, pp. 145–83.

European Commission 2006. 'Impact Assessment on the Proposal for a Directive on the Exercise of Shareholders' Voting Rights', SEC(2006)181, available at http://register.consilium.eu.int/pdf/en/06/st05/st05217-ad01.en06.pdf.

European Parliament 2012. Dissenting Opinions in the Supreme Courts of the Member States – Study, available at www.europarl.europa.eu/committees/fr/studiesdownload.html?languageDocument=EN&file=78915.

Evans, Peter and James E. Rauch 1999. 'Bureaucracy and Growth: A Cross-National Analysis of the Effects of "Weberian" State Structures on Economic Growth', *American Sociological Review*, vol. 64, 748–65.

Evans-Jones, Robin 1998. 'Receptions of Law, Mixed Legal Systems and the Myth of the Genius of Scots Private Law', *Law Quarterly Review*, vol. 114, 228–49.

Evans-Pritchard, E. E. 1963. *The Comparative Method in Social Anthropology*, London: Athlone Press.

Ewald, William 1995a. 'Comparative Jurisprudence (I): What Was It Like to Try a Rat?', *University of Pennsylvania Law Review*, vol. 143, 1898–2149.

Ewald, William 1995b. 'Comparative Jurisprudence (II): The Logic of Legal Transplants', *American Journal of Comparative Law*, vol. 43, 489–510.

Ewald, William 1998. 'The Jurisprudential Approach to Comparative Law: A Field Guide to "Rats"', *American Journal of Comparative Law*, vol. 46, 701–7.

Fairgrieve, Duncan 2003. *State Liability in Tort: A Comparative Study*, Oxford: Oxford University Press.

Farnsworth, E. Allan 2006. 'Comparative Contract Law', in Mathias Reimann and Reinhard Zimmermann (eds.), *The Oxford Handbook of Comparative Law*, Oxford: Oxford University Press, pp. 899–933.

Fathally, Jabeur and Nicola Mariani 2008. *Les Systèmes Juridiques dans le Monde*, 2nd edn, Montréal: Wilson & Lafleur.

Faundez, Julio 2010. 'Rule of Law or Washington Consensus: The Evolution of the World Bank's Approach to Legal and Judicial Reform', in Amanda Perry-Kessaris (ed.), *Law in the Pursuit of Development*, London: Routledge, pp. 180–201.

Faundez, Julio 2011. 'Legal Pluralism and International Development Agencies: State Building or Legal Reform', *Hague Journal on the Rule of Law*, vol. 3, 18–38 (also published in Brian Z. Tamanaha (ed.), *Legal Pluralism and Development: Scholars and Practitioners in Dialogue*, Cambridge: Cambridge University Press, 2012, pp. 177–96).

Faust, Florian 2006. 'Comparative Law and Economic Analysis of Law', in Mathias Reimann and Reinhard Zimmermann (eds.), *The Oxford Handbook of Comparative Law*, Oxford: Oxford University Press, pp. 837–65.

Fauvarque-Cosson, Bénédicte 2007. *The Rise of Comparative Law: A Challenge for Legal Education in Europe*, Groning: Europa Law Publishing.

Fauvarque-Cosson, Bénédicte and Anne-Julie Kerhuel 2009. 'Is Law an Economic Contest? French Reactions to the Dong Business World Bank Reports and Economic Analysis of Law', *American Journal of Comparative Law*, vol. 57, 811–25.

Fazio, Silvia 2007. *The Harmonization of International Commercial Law*, Alphen aan den Rijn: Kluwer.

Fedderke, Johannes W., Raphael De Kadt and John Luiz 2001. 'Indicators of Political Liberty, Property Rights and Political Instability in South Africa', *International Review of Law and Economics*, vol. 21, 103–34.

Fedderke, Johannes W. and Julia Garlick 2011. 'Measuring Institutions: Indicators of Political and Property Rights in Malawi', Working Paper available at http://ssrn.com/abstract=1809887.

Fedtke, Jörg 2008. 'Constitutional Transplants: Returning to the Garden', *Current Legal Problems*, vol. 61, 49–93.

Feeley, Malcolm M. 1997. 'Comparative Criminal Law for Criminologists: Comparing for What Purpose?', in David Nelken (ed.), *Comparing Legal Cultures*, Aldershot: Dartmouth, pp. 93–104.

Fein, Helen 1987. 'More Murder in the Middle: Life-Integrity Violations and Democracy in the World', *Human Rights Quarterly*, vol. 18, 170–91.

Fekete, Balázs 2011. 'Cultural Comparative Law?', in Peter Cserne and Miklos Könczöl (eds.), *Legal and Political Theory in the Post-National Age*, Frankfurt: Peter Lang, pp. 40–51.

Feld, Lars P. and Stefan Voigt 2003. 'Economic Growth and Judicial Independence: Cross-country Evidence Using a New Set of Indicators', *European Journal of Political Economy*, vol. 19, 497–527.

Feldman, Eric 2000a. 'Blood Justice, Courts, Conflict and Compensation in Japan, France and the United States', *Law and Society Review*, vol. 34, 651–702.

Feldman, Eric 2000b. *The Ritual of Rights in Japan: Law, Society and Health Policy*, Cambridge: Cambridge University Press.

Feldman, Eric 2009. 'Why Patients Sue Doctors: The Japanese Experience', *Journal of Law, Medicine and Ethics*, vol. 37, 792–99.

Feng, Yi 2003. *Democracy, Governance, and Economic Performance: Theory and Evidence*, Cambridge: MA, MIT Press.

Ferejohn, John, Frances Rosenbluth, and Charles Shipan 2007. 'Comparative Judicial Politics', in Carles Boix and Susan C. Stokes (eds.), *The Oxford Handbook of Comparative Politics*, Oxford: Oxford University Press, pp. 727–51.

Ferguson, Niall 2011. *Civilization: The West and the Rest*, New York: Penguin Press.

Ferguson, Niall 2012. *The Great Degeneration: How Institutions Decay and Economies Die*, London: Allen Lane.

Fernandez, Patricio and Giacomo Ponzetto 2012. 'Stare Decisis: Rhetoric and Substance', *Journal of Law, Economics and Organization*, vol. 28, 313–36.

Ferrando, Tomaso 2013. 'Codes of Conduct as Private Legal Transplant: The Case of European Extractive MNEs', *European Law Journal*, vol. 19, 799–821.

Ferreira, Daniel, David Kershaw, Tom Kirchmaier and Edmund-Philipp Schuster 2013. 'Shareholder Empowerment and Bank Bailouts', ECGI – Finance Working Paper No. 345/2013, available at http://ssrn.com/abstract=2170392.

Ferreres Comella, Victor 2011. 'The Rise of Specialised Constitutional Courts', in Tom Ginsburg and Rosalind Dixon (eds.), *Research Handbook in Comparative Constitutional Law*, Cheltenham: Edward Elgar, pp. 265–77.

Figueroa, Dante 2011. 'Current Constitutional Developments in Latin America', *International Legal Research Informer*, Summer 2011, pp. 8–18.

Fikentscher, Wolfgang 1975–77. *Methoden des Rechts in Vergleichender Darstellung*, five volumes, Tübingen: Mohr.

Fikentscher, Wolfgang 2004. *Modes of Thought: A Study in the Anthropology of Law and Religion*, Tübingen: Mohr Siebeck.

Fikentscher, Wolfgang 2009. *Law and Anthropology: Outlines, Issues, Suggestions*, Munich: Beck.

Fineman, Martha L. 1988. 'Contexts and Comparisons' (book review of *Abortion and Divorce in Western Law* by Mary Ann Glendon), *University of Chicago Law Review*, vol. 55, 1431–44.

Finkin, Matthew W. 2006. 'Comparative Labour Law', in Mathias Reimann and Reinhard Zimmermann (eds.), *The Oxford Handbook of Comparative Law*, Oxford: Oxford University Press, pp. 1131–60.

Finlay, Jocelyn E., David Canning and June Y. T. Po 2012. 'Reproductive Health Laws Around the World', PGDA Working Paper, available at www.hsph.harvard.edu/pgda/WorkingPapers/2012/PGDA_WP_96.pdf.

Finnegan, David Louis 2006. 'Applied Comparative Law and Judicial Reform', *Thomas M. Cooley Journal of Practical and Clinical Law*, vol. 8, 97–132.

Fischer-Lescano, Andreas and Gunther Teubner 2004. 'Regime-Collisions: The Vain Search for Legal Unity in the Fragmentation of Global Law', *Michigan Journal of International Law*, vol. 25, 999–1045.

Fish, M. Steven 2011. *Are Muslims Distinctive? A Look at the Evidence*, New York: Oxford University Press.

Fish, M. Steven and Matthew Kroenig 2009. *The Handbook of National Legislatures: A Global Survey*, New York: Cambridge University Press.

Fiske, Alan Page 1991. *Structures of Social Life: The Four Elementary Forms of Human Relations*, New York: Free Press.

Flanagan, Brian and Sinead Ahern 2011. 'Judicial Decision-Making and Transnational Law: A Survey of Common-Law Supreme Court Judges', *International and Comparative Law Quarterly*, vol. 60, 1–28.

Fletcher, George P. 1998. 'Comparative Law as a Subversive Discipline', *American Journal of Comparative Law*, vol. 46, 683–700.

Fletcher, George P. 2007. *The Grammar of Criminal Law: American, Comparative, and International: Volume One: Foundations*, Oxford: Oxford University Press.

Forster, Marc 1995. 'Functions and Practice of Legal Citing: Towards a Uniform International Quotation System', *International Journal of Legal Information*, vol. 23, 149–68.

Foster, Jacob 2010. 'The Use of Foreign Law in Constitutional Interpretation: Lessons from South Africa', *University of San Francisco Law Review*, vol. 45, 79–139.

Foster, Nicholas H. D. 2007. 'Comparative Commercial Law: Rules or Context?', in Esin Örücü and David Nelken (eds.), *Comparative Law: A Handbook*, Oxford: Hart, pp. 263–85.

Foster, Nicholas H. D. 2010. 'Islamic Perspectives on the Law of Business Organisations I: An Overview of the Classical Sharia and a Brief Comparison of the Sharia Regimes with Western-Style Law', *European Business Organization Law Review*, vol. 11, 3–34.

Foster, Nicholas H. D. 2012. 'Commerce, Inter-Polity Legal Conflict and the Transformation of Civil and Commercial Law in the Ottoman Empire', in Eugene Cotran and Martin W. Lau (eds.), *Yearbook of Islamic and Middle Eastern Law*, Leiden: Brill, vol. 17, pp. 1–47.

Foucault, Michel 1977. *Discipline and Punish: The Birth of the Prison*, London: Allen Lane.

Fox, Eleanor 2002. 'Global Markets, National Law, and the Regulation of Business – A View from the Top', in Michael Likosky (ed.), *Transnational Legal Processes: Globalisation and Power Disparities*, London: Butterworths, pp. 135–47.

Frankenberg, Günter 1985. 'Critical Comparisons: Re-thinking Comparative Law', *Harvard International Law Journal*, vol. 26, 411–55.

Frankenberg, Günter 1997. 'Stranger Than Paradise: Identity & Politics in Comparative Law', *Utah Law Review*, 259–74.

Frankenberg, Günter 2006a. 'How to Do Projects with Comparative Law – Notes of an Expedition to the Common Core', *Global Jurist Advances*, vol. 6, issue 2, article 1 (reprinted in Mauro Bussani and Ugo Mattei (eds.), *Opening Up European Law*, Durham, NC: Carolina Academic Publishers, 2007, pp. 17–48, and Pier Giuseppe Monateri (ed.), *Methods of Comparative Law*, Cheltenham: Edward Elgar, pp. 120–43).

Frankenberg, Günter 2006b. 'Comparing Constitutions: Ideas, Ideals, and Ideology – Toward a Layered Narrative', *International Journal of Constitutional Law*, vol. 4, 439–59.

Frankenberg, Günter 2012a. 'Constitutional Transfer: The IKEA Theory revisited', *International Journal of Constitutional Law*, vol. 8, 563–79.

Frankenberg, Günter 2012b. 'Comparative Constitutional Law', in Mauro Bussani and Ugo Mattei (eds.), *Cambridge Companion to Comparative Law*, Cambridge: Cambridge University Press, pp. 171–90.

Freeden, Michael and Andrew Vincent 2013. 'Introduction: The Study of Comparative Political Thought', in Michael Freeden and Andrew Vincent (eds.), *Comparative Political Thought*, Abingdon: Routledge, pp. 1–23.

Friedman, Lawrence M. 1975. *The Legal System: A Social Science Perspective*, New York: Russell Sage Foundation.

Friedman, Lawrence M. 1994. 'Is There a Modern Legal Culture?', *Ratio Juris*, vol. 7, 117–31.

Friedman, Lawrence M. 1996. 'Borders: On the Emerging Sociology of Transnational Law', *Stanford Journal of International Law*, vol. 32, 65–90.

Friedman, Lawrence M. 1997. 'The Concept of Legal Culture: A Reply', in David Nelken (ed.), *Comparing Legal Cultures*, Aldershot: Dartmouth, pp. 33–9.

Friedman, Lawrence M. 2001. 'Erewhon: The Coming Global Legal Order', *Stanford Journal of International Law*, vol. 37, 347–64.

Friedmann, Wolfgang 1959. *Law in a Changing Society*, 2nd edn, Berkeley: University of California Press.

Fromont, Michel 2005. *Grands Systèmes de Droit Étrangers*, 5th edn, Paris: Dalloz.

Fukuyama, Francis 1989. 'The End of History?', *The National Interest*, Summer 1989, pp. 3–18.

Fukuyama, Francis 1992, *The End of History and the Last Man*, New York: Free Press.

Fukuyama, Francis 2007. 'Development and the Limits of Institutional Design', in Natalia Dinello and Vladimir Popov (eds.), *Political Institutions and Development: Failed Expectations and Renewed Hopes*, Cheltenham: Edward Elgar, pp. 21–42.

Fukuyama, Francis 2008. 'Do Defective Institutions Explain the Gap Between the United States and Latin America?', in Francis Fukuyama (ed.), *Falling Behind: Explaining the Development Gap Between Latin America and the United States*, New York: Oxford University Press, pp. 194–221.

Fukuyama, Francis 2010. 'The "End of History" 20 Years Later', *New Perspectives Quarterly*, vol. 27, 7–10.

Fukuyama, Francis 2013. 'What Is Governance?', *Governance*, vol. 26, 347–68.

Fyzee, Asaf A. A. and Tahir Mahmood 2008. *Outlines of Muhammadan Law*, New Delhi: Oxford University Press.

Gaakeer, Jeanne 2012. 'Iudex Translator: The Reign of Finitude', in Pier Giuseppe Monateri (ed.), *Methods of Comparative Law*, Cheltenham: Edward Elgar, pp. 252–69.

Galanter, Marc 1993. 'The Debased Debate on Civil Justice', *Denver University Law Review*, vol. 71, 77–113.

Galanter, Marc 1994. 'Predators and Parasites: Lawyer-Bashing and Civil Justice', *Georgia Law Review*, vol. 28, 633–81.

Galdia, Marcus 2009. *Legal Linguistics*, Frankfurt: Peter Lang.

Galligan, Denis J. 2003. 'Legal Failure: Law and Social Norms in Post-Communist Europe', in Denis J. Galligan and Marina Kurkchiyan (eds.), *Law and Informal Practices: The Post-Communist Experience*, Oxford: Oxford University Press, pp. 1–23.

Gambaro, Antonio 2007. 'Interpretation of Multilingual Legislative Texts', *Electronic Journal of Comparative Law*, vol. 11.3, available at www.ejcl.org/113/article113–4.pdf.

Gambaro, Antonio and Rodolfo Sacco 2002. *Systemi Giuridici Comparati*, Turin: UTET.

Gannon, Martin J. and Rajnandini Pillai 2010. *Understanding Global Cultures*, Los Angeles: Sage.

Garapon, Antoine 2010. 'A New Approach for Promoting Judicial Integrity', in Randall Peerenboom (ed.), *Judicial Independence in China*, Cambridge: Cambridge University Press, pp. 37–51.

Garapon, Antoine and Ioannis Papadopoulos 2003. *Juger en Amérique et en France*, Paris: Odile Jacob.

Garcia-Villegas, Mauricio 2006. 'Comparative Sociology of Law: Legal Fields, Legal Scholarships, and Social Sciences in Europe and the United States', *Law and Social Inquiry*, vol. 31, 343–82.

Gardner, James A. 1980. *Legal Imperialism: American Lawyers and Foreign Aid in Latin America*, Madison: University of Wisconsin Press.

Garland, David 1990. *Punishment and Modern Society: A Study in Social Theory. Studies in Crime and Justice*, Oxford: Clarendon.

Garland, David 2001. *The Culture of Control: Crime and Social Order in Contemporary Society*, Chicago: Chicago University Press.

Garland, David 2007. 'The Peculiar Forms of American Capital Punishment', *Social Research*, vol. 74, 435–64.

Garoupa, Nuno 2004. 'Regulation of Professions in the US and Europe: A Comparative Analysis', *American Law & Economics Association Annual Meetings*, Paper 42.

Garoupa, Nuno 2011. 'The Law and Economics of Legal Parochialism', *University of Illinois Law Review*, 1517–29.

Garoupa, Nuno and Anthony Ogus 2006. 'A Strategic Interpretation of Legal Transplants', *Journal of Legal Studies*, vol. 35, 339–59.

Garoupa, Nuno and Tom Ginsburg 2011. 'Hybrid Judicial Career Structures: Reputation versus Legal Tradition', *Journal of Legal Analysis*, vol. 3, 411–48.

Garoupa, Nuno and Carlos Gómez Ligüerre 2011. 'The Syndrome of the Efficiency of the Common Law', *Boston University Journal of International Law*, vol. 29, 287–335.

Garoupa, Nuno and Carlos Gómez Ligüerre 2012. 'The Evolution of the Common Law and Efficiency', *Georgia Journal of International and Comparative Law*, vol. 40, 307–40.

Garoupa, Nuno and Mariana Pargendler 2013. 'A Law and Economics Perspective on Legal Families', Illinois Public Law Research Paper 13-11, available at http://ssrn.com/abstract=2104443.

Gaudreault-DesBiens, Jean-François 2010. 'Religious Courts, Personal Federalism, and Legal Transplants', in Rex Ahdar and Nicholas Aroney (eds.), *Shari'a in the West*, Oxford: Oxford University Press.

Gauri, Varun 2009. 'How Do Local-Level Legal Institutions Promote Development? An Exploratory Essay', World Bank Justice and Development Working Paper Series No. 6/2009.

Geddes, Barbara 2007. 'What Causes Democratization?', in Carles Boix and Susan C. Stokes (eds.), *The Oxford Handbook of Comparative Politics*, Oxford: Oxford University Press, pp. 317–39.

Geeroms, Sofie M.F. 2002. 'Comparative Law and Legal Translation: Why the Terms Cassation, Revision and Appeal Should Not Be Translated ...', *American Journal of Comparative Law*, vol. 50, 201–28.

Geertz, Clifford 1983. *Local Knowledge: Further Essays in Interpretive Anthropology*, New York: Basic Books.

Gelter, Martin and Mathias Siems 2012. 'Networks, Dialogue or One-Way Traffic? An Empirical Analysis of Cross-Citations Between Ten European High Courts', *Utrecht Law Review*, vol. 8, 88–99.

Gelter, Martin and Mathias Siems 2013. 'Language, Legal Origins, and Culture before the Courts: Cross-Citations between Supreme Courts in Europe', *Supreme Court Economic Review*, vol. 21, forthcoming.

Gelter, Martin and Mathias Siems 2014. 'Citations to Foreign Courts – Illegitimate and Superfluous, or Unavoidable? Evidence from Europe', *American Journal of Comparative Law*, vol. 62, 35–85.

Gephart, Werner 2011. *Law as Culture: For a Study of Law in the Process of Globalization from the Perspective of the Humanities*, Frankfurt: Vittorio Klostermann.

Gerber, David J. 2001. 'Sculpting the Agenda of Comparative Law: Ernst Rabel and the Façade of Language', in Annelise Riles (ed.), *Rethinking the Masters of Comparative Law*, Oxford: Hart, pp. 190–208.

Gerber, David J. 2004. 'The Common Core of European Private Law: The Project and Its Books', *American Journal of Comparative Law*, vol. 52, 995–1001.

Giaro, Tomasz 2003. 'Westen im Osten – Modernisierung Osteuropäischer Rechte bis zum Zweiten Weltkrieg', *Rechtsgeschichte*, 123–39.

Gibbs, James Lovell 1981. 'Law in Radically Different Countries: An Experimental Course on Comparative Law', *American Behavioral Scientist*, vol. 25, 37–42.

Gibson, James L. and Gregory A. Caldeira 1996. 'The Legal Cultures of Europe', *Law and Society Review*, vol. 30, 55–86.

Gilardi, Fabrizio 2005. 'The Institutional Foundations of Regulatory Capitalism: The Diffusion of Independent Regulatory Agencies in Western Europe', *The Annals of the American Academy of Political and Social Sciences*, vol. 598, 84–101.

Gillespie, John Stanley 2006. *Transplanting Commercial Law Reform: Developing a Rule of Law in Vietnam*, London: Ashgate.

Gillespie, John Stanley and Pip Nicholson (eds.) 2012. *Law and Development and the Global Discourses of Legal Transfers*, Cambridge: Cambridge University Press.

Gilpin, Robert 2001. *Global Political Economy*, Princeton: Princeton University Press.

Gilson, Ronald J. 2001. 'Globalizing Corporate Governance: Convergence of Form or Function', *America Journal of Comparative Law*, vol. 49, 329–57.

Gilson, Ronald J. and Curtis J. Milhaupt 2011. 'Economically Benevolent Dictators: Lessons for Developing Democracies', *American Journal of Comparative Law*, vol. 59, 227–88.

Ginsburg, Tom 2000. 'Does Law Matter for Economic Development? Evidence from East Asia', *Law and Society Review*, vol. 34, 829–56.

Ginsburg, Tom 2003. *Judicial Review in New Democracies: Constitutional Courts in Asian Cases*, Cambridge: Cambridge University Press.

Ginsburg, Tom 2010a. 'The Politics of Courts in Democratization', in James J. Heckman, Robert L. Nelson and Lee Cabatingan (eds.), *Global Perspectives on the Rule of Law*, Abingdon: Routledge, pp. 175–91.

Ginsburg, Tom 2010b. 'Constitutional Specificity, Unwritten Understandings and Constitutional Agreement', in András Sajo and Renáta Uitz (eds.), *Constitutional Topography: Values and Constitutions*, The Hague: Eleven International Publishing, pp. 69–93.

Ginsburg, Tom 2010c. 'Judicial Independence in East Asia: Lessons for China', in Randall Peerenboom (ed.), *Judicial Independence in China*, Cambridge: Cambridge University Press, pp. 247–59.

Ginsburg, Tom 2012. 'Constitutional Law and Courts', in David S. Clark (ed.), *Comparative Law and Society*, Cheltenham: Edward Elgar, pp. 290–309.

Ginsburg, Tom and Glenn Hoetker 2006. 'The Unreluctant Litigant? An Empirical Analysis of Japan's Turn to Litigation', *Journal of Legal Studies*, vol. 35, 31–59.

Ginsburg, Tom and Tamir Moustafa 2008. 'Introduction: The Function of Courts in Authoritarian Politics', in Tom Ginsburg and Tamir Moustafa (eds.), *Rule by Law: The Politics of Courts in Authoritarian Regimes*, Cambridge: Cambridge University Press, pp. 1–22.

Ginsburg, Tom and Rosalind Dixon 2011. 'Introduction', in Tom Ginsburg and Rosalind Dixon (eds.), *Research Handbook in Comparative Constitutional Law*, Cheltenham: Edward Elgar, pp. 1–15.

Ginsburg, Tom, Zachary Elkins, and James Melton 2012. 'Do Executive Term Limits Cause Constitutional Crises?', in Tom Ginsburg (ed.), *Comparative Constitutional Design*, Cambridge: Cambridge University Press, pp. 350–80.

Ginsburg, Tom and Mila Versteeg 2013. 'Why Do Countries Adopt Constitutional Review?', *Journal of Law, Economics, and Organization*, forthcoming.

Girling, Evi 2005. 'European Identity and the Mission Against the Death Penalty in the United States', in Austin Sarat and Christian Boulanger (eds.), *The Cultural Lives of Capital Punishment*, Stanford, CA: Stanford University Press, pp. 112–28.

Glanert, Simone 2012. 'Method?', in Pier Giuseppe Monateri (ed.), *Methods of Comparative Law*, Cheltenham: Edward Elgar, pp. 61–81.

Gleditsch, Kristian Skrede and Michael D. Ward 2008. 'Diffusion and the Spread of Democratic Institution', in Beth A. Simmons, Frank Dobbin and Geoffrey Garrett (eds.), *The Global Diffusion of Market and Democracy*, Cambridge: Cambridge University Press, pp. 261–302.

Glendon, Mary Ann 1987. *Abortion and Divorce in Western Law: American Failures, European Challenges*, Cambridge, MA: Harvard University Press.

Glendon, Mary Ann 2007. 'Plato as Statesman', *First Things*, November 2007, available at www.firstthings.com/article/2007/10/002-plato-as-statesman-13.

Glendon, Mary Ann, Paolo G. Carozza and Colin B. Picker 2008. *Comparative Legal Traditions in a Nutshell*, 3rd edn, St Paul, MN: West.

Glenn, H. Patrick 2001. 'Are Legal Systems Incommensurable?', *American Journal of Comparative Law*, vol. 49, 133–45.

Glenn, H. Patrick 2003. 'The Nationalist Heritage', in Pierre Legrand and Roderick Munday (eds.), *Comparative Legal Studies: Traditions and Transitions*, Cambridge: Cambridge University Press, pp. 76–99.

Glenn, H. Patrick 2004. 'Legal Cultures and Legal Traditions', in Mark Van Hoecke (ed.), *Epistemology and Methodology of Comparative Law*, Oxford: Hart, pp. 7–20.

Glenn, H. Patrick 2005. *On Common Laws*, Oxford: Oxford University Press.

Glenn, H. Patrick 2006. 'Transnational Common Laws', *Fordham International Law Journal*, vol. 29, 457–71.

Glenn, H. Patrick 2007. 'Com-paring' in Esin Örücü and David Nelken (eds.) *Comparative Law: A Handbook*, Oxford: Hart, pp. 91–108.

Glenn, H. Patrick 2009. 'Cosmopolitan Legal Orders', in Andrew Halpin and Voljer Roeben (eds.), *Theorising the Global Legal Order*, Oxford: Hart, pp. 25–37.

Glenn, H. Patrick 2010a. *Legal Traditions of the World*, 4th edn, Oxford: Oxford University Press.

Glenn, H. Patrick 2010b. 'A Western Legal Tradition?', in Janet Walker and Oscar G. Chase (eds.), *Common Law, Civil Law and the Future of Categories*, Markham: LexisNexis Canada, pp. 601–19.

Glenn, H. Patrick 2011. 'Sustainable Diversity in Law', *Hague Journal on the Rule of Law*, vol. 3, 39–56 (also published in Brian Z. Tamanaha (ed.), *Legal Pluralism and Development: Scholars and Practitioners in Dialogue*, Cambridge: Cambridge University Press, 2012, pp. 95–111).

Glenn, H. Patrick 2013. *The Cosmopolitan State*, Oxford: Oxford University Press.

Glinavos, Ioannis 2010. *Neoliberalism and the Law in Post Communist Transition: The Evolving Role of Law in Russia's Transition to Capitalism*, Abingdon: Routledge.

Gluckman, Max 1955. *The Judicial Process among the Barotse of Northern Rhodesia*, Glencoe, IL: The Free Press.

Goddard, Christopher 2009. 'Where Legal Cultures Meet: Translating Confrontation into Coexistence', *Investigationes Linguisticae*, vol. 17, 168–205.

Goderis, Benedikt and Mila Versteeg 2013. 'Transnational Constitutions: A Conceptual Framework', in Denis Galligan and Mila Versteeg (eds.), *Social and Political Foundations of Constitutions*, Cambridge: Cambridge University Press, pp. 103–33.

Goertz, Gary and James Mahoney 2012. *A Tale of Two Cultures: Qualitative and Quantitative Research in the Social Sciences*, Princeton: Princeton University Press.

Goff of Chieveley, Lord 1997. 'The Future of the Common Law', *International and Comparative Law Quarterly*, vol. 46, 745–60.

Goldman, David 2008. *Globalisation and the Western Legal Tradition: Recurring Patterns of Law and Authority*, Cambridge: Cambridge University Press.

Goldschmidt, Walter 1966. *Comparative Functionalism: An Essay in Anthropological Theory*, Berkeley: University of California Press.

Goldstein, Leslie Friedman 2001. *Constituting Federal Sovereignty: The European Union in Comparative Context*, Baltimore: Johns Hopkins University Press.

Goldsworthy, Jeffrey 2006. 'Questioning the Migration of Constitutional Ideas: Rights, Constitutionalism and the Limits of Convergence', in Sujit Choudhry (ed.), *The Migration of Constitutional Ideas*, Cambridge: Cambridge University Press, pp. 115–41.

Goldsworthy, Jeffrey (ed.), 2007. *Interpreting Constitutions: A Comparative Study*, Oxford: Oxford University Press.

Goldsworthy, Jeffrey 2012. 'Constitutional Interpretation', in Michel Rosenfeld and Andras Sajo (eds.), *The Oxford Handbook of Comparative Constitutional Law*, Oxford: Oxford University Press, pp. 689–717.

Goldthorpe, John H. 1997. 'Current Issues in Comparative Macrosociology: A Debate on Methodological Issues', *Comparative Social Research*, vol. 16, 1–26.

Gompers, Paul A., Joy L. Ishii and Andrew Metrick 2003. 'Corporate Governance and Equity Prices', *Quarterly Journal of Economics*, vol. 118, 107–55.

Goode, Roy 1998. *Commercial Law in the Next Millennium*, London: Sweet & Maxwell.

Goode, Roy 2005. 'Rule, Practice, and Pragmatism in Transnational Commercial Law', *International and Comparative Law Quarterly*, vol. 54, 539–62.

Goode, Roy, Herbert Kronke and Ewan McKendrick 2007. *Transnational Commercial Law: Text, Cases, and Materials*, Oxford: Oxford University Press.

Goodhart, Michael 2005. *Democracy as Human Rights: Freedom and Equality in the Age of Globalization*, New York: Routledge.

Goodin, Robert E. 1996. 'Designing Constitutions: The Political Constitution of a Mixed Commonwealth', in Richard Bellamy and Dario Castiglione (eds.), *Constitutionalism in Transformation: European and Theoretical Perspectives*, Oxford: Blackwell, pp. 223–34.

Goodpaster, Gary 2007. 'Law Reform in Developing Countries', in Tim Lindsey (ed.), *Law Reform in Developing and Transition States*, London: Routledge, pp. 106–39.

Gopal, Mohan 2009. 'Development and Implementation of Reform Initiatives to Ensure Effective Judiciaries', in Asia Pacific Judicial Forum (ed.), *Searching for Success in Judicial Reform: Voices from the Asia Pacific Experience*, Oxford: Oxford University Press, pp. 45–77.

Gordley, James 2003. 'The Universalist Heritage', in Pierre Legrand and Roderick Munday (eds.), *Comparative Legal Studies: Traditions and Transitions*, Cambridge: Cambridge University Press, pp. 31–45.

Gordley, James and Arthur Taylor von Mehren 2006. *An Introduction to the Comparative Study of Private Law: Readings, Cases, Materials*, Cambridge: Cambridge University Press.

Gordon, Richard K. 2010. 'On the Use and Abuse of Standards for Law: Global Governance and Offshore Financial Centers', *North Carolina Law Review*, vol. 88, 501–94.

Grajzl, Peter and Valentina Dimitrova-Grajzl 2009. 'The Choice in the Lawmaking Process: Legal Transplants vs. Indigenous Law', *Review of Law and Economics*, vol. 5, 615–60.

Gramatikov, Martin and Robert B. Porter 2011. 'Yes, I Can: Subjective Legal Empowerment', *Georgetown Journal on Poverty Law and Policy*, vol. 18, 169–99.

Grande, Elisabetta 2012. 'Comparative Criminal Justice', in Mauro Bussani and Ugo Mattei (eds.), *Cambridge Companion to Comparative Law*, Cambridge: Cambridge University Press, pp. 191–209.

Graziadei, Michele 2003. 'The Functionalist Heritage', in Pierre Legrand and Roderick Munday (eds.), *Comparative Legal Studies: Traditions and Transitions*, Cambridge: Cambridge University Press, pp. 100–27.

Graziadei, Michele 2006. 'Comparative Law as the Study of Transplants and Receptions', in Mathias Reimann and Reinhard Zimmermann (eds.), *The Oxford Handbook of Comparative Law*, Oxford: Oxford University Press, pp. 441–74.

Graziadei, Michele 2009. 'Legal Transplants and the Frontiers of Legal Knowledge', *Theoretical Inquiries in Law*, vol. 10, 723–43.

Grechenig, Kristoffel and Martin Gelter 2008. 'The Transatlantic Divergence in Legal Thought: American Law and Economics vs. German Doctrinalism', *Hastings International and Comparative Law Review*, vol. 31, 295–360.

Green, Alan 2011. 'Institutions Matter, but in Surprising Ways: New Evidence on Institutions in Africa', *KYKLOS*, vol. 64, 87–105.

Greenberg, David and Valerie West 2008. 'Siting the Death Penalty Internationally', *Law and Social Inquiry*, vol. 33, 295–343.

Greenhouse, Carol J., Barbara Yngvesson and David M. Engel 1994. *Law and Community in Three American Towns*, Ithaca, NY: Cornell University Press.

Griffiths, Anne 2009a. 'Law, Space, and Place: Reframing Comparative Law and Legal Anthropology', *Law and Social Inquiry*, vol. 34, 495–507.

Griffiths, Anne 2009b. 'Anthropological Perspectives on Legal Pluralism and Governance in a Transnational World', in Michael Freeman and David Napier (eds.), *Law and Anthropology*, Oxford: Oxford University Press, pp. 164–86.

Griffiths, John 1986. 'What is Legal Pluralism?', *Journal of Legal Pluralism and Unofficial Law*, vol. 24, 1–55.

Griffiths, John, Heleen Weyers and Mauric Adams 2008. *Euthanasia and Law in Europe*, Oxford: Hart.

Grondona, Mariano 2000. 'A Cultural Typology of Economic Development', in Lawrence E. Harrison and Samuel P. Huntington (eds.), *Culture Matters: How Values Shape Human Progress*, New York: Basic Books, pp. 44–55.

Groppi, Tania and Marie-Claire Ponthoreau (eds.) 2013. *The Use of Foreign Precedents by Constitutional Judges*, Oxford: Hart.

Grossfeld, Bernhard 1990. *The Strength and Weakness of Comparative Law*, Oxford: Clarendon.

Grossfeld, Bernhard 2003. 'Comparatists and languages', in Pierre Legrand and Roderick Munday (eds.), *Comparative Legal Studies: Traditions and Transitions*, Cambridge: Cambridge University Press, pp. 154–94.

Grossfeld, Bernhard 2005. *Core Questions of Comparative Law*, Durham, NC: Carolina.

Grossfeld, Bernhard and Edward J. Eberle 2003. 'Patterns of Order in Comparative Law: Discovering and Decoding Invisible Powers', *Texas International Law Journal*, vol. 38, 291–316.

Grundmann, Stefan 2009. 'The Fault Principle as the Chameleon of Contract Law: A Market Function Approach', *Michigan Law Review*, vol. 107, 1583–99.

Guarnieri, Carlo 2010. 'Judicial Independence in Authoritarian Regimes: Lessons from Continental Europe', in Randall Peerenboom (ed.), *Judicial Independence in China*, Cambridge: Cambridge University Press, pp. 234–46.

Guarnieri, Carlo and Patrizia Pederzoli 2001. *The Power of Judges, A Comparative Study of Courts and Democracy*, Oxford: Oxford University Press.

Guillet, David 2005. 'Customary Law and the Nationalist Project in Spain and Peru', *Hispanic American Historical Review*, vol. 85, 81–114.

Gulliver, Philip H. 1979. *Disputes and Negotiations: A Cross-Cultural Perspective*. New York: Academic Press.

Gutteridge, Harold Cooke 1949. *Comparative Law: An Introduction to the Comparative Method of Legal Study and Research*, Cambridge: Cambridge University Press.

Guzman, Andrew 2008. *How International Law Works: A Rational Choice Theory*, Oxford: Oxford University Press.

Haber, Stephen and Victor Menaldo 2011. 'Do Natural Resources Fuel Authoritarianism? A Reappraisal of the Resource Curse', *American Political Science Review*, vol. 105, 1–26.

Hacker, Jacob 2002. *The Divided Welfare State: The Battle Over Public and Private Social Benefits in the United States*, Cambridge: Cambridge University Press.

Hadfield, Gillian K. 2008. 'The Levers of Legal Design: Institutional Determinants of the Quality of Law', *Journal of Comparative Economics*, vol. 36, 43–73.

Haggard, Stephan, Andrew MacIntyre and Lydia Tiede 2008. 'The Rule of Law and Economic Development', *Annual Review of Political Science*, vol. 11, 205–34.

Halberstam, Daniel and Mathias Reimann 2012. 'General Report', in Daniel Halberstam, Mathias Reimann and Jorge Sanchez-Cordero (eds.), *Federalism and Legal Unification: A Comparative Empirical Investigation of Twenty Systems*, Paris: International Academy of Comparative Law, pp. 1–56.

Haley, John Owen 1978. 'The Myth of the Reluctant Litigant', *Journal of Japanese Studies*, vol. 4, 359–90.

Haley, John Owen 1998. *The Spirit of Japanese Law*. Athens, GA: University of Georgia Press.

Haley, John Owen 2002, 'Litigation in Japan: A New Look at Old Problems', *Willamette Journal of International Law and Dispute Resolution*, vol. 10, 121–42.

Hall, Jerome 1963. *Comparative Law and Social Theory*, Binghamton, NY: Louisiana State University Press.

Hall, Mark A. and Ronald F. Wright 2008. 'Systematic Content Analysis of Judicial Opinions', *California Law Review*, vol. 96, 63–122.

Hall, Peter A. and David Soskice 2001. 'An Introduction to Varieties of Capitalism', in Peter A. Hall and David Soskice (eds.), *Varieties of Capitalism: The Institutional Foundations of Comparative Advantage*, Oxford: Oxford University Press, pp. 1–68.

Hall, Peter A. and Daniel W. Gingerich 2009. 'Varieties of Capitalism and Institutional Complementarities in the Political Economy: An Empirical Analysis', *British Journal of Political Science*, vol. 39, 449–82.

Halliday, Terence C. 2010, 'The Fight for Basic Legal Freedoms', in James J. Heckman, Robert L. Nelson and Lee Cabatingan (eds.), *Global Perspectives on the Rule of Law*, Abingdon: Routledge, pp. 210–40.

Halliday, Terence C. and Lucien Karpik (eds.) 1998. *Lawyers and the Rise of Western Political Liberalism: Legal Professions and the Constitution of Modern Politics*, Oxford: Oxford University Press.

Halliday, Terence C., Lucien Karpik and Malcolm M. Feeley (eds.) 2007. *Fighting for Political Freedom: Comparative Studies of the Legal Complex for Political Change*, Oxford: Hart.

Halpérin, Jean-Louis 2010a. 'Western Legal Transplants and India', *Jindal Global Law Review*, vol. 2, 14–40.

Halpérin, Jean-Louis 2010b. 'The Concept of Law: A Western Transplant?', *Theoretical Inquiries in Law*, vol. 10, 333–54.

Halperin, Morton H., Joseph T. Siegle and Michael M. Weinstein 2010. *The Democracy Advantage: How Democracies Promote Prosperity and Peace*, New York: Routledge.

Hamilton, V. Lee and Joseph Sanders 1992. *Everyday Justice: Responsibility and the Individual in Japan and the United States*, New Haven: Yale University Press.

Hammel, Andrew, 2010. *Ending the Death Penalty: The European Experience in Global Perspective*, London: Palgrave.

Hammel, E. A. 1980. 'The Comparative Method in Anthropological Perspective', *Comparative Studies in Society and History*, vol. 22, 145–55.

Hanretty, Chris 2011. 'On the Specificity of Constitutions', Working Paper, available at http://chrishanretty.co.uk/blog/wp-content/uploads/2011/04/article2.pdf.

Hansmann, Henry and Reinier Kraakman 2001, 'The End of History for Corporate Law', *Georgetown Law Journal*, vol. 88, 439–68.

Hantrais, Linda 2009. *International Comparative Research: Theory, Methods and Practice*, Basingstoke and New York: Palgrave Macmillan and St Martin's Press.

Harding, Andrew 2001. 'Comparative Law and Legal Transplantation in South East Asia: Making Sense of the "Nomic Din"', in David Nelken and Johannes Feest (eds.), *Adapting Legal Culture*, Oxford: Hart, pp. 199–222.

Harding, Andrew 2002. 'Global Doctrine and Local Knowledge: Law in South East Asia', *International and Comparative Law Quarterly*, vol. 51, 35–53.

Harding, Andrew and Connie Carter 2003. 'The Singapore Model of Law and Development: Cutting Through Complexity', in John Hatchard and Amanda Perry-Kessaris (eds.), *Law and Development: Facing Complexity in the 21st Century*, London: Cavendish, pp. 191–206.

Harding, Andrew and Peter Leyland 2007. 'Comparative Law in Constitutional Context', in Esin Örücü and David Nelken (eds.), *Comparative Law: A Handbook*, Oxford: Hart, pp. 313–38.

Harding, Andrew, Peter Leyland and Tania Groppi 2008. 'Constitutional Courts: Forms, Functions and Practice in Comparative Perspective', *Journal of Comparative Law*, vol. 3, 1–21.

Harding, Andrew and Penelope Nicholson 2011. 'New Courts in Asia: Law, Development and Judicialization', in Andrew Harding and Penelope Nicholson (eds.), *New Courts in Asia*, London: Routledge, pp. 1–27.

Hartmann, Michael and Agnieszka Klonowiecka-Milart 2011. 'Lost in Translation: Legal Transplants without Consensus-based Adaptation', in Whit Mason (ed.), *The Rule of Law in Afghanistan: Missing in Inaction*, Cambridge: Cambridge University Press, pp. 266–98.

Harvey, David 1989a. *The Condition of Postmodernity*, Oxford: Blackwell.

Harvey, David 1989b. 'Editorial: A Breakfast Vision', *Geographical Review*, vol. 3, 1.

Hawken, Angela and Gerardo L. Munck 2011. 'Does the Evaluator Make a Difference? Measurement Validity in Corruption Research', Committee on Concepts and Methods Working Paper Series 48.

Hay, Colin 2004. 'Common Trajectories, Variable Paces, Divergent Outcomes? Models of European Capitalism Under Conditions of Complex Economic Interdependence', *Review of International Political Economy*, vol. 11, 231–62.

Hay, Colin 2011. 'Globalization's Impact on States', in John Ravenhill (ed.), *Global Political Economy*, 3rd edn, Oxford: Oxford University Press, pp. 312–44.

Hayo, Bernd and Stefan Voigt 2007. 'Explaining De Facto Judicial Independence', *International Review of Law and Economics*, vol. 27, 269–90.

Head, John W. 2010. 'Feeling the Stones When Crossing the River: The Rule of Law in China', *Santa Clara Journal of International Law*, vol. 7, 25–83.

Head, John W. 2011. *Great Legal Traditions: Civil Law, Common Law, and Chinese Law in Historical Perspective*, Durham, NC: Carolina University Press.

Headley, John M. 2008. *The Europeanization of the World: On the Origins of Human Rights and Democracy*, Princeton: Princeton University Press.

Henderson, Keith 2010. 'Half-way Home and a Long Way to Go: China's Rule of Law Evolution and the Global Road to Judicial Independence, Impartiality and Integrity', in Randall Peerenboom (ed.), *Judicial Independence in China*, Cambridge: Cambridge University Press, pp. 23–36.

Hendley, Kathryn 2004. 'The Rule of Law and Economic Development in a Global Era', in Austin Sarat (ed.), *The Blackwell Companion to Law and Society*, Malden MA: Blackwell, pp. 605–23.

Hendley, Kathryn 2006. 'Assessing the Rule of Law in Russia', *Cardozo Journal of International and Comparative Law*, vol. 14, 347–91.

Hendley, Kathryn 2009. '"Telephone Law" and the "Rule of Law": The Russian Case', *Hague Journal on the Rule of Law*, vol. 1, 241–62.

Hendley, Kathryn 2013. 'Too Much of a Good Thing? Assessing Access to Civil Justice in Russia', *Slavic Review*, vol. 72, 802–27.

Hendry, Jennifer 2013. 'Legal Pluralism and Normative Transfer', in Günter Frankenberg (ed.), *Order from Transfer: Comparative Constitutional Design and Legal Culture*, Cheltenham: Edward Elgar, 153–70.

Henrich, Joseph, Steven J. Heine and Ara Norenzayan 2010. 'The Weirdest People in the World?', *Behavioral and Brain Sciences*, vol. 33, 61–83.

Heringa, Aalt Willem and Bram Akkermans (eds.) 2011. *Educating European Lawyers*, Antwerp: Intersentia.

Herings, P. Jean-Jacques and Arnald J. Kanning 2008. 'Harmonization of Private Law on a Global Level', *International Review of Law and Economics*, vol. 28, 256–61.

Hermida, Julian 2004. 'Convergence of Civil Law and Common Law Contracts in the Space Field', *Hong Kong Law Review*, vol. 34, 338–74.

Herrmann, Benedikt, Christian Thöni and Simon Gächter 2008. 'Antisocial Punishment Across Societies', *Science*, vol. 319, 1362–7.

Hertel, Christian 2009. 'Legal Systems of the World – An Overview', *Notarius International*, 128–41.

Hertogh, Marc 2010. 'The Curious Case of Dutch Legal Culture: A Reassessment of Survey Evidence', *Journal of Comparative Law*, vol. 5, 146–68.

Heydebrand, Wolf 2001. 'From Globalisation of Law to Law under Globalisation', in David Nelken and Johannes Feest (eds.), *Adapting Legal Culture*, Oxford: Hart, pp. 117–37.

Hill, Claire A. and Christopher King 2004. 'How Do German Contracts Do as Much with Fewer Words?', *Chicago-Kent Law Review*, vol. 79, 889–926.

Hill, Jonathan 1989. 'Comparative Law, Law Reform and Legal Theory', *Oxford Journal of Legal Studies*, vol. 9, 101–15.

Hiller, Jack and Bernhard Grossfeld 2002. 'Comparative Legal Semiotics and the Divided Brain: Are We Producing Half-Brained Lawyers?', *American Journal of Comparative Law*, vol. 50, 175–200.

Hirschl, Ran 2004. *Towards Juristocracy: The Origins and Consequences of the New Constitutionalism*, Cambridge MA: Harvard University Press.

Hirschl, Ran 2006. 'On the Blurred Methodological Matrix of Comparative Constitutional Law', in Sujit Choudhry (ed.), *The Migration of Constitutional Ideas*, Cambridge: Cambridge University Press, pp. 39–66.

Hirschl, Ran 2008. 'The Judicialization of Mega-Politics and the Rise of Political Courts', *Annual Review of Political Science*, vol. 11, 93–118.

Hirschl, Ran 2011. 'Comparative Constitutional Law and Religion', in Tom Ginsburg and Rosalind Dixon (eds.), *Research Handbook in Comparative Constitutional Law*, Cheltenham: Edward Elgar, pp. 422–40.

Hobe, Stephan 2002. 'Globalisation: A Challenge to the Nation State and International Law', in Michael Likosky (ed.), *Transnational Legal Processes: Globalisation and Power Disparities*, London: Butterworths, pp. 378–91.

Hobsbawm, Eric and Terence Ranger (eds.), 1983. *The Invention of Tradition*, Cambridge: Cambridge University Press.

Hobson, John M. 2004. *The Eastern Origins of Western Civilisation*, Cambridge: Cambridge University Press.

Hodges, Christopher 2010. 'Collective Redress in Europe: The New Model', *Civil Justice Quarterly*, 370–96.

Hodges, Christopher, Stefan Vogenauer and Magdalena Tulibacka 2010. 'The Oxford Study on Costs and Funding of Civil Litigation', in Christopher Hodges, Stefan Vogenauer and Magdalena Tulibacka (eds.), *The Costs and Funding of Civil Litigation: A Comparative Study*, Oxford: Hart, pp. 3–186.

Hoffmann, Hermann and Andreas Maurer 2010. 'Entstaatlichung der Justiz: Empirische Belege zum Bedeutungsverlust staatlicher Gerichte für internationale Wirtschaftsstreitigkeiten', *Zeitschrift für Rechtssoziologie*, vol. 31, 279–302.

Hol, Antoine M. 2009. 'Internationalisation and Legitimacy of Decisions by the Highest Courts', in Sam Muller and Marc Loth (eds.), *Highest Courts and the Internationalisation of Law: Challenges and Changes*, Hague Academic Press, pp. 77–86.

Hol, Antoine M. 2012. ' Highest Courts and Transnational Interaction – Introductory and Concluding Remarks', *Utrecht Law Review*, vol. 8, 1–7.

Holder, Jane and Carolyn Harrison (ed.) 2003. *Law and Geography*, Oxford: Oxford University Press.

Holmes, Oliver Wendell 1897. 'The Path of Law', *Harvard Law Review*, vol. 10, 457–78.

Holzinger, Katharina, Christoph Knill and Bas Arts (eds.) 2008. *Environmental Policy Convergence in Europe*, Cambridge: Cambridge University Press.

Hondius, Ewould 2007. 'Precedent and the Law', *Electronic Journal of Comparative Law*, vol. 11.3.

Hondius, Ewoud 2011. 'Towards a European Palandt', *European Review of Private Law*, vol. 5, 483–88.

Hood, Christopher 2000. 'Paradoxes of Public-sector Managerialism, Old Public Management and Public Service Bargains', *International Public Management Journal*, vol. 3, 1–22.

Hood, Roger and Carolyn Hoyle 2008. *The Death Penalty: A Worldwide Perspective*, 4th edn, Oxford: Oxford University Press.

Hopkins, Terence K. and Immanuel Wallerstein 1967. 'The Comparative Study of National Societies', *Social Science Information*, vol. 6, 25–58.

Horwitz, Morton J. 2009. 'Constitutional Transplants', *Theoretical Inquiries in Law*, vol. 10, 535–60.

Huang, Peter Henry 2010. 'Happiness Studies and Legal Policy', *Annual Review of Law and Social Science*, vol. 6, 405–32.

Huber, Peter 2006. 'Comparative Sales Law', in Mathias Reimann and Reinhard Zimmermann (eds.), *The Oxford Handbook of Comparative Law*, Oxford: Oxford University Press, pp. 937–67.

Hughes, Owen E. 2003. *Public Management and Administration: An Introduction*, 3rd edn, Houndmills: Palgrave.

Humphreys, Stephen 2010. *Theatre of the Rule of Law*, Cambridge: Cambridge University Press.

Huneeus, Alexandra, Javier A. Couso and Rachel Sieder (eds.) 2010. *Cultures of Legality: Judicialization and Political Activism in Latin America*, Cambridge: Cambridge University Press.

Huneeus, Carlos, Fabiola Berrios and Rodrigo Cordero 2007. 'Legislatures in Presidential Systems: The Latin American Experience', in David Arter (ed.), *Comparing and Classifying Legislatures*, London: Routledge, pp. 147–68.

Huntington, Samuel 1993. 'The Clash of Civilizations', *Foreign Affairs*, vol. 72, 22–49.

Huntington, Samuel 1996. *The Clash of Civilizations and the Remaking of the World Order*, London: Simon & Schuster.

Hurrell, Andrew J. 1995. 'Explaining the Resurgence of Regionalism in World Politics', *Review of International Studies*, vol. 21, 331–58.

Husa, Jaakko 2003. 'Farewell to Functionalism or Methodological Tolerance?', *Rabels Zeitschrift für Ausländisches und Internationales Privatrecht*, vol. 67, 419–47.

Husa, Jaakko 2004. 'Classification of Legal Families Today. Is it Time for a Memorial Hymn?', *Revue Internationale de Droit Comparé*, 11–38.

Husa, Jaakko 2006. 'Methodology of Comparative Law Today: From Paradoxes to Flexibility?', *Revue Internationale de Droit Comparé*, 1095–117.

Husa, Jaakko 2007. 'About the Methodology of Comparative Law – Some Comments Concerning the Wonderland . . . ', Maastricht Working Papers 2007–5.

Husa, Jaakko 2009. 'Nicht nur Juristische Auslandsforschung: Rechtsvergleichung als Rechtsphilosophie', *Rechtstheorie*, vol. 40, 1–20.

Husa, Jaakko 2011a. 'Comparative Law, Legal Linguistics, and Methodology of Legal Doctrine', in Mark Van Hoecke (ed.), *Methodologies of Legal Research*, Oxford: Hart, pp. 209–28.

Husa, Jaakko 2011b. 'The False Dichotomy between Theory and Practice: Lessons from Comparative Law', in Claes Peterson (ed.), *Rechtswissenschaft als Juristische Doktrin*, Stockholm: Olin Foundation for Legal History, pp. 105–28.

Husa, Jaakko 2011c. 'Metamorphosis of Functionalism – or Back to Basics?', *Maastricht Journal of European and Comparative Law*, vol. 18, 548–53.

Husa, Jaakko 2012. 'The Method is Dead, Long Live the Methods! European Polynomia and Pluralist Methodology', *Legisprudence*, vol. 5, 249–71.

Husa, Jaakko 2013. 'Functional Method in Comparative Law – Much Ado About Nothing?', *European Property Law Journal*, vol. 2, 4–21.

Husa, Jaakko, Kimmo Nuotio and Heikki Pihlajamäki (eds.) 2008. *Nordic Law – Between Tradition and Dynamism*, Antwerp-Oxford: Intersentia.

Hutchinson, Allan C. and Patrick J. Monahan 1984. 'Law, Politics, and the Critical Legal Scholars: The Unfolding Drama of American Legal Thought', *Stanford Law Review*, vol. 36, 199–245.

Huxley, Andrew 1997. 'Golden Yoke, Silken Text', *Yale Law Journal*, vol. 106, 1885–951.

Huxley, Andrew 2007. 'Jeremy Bentham on Legal Transplants', *Journal of Comparative Law*, vol. 2, 177–88.

Hyland, Richard 1996. 'Comparative Law', in Dennis Patterson (ed.), *A Companion to Philosophy of Law and Legal Theory*, Chichester: Wiley-Blackwell, pp. 184–99.

Hyland, Richard 2009. *Gifts, A Study in Comparative Law*, Oxford: Oxford University Press.

IDEA 2008. 'Electoral System Design: The New International IDEA Handbook', available at www.idea.int/esd/.

Inoue, Kyoko 1991. *MacArthur's Japanese Constitution*, Chicago: Chicago University Press.

Inoue, Kyoko 2002. 'From Individual Dignity to Respect for Jinkaku – Continuity and Change in the Concept of the Individual in Modern Japan', in Michael Likosky (ed.), *Transnational Legal Processes: Globalisation and Power Disparities*, London: Butterworths, pp. 295–315.

International Council of Human Rights and Transparency International 2009. *Corruption and Human Rights: Making the Connection*, Geneva: ICHRR.

Islamic Republic of Afghanistan 2008. *Afghanistan National Development Strategy 2008–2013*, available at www.undp.org.af/Publications/KeyDocuments/ANDS_Full_Eng.pdf.

IUC Global Legal Standards Research Group 2009. 'IUC Independent Policy Report: At the End of the End of History – Global Legal Standards: Part of the Solution or Part of the Problem?', *Global Jurist*, vol. 9, issue 3, article 2.

Ivanyna, Maksym and Anwar Shah 2011. 'Citizen-centric Governance Indicators: Measuring and Monitoring Governance By Listening to the People', *CESifo Forum*, vol. 12, 59–71.

Jackson, Howell E. and Mark J. Roe 2009. 'Public and Private Enforcement of Securities Laws: Resource-Based Evidence', *Journal of Financial Economics*, vol. 93, 207–38.

Jackson, Jonathan et al. (eight co-authors) 2011. 'Developing European Indicators of Trust in Justice', *European Journal of Criminology*, vol. 8, 267–85.

Jackson, Vicki C. 2010. *Constitutional Engagement in a Transnational Era*, Oxford: Oxford University Press.

Jackson, Vicki C. 2012. 'Comparative Constitutional Law: Methodologies', in Michel Rosenfeld and Andras Sajo (eds.), *The Oxford Handbook of Comparative Constitutional Law*, Oxford: Oxford University Press, pp. 54–74.

Jacob, Herbert, Erhard Blankeburg, Herbert Kritzer, Doris Marie Provine and Jospeph Sanders 1996. *Courts, Law, and Politics in Comparative Perspective*, New Haven: Yale University Press.

Jacobs, David and Jason T. Carmichael 2002. 'The Political Sociology of the Death Penalty: A Pooled Time-Series', *American Sociological Review*, vol. 67, 109–31.

Jagtenberg, Bob and Annie de Roo 2009. 'From Traditional Judicial Styles to Verdict Industries Inc.', in Nick Huls, Maurice Adams and Jacco Bomhoff (eds.), *The Legitimacy of Highest Courts' Rulings: 'Judicial Deliberations' and Beyond*, The Hague: TMC Asser Press, pp. 301–22.

Jameson, Fredric 1991. *Postmodernism, or, The Cultural Logic of Late Capitalism*, Durham, NC: Duke University Press.

Jamin, Christophe 2002. 'Saleilles' and Lambert's Old Dream Revisited', *American Journal of Comparative Law*, vol. 50, 701–18.

Jauffret-Spinosi, Camille and René David 2002. *Les Grands Systèmes de Droit Contemporains*, 11th edn, Paris: Dalloz.

Jemielniak, Joanna and Przemyslaw Mikłaszewicz 2010. 'Capturing the Change: Universalising Tendencies in Legal Interpretation', in Joanna Jemielniak and Przemyslaw Mikłaszewicz (eds.), *Interpretation of Law in the Global World: From Particularism to a Universal Approach*, Heidelberg: Springer, pp. 1–30.

Jessup, Philip C. 1956. *Transnational Law*, New Haven: Yale University Press.

Jettinghoff, Alex 2001. 'State Formation and Legal Change: On the Impact of International Politics', in David Nelken and Johannes Feest (eds.), *Adapting Legal Culture*, Oxford: Hart, pp. 99–116.

Johnson, David T. 2001. *The Japanese Way of Justice: Prosecuting Crime in Japan*, Oxford: Oxford University Press.

Johnson, David T. 2010. 'Chinese Executions and the Japanese Dog That Did Not Bark', available at http://japanfocus.org/-David_T_-Johnson/3355.

Johnson, David T. and Franklin E. Zimring 2009. *The Next Frontier: National Development, Political Change, and the Death Penalty in Asia*, New York: Oxford University Press.

Joireman, Sandra Fullerton 2004. 'Colonization and the Rule of Law: Comparing the Effectiveness of Common Law and Civil Law Countries', *Constitutional Political Economy*, vol. 15, 315–38.

Jones, Gareth 1983. 'The Recovery of Benefits Gained from a Breach of Contract', *Law Quarterly Review*, vol. 99, 443–60.

Jones, Owen D. 2001. 'Proprioception, Non-Law, and Biolegal History', *Florida Law Review*, vol. 53, 831–74.

Jones, Trevor and Tim Newburn 2007. *Policy Transfer and Criminal Justice: Exploring US Influence over British Crime Control Policy*, Maidenhead: Open University Press.

Jordan, Cally 2013. 'How International Finance Really Works', *Law and Financial Markets Review*, vol. 7, 256–66.

Jordana, Jacint, David Levi-Faur and Xavier Fernández i Marín 2011. 'The Global Diffusion of Regulatory Agencies: Channels of Transfer and Stages of Diffusion', *Comparative Political Studies*, vol. 44, 1343–69.

Jowell, Roger 1998. 'How Comparative is Comparative Research?', *American Behavioral Scientists*, vol. 42, 168–77.

Jowell, Roger, Caroline Roberts, Rory Fitzgerald and Gillian Eva (eds.) 2007. *Measuring Attitudes Cross-Nationally: Lessons from the European Social Survey*, London: Sage.

Jreisat, Jamil 2012. *Globalism and Comparative Public Administration*, Boca Rato, FL: CRC Press.

Juenger, Friedrich K. 2000. 'The Lex Mercatoria and Private International Law', *Louisiana Law Review*, vol. 60, 1133–50.

Jupp, John 2013. 'Legal Transplants as Solutions for Criminal Law Reform in Post-Intervention States: Afghanistan's Interim Criminal Procedure Code 2004', *American Journal of Comparative Law*, vol. 61, 51–91.

Juwana, Hikmahanto 2006. 'Human Rights in Indonesia', in Randall Peerenboom, Carole J. Petersen and Albert H. Y. Chen (eds.), Routledge, *Human Rights in Asia*, London and New York, pp. 364–83.

Kadner Grazio, Thomas, 2009. *Comparative Contract Law*, New York: Palgrave.

Kagan, Robert A. 2001. *Adversarial Legalism: The American Way of Law*. Cambridge, MA: Harvard University Press.

Kagan, Robert A. 2007. 'American and European Ways of Law: Six Entrenched Differences', in Volkmar Gessner and David Nelken (eds.), *European Ways of Law*, Oxford: Hart, pp. 41–70.

Kahn, Jeffrey 2005. 'The Search for the Rule of Law in Russia', *Georgetown Journal of International Law*, vol. 37, 353–409.

Kahn, Paul W. 2003. 'Comparative Constitutionalism in a New Key', *Michigan Law Review*, vol. 101, 2677–705.

Kahn-Freund, Otto 1974. 'On Use and Misuse of Comparative Law', *Modern Law Review*, vol. 37, 1–27.

Kahn-Freund, Sir Otto, Claudine Levy and Bernard Rudden 1979. *A Sourcebook on French Law*, 2nd edn, Oxford: Clarendon.

Kakouris, Constantinos N. 1994. 'Use of the Comparative Method by the Court of Justice of the European Communities', *Pace International Law Review*, vol. 6, 267–83.

Kamba, W. C. 1974. 'Comparative Law: A Theoretical Framework', *International and Comparative Law Quarterly*, vol. 23, 485–519.

Karhu, Juha 2004. 'How to Make Comparable Things: Legal Engineering at the Service of Comparative Law', in Mark Van Hoecke (ed.), *Epistemology and Methodology of Comparative Law*, Oxford: Hart, pp. 79–89.

Karton, Joshua D. H. 2013. *The Culture of International Arbitration and The Evolution of Contract Law*, Oxford: Oxford University Press.

Kayaalp, Ebru 2012. 'Torn in Translation: An Ethnographic Study of Regulatory Decision-making in Turkey', *Regulation & Governance*, vol. 6, 225–41.

Keck, Margaret E. and Kathryn Sikkink 1998. *Activists Beyond Borders: Advocacy Networks in International Politics*. Ithaca, NY: Cornell University Press.

Keep, Helen and Rob Midgley 2007. 'The Emerging Role of Ubuntu-botho in Developing a Consensual South African Legal Culture', in Fred Bruinsma and David Nelken (eds.), *Explorations in Legal Culture, Recht der Werkelijkheid* (special issue), pp. 29–56.

Kelemen, R. Daniel 2011. *Eurolegalism: The Transformation of Law and Regulation in the European Union*, Cambridge, MA: Harvard University Press.

Kelemen, R. Daniel and Eric C. Sibbitt 2002. 'The Americanization of Japanese Law', *University of Pennsylvania Journal of International Economic Law*, vol. 23, 269–323.

Kelley, Thomas A. 2007. 'Exporting Western Law to the Developing World: The Troubling Case of Niger', *Global Jurist*, vol. 7, issue 3, article 8.

Kelley, Thomas A. 2008. 'Unintended Consequences of Legal Westernization in Niger: Harming Contemporary Slaves by Reconceptualizing Property', *American Journal of Comparative Law*, vol. 56, 999–1038.

Kelsen, Hans 1942. 'Judicial Review of Legislation: A Comparative Study of the Austrian and the American Constitution', *Journal of Politics*, vol. 4, 183–200.

Kennedy, David 1997. 'New Approaches to Comparative Law: Comparativism and International Governance', *Utah Law Review*, 545–637.

Kennedy, David 2002. 'The International Human Rights Movement: Part of the Problem?', *Harvard Human Rights Journal*, vol. 15, 101–25.

Kennedy, David 2003a. 'Two Globalizations of Law & Legal Thought: 1850–1968', *Suffolk University Law Review*, vol. 36, 631–79.

Kennedy, David 2003b. 'Law and Developments', in John Hatchard and Amanda Perry-Kessaris (eds.), *Law and Development: Facing Complexity in the 21st Century*, London: Cavendish, pp. 17–26.

Kennedy, David 2008. 'The "Rule of Law", Political Choices, and Development Common Sense', in David M. Trubek and Alvaro Santos (eds.), *The New Law and Economic Development*, Cambridge: Cambridge University Press, pp. 95–173.

Kennedy, Duncan 2012. 'Political Ideology and Comparative Law', in Mauro Bussani and Ugo Mattei (eds.), *Cambridge Companion to Comparative Law*, Cambridge: Cambridge University Press, pp. 35–56.

Kenney, Sally J. 2000. 'Supreme Court Référendaires at the European Court of Justice and Law Clerks at the U.S. Supreme Court', *Comparative Political Studies*, vol. 33, 593–625.

Kenworthy, Lane 2010. 'Institutions, Wealth, and Inequality', in Glenn Morgan, John L. Campbell, Colin Crouch, Ove Kaj Pedersen and Richard Whitley (eds.), *The Oxford Handbook of Comparative Institutional Analysis*, Oxford: Oxford University Press, pp. 399–420.

Kern, Christoph A. 2007. *Justice between Simplification and Formalism*, Tübingen: Mohr Siebeck.

Kern, Christoph A. 2009. Der Doing-Business Report der Weltbank – Fragwürdige Quantifizierung Rechtlicher Qualität?, *Juristenzeitung*, 498–504.

Kessler, Amalia D. 2011. 'The Making and Debunking of Legal Tradition', *Roger Williams University Law Review*, vol. 16, 129–32.

Kfir, Isaac 2013. 'An Imperfect Solution to Afghan Reconciliation – An Afghan Truth Commission', *Penn State Journal of Law and International Affairs*, forthcoming.

Khan, Rahmatulla and Sushil Kumar 1971. Parts I and II, in Indian Law Institute (ed.), *An Introduction to the Study of Comparative Law*, Bombay: N. M. Tripathi.

Kiefel, Mr. Justice 2000. 'Guarantees by Family Members and Spouses: Garcia and a German Perspective', *Australian Law Journal*, vol. 74, 692–706.

Kiikeri, Markku 2001, *Comparative Legal Reasoning and European Law*, Dodrecht: Kluwer.

Kim, Kensie 2010. 'Mixed Systems in Legal Origins Analysis', *Southern California Law Review*, vol. 83, 693–728.

King, Michael 1997. 'Comparing Legal Cultures in the Quest for Law's Identity', in David Nelken (ed.), *Comparing Legal Cultures*, Aldershot: Dartmouth, pp. 119–34.

Kinoshita, Tsuyoshi 2001. 'Legal System and Legal Culture in Japan', *Zeitschrift für Japanisches Recht*, vol. 11, 7–36.

Kirchgässner, Gebhard 2011. 'Econometric Estimates of Deterrence of the Death Penalty: Facts or Ideology?', *Kyklos*, vol. 64, 448–78.

Kirshner, Jodie 2012. 'Why is the U.S. Abdicating the Policing of Multinational Corporations to Europe?: Extraterritoriality, Sovereignty, and the Alien Tort Statute', *Berkeley Journal of International Law*, vol. 30, 259–302.

Kiser, Edgar and Michael Hechter 1991. 'The Role of General Theory in Comparative-Historical Sociology', *American Journal of Sociology*, vol. 97, 1–30.

Kitagawa, Zentaro 2006. 'Development of Comparative Law in East Asia', in Mathias Reimann and Reinhard Zimmermann (eds.), *The Oxford Handbook of Comparative Law*, Oxford: Oxford University Press, pp. 237–60.

Klami, Hannu Tapani 1981. *Comparative Law and Legal Concepts: The Methods and Limits of Comparative Law and Its Connection with Legal Theory*, Vammala: Oikeustiede-Jurisprudentia XIV.

Klasing, Mariko J. 2013. 'Cultural Dimensions, Collective Values and their Importance for Institutions', *Journal of Comparative Economics*, vol. 41, 447–67.

Kleinfeld, Joshua 2011. 'The Concept of Evil in American and German Criminal Punishment', available at http://works.bepress.com/joshua_kleinfeld/2/.

Kleinheisterkamp, Jan 2006. 'Development of Comparative Law in Latin America', in Mathias Reimann and Reinhard Zimmermann (eds.), *The Oxford Handbook of Comparative Law*, Oxford: Oxford University Press, pp. 261–301.

Klerman, Daniel M. and Paul G. Mahoney 2007. 'Legal Origin?', *Journal of Comparative Economics*, vol. 35, 278–93.

Klerman, Daniel M., Paul G. Mahoney, Holger Spamann and Mark I. Weinstein 2011. 'Legal Origin or Colonial History?', *Journal of Legal Analysis*, vol. 3, 379–409.

Klimas, Tadas 2006. *Comparative Contract Law: A Transystemic Approach With an Emphasis on the Continental Law: Cases, Text and Materials*, Durham, NC: Carolina Academic Press Law Casebook.

Klug, Heinz 2005. 'Transnational Human Rights: Exploring the Persistence and Globalization of Human Rights', *Annual Review of Law and Social Science*, vol. 1, 85–103.

Koch, Charles H. 2003. 'Envisioning a Global Legal Culture', *Michigan Journal of International Law*, vol. 25, 1–76.

Koch, Charles H. 2004. 'The Advantages of the Civil Law Judicial Design as The Model for Emerging Legal Systems', *Indiana Journal of Global Legal Studies*, vol. 11, 139–60.

Kogut, Bruce and Charles Ragin 2006. 'Exploring Complexity When Diversity Is Limited: Institutional Complementarity in Theories of Rule of Law and National Systems Revisited', *European Management Review*, vol. 3, 44–59.

Kokott, Juliane and Martin Kaspar 2012. 'Ensuring Constitutional Efficacy', in Michel Rosenfeld and Andras Sajo (eds.), *The Oxford Handbook of Comparative Constitutional Law*, Oxford: Oxford University Press, pp. 795–815.

Komarek, Jan 2011. 'Judicial Lawmaking and Precedent in Supreme Courts', LSE Law, Society and Economy Working Papers, 04–2011.

Konzelmann, Sue and Marc Fovargue-Davies (eds). 2013. *Banking Systems in Crisis: The Faces of Liberal Capitalism*, London: Routledge.

Koopmans, Tim 2003. *Courts and Political Institutions: A Comparative View*, Cambridge: Cambridge University Press.

Kötz, Hein 1987. 'Taking Civil Codes Less Seriously', *Modern Law Review*, vol. 50, 1–15.

Kötz, Hein 1990. 'Scholarship and the Courts: A Comparative Survey', in David S. Clark (ed.), *Comparative and Private International Law: Essay in Honour of J. H. Merryman on his Seventieth Birthday*, pp. 183–95.

Kötz, Hein 2003. 'Civil Justice Systems in Europe and the United States', *Duke Journal of Comparative and International Law*, vol. 13, 61–78.

Kötz, Hein 2010. 'The Jurisdiction of Choice: England and Wales or Germany?', *European Review of Private Law*, vol. 6, 1243–57.

Kovac, Mitja 2011. *Comparative Contract Law and Economics*, Cheltenham: Edward Elgar.

Krause, Harry D. 2006. 'Comparative Family Law', in Mathias Reimann and Reinhard Zimmermann (eds.), *The Oxford Handbook of Comparative Law*, Oxford: Oxford University Press, pp. 1099–129.

Kravets, Erik 2010. 'Discovery: Should U.S. Civil Procedure be "Germanized"?', *DAJV Newsletter*, p. 154.

Krever, Tor 2011. 'The Legal Turn in Late Development Theory: The Rule of Law and the World Bank's Development Model', *Harvard International Law Journal*, vol. 52, 288–319.

Krever, Tor 2013. 'Quantifying Law: Legal Indicator Projects and the Reproduction of Neo-liberal Common Sense', *Third World Quarterly*, vol. 34, 131–50.

Krishnan Jayanth K. 2012. 'Academic SAILERS: The Ford Foundation and the Efforts to Shape Legal Education in Africa, 1957–1977', *American Journal of Legal History*, vol. 52, 262–324.

Krishnan, Jayanth K. and C. Raj Kumar 2011. 'Delay in Process, Denial of Justice: The Jurisprudence and Empirics of Speedy Trials in Comparative Perspective', *Georgetown Journal of International Law*, vol. 42, 747–84.

Kritzer, Herbert M. (ed.) 2002. *Legal Systems of the World, A Political and Cultural Encyclopedia*, Santa Barbara, CA: ABC Clio.

Kritzer, Herbert M. 2008. 'To Lawyer or Not to Lawyer: Is That the Question?', *Journal of Empirical Legal Studies*, vol. 5, 875–906.

Kroncke, Jedidiah 2012. 'Law and Development as Anti-Comparative Law', *Vanderbilt Journal of Transnational Law*, vol. 45, 477–555.

Krygier, Martin 2011. 'Approaching the Rule of Law', in Whit Mason (ed.), *The Rule of Law in Afghanistan. Missing in Inaction*, Cambridge: Cambridge University Press, pp. 35–49.

Krygier, Martin 2012. 'Rule of Law', in Michel Rosenfeld and Andras Sajo (eds.), *The Oxford Handbook of Comparative Constitutional Law*, Oxford: Oxford University Press, pp. 233–49.

Kühn, Zdenek 2006. 'Development of Comparative Law in Central and Eastern Europe', in Mathias Reimann and Reinhard Zimmermann (eds.), *The Oxford Handbook of Comparative Law*, Oxford: Oxford University Press, pp. 216–36.

Kumar, C. Raj 2011. *Corruption and Human Rights in India: Comparative Perspectives on Transparency and Good Governance*, Oxford: Oxford University Press.

Kuper, Adam 1999. *Culture: The Anthropologists Account*, Cambridge, MA: Harvard University Press.

Kuran, Timur 2005. 'The Absence of the Corporation in Islamic Law: Origins and Persistence', *American Journal of Comparative Law*, vol. 53, 785–834.

Kuran, Timur 2010a. *The Long Divergence: How Islamic Law Held Back the Middle East*, Princeton: Princeton University Press.

Kuran, Timur 2010b. 'The Rule of Law in Islamic Thought and Practice', in James J Heckman, Robert L. Nelson and Lee Cabatingan (eds.), *Global Perspectives on the Rule of Law*, Abingdon: Routledge, pp. 71–89.

Kurkchiyan, Marina 2007. 'The Impact of the Transition on the Role of Law in Russia', in Fred Bruinsma and David Nelken (eds.), *Explorations in Legal Culture, Recht der Werkelijkheid* (special issue), pp. 75–93.

Kurkchiyan, Marina 2009. 'Russian Legal Culture: An Analysis of Adaptive Response to an Institutional Transplant', *Law and Social Inquiry*, vol. 34, 337–64.

Kurkchiyan, Marina 2010. 'Russia and China: A Comparative Perspective on the Post-Communist Transition', FLJS Working Paper.

Kurtz, Marcus J. and Andrew Schrank 2007. 'Growth and Governance: Models, Measures, and Mechanisms', *The Journal of Politics*, vol. 69, 538–54.

La Porta, Rafael, Florencio Lopez-de-Silanes, Andrei Shleifer and Robert Vishny 1998. 'Law and Finance', *Journal of Political Economy*, vol. 106, 1113–55.

La Porta, Rafael, Florencio Lopez-de-Silanes, Christian Pop-Eleches and Andrei Shleifer 2004. 'Judicial Checks and Balances', *Journal of Political Economy*, vol. 11, 445–70.

La Porta, Rafael, Florencio Lopez-de-Silanes and Andrei Shleifer 2006. 'What Works in Securities Laws', *Journal of Finance*, vol. 61, 1–32.

La Porta, Rafael, Florencio Lopez-de-Silanes and Andrei Shleifer 2008. 'The Economic Consequences of Legal Origins', *Journal of Economic Literature*, vol. 46, 285–332.

Labov, William 2007. 'Transmission and Diffusion', *Language*, vol. 83, 344–87.

Lacey, Nicola 2008. *The Prisoners' Dilemma: Political Economy and Punishment in Contemporary Democracies*, Cambridge: Cambridge University Press.

Lacey, Nicola 2011. 'Why Globalisation doesn't Spell Convergence: Models of Institutional Variation and the Comparative Political Economy of Punishment', in Adam Crawford (ed.), *International and Comparative Criminal Justice and Urban Governance*, Cambridge: Cambridge University Press, pp. 214–50.

Ladeur, Karl-Heinz 2004. 'Methodology and European Law – Can Methodology Change so as to Cope with the Multiplicity of the Law?', in Mark Van Hoecke (ed.), *Epistemology and Methodology of Comparative Law*, Oxford: Hart, pp. 91–122.

Laithier, Yves-Marie 2009. *Droit Comparé*, Paris: Dalloz.

Lalenis, Konstantinos, Martin de Jong and Virginie Mamadouh 2002. 'Families of Nations and Institutional Transplantation', in Martin de Jong, Konstantinos Lalenis and Virginie Mamadouh (eds.), *The Theory and Practice of Institutional Transplantation*, Dordrecht: Kluwer, pp. 33–52.

Lambert, Édouard 1903. *La Fonction du Droit Civil Comparé. Tome Ier: Les Conceptions Étroites ou Unilatérales*, Paris: V. Giard & E. Brière.

Lambert, Édouard 1905. 'Congrès International de Droit Comparé, Tenu à Paris du 31 Juillet au 4 Août 1900', *Procès-verbaux des Séances et Documents*, vol. I, pp. 26–60, available at http://archive.org/details/congrsinternati00compgoog.

Landau, David 2010. 'Political Institutions and Judicial Role in Comparative Constitutional Law', *Harvard International Law Journal*, vol. 51, pp. 319–77.

Landman, Todd 2002. 'Comparative Politics and Human Rights', *Human Rights Quarterly*, vol. 24, 890–923.

Landman, Todd 2008. *Issues and Methods in Comparative Politics: An Introduction*, 3rd edn, London: Routledge.

Landman, Todd and Edzia Carvalho 2010. *Measuring Human Rights*, London: Routledge.

Lando, Henrik and Caspar Rose 2003. 'The Myth Of Specific Performance in Civil Law Countries', *American Law & Economics Association Annual Meetings*, available at http://law.bepress.com/alea/14th/art15.

Lang, Andrew 2011. *World Trade Law after Neoliberalism: Reimagining the Global Economic Order*, Oxford: Oxford University Press.

Langer, Maximo 2004. 'From Legal Transplants to Legal Translations: The Globalization of Plea Bargaining and the Americanization Thesis in Criminal Procedure', *Harvard International Law Journal*, vol. 45, 1–64.

Lasser, Mitchel 1998. '"Lit. Theory" Put to the Test: A Comparative Literary Analysis of American Judicial Tests and French Judicial Discourse', *Harvard Law Review*, vol. 111, 689–770.

Lasser, Mitchel 2003. 'The Question of Understanding', in Pierre Legrand and Roderick Munday (eds.), *Comparative Legal Studies: Traditions and Transitions*, Cambridge: Cambridge University Press, pp. 197–239.

Lasser, Mitchel 2009a. *Judicial Deliberations: A Comparative Analysis of Judicial Transparency and Legitimacy*, Oxford: Oxford University Press.

Lasser, Mitchel 2009b. *Judicial Transformations: The Rights Revolution in the Courts of Europe*, Oxford: Oxford University Press.

Latour, Bruno 1996. *Aramis or the Love of Technology*, Cambridge, MA: Harvard University Press.

Latour, Bruno 2005. *Reassembling the Social*, Oxford: Oxford University Press.

Launay, Ribert 2001. 'Montesquieu: The Spectre of Despotism and the Origins of Comparative Law', in Annelise Riles (ed.), *Rethinking the Masters of Comparative Law*, Oxford: Hart, pp. 22–39.

Lauterpacht, Hersch 1927. *Private Law Sources and Analogies of International Law*, London: Longmans.

Law, David S. 2008. 'Globalization and the Future of Constitutional Rights', *Northwestern University Law Review*, vol. 102, 1277–349.

Law, David S. 2011a. 'Why Has Judicial Review Failed in Japan?', *Washington University Law Review*, vol. 88, 1425–66.

Law, David S. 2011b. 'Constitutions', in Peter Cane and Herbert Kritzer (eds.), *Oxford Handbook of Empirical Legal Studies*, Oxford: Oxford University Press, pp. 376–98.

Law, David S. and Mila Versteeg 2011. 'The Evolution and Ideology of Global Constitutionalism', *California Law Review*, vol. 99, 1163–253.

Law, David S. and Mila Versteeg 2012. 'The Declining Influence of the US Constitution', *New York University Law Review*, vol. 87, 762–858.

Lawless, Robert M., Jennifer K. Robbennolt and Thomas S. Ulen 2009. *Empirical Methods in Law*, New York: Aspen.

Lawson, F.H. 1977. *Selected Essays, Volume II: The Comparison*, Amsterdam: North-Holland.

Lee, Hoong Phun 2011. 'The Judiciary: A Comparative Conspectus', in Hoong Phun Lee (ed.), *Judiciaries in Comparative Perspective*, Cambridge: Cambridge University Press, pp. 533–41.

Lee, Sang M. and David L. Olson 2010. *Convergenomics: Strategic Innovation in the Convergence Era*, Farnham: Gower.

Legeais, Raymond 2008. *Grands Systèmes de Droit Contemporains: Approche Comparative*, 2nd edn, Paris: Litec.

Legrand, Pierre 1995. 'Strange Power of Words: Codification Situated', *Tulane European and Civil Law Forum*, 1–34.

Legrand, Pierre 1996. 'European Legal Systems Are Not Converging', *The International and Comparative Law Quarterly*, vol. 45, 52–81.

Legrand, Pierre 1997a. 'Against a European Civil Code', *The Modern Law Review*, vol. 60, 44–63.

Legrand, Pierre 1997b. 'The Impossibility of Legal Transplants', *Maastricht Journal of European and Comparative Law*, vol. 4, 111–24.

Legrand, Pierre 1998a. 'Codification and the Politics of Exclusion: A Challenge for Comparativists', *UC Davis Law Review*, vol. 31, 779–807.

Legrand, Pierre 1998b. 'Are Civilians Educatable?', *Legal Studies*, vol. 18, 216–30.

Legrand, Pierre 1998c. 'Counterpoint: Law is also Culture', in Franco Ferrari (ed.), *The Unification of International Commercial Law*, Baden-Baden: Nomos, pp. 245–55.

Legrand, Pierre 1999. *Fragments on Law-as-Culture*, Deventer: W. E. J. Willink.

Legrand, Pierre 2001a. 'What "Legal Transplants?"', in David Nelken and Johannes Feest (eds.), *Adapting Legal Culture*, Oxford: Hart, pp. 55–70.

Legrand, Pierre 2001b. 'The Return of the Repressed, Moving Comparative Legal Studies Beyond Pleasure', *Tulane Law Review*, vol. 75, 1033–51.

Legrand, Pierre 2002. 'On the Unbearable Localness of Law: Academic Fallacies and Unseasonable Observations', *European Review of Private Law*, vol. 10, 61–76.

Legrand, Pierre 2003. 'The Same and the Different', in Pierre Legrand and Roderick Munday (eds.), *Comparative Legal Studies: Traditions and Transitions*, Cambridge: Cambridge University Press, pp. 240–311.

Legrand, Pierre 2005. 'Paradoxically, Derrida: For a Comparative Legal Studies', *Cardozo Law Review*, vol. 27, 631–717.

Legrand, Pierre 2006a. 'Antivonbar', *Journal of Comparative Law*, vol. 1, 13–40.

Legrand, Pierre 2006b. 'Comparative Legal Studies and the Matter of Authenticity', *Journal of Comparative Law*, vol. 1, 371–460.

Legrand, Pierre 2006c. 'On the Singularity of Law', *Harvard International Law Journal*, vol. 47, 517–30.

Legrand, Pierre 2007a. 'Comparative Law', in David S. Clark (ed.), *Encyclopedia of Law and Society*, Los Angeles: Sage, pp. 220–3.

Legrand, Pierre 2007b. 'Book review: *The Oxford Handbook of Comparative Law*', *Journal of Comparative Law*, vol. 2, p. 253.

Legrand, Pierre 2009. 'Econocentrism', *University of Toronto Law Journal*, vol. 59, 215–22.

Legrand, Pierre 2011. *Le Droit Comparé*, 4th edn, Paris: Presses Universitaires de France.

Lele, Priya and Mathias Siems 2007. 'Shareholder Protection: A Leximetric Approach', *Journal of Corporate Law Studies*, vol. 7, 17–50.

Lemmens, Koen 2012. 'Comparative Law as an Act of Modesty: A Pragmatic and Realistic Approach to Comparative Legal Scholarship', in Maurice Adams and Jacco Bomhoff (eds.), *Practice and Theory in Comparative Law*, Cambridge: Cambridge University Press, pp. 302–25.

Levasseur, Alain A. 2008. *Comparative Law of Contracts: Cases and Materials*, Durham, NC: Carolina University Press.

Levi Faur, David 2005. 'The Global Diffusion of Regulatory Capitalism', *The Annals of the American Academy of Political and Social Sciences*, vol. 598, 12–32.

Levitsky, Steven and Lucan A. Way 2010. *Competitive Authoritarianism, Hybrid Regimes After the Cold War*, Cambridge: Cambridge University Press.

Levy, Ernst 1950. 'The Reception of Highly Developed Legal Systems by Peoples of Different Cultures', *Washington Law Review*, vol. 25, 233–45.

Liamputtong, Pranee 2010. *Performing Qualitative Cross-Cultural Research*, Cambridge: Cambridge University Press.

Libman, Alexander 2012. 'Democracy and Growth: Is the Effect Nonlinear?', *The Economic Research Guardian*, vol. 2, 99–120.

Licht, Amir, Chanan Goldschmidt and Shalom H. Schwartz 2005. 'Culture, Law, and Corporate Governance', *International Review of Law and Economics*, vol. 25, 229–55.

Licht, Amir, Chanan Goldschmidt, and Shalom H. Schwartz 2007. 'Culture Rules: The Foundations of the Rule of Law and Other Norms of Governance', *Journal of Comparative Economics*, vol. 35, 659–88.

Liebman, Benjamin L. 2013. 'China's Courts: Restricted Reform', in David Kennedy and Joseph E. Stiglitz (eds.), *Law and Economics with Chinese Characteristics: Institutions for Promoting Development in the Twenty-First Century*, Oxford: Oxford University Press, pp. 568–82.

Lijphart, Arend 1971. 'Comparative Politics and the Comparative Method', *American Political Science Review*, vol. 65, 682–93.

Lijphart, Arend 1999. *Patterns of Democracy: Government Forms and Performance in Thirty-Six Countries*, New Haven: Yale University Press.

Lin, Li-Wen 2009. 'Legal Transplants Through Private Contracting: Codes of Vendor Conduct in Global Supply Chains as an Example', *American Journal of Comparative Law*, vol. 57, 711–44.

Lindsey, Tim (ed.) 2007. *Law Reform in Developing and Transition States*, London: Routledge.

Linos, Katerina 2007. 'How Can International Organizations Shape National Welfare States? Evidence From Compliance With European Union Directives', *Comparative Political Studies*, vol. 40, 547–70.

Linos, Katerina 2013. *The Democratic Foundations of Policy Diffusion: How Health, Family, and Employment Laws Spread Across Countries*, Oxford: Oxford University Press.

Linz, Juan J. 1990. 'The Perils of Presidentialism', *Journal of Democracy*, vol. 1, pp. 51–69.

Linz, Juan J. and Alfred Stepan 1996. *Problems of Democratic Transition and Consolidation: Southern Europe, South America and Post Communist Europe*, Baltimore, MD: Johns Hopkins University Press.

Lipset, Martin Seymour 1959, 'Some Social Requisites of Democracy, Economic Development, and Political Legitimacy', *American Political Science Review*, vol. 53, 69–105.

Lipset, Martin Seymour 1973. *The First New Nation: The United States in Historical & Comparative Perspective*, New York: Norton.

Lipset, Martin Seymour 1996. *American Exceptionalism*, New York: Norton.

López-Medina, Diego 2012. 'The Latin American and Caribbean Legal Traditions', in Mauro Bussani and Ugo Mattei (eds.), *Cambridge Companion to Comparative Law*, Cambridge: Cambridge University Press, pp. 244–367.

Losano, Mario G. 2000. *I Grandi Sistemi Giuridici: Introduzione ai Diritti Europei ed Extraeuropei*, Rome: Laterza.

Loth, Marc A. 2009, 'Courts in a Quest for Legitimacy: A Comparative Approach', in Nick Huls, Maurice Adams and Jacco Bomhoff (eds.), *The Legitimacy of Highest Courts' Rulings: 'Judicial Deliberations' and Beyond*, The Hague: TMC Asser Press, pp. 267–88.

Low, Gary 2012. 'The (Ir)Relevance of Harmonization and Legal Diversity to European Contract Law: A Perspective from Psychology', *European Review of Private Law*, vol. 18, 285–305.

Lubman, Stanley B. 1999. *Bird in a Cage: Legal Reform in China after Mao*, Stanford: Stanford University Press.

Lundmark, Thomas 2001. 'Verbose Contracts', *American Journal of Comparative Law*, vol. 49, 121–32.

Lundmark, Thomas 2012. *Charting the Divide Between Common and Civil Law*, Oxford: Oxford University Press.

Luts, L. A. 2011. 'Typologies of Modern Legal Systems of the World', in William E. Butler, Oleksiy V. Kresin and Iu. S. Shemshuchenko (eds.), *Foundations of Comparative Law: Methods and Typologies*, London: Wildy, Simmonds and Hill Publishing, pp. 36–52 (also in *Journal of Comparative Law*, vol. 5 (2010), 28–40).

Macaulay, Stewart 1963. 'Non-Contractual Relations in Business: A Preliminary Study', *American Sociological Review*, vol. 28, 55–67.

MacCormick, D. Neil and Robert S. Summers (eds.) 1991. *Interpreting Statutes: A Comparative Study*, Aldershot: Dartmouth.

MacCormick, D. Neil and Robert S. Summers, 1997. 'Introduction' and 'Further General Reflections and Conclusions', in D. Neil MacCormick and Robert S. Summers (eds.), *Interpreting Precedents*, Aldershot: Ashgate, pp. 1–15 and 531–50.

Macfarlane, Alan 2004. 'To Contrast and Compare', in Vinay Kumar Srivastava (ed.), *Methodology and Fieldwork*, Delhi: Oxford University Press, pp. 94–111.

MacNeil, Iain and Li Xiao 2006. 'Comply or Explain: Market Discipline and Non-Compliance with the Combined Code', *Corporate Governance: An International Review*, vol. 14, 486–96.

Mahoney, James 1999. 'Nominal, Ordinal, and Narrative Appraisal in Macrocausal Analysis', *American Journal of Sociology*, vol. 104, 1154–96.

Mahoney, James and Dietrich Rueschemeyer (eds.) 2003. *Comparative Historical Analysis in the Social Sciences*, Cambridge: Cambridge University Press.

Mahoney, Paul G. 2001. 'The Common Law and Economic Growth: Hayek Might be Right', *Journal of Legal Studies*, vol. 30, 503–24.

Maine, Sir Henry 1861. *Ancient Law*, London: Humphrey Milford.

Mair, Peter 1996. 'Comparative Politics: An Overview', in Robert Gooden and Hans-Dieter Klingemann (eds.), *A New Handbook of Political Science*. Oxford: Oxford University Press, pp. 309–35.

Maitland, Frederic William 1936. *The Forms of Action at Common Law: A Course of Lectures* (edited by A. H. Chaytor and W. J. Whittaker), Cambridge: Cambridge University Press.

Mak, Elaine 2011. 'Why Do Dutch and UK Judges Cite Foreign Law?', *Cambridge Law Journal*, vol. 70, 420–50.

Makdisi, George 1981. *The Rise of Colleges: Institutions of Higher Learning in Islam and the West*, Edinburgh: Edinburgh University Press.

Makdisi, George 1985–86. 'The Guilds of Law in Medieval Legal History: An Inquiry into the Origins of the Inns of Court', *Cleveland State Law Review*, vol. 34, 3–18.

Makdisi, John A. 1999. 'The Islamic Origins of The Common Law', *North Carolina Law Review*, vol. 77, 1635–739.

Malinowski, Bronislaw 1926. *Crime and Custom in Savage Society*, Totowa, NJ: Rowman & Allanheld.

Mallat, Chibli 2007. *Introduction to Middle Eastern Law*, Oxford: Oxford University Press.

Mamdani, Mahmood 1996. *Citizen and Subject: Contemporary Africa and the Legacy of Late Colonialism*, Princeton: Princeton University Press.

Mamlyuk, Boris N. and Ugo Mattei 2011. 'Comparative International Law', *Brooklyn Journal of International Law*, vol. 36, 385–452.

Mancuso, Salvatore 2008. 'The New African Law: Beyond the Difference Between Common Law and Civil Law', *Annual Survey of International & Comparative Law*, vol. 14, iss. 1, article 4.

Mancuso, Salvatore 2009. 'Legal Transplants and Economic Development: Civil Law Vs. Common Law?', in J. C. Oliveira and P. Cardinal (eds.), *One Country, Two Systems, Three Legal Orders – Perspectives of Evolution*, Berlin: Springer, pp. 75–89.

Manning, Nick and Ian Shaw 1999. 'The Transferability of Welfare Models: A Comparison of the Scandinavian and State Socialist Models in Relation to Finland and Estonia', in C. Jones Finer (ed.), *Transnational Social Policy*, Oxford: Blackwell, pp. 120–38.

March, James G. and Johan P. Olsen 2006. 'Elaborating the "New Institutionalism"', in R. A. W. Rhodes, Sarah A. Binder and Bert A. Rockman (eds.), *The Oxford Handbook of Political Institutions*, Oxford: Oxford University Press, pp. 3–20.

Marchenko, M. N. 2011. 'Legal Systems of the Modern World: Problems of Identification', in William E. Butler, Oleksiy V. Kresin and Iu. S. Shemshuchenko (eds.), *Foundations of Comparative Law: Methods and Typologies*, London: Wildy, Simmonds and Hill Publishing, pp. 276–303.

Marcus, Richard 2010. 'Exceptionalism and Convergence: Form Versus Content and Categorical Views of Procedure', in Janet Walker and Oscar G. Chase (eds.), *Common*

Law, Civil Law and the Future of Categories, Markham: LexisNexis Canada, pp. 521–38.

Markesinis, Basil 1990a. 'Comparative Law – A Subject in Search of an Audience', *Modern Law Review*, vol. 53, 1–21.

Markesinis, Basil 1990b. 'Litigation-Mania in England, Germany and the USA: Are We So Very Different?', *Cambridge Law Journal*, vol. 49, 233–76.

Markesinis, Basil 1993. 'The Destructive and Constructive Role of the Comparative Lawyer', *Rabels Zeitschrift für Ausländisches und Internationales Privatrecht*, vol. 57, 438–48.

Markesinis, Basil 1994. 'A Matter of Style', *Law Quarterly Review*, vol. 110, 607–28.

Markesinis, Sir Basil 2000. 'Our Debt to Europe: Past, Present and Future', in Sir Basil Markesinis (ed.), *The Coming Together of the Common Law and the Civil Law*, Oxford: Hart, pp. 37–66.

Markesinis, Sir Basil 2003. *Comparative Law in the Courtroom and Classroom: The Story of the Last Thirty-Five Years*, Oxford: Hart.

Markesinis, Sir Basil 2006. 'Judicial Mentality: Mental Disposition or Outlook as a Factor. Impeding Recourse to Foreign Law', *Tulane Law Review*, vol. 80, 1325–75.

Markesinis, Sir Basil 2009. 'Goethe, Bingham, and the Gift of an Open Mind', in Mads Andenas and Duncan Fairgrieve (eds.), *Tom Bingham and the Transformation of the Law: A Liber Amicorum*, Oxford: Oxford University Press, pp. 729–50.

Markesinis, Sir Basil and Jörg Fedtke 2005. 'The Judge as Comparatist', *Tulane Law Review*, vol. 80, 11–167.

Markesinis, Sir Basil and Jörg Fedtke (eds.) 2006. *Judicial Recourse to Foreign Law*, London: UCL Press.

Markesinis, Sir Basil and Jörg Fedtke 2009. *Engaging with Foreign Law*, Oxford: Hart.

Markesinis, Sir Basil, Jean-Bernard Auby, Dagmar Coester-Waltjen and Simon Deakin 1999. *Tortious Liability of Statutory Bodies: A Comparative and Economic Analysis of Five English Cases*, Oxford: Hart.

Marrani, David 2010. 'Confronting the Symbolic Position of the Judge in Western European Legal Traditions: A Comparative Essay', *European Journal of Legal Studies*, vol. 3, 45–75.

Marsh, Peter D. V. 1994. *Comparative Contract Law: England, France, Germany*, London: Gower.

Martins, Mark 2011. 'Rule of Law in Iraq and Afghanistan? One Harvard Law Grad's View', available at www.law.harvard.edu/news/spotlight/terrorism-and-national-security/related/martins-hls-mof-remarks-18-apr-2011.pdf.

Maslen, Susan 1998. 'Japan and The Rule of Law', *UCLA Pacific Basin Law Journal*, vol. 16, 281–95.

Mason, Anthony F. 2000. 'Contract, Good Faith and Equitable Standards in Fair Dealing', *Law Quarterly Review*, vol. 116, 66–94.

Mason, Whit (ed.) 2011. *The Rule of Law in Afghanistan: Missing in Inaction*, Cambridge: Cambridge University Press.

Massenot, Baptiste 2011. 'Financial Development in Adversarial and Inquisitorial Legal Systems', *Journal of Comparative Economics*, vol. 39, 602–8.

Matsuo, Hiroshi 2004. 'Reception of Law and Civil Law Traditions', in Guenther Doeker-Mach and Klaus A. Ziegert (eds.), *Law and Legal Culture in Comparative Perspective*, Stuttgart: Franz Steiner Verlag, pp. 50–9.

Mattei, Ugo 1994. 'Why the Wind Changed: Intellectual Leadership in Western Law', *American Journal of Comparative Law*, vol. 42, 195–218.

Mattei, Ugo 1997a. *Comparative Law and Economics*, Ann Arbor: University of Michigan Press.

Mattei, Ugo 1997b. 'Three Patterns of Law: Taxonomy and Change in the World's Legal Systems', *American Journal of Comparative Law*, vol. 45, 5–44.

Mattei, Ugo 1998. 'An Opportunity Not to Be Missed: The Future of Comparative Law in the United States', *American Journal of Comparative Law*, vol. 46, 709–18.

Mattei, Ugo 2001. 'The Comparative Jurisprudence of Schlesinger and Sacco: A Study of Legal Influence', in Annelise Riles (ed.), *Rethinking the Masters of Comparative Law*, Oxford: Hart, pp. 238–56.

Mattei, Ugo 2002. 'Patterns of African Constitutions in the Making', in Michael Likosky (ed.), *Transnational Legal Processes: Globalisation and Power Disparities*, London: Butterworths, pp. 275–94.

Mattei, Ugo 2003. 'A Theory of Imperial Law: A Study of U.S. Hegemony and the Latin Resistance', *Indiana Journal of Global Legal Studies*, vol. 10, 383–448.

Mattei, Ugo 2007. 'Access to Justice. A Renewed Global Issue?', *Electronic Journal of Comparative Law*, vol. 11.3.

Mattei, Ugo and Pier Giuseppe Monateri 1997. *Introduzione Breve al Diritto Comparato*, Padova: Cedam.

Mattei, Ugo and Anna di Robilant 2001. 'The Art and Science of Critical Scholarship: Postmodernism and International Style in the Legal Architecture of Europe', *Tulane Law Review*, vol. 75, 1054–91.

Mattei, Ugo and Laura Nader 2008. *Plunder: When the Rule of Law is Illegal*, Oxford: Wiley-Blackwell.

Mattei, Ugo, Teemu Ruskola and Antonio Gidi 2009. *Schlesinger's Comparative Law*, 7th edn, New York: Foundation Press.

Mattila, Heikki E. S. 2006. *Comparative Legal Linguistics*, Hampshire: Ashgate.

Mautner, Menachem 2011. *Law & The Culture of Israel*, Oxford: Oxford University Press.

Maxeiner, James R., Gyooho Lee, Armin Weber and Harriet Weber 2010. *Practical Global Civil Procedure: United States-Germany-Korea*, Durham, NC: Carolina Academic Press.

Maxeiner, James R., Gyooho Lee, Armin Weber and Harriet Weber 2011. *Failures of American Civil Justice in International Perspective*, Cambridge: Cambridge University Press.

Mayeda, Graham 2006. 'Appreciate the Difference: The Role of Different Domestic Norms in Law and Development Reform: Lessons from China and Japan', *McGill Law Journal*, vol. 51, 547–98.

McAuliffe, Padraig 2010. 'Transitional Justice and the Rule of Law: The Perfect Couple or Awkward Bedfellows?', *Hague Journal on the Rule of Law*, vol. 2, 127–54.

McAuslan, Patrick 2003. *Bringing the Law Back In: Essays in Land Law and Development*, Aldershot: Ashgate.

McBarnet, Doreen 2002. 'Transnational Transactions: Legal Work, Cross-border Commerce and Global Regulation', in Michael Likosky (ed.), *Transnational Legal Processes: Globalisation and Power Disparities*, London: Butterworths, pp. 98–113.

McConnaughay, Philip J. 1999. 'The Risks and Virtues of Lawlessness: A "Second Look" at International Commercial Arbitration', *Northwestern University Law Review*, vol. 93, 453–523.

McCorquodale, Robert 2010. 'Business, the International Rule of Law and Human Rights', in Robert McCorquodale (ed.), *The Rule of Law in International and Comparative Context*, London: BIICL, pp. 27–47.

McCrudden, Christopher 2007. 'Judicial Comparativism and Human Rights', in Esin Örücü and David Nelken (eds.), *Comparative Law: A Handbook*, Oxford: Hart, pp. 371–97.

McEldowney, John 2010. 'Hybridization: A Study in Comparative Constitutional Law', *Penn State International Law Review*, vol. 28, 327–55.

McEvoy, Sebastian 2012. 'Descriptive and Purposive Categories of Comparative Law', in Pier Giuseppe Monateri (ed.), *Methods of Comparative Law*, Cheltenham: Edward Elgar, pp. 144–62.

McGann, Anthony J. 2007. 'Social Choice and Comparing Legislatures: Constitutional versus Institutional Constraints', in David Arter (ed.), *Comparing and Classifying Legislatures*, London: Routledge, pp. 186–204.

McGrew, Anthony 2011. 'The Logics of Economic Globalisation', in John Ravenhill (ed.), *Global Political Economy*, 3rd edn, Oxford: Oxford University Press, pp. 275–311.

McKendrick, Ewan 1999. 'Good Faith: A Matter of Principle', in A. D. M. Forte (ed.), *Good Faith in Contract and Property Law*, Oxford: Hart, pp. 39–62.

McPherson, Bruce H. 2007. *The Reception of English Law Abroad*, Brisbane: Supreme Court of Queensland Library.

Melton, James, Zachary Elkins, Tom Ginsburg and Kalev Leetaru 2013. 'On the Interpretability of Law: Lessons from the Decoding of National Constitutions', *British Journal of Political Science*, vol. 43, 399–423.

Menski, Werner 2006. *Comparative Law in a Global Context*, 2nd edn, Cambridge: Cambridge University Press.

Menski, Werner 2007. 'Beyond Europe', in Esin Örücü and David Nelken (eds.), *Comparative Law: A Handbook*, Oxford: Hart, pp. 189–216.

Merino Acuña, Roger 2012. *Comparative Law from Below: The Construction of a Critical Project in Comparative Legal Studies*, Saarbrücken: LAP Lambert Academic Publishing.

Merry, Sally Engle 2003. 'Human Rights Law and the Demonization of Culture (And Anthropology Along the Way)', *PoLAR: Political and Legal Anthropology Review*, vol. 26, 55–76.

Merry, Sally Engle 2004. 'Colonial and Postcolonial Law', in Austin Sarat (ed.), *The Blackwell Companion to Law and Society*, Malden, MA: Blackwell, pp. 569–88.

Merry, Sally Engle 2006. *Human Rights and Gender Violence: Translating International Law into Local Justice*. Chicago, IL: University of Chicago Press.

Merry, Sally Engle 2010. 'What is Legal Culture? An Anthropological Perspective', *Journal of Comparative Law*, vol. 5, 40–58.

Merryman, John Henry 1996. 'The French Deviation', *American Journal of Comparative Law*, vol. 44, 109–19.

Merryman, John Henry 1999. *The Loneliness of the Comparative Lawyer – And Other Essays in Foreign and Comparative Law*, The Hague: Kluwer.

Merryman, John Henry, David S. Clark and Lawrence M. Friedman 1979. *Law and Social Change in Mediterranean Europe and Latin America*. Stanford: Stanford Studies in Law and Development.

Merryman, John Henry and Rogelio Pérez-Perdomo 2007. *The Civil Law Tradition*, 3rd edn, Stanford: Stanford University Press.

Merton, Robert K., David L. Sills and Stephen M. Stigler 1984. 'The Kelvin Dictum and Social Science: An Excursion into the History of an Idea', *Journal of the History of the Behavioral Sciences*, vol. 20, 319–31.

Meuwese, Anne and Mila Versteeg 2012. 'Quantitative Methods for Comparative Constitutional Law', in Maurice Adams and Jacco Bomhoff (eds.), *Practice and Theory in Comparative Law*, Cambridge: Cambridge University Press, pp. 230–57.

Michaels, Ralf 2006. 'The Functional Method of Comparative Law', in Mathias Reimann and Reinhard Zimmermann (eds.), *The Oxford Handbook of Comparative Law*, Oxford: Oxford University Press, pp. 339–82.

Michaels, Ralf 2007. 'The True Lex Mercatoria: Law Beyond the State', *Indiana Journal of Global Legal Studies*, vol. 14, 447–68.

Michaels, Ralf 2009a. 'Comparative Law by Numbers? Legal Origins Thesis, Doing Business Report, and The Silence of Traditional Comparative Law', *American Journal of Comparative Law*, vol. 57, 765–95.

Michaels, Ralf 2009b. 'Global Legal Pluralism', *Annual Review of Law and Social Science*, vol. 5, 243–62.

Michaels, Ralf 2013a. 'Make or Buy – A New Look at Legal Transplants', in Horst Eidenmüller (ed.), *Regulatory Competition in Contract Law and Dispute Resolution*, Munich: Beck, pp. 27–41.

Michaels, Ralf 2013b. '"One Size Can Fit All" – Some Heretical Thoughts on the Mass Production of Legal Transplants', in Günter Frankenberg (ed.), *Order from Transfer: Comparative Constitutional Design and Legal Culture*, Cheltenham: Edward Elgar, pp. 56–78.

Mikhail, John 2009. 'Is the Prohibition of Homicide Universal? Evidence from Comparative Criminal Law', *Brooklyn Law Review*, vol. 75, 497–515.

Milhaupt, Curtis 2001. 'Creative Norm Destruction: The Evolution of Nonlegal Rules in Japanese Corporate Governance', *University of Pennsylvania Law Review*, vol. 149, 2083–129.

Milhaupt, Curtis 2009. 'Beyond Legal Origin: Rethinking Law's Relationship to the Economy – Implications for Policy', *American Journal of Comparative Law*, vol. 57, 831–45.

Milhaupt, Curtis and Katharina Pistor 2008. *Law & Capitalism: What Corporate Crises Reveal About Legal Systems and Economic Development Around the World*, Chicago: Chicago University Press.

Mill, John Stuart 2006 (1843), 'Of the Four Methods of Experimental Inquiry', in Alan Sica (ed.), *Comparative Methods in the Social Sciences*, London: Sage, pp. 105–23.

Miller, Jonathan M. 2003. 'A Typology of Legal Transplants: Using Sociology, Legal History, and Argentine Examples to Explain the Transplant Process', *American Journal of Comparative Law*, vol. 51, 839–85.

Miller, Lucinda 2011. *The Emergence of EU Contract Law: Exploring Europeanization*, Oxford: Oxford University Press.

Mirow, Matthew C. 2004. *Latin American Law: A History of Private Law and Institutions in Spanish America*, Austin, TX: University of Texas Press.

Mirow, Matthew C. 2005. 'The Code Napoléon: Buried But Ruling in Latin America', *Denver Journal of International Law and Policy*, vol. 33, 179–94.

Mitchell, Sara McLaughlin and Emilia Justyna Powell 2011. *Domestic Law Goes Global: Legal Traditions and International Courts*, Cambridge: Cambridge University Press.

Mitton, Todd 2013. 'The Wealth of Subnations: Geography, Institutions, and Within-Country Development', Working Paper, available at http://ssrn.com/abstract=2239402.

Möllers, Thomas and Andreas Heinemann (eds.) 2008. *The Enforcement of Competition Law in Europe*, Cambridge: Cambridge University Press.

Momirov, Aleksandar and Andria Naudé Fourie 2009. 'Vertical Comparative Law Methods: Tools for Conceptualising the International Rule of Law', *Erasmus Law Review*, vol. 2, 291–309.

Mommsen, Wolfgang J. 1992. 'Introduction', in Wolfgang J. Mommsen and J. A. de Moor (eds.), *European Expansion and Law*, Oxford: Berg, pp. 1–14.

Monateri, Pier Giuseppe 1998. 'Everybody's Talking. The Future of Comparative Law', *Hastings International and Comparative Law Review*, vol. 21, 825–46.

Monateri, Pier Giuseppe 1999. 'Black Gaius – A Quest for the Multicultural Origins of the "Western Legal Tradition"', *Hastings Law Journal*, vol. 50, 1–72.

Monateri, Pier Giuseppe 2003. 'The Weak Law: Contaminations and Legal Cultures', *Transnational Law & Contemporary Problems*, vol. 13, 575–92.

Monateri, Pier Giuseppe 2012. 'Methods in Comparative Law. An Intellectual Overview', in Pier Giuseppe Monateri (ed.), *Methods of Comparative Law*, Cheltenham: Edward Elgar, pp. 7–24.

Montesquieu, Charles de Secondat, Baron 1914 (1748). *The Spirit of Laws*, London: G. Bell & Sons.

Moore, Barrington 1993. *Social Origins of Dictatorship and Democracy: Lord and Peasant in the Making of the Modern World*, Boston, MA: Beacon Press.

Moore, Sally Falk 1986a. *Law as Process: An Anthropological Approach*, New York: Routledge.

Moore, Sally Falk 1986b. 'Legal Systems of the World: An Introductory Guide to Classifications, Typological Interpretations, and Bibliographic Resources', in Leon Lipson and Stanton Wheeler (eds.), *Law and the Social Sciences*, New York: Russell Sage, pp. 11–62.

Moore, Sally Falk 1996. 'Doctrine as Determinism: A New Old Grand Theory' (review of Fikentscher, *Modes of Thought*), *Rechtshistorisches Journal*, vol. 15, 447–61.

Moore, Sally Falk 2005. *Law and Anthropology: A Reader*, Malden, MA: Blackwell.

Moore Dickerson, Claire 2010. 'OHADA on The Ground: Harmonizing Business Laws in Three Dimensions', *Tulane European and Civil Law Forum*, vol. 25, 103–18.

Moran, Mayo 2006. 'Inimical to Constitutional Values: Complex Migrations of Constitutional Rights', in Sujit Choudhry (ed.), *The Migration of Constitutional Ideas*, Cambridge: Cambridge University Press, pp. 233–55.

Moss, Giuditta Cordero 2007. 'International Contracts between Common Law and Civil Law: Is Non-state Law to Be Preferred? The Difficulty of Interpreting Legal Standards Such as Good Faith', *Global Jurist*, vol. 7, issue 1, article 3.

Mousourakis, George 2006. *Perspectives on Comparative Law and Jurisprudence*, Auckland: Pearson.

Muir Watt, Horatia 2000. 'La Function Subversive du Droit Comparé', *Revue Internationale de Droit Comparé*, 503–27.

Muir Watt, Horatia 2006. 'Globalization and Comparative Law', in Mathias Reimann and Reinhard Zimmermann (eds.), *The Oxford Handbook of Comparative Law*, Oxford: Oxford University Press, pp. 579–607.

Muir Watt, Horatia 2011. 'The Epistomological Function of "La Doctrine"', in Mark Van Hoecke (ed.), *Methodologies of Legal Research*, Oxford: Hart, pp. 123–31.

Muir Watt, Horatia 2012. 'Further Terrains for Subversive Comparison: The Field of Global Governance and the Public/Private Divide', in Pier Giuseppe Monateri (ed.), *Methods of Comparative Law*, Cheltenham: Edward Elgar, pp. 270–88.

Mullenix, Linda S. 2010. 'American Exceptionalism and Convergence Theory: Are We There Yet?', in Janet Walker and Oscar G. Chase (eds.), *Common Law, Civil Law and the Future of Categories*, Markham: LexisNexis Canada, pp. 41–62.

Munger, Frank 2012. 'Globalization through the Lens of Palace Wars: What Elite Lawyers' Careers Can and Cannot Tell Us about Globalization of Law', *Law and Social Inquiry*, vol. 37, 476–99.

Murray, Peter 2007. *Real Estate Conveyancing in 5 European Union Member States: A Comparative Study*, available at www.cnue-nouvelles.be/en/000/actualites/murray-report-final.pdf.

Nader, Laura 2006. 'Promise or Plunder? A Past and Future Look at Law and Development', in *World Bank Legal Review: Law and Justice for Development*, Rotterdam and New York: Kluwer Law International, vol. 2, pp. 87–111 (also in *Global Jurist*, vol. 7, issue 2 (Frontiers), article 1).

Nader, Laura 2009. 'Law and the Frontiers of Illegalities', in Franz von Benda-Beckmann, Keebet von Benda-Beckmann and Anne Griffiths (eds.), *The Power of Law in a Transnational World. Anthropological Enquiries*, Oxford and New York: Berghahn Books, pp. 54–73.

Nader, Laura and Harry F. Todd Jr. 1978. *The Disputing Process – Law in Ten Societies*, New York: Columbia University Press.

Nardulli, Peter F., Buddy Peyton and Joseph Bajjalieh 2013. 'Conceptualizing and Measuring Rule of Law Constructs, 1850–2010, *Journal of Law and Courts*, vol. 1, 139–92.

Naroll, Raoul 1965. 'Galton's Problem: The Logic of Cross Cultural Analysis', *Social Research*, vol. 32, 428–51.

Nelken, David 1995. 'Disclosing/Invoking Legal Culture: An Introduction', *Social and Legal Studies*, vol. 7, 435–52.

Nelken, David 1997. 'Puzzling Out Legal Culture: A Comment on Blankenburg', in David Nelken (ed.), *Comparing Legal Cultures*, Aldershot: Dartmouth, pp. 69–92.

Nelken, David (ed.) 2000. *Contrasting Criminal Justice: Getting from Here to There*, Aldershot: Ashgate.

Nelken, David 2001. 'Towards a Sociology of Legal Adaptation', in David Nelken and Johannes Feest (eds.), *Adapting Legal Culture*, Oxford: Hart, pp. 7–54.

Nelken, David 2002. 'Legal Transplants and Beyond: Of Disciplines and Metaphors', in Andrew Harding and Esin Örücü (eds.), *Comparative Law in the 21st Century*, New York: Kluwer, pp. 19–34.

Nelken, David 2003a. 'Comparatists and transferability', in Pierre Legrand and Roderick Munday (eds.), *Comparative Legal Studies: Traditions and Transitions*, Cambridge: Cambridge University Press, pp. 437–66.

Nelken, David 2003b. 'Beyond Compare? Criticizing "The American Way of Law"', *Law and Social Inquiry*, vol. 28, 799–831.

Nelken, David 2004a. 'Using the Concept of Legal Culture', *Australian Journal of Legal Philosophy*, vol. 29, 1–28.

Nelken, David 2004b. 'Comparing Legal Cultures', in Austin Sarat (ed.), *The Blackwell Companion to Law and Society*, Malden MA: Blackwell, pp. 113–27.

Nelken, David 2006. 'Signaling Conformity: Changing Norms in Japan and China', *Michigan Journal of International Law*, vol. 27, 933–72.

Nelken, David 2007a. 'Comparative Law and Comparative Legal Studies' and 'Defining and Using the Concept of Legal Culture', in Esin Örücü and David Nelken (eds.), *Comparative Law: A Handbook*, Oxford: Hart, pp. 3–42 and 109–32.

Nelken, David 2007b. 'Three Problems in Employing the Concept of Legal Culture', in Fred Bruinsma and David Nelken (eds.), *Explorations in Legal Culture, Recht der Werkelijkheid (special issue)*, pp. 11–28.

Nelken, David 2009. 'Comparative Criminal Justice – Beyond Ethnocentricism and Relativism', *European Journal of Criminology*, vol. 6, 291–311.

Nelken, David 2010. *Comparative Criminal Justice*, Los Angeles: Sage.

Nelken, David (ed.) 2011. *Comparative Criminal Justice and Globalization*, Farnham: Ashgate.

Nelken, David 2012. 'Legal Cultures', in David S. Clark (ed.), *Comparative Law and Society*, Cheltenham: Edward Elgar, pp. 310–27.

Newman, Graeme 1976/2008. *Comparative Deviance: Perception and Law in Six Cultures*, New Brunswick: Transaction Publishers.

Newman, Katherine S. 1983. *Law and Economic Organization: A Comparative Study of Preindustrial Studies*, Cambridge: Cambridge University Press.

Ngugi, Joel M. 2006. 'The World Bank and the Ideology of Reform and Development in International Economic Development Discourse', *Cardozo Journal of International and Comparative Law*, vol. 14, 313–45.

Nicola, Fernanda G. 2010. 'Family Law Exceptionalism in Comparative Law', *American Journal of Comparative Law*, vol. 58, 777–810.

Nielsen, Lynge 2011. 'Classifications of Countries Based on Their Level of Development: How it is Done and How it Could be Done', IMF Working Paper WP/11/31, available at www.imf.org/external/pubs/ft/wp/2011/wp1131.pdf.

Nijzink, Lia, Shaheen Mozaffar and Elisabete Azevedo 2007. 'Parliaments and the Enhancement of Democracy on the African Continent: An Analysis of Institutional Capacity and Public Perceptions', in David Arter (ed.), *Comparing and Classifying Legislatures*, London: Routledge, pp. 54–78.

Nisbett, Richard E. 2003. *The Geography of Thought: How Asians and Westerners Think Differently . . . And Why*. New York: The Free Press.

Noda, Yoshiyuki 1975. 'Quelques Réflexions sur le Fondement du Droit Comparé: Essai d'une Recherche Anthropologique du Fondement du Droit Compare', in *Aspects Nouveaux de la Pensée Juridique. Recueil d'Éludés en Hommage à Marc Ancel*, Paris: Pedone, vol. 1, pp. 23–41.

Nolan, James L. 2009. *Legal Accents, Legal Borrowing: The International Problem-Solving Court Movement*, Princeton: Princeton University Press.

North, Douglass C. 1990. *Institutions, Institutional Change and Economic Performance*, Cambridge: Cambridge University Press.

North, Douglass C., John Joseph Wallis, Barry R. Weingast 2009. *Violence and Social Orders: A Conceptual Framework for Interpreting Recorded Human History*, Cambridge: Cambridge University Press.

Nottage, Luke 2010. 'Comment on Civil Law, and Common Law: Two Different Paths Leading to the Same Goal', *Victoria University of Wellington Law Review*, vol. 32, 843–51.

Nussbaum, Martha 2011. *Creating Capabilities: The Human Development Approach*, Cambridge, MA: Harvard University Press.

O'Hara, Erin and Larry E. Ribstein 2009. *The Law Market*, Oxford: Oxford University Press.

Obiora, L. Amede 1998. 'Toward an Auspicious Reconciliation of International and Comparative Analyses', *American Journal of Comparative Law*, vol. 46, 669–82.

Oda, Hiroshi 2009. *Japanese Law*, 3rd edn, Oxford: Oxford University Press.

Odinkalu, Chidi Anselm 2006. 'Poor Justice or Justice for the Poor? A Policy Framework for Reform of Customary and Informal Justice Systems in Africa', in *World Bank Legal Review: Law and Justice for Development*, Rotterdam–New York: Kluwer Law International, vol. 2, 141–65.

OECD 2004. 'Organisation for Economic Co-operation and Development, Principles on Corporate Governance', available at www.oecd.org/dataoecd/32/18/31557724.pdf.

Ogus, Anthony 1999. 'Competition between National Legal Systems: A Contribution of Economic Analysis to Comparative Law', *International and Comparative Law Quarterly*, vol. 48, 405–18.

Ogus, Anthony 2002. 'The Economic Basis of Legal Culture: Networks and Monopolization', *Oxford Journal of Legal Studies*, vol. 22, 419–34.

Ogus, Anthony 2004. 'Comparing Regulatory Systems: Institutions, Processes and Legal Forms in Industrialised Countries', in Paul Cook, Colin Kirkpatrick, Martin Minogue and David Parker (eds.), *Leading Issues in Competition, Regulation and Development*, Cheltenham: Edward Elgar, pp. 146–64.

Ogus, Anthony 2006. *Costs and Cautionary Tales: Economic Insights for the Law*, Oxford: Hart.

Ohmae, Kenichi 1990. *The Borderless World*, London: Collins.

Ohnesorge, John K. M. 2007. 'The Rule of Law', *Annual Review of Law and Social Science*, vol. 3, 99–114.

Ohnesorge, John K. M. 2009. 'Legal Origins and the Tasks of Corporate Law in Economic Development: A Preliminary Exploration', *BYU Law Review*, 1619–34.

Oksamytnyi, V. V. 2011, 'Legal Systems of the Modern World: Problems of Identification', in William E. Butler, Oleksiy V. Kresin and Iu. S. Shemshuchenko (eds.), *Foundations of Comparative Law: Methods and Typologies*, London: Wildy, Simmonds and Hill Publishing, pp. 53–83 (also in *Journal of Comparative Law*, vol. 5 (2010), 41–64).

Olson, Greta 2010. 'De-Americanizing Law and Literature Narratives: Opening Up the Story', *Law and Literature*, vol. 22, 338–64.

Olsson, Ola 2009. 'On the Democratic Legacy of Colonialism', *Journal of Comparative Economics*, vol. 37, 534–51.

Örücü, Esin 1999. *Critical Comparative Law: Considering Paradoxes for Legal Systems in Transition*, Deventer: Kluwer.

Örücü, Esin 2002. 'Law as Transposition', *International and Comparative Law Quarterly*, vol. 51, 205–23.

Örücü, Esin 2004a. *The Enigma of Comparative Law: Variations on a Theme for the Twenty-First Century*, Leiden: Martinus Nijhoff.

Örücü, Esin 2004b. 'Family Trees for Legal Systems: Towards a Contemporary Approach', in Mark Van Hoecke (ed.), *Epistemology and Methodology of Comparative Law*, Oxford: Hart, pp. 359–75.

Örücü, Esin 2006a. 'Methodological Aspects of Comparative Law', *European Journal of Law Reform*, vol. 8, 29–42.

Örücü, Esin 2006b. 'A Synthetic and Hyphenated Legal System: The Turkish Experience', *Journal of Comparative Law*, vol. 1, 261–81.

Örücü, Esin 2007. 'Developing Comparative Law', 'A General View of "Legal Families" and of "Mixing Systems"', 'Comparative Law in Practice: The Courts and the Legislator' and 'A Project: Comparative Law in Action', in Esin Örücü and David Nelken (eds.) *Comparative Law: A Handbook*, Oxford: Hart, pp. 43–65, 169–87, 411–33, 435–49.

Örücü, Esin 2008. 'What is a Mixed Legal System: Exclusion or Expansion?', *Journal of Comparative Law*, vol. 3, 34–52.

Örücü, Esin and David Nelken (eds.) 2007. *Comparative Law: A Handbook*, Oxford: Hart.

Ostien, Philip and Albert Dekker 2010. 'Sharia and National Law in Nigeria', in Jan Michiel Otto (ed.), *Sharia and National Law*, Leiden: Leiden University Press, pp. 553–612.

Otterbein, Keith F. 1986. *The Ultimate Coercive Sanction: A Cross Cultural Study of Capital Punishment*. New Haven: HRAF Press.

Oxner, Sandra E. 2003. 'The Quality of Judges', in *World Bank Legal Review: Law and Justice for Development*, Rotterdam-New York: Kluwer Law International, vol. 1, pp. 307–76.

Özsunay, Ergun 2011. 'Legal Culture and Legal Transplants – Turkish National Report', *Isaidat Law Review*, vol. 1, 1121–37.

Pagano, Marco and Paolo Volpin 2001. 'The Political Economy of Finance', *Oxford Review of Economic Policy*, vol. 17, 502–19.

Pakes, Francis 2012. 'Comparative Criminology', in David S. Clark (ed.), *Comparative Law and Society*, Cheltenham: Edward Elgar, pp. 61–76.

Palmer, Vernon Valentine 2004. 'From Lerotholi to Lando: Some Examples of Comparative Law Methodology', *Global Jurist Frontiers*, vol. 4, issue 2, article 1.

Palmer, Vernon Valentine 2008. 'Two Rival Theories of Mixed Legal Systems', *Journal of Comparative Law*, vol. 3, 7–33.

Palmer, Vernon Valentine (ed.) 2012. *Mixed Jurisdictions Worldwide: The Third Legal Family*, 2nd edn, Cambridge: Cambridge University Press.

Panditaratne, Dinusha 2006. 'Uncovering Rights in the USA: Gauging the Gap Rightlessness in India', in Randall Peerenboom, Carole J. Petersen and Albert H. Y. Chen (eds.), *Human Rights in Asia*, London and New York: Routledge, pp. 384–412.

Pangalangan, Raul C. 2006. 'The Philippines: The Persistence of Rights Discourse Vis-à-vis Substantive Social Claims', in Randall Peerenboom, Carole J. Petersen and Albert H. Y. Chen (eds.), *Human Rights in Asia*, London and New York: Routledge, pp. 346–63.

Pardolesi, Roberto and Massimiliano Granieri 2012. 'The Future of Law Professors and Comparative Law', Working Paper, available at www.law-economics.net/?page_id=571.

Pargendler, Mariana 2012a. 'Politics in the Origins: The Making of Corporate Law in Nineteenth Century Brazil', *American Journal of Comparative Law*, vol. 60, 805–49.

Pargendler, Mariana 2012b. 'The Rise and Decline of Legal Families', *American Journal of Comparative Law*, vol. 60, 1043–74.

Parker, Jeffrey S. 2009. 'Comparative Civil Procedure and Transnational "Harmonization": A Law-And-Economics Perspective', Working Paper, available at http://ssrn.com/abstract=1325013.

Parrish, Austen L. 2007. 'Storm in a Teacup: The U.S. Supreme Court's Use of Foreign Law', *University of Illinois Law Review*, 637–80.

Parsons, Talcott 1951. *The Social System*, New York: Free Press.

Parsons, Talcott 1966. *Societies: Evolutionary and Comparative Perspectives*, Englewood Cliffs, NJ: Prentice-Hall.

Pattison, Patricia and Daniel Herron 2003. 'The Mountains are High and the Emperor is Far Away: Sanctity of Contract in China', *American Business Law Journal*, vol. 40, 459–510.

Paul, James C. N. 2003. 'Foreword: Law and Development and Peter Slinn', in John Hatchard and Amanda Perry-Kessaris (eds.), *Law and Development: Facing Complexity in the 21st Century*, London: Cavendish, pp. vii–xxiii.

Peabody, Dean 1985. *National Characteristics*, Cambridge: Cambridge University Press.

Peck, Jamie 2011. 'Geographies of Policy: From Transfer-diffusion to Mobility-mutation', *Progress in Human Geography*, vol. 35, 773–97.

Pedersen, Ove Kaj 2010. 'Institutional Competitiveness: How Nations Came to Compete', in Glenn Morgan, John L. Campbell, Colin Crouch, Ove Kaj Pedersen and Richard Whitley (eds.), *The Oxford Handbook of Comparative Institutional Analysis*, Oxford: Oxford University Press, pp. 625–57.

Peerenboom, Randall 2002. *China's Long March Toward Rule of Law*, Cambridge: Cambridge University Press.

Peerenboom, Randall 2003. 'The X-Files: Past and Present Portrayals of China's Alien "Legal System"', *Washington University Global Studies Law Review*, vol. 2, 37–95.

Peerenboom, Randall 2006. 'An Empirical Overview of Rights Performance in Asia, France, and the USA: The Dominance of Wealth in the Interplay of Economics, Culture, Law, and Governance', in Randall Peerenboom, Carole J. Petersen and Albert H. Y. Chen (eds.), *Human Rights in Asia*, London and New York: Routledge, pp. 1–64.

Peerenboom, Randall 2010a. 'Introduction' and 'Common Myths and Unfounded Assumptions: Challenges and Prospects for Judicial Independence in China', in Randall Peerenboom (ed.), *Judicial Independence in China*, Cambridge: Cambridge University Press, pp. 1–22 and pp. 69–94.

Peerenboom, Randall 2010b. 'The Political Economy of Rule of Law in Middle-Income Countries: A Comparison of Eastern Europe and China', *UCLA Pacific Basin Law Journal*, vol. 28, 64–106.

Peerenboom, Randall 2013. 'Toward a Methodology for Successful Legal Transplants', *Chinese Journal of Comparative Law*, vol. 1, 4–20.

Peerenboom, Randall, André Nollkaemper, Andre and Michael Zürn 2012. 'Conclusion: From Rule of Law Promotion to Rule of Law Dynamics', in Michael Zürn, André Nollkaemper and Randall Peerenboom (eds.), *Rule of Law Dynamics: In an Era of International and Transnational Governance*, Cambridge: Cambridge University Press, pp. 305–24.

Pei, Minxin, Guoyan Zhang, Fei Pei and Lixin Chen 2010. 'A Survey of Commercial Litigation in Shanghai Courts', in Randall Peerenboom (ed.), *Judicial Independence in China*, Cambridge: Cambridge University Press, pp. 221–33.

Pejovic, Caslav 2001. 'Civil Law, and Common Law: Two Different Paths Leading to the Same Goal', *Victoria University of Wellington Law Review*, vol. 32, 817–41.

Peppers, Todd C. 2006. *Courtiers of the Marble Palace: The Rise and Influence of the Supreme Court Law Clerk*, Stanford, CA: Stanford University Press.

Pérez-Perdomo, Rogelio and Lawrence Friedman 2003. 'Latin Legal Cultures in the Age of Globalization', in Lawrence M. Friedman and Rogelio Pérez-Perdomo (eds.), *Legal Culture in the Age of Globalization: Latin America and Latin Europe*, Stanford: Stanford University Press, pp. 1–19.

Perju, Vlad 2012. 'Constitutional Transplants, Borrowing, and Migrations', in Michel Rosenfeld and Andras Sajo (eds.), *The Oxford Handbook of Comparative Constitutional Law*, Oxford: Oxford University Press, pp. 1304–27.

Perry-Kessaris, Amanda 2002. 'The Relationship between Legal Systems and Economic Development: Integrating Economic and Cultural Approaches', *Journal of Law and Society*, vol. 29, 282–307.

Perry-Kessaris, Amanda 2003. 'Finding and Facing Facts about Legal Systems and Foreign Direct Investment in South Asia', *Legal Studies*, vol. 23, 649–89.

Perry-Kessaris, Amanda 2011. 'Prepare Your Indicators: Economics Imperialism on the Shores of Law and Development', *International Journal of Law in Context*, vol. 7, 401–21.

Persson, Torsten and Guido Tabellini 2003. *The Economic Effect of Constitutions*, Cambridge, MA: MIT Press.

Peters, Anne and Heiner Schwenke 2000. 'Comparative Law Beyond Post-modernism', *International and Comparative Law Quarterly*, vol. 49, 800–34.

Peters, Guy 1998. *Comparative Politics, Theory and Method*, New York: NYU University Press.

Petersen, Carole J. 2006. 'From British Colony to Special Administrative Region of China: Embracing Human Rights in Hong Kong', in Randall Peerenboom, Carole J. Petersen and Albert H. Y. Chen (eds.), *Human Rights in Asia*, London and New York: Routledge, pp. 224–64.

Petherbridge, Lee and David Schwartz 2012. 'An Empirical Assessment of the Supreme Court's Use of Legal Scholarship', *Northwestern University Law Review*, vol. 106, 995–1031.

Pettai, Vello and Ülle Madise 2007. 'The Baltic Parliaments: Legislative Performance from Independence to EU Accession', in David Arter (ed.), *Comparing and Classifying Legislatures*, London: Routledge, pp. 34–53.

Phillips, Emma 2007. 'The War on Civil Law? The Common Law as a Proxy for the Global Ambition of Law and Economics', *Wisconsin International Law Journal*, vol. 24, 915–59.

Picciotto, Sol 2011. *Regulating Global Corporate Capitalism*, Cambridge: Cambridge University Press.

Piché, Catherine 2009. 'The Cultural Analysis of Class Action Law', *Journal of Civil Law Studies*, vol. 2, 101–45.

Piers, Maud 2011. 'Good Faith in English Contract Law – Could a Rule Become a Principle?', *Tulane European & Civil Law Forum*, vol. 26, 123–69.

Pimentel, David 2010. 'Rule of Law Reform Without Cultural Imperialism? Reinforcing Customary Justice Through Collateral Review in Southern Sudan', *Hague Journal on the Rule of Law*, vol. 2, 1–28.

Pimentel, David 2011. 'Legal Pluralism and the Rule of Law: Can Indigenous Justice Survive?', *Harvard International Review*, vol. 32/2, 32.

Pinotti, Paolo 2012. 'Trust, Regulation and Market Failures', *The Review of Economics and Statistics*, vol. 94, 650–8.

Pistor, Katharina 2002. 'The Standardization of Law and Its Effect on Developing Economies', *American Journal of Comparative Law*, vol. 50, 97–130.

Pistor, Katharina 2005. 'Legal Ground Rules in Coordinated and Liberal Market Economies', in Klaus Hopt et al. (eds.), *Corporate Governance in Context: Corporations, States and Markets in Europe, Japan and the U.S.*, Oxford: Oxford University Press, pp. 249–80.

Pistor, Katharina 2009. 'Rethinking the "Law and Finance" Paradigm', *BYU Law Review*, 1647–70.

Pistor, Katharina and Philip A. Wellons 1999. *The Role of Law and Legal Institutions in Asian Economic Development, 1960–1995*, New York: Oxford University Press.

Pistor, Katharina, Antara Haldar and Amrit Amirapu 2010. 'Social Norms, Rule of Law, and Gender Reality', in James J. Heckman, Robert L. Nelson and Lee Cabatingan (eds.), *Global Perspectives on the Rule of Law*, Abingdon: Routledge, pp. 241–78.

Pizzorusso, Alessandro 1988. 'The Law-Making Process as a Juridical and Political Activity', in Alessandro Pizzorusso (ed.), *Law in the Making: A Comparative Survey*, New York: Springer, pp. 1–87.

Popova, Maria 2012. *Politicized Justice in Emerging Democracies: A Study of Courts in Russia and Ukraine*, Cambridge: Cambridge University Press.

Popper, Sir Karl 1963. *Conjectures and Refutations*, London: Routledge.

Posner, Eric A. and Adrian Vermeule 2012. 'Tyrannophobia', in Tom Ginsburg (ed.), *Comparative Constitutional Design*, Cambridge: Cambridge University Press, pp. 317–49.

Posner, Richard A. 1996. *Law and Legal Theory in England and America*, Oxford: Clarendon.

Pospisil, Leopold 1971. *Anthropology of Law: A Comparative Theory*, New York: Harper & Row.

Post, Albert Hermann 1884. *Die Grundlagen des Rechts und die Grundzüge seiner Entwicklungsgeschichte: Leitgedanken für den Aufbau einer Allgemeinen Rechtswissenschaft auf Sociologischer Basis*, Oldenburg: Schulze.

Pound, Roscoe, 1921. *The Spirit of the Common Law*, Boston, MA: Marshall Jones.

Pound, Roscoe 1951. 'Philosophy of Law and Comparative Law', *University of Pennsylvania Law Review*, vol. 100, 1–19.

Pozzo, Barbara 2012. 'Comparative Law and Language', in Mauro Bussani and Ugo Mattei (eds.), *Cambridge Companion to Comparative Law*, Cambridge: Cambridge University Press, pp. 88–113.

Prada, Mariana and Michael Trebilcock 2009. 'Path Dependence, Development, and the Dynamics of Institutional Reform', *University of Toronto Law Journal*, vol. 59, 341–79.

Prebisch, Raúl 1959. 'Commercial Policy in the Underdeveloped Countries', *American Economic Review*, vol. 49, 251–73.

Procaccia, Uriel 2007. *Russian Culture, Property Rights and the Market Economy*, Cambridge: Cambridge University Press.

Przeworski, Adam and Henry Teune 1970. *The Logic of Comparative Social Inquiry*, London: Wiley.

Przeworski, Adam and Fernando Limongi 1993. 'Political Regimes and Economic Growth', *Journal of Economic Perspectives*, vol. 7 (summer), 51–69.

Qian, X. Y. 2010. 'Traditional Chinese Law v. Weberian Legal Rationality', *Max Weber Studies*, vol. 10, 29–45.

Quraishi, Asifa 2006. 'Interpreting the Qur'an and the Constitution: Similarities in the Use of Text, Tradition and Reason in Islamic and American Jurisprudence', *Cardozo Law Review*, vol. 28, 67–121.

Radcliffe-Brown, Alfred 1951. 'The Comparative Method in Social Anthropology', *Journal of the Royal Anthropological Institute*, vol. 81, 15–22.

Ragin, Charles C. 1987. *The Comparative Method*, Berkeley: University of California Press.

Ragin, Charles C. 1998. 'The Logic of Qualitative Comparative Analysis', *International Review of Social History*, vol. 43, 105–24.

Rajagopal, Balakrishnan 2003. *International Law from Below: Developing Social Movements and Third World Resistance*, Cambridge: Cambridge University Press.

Rajan, Raghuram G. and Luigi Zingales 2003. 'The Great Reversals: The Politics of Financial Development in the Twentieth Century', *Journal of Financial Economics*, vol. 69, 5–50.

Ramseyer, J. Mark 1984–85. 'The Costs of the Consensual Myth: Antitrust Enforcement and Institutional Barriers to Litigation in Japan', *Yale Law Journal*, vol. 94, 604–45.

Ramseyer, J. Mark 1988. 'Reluctant Litigant Revisited. Rationality and Disputes in Japan', *Journal of Japanese Studies*, vol. 14, 111–23.

Ramseyer, J. Mark 1994. 'The Puzzling (In)Dependence of Courts: A Comparative Approach', *Journal of Legal Studies*, vol. 23, 721–47.

Ramseyer, J. Mark 2009. 'Mixing-and-Matching Across (Legal) Family Lines', *BYU Law Review*, 1701–12.

Ramseyer, J. Mark and Eric B. Rasmusen 2003. *Measuring Judicial Independence: The Political Economy of Judging in Japan*, Chicago: Chicago University Press.

Ramseyer, J. Mark and Eric B. Rasmusen 2010. 'Comparative Litigation Rates', Harvard John M. Olin Discussion Paper No. 681, available at www.law.harvard.edu/programs/olin_center/papers/681_Ramseyer.php.

Ravenhill, John 2011. 'Regional Trade Agreements', in John Ravenhill (ed.), *Global Political Economy*, 3rd edn, Oxford: Oxford University Press, pp. 173–212.

Raynouard, Arnaud and Anne-Julie Kerhuel 2011, 'Measuring the Law: Sécurité Juridique as a Watermark', *International Journal of Disclosure and Governance*, vol. 8, 360–79.

Read, James S. 2000. 'Law in Africa: Back to the Future?', in Ian Edge (ed.), *Comparative Law in Global Perspective*, New York: Transnational Publishers, pp. 173–98.

Reamey, Gerald S. 2010. 'Innovation or Renovation in Criminal Procedure: Is the World Moving Toward a New Model of Adjudication?', *Arizona Journal of International and Comparative Law*, vol. 27, 683–746.

Reimann, Mathias (ed.) 1993. *The Reception of Continental Ideas in the Common Law World*, Berlin: Duncker & Humblot.

Reimann, Mathias 1996. 'The End of Comparative Law as an Autonomous Subject', *Tulane European and Civil Law Forum*, vol. 11, 49–72.

Reimann, Mathias 2001. 'Beyond National Systems: A Comparative Law for the International Age', *Tulane Law Review*, vol. 75, 1103–20.

Reimann, Mathias 2002. 'The Progress and Failure of Comparative Law in the Second Half of the Twentieth Century', *American Journal of Comparative Law*, vol. 50, 671–700.

Reimann, Mathias 2003. 'Liability for Defective Products at the Beginning of the Twenty-First Century: Emergence of a Worldwide Standard?', *American Journal of Comparative Law*, vol. 51, 751–838.

Reimann, Mathias 2006. 'Comparative Law and Private International Law', in Mathias Reimann and Reinhard Zimmermann (eds.), *The Oxford Handbook of Comparative Law*, Oxford: Oxford University Press, pp. 1363–96.

Reitz, John C. 1998. 'How to Do Comparative Law', *American Journal of Comparative Law*, vol. 46, 617–36.

Reitz, John C. 2002. 'Doubts about Convergence: Political Economy as an Impediment to Globalization', *Transnational Law and Contemporary Problems*, vol. 12, 139–59.

Reitz, John C. 2007. 'Political Economy and Contract Law', in Reiner Schulze (ed.), *New Features in Contract Law*, Munich: Sellier, pp. 247–76.

Reitz, John C. 2009. 'Legal Origins, Comparative Law, and Political Economy', *American Journal of Comparative Law*, vol. 57, 847–62.

Reitz, John C. 2012. 'Comparative Law and Political Economy', in David S. Clark (ed.), *Comparative Law and Society*, Cheltenham: Edward Elgar, pp. 105–32.

Remaud, Olivier 2013. 'On Vernacular Cosmopolitanisms, Multiple Modernities, and the Task of Comparative Thought', in Michael Freeden and Andrew Vincent (eds.), *Comparative Political Thought*, Abingdon: Routledge, pp. 141–57.

Resnik, Judith 2010. 'Managerial Judges, Jeremy Bentham and the Privatization of Adjudication', in Janet Walker and Oscar G. Chase (eds.), *Common Law, Civil Law and the Future of Categories*, Markham: LexisNexis Canada, pp. 205–24.

Reynolds, Andrew 2011. *Designing Democracy in a Dangerous World*, Oxford: Oxford University Press.

Reynolds, Thomas and Arturo Flores 1989. *Foreign Law: Current Sources of Basic Legislation in Jurisdictions of the World*, Littleton, CO: Rothman.

Rhodes, Rod 1997. *Understanding Governance*, Buckingham: Open University Press.

Richter, Melvin 1969. 'Comparative Political Analysis in Montesquieu and Tocqueville', *Comparative Politics*, vol. 1, 129–60.

Riesenfeld, Stefan A. and Walter J. Pakter 2001. *Comparative Law Casebook*, Ardsley, NY: Transnational Publishers.

Rigobon, Roberto and Dani Rodrik 2005.'Rule of Law, Democracy, Openness, and Income: Estimating the Interrelationships', *Economics of Transition*, vol. 13, 533–64.

Riles, Annelise 1999. 'Wigmore's Treasure Box: Comparative Law in the Era of Information', *Harvard International Law Journal*, vol. 40, 221–83.

Riles, Annelise 2001. 'Encountering Amateurism: John Henry Wigmore and the Uses of American Formalism', in Annelise Riles (ed.), *Rethinking the Masters of Comparative Law*, Oxford: Hart, pp. 94–126.

Riles, Annelise 2006. 'Comparative Law and Socio-Legal Studies', in Mathias Reimann and Reinhard Zimmermann (eds.), *The Oxford Handbook of Comparative Law*, Oxford: Oxford University Press, pp. 775–813.

Riles, Annelise 2008. 'The Anti-Network: Private Global Governance, Legal Knowledge, and the Legitimacy of the State', *American Journal of Comparative Law*, vol. 56, 605–30.

Rios-Figueroa, Julio and Matthew M. Taylor 2006. 'Institutional Determinants of the Judicialisation of Policy in Brazil and Mexico', *Journal of Latin American Studies*, vol. 38, 739–66.

Rittich, Kerry 2004. 'The Future of Law and Development: Second Generation Reforms and the Incorporation of the Social', *Michigan Journal of International Law*, vol. 26, 199–243.

Roberts, Anthea 2011. 'Comparative International Law? The Role of National Courts in Creating and Enforcing International Law', *International and Comparative Law Quarterly*, vol. 60, 57–92.

Roberts, Paul 2007. 'Comparative Law for International Criminal Justice', in Esin Örücü and David Nelken (eds.), *Comparative Law: A Handbook*, Oxford: Hart, pp. 339–70.

Robinson, Paul H. and Robert Kurzban and Owen D. Jones 2007. 'The Origins of Shared Intuitions of Justice', *Vanderbilt Law Review*, vol. 60, pp. 1633–88.

Rodriguez-Garavito, César A. 2005. 'Nike's Law: The Anti-Sweatshop Movement, Transnational Corporations, and the Struggle over International Labor Rights in the Americas', in Boaventura de Sousa Santos and César A. Rodriguez-Garavito (eds.), *Law and Globalization from Below: Towards a Cosmopolitan Legality*, Cambridge: Cambridge University Press, pp. 1–26.

Rodrik, Dani 2006. 'Goodbye Washington Consensus, Hello Washington Confusion? A Review of the World Bank's Economic Growth in the 1990s: Learning from a Decade of Reform', *Journal of Economic Literature*, vol. 44, 973–87.

Rodrik, Dani 2007. *One Economics, Many Recipes: Globalization, Institutions, and Economic Growth*, Princeton: Princeton University Press.

Rodrik, Dani, Arvind Subramanian and Francesco Trebbi 2004. 'Institutions Rule: The Primacy of Institutions over Geography and Integration in Economic Development', *Journal of Economic Growth*, vol. 9, 131–65.

Roe, Mark J. 1993. 'Some Differences in Corporate Structure in Germany, Japan, and the United States', *Yale Law Journal*, vol. 102, 1927–2003.

Roe, Mark J. 1997. 'Path Dependence, Political Options, and Governance Systems', in Klaus J. Hopt and Eddy Wymeersch (eds.), *Comparative Corporate Governance – Essays and Materials*, Berlin: de Gruyter, pp. 165–84.

Roe, Mark J. 2000. 'Political Preconditions to Separating Ownership from Corporate Control', *Stanford Law Review*, vol. 53, 539–606.

Roe, Mark J. 2009. 'Juries and the Political Economy of Legal Origin', in Michel Tison et al. (eds.), *Perspectives in Company Law and Financial Regulation*, Cambridge: Cambridge University Press, pp. 583–603.

Roe, Mark J. and Jordan I. Siegel 2011. 'Political Instability: Effects on Financial Development, Roots in the Severity of Economic Inequality', *Journal of Comparative Economics*, vol. 39, 279–309.

Rogers, Everett M. 1962. *Diffusion of Innovations*, New York: Free Press.

Romano, Cesare P. R. 2003. 'The Americanization of International Litigation', *Ohio State Journal on Dispute Resolution*, vol. 19, 89–119.

Root, Hilton J. and Karen May 2008. 'Judicial Systems and Economic Development', in Tom Ginsburg and Tamir Moustafa (eds.), *Rule by Law: The Politics of Courts in Authoritarian Regimes*, Cambridge: Cambridge University Press, pp. 304–25.

Rose, Carol M. 2010. 'Invasions, Innovation, Environment', in Benjamin D. Barros (ed.), *Hernando de Soto and Property in a Market Economy*, Farnham: Ashgate, pp. 21–40.

Rose, Paul 2001. 'EU Company Law Convergence Possibilities after Centros', *Transnational Law and Contemporary Problems*, vol. 11, 121–39.

Rose, Richard 1991. 'Comparing Forms of Comparative Analysis', *Political Studies*, vol. 39, 446–62.

Rose, Richard 1993. *Lesson-Drawing in Public Policy: A Guide to Learning across Time and Space*, Chatham: Chatham House.

Rose, Richard 2005. *Learning from Comparative Public Policy: A Practical Guide*, London: Routledge.

Rose-Ackermann, Susan 1995. *Controlling Environmental Policy: The Limits of Public Law in Germany and the United States*, New Haven, CT: Yale University Press.

Rosen, Lawrence 1989. *The Anthropology of Justice: Law as Culture in Islamic Society*, Cambridge: Cambridge University Press.

Rosen, Lawrence 2000. *The Justice of Islam*, Oxford: Oxford University Press.

Rosen, Lawrence 2006. *Law as Culture: An Invitation*, Princeton: Princeton University.

Rosen, Lawrence 2012. 'Comparative Law and Anthropology', in Mauro Bussani and Ugo Mattei (eds.), *Cambridge Companion to Comparative Law*, Cambridge: Cambridge University Press, pp. 75–87.

Rosenfeld, Michel 2012. 'Constitutional Identity', in Michel Rosenfeld and Andras Sajo (eds.), *The Oxford Handbook of Comparative Constitutional Law*, Oxford: Oxford University Press, pp. 756–76.

Rubin, Paul 1994. 'Growing a Legal System in the Post-Communist Economies', *Cornell International Law Journal*, vol. 27, 1–47.

Rubin, Edward 2000. 'Administrative Law and the Complexity of Culture', in Anne Seidman, Robert Seidman, and Janice Payne (eds.), *Legislative Drafting for Market Reform: Some Lessons from China*, Hampshire: Macmillan, pp. 88–108.

Rubin, Jared 2010. 'Bills of Exchange, Interest Bans, and Impersonal Exchange in Islam and Christianity', *Explorations in Economic History*, vol. 47, 213–27.

Rueschemeyer, Dietrich, Evelyne H. Stephens and John D. Stephens 1992. *Capitalist Development and Democracy*, Chicago, IL: University of Chicago Press.

Rühl, Giesela 2013. 'The Choice of Law Framework For Efficient Regulatory Competition in Contract Law', in Horst Eidenmüller (ed.), *Regulatory Competition in Contract Law and Dispute Resolution*, Munich: Beck, pp. 287–303.

Ruskola, Teemu 2002. 'Legal Orientalism', *Michigan Law Review*, vol. 101, 179–234.

Ruskola, Teemu 2003. 'Law Without Law, Or is "Chinese Law" an Oxymoron?', *William and Mary Bill of Rights Journal*, vol. 11, 655–70.

Ruskola, Teemu 2012. 'The East Asian Tradition', in Mauro Bussani and Ugo Mattei (eds.), *Cambridge Companion to Comparative Law*, Cambridge: Cambridge University Press, pp. 257–80.

Ruskola, Teemu 2013. *Legal Orientalism: China, the United States and Modern Law*, Cambridge, MA: Harvard University Press.

Sacco, Rodolfo 1990. *Introduzione al Diritto Comparato*, 4th edn, Turin: Giappichelli.

Sacco, Rodolfo 1991. 'Legal Formants: A Dynamic Approach to Comparative Law', *American Journal of Comparative Law*, vol. 39, 1–34 and 343–401.

Sacco, Rodolfo 1995. 'Mute Law', *American Journal of Comparative Law*, vol. 43, 455–67.

Sacco, Rodolfo 2000. 'One Hundred Years of Comparative Law', *Tulane Law Review*, vol. 75, 1159–76.

Sacco, Rodolfo 2001. 'Diversity and Uniformity in the Law', *American Journal of Comparative Law*, vol. 9, 171–89.

Sachs, Jeffrey 2008. *Common Wealth: Economics for a Crowded Planet*, New York: Penguin.

Sachs, Jeffrey, Clifford Zinnes and Yair Eilat 2000. 'Systemic Transformation in Transition Economies. Volume II. Benchmarking Competitiveness in Transition Economies', CAER Discussion Papers, Harvard University for International Development.

Said, Edward W. 1979. *Orientalism*, New York: Vintage.

Saidov, Akmal Kh. 2003. *Comparative Law*, London: Wildy.

Saleilles, Raymond 1900. 'Conception et Objet de la Science du Droit Compare', *Bulletin de la Société de Législation Comparée*, 383–405.

Samuel, Geoffrey 1998. 'Comparative Law and Jurisprudence', *International and Comparative Law Quarterly*, vol. 47, 817–36.

Samuel, Geoffrey 2004. 'Epistemology and Comparative Law: Contributions from The Sciences and Social Sciences', in Mark Van Hoecke (ed.), *Epistemology and Methodology of Comparative Law*, Oxford: Hart, pp. 35–77.

Samuel, Geoffrey 2007. 'Taking Methods Seriously (Part 1)' and 'Taking Methods Seriously (Part 2)', *Journal of Comparative Law*, vol. 2, 94–119 and 210–37.

Samuel, Geoffrey 2008. 'Is Law Really a Social Science? A View From Comparative Law', *Cambridge Law Journal*, vol. 67, 288–321.

Samuel, Geoffrey 2009. 'Form, Structure and Content in Comparative Law', in Eleanor Cashin Ritaine et al. (eds.), *Legal Engineering and Comparative Law*, Zurich: Schulthess, pp. 27–50.

Samuel, Geoffrey 2012. 'All that Heaven Allows: Are Transnational Codes a "Scientific Truth" or Are They Just a Form of Elegant "Pastiche"?', in Pier Giuseppe Monateri (ed.), *Methods of Comparative Law*, Cheltenham: Edward Elgar, pp. 165–91.

Sandefur, Rebecca L. 2009. 'The Fulcrum Point of Equal Access to Justice: Legal and Nonlegal Institutions of Remedy', *Loyola of Los Angeles Law Review*, vol. 42, 949–78.

Sandulli, Aldo 1998. *La Proporzionalità dell'Azione Amministrativa*, Padova: Cedam.

Santos, Alvaro 2006. 'The World Bank's Uses of the "Rule of Law" Promise in Economic Development', in David M. Trubek and Alvaro Santos (eds.), *The New Law and Economic Development: A Critical Appraisal*, Cambridge: Cambridge University Press, pp. 253–300.

Santos, Boaventura de Sousa 2002. 'Toward a Multicultural Conception of Human Rights', in Berta Hernández-Truyol (ed.), *Moral Imperialism. A Critical Anthology*, New York: NYU Press, pp. 39–60.

Santos, Boaventura de Sousa 2004. *Toward a New Legal Common Sense: Law, Globalization, and Emancipation*, 2nd edn, London: Butterworths.

Santos, Boaventura de Sousa 2005. 'Beyond Neoliberal Governance: The World Social Forum as Subaltern Cosmopolitan Politics and Legality' and 'Two Democracies, Two Legalities: Participatory Budgeting in Porto Alegre, Brazil', in Boaventura de Sousa Santos and César A. Rodriguez-Garavito (eds.), *Law and Globalization from Below: Towards a Cosmopolitan Legality*, Cambridge: Cambridge University Press, pp. 29–63 and 310–38.

Santos, Boaventura de Sousa and César A. Rodriguez-Garavito 2005. 'Law, Politics, and the Subaltern in Counter-Hegemonic Globalization', in Boaventura de Sousa Santos and César A. Rodriguez-Garavito (eds.), *Law and Globalization from Below: Towards a Cosmopolitan Legality*, Cambridge: Cambridge University Press, pp. 1–26.

Sarat, Austin and Jonathan Simon 2003. 'Cultural Analysis, Cultural Studies, and the Situation of Legal Scholarship', in Austin Sarat and Jonathan Simon (eds.), *Cultural Analysis, Cultural Studies, and the Law*, Durham, NC: Duke University Press.

Sarat, Austin and Jürgen Martschukat 2011. 'Introduction: Transatlantic Perspectives on Capital Punishment: National Identity, the Death Penalty, and the Prospects for Abolition', in Austin Sarat and Jürgen Martschukat (ed.), *Is the Death Penalty Dying? European and American Perspectives*, Cambridge, Cambridge University Press, pp. 1–13.

Sarfaty, Galit A. 2009. 'Measuring Justice: Internal Conflict over the World Bank's Empirical Approach to Human Rights', in Kamari Clarke and Mark Goodale (eds.), *Mirrors of Justice: Law and Power in the Post-Cold War Era*, Cambridge: Cambridge University Press, pp. 131–46.

Sarkar, Rumu 2009. *International Development Law: Rule of Law, Human Rights, and Global Finance*, Oxford: Oxford University Press.

Sartori, Giovanni 1970. 'Concept Misformation in Comparative Politics', *American Political Science Review*, vol. 64, 1033–53.

Sartori, Giovanni 1991. 'Comparing and Miscomparing', *Journal of Theoretical Politics*, vol. 3, 243–57.

Sartori, Giovanni 1997. *Comparative Constitutional Engineering: An Inquiry into Structure, Incentives and Outcomes*, 2nd edn, New York: NYU Press.

Saunders, Cheryl 2006. 'Comparative Constitutional Law in the Courts: Is There a Problem?', *Current Legal Problems*, vol. 59, 91–127.

Saunders, Cheryl 2009. 'Towards a Global Constitutional Gene Pool', *National Taiwan University Law Review*, vol. 4, 1–38.

Sauser-Hall, Georges 1913. *Function et méthode du droit comparé*, Geneva: Kündig.

Saussy, Haun (ed.) 2006. *Comparative Literature in an Age of Globalization*, Baltimore: Johns Hopkins University Press.

Sawyer, Jack 1967–68. 'Dimensions of Nations – Size, Weather, and Politics', *American Journal of Sociology*, vol. 73, 145–72.

Schäffer, Heinz and Attila Racz (ed.) 1990. *Quantitative Analyses of Law – A Comparative Empirical Study: Sources of Law in Eastern and Western Europe*, Budapest: Akademiai Kiado.

Schauer, Frederick 2012. 'Comparative Constitutional Compliance: Notes towards a Research Agenda', in Maurice Adams and Jacco Bomhoff (eds.), *Practice and Theory in Comparative Law*, Cambridge: Cambridge University Press, pp. 212–29.

Schieck, Dagmar 2010. 'Comparative Law and European Harmonisation – a Match Made in Heaven or Uneasy Bedfellows?', *European Business Law Review*, 203–25.

Schimmelfennig, Frank 2012. 'A Comparison of the Rule of Law Promotion Policies of Major Western Powers', in Michael Zürn, André Nollkaemper and Randall Peerenboom (eds.), *Rule of Law Dynamics: In an Era of International and Transnational Governance*, Cambridge: Cambridge University Press, pp. 111–32.

Schlesinger, Rudolf B. (ed.) 1968. *Formation of Contracts: A Study of the Common Core of Legal Systems*, Dobbs Ferry: Oceana.

Schlesinger, Rudolf B. 1995. 'The Past and Future of Comparative Law', *American Journal of Comparative Law*, vol. 43, 477–81.

Schmeidl, Susanne 2011. 'Engaging Traditional Justice Mechanisms in Afghanistan: State-building Opportunity or Dangerous Liaison?', in Whit Mason (ed.), *The Rule of Law in Afghanistan: Missing in Inaction*, Cambridge: Cambridge University Press, pp. 149–71.

Schmid, Christoph U. 2009. 'Legal Services in Conveyancing: A European Comparison', in Antonina Bakardjieva Engelbrekt and Joakim Nergelius (eds.), *New Directions in Comparative Law*, Cheltenham: Edward Elgar, pp. 185–200.

Schneider, Carl E. 2010. 'At Law: America as Pattern and Problem', *The Hastings Center Report*, vol. 30, 20–1.

Schneider, Eric C. 1995. 'Deconstructing Principles Foundational to the Paradox of Freedom – A Comparative Study of United States and German Subversive Party Decisions', *DePaul Law Review*, vol. 34, 621–62.

Schnitzer, Adolf 1961. *Vergleichende Rechtslehre I*, 2nd edn, Basel: Basel Recht und Gesellschaft.

Schnyder, Gerhard and Mathias Siems 2013. 'The Ordoliberal Variety of Neoliberalism', in Sue Konzelmann and Marc Fovargue-Davies (eds.), *The Faces of Liberal Capitalism: Banking Systems in Crisis*, London: Routledge, pp. 250–68.

Schön, Wolfgang 2005. 'Playing Different Games? Regulatory Competition in Tax and Company Law Compared', *Common Market Law Review*, vol. 42, 331–65.

Schütze, Robert 2009. *From Dual To Cooperative Federalism: The Changing Structure Of European Law*, Oxford: Oxford University Press.

Scoffoni, Guy 2006. 'The Protection of Human Rights in France: A Comparative Perspective', in Randall Peerenboom, Carole J. Petersen and Albert H. Y. Chen, *Human Rights in Asia*, London and New York: Routledge, pp. 65–82.

Seidman, Ann and Robert B. Seidman 2007. 'Law, Social Change, Development: The Fatal Race – Causes and Solutions', in Ann Seidman, Robert B. Seidman, Pumzo

Mbana, and Hanson Hu Li (eds.), *Africa's Challenge*, Asmara: Africa World Press, pp. 19–50.

Sellers, Mortimer 2010. 'An Introduction to the Rule of Law in Comparative Perspective', in Mortimer Sellers and Tadeusz Tomaszewski (eds.), *The Rule of Law in Comparative Perspective*, Heidelberg: Springer, pp. 1–9.

Sen, Amartya 1999. *Development as Freedom*, New York: Knopf.

Sen, Amartya 2006. 'What is the Role of Legal and Judicial Reform in the Development Process?', in *World Bank Legal Review: Law and Justice for Development*, Rotterdam and New York: Kluwer Law International, vol. 2, pp. 33–49.

Sen, Amartya 2009. *The Idea of Justice*, London: Allen Lane.

Senn, Myriam 2011. *Non-State Regulatory Regimes: Understanding Institutional Transformation*, Heidelberg: Springer.

Shalakany, Amr 2001. 'Sanhuri, and the Historical Origins of Comparative Law in the Arab World (or How Sometimes Losing Your Asalah Can be Good for You)', in Annelise Riles (ed.), *Rethinking the Masters of Comparative Law*, Oxford: Hart, pp. 152–88.

Shapiro, Martin 1981. *Courts: A Comparative and Political Analysis*, Chicago: Chicago University Press.

Shapiro, Martin 1990. 'Lawyers, Corporations and Knowledge', *American Journal of Comparative Law*, vol. 38, 683–716.

Shapiro, Martin and Alec Stone Sweet 2002. *On Law, Politics & Judicialization*, Oxford: Oxford University Press.

Sharma, Arvin 2006. *Are Human Rights Western?: A Contribution to the Dialogue of Civilizations*, Oxford: Oxford University Press.

Shavell, Steven 1987. *Economics of Accident Law*, Cambridge, MA: Harvard University Press.

Shavell, Steven 2006. 'Specific Performance versus Damages for Breach of Contract: An Economic Analysis', *Texas Law Review*, vol. 84, 831–76.

Shigenori, Matsui 2006. 'The Protection of "Fundamental Human Rights" in Japan', in Randall Peerenboom, Carole J. Petersen and Albert H. Y. Chen (eds.), *Human Rights in Asia*, London and New York: Routledge, pp. 121–57.

Shin, Doh Chull 2011. *Confucianism and Democratization in East Asia*, Cambridge: Cambridge University Press.

Shirley, Mary M. 2008. *Institutions and Development*, Cheltenham: Edward Elgar.

Sica, Alan 2006, 'Editor's Introduction: Comparative Methodology: Its Origins and Prospects', in Alan Sica (ed.), *Comparative Methods in the Social Sciences*, London: Sage, pp. xix–xxxii.

Siems, Mathias 2002. 'No Risk, No Fun? Should Spouses be Advised before Committing to Guarantees? A Comparative Analysis', *European Review of Private Law*, vol. 10, 509–28.

Siems, Mathias 2003. 'Disgorgement of Profits for Breach of Contract – A Comparative Analysis', *Edinburgh Law Review*, vol. 7, 27–59.

Siems, Mathias 2004a. 'Unevenly Formed Contracts: Ignoring the Mirror of Offer and Acceptance', *European Review of Private Law*, vol. 12, 771–88.

Siems, Mathias 2004b. 'The Rules on Conflict of Laws in the European Takeover Directive', *European Company and Financial Law Review*, 458–76.

Siems, Mathias 2004c. 'The Divergence of Austrian and German Commercial Law – What Kind of Commercial Law Do We Need in a Globalised Economy?', *International Company and Commercial Law Review*, 273–8.

Siems, Mathias 2005. 'Numerical Comparative Law – Do We Need Statistical Evidence in Law in Order to Reduce Complexity?', *Cardozo Journal of International and Comparative Law*, vol. 13, 521–40.

Siems, Mathias 2006. 'Legal Adaptability in Elbonia', *International Journal of Law in Context*, vol. 2, 393–408.

Siems, Mathias 2007a. 'Legal Origins: Reconciling Law & Finance and Comparative Law', *McGill Law Journal*, vol. 52, 55–81.

Siems, Mathias 2007b. 'The End of Comparative Law', *Journal of Comparative Law*, vol. 2/2, 133–50.

Siems, Mathias 2007c. 'The Adjudication of the German Federal Supreme Court (BGH) in the Last 55 Years – A Quantitative and Comparative Approach', *Oxford University Comparative Law Forum*, vol. 4, available at http://ouclf.iuscomp.org/articles/siems.shtml.

Siems, Mathias 2008a. *Convergence in Shareholder Law*, Cambridge: Cambridge University Press.

Siems, Mathias 2008b. 'Legal Originality', *Oxford Journal of Legal Studies*, vol. 28, 147–64.

Siems, Mathias 2008c. 'Shareholder Protection Around the World ('Leximetric II')', *Delaware Journal of Corporate Law*, vol. 33, 111–47.

Siems, Mathias 2009a. 'The Taxonomy of Interdisciplinary Legal Research: Finding the Way out of the Desert', *Journal of Commonwealth Law and Legal Education*, vol. 7, 5–17.

Siems, Mathias 2009b. 'Regulatory Competition in Partnership Law', *International and Comparative Law Quarterly*, vol. 58, 767–802.

Siems, Mathias 2010a. 'Citation Patterns of the German Federal Supreme Court and of the Court of Appeal of England and Wales', *King's Law Journal*, vol. 21, 152–71.

Siems, Mathias 2010b. 'Convergence in Corporate Governance: A Leximetric Approach', *The Journal of Corporation Law*, vol. 35, 729–56.

Siems, Mathias 2010c. 'The Web of Creditor and Shareholder Protection: A Comparative Legal Network Analysis', *Arizona Journal of International and Comparative Law*, vol. 27, 747–84.

Siems, Mathias 2011. 'Measuring the Immeasurable: How to Turn Law into Numbers', in Michael Faure and Jan Smits (eds.), *Does Law Matter? On Law and Economic Growth*, Cambridge: Intersentia, pp. 115–36.

Siems, Mathias and Simon Deakin 2010. 'Comparative Law and Finance: Past, Present and Future Research', *Journal of Institutional and Theoretical Economics (JITE)*, vol. 166, 120–40.

Siems, Mathias and Daithi MacSithigh 2012. 'Mapping Legal Research', *Cambridge Law Journal*, vol. 71, 651–76.

Siems, Mathias and David Cabrelli (eds.) 2013. *Comparative Law: A Case-Based Approach*, Oxford: Hart.

Siems, Mathias and Oscar Alvarez Macotela 2014. 'The OECD Principles of Corporate Governance in Emerging Economies: A Successful Example of Networked Governance?', in Mark Fenwick, Stefan Wrbka and Steven Van Uytsel (eds.),

Networked Governance, Transnational Business and the Law, Berlin: Springer, pp. 257–84.

Silverstein, Gordon 2008. 'Singapore: The Exception That Proves Rules Matter', in Tom Ginsburg and Tamir Moustafa (eds.), *Rule by Law: The Politics of Courts in Authoritarian Regimes*, Cambridge: Cambridge University Press, pp. 73–101.

Simmons, Beth A. 2009. *Mobilizing Human Rights: International Law in Domestic Politics*, Cambridge: Cambridge University Press.

Singh, Jerome Amir, Michelle Govender, and Edward J. Mills 2007. 'Do Human Rights Matter to Health?', *Lancet*, vol. 370, 521–27.

Skaaning, Svend-Erik 2010. 'Measuring the Rule of Law', *Political Research Quarterly*, vol. 63, 449–60.

Skocpol, Theda and Margaret Somers 1980. 'The Uses of Comparative History in Macrosocial Inquiry', *Comparative Studies in Society and History*, vol. 22, 174–97.

Slaughter, Anne-Marie 1997. 'The Real New World', *Foreign Affairs*, vol. 76, 183–97.

Slaughter, Anne-Marie 2003. 'A Global Community of Courts', *Harvard International Law Journal*, vol. 44, 191–219.

Smelser, Neil J. 1976. *Comparative Methods in the Social Sciences*, Englewood Cliffs NJ: Prentice-Hall.

Smith, Marcus 2013. 'The Vindication of an Owner's Rights to Intangible Property', *Journal of International Banking and Financial Law*, vol. 7, 412–7.

Smith, Stephen A. 2010. 'Comparative Legal Scholarship as Ordinary Legal Scholarship', *Journal of Comparative Law*, vol. 5/2, 331–56.

Smithey, Shannon Ishiyama 2001. 'A Tool, Not a Master: The Use of Foreign Case Law in Canada and South Africa', *Comparative Political Studies*, vol. 34, 1188–211.

Smits, Jan M. 2002a. *The Making of European Private Law: Towards a Ius Commune Europaeum as a Mixed Legal System*, Antwerp: Intersentia.

Smits, Jan M. 2002b. 'The Harmonisation of Private Law in Europe: Some Insights From Evolutionary Theory', *Georgia Journal of International and Comparative Law*, vol. 31, 79–99.

Smits, Jan M. (ed.) 2006a. *Elgar Encyclopaedia of Comparative Law*, Cheltenham: Edward Elgar – cited EE 2006.

Smits, Jan M. 2006b. 'Comparative Law and Its Influence on National Legal Systems', in Mathias Reimann and Reinhard Zimmermann (eds.), *The Oxford Handbook of Comparative Law*, Oxford: Oxford University Press, pp. 513–38.

Smits, Jan M. 2007a. 'Convergence of Private Law in Europe: Towards a New Ius Commune?', in Esin Örücü and David Nelken (eds.), *Comparative Law: A Handbook*, Oxford: Hart, pp. 219–40.

Smits, Jan M. 2007b. 'Legal Culture as Mental Software, or: How to Overcome National Legal Culture?', in Thomas Wilhemsson, Elina Paunio and Annika Pohjolainen (eds.), *Private Law and the Many Cultures of Europe*, The Hague: Kluwer Law International, pp. 133–43.

Smits, Jan M. 2010a. 'The Complexity of Transnational Law: Coherence and Fragmentation of Private Law', *Electronic Journal of Comparative Law*, available at www.ejcl.org/143/art143--14.pdf.

Smits, Jan M. 2010b. 'European Private Law and the Comparative Method', in Christian Twigg-Flessner (ed.), *The Cambridge Companion to European Union Private Law*, Cambridge: Cambridge University Press, pp. 33–43.

Smits, Jan M. 2010c. 'Beyond Euroscepticism: On the Choice of Legal Regimes as Empowerment of Citizens', *Utrecht Law Review*, vol. 6, 68–74.

Smits, Jan M. 2011. 'Is Law a Parasite? An Evolutionary Explanation of Differences Among Legal Traditions', *Review of Law and Economics*, vol. 7, 791–804.

Smits, Jan M. (ed.) 2012. *Elgar Encyclopaedia of Comparative Law*, 2nd edn, Cheltenham: Edward Elgar – cited EE 2012.

Smits, Jan M. 2013. 'A Radical View of Legal Pluralism', in Leone Niglia (ed.), *Pluralism and European Private Law*, Oxford: Hart, pp. 161–71.

Snyder, Francis G. 1981. *Capitalism and Legal Change: An African Transformation*, New York: Academic Press.

Snyder, Francis G. 1999. 'Governing Economic Globalisation: European Law and Global Legal Pluralism', *European Law Journal*, vol. 5, 334–74.

Somma, Alessandro 2006. *Introducción Crítica al Derecho Comparado*, Lima: Ara Editores.

Somma, Alessandro 2007. 'At the Patient's Beside? Considerations on the Methods of Comparative Law', *The Cardozo Electronic Law Bulletin*, vol. 13, available at www.jus.unitn.it/cardozo/Review/2007/somma2.pdf.

Sommerer, Thomas, Katharina Holzinger and Christoph Knill 2008. 'The Pair Approach: What Causes Convergence of Environmental Policies?', in Katharina Holzinger, Christoph Knill and Bas Arts (eds.), *Environmental Policy Convergence in Europe*, Cambridge: Cambridge University Press, pp. 144–95.

Spamann, Holger 2009. 'Contemporary Legal Transplants: Legal Families and the Diffusion of (Corporate) Law', *BYU Law Review*, 1813–78.

Spamann, Holger 2010. 'The "Antidirector Rights Index" Revisited', *Review of Financial Studies*, vol. 23, 468–83.

Spencer, Herbert 1873–81. *Descriptive Sociology; or Groups of Sociological Facts*, eight parts, London: Williams & Norgate.

Stahnke, Tad and Robert Blitt 2005. *The Religion-State Relationship and the Right to Freedom of Religion or Belief: A Comparative Textual Analysis of the Constitutions of Predominantly Muslim Countries*, United States Commission on International Religious Freedom.

Starr, June 1978. *Dispute and Settlement in Rural Turkey: An Ethnography of Law*, Leiden: EJ Brill.

Steger, Manfred 2009. *Globalization: A Very Short Introduction*, Oxford: Oxford University Press.

Steiner, Eva 2010. *French Law: A Comparative Approach*, Oxford: Oxford University Press.

Steiner, Henry J. and Philip Alston 2000. *International Human Rights in Context: Law, Politics, Morals*, 2nd edn, Oxford: Clarendon.

Steinmetz, George 2004. 'Odious Comparisons: Incommensurability, the Case Study, and "Small N's" in Sociology', *Sociological Theory*, vol. 22, 371–400.

Steinmo, Sven 1993. *Taxation and Democracy*, New Haven, CT: Yale University Press.

Stephan, Paul B. 1999. 'The Futility of Unification and Harmonization in International Commercial Law', *Virginia Journal of International Law*, vol. 39, 743–97.

Stephenson, Matthew 2000. 'A Trojan Horse Behind Chinese Walls? Problems and Prospects of U.S.-Sponsored "Rule of Law" Reform Projects in the People's Republic of China', *UCLA Pacific Basin Law Journal*, vol. 18, 64–97.

Stern, Rachel E. 2013. *Environmental Litigation in China: A Study in Political Ambivalence*, Cambridge: Cambridge University Press.

Stiefel, Ernst C. and James R. Maxeiner 1994. 'Civil Justice Reform in the United States – Opportunity for Learning from "Civilized" European Procedure Instead of Continued Isolation?', *American Journal of Comparative Law*, vol. 42, 147–62.

Stiglitz, Joseph E., Amartya Sen and Jean-Paul Fitoussi 2008. 'Report by the Commission on the Measurement of Economic Performance and Social Progress', available at www.stiglitz-sen-fitoussi.fr.

Stone Sweet, Alec 2000. *Governing with Judges*, Oxford: Oxford University Press.

Stone Sweet, Alec 2004. *The Judicial Construction of Europe*, Oxford: Oxford University Press.

Stone Sweet, Alec 2006. 'The New Lex Mercatoria and Transnational Governance', *Journal of European Public Policy*, vol. 13, 627–46.

Stramignoni, Igor 2002. 'The King's One Too Many Eyes: Language, Thought, and Comparative Law', *Utah Law Review*, 739–73.

Strange, Susan 1996. *The Retreat of the State. The Diffusion of Power in the World Economy*, Cambridge: Cambridge University Press.

Streeck, Wolfgang 2006. 'The Study of Organized Interests: Before "The Century" and After', in Colin Crouch and Wolfgang Streeck (eds.), *The Diversity of Democracy*, Cheltenham: Edward Elgar, pp. 3–45.

Struck, Peter H. 2008. 'Tort Reform Kiwi-Style', *Yale Law and Policy Review*, vol. 27, 187–203.

Stulz, René M. and Rohan Williamson 2003. 'Culture, Openness, and Finance', *Journal of Financial Economcis*, vol. 70, 313–49.

Sturgess, Garry and Philip Chupp 1988. *Judging the World: Law and Politics in the World's Leading Courts*, Sydney: Butterworths.

Sucharitkul, Sompong 1998. 'Thai Law and Buddhist Law', *American Journal of Comparative Law*, vol. 46, 69–86.

Sunde, Jørn Øyrehagen 2010. 'Champagne at the Funeral – an Introduction to Legal Culture' and 'The Art of being Artful – the Complex Reception of Law', in Jørn Øyrehagen Sunde and Knut Einar Skodin (eds.), *Rendezvous of European Legal Cultures*, Bergen: Fagbokforlaget, pp. 11–28 and pp. 29–43.

Svensson, Måns and Stefan Larsson 2009. 'Social Norms and Intellectual Property: Online Norms and the European Legal Development', Research Report in Sociology of Law, available at http://ssrn.com/abstract=1598288.

Swank, Duane 2002. *Global Capital, Political Institutions, and Policy Change in Developed Welfare States*, New York: Cambridge University Press.

Tamanaha, Brian Z. 1993a. *Understanding Law in Micronesia: An Interpretive Approach to Transplanted Law*, Leiden: Brill.

Tamanaha, Brian Z. 1993b. 'The Folly of the "Social Scientific" Concept of Legal Pluralism', *Journal of Law and Society*, vol. 20, 192–217.

Tamanaha, Brian Z. 2000. 'A Non-Essentialist Version of Legal Pluralism', *Journal of Law and Society*, vol. 27, 296–321.

Tamanaha, Brian Z. 2001. *A General Jurisprudence of Law and Society*, Oxford: Oxford University Press.

Tamanaha, Brian Z. 2004. *On the Rule of Law*, Cambridge: Cambridge University Press.

Tamanaha, Brian Z. 2008. 'Understanding Legal Pluralism: Past to Present, Local to Global', *Sydney Law Review*, vol. 30, 375–411.

Tamanaha, Brian Z. 2011a. 'The Rule of Law and Legal Pluralism in Development', *Hague Journal on the Rule of Law*, vol. 3, 1–17 (also published in Brian Z. Tamanaha (ed.), *Legal Pluralism and Development: Scholars and Practitioners in Dialogue*, Cambridge: Cambridge University Press, 2012, pp. 34–49).

Tamanaha, Brian Z. 2011b. 'The Primacy of Society and the Failure of Law and Development', *Cornell International Law Journal*, vol. 44, 209–47.

Tamanaha, Brian Z. 2011c. 'What is "General" Jurisprudence? A Critique of Universalistic Claims by Philosophical Concepts of Law', *Transnational Legal Theory*, vol. 2, 287–308.

Tasikas, Vasilios 2007. 'Developing the Rule of Law in Afghanistan: The Need for a New Strategic Paradigm', *The Army Lawyer*, July 2007, pp. 45–60.

Tate, Jay 2001. 'National Varieties of Standardization', in Peter A. Hall and David Soskice (eds.), *Varieties of Capitalism: The Institutional Foundations of Comparative Advantage*, Oxford: Oxford University Press, pp. 442–73.

Taylor, Veronica 2007. 'The Law Reform Olympics: Measuring the Effects of Law Reform in Transition Economies', in Tim Lindsey (ed.), *Law Reform in Developing and Transition States*, London: Routledge, pp. 83–105.

Teitel, Ruti 2004. 'Book Review: Comparative Constitutional Law in a Global Age', *Harvard Law Review*, vol. 117, 2570–96.

Tetley, William 2000. 'Mixed Jurisdictions: Common Law vs. Civil Law (Codified and Uncodified)', *Louisiana Law Review*, vol. 60, 677–738.

Teubner, Gunther 1997. 'Global Bukowina: Legal Pluralism in the World Society', in Gunter Teubner (ed.), *Global Law Without a State*, Dartmouth: Aldershot, pp. 3–28.

Teubner, Gunther 1998. 'Legal Irritants: Good Faith in British Law or How Unifying Law Ends Up in New Divergences', *Modern Law Review*, vol. 61, 11–32.

Thomas, Melissa A. 2010. 'What Do the Worldwide Governance Indicators Measure?', *European Journal of Development Research*, vol. 22, 31–54.

Thomson, Joseph 1999. 'Good Faith in Contracting: A Sceptical View', in A.D.M. Forte (ed.), *Good Faith in Contract and Property*, Oxford: Hart, pp. 63–76.

Tilburg Institute for Interdisciplinary Studies of Civil Law and Conflict Resolution Systems (ed.) 2009. *A Handbook of Measuring the Cost and Quality of Paths to Justice*, Apeldoorn: Maklu.

Tilly, Charles 1984. *Big Structures, Large Processes, Huge Comparisons*, New York: Russell Sage.

Toharia, Jose Juan 2001. 'Exploring Legal Culture', in Robert W. Gordon and Morton J. Horwitz (eds.), *Law, Society, and History: Themes in the Legal Sociology and Legal History of Lawrence M. Friedman*, Cambridge: Cambridge University Press, pp. 90–100.

Toynbee, Arnold J. 1934–61. *A Study of History*, 12 volumes, Oxford: Oxford University Press.

Trakman, Leon E. 2011. 'A Plural Account of the Transnational Law Merchant', *Transnational Legal Theory*, vol. 2, 309–45.

Trebilcock, Michael J. and Ronald J. Daniels 2008. *Rule of Law Reform and Development*, Cheltenham: Edward Elgar.

Trebilock, Michael J. and Paul-Erik Veel 2008. 'Property Rights and Development: The Contingent Case for Formalization', *University of Pennsylvania Journal of International Law*, vol. 30, 397–481.

Treitel, Guenter Heinz 1988. *Remedies for Breach of Contract: A Comparative Account*, Oxford: Clarendon.

Triandis, Harry C. 1994. *Culture and Social Behaviour*, New York: McGraw-Hill.

Trubek, David M. 2001. 'Law and Development', in Neil J. Smelser and Paul B. Baltes (eds.), *International Encyclopedia of the Social & Behavioral Sciences*, Oxford: Pergamon, pp. 8443–6.

Trubek, David M. 2007. 'The Owl and the Pussy-cat: Is There a Future for Law and Development?', *Wisconsin International Law Journal*, vol. 25, 235–42.

Trubek, David M. and Marc Galanter 1974. 'Scholars in Self-Estrangement: Some Reflections on the Crisis in Law and Development Studies in the United States', *Wisconsin Law Review*, 1062–95.

Trubek, David M. and Alvaro Santos 2006. 'Introduction: The Third Moment in Law and Development Theory and the Emergence of a New Critical Practice', in David M. Trubek and Alvaro Santos (eds.), *The New Law and Economic Development: A Critical Appraisal*, Cambridge: Cambridge University Press, pp. 1–18.

Turner, Bryan S. 2011. *Religion and Modern Society: Citizenship, Secularisation and the State*, Cambridge: Cambridge University Press.

Tushnet, Mark 1991. 'Critical Legal Studies: A Political History', *Yale Law Journal*, vol. 100, 1515–44.

Tushnet, Mark 2006a. 'Comparative Constitutional Law', in Mathias Reimann and Reinhard Zimmermann (eds.), *The Oxford Handbook of Comparative Law*, Oxford: Oxford University Press, pp. 1225–57.

Tushnet, Mark 2006b. 'Some Reflections on Method in Comparative Constitutional Law', in Sujit Choudhry (ed.), *The Migration of Constitutional Ideas*, Cambridge: Cambridge University Press, pp. 67–83.

Tushnet, Mark 2009. 'The Inevitable Globalization of Constitutional Law', *Virginia Journal of International Law*, vol. 49, 985–1006.

Twining, William 1997. *Law in Context: Enlarging a Discipline*, Oxford: Clarendon.

Twining, William 1999. 'Mapping Law', *Northern Ireland Legal Quarterly*, vol. 50, 12–49.

Twining, William 2000a. *Globalisation and Legal Theory*, London: Butterworths.

Twining, William 2000b. 'Comparative Law and Legal Theory: The Country and Western Tradition', in Ian Edge (ed.), *Comparative Law in Global Perspective*, New York: Transnational Publishers, pp. 21–76.

Twining, William 2002. 'Generalizing about Law: The Case of Legal Transplants', Tilburg-Warwick Lectures, available at www.ucl.ac.uk/laws/jurisprudence/docs/others/twi_til_4.pdf.

Twining, William 2004. 'Diffusion of Law: A Global Perspective', *Journal of Legal Pluralism*, vol. 49, 1–45.

Twining, William 2005. 'Social Science and Diffusion of Law', *Journal of Law and Society*, vol. 32, 203–40.

Twining, William 2007. 'Globalisation and Comparative Law', in Esin Örücü and David Nelken (eds.), *Comparative Law: A Handbook*, Oxford: Hart, pp. 69–89.

Twining, William 2009a. *General Jurisprudence: Understanding Law from a Global Perspective*, Cambridge: Cambridge University Press.

Twining, William 2009b. 'Implications of Globalisation for Law as a Discipline', in Andrew Halpin and Voljer Roeben (eds.), *Theorising the Global Legal Order*, Oxford: Hart, pp. 39–59.

Twining, William et al. 2006. 'A Fresh Start for Comparative Legal Studies? A Collective Review of Patrick Glenn's Legal Traditions of the World, 2nd Edition', *Journal of Comparative Law*, vol. 1, 100–76.

Ubink, Janine and Benjamin van Rooij 2011. 'Towards Customary Legal Empowerment: An Introduction', in Janine Ubink and Thomas McInerney (eds.), *Customary Justice: Perspectives on Legal Empowerment*, Rome: International Development Law Organization, pp. 7–27.

UN (United Nations) 2010. *Guidance Note of the Secretary General on Democracy.*

UN General Assembly 1993. *World Conference on Human Rights, Vienna Declaration and Programme of Action.*

UNCTAD 2006. *UNCTAD: A Brief Historical Overview*, available at www.transnational. deusto.es/IP2011/docs/unctad%20history.pdf.

Unidroit 2003. *Principles of Transnational Civil Procedure.*

Upham, Frank K. 1987. *Law & Social Change in Postwar Japan*, Cambridge, MA: Harvard University Press.

Upham, Frank K. 1998. 'Weak Legal Consciousness as Invented Tradition', in Stephen Vlastos (ed.), *Mirror of Modernity: Invented Traditions of Modern Japan*, Berkeley: University of California Press, pp. 48–64.

Upham, Frank K. 2005. 'Political Lackeys or Faithful Public Servants? Two Views of the Japanese Judiciary', *Law and Social Inquiry*, vol. 30, 421–55.

Upham Frank K. 2009. 'From Demsetz to Deng: Speculations on the Implications of Chinese Growth for Law and Development Theory', *NYU Journal of International Law and Politics*, vol. 41, 551–602.

Uslander, Eric M. 2008. *Corruption, Inequality, and the Rule of Law*, Cambridge: Cambridge University Press.

Utter, Robert F. and David C. Lundsgaard 1993. 'Judicial Review in the New Nations of Central and Eastern Europe: Some Thoughts from a Comparative Perspective', *Ohio State Law Journal*, vol. 54, 559–606.

Uzelac, Alan 2010. 'Survival of the Third Legal Tradition?', in Janet Walker and Oscar G. Chase (eds.), *Common Law, Civil Law and the Future of Categories*, Markham: LexisNexis Canada, pp. 377–96.

Vagts, Detlev F. 2000. 'Comparative Company Law – The New Wave', in Rainer J. Schweizer, Herbert Burkert and Urs Gasser (eds.), *Festschrift für Jean Nicolas Druey*, Zurich: Schulthess, pp. 595–605.

Valcke, Catherine 2004. 'Comparative Law as Comparative Jurisprudence – The Comparability of Legal Systems', *American Journal of Comparative Law*, vol. 52, 713–40.

Valcke, Catherine 2009a. 'On Comparing French and English Contract Law: Insights from Social Theory', *Journal of Comparative Law*, vol. 4, 69–95.

Valcke, Catherine 2009b. 'Contractual Interpretation at Common Law and Civil Law: An Exercise in Comparative Legal Rhetoric', in Jason W. Neyers, Richard Bronaugh and Stephen G. A. Pitel (eds.), *Exploring Contract Law*, Oxford: Hart, pp. 77–114.

Valcke, Catherine 2012. 'Reflections on Comparative Law Methodology – Getting Inside Contract Law', in Maurice Adams and Jacco Bomhoff (eds.), *Practice and Theory in Comparative Law*, Cambridge: Cambridge University Press, pp. 22–48.

van Aeken, Koen 2012. 'Civil Court Litigation and Alternative Dispute Resolution', in David S. Clark (ed.), *Comparative Law and Society*, Cheltenham: Edward Elgar, pp. 216–34.

van Boom, Willem H. 2012. 'Torts, Courts, and Legislatures: Comparative Remarks on Civil Law Codifications of Tort Law', in T. T. Arvind and Jenny Steele (eds.), *Tort Law and the Legislature – Common Law, Statute and the Dynamics of Legal Change*, Oxford: Hart, pp. 17–30.

van Caenegem, Raoul C. 1987. *Legislators, Judges, Professors*, Cambridge: Cambridge University Press.

van Caenegem, Raoul C. 2002. *European Law in the Past and the Future*, Cambridge: Cambridge University Press.

van Dam 2013. *European Tort Law*, 2nd edn, Oxford: Oxford University Press.

Van de Walle, Nicolas 2001. *African Economies and the Politics of Permanent Crisis, 1979–1999*, Cambridge: Cambridge University Press.

van den Baembussche, A. A. 1989. 'Historical Explanation and Comparative Method: Toward a Theory of the History of Society', *History and Theory*, vol. 28, 1–24.

van der Walt, Lirieka Meintjes 2006. 'Comparative Method: Comparing Legal Systems and/or Legal Cultures?', *Speculum Juris*, 51–64.

van Erp, Sjef 1999. 'European Private Law: Postmodern Dilemmas and Choices. Towards a Method of Adequate Comparative Legal Analysis', *Electronic Journal of Comparative Law*, vol. 3.1.

van Erp, Sjef 2006. 'Comparative Property Law', in Mathias Reimann and Reinhard Zimmermann (eds.), *The Oxford Handbook of Comparative Law*, Oxford: Oxford University Press, pp. 1043–70.

van Erp, Sjef 2007. 'Comparative Private Law in Practice: The Process of Law Reform' in Esin Örücü and David Nelken (eds.), *Comparative Law: A Handbook*, Oxford: Hart, pp. 399–409.

van Essen, Marc, Peter-Jan Engelen, and Michael Carney 2013. 'Does "Good" Corporate Governance Help in a Crisis? The Impact of Country- and Firm-Level Governance Mechanisms in the European Financial Crisis', *Corporate Governance: An International Review*, vol. 21, 201–24.

van Genugten, Willem 2012, ' The Universalization of Human Rights: Reflections on Obstacles and the Way Forward', in Sonja Zweegers and Afke de Groot (eds.), *Global Values in a Changing World*, Amsterdam: KIT Publishers, pp. 205–36.

Van Hoecke, Mark 2004. 'Deep Level Comparative Law', in Mark Van Hoecke (ed.), *Epistemology and Methodology of Comparative Law*, Oxford: Hart, pp. 165–95.

Van Hoecke, Mark and Mark Warrington 1998. 'Legal Cultures, Legal Paradigms and Legal Doctrine: Towards a New Model for Comparative Law', *International and Comparative Law Quarterly*, vol. 47, 495–536.

Vanderlinden, Jacques 1995. *Comparer les droit*, Diegem: E. Story-Scientia.

Vanderlinden, Jacques 2002. 'Religious Laws as Systems of Law – A Comparatist's View', in Andrew Huxley (ed.), *Religion, Law and Tradition: Comparative Studies in Religious Law*, London: Routledge, pp. 165–82.

Varano, Vicenzo and Vittoria Barsotti 2010. *La Tradizione Giuridica Occidentale – Volume I: Testo e Materiali per un Confronto Civil Law Common Law*, 4th edn, Turin: Giappichelli.

Varga, Csaba 2007. 'Comparative Legal Cultures. Renewal by Transforming into a Genuine Discipline', *Acta Juridica Hungarica*, vol. 48, 95–113.

Varga, Csaba 2010. 'Taxonomy of Law and Legal Mapping, Patterns and Limits of the Classification of Legal Systems', *Acta Juridica Hungarica*, vol. 51, 253–72.

Varshney, Ashutosh 2007. 'Ethnicity and Ethnic Conflict', in Carles Boix and Susan C. Stokes (eds.), *The Oxford Handbook of Comparative Politics*, Oxford: Oxford University Press, pp. 274–94.

Voermans, Wim 2011, 'Styles of Legislation and their Effects', *Statute Law Review*, vol. 32, 38–53.

Vogel, David 2012. *The Politics of Precaution: Regulating Health, Safety and Environmental Risks in Europe and the United States*, Princeton: Princeton University Press.

Vogel, Frank E. 2006. 'Contract Law of Islam and the Arab Middle East', in *International Encyclopedia of Comparative Law*, vol. VII, Contract in General, Tübingen: Mohr Siebeck, ch. 7.

Vogenauer, Stefan 2001. *Die Auslegung von Gesetzen in England und auf dem Kontinent*, Tübingen: Mohr Siebeck.

Vogenauer, Stefan 2005. 'An Empire of Light? Learning and Lawmaking in the History of German Law', *Cambridge Law Journal*, vol. 64, 481–500.

Vogenauer, Stefan 2006. 'Sources of Law and Legal Method in Comparative Law', in Mathias Reimann and Reinhard Zimmermann (eds.), *The Oxford Handbook of Comparative Law*, Oxford: Oxford University Press, pp. 869–98.

Vogenauer, Stefan 2008. *Civil Justice Survey 2008*, available at http://denning.law.ox.ac.uk/iecl/ocjsurvey.shtml.

Vogenauer, Stefan 2013. 'Regulatory Competition Through Choice of Contract Law and Choice of Forum in Europe: Theory and Empirical Evidence', *European Review of Private Law*, vol. 21, 13–78.

Vogler, Richard 2005. *A World View of Criminal Justice*, Aldershot: Ashgate.

Voigt, Stefan 2008. 'Are International Merchants Stupid? Their Choice of Law Sheds Doubt on the Legal Origin Theory', *Journal of Empirical Legal Studies*, vol. 5, 1–20.

Voigt, Stefan 2009a. 'Explaining Constitutional Garrulity', *International Review of Law and Economics*, vol. 29, 290–303.

Voigt, Stefan 2009b. 'How to Measure the Rule of Law', Working Paper, available at http://ssrn.com/abstract=1420287.

Voigt, Stefan 2012. 'On the Optimal Number of Courts', *International Review of Law and Economics*, vol. 32, 49–62.

von Benda-Beckmann, Franz 2006. 'The Multiple Edges of Law: Dealing with Legal Pluralism in Development Practice', in *World Bank Legal Review: Law and Justice for Development*, Rotterdam and New York: Kluwer Law International, vol. 2, 51–86.

von Benda-Beckmann, Franz 2009. 'Human Rights, Cultural Relativism and Legal Pluralism', in Franz von Benda-Beckmann, Keebet von Benda-Beckmann and Anne Griffiths (eds.), *The Power of Law in a Transnational World. Anthropological Enquiries*, Oxford and New York: Berghahn Books, pp. 115–34.

von Benda-Beckmann, Franz, Keebet von Benda-Beckmann and Anne Griffiths 2009a. 'Introduction', in Franz von Benda-Beckmann, Keebet von Benda-Beckmann and Anne Griffiths (eds.), *The Power of Law in a Transnational World. Anthropological Enquiries*, Oxford and New York: Berghahn Books, pp. 1–29.

von Benda-Beckmann, Franz, Keebet von Benda-Beckmann and Julia Eckert 2009b. 'Rules of Law and Laws of Ruling: Law and Governance between Past and Future', in Franz von Benda-Beckmann, Keebet von Benda-Beckmann and Julia Eckert (eds.), *Rules of Law and Laws of Ruling*, Farnham: Ashgate, pp. 1–30.

von Benda-Beckmann, Keebet 2009. 'Balancing Islam, Adat and the State', in Franz von Benda-Beckmann, Keebet von Benda-Beckmann and Anne Griffiths (eds.), *The Power of Law in a Transnational World. Anthropological Enquiries*, Oxford and New York: Berghahn Books, pp. 216–35.

von Mehren, Arthur T. 2010. 'The U.S. Legal System: Between the Common Law and Civil Law Legal Traditions', Discussion Paper.

von Staden, Andreas 2013. 'The Democratic Legitimacy of Judicial Review Beyond the State: Normative Subsidiarity and Judicial Standards of Review', *International Journal of Constitutional Law*, vol. 10, 1023–49.

von Wangenheim 2011. 'Evolutionary Theories in Law and Economics and Their Use for Comparative Legal Theory', *Review of Law and Economics*, vol. 7, 737–65.

von Werder, Axel, Till Talaulicar and Georg L. Kolat 2005. 'Compliance with the German Corporate Governance Code: An Empirical Analysis of the Compliance Statements by German Listed Companies', *Corporate Governance: An International Review*, vol. 13, 178–87.

Vorrasi, Kenneth M. 2004. 'England's Reform to Alleviate the Problems of Civil Process: A Comparison of Judicial Case Management in England and the United States', *Journal of Legislation*, vol. 30, 361–87.

Wacquant, Loïc 2009. *Punishing the Poor: The Neoliberal Government of Social Insecurity*, Durham, NC: Duke University Press.

Waelde, Thomas W. and James L. Gunderson 1994. 'Legislative Reform in Transitional Economies: Western Transplants – A Short Cut to Social Market Economy Status?', *International and Comparative Law Quarterly*, vol. 43, 347–78.

Wagner, Gerhard 2006. 'Comparative Tort Procedure', in Mathias Reimann and Reinhard Zimmermann (eds.), *The Oxford Handbook of Comparative Law*, Oxford: Oxford University Press, pp. 1003–41.

Wagner, Gerhard 2013. 'Dispute Resolution as a Product: Competition between Civil Justice Systems', in Horst Eidenmüller (ed.), *Regulatory Competition in Contract Law and Dispute Resolution*, Munich: Beck, pp. 347–422.

Wagnleitner, Reinhold 1994. *Coca-Colonization and the Cold War*, Chapel Hill: University of North Carolina Press.

Wai, Robert 2002. 'Transnational Liftoff and Juridical Touchdown: The Regulatory Function of Private International Law in an Era of Globalization', *Columbia Journal of Transnational Law*, vol. 40, 209–74.

Waldock, Humphrey 1962. 'General Course of Public International Law', *Recueil des Cours*, vol. 106 (1962-II), iss. 1.

Walker, Jack 1969. 'The Diffusion of Innovations among the American States', *American Politcal Science Review*, vol. 63, 880–99.

Wallerstein, Immanuel 1979. *The Capitalist World Economy*, Cambridge: Cambridge University Press.

Wang, Liming and Chuanxi Xu 1999. 'Fundamental Principles of Chinese Contract Law', *Columbia Journal of Asian Law*, vol. 13, 1–34.

Watson, Alan 1976. 'Legal Transplants and Law Reform', *Law Quarterly Review*, vol. 92, 79–84.

Watson, Alan 1993. *Legal Transplants: An Approach to Comparative Law*, 2nd edn, Athens: University of Georgia Press.

Watson, Alan 1994. 'The Importance of "Nutshells"', *American Journal of Comparative Law*, vol. 42, 1–23.

Watson, Alan 2007. *Law, Society, Reality*, Lake Mary, FL: Vandeplas.

Watt, Gary 2012. 'Comparison as Deep Appreciation', in Pier Giuseppe Monateri (ed.), *Methods of Comparative Law*, Cheltenham: Edward Elgar, pp. 82–103.

Weber, Max 1978. *Economy and Society*, Berkeley: University of California Press.

Weber, Max 2008. *The Protestant Ethic and the Spirit of Capitalism*, New York: Norton.

Weingast, Barry R. 2010. 'Why Developing Countries Prove so Resistant to the Rule of Law', in James J. Heckman, Robert L. Nelson and Lee Cabatingan (eds.), *Global Perspectives on the Rule of Law*, Abingdon: Routledge, pp. 27–51.

Weinshall-Margel, Keren 2011. 'Attitudinal and Neo-Institutional Models of Supreme Court Decision Making: An Empirical and Comparative Perspective from Israel', *Journal of Empirical Legal Studies*, vol. 8, 556–86.

Weiss, Gunther A. 2000. 'The Enchantment of Codification in the Common Law World', *Yale Journal of International Law*, vol. 25, 435–532.

Weiss, Linda 2010. 'The State in the Economy: Neoliberal or Neoactivist?', in Glenn Morgan, John L. Campbell, Colin Crouch, Ove Kaj Pedersen and Richard Whitley (eds.), *The Oxford Handbook of Comparative Institutional Analysis*, Oxford: Oxford University Press, pp. 183–209.

Wells, Michael 1994. 'French and American Judicial Opinions', *Yale Journal of International Law*, vol. 19, 81–133.

Welzel, Christian and Ronald Inglehart 2007. 'Mass Beliefs and Democratic Institutions', in Carles Boix and Susan C. Stokes (eds.), *The Oxford Handbook of Comparative Politics*, Oxford: Oxford University Press, pp. 297–316.

West, Mark D. 2001. 'The Puzzling Divergence of Corporate Law: Evidence and Explanations from Japan and the United States', *University of Pennsylvania Law Review*, vol. 149, 528–601.

Weyland, Kurt (ed.) 2004. *Learning from Foreign Models in Latin American Policy Reform*, Washington DC: Woodrow Wilson Center Press.

Weyrauch, Walter O. (ed.) 2001. *Gypsy Law: Romani Legal Traditions and Culture*, Berkeley: University of California Press.

White, Ahmed A. 2001. 'Max Weber and the Uncertainties of Categorical Comparative Law', in Annelise Riles (ed.), *Re-thinking the Masters of Comparative Law*, Oxford: Hart, pp. 40–57.

Whitman, James Q. 1987. 'Commercial Law and the American Volk: A Note on Llewellyn's German Sources for the Uniform Commercial Code', *Yale Law Journal*, vol. 97, 156–75.

Whitman, James Q. 2003a. *Harsh Justice: Criminal Punishment and the Widening Divide Between America and Europe.* New York: Oxford University Press.

Whitman, James Q. 2003b. 'The Neo-Romantic Turn', in Pierre Legrand and Roderick Munday (eds.), *Comparative Legal Studies: Traditions and Transitions*, Cambridge: Cambridge University Press, pp. 312–44.

Whitman, James Q. 2004. 'The Two Western Cultures of Privacy: Dignity Versus Liberty', *Yale Law Journal*, vol. 113, 1151–221.

Whitman, James Q. 2005a. 'The Comparative Study of Criminal Punishment', *Annual Review of Law and Social Science*, vol. 1, 17–34.

Whitman, James Q. 2005b. 'Response to Garland', *Punishment and Society*, vol. 7, 389–96.

Whitman, James Q. 2007. 'Consumerism Versus Producerism: A Study in Comparative Law', *Yale Law Journal*, vol. 117, 340–406.

Whittaker, Simon 2005. *Liability for Products: English, French law and European Harmonization*, Oxford: Oxford University Press.

Whytock, Christopher A. 2009. 'Legal Origins, Functionalism, and the Future of Comparative Law', *BYU Law Review*, 1879–906.

Wiarda, Howard J. and Jonathan T. Polk 2012. 'Separation of Legislative and Executive Governmental Powers', in David S. Clark (ed.), *Comparative Law and Society*, Cheltenham: Edward Elgar, pp. 157–74.

Widner, Jennifer 1998. 'Comparative Politics and Comparative Law', *American Journal of Comparative Law*, vol. 46, 739–49.

Wieacker, Franz 1990. 'Foundations of European Legal Culture', *American Journal of Comparative Law*, vol. 38, 1–29.

Wiegand, Wolfgang 1991. 'The Reception of American Law in Europe', *American Journal of Comparative Law*, vol. 39, 229–48.

Wiegand, Wolfgang 1996. 'Americanization of Law: Reception or Convergence?', in Lawrence M. Friedman and Harry N. Scheiber (eds.), *Legal Culture and the Legal Profession*, Boulder, CO: Westview Press, pp. 137–52.

Wielsch, Dan 2012. 'Global Law's Toolbox: How Standards Form Contracts', *American Journal of Comparative Law*, vol. 60, 1075–104.

Wiener, Jarrod 1999. *Globalization and the Harmonization of Law*, London: Pinter.

Wigmore, John Henry 1928. *A Panorama of the World's Legal Systems*, St Paul: West Publishing.

Wigmore, John Henry 1941. *A Kaleidoscope of Justice*, Washington: Washington Law Book Co.

Williamson, John 1989. 'What Washington Means by Policy Reform', in John Williamson (ed.), *Latin American Readjustment: How Much has Happened*, Washington: Institute for International Economics.

Williamson, Oliver E. 2000. 'The New Institutional Economics: Taking Stock, Looking Ahead', *Journal of Economic Literature*, vol. 38, 595–613.

Wollschläger, Christian 1997. 'Historical Trends of Civil Litigation in Japan, Arizona, Sweden and Germany: Japanese Legal Culture in Light of Judicial Statistics', in Harald Baum (ed.), *Japan: Economic Success and Legal System*, New York: De Gruyter, pp. 89–142.

Wollschläger, Christian 1998. 'Exploring Global Landscapes of Litigation Rates', in Jürgen Brand and Dieter Strempel (eds.), *Soziologie des Rechts: Festschrift für Erhard Blankenburg zum 60. Geburtstag*, Baden-Baden: Nomos, pp. 577–88.

Wood, Geof and Ian Gough 2006. 'A Comparative Welfare Regime Approach to Global Social Policy', *World Development*, vol. 34, 1696–712.

Woodman, Gordon R. 2008. 'The Possibilities of Co-Existence of Religious Laws with Other Laws', in Rubya Mehdi, Hanne Petersen, Erik Reenberg Sand and Gordon R. Woodman (eds.), *Law and Religion in Multicultural Societies*, Copenhagen: DJØF Publishing, pp. 23–42.

World Bank Independent Evaluation Group (IEG) 2008. *Doing Business: An Independent Evaluation. Taking the Measure of the World Bank-IFC Doing Business Indicators.*

World Commission on Environment and Development 1987. *Our Common Future*, Oxford: Oxford University Press.

World Development Report 2002. *Building Institutions for Markets*, Oxford: Oxford University Press.

Worthington, Sarah 2011. 'The Unique Charm of the Common Law', *European Review of Private Law*, vol. 19, 345–61.

Wrbka, Stefan, Steven Van Uytsel and Mathias Siems (eds.) 2012. *Collective Actions: Enhancing Access to Justice and Reconciling Multilayer Interests?*, Cambridge: Cambridge University Press.

Wyler, Lyana Sun and Kenneth Katzman 2010. 'Afghanistan: U.S. Rule of Law and Justice Sector Assistance', Congressional Research Service R41484.

Wymmersch, Eddy 2009. 'Comparative Study of the Company Types in Selected EU States', *European Company and Financial Law Review*, vol. 6, 71–124.

Xanthaki, Helen 2008. 'Legal Transplants in Legislation: Defusing the Trap', *International and Comparative Law Quarterly*, vol. 57, 659–73.

Xanthaki, Helen 2012. 'Editorial: Burying the Hatchet Between Common and Civil Law Drafting Styles in Europe', *Legisprudence*, vol. 6, 133–48.

Xu, Chenggang 2011. 'The Fundamental Institutions of China's Reforms and Development', *Journal of Economic Literature*, vol. 49, 1076–151.

Xu, Guangdong 2011. 'The Role of Property Law in Economic Growth', in Michael Faure and Jan Smits (eds.), *Does Law Matter? On Law and Economic Growth*, Cambridge: Intersentia, pp. 331–83.

Yao, Yang and Linda Yueh 2009. 'Law, Finance, and Economic Growth in China: An Introduction', *World Development*, vol. 37, 753–62.

Yap, Po-Jen 2005. 'Transnational Constitutionalism in the United States: Toward a Worldwide Use of Interpretive Modes of Comparative Reasoning', *University of San Francisco Law Review*, vol. 39, 999–1044.

Yeates, Nicola and Chris Holden (eds.) 2009. *The Global Social Policy Reader*, Bristol: Policy Press.

Yeazell, Stephen C. 1987. *From Medieval Group Litigation to the Modern Class Action*, New Haven: Yale University Press.

Yildirim, Seval 2005. 'Aftermath of a Revolution: A Case Study of Turkish Family Law', *Pace International Law Review*, vol. 17, 347–71.

Young, Katharine G. 2012. *Constituting Economic and Social Rights*, Oxford: Oxford University Press.

Yulin, Fu and Randall Peerenboom 2010. 'A New Analytical Framework for Understanding and Promoting Judicial Independence', in Randall Peerenboom (ed.), *Judicial Independence in China*, Cambridge: Cambridge University Press, pp. 95–133.

Yusuf, Hakeem O. 2010. *Transitional Justice, Judicial Accountability and the Rule of Law*, Abingdon: Routledge.

Zakaria, Fareed 2003. *The Future of Freedom: Illiberal Democracy at Home and Abroad*, New York: Norton.

Zaring, David 2006. 'The Use of Foreign Decisions by Federal Courts: An Empirical Analysis', *Journal of Empirical Legal Studies*, vol. 3, 297–331.

Zekoll, Joachim 2006. 'Comparative Civil Procedure', in Mathias Reimann and Reinhard Zimmermann (eds.), *The Oxford Handbook of Comparative Law*, Oxford: Oxford University Press, pp. 1327–62.

Zelditch, Morris 1971. 'Intelligible Comparisons', in Ivan Vallier (ed.), *Comparative Methods in Sociology*, Berkeley: University of California Press, pp. 267–307.

Zenzo-Zencovich, Vicenzo and Noah Vardi 2008. 'European Union Law as a Legal System in a Comparative Perspective', *European Business Law Review*, 243–65.

ZERP 2007. Study for the European Commission (COMP/2006/D3/003), DG Competition led by the Centre of European Law and Politics (ZERP) at Bremen University, available at http://ec.europa.eu/competition/sectors/professional_services/studies/studies.html.

Zhu, Suli 2010. 'The Party and the Courts', in Randall Peerenboom (ed.), *Judicial Independence in China*, Cambridge: Cambridge University Press, pp. 52–68.

Ziegert, Klaus A. 2004. '"With Law the Land Shall Be Built" – The Case of Changing Norms Seriously', in Guenther Doeker-Mach and Klaus A. Ziegert (eds.), *Law and Legal Culture in Comparative Perspective*, Stuttgart: Franz Steiner Verlag, pp. 142–71.

Zimmermann, Andreas, Christian Tomuschat and Karin Oellers-Frahm 2006. *The Statute of the International Criminal Court: A Commentary*, Oxford: Oxford University Press.

Zimmermann, Reinhard 1996. 'Savigny's Legacy: Legal History, Comparative Law, and the Emergence of a European Legal Science', *Law Quarterly Review*, vol. 112, 576–605.

Zimmermann, Reinhard 2001. *Roman Law, Contemporary Law, European Law: The Civilian Tradition Today*, Oxford: Oxford University Press.

Zimmermann, Reinhard 2006. 'Comparative Law and the Europeanization of Private Law', in Mathias Reimann and Reinhard Zimmermann (eds.), *The Oxford Handbook of Comparative Law*, Oxford: Oxford University Press, pp. 539–78.

Zimmermann, Reinhard and Daniel Visser (eds.) 1996. *Southern Cross: Civil Law and Common Law in South Africa*, Oxford: Clarendon.

Zimmermann, Reinhard and Simon Whittaker (eds.) 2000. *Good Faith in European Contract Law*, Cambridge; Cambridge University Press.

Zimring, Franklin E. 2003. *The Contradictions of American Capital Punishment*, Oxford: Oxford University Press.

Zweigert, Konrad 1969. *Einführung in die Rechtsvergleichung auf dem Gebiete des Privatrechts*, Band 1, Tübingen: Mohr Siebeck.

Zweigert, Konrad and Hein Kötz 1996. *Einführung in die Rechtsvergleichung auf dem Gebiete des Privatrechts*, 3rd edn, Tübingen: Mohr Siebeck.

Zweigert, Konrad and Hein Kötz 1998. *An Introduction to Comparative Law*, 3rd edn, Oxford: Clarendon.

Zywicki, Todd J. and Edward Peter Stringham 2011. 'Common Law and Economic Efficiency', in Francesco Parisi (ed.), *Production of Legal Rules*, Cheltenham: Edward Elgar, pp. 107–31.

Index

Page numbers in italics refer to tables.

abortion law, culture and, 104–5
academic research *see* scholarship
access to justice
    civil litigation, 135–6
    quality measurement, 177–8, *178*
    rule of law and, 269
adaptability of law, criteria for, *123*
administrative law, classification, 90
Afghanistan, rule of law, *269*, 269, 273–5
African legal systems
    classification, 77, 83
    classification critiqued, 83–4
    customary law, 86–7
    parallel systems, 92
aggregated data, use of, 179–86, 306
American Anthropological Association
    on universal human rights, 307–8
'Americanisation' *see* United States law
Anglo-American law *see* common law systems
        English law United States law
anthropology
    aggregated data, use of, 306
    functionalism, 25–6
    'Galton's problem' as to cultural similarity,
        305
    'implicit comparative law', 301–2
    lawyers as anthropologists, 34–5
    legal classifications, 304–5
    legal universalities and singularities, 305–9
    and less developed legal systems, 27–8
    perspective on legal comparison, 36–7
appeal courts, civil/common law comparison,
    49–50
areas of law
    focus of study on, *7*, 7
    suitability for study, 28 *see also specific areas*
        of law

Aristotle
    on constitutions, 11, 293
    legal theory, 28–9
Arminjon, Pierre
    classification of legal systems, 77
Arrighetti, Alessandro
    on contract law, 136–7
Arvind, T. T.
    on Germany and French Civil Code,
        157–8
    on legal transplants, 199
Asian legal systems
    capital punishment, 143
    classification critiqued, 83–4
    Far Eastern legal family, 80–2
    mixed classification, 87–8
    orientalism controversy, 80–2
Atiyah, Patrick
    on civil litigation rates, 129
Austin, John
    on commonality between laws, 100
Ayres, Ian
    on legal transplants, 209

Banakar, Reza
    on core themes of comparative law, 11
Banakas, Stathis
    on awareness of differing understandings of
        law, 18–19
Barak, Aharon
    on citation of foreign judgments, 148
Bartie, Susan
    on US scholarship, 67
Baudenbacher, Carl
    on citation of foreign judgments, 148
Baxi, Upendra
    typology of globalisation, 194

Beck, Thorsten
    on adaptability of law, 122
Bell, John
    on 'immersion' in foreign law, 105
    on traditional comparative method, 34
Benda-Beckmann, Franz von
    on legal pluralism, 107
Benedict, Ruth
    legal anthropology, 307–8
Berman, Harold
    on Christianity and law, *125*, 125
Berman, Paul Schiff
    on transnational law, 258
Bingham, Lord
    on citation of foreign judgments, 148–9
    human rights and rule of law, 267
Black, Donald
    on similarities and differences between
        systems, 160
Blankenburg, Erhard
    on civil litigation rates, 129–30, 131
Bloch, Maurice
    legal anthropology, 306–7
Boas, Franz
    legal anthropology, 307–8
Bogdan, Michael
    analytical approach to comparative law, 5–6
    on law and society, 138–9
    on policy evaluations, 23
Bohannan, Paul
    legal anthropology, 304, 307–8
Burke, John
    on convergence of laws, 238
business law *see* commercial law
Bussani, Mauro
    analytical approach to comparative law, *6*

Caldeira, Gregory
    on legal cultures, 310
Canivet, Guy
    on citation of foreign judgments, 148
capital punishment *see* criminal law
Carney, William
    on influence of other legal systems, 156–7
Cartesian logic and civil law systems, 99
causal relationship between law and society
    examples of, 125–7
    law and religion in relation, *125*, 125
    mirror view, 121–4, *123*
Cavadino, Michael
    on criminal punishment, 143–4

Centre for Business Research (CBR)
        (University of Cambridge)
    on quality of rules, 171
    on shareholder protection, *236*, 236
Charny, David
    on convergence of laws, 233–4
Chinese law
    changes in legal culture, 81–2
    classification, 77–8
    functional comparison with foreign laws,
        36
    mixed classification, 87–8
    as mixed system, 89
    rule of law, *269*, 269–71, 276
    as vertically divided system, 90–1
    Western law compared, 101–2
    Western perspectives on, 16–17
Chomsky, Noam
    on universality, 29
Christianity
    and capital punishment, 142–3
    causal relationship with law, *125*, 125
    influence on law, 142–3
    law and culture, 102–3
    legal classifications, 77
    legal principles, 28–9
citation of foreign judgments
    econometric analysis, 152–3, *153*,
        154
    non-quantitative research, 147–9
    numerical analysis, *151*
    quantitative research, 150–2
civil/common law comparison
    business regulation, 183–4
    and classification of legal systems, 79–80
    consideration of degree of difference or
        similarity, 16
    contract law *see* contract law
    convergence within Western legal tradition,
        68–70, 79
    core areas of division, 43–4
    courts *see* courts
    economic performance, 300–1
    judgments, 57–8, 161–4
    key issues summarised, 70–1
    legal scholarship, 47–8
    linkage of countries, 166
    statute law and interpretation, 44–6
    vertically divided systems, 90
civil law systems
    and Cartesian logic, 99

classification, 77–80, 83, 87
codification, 44–6
common law systems compared *see*
     civil/common law comparison
diversity within European systems, 64–5
dominance of, 41
historical origins, 42
legal scholarship's role, 47–8
linkage of countries, 166
mixed systems, 87
Roman law and, 68
society in relation, 138–40
terminology, 41–2
transplantation, 42, 202–3
as vertically divided system, 91
civil litigation
     access to justice, 135–6
     alternative dispute resolution, 128
     legal anthropology, 306
     personnel involved in, 132–6
     rates of, 128–32
     socio-legal comparative research, 127–8
civil proceedings, civil/common law
     comparison, 51–2
classification of legal systems *see* legal systems
codification of laws, civil/common law
     comparison, 44–8
Cohen-Tanugi, Laurent
     on civil litigation, 127
Cohn, Margit
     typology of legal transplants, 198, 200
Collins, Hugh
     on civil law and Cartesian logic, 99
colonialism
     and codification of laws, 44
     and legal transplants, 42, 43, 78–9, 83,
         205–7
     post-colonial transplants, 207–11 *see also*
         non-colonial countries
commercial law
     aggregated data, 182–6
     application in social context, 136–8
     in causal relationship with social change,
         138–40
     codification, 44
     ease of doing business ranking, *183*
     parallel systems, 92
     socio-legal comparative research,
         136
     transnational law, 249, 250, 251–5
     vertically divided systems, 90–1

Common Core project
     functionalism and universalism within,
         31–3
     good faith study, 61
common law systems
     civil law systems compared *see* civil/
         common law comparison
     classification, 77–80, 83, 98–9
     codification, 44–6
     comparison between, 16
     dominance of, 41
     English law and US law contrasted, 65–8
     historical origins, 43
     Islamic law compared, 80, 305
     legal scholarship's role, 48
     linkage of countries, 166
     rationality of, 305
     Roman law and, 68
     society in relation, 138–40
     superiority of, 235
     terminology, 41–2
     transplantation, 43
company law
     application of, 137–8
     convergence of laws, 191, 233–8, 239–40,
         241–2
     divergence of laws, 158–9
     legal transplants, 198–9
     measurement of similarities and differences,
         164
     place of incorporation, 228
     regionalisation, 229, 230
     shareholder protection *see* shareholder
         protection
     society in relation, 138–40
     socio-legal perspective, 137
     vertically divided systems, 90–1
comparative law
     content and structure of present study,
         9–10
     cosmopolitan nature of, 1
     future of
         author's analytical approach, 313
         conclusions as to, 316–17
     global *see* global comparative law
     historical origins of, 11–12
     interdisciplinary dimension of, 7–9
     method *see* comparative method
     methodological focus of present study, 6–7
     as open subject, 285
     purposes of, 2–5, *3*

comparative law (*cont.*)
 rationale for, 1–5
 scholarship *see* scholarship
 scope of, 5–10
 thought process of, 1–2
 'traditional comparative law' generally,
  11–12 *see also* 'implicit comparative
  law'
comparative method
 awareness of differing understandings of
  law, 18–20
 choice of countries, 15–16
 choice of research questions, 13–15
 comparative analysis stage, 20–2
 'critical' method *see* 'critical comparative
  law'
 critical policy evaluation stage
  critiques of, 39
  inclusion in comparative analysis, 22–3
  policy recommendations, 23
 critiques of, 33–9, 116–17
 'deep-level' method *see* 'deep-level'
  comparative law
 description of laws, 16–20
 descriptive perspectives within, 16–17
 example from comparative tort law, 24–5
 explanation of legal variation, 20–2
 functionalism *see* functionalism
 future of, 314–16
 identification of legal variation, 20
 key issues summarised, 40
 numerical method *see* numerical
  comparative law
 postmodern *see* postmodern comparative
  law
 preliminary considerations stage, 13–16
 simplicity of method critiqued, 33–5
 socio-legal method *see* socio-legal
  comparative law
 stages of, 13
 traditional method and other forms in
  relation, 95–6
 translation of foreign legal terms, 17–18
 universalism *see* universalism
 Western-centric focus critiqued, 35–7
conceptual research and comparative
  approach, 290–1
constitutional law
 Aristotle's analysis of, 11, 293
 classification, 90
 convergence of laws, 234–8, 240

law and politics, 114–15
length of constitution, 161
quantitative research on, 167
suitability for study, 28
transnational law, 250
consumer law, Christianity and, *125*, 125
contract law
 application of, 136–7
 civil/common law comparison
  conclusions as to comparison, 63–4
  contract formation, 59–60, 99–100
  contractual remedies, 62–3
  general comparisons, 58–9
  good faith, 60–1
  pre-contractual duties, 60–1
  society in relation to law, 138–40
 philosophical conceptions of, 99–100
 society in relation, 138–40
 suitability for study, 28
 vertically divided systems, 90–1
convergence of laws
 examples of, 191, 234–8
 forces for, 230–1, *231*, 232
 meaning of, 233–4
 movement towards, 223
 normative and positive viewpoints as to,
  238–42 *see also* law across borders
conveyancing services, aggregated data, 180–1
Cooter, Bob
 on law and economic development, 262–3
corporate governance *see* shareholder
  protection
Cossmann, Brenda
 on law and politics, 115
Cotterrell, Roger
 on law and culture, 104
 on legal transplants, 198–9
courts
 civil/common law comparison
  civil proceedings, 51–2
  civil trials, roles of persons involved, 52–5
  conclusions as to comparison, 58
  judges, 50–1, 52–3
  judges' law-making role, 46–7
  judgments, 57–8, 161–4
  juries, 51
  law of evidence, 53–4
  types of courts, 48–50
  writing of judgments, 55–7
 duration of proceedings, *175*
 juries, 51

lawyers *see* lawyers
numerical comparative analysis, 172–6
role in development of law, 14 *see also*
    judges
creditor protection
    quality of rules, 168–9
criminal law
    application in social context, 140–1
    death penalty, application of, 140–4
    imprisonment and political economy in
        relation, *144*
    law and culture, 102–3
    legal anthropology, 307
    opinion surveys, 177
    socio-legal comparative research, 136
    universal concepts of, 100
'critical comparative law'
    'deep-level' approaches distinguished, 98
    law as discourse, 109–14
    law as political arena, 114–16
    meaning of, 108–9
critical policy evaluation *see* comparative
    method
cross-border law *see* law across borders
cultural understanding of legal systems, 302–5
culturally embedded law
    'law and development' in relation, 276–7
    normative approaches, 104–5
    positivist approaches, 101–3 *see also* legal
        culture
culture and legal mentalities, 309–11
Curran, Vivian Grosswald
    on 'immersion' in foreign law, 106
    on universality, 29
customary law and Western legal tradition,
    86–7, 89

Dakolias, Maria
    on civil litigation, 128
Dalhuisen, Jan
    on convergence of laws, 223
Dam, Kenneth
    on law and economic development, 262–3
Damaška, Mirjan
    on organisation of authority, 50
David, René
    analytical approach to comparative law, 5–6
    classification of legal systems, 77–8
    on legal transplants, 208–9
Dawson, John
    on court systems, 14

de Coninck, Julie
    legal anthropology, 307
de Cruz, Peter
    analytical approach to comparative law, 5–6
    classification of legal systems, 79
    on correct perspective, 16–17
    on critical policy evaluation, 22
de Soto, Hernando
    on law and economic development, 262–3
de Tocqueville, Alexis
    on legal and political institutions, 293–4
death penalty *see* criminal law
'deep-level' comparative law
    'critical' approaches distinguished, 98
    'immersion' into foreign legal system, 105–7
    law as culturally embedded
        normative approaches, 104–5
        positivist approaches, 101–3
    law as reflecting jurisprudential concepts,
        98–101
    legal pluralism, 107–8
    meaning of, 98
Deffains, Bruno
    on trust in judicial institutions, 177
Delmas-Marty, Mireille
    on transnational law, 258
Demleitner, Nora
    on critical comparative law, 110
Derrett, Duncan
    classification of legal systems, 77, 79
Descartes, René
    Cartesian logic and civil law systems, 99
description of laws *see* comparative method
developing countries
    aggregated data, 180
    civil litigation, 128
    suitability for study, 16, 36
    Western law compared, 27–8 *see also* 'law
        and development'
Dezalay, Yves
    on legal transplants, 208
    on transnational commercial law, 255
Dignan, James
    on criminal punishment, 143–4
dispute resolution *see* civil litigation
Djankov, Simeon
    quality measurement of courts, 174–6
    on quality of rules, 170–1
Doh Chull Shin
    on public attitudes to government, 311
domestic laws *see* national laws

Draft Common Frame of Reference (DCFR)
  statutory sources for, 156
  top ten words, *157*
Durkheim, Émile
  on law and society, 302

economic development *see* 'law and
    development'
economic policy evaluation, 297
Ehrmann, Henry
  on opinion surveys, 176
English language translation of foreign terms,
    18
English law
  classification, 77–8
  colonialism, 205–7
  distinctiveness, 74
  influence of, 43–4
  journal references to 'English law', 155–6
  legal reasoning compared, 21
  legal scholarship's role, 48
  legal terminology compared, 161
  legal thought, 67
  as mixed system, 88–9
  religion and law, 102
  and Roman law, 68
  society in relation, 124
  United States law contrasted, 65–8
  as vertically divided system, 90, 91
Euro-Justis
  use of opinion surveys, 177
Europe, legal transplants in
  Americanisation, 203–5
  inter-European transplants, 202–3
European Commission for the Efficiency of
    Justice (CEPEJ)
  on opinion surveys, 176
  on quality of judicial systems, 172–3
European Social Survey
  use of opinion surveys, 176–7
European Union law
  Draft Common Frame of Reference,
    statutory sources for, 156
  as example of regionalisation, 244–7
  legal pluralism, 108
  movement towards towards multi-level
    governance, 247–8
  national implementation of laws, 156–7,
    160
  opinion surveys, 176
  variation within national laws, 164

Evans-Pritchard, E. E.
  legal anthropology, 308
evidence, law of, 53–4
Ewald, William
  on comparative analysis, 20
  on jurisprudential approach to comparative
    law, 99
executions *see* criminal law

family law
  Christianity and, *125*, 125
  culture and, 250
  parallel systems, 92
  politics and, 114–15
  religion and, 126
  society in relation, 124
  suitability for study, 28
  transnational law, 250
Fedtke, Jörg
  on citation of foreign judgments, 149
  on critical comparative law, 112
  focus on major legal systems, 16
  on less developed legal systems, 27–8
Feldman, Eric
  on civil litigation rates, 132
Ferguson, Niall
  on rule of law, 267
Fikentscher, Wolfgang
  on comparative methods of law, 98–9
  legal anthropology, 304
film studies, insights on law and culture, 102
Fletcher, George
  on commonality between laws, 100
  on critical comparative law, 113
foreign laws *see* legal systems; national laws
Foster, Nick
  on law and society, 139
Frankenberg, Günter
  on convergence of laws, 235
  on critical comparative law, 110
Fraser Institute
  use of aggregated data, 179–80
Freedom House
  Freedom in the World report, 173
French law
  classification, 77
  codification, 44
  in comparative law books, 16
  influence of, 43–4
  journal references to 'French law', 155–6
  legal scholarship's role, 48

as mixed system, 88–9
society in relation, 124
statutory interpretation, 45
translation into English, 18
as vertically divided system, 90, 91
Friedman, Lawrence
on convergence of laws, 223
on legal culture, 120, 121
Fukuyama, Francis
on 'end of history', 222–3
functionalism
assumption that all societies share same
social problems, 38
Common Core project as example, 31–3
in comparative law, 26–7
critiques of, 37–9
focus on legal similarities, 37
limitations of, 27–8
limitations of strict functionalist view,
38–9
in other disciplines, 25–6
as starting point for research, 14–15

Galanter, Marc
on legal transplants, 197–8
Galton, Francis
on cultural similarity, 305
Garland, David
on capital punishment, 142
on culture and criminal law, 103
Garth, Bryant
on legal transplants, 208
on transnational commercial law, 255
Geertz, Clifford
legal anthropology, 304
Gerber, David
Common Core project, 31
German law
classification, 77–8
in comparative law books, 16
culturally embedded law, 102–3
influence of, 43–4
journal references to 'German law', 155–6
legal profession, 54, 55
legal scholarship's role, 47–8
legal terminology compared, 161
as mixed system, 88–9
society in relation, 124
translation of foreign legal terms,
155
as vertically divided system, 90, 91

Gibson, James
on legal cultures, 310
Gilson, Ronald
on convergence of laws, 233–4
Ginsburg, Tom
on civil litigation rates, 132
on similarities and differences between
systems, 160–1
Glendon, Mary Ann
on interdisciplinary dimension of
comparative law, 7–8
on law and culture, 104–5
Glenn, Patrick
classification of legal systems, 79, 84–5, 93
on legal transplants, 202
on 'wrong' laws, 281
global comparative law
author's analytical approach, 190
legal transplants *see* legal transplants
meaning of, 189–90
globalisation
human rights law *see* human rights law
law across borders *see* law across borders
and private international law, 227–30
and public international law, 224–7
typology of, 194 *see also* law across borders
Gluckman, Max
legal anthropology, 306
Goethe, Johann Wolfgang von
on universality, 29
Goldschmidt, Walter
on functionalism, 25–6
Gompers, Paul
on company law, 137–8
good faith
civil/common law comparison, 60–1
transplantation, 61
Goode, Roy
on transnational law, 249
government liability law, philosophical
conceptions of, 100
Graziadei, Michele
on legal transplants, 198
Grossfeld, Bernhard
on law and culture, 101–2
Gulliver, Philip
legal anthropology, 304
Gutteridge, Harold
analytical approach to comparative law, 5–6
on convergence of laws, 238
on meaning of 'comparative law', 5

Haley, John
  on civil litigation rates, 131–2
Hall, Jerome
  on commonality between laws, 100
Hall, Mark
  on content analysis of court decisions, 161
Hall, Peter
  on 'varieties of capitalism', 298–9
Hansmann, Henry
  on convergence of laws, 223, 235, 239–40
Hantrais, Linda
  on comparative analysis, 20, 314
Harvey, David
  geographical perspective on legal transplants, 201–2
Hay, Colin
  on convergence of laws, 233–4
Hendley, Kathryn
  on rule of law in Russia, 272–3
historical research and comparative approach, 289–91
Hodges, Chris
  on civil litigation, 135
Hoetker, Glenn
  on civil litigation rates, 132
Hofstede, Geert
  on national cultures, 309, 310
Holmes, Oliver Wendell
  on contractual remedies, 62
Human Relations Area Files project (Yale University)
  use of aggregated data, 306
human rights law
  citation of foreign judgments, 148
  global role of, 217–20
  globalisation, debate as to, 216–17
  and judicial review in Western legal systems, 214–16
  legal anthropology, 306–7
  quality of legal institutions, 173
  quantitative research on transplantation, 218
  and rule of law, 267
Husa, Jaakko
  on classifying legal systems, 74–5
Huxley, Andrew
  on choice of legal systems, 15
Hyland, Richard
  on convergence of laws, 238
  on 'immersion' in foreign law, 105

'implicit comparative law'
  anthropology *see* anthropology
  author's analytical approach, 285, 287
  future of, 313–14
  key issues summarised, 312
  psychology *see* psychology
  social sciences *see* social sciences
imprisonment *see* criminal law
interdisciplinary approach
  in comparative law, 7–9
  and traditional method, 19
international law, comparative law applied to, 4–5
investor protection *see* shareholder protection
Islamic law
  classification, 75–8, *76*
  commercial law and society in relation, 140
  common law compared, 80, 305
  criminal law, 103, 140–1
  lawyers, 133
  parallel systems, 92
  post-colonialism and, 209–10
  rationality of, 303, 305
  rule of law and, 281
  as vertically divided system, 90–1
  vertically divided systems, 90
  Western law compared, 103

Jackson, Howell
  quality measurement of investor protection, 174
Japanese law
  classification, 78
  legal profession, 54
  transplantation into, 42, 86, 158–9
Jhering, Rudolph von
  on legal transplants, 192
Jones, Owen
  legal anthropology, 307
judges
  civil litigation role, 132–6
  in civil trials, 52–3
  education and training, 50–1
  law-making role, 46–7
  number of, 50
  opinion surveys as to, 177
  quality measurement, 173–4
judgments, civil/common law comparison, 57–8, 161–4
judicial review and human rights law, 214–16

Jung, Carl
  on universality, 29
juries, civil/common law comparison,
  51

Kagan, Robert
  on American exceptionalism, 65, 67–8
Kahn-Freund, Otto
  on legal transplants, 199
Kennedy, David
  on law and politics, 115–16
Kirchgässner, Gebhard
  on capital punishment, 142
knowledge and understanding
  awareness of differing understandings,
    18–20
  as purpose of comparative law, 2–3
  translation of foreign legal terms,
    controversy as to, 17–18 *see also* legal
    systems, classification
Kötz, Hein
  analytical approach to comparative law,
    5–6
  classification of legal systems, 77–8,
    83
  on critical policy evaluation, 5–6
  on tort law, 24–5
  on universality, 30
Kraakman, Reinier
  on convergence of laws, 223, 235, 239–40
Kuran, Timur
  on Islamic law and society, 140

La Porta, Rafael
  classification of legal systems, 78–9, 83
  on quality of legal rules, 168–72
Lambert, Édouard
  emphasis on legal commonality, 30–1
Lasser, Mitchell
  on critical comparative law, 109–10
  on US and French written judgments, 56–7
Latin American legal systems, classification
  critiqued, 83–4
Latour, Bruno
  legal anthropology, 307–8
  on legal transplants, 196
law across borders
  author's analytical approach, 222
  claims for decline of national borders, 222–4
  convergence of laws *see* convergence of laws
  key issues summarised, 258–9

regionalisation *see* regionalisation
transnationalisation *see* transnationalisation
  see also convergence of laws
'law and development'
  author's analytical approach, 260
  critiques of, 275–6
  development of concept, 260–5
  key issues summarised, 282–3
  national culture in relation, 276–7
  New Institutional Economics, 299–300
  policy choices, analysis of, 297
  and rule of law
    examples, 269–75
    terminology, typology and purpose,
      265–9
  'top-down' approaches critiqued, 277–9
  use of 'wrong' legal rules and institutions,
    281–2
  Western legal systems used inappropriately,
    279–81
'law and finance' research, 300
Law, David
  on transplanted human rights law,
    218
lawyers
  as anthropologists, 34–5
  civil litigation role, 132–6
  public responsibility, 55
  qualifications, 54
  responsibility to clients, 54–5
  role of, 54
legal anthropology *see* anthropology
legal culture
  legal families in relation, 120–1
  meanings of, 119–20
  as nationally defined, 120–1
legal families
  classification *see* legal systems
  distinctiveness within, 74
  focus of study on, 6–7, 41
  looseness of concept, 73–4
  rationales for concept, 73–4
legal journals, usage of legal terms,
  155–6
legal mentalities, measurement of, 309–11
legal 'myths', refutation of, 19
'legal orientalism', 80–2
legal pluralism and 'deep-level' comparative
  law, 107–8
legal profession *see* lawyers
legal scholarship *see* scholarship

legal systems
  choice for comparison, 16
  classification
    author's analytical approach, 72
    bases for, 74–5
    chronological overview of schemes, 88
    differences overemphasised, 80–2
    geographic basis, 80
    historically-based schemes, 77, 78–9
    horizontally divided (bijural) systems, 89
    hybrid systems, 85–93
    key issues summarised, 93–4
    legal technique as basis, 78
    main classifications, *76*, 75–7, 79
    main commonalities, 79–80
    mixed systems, 79–80, 85–9
    orientalism controversy, 80–2
    parallel (transnational) systems, 92–3
    'political law'-based systems, 78
    'professional law'-based systems, 78
    racially-based schemes, *76*, 75–7
    reasons for, 73–4
    religion-based schemes, *76*, 75–7, 80
    similarities overemphasised, 82–5
    taxonomic methodology, 72–3
    'traditional law'-based systems, 78
    vertically divided systems, 89–92 *see also*
      legal families
  differences
    overemphasis on, 80–2
    summary of, *38*
  focus of study on, *7*
  'immersion' into foreign system, 105–7
  knowledge and understanding of, 3
  radically different systems as suitable for
    study, 16, 27–8, 36
  research focus on major systems, 16
  similarities
    overemphasis on, 82–5
    summary of, *38*
legal transplants
  author's analytical approach, 191
  categories of, 192–3
  colonialism and, 42, 43, 78–9, 83, 205–7
  conceptual research, 191
  in Europe
    Americanisation, 203–5
    inter-European transplants, 202–3
  good faith, 61
  historical overview, 201–2
  human rights law *see* human rights law

key issues summarised, 220–1
non-colonial countries
  operation of legal transplants, 212–13
  transplanted formal law, 211–12
numerical comparative analysis *see*
  numerical comparative law
operation in transplant country
  differing views as to, 195
  functions in modified way (intermediate
    view), 197–200
  legal transplants are harmful (negative
    view), 196–7
  transplanted texts reinterpreted (negative
    view), 196
  work as in origin country (positive view),
    195–6
post-colonialism, 207–11
rationales for transplant
  benefits for origin country, 193–4
  benefits for transplant country, 192–3
  diffusion of law, 194–5
typologies, 198, 200
voluntary transplant, 42 *see also* law across
  borders
Legrand, Pierre
  on comparative analysis, 20
  on convergence of laws, 240–1
  on core themes of comparative law, 9
  on critical comparative law, 110–12, 114
  on interdisciplinary dimension of
    comparative law, 9
  on legal transplants, 196
  on multi-level governance, 247
Levy, Ernst
  on legal transplants, 199
Licht, Amir
  on legal cultures, 310
Linnaean taxonomic methodology, use of,
  72–3
Lundmark, Thomas
  on similarities and differences between
    systems, 160

MacCormick, Neil
  on effect of judgments, 58
Macey, Jonathan
  on legal transplants, 209
Maine, Sir Henry
  on evolution of legal systems, 21, 261
Makdisi, John
  on legal transplants, 206

Malinowski, Bronislaw
  legal anthropology, 306
Markesinis, Sir Basil
  on citation of foreign judgments, 149
  on critical comparative law, 112
  focus on major legal systems, 16
  on legal transplants, 195–6
  on less developed legal systems, 27–8
  on tortious liability of statutory bodies, 23
Mattei, Ugo
  analytical approach to comparative law, 6
  classification of legal systems, 78
  on interdisciplinary dimension of
    comparative law, 7–8
  on similarities and differences between
    systems, 164
  on traditional comparative method, 34
Mautner, Menachem
  on Israeli law and culture, 102
Mavčič, Arne
  on transplanted human rights law, 218
Measuring Access to Justice
  use of opinion surveys, 177–8
Menski, Werner
  classification of legal systems, 83
Merry, Sally Engle
  legal anthropology, 306–7
Merryman, John Henry
  on civil litigation, 127
  classification of legal systems, 84
methodological focus of present study,
    6–7
methodology see comparative method
Milhaupt, Curtis
  on convergence of laws, 233–4
  on law and society, 139
Mill, John Stuart
  on choice of variables for comparison,
    291–2
Monateri, Pier Giuseppe
  on legal transplants, 206
Montesquieu, Charles-Louis de Secondat,
    Baron de La Brède et de
  on national consciousness and law, 11,
    121–2, 293
multi-level governance, movement towards,
    247–8

Nader, Laura
  legal anthropology, 306
Nardulli, Peter

on similarities and differences between
    systems, 160
national borders see law across borders
national laws
  choice for comparison, 15–16
  common consciousness as basis for, 114,
    121–2
  comparative description of, 16–20
  comparative law applied to, 3–4
  distinctiveness within legal families,
    74
  and foreign laws see law across borders; legal
    transplants
  knowledge and understanding of, 2–3
  legal anthropology see anthropology
  translation of legal terms, 17–18 see also
    specific national laws
Nelken, David
  analytical approach to comparative law,
    5–6
  on civil litigation rates, 130–1
  on interdisciplinary dimension of
    comparative law, 5–6
  on legal culture, 119–20
Netherlands Council for the Judiciary
  on quality of judicial systems, 172–3
New Institutional Economics
  on law and economic development,
    299–300
Newman, Katherine
  legal anthropology, 304
Noda, Yoshiyuki
  on universality, 29
Nolde, Boris
  classification of legal systems, 77
non-colonial countries
  operation of legal transplants, 212–13
  transplanted formal law, 211–12
normative approaches to culturally-based
    comparisons, 104–5
numerical comparative law
  author's analytical approach, 146
  citation of foreign judgments, 150–2
  combining of approaches and datasets,
    179–86
  impact of foreign legal ideas, measurement
    of, 147
  key issues summarised, 186–7
  and legal mentalities, measurement of,
    309–11
  meaning of, 146

numerical comparative law (*cont.*)
    measurement of quality of legal rules and
        institutions
        approaches to, 167–8
        courts and other institutions, 172–6
        legal rules, 168–72
    measurement of similarities and differences
        formal features of legal system, 160–4
        purpose of, 159–60
        substance of legal rules, 164–7
    methods and topics overviewed, *147*
    opinion surveys on law and law
        enforcement, 176–9

Ogus, Anthony
    on regulatory competition, 229, 230
O'Hara, Erin
    on global 'law market', 228–9
opinion surveys
    measurement of legal mentalities, 311
    numerical comparative law, 176–9
Örücü, Esin
    analytical approach to comparative law,
        5–6
    on citation of foreign judgments, 150
    classification of legal systems, 89–90
Otterbein, Keith
    legal anthropology, 304
Oxner, Sandra
    on opinion surveys, 176
    on quality of judges, 173–4

Parsons, Talcott
    on functionalism, 25–6
Perry-Kessaris, Amanda
    on legal cultures, 310–11
philosophical conceptions of law, 98–101
Pistor, Katharina
    on law and society, 139
    on legal transplants, 198–9
policy evaluation
    legal systems *see* comparative method
    state policies, 297
political economy *see entries at* social, socio-
Political Risk Services
    Political Risk Index, 173
politics
    'implicit comparative law' *see* states
    law as political arena, 114–16
    Montesquieu's comparison of political
        systems, 11

political institutions, numerical comparative
        analysis, 114–16
'political law'-based systems, 78
Polity IV Project
    survey on forms of government, 294
Popova, Maria
    on rule of law in Russia, 273
Popper, Karl
    on growth of scientific knowledge,
        73–4
positive law
    comparative method, 18–20
    convergence of laws, 238–42
    culturally embedded law, 101–3
Posner, Eric
    on public attitudes to government,
        311
Posner, Richard
    on citation of judgments, 162
    on civil litigation, 132–3, 134
Post, Albert Hermann
    legal anthropology, 306
post-colonial legal transplants, 207–11
postmodern comparative law
    author's analytical approach, 97
    definitional issues, 97–8
    key issues summarised, 116–18
    specific approaches, 98 *see also* 'critical
        comparative law'; 'deep-level'
        comparative law
Pound, Roscoe
    on judges' law-making role, 45
    on philosophical method of comparative
        law, 98–9
pre-contractual duties, civil/common law
        comparison, 60–1
precedent, role of, 57–8
private international law
    choice of, 227–8
    controversy as to private law-making, 255–8
    globalisation and, 227–30
    models of, 227
    regulatory competition, 228–30
Procaccia, Uriel
    on Russian law and culture, 102
psychology
    'implicit comparative law', 301–2
    measurement of legal mentalities, 309–11
public international law, globalisation and,
        224–7
public opinion *see* opinion surveys

qualitative research
    choice of units for comparison, 292
    Qualitative Comparative Analysis (QCA),
        290
    use of, 288–9
quantitative research
    choice of units for comparison, 292
    historical research and, 289–91
    use of, 288–9

Rabel, Ernst
    on awareness of differing understandings of
        law, 18–19
    on functionalism, 14–15
Racz, Attila
    on similarities and differences between
        systems, 160
Radcliffe-Brown, Alfred
    legal anthropology, 306
Ragin, Charles
    Qualitative Comparative Analysis (QCA),
        290
Ramseyer, Mark
    on civil litigation rates, 131–2
    on refutation of legal 'myths', 19
regionalisation
    forces for, 230–2
    meaning of, 242–4
    multi-level governance, 247–8
regulatory competition in private international
        law, 228–30
Reitz, John
    on commercial law, 139–40
    on interdisciplinary dimension of
        comparative law, 7–8
religion
    causal relationship with law, *125*,
        125–7
    classification of, 72
    Hindu law, 91, 210
    insights on law and culture, 102
    legal anthropology, 305
    legal classifications, 89
    parallel legal systems, 92
    transnational law, 250 *see also* Christianity;
        Islamic law
research method *see* comparative method
Ribstein, Larry
    on global 'law market', 228–9
Roe, Mark
    on law and society, 139

quality measurement of investor protection,
        174
Roman law
    civil law's origins in, 42
    classification, 77
    continued influence of, 68
Rose, Paul
    on convergence of laws, 233–4
Rosen, Lawrence
    on culture and criminal law, 103
Roussey, Ludivine
    on trust in judicial institutions, 177
Rule of Law Index
    aggregated data, 181
    selected countries, *182*
rule of law programmes
    examples, 269–75
    functions of, *269*
    human rights and, 267
    terminology, typology and purpose,
        265–9
Ruskola, Teemu
    on classifying legal systems, 82
Russian law
    classification, 77–8
    law and culture, 102
    mixed classification, 87–8
    rule of law, *269*, 269, 271–3

Sacco, Rodolfo
    on English and French contract law,
        59–60
    on traditional comparative method, 34
Sachs, Jeffrey
    use of aggregated data, 179–80
Saidov, Akmal
    classification of legal systems, 79
Saleilles, Raymond
    emphasis on legal commonality, 30–1
Samuel, Geoffrey
    on interdisciplinary dimension of
        comparative law, 9
    on 'internal structures of legal knowledge',
        100
    on legal scholarship's role, 48
Sandefur, Rebecca
    on civil litigation rates, 129
Santos, Boaventura de Sousa
    on globalisation, 189–90
Sauser-Hall, Georges
    classification of legal systems, *76*, 75–7

Savigny, Friedrich Carl von
  on national consciousness and law, 114,
    121–2
Scandinavia see Nordic legal family
Schäfer, Hans-Bernd
  on law and economic development, 262–3
Schäffer, Heinz
  on similarities and differences between
    systems, 160
Schlesinger, Rudolf
  Common Core project, 31
Schnitzer, Adolf
  classification of legal systems, 77
scholarship
  differing approaches to comparative law,
    5–6, 6, 11
  foreign scholarship, measurement of
    influence of, 154–6
  'traditional comparative law', 11, 33–9
Sen, Amartya
  on law and economic development, 265
Shapiro, Martin
  on commonality between laws, 100
shareholder protection
  convergence of laws, 229, 236, 239–40
  differences matrix, 165
  functional analysis of legal rules, 164–7
  influence of foreign legal systems, 158–9
  legal culture and, 310
  quality measurement, 174
  quality of rules, 168–9
  shareholder primacy, 235
  shareholder rights, 169
  transnational law, 236
Siems, Mathias
  on citation of foreign judgments, 150–4
Slaughter, Anne-Marie
  on global community of courts, 148
Smith, Stephen
  on critical comparative law, 113
social policy evaluation, 297
social sciences
  applicability of comparative method, 287
  choice of units of comparison, 291–2
  historical research and comparative
    approach, 289–91
  'implicit comparative law', 301–2
  rationales for comparative approach, 287–8
  types of comparative research, 288–9
  understanding of legal systems, 302–5
socialist law, classification, 77–8, 79, 80

socio-legal comparative law
  author's analytical approach, 119
  civil litigation see civil litigation
  commercial law see commercial law
  criminal law see criminal law
  elements of, 119–20
  key issues summarised, 144–5
  legal culture concept see legal culture
sociology
  functionalism, 25–6
  and less developed legal systems, 27–8 see
    also causal relationship between law
    and society; culturally embedded law;
    legal culture
Soskice, David
  on 'varieties of capitalism', 298–9
states
  'best' form of government, 293–5
  borders see law across borders
  classification by policy choices, 297
  comparative studies, 292
  laws see national laws
  'state in action', 295–7
statute law and interpretation
  civil/common law comparison, 44–6
  foreign statute law, measurement of
    influence of, 156–9
statutory bodies, tortious liability, 23
Stirton, Lindsay
  on Germany and French Civil Code, 157–8
Stramignoni, Igor
  on 'immersion' in foreign law, 106
Summers, Robert
  on effect of judgments, 58
Swiss law
  citation of foreign judgments, 148
  in comparative law books, 16
  statutory interpretation, 45
  tort law comparison, 24–5

taxonomic methodology, use of, 72–3
Teubner, Gunther
  on good faith, 61
Third World countries
  'law and development' see 'law and
    development'
  Western law compared, 27–8
Todd, Harry
  legal anthropology, 306
tort law
  example of comparative method, 24–5

liability of statutory bodies, 23
suitability for study, 28
'traditional comparative law' generally, 11
traditional comparative method *see*
            comparative method
translation of foreign legal terms
controversy as to, 17–18
quantitative research on, 155
transnationalisation
commercial law examples, 251–5
forces for, 230–2
meaning of, 249–51
private law-making, controversy as to,
            255–8
Transparency International
use of aggregated data, 179–80
use of opinion surveys, 176
trust law
religion and, 102
Twining, William
on core themes of comparative law, 11
typology of legal transplants, 200, *201*

understanding *see* knowledge and
            understanding
United States Agency for International
            Development (USAID)
use of aggregated data, 180
United States law
academic references to foreign laws, 155–6
'Americanisation', 158–9, 203–5
citation of foreign judgments, 147–9
codification, 44
critical legal studies movement, 108–9,
            114
English law compared, 65–8
and foreign statute law, 156
functional comparison with foreign laws, 36
influence of, 43–4
legal process compared to English law, 65–6
legal profession, 54
legal thought, 67
legal transplants in Europe, 203–5
as mixed system, 89
religion and law, 102–3
translation of foreign legal terms, 155
as vertically divided system, 90, 91
universalism
Common Core project as example, 31–3
in comparative law, 29–31
in other disciplines, 28–9

Upham, Frank
on civil litigation rates, 131–2

Valcke, Catherine
contract formation, 99–100
Vanderlinden, Jacques
on classifying legal systems, 73
Vermeule, Adrian
on public attitudes to government, 311
Versteeg, Mila
on constitutional laws, 167
on transplanted human rights law, 218
Voigt, Stefan
quality measurement of high courts, 174

Watson, Alan
on legal transplants, 195, 196
Watt, Gary
on convergence of laws, 238
on law and religion, 102
Watt, Horatia Muir
on law and culture, 104
Weber, Max
historical and conceptual research method,
            290–1
on law and economic development, 261, 267
typology of socio-legal systems, 303–4
Wells, Michael
on US and French written judgments, 56–7
West, Mark
on US and Japanese commercial law, 158–9
Western legal tradition
and capitalism, 267
Chinese law compared, 101–2
colonialism *see* colonialism
convergence of civil law and common law,
            68–70, 79
and customary law, 86–7, 89
developing countries' law compared, 27–8
focus on, 27
Islamic law compared, 103
law and development in relation, 277–9
and 'legal orientalism', 80–2
legal pluralism, 108
legal transplants *see* legal transplants
mismatch with developing countries' laws,
            279–81
non-Western origins, 206
perspectives on other laws, 16–17
'rule of professional law', 78
Western-centric focus critiqued, 35–7, 82

Whitman, James
  on criminal law, 140–1
Wigmore, John Henry
  classification of legal systems, 75–7, *76*
  emphasis on legal commonality,
    30–1
  interdisciplinary approach by, 19
Wolff, Martin
  classification of legal systems, 77
World Bank
  on law and economic development, 263–4,
    280
  on quality of legal institutions, 172
  use of aggregated data, 179–80, 182–6
  use of opinion surveys, 177
World Economic Forum (WEF)
  use of opinion surveys, 177
World Justice Project (WJP)
  use of aggregated data, 181

World Values Survey
  use of opinion surveys, 176–7
Wright, Ronald
  on content analysis of court decisions, 161
'wrong' legal rules and institutions, 281–2

Zaring, David
  on citation of foreign judgments, 150
Zentrum für Europäische Rechtspolitik
    (University of Bremen, ZERP)
  use of aggregated data, 180–1
Zimmermann, Reinhard
  on legal scholarship, 67
Zweigert, Konrad
  analytical approach to comparative law, 5–6
  classification of legal systems, 77–8, 83
  on critical policy evaluation, 22–3
  on tort law, 24–5
  on universality, 30